CERTIFICATE
PHYSICS

In accordance with the latest syllabus prescribed by the Council for the Indian Certificate of Secondary Education Examination, New Delhi.

CERTIFICATE PHYSICS

Class X

Edition-Coordinator
Cosmic Strands e-publishing Pvt. Ltd.

Lee She Kayan
(M.Sc., B.Ed.)
Department of Physics
Don Bosco School, **Siliguri**

Dharmendra Pant
M.Sc. (Honors); M.Ed.
H.O.D. Physics
St. Xavier's Senior Secondary School, **Chandigarh**

OSWAL PUBLISHERS
1/12, Sahitya Kunj, M. G. Road, Agra-282 002

No Part of this book can be reproduced in any form or by any means without the prior written permission of the publisher.

Edition : 2019

ISBN : 978-93-87660-80-9

OSWAL PUBLISHERS

Head office	:	1/12, Sahitya Kunj, M.G. Road, Agra-282 002
Phone	:	(0562) 2527771- 4, +91 75340 77222
Order at	:	contact@oswalpublishers.com, sales@oswalpublishers.com
Website	:	www.oswalpublishers.com
Facebook link	:	https://www.facebook.com/oswalpublishersindia
Available at	:	amazon.in, Flipkart, snapdeal

PREFACE

Physics is a branch of science that deals with the study of mechanics of naturally occurring phenomenon, such as the interactions of matter and energy. Its study involves experiments with qualitative as well as quantitative measures.

With immense pleasure, we present the Textbook of Certificate Physics, which has been designed in accordance with the latest syllabus for class X, as prescribed by the Council for the Indian School Certificate Examination (ICSE). The main objective of writing this book is to present the subject matter at an elementary level with an interesting approach.

The textbook covers the theoretical, practical and applied aspects of each chapter in a simplified manner. Several illustrations have been included in each chapter for a better understanding of the subject. In the beginning of each chapter, a 'Learning path' has been incorporated, which broadly highlights the topics covered in the chapter. There is a 'Do you know?' section in every chapter, which states certain interesting facts which would be fascinating for the students. Definitions, laws and important terms have been emphasized by using the Italics and Bold format. Examples and note points have been placed in a particular layout to make them stand out.

There are a number of solved examples along with the exercise section that aids in analyzing the entire content of the section. The exercise section includes multiple choice questions, short and long answer type questions and numerical problems for the students' practice. Hints and solutions have been provided for selective questions. Questions from a few previous years' examination papers have also been included in each chapter for students to understand the pattern of the questions asked in the board examination.

Sincere thanks to all the teachers who have provided their valuable feedback for this text book.

We would like to express our gratitude towards 'Oswal Publishers' for their co-operation, guidance and assistance in bringing out this book to our entire satisfaction.

Suggestions and feedback from all readers for the further improvement of this book in its subsequent editions are welcome.

Authors

SYLLABUS CLASS - X

There will be one paper of two hours duration carrying 80 marks and Internal Assessment of practical work carrying 20 marks.

The paper will be divided into two sections, Section I (40 marks) and Section II (40 marks).

Section I (compulsory) will contain short answer questions on the entire syllabus.

Section II will contain six questions. Candidates will be required to answer any four of these six questions.

Note : Unless otherwise specified, only S. I. Units are to be used while teaching and learning, as well as for answering questions.

1. Force, Work, Power and Energy

(i) Turning forces concept; moment of a force; forces in equilibrium; centre of gravity; [discussions using simple examples and simple numerical problems].

Elementary introduction of translational and rotational motions; moment (turning effect) of a force, also called torque and its cgs and SI units; common examples - door, steering wheel, bicycle pedal, etc.; clockwise and anti-clockwise moments; conditions for a body to be in equilibrium (translational and rotational); principle of moment and its verification using a metre rule suspended by two spring balances with slotted weights hanging from it; simple numerical problems; Centre of gravity (qualitative only) with examples of some regular bodies and irregular lamina.

(ii) Uniform circular motion.

As an example of constant speed, though acceleration (force) is present. Differences between centrifugal and centripetal force.

(iii) Work, energy, power and their relation with force.

Definition of work. $W = FS\cos\theta$; special cases of $\theta = 0°$, $90°$. $W = mgh$. Definition of energy, energy as work done. Various units of work and energy and their relation with SI units.[erg, calorie, kW h and eV]. Definition of Power, $P=W/t$; SI and cgs units; other units, kilowatt (kW), megawatt (MW) and gigawatt (GW); and horse power (1 hp = 746 W) [Simple numerical problems on work, power and energy].

(iv) Different types of energy (e.g. chemical energy, Mechanical energy, heat energy, electrical energy, nuclear energy, sound energy, light energy).

Mechanical energy: potential energy $U = mgh$ (derivation included) gravitational PE, examples; kinetic energy $K = \frac{1}{2}mv^2$ (derivation included); forms of kinetic energy: translational, rotational and vibrational - only simple examples. [Numerical problems on K and U only in case of translational motion]; qualitative discussions of electrical, chemical, heat, nuclear, light and sound energy, conversion from one form to another; common examples.

(v) Machines as force multipliers; load, effort, mechanical advantage, velocity ratio and efficiency; simple treatment of levers, pulley systems showing the utility of each type of machine.

Functions and uses of simple machines : Terms– effort E, load L, mechanical advantage MA = L/E, velocity ratio $VR = V_E/V_L = d_E/d_L$, input (W_i), output (W_o), efficiency (η), relation between η and MA,VR (derivation included); for all practical machines $\eta <1$; MA < VR.

Lever : principle. First, second and third class of levers; examples: MA and VR in each case. Examples of each of these classes of levers as also found in the human body.

Pulley system : single fixed, single movable, block and tackle; MA, VR and η in each case.

(vi) Principle of Conservation of energy.

Statement of the principle of conservation of energy; theoretical verification that $U + K$ = constant for a freely falling body. Application of this law to simple pendulum (qualitative only); [simple numerical problems].

2. Light

(i) Refraction of light through a glass block and a triangular prism - qualitative treatment of simple applications such as real and apparent depth of objects in water and apparent bending of sticks in water. Applications of refraction of light.

Partial reflection and refraction due to change in medium. Laws of refraction; the effect on speed (V), wavelength (λ) and frequency (f) due to refraction of light; conditions for a light ray to pass undeviated. Values of speed of light (c) in vacuum, air, water and glass; refractive index $\mu = c/V$, $V = f\lambda$. Values of μ for common substances such as water, glass and diamond; experimental verification; refraction through glass block; lateral displacement; multiple images in thick glass plate/mirror; refraction through a glass prism simple applications : real and apparent depth of objects in water; apparent bending of a stick under water. (Simple numerical problems and approximate ray diagrams required).

(ii) Total internal reflection: Critical angle; examples in triangular glass prisms; comparison with reflection from a plane mirror (qualitative only). Applications of total internal reflection.

Transmission of light from a denser medium (glass/ water) to a rarer medium (air) at different angles of incidence; critical angle (C) $\mu = 1/\sin C$. Essential *conditions for total internal reflection. Total internal reflection in a triangular glass prism; ray diagram, different cases - angles of prism (60°, 60°, 60°), (60°, 30°, 90°), (45°, 45°, 90°); use of right angle prism to obtain δ = 90° and 180° (ray diagram); comparison of total internal reflection from a prism and reflection from a plane mirror.*

(iii) Lenses (converging and diverging) including characteristics of the images formed (using ray diagrams only); magnifying glass; location of images using ray diagrams and thereby determining magnification.

(iv) Types of lenses (converging and diverging), convex and concave, action of a lens as a set of prisms; technical terms; centre of curvature, radii of curvature, principal axis, foci, focal plane and focal length,; detailed study of refraction of light in spherical lenses through ray diagrams; formation of images - principal rays or construction rays; location of images from ray diagram for various positions of a small linear object on the principal axis; characteristics of images. Sign convention and direct numerical problems using the lens formula are included.(derivation of formula not required)

Scale drawing or graphical representation of ray diagrams not required.

Power of a lens (concave and convex) – [simple direct numerical problems] : magnifying glass or simple microscope : location of image and magnification from ray diagram only [formula and numerical problems <u>not</u> included]. Applications of lenses.

(v) Using a triangular prism to produce a visible spectrum from white light; Electromagnetic spectrum. Scattering of light.

Deviation produced by a triangular prism; dependence on colour (wavelength) of light; dispersion and spectrum; electromagnetic spectrum: broad classification (names only arranged in order of increasing wavelength); properties common to all electromagnetic radiations; properties and uses of infrared and ultraviolet radiation. Simple application of scattering of light e.g. blue colour of the sky.

3. Sound

(i) Reflection of Sound Waves; echoes: their use; simple numerical problems on echoes.

Production of echoes, condition for formation of echoes; simple numerical problems; use of echoes by bats, dolphins, fishermen, medical field. SONAR.

(ii) Natural vibrations, Damped vibrations, Forced vibrations and Resonance – a special case of forced vibrations. *Meaning and simple applications of natural, damped, forced vibrations and resonance.*

(iii) Loudness, pitch and quality of sound :

Characteristics of sound: loudness and intensity; subjective and objective nature of these properties; sound level in db (as unit only); noise pollution; interdependence of : pitch and frequency; quality and waveforms (with examples).

4. Electricity and Magnetism

(i) Ohm's Law; concepts of emf, potential difference, resistance; resistances in series and parallel, internal resistance.

Concepts of pd (V), current (I), resistance (R) and charge (Q). Ohm's law: statement, $V = IR$; SI units; experimental verification; graph of V vs I and resistance from slope; ohmic and non-ohmic resistors, factors affecting resistance (including specific resistance) and internal resistance; super conductors, electromotive force (emf); combination of resistances in series and parallel and derivation of expressions for equivalent resistance. Simple numerical problems using the above relations. [Simple network of resistors].

(ii) Electrical power and energy.

Electrical energy; examples of heater, motor, lamp, loudspeaker, etc. Electrical power; measurement of electrical energy, $W = QV = VIt$ from the definition of pd. Combining with ohm's law $W = VIt = I^2 Rt = (V^2/R)t$ and electrical power $P = (W/t) = VI = I^2R = V^2/R$. Units : SI and commercial; Power rating of common appliances, household consumption of electric energy; calculation of total energy consumed by electrical appliances; $W = Pt$ (kilowatt × hour = kW h), [simple numerical problems].

(iii) Household circuits – main circuit; switches; fuses; earthing; safety precautions; three-pin plugs; colour coding of wires.

House wiring (ring system), power distribution; main circuit (3 wires-live, neutral, earth) with fuse / MCB, main switch and its advantages – circuit diagram; two-way switch, staircase wiring, need for earthing, fuse, 3-pin plug and socket; Conventional location of live, neutral and earth points in 3 pin plugs and sockets. Safety precautions, colour coding of wires.

(iv) Magnetic effect of a current (principles only, laws not required); electromagnetic induction (elementary); transformer.

Oersted's experiment on the magnetic effect of electric current; magnetic field (B) and field lines due to current in a straight wire (qualitative only), right hand thumb rule – magnetic field due to a current in a loop; Electromagnets: their uses; comparisons with a permanent magnet; Fleming's Left Hand Rule, the DC electric motor- simple sketch of main parts (coil, magnet, split ring commutators and brushes); brief description and type of energy transfer(working not required): Simple introduction to electromagnetic induction; frequency of AC in house hold supplies, Fleming's Right Hand Rule, AC Generator – Simple sketch of main parts, brief description and type of energy transfer(working not required). Advantage of AC over DC. Transformer- its types, characteristics of primary and secondary coils in each type (simple labelled diagram and its uses).

5. Heat

(i) Calorimetry: meaning, specific heat capacity; principle of method of mixtures; Numerical Problems on specific heat capacity using heat loss and gain and the method of mixtures.

Heat and its units (calorie, joule), temperature and its units (°C, K); thermal (heat) capacity $C' = Q/\Delta T$... (SI unit of C): Specific heat Capacity $C = Q/m\Delta T$ (SI unit of C) Mutual relation between Heat Capacity and Specific Heat capacity, values of C for some common substances (ice, water and copper). Principle of method of mixtures including mathematical statement. Natural phenomenon involving specific heat. Consequences of high sp. heat of water. [Simple numerical problem].

(ii) Latent heat; loss and gain of heat involving change of state for fusion only.

Change of phase (state); heating curve for water; latent heat; sp latent heat of fusion (SI unit). Simple numerical problems. Common physical phenomena involving latent heat of fusion.

6. Modern Physics

(i) Radioactivity and changes in the nucleus; background radiation and safety precautions.

Brief introduction (qualitative only) of the nucleus, nuclear structure, atomic number (Z), mass number (A). Radioactivity as spontaneous disintegration. α, β and γ – their nature and properties; changes within the nucleus. One example each of α and β decay with equations showing changes in Z and A. Uses of radioactivity – radio isotopes. Harmful effects. Safety precautions. Background radiation.

Radiation : X-rays; radioactive fallout from nuclear plants and other sources.

Nuclear Energy: working on safe disposal of waste. Safety measures to be strictly reinforced.

(ii) Nuclear fission and fusion; basic introduction and equations.

A NOTE ON SI UNITS

SI units (*Systeme International d'Unites*) were adopted internationally in 1968.

Fundamental units

The system has seven fundamental (or basic) units, one for each of the fundamental quantities.

Fundamental quantity	Unit	
	Name	Symbol
Mass	kilogram	kg
Length	metre	m
Time	second	s
Electric current	ampere	A
Temperature	kelvin	K
Luminous intensity	candela	cd
Amount of substance	mole	mol

Derived units

These are obtained from the fundamental units by multiplication or division; no numerical factors are involved. Some derived units with complex names are :

Derived quantity	Unit	
	Name	Symbol
Volume	cubic metre	m^3
Density	kilogram per cubic metre	$kg.m^{-3}$
Velocity	metre per second	$m.s^{-1}$
Acceleration	metre per second squared	$m.s^{-2}$
Momentum	kilogram metre per second	$kg.m.s^{-1}$

Some derived units are given special names due to their complexity when expressed in terms of the fundamental units, as below :

Derived quantity	Unit	
	Name	Symbol
Force	newton	N
Pressure	pascal	Pa
Energy, Work	joule	J
Power	watt	W
Frequency	hertz	Hz
Electric charge	coulomb	C
Electric resistance	ohm	Ω
Electromotive force	volt	V

When the unit is named after a person, the symbol has a capital letter.

Standard prefixes

Decimal multiples and submultiples are attached to units when appropriate, as below :

Multiple	Prefix	Symbol
10^9	giga	G
10^6	mega	M
10^3	kilo	k
10^{-1}	deci	d
10^{-2}	centi	c
10^{-3}	milli	m
10^{-6}	micro	µ
10^{-9}	nano	n
10^{-12}	pico	p
10^{-15}	femto	f

INTERNAL ASSESSMENT OF PRACTICAL WORK

Candidates will be asked to carry out experiments for which instructions will be given. The experiments may be based on topics that are not included in the syllabus but theoretical knowledge will not be required. A candidate will be expected to be able to follow simple instructions, to take suitable readings and to present these readings in a systematic form. He/she may be required to exhibit his/her data graphically. Candidates will be expected to appreciate and use the concepts of least count, significant figures and elementary error handling.

Note : Teachers may design their own set of experiments, preferably related to the theory syllabus. A comprehensive list is suggested below.

1. Lever : There are many possibilities with a meter rule as a lever with a load (known or unknown) suspended from a point near one end (say left), the lever itself pivoted on a knife edge, use slotted weights suspended from the other (right) side for effort.

   Determine the mass of a metre rule using a spring balance or by balancing it on a knife edge at some point away from the middle and a 50 g weight on the other side. Next pivot (F) the metre rule at the 40 cm, 50 cm and 60 cm mark, each time suspending a load L or the left end and effort E near the right end. Adjust E and or its position so that the rule is balanced. Tabulate the position of L, F and E and the magnitudes of L and E and the distances of load arm and effort arm. Calculate MA = L/E and VR = effort arm/load arm. It will be found that MA <VR in one case, MA = VR in another and MA > VR in the third case. Try to explain why this is so. Also try to calculate the real load and real effort in these cases.

2. Determine the VR and MA of a given pulley system.

3. Trace the course of different rays of light refracting through a rectangular glass slab at different angles of incidence, measure the angles of incidence, refraction and emergence. Also measure the lateral displacement.

4. Determine the focal length of a convex lens by (a) the distant object method and (b) using a needle and a plane mirror.

5. Determine the focal length of a convex lens by using two pins and formula $f = uv/(u + v)$.

6. For a triangular prism, trace the course of rays passing through it, measure angles i_1, i_2, A and δ. Repeat for four different angles of incidence (say $i_1 = 40°, 50°, 60°$ and $70°$). Verify $i_1 + i_2 = A + \delta$ and $A = r_1 + r_2$.

7. For a ray of light incident normally ($i_1 = 0$) on one face of a prism, trace course of the ray. Measure the angle δ. Explain briefly. Do this for prisms with A = 60°, 45° and 90°.

8. Calculate the sp. heat of the material of the given calorimeter, from the temperature readings and masses of cold water, warm water and its mixture taken in the calorimeter.

9. Determination of sp. heat of a metal by method of mixtures.

10. Determination of specific latent heat of ice.

11. Using a simple electric circuit, verify Ohm's law. Draw a graph, and obtain the slope.

12. Set up model of household wiring including ring main circuit. Study the function of switches and fuses.

Teachers may feel free to alter or add to the above list. The students may perform about 10 experiments. Some experiments may be demonstrated.

EVALUATION

The practical work/project work are to be evaluated by the subject teacher and by an External Examiner. (The External Examiner may be a teacher nominated by the Head of the school, who could be from the faculty, **but not teaching the subject in the relevant section/class.** For example, a teacher of Physics of Class VIII may be deputed to be an External Examiner for Class X, Physics projects.)

The Internal Examiner and the External Examiner will assess the practical work/project work independently.

Award of marks (20 Marks)

Subject Teacher (Internal Examiner)   10 marks
External Examiner   10 marks

The total marks obtained out of 20 are to be sent to the Council by the Head of the school.

The Head of the school will be responsible for the entry of marks on the mark sheets provided by the Council.

CONTENTS

1. Force — 13-29
2. Work, Power and Energy — 30-50
3. Machines — 51-67
4. Refraction of Light at Plane Surfaces — 68-94
5. Refraction of Light Through a Lens — 95-120
6. The Electromagnetic Spectrum — 121-133
7. Sound — 134-156
8. Electric Current — 157-178
9. Electrical Energy and Household Circuits — 179-199
10. Electromagnetism — 200-224
11. Heat — 225-244
12. Modern Physics — 245-263

1

FORCE

LEARNING OUTCOMES
- Torque, Equilibrium and Centre of Gravity.
- Uniform Circular Motion : Centripetal Force and Centrifugal Force.

The word 'force' is used commonly in our everyday life. Generally, we say that we use force to walk, to talk, to lift objects, to push or pull objects or to even change the shape of objects. Some common examples include pulling a rope, pushing a pin on a paper, squeezing a lemon, stretching a rubber band, lifting a bucket of water and so on.

In physics, force is the cause of the change of state of rest or state of motion in a body, or it is used to denote an action that deforms a body.

Force is an external influence that changes, or tends to change, the state of rest or motion of a body or deforms a body; that is, changes its shape and size.

Force is a vector quantity. Its S.I. unit is Newton.

(A) TORQUE, EQUILIBRIUM AND CENTRE OF GRAVITY

1.1 TRANSLATIONAL AND ROTATIONAL MOTION

A rigid body is a body that does not get deformed under the action of a force. Ideally, no real body is truly rigid; however, wood, stone, metals, glass and so on can be regarded as rigid bodies.

A rigid body can have two types of motion, translational and rotational.

1. Translational motion : It is also called *linear motion*. In translational motion, the body moves along a straight-line path in the direction of force applied.

In this type of motion, the rigid body is not pivoted or fixed in any way, and every particle of the body has the same displacement.

Examples : Motion of a rectangular wooden block down the inclined plane, a car moving on a straight road, a ball rolling on the floor in a straight line path (Fig. 1.1) and so on.

Fig. 1.1 : Translational motion.

2. Rotational motion : This type of motion occurs when the force is applied on a body that is pivoted or fixed in some way (Fig. 1.2). The rotation may occur around a fixed axis, such as the rotation of a ceiling fan, or the rotation may occur along with the oscillation of the axis, such as the rotation of an oscillating table fan.

Examples : Rotation of a potter's wheel, a merry-go-round, a spinning top, movement of a door around the hinges, a wheel of a vehicle and so on.

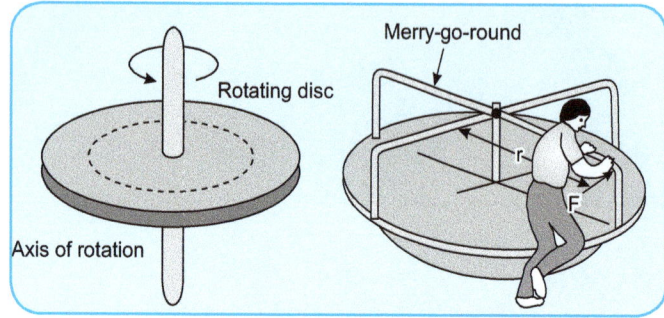

Fig. 1.2 : Rotational motion.

In general, the motion of a rigid body is a combination of translational and rotational motion.

The turning or rotational effects of a force shall be discussed in the following sections.

1.2 MOMENT OR TURNING EFFECTS OF A FORCE/TORQUE

Consider a rigid body fixed at a point O on which a force F acts at a point P (Fig. 1.3). Point P is called the *point of action of the force*. An imaginary line passing through the point of action of force and drawn in the same direction in which the force acts is called the *line of action of force*. XY is the line of action of force.

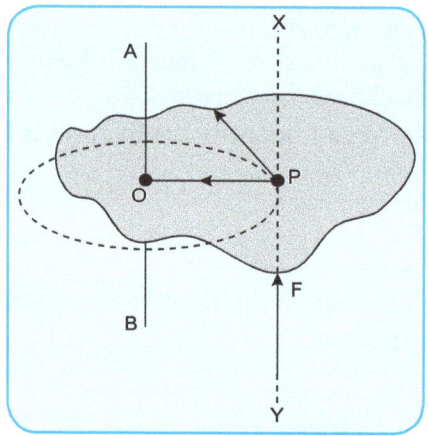

Fig. 1.3 : Moment of force.

When the line of action passes through the point of action, the force is unable to produce linear motion in the body as the body is pivoted, but it is capable of turning or rotating the body about a vertical axis passing through the point O, as shown by line AOB. This vertical axis is known as *axis of rotation* and the turning effect is known as *moment of force or torque*. It is represented by the symbol τ (tau). Torque is created when the line of action of a force does not pass through the centre of rotation.

The moment of a force or torque on a body is the turning effect of force acting on the body about the point or axis of rotation.

Factors Affecting the Moment of a Force

The two factors affecting the moment or turning of a force are as follows :
1. The magnitude of the force (F) applied.
2. The perpendicular distance of line of action of the force (XY) from the point of action or axis of the rotation (AOB).

In Fig. 1.3, OP is a perpendicular drawn from the point O on the line of action of force. This represents the distance between the line of action of force, *i.e.* XY and the axis of rotation, *i.e.* AOB.

The moment of force or torque about a point is measured by the product of the magnitude of the force and the perpendicular distance of the line of action of force from the axis of rotation.

Moment of force about the point O = Force × Perpendicular distance of force from the point O

$$\tau = F \times OP$$

The farther the line of action from the axis of rotation, the more is the turning of a body. In other words, when the perpendicular distance of line of action of force is maximum from the axis of rotation, then the given amount of force will produce the maximum torque to turn the body.

Units of Moment of Force/Torque

Unit of moment of force = Unit of force × Unit of distance

As the SI unit of force is newton and that of distance is metre, the SI unit of moment of force is newton × metre (N m).

The CGS unit of moment of force is dyne cm.

If the gravitational unit of force is considered, then the units of torque are kgf m and gf cm in the SI and CGS unit, respectively.

Relation between the units :
$$1 \text{ N m} = 10^5 \text{ dyne} \times 10^2 \text{ cm}$$
$$= 10^7 \text{ dyne cm}$$
$$1 \text{ kgf m} = 9.8 \text{ N m}$$
$$1 \text{ gf cm} = 980 \text{ dyne cm}$$

Torque is a *vector* quantity. Its magnitude is equal to the product of force and the perpendicular distance, and the direction is normal to the plane containing the perpendicular distance and the force.

Clockwise and Anticlockwise Moments

The direction of rotation produced on a body can be either clockwise or anticlockwise. It depends on the direction of the force applied and the point of application of force. In Fig. 1.4, $r_\perp$ represents perpendicular distance from the centre to the line of action of the force. If the force is applied at the point P in the upward direction as shown, the body will rotate in the anticlockwise direction and the moment of force is called *anticlockwise moment*. It is taken as *positive*. Conversely, if the force at point P is applied in the downward direction, then the body will rotate in the clockwise direction and the moment of force is called *clockwise moment*. It is considered *negative*.

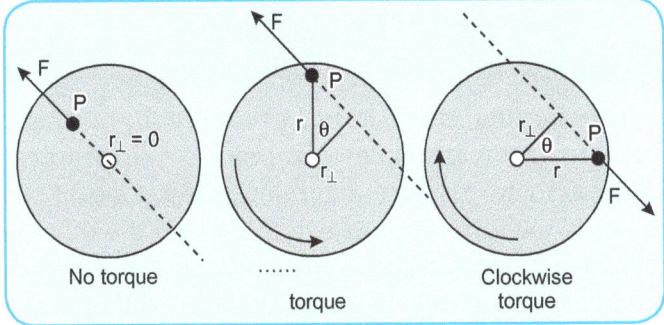

Fig. 1.4 : Anticlockwise and clockwise moments.

Examples of turning effect of force

1. Opening and shutting a door : A door is attached on one side to the hinges. A vertical line drawn through the hinges forms its axis of rotation.

To open or close a door, we apply a force on its handle (*i.e.* normal to the door). The handle is provided at the other free end of the door, (at point A) so that the distance from the hinges is more, as shown in Fig. 1.5. If we apply a force at a point somewhere in the middle of the door (point B) or near to the hinges, a much greater force is required to open or (point C) close the door, and if we apply a force on the hinges of the door, the door will not open or close even if the magnitude of force is large, because the line of action is passing through the point of rotation. The handles being at a large perpendicular distance from the hinges of the door, comparatively a much smaller force is required to be applied on the handles to open or close the doors. A smaller force on the handle at the free end will produce the same turning effect as a larger force on the handle if it is located nearer to the hinges. It is due to this reason the handle is provided near the free end of the door.

2. Turning of a see-saw : In a see-saw, the fulcrum at the centre is the axis of rotation. If two children of roughly the same weight sit on the two ends of a see-saw, at points equidistant from the fulcrum, then the see-saw is in equilibrium as the two children exert an equal force (due to their weight) in opposite direction.

However, if on one side of the see-saw a child is sitting and on the other side an adult person with heavier weight is sitting, as shown in Fig. 1.6(a), then due to the greater force of the adult person, the see-saw will turn anticlockwise. To maintain an equilibrium or balance Fig. 1.6(b), the adult person needs to sit closer to the fulcrum, as this decreases the perpendicular distance of line of action of force from the axis of rotation (resulting in a lesser turning effect).

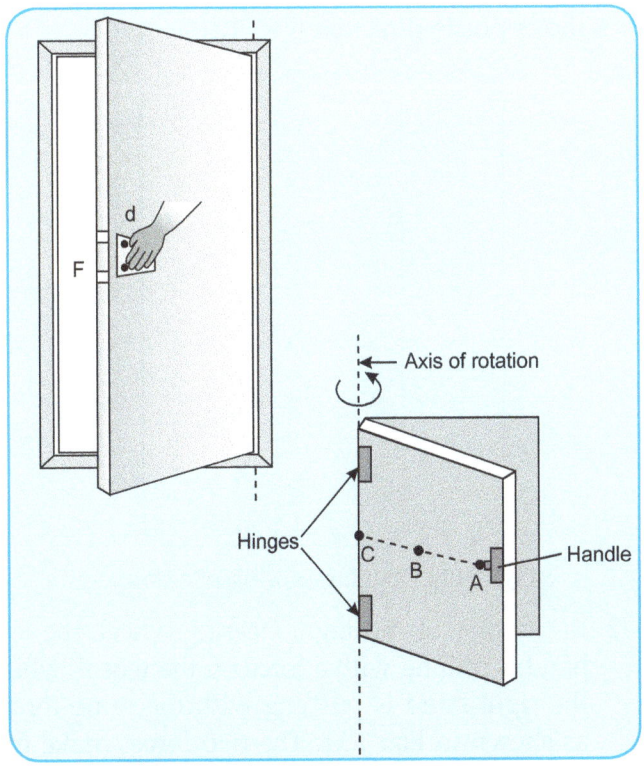

Fig. 1.5 : Opening/shutting a door.

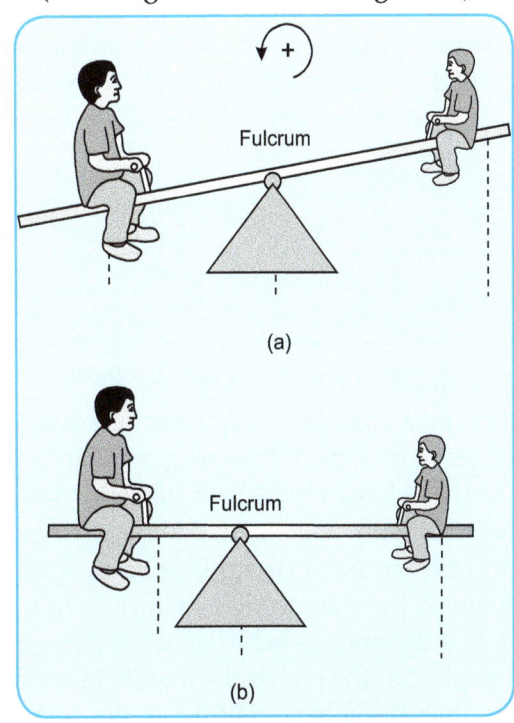

Fig. 1.6 : Turning a see-saw.

3. Turning of a steering wheel : A driver has to turn the steering wheel to change the direction of a moving vehicle. A line passing through the centre of the wheel will form its axis of rotation. For turning a steering wheel, a force needs to be applied tangentially (*i.e.* normally on the axis of rotation) on its rim, because the perpendicular distance is maximum at the rim from the axis of rotation. By changing the point of application of force on the wheel, its rotation can be changed, without changing the direction of the force.

If a force is applied at point A on the wheel (*i.e.* at the bottom from the left direction), then the wheel rotates in anticlockwise direction, whereas if a force is applied at point B on the wheel (*i.e.* at the top), in the same direction, then the wheel rotates clockwise (Fig. 1.7).

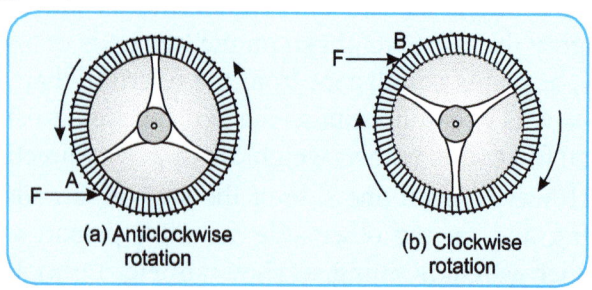

Fig. 1.7 : Point of application of force in case of a steering wheel.

4. Rotation of a bicycle wheel : In a bicycle, the axle of the wheel is the axis of rotation. The pedal is kept at a distance from the axle of the wheel so that the perpendicular distance from the line of action to the axis of rotation is large (Fig. 1.8). Due to this, a small force applied on the pedals can rotate the wheels.

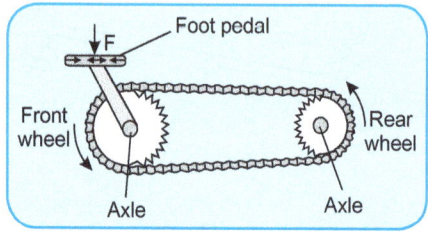

Fig. 1.8 : Turning of a bicycle wheel.

5. Turning a spanner : A spanner or a wrench is a tool used for tightening or loosening a nut. It has a long handle so that a large torque is produced when a force is applied normally at its end. As the perpendicular distance from the point of application of force being large, a small force is needed to turn a nut. When the end of a spanner is held by hand, such that the force is applied at the end of the handle in an upward direction, then the spanner is turned anticlockwise to loosen a nut. If the direction of force is opposite (*i.e.* in a downward direction), then the spanner is turned clockwise to tighten a nut (Fig. 1.9).

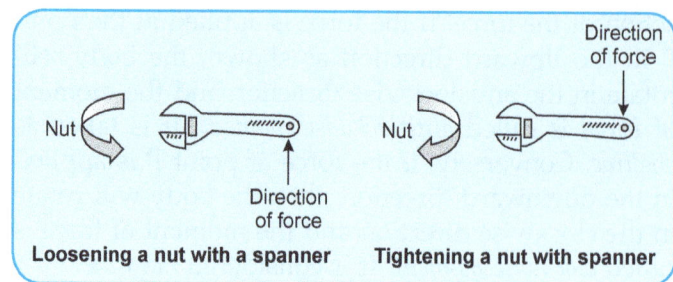

Fig. 1.9 : Turning a spanner.

Couple

The turning effect is not produced by a single force. In all the examples discussed, a pair of forces is required to produce a turning effect. One of the forces is the force applied externally and the other is the reaction force at the fixed or pivoted point, which is equal in magnitude to the applied force but opposite in direction. This pair of forces acting together to turn the body in the same direction constitute a *couple*.

A pair of equal and opposite parallel forces whose lines of action are not the same constitute a couple.

A couple is always needed to produce a turning effect or rotation. A couple can be balanced by an equal and opposite couple (*i.e.* an equal couple but acting in the opposite direction).

Examples :

1. To open a door, the applied force is the force exerted on the handle of the door and the reaction force is the force acting on the hinges in the opposite direction (Fig. 1.10).

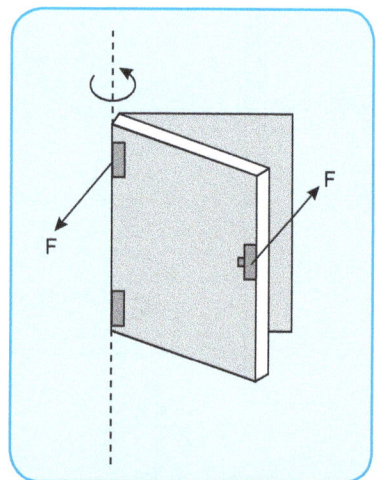

Fig. 1.10 : Opening/closing of a door.

2. In the case of turning a steering wheel, the left hand is pulling with a force on the wheel, while the right hand is pushing with the same force, as shown in Fig. 1.11. The two forces make the wheel turn in an anticlockwise direction.

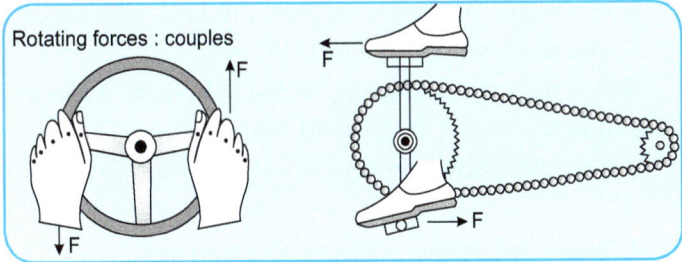

Fig. 1.11 : Turning a steering wheel and rotation of a bicycle wheel.

3. Similarly, to rotate the wheel of a bicycle, a force is applied by pushing one pedal forward and the other pedal backward (Fig. 1.11).

Other examples where a pair of forces or a couple is needed for rotation are turning a tap, tightening a cap of a bottle, winding of a clock, turning a key in the lock, turning a wrench, rotation of a merry-go-round and so on.

Moment of Couple :

The moment of a couple is equal to the product of either of the two forces and the perpendicular distance between the line of action of both the forces.

This can be illustrated by Fig. 1.12. Consider a bar PQ pivoted in the middle at a point O. At the two ends P and Q of the bar, two equal and opposite forces of magnitude F are exerted. The perpendicular distance between the two forces is called the couple arm, denoted by d. Each force has the turning effect on the bar in the same direction (anticlockwise in the figure). These two forces form a couple and rotate the bar around the fixed point O.

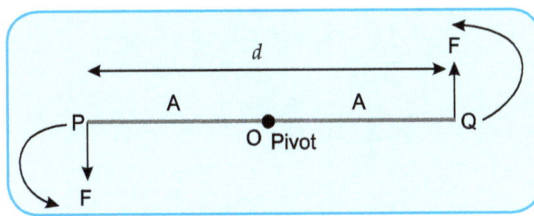

Fig. 1.12 : Moment of couple.

Now, moment of force at the end P = F × OP (anticlockwise)

Moment of force at the end Q = F × OQ (anticlockwise).

Total moment of the couple
= (F × OP) + (F × OQ)
= F × (OP + OQ)
= F × d (anticlockwise)
= Either force × Couple arm (perpendicular distance between the two forces).

The units of moment of couple are same as that of the torque; that is, N m and dyne cm in the SI and CGS system, respectively.

1.3. EQUILIBRIUM OF RIGID BODIES

A rigid body is said to be in a state of equilibrium when the resultant of number of forces (two or more) acting on the body is zero such that the state of the body, whether rest or motion, remains unchanged.

In other words, we can say, a body in equilibrium has balanced forces acting on it.

Types of Equilibrium

The equilibrium is of two types : (1) static equilibrium and (2) dynamic equilibrium.

1. Static equilibrium : A body is said to be in static equilibrium if it remains in a state of rest under the influence of applied forces.

Examples :

(a) A cup lying on the table. The force exerted by the weight of the cup in the downward direction is balanced by the reaction force of the table in the opposite direction; i.e., vertically upwards. The cup remains in its state of rest as the resultant force is zero. It is thus in static equilibrium.

(b) If a wooden block placed on a desk is pushed on the left side and the right side along the same line with an equal force, the block does not move because the two forces applied on the block are equal and opposite in direction and thus the net force is zero.

(c) A beam balance is in static equilibrium when the anticlockwise moment of force on its left pan balances the clockwise moment of force on its right pan. The beam has zero rotational motion in this state.

2. Dynamic equilibrium : A body is said to be in dynamic equilibrium if it remains in a state of *motion* under the influence of applied forces.

Examples :

(a) The revolution of Earth around the Sun. The gravitational force of attraction provides the force necessary for the motion of Earth. The resultant of the two forces is zero.

(b) The movement of electrons around the nucleus of an atom. Here also the force of attraction provides the force necessary for the motion of electrons.

Conditions for Equilibrium

The following two conditions are needed to be satisfied for a body to be in equilibrium :

1. *The resultant of all the external forces acting on a rigid body must be zero.*
2. *The resultant of all the external moment of forces or torque acting on a rigid body about its point of rotation must be zero; i.e., the sum of all anticlockwise moments must be equal to the sum of all clockwise moments about the same point.*

1.4 PRINCIPLE OF MOMENTS

If a body is in equilibrium under the action of a number of forces, then the algebraic sum of the moments of the forces about any point on the body is equal to zero.

According to the principle of moments, *the algebraic sum of anticlockwise moments is equal to the sum of clockwise moments when a number of forces act on a rigid body in equilibrium.*

The anticlockwise moment is considered positive, whereas the clockwise moment is considered negative while calculating the algebraic sum.

A beam balance is a device that works on the principle of moments.

Verification of Principle of Moments

Take a metre scale and suspend it horizontally with the help of a strong thread from a fixed support. Suspend two spring balances with certain amount of weights attached to them from either side of the scale. Let the weights on the left and right sides be W_1 and W_2, respectively (Fig. 1.13). The scale will tilt on the side where the weight is more. Adjust the distance of the two balances from the fixed support such that the scale becomes horizontal.

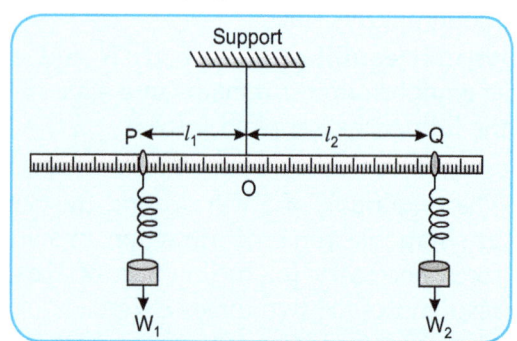

Fig. 1.13 : Verification of principle of moments.

Let the distance between the support and weight W_1 be l_1 and let the distance between the support and weight W_2 be l_2.

The weight W_1 tends to turn the scale anticlockwise, thus the anticlockwise moment is $W_1 \times l_1$.

The weight W_2 tends to turn the scale clockwise, thus, the clockwise moment is $W_2 \times l_2$.

When the scale is adjusted to the horizontal position, it is in equilibrium. It is found that,

Anticlockwise moment = Clockwise moment

i.e. $W_1 \times l_1 = W_2 \times l_2$

It thus verifies the principle of moments.

1.5 CENTRE OF GRAVITY

It is known that the Earth attracts every body or particle towards its centre through the force of gravity due to the weight of a body. A rigid body of weight W can be considered to be made up of a number of minute particles, each particle of weight w (Fig. 1.14).

As the size of a body is quite small compared to the size of the Earth, the pull of gravity due to weight w acting on the particles can be considered parallel to each other such that the sum of all the parallel forces is equal to the entire weight W of the body. These individual parallel forces act in the same direction (*i.e.* vertically downwards). The force due to weight W will act at a point G such that the algebraic sum of moments about the point G due to the weight w of each particle is zero. The point G where the net force is zero is called the *centre of gravity of a body*. The weight W of a body is considered as a single force acting vertically downwards through the centre of gravity G of the body. Thus,

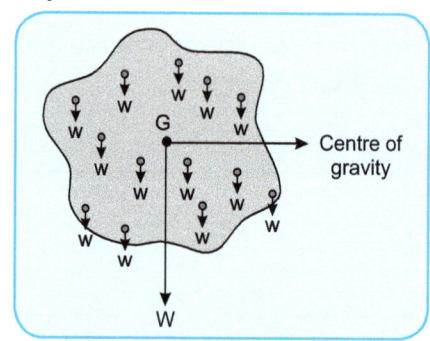

Fig. 1.14. : Centre of gravity.

Centre of gravity (C.G.) of a rigid body is defined as the point at which the entire weight of the body acts and the algebraic sum of moments of weights of particles constituting the body is zero about this point.

The position of C.G. of a body of a given mass depends on the *shape of the body and distribution of its mass*. Depending on these two factors, the C.G. may lie within the body or outside where there is no material. Also, if a body is deformed, the position of its C.G. changes.

FORCE

Examples:
1. The C.G. of a uniform bar or rod lies at the midpoint of its axis.
2. The C.G. of a ring lies at its centre where there is no material.
3. A wire has its C.G. at its midpoint. But if the wire is bent in the form of a circle, its C.G. will be at the centre of the circle; *i.e.*, the position of C.G. changes.

Centre of Gravity of Regular Bodies

Regular or homogeneous bodies have a definite geometrical shape and uniform distribution of mass. If a body has a regular geometrical shape and its mass distribution or density is uniform, then, in most cases, its C.G. coincides with its geometrical centre. The position of C.G. for a few regular bodies is given in the Fig. 1.15 and Table 1.1.

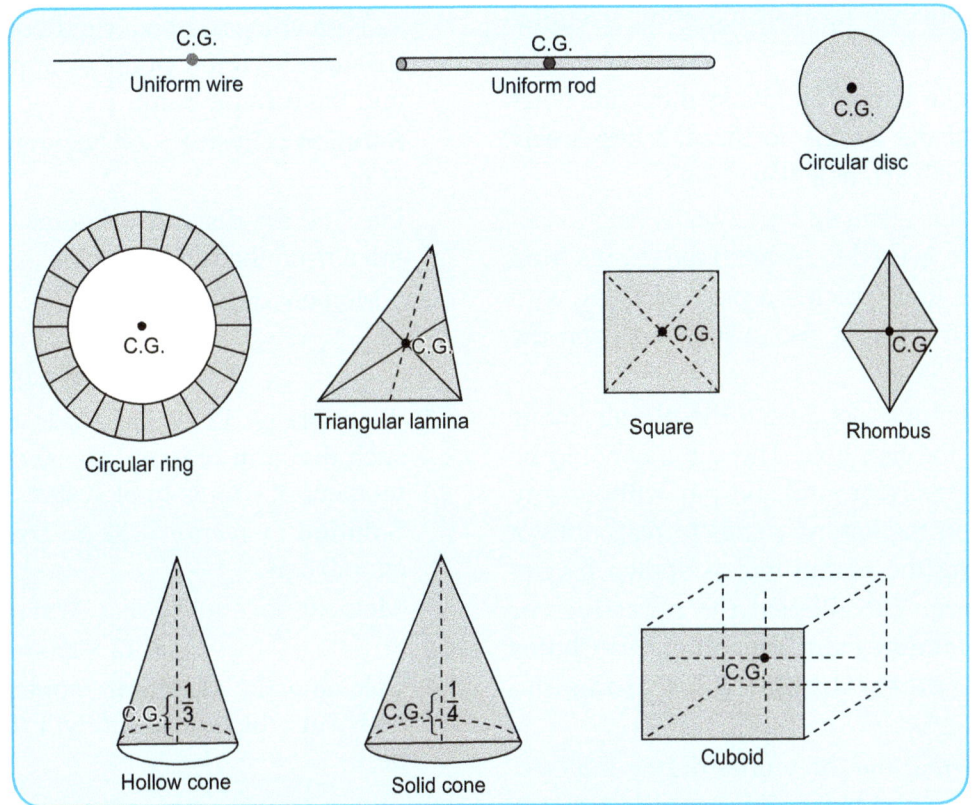

Fig. 1.15 : Centre of gravity of some regular bodies.

Table 1.1 : The shape and position of C.G. for a few regular bodies

Shape of the object	Position of centre of gravity
Uniform straight wire	Midpoint of the wire.
Uniform beam or rod	Midpoint of the axis of rod.
Circular disc or ring	Geometric centre.
Sphere (solid or hollow)	Geometric centre.
Cylinder	Midpoint on the axis of cylinder.
Solid cone	At a height, 1/4th from its base on its axis.
Hollow cone	At a height, 1/3rd from its base on its axis.
Triangular lamina	Centroid–the point of intersection of medians.
Rectangular lamina or square	Point of intersection of its diagonals.
Rhombus (or parallelogram)	Point of intersection of its diagonals.
Cube or cuboid	Midpoint of the line joining the centres of opposite sides.

Balance point due to centre of gravity : Each body can be balanced by supporting it at its centre of gravity. When a body is freely suspended from a point, it comes to rest in such a position that its centre of gravity lies vertically below the point of suspension. For example, we often try to balance a notebook on the tip of our finger at its centre. Similarly, an object can be balanced on a knife by keeping it exactly below the centre of gravity of the object.

Centre of Gravity of an Irregular Body (or Lamina)

Unlike regular bodies, it is difficult to locate the centre of gravity of irregular bodies.

Procedure for Determining the C.G. of an Irregular Lamina :

Take an irregular lamina and make three fine holes near the edges of the lamina so that it hangs freely when pivoted from each hole (Fig. 1.16).

A pin or a nail is clamped horizontally on a retort stand, and this pin is used to suspend the lamina from its hole. A plumb line, which is a piece of string with weight hanging from it, is also suspended from the same point.

Suppose the lamina along with the plumb line is suspended from the first hole. The lamina should be able to oscillate freely around the pin without any obstruction. When the lamina comes to rest, draw a straight line along the plumb line as shown by the dotted line in Fig. 1.16. Repeat the procedure of suspension of lamina from the other two holes and draw two other straight lines along the plumb line.

It is observed that the three lines drawn intersect each other at a common point. This common point is the centre of gravity of this lamina.

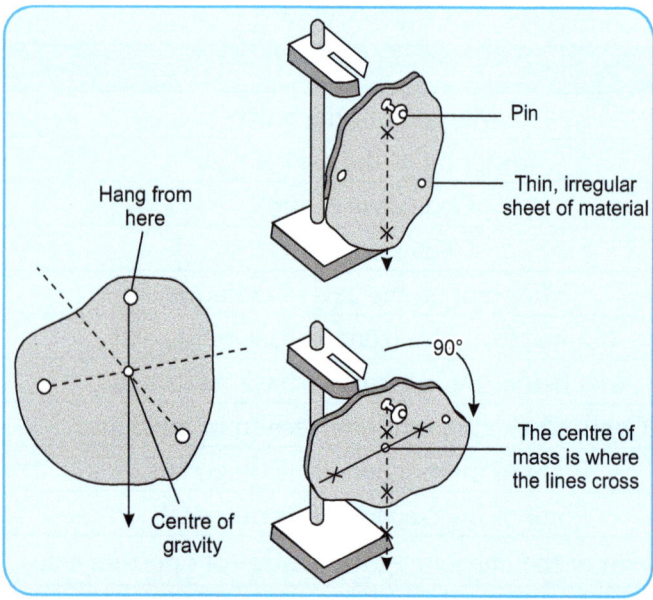

Fig. 1.16. : Centre of gravity of an irregular lamina.

ILLUSTRATIVE EXAMPLES

1. A rigid body is pivoted at a point. A force of 30 dyne acts on it at a distance of 65 cm from the pivot. Calculate the moment of force.

   Solution : Given F = 30 dyne, r = 65 cm
   Moment of force = Force × Distance
   $$F \times r = 30 \times 65 = 1{,}950 \text{ dyne cm}$$

2. A force of 60 N produces a moment of force of 12 N m at a point on a rigid body. Calculate the distance between point of application of force and the turning point.

   Solution : Given F = 60 N, moment of force = 12 N m
   Let r be the distance of point of application of force from the turning point.
   Moment of force = F × r
   i.e.   12 = 60 × r
   ∴ r = 12/60 = 0.2 m

3. A couple of 12 N force acts on a rigid body such that arm of couple is 60 cm. Calculate the moment of couple in SI system.

   Solution : Given F = 12 N, arm of couple = 60 cm = 0.6 m
   Moment of couple = F × Arm of couple
   = 12 × 0.6 = 7.2 N m

4. Calculate the resultant moment of the given body. In which direction will the turning effect be ?

   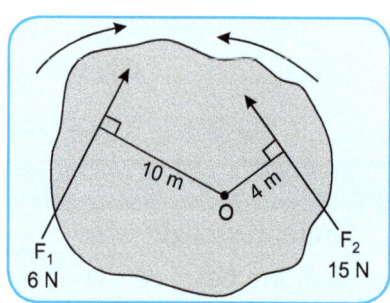

   Solution : From the figure, force F_1 will produce clockwise moment whereas force F_2 will produce anticlockwise moment.
   Clockwise moment = $-F_1 \times r = -6 \times 10 = -60$ N m
   Anticlockwise moment = $F_2 \times r = 15 \times 4 = 60$ N m
   Resultant moment = Anticlockwise moment + Clockwise moment = 60 − 60 = 0
   As the resultant moment is zero, the body will not turn.

5. A metre scale is balanced at its midpoint by suspending two weights A and B of magnitude 50 gf and 25 gf as shown in the figure. Find the

mark on the scale from where the weight B is suspended.

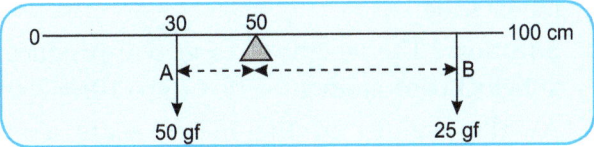

Solution : Given $W_1 = 50$ gf, from the figure, $l_1 = 50$ cm $- 30$ cm $= 20$ cm, $W_2 = 25$ gf.
According to the principle of moments, we have
$$W_1 \times l_1 = W_2 \times l_2$$
i.e. $\qquad 50 \times 20 = 25 \times l_2$
∴ $\qquad l_2 = 1{,}000/25 = 40$ cm

This is the distance of point B from the midpoint of the scale.
Thus, the mark on the scale from where point B is suspended is $50 + 40 = 90$ cm.

6. A uniform metre scale is balanced on a wedge placed under its 40 cm mark at point O. At points A and B, weights of magnitude 60 gf and 20 gf, respectively, are suspended. The scale is balanced by suspending a weight W at the point C. Calculate the value of weight W.

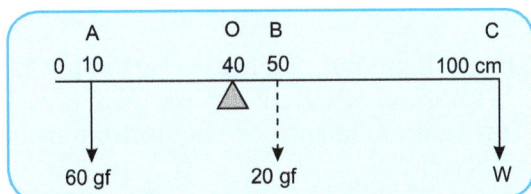

Solution : From the figure, the weight at point A will produce anticlockwise moment whereas the weights at point B and C will produce clockwise moments.
Anticlockwise moment
$\qquad = 60$ gf $\times (40 - 10)$ cm
$\qquad = 1{,}800$ gf cm
Clockwise moment
$\qquad = 20$ gf $\times (50-40)$ cm $+ W$ gf $\times (100-40)$ cm
$\qquad = 200$ gf cm $+ 60W$ gf cm
According to the principle of moments, we know
Clockwise moment $=$ Anticlockwise moment
$\qquad 60W + 200 = 1{,}800$
i.e. $\qquad 60W = 1{,}600$
∴ $\qquad W = 1{,}600/60 = 26.66$ gf

7. The handle of a spanner is 25 cm long and can tighten a nut if a force of 200 N is applied. If the magnitude of force applied is 120 N, what is the length of the handle required to tighten the nut?
Solution : Given $l_1 = 25$ cm $= 0.25$ m, $F_1 = 200$ N, $F_2 = 120$ N
Let l_2 be the length of the handle required to tighten the nut.
From the first case,
Moment of force $= F_1 \times l_1 = 200 \times 0.25 = 50$ N m
In the second case,
$\qquad$ Moment of force $= F_2 \times l_2$
i.e. $\qquad 50 = 120 \times l_2$
∴ $\qquad l_2 = 120/50 = 2.4$ m

8. In the figure given below, two forces each of magnitude 5 N are acting at points P and Q separated by a distance of 20 cm in opposite directions. Calculate the resultant moment of the two forces at point (a) P, (b) Q and (c) O, situated exactly at the middle of the two forces.

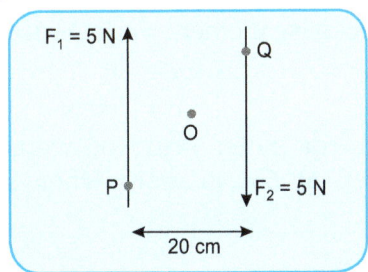

Solution : From the given figure, $F_1 = 5$ N, $F_2 = 5$ N, $r = 20$ cm $= 0.2$ m
(a) Moment of force F_1 at point P $= 0$ (because perpendicular distance of line of action of F_1 from point P is zero)
Moment of force F_2 at point P $= 5$ N $\times 0.2$ m $= 1$ N m
Total moment of force at point P
$\qquad = 1$ N m clockwise
(b) Moment of force F_1 at point
$\qquad Q = 5$ N $\times 0.2$ m $= 1$ N m
Moment of force F_2 at point Q $= 0$ (because perpendicular distance of line of action of F_2 from point Q is zero)
Total moment of force at point Q $= 1$ N m clockwise.
(c) Perpendicular distance of point O from either of the forces $= (1/2) \times 20 = 10$ cm $= 0.1$ m
Moment of force F_1 at point O $= 5 \times 0.1 = 0.5$ N m
Moment of force F_2 at point O $= 5 \times 0.1 = 0.5$ N m
Total moment of force at point O $= 1$ N m clockwise

9. The figure below shows a balanced see-saw that is 4 m long and pivoted at the centre. A force of 40 N is applied at the end of the see-saw and another force F is applied at a distance of 1.6 m from the opposite end on the other side of the pivot. Calculate the force F.

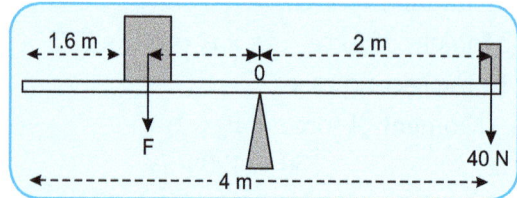

Solution : The pivot is at the centre of 4 m long see-saw, *i.e.* at 2 m point.
The force F will produce anticlockwise moment
$$= F \times (2 - 1.6) \text{ m} = F \times 0.4$$
The force 40 N will produce clockwise moment
$$= 40 \times (4 - 2) \text{ m} = 80 \text{ N m}$$
As the see-saw is balanced, we know
Anticlockwise moment = Clockwise moment
i.e. $\qquad F \times 0.4 = 80$
∴ $\qquad F = 200 \text{ N}$

10. A uniform meter scale of weight 50 gf is balanced at 60 cm mark when a weight of 15 gf is suspended at its 10 cm mark. Where must a weight of 100 gf be suspended to balance the meter scale.

Solution : The weight of 15 gf will produce an anticlockwise moment $= 15 \times (60 - 10) = 750$ gf
As the weight of the metre scale acts at its midpoint (*i.e.* 50 m), the anticlockwise moment produced by the weight of the scale
$$= 50 \times (60 - 50) = 500 \text{ gf}.$$
Total anticlockwise moment
$$= 750 + 500 = 1,250 \text{ gf}$$
Let x be the point where the 100 gf weight is suspended. It would lie on the other side of the pivot and will produce a clockwise moment.
Clockwise moment $= 100 \times (x - 60)$
In a balanced scale, we know
Clockwise moment = Anticlockwise moment
i.e. $\qquad 100 (x - 60) = 1,250$
$\qquad 100 x = 1,250 + 6,000 = 7,250$
∴ $\qquad x = 72.50 \text{ cm}$

Thus, the weight of 100 gf must be suspended from 72.50 cm mark of the meter scale to balance it.

EXERCISE 1(A)

1. What is meant by rotational motion? How is it different from translational motion?
2. Give few examples of rotational motion.
3. What is meant by the term 'moment of a force'?
4. What is the S.I. unit of the moment of force ?
5. Is moment of a force scalar or a vector quantity?
6. Name the factors affecting the turning effect of a body.
7. What is the expression for calculating the moment of force about a point?
8. Keeping the magnitude of the force applied constant, how will you increase and decrease the turning effect of a force about a given axis of rotation?
9. State the direction of a torque.
10. State the gravitational units of torque.
11. If the moment of force is assigned a negative sign, then will the turning tendency of the force be clockwise or anticlockwise?
    Ans : Clockwise
12. Will a door open if a force is applied on its hinges?
13. Why is the handle of a door provided at its free end away from the hinges?
14. If one light and one heavy person are to sit on a see-saw, what should be their positions to maintain a balance or equilibrium around the fulcrum?
    Ans : The heavier person needs to sit closer to the fulcrum as compared to the lighter person, on the opposite side.
15. Which of these would be easier to turn : a steering wheel of small diameter and a steering wheel of large diameter?
    Ans : Large diameter
16. Why does a wrench has a long handle?
17. In the digram given below, a force F is applied on a bicycle tyre at two different points as shown in figure A and B. Which of these wheels will have a more turning effect? If the two wheels need to have equal turning effect, how should the force be changed ?

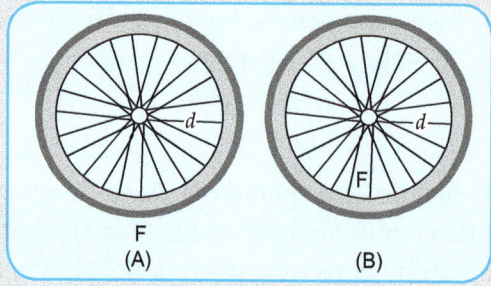

Ans : Wheel A, as the perpendicular distance between the turning point and point of application of force is more. To have the same turning effect, the magnitude of force needs to be increased on wheel B

18. In the figure below, A, B, C and D are forces of equal magnitudes around a point O. The distances of forces A, B, C and D from point O are 3 cm, 7 cm, 1.5 cm and 4.5 cm, respectively. Among these forces,
    (a) Which force has the greatest moment about point O?
    (b) Which force has the smallest moment about point O?

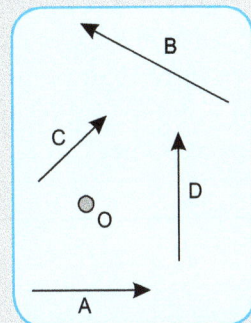

Ans : (a) Force B, due to maximum perpendicular distance, (b) Force C, due to least perpendicular distance

19. What is meant by the term 'couple'?
20. Give two examples of couple action.
21. Explain the action of couple as applied on a steering wheel of a car.
22. Define moment of couple. What are its units?
23. Derive an expression for moment of couple.
24. Define equilibrium.
25. What are the two types of equilibrium?
26. State the two conditions necessary for a body to be in equilibrium.
27. Give two examples each of static and dynamic equilibrium.
28. State the principle of moments. Name a device that works on this principle.
29. Describe an experiment to verify the principle of moments.
30. What is meant by the term 'centre of gravity of a body'?
31. On what factor does the position of the centre of gravity of a body depend?
32. Where is the centre of gravity of a uniform ring situated?
33. The position of centre of gravity of a body remains unchanged even when the body is deformed. Is this statement true or false?
    Ans : False
34. Where does the position of centre of gravity lie for (a) a circular lamina and (b) a triangular lamina?
35. Give an example of a body where the centre of gravity does not lie within the material of the body.
36. In the figure given below, there are three bodies of different shapes. On each diagram, draw lines to indicate the position of centre of gravity.

37. How will you determine the centre of gravity for an irregular lamina?
38. In a beam balance when the beam is balanced in a horizontal position, it is in .... equilibrium.
    Ans : Static

MULTIPLE CHOICE QUESTIONS

1. Which of these moments is considered negative?
   (a) Anticlockwise moment
   (b) Clockwise moment
   (c) Both of these
   (d) None of these
   Ans : (b)

2. The unit of moment of couple is :
   (a) N   (b) N m
   (c) N m^{-1} (d) N m^2
   Ans : (b)

3. When a body is in equilibrium
   (a) Sum of anticlockwise moments > Sum of clockwise moments
   (b) Sum of anticlockwise moments < Sum of clockwise moments
   (c) Sum of anticlockwise moments = Sum of clockwise moments
   (d) None of the above
   Ans : (c)

4. A couple constitutes :
   (a) A pair of equal and opposite forces whose lines of action are same
   (b) A pair of equal and like forces whose lines of action are same
   (c) A pair of equal and opposite forces whose lines of action are not same
   (d) A pair of equal and like forces whose lines of action are not same
   Ans : (c)

5. The centre of gravity of a hollow sphere lies :
   (a) at its topmost point
   (b) at its lowermost point
   (c) at any point on its surface
   (d) at its geometric centre
   Ans : (d)

NUMERICAL PROBLEMS

1. A force of 5 N is applied at a perpendicular distance of 0.2 m from a pivoted point. Calculate the moment of force.
   Ans : 1 N m
2. The moment of force of 8 N about a fixed point is 4 N m. Calculate the distance of the point from the line of action of force.
   Ans : 0.5 m
3. A nut can be opened by a wrench of length 50 cm with a force of 120 N. If a smaller force of 75 N is applied, what will the required length of the handle of the wrench?
   Ans : 80 cm
4. In the figure, a bicycle wheel of circumference 8 m is shown. A force of 4 N is applied at the point P in the direction shown. Calculate the moment of force at (a) point O and (b) point Q.

   Ans : (a) 5.09 m in anticlockwise direction, (b) 10.18 m in anticlockwise direction.
5. Two forces of equal magnitude are acting on a uniform bar AB of length 6 m, which is pivoted in the centre as shown in the figure. Determine the magnitude of moment of force (a) at the end A, (b) at the end B and (c) total moment of couple.

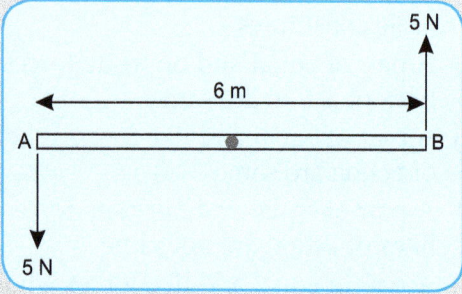

   Ans : (a) 15 N m anticlockwise, (b) 15 N m anticlockwise, (c) 30 N m anticlockwise
6. Two forces each of 5 N act vertically upwards and downwards, respectively, on the two ends of a uniform metre rule that is placed at its midpoint as shown in the diagram. Determine the magnitude of the resultant moment of these forces about the midpoint.

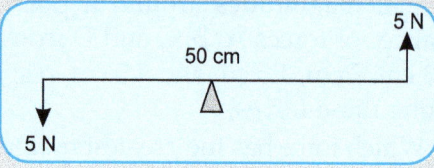

   Ans : 2.5 N m in anticlockwise direction.
7. Two forces $F_1 = 5$ N and $F_2 = 8$ N are acting at points P and Q of a rod pivoted at a point O such that OP = 8 m and OQ = 2 m. Calculate the (a) moment of force F_1 at point O, (b) moment of force F_2 at point O and (c) total moment of the two forces at point O.

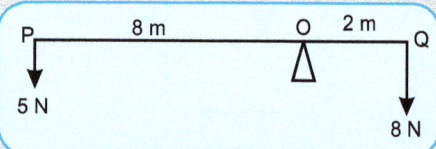

   Ans : (a) 40 N m anticlockwise, (b) 16 N m clockwise, (c) 24 N m anticlockwise.
8. Two equal and unlike parallel forces of magnitude 12 N act on a rigid body, such that the moment of couple is 10 N m. Calculate the arm of couple.
   Ans : 0.833 m
9. A nut is opened by a wrench of length 20 cm. If the least force required is 2 N, find the moment of force needed to loosen the nut.
   Ans : 0.4 N m
10. A steering wheel with a radius of 0.3 m is rotated anticlockwise by applying two forces each of magnitude 8 N. Calculate the moment of the couple applied.
    Ans : 4.8 N m
11. A uniform metre scale is pivoted at its midpoint. A weight of 20 gf is suspended from end of the scale. Where should a weight of 50 gf be suspended to keep the scale horizontal.
    Ans : At a distance 20 cm from the midpoint
12. A uniform metre scale is balanced at 60 cm mark, when weights of 5 gf and 40 gf are suspended from 10 cm mark and 80 cm mark, respectively. Calculate the weight of the meter scale.
    Ans : 55 gf

13. A uniform metre scale weighing 100 gf is pivot at a point O, a 25 cm mark. A 80 gf weight is hung from 10 cm mark and a 30 gf weight is hung from 70 cm mark as shown in the figure. Calculate (a) the total anticlockwise moment about point O, (b) the total clockwise moment about point O and (c) the net resultant moment.

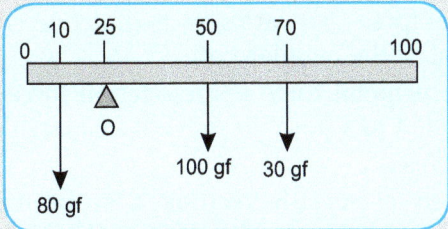

Ans : (a) 1,200 gf cm, (b) 3,850 gf cm, (c) 2,650 gf cm anticlockwise.

14. A uniform metre scale of mass 50 g is balanced on the edge of a knife at mark 60 cm by suspending an unknown mass at the 80 cm mark. Find the value of the unknown mass.
Ans : 25 g

15. A see-saw of 8 m long is balanced in the middle. Two children of mass 30 kgf and 40 kgf are sitting on the same side of the fulcrum at a distance of 1.5 m and 3.5 m, respectively, from the fulcrum. At what distance must an adult person of weight 60 kgf sit from the fulcrum so as to balance the see-saw?
Ans : 3.08 m from fulcrum on the opposite side of children.

16. A uniform metre scale of weight 20 gf is pivoted at its zero mark. Calculate (a) the moment of force that depresses the scale and (b) what would be the magnitude of least force applied on it to make it horizontal?
Ans : (a) 1,000 gf cm, (b) 10 gf force upwards at the 100 cm mark.

17. A uniform metre scale can be balanced at the 70 cm mark when a mass of 0.05 kg is hung from the 94 cm mark. (a) Draw the diagram of the arrangement and (b) find the mass of the metre scale.
Ans : (b) 0.06 kg.

18. A boy of mass 30 kg is sitting at a distance of 2 m from the middle of a see-saw. Where should a boy of mass 40 kg sit so as to balance the see-saw ?
Ans : 1.5 m from the middle on the other side.

(B) UNIFORM CIRCULAR MOTION

1.6 UNIFORM CIRCULAR MOTION

Circular motion is the simplest type of rotational motion. It is commonly seen in both microscopic and macroscopic systems. Motion of the electron, planetary motion and rotation of tyres are common examples of circular motion. It is a type of motion exhibited by a particle or set of particles moving around a fixed point at a constant distance from that point. Circular motion should not be interpreted as motion of a particle in a perfect circle; for instance, elliptical motion and rounding a curve in a car are also examples of circular motion.

The motion of a body or particle is said to be uniform circular motion when it moves with a constant speed in a circular path.

In a uniform circular motion, the particle travels equal distances in equal intervals of time along the circular path. Although the speed remains constant, its direction changes continuously at each point of the circular path. This implies that the velocity of the particle changes continuously and thus there is acceleration in circular motion.

The change in direction of motion of particle(s) in a circular path at each point can be demonstrated by a simple experiment.

Experiment :

Take a thread and tie a small piece of stone at one of its ends. Hold the other end of the thread and move it in a horizontal circular path. Now, release the stone. It is observed that the stone moves in a straight line.

If the stone is released at different positions in this experiment, it is observed that every time when the stone is released, it moves in a straight line in a direction perpendicular or tangential to the path at the position where it is released (Fig. 1.17).

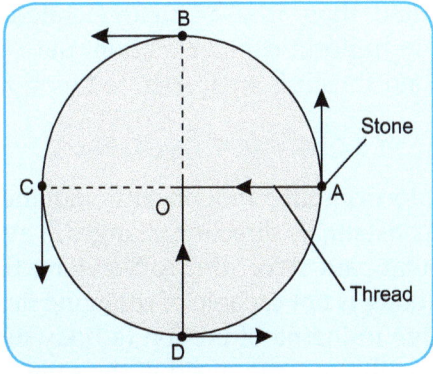

Fig. 1.17 : Uniform circular motion.

Direction of velocity at any instant in a circular path :

Suppose a particle is moving in a clockwise direction in a circular path as shown in the Fig. 1.18. Let its speed be v. As the motion of the particle is uniform, it will cover distances AB, BC, CD and DA, which represent each quarter of a circle in equal intervals of time. Let T be the total time taken by the particle to cover one round of circular path and let t be the time taken to cover each quarter of the circle. Thus, time taken to cover the distances AB, BC, CD and DA is $t = \dfrac{T}{4}$.

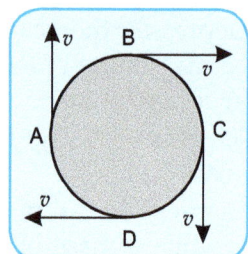

Fig. 1.18 : Direction of velocity at any instant in a circular path.

The direction of motion of the particle is different at each point and at any given point, it is represented by the tangent drawn at that point of the circular path. As shown in Fig. 1.18, at the point A, the direction of motion of particle is towards north. Once the particle covers one-quarter of the circle (*i.e.* distance AB), its direction of motion at point B is towards east. After completing another quarter of circle, or in total the distance of half circle, the particle is at point C, where the direction of its motion is towards south. Now, the particle covers another quarter, or in total three-quarters of the circular path, and reaches point D. Here the direction of motion of the particle is towards west.

Even though the speed of the particle is constant, velocity changes, (due to continuous change in direction). Therefore, the motion along the circular path is said to be accelerated.

NOTE
In uniform linear motion, the velocity of a body is constant and thus, it is an unaccelerated motion, whereas in uniform circular motion, the velocity is variable and thus it is an accelerated motion.

1.7 CENTRIPETAL FORCE

In a uniform circular motion, although the speed of a body is constant, its direction changes at every point in the circular path. According to Newton's first law of motion, a body is not capable of changing its direction by itself due to inertia of motion (a body tends to be in motion with the same speed in the same direction) unless an external force is applied on it. Thus, the body moving in a circular motion must be under the action of some force, which is termed as *centripetal force*.

The force which acts on a body moving in a circular path and is directed towards the centre around which body is moving is known as centripetal force.

The word 'centripetal' means 'centre seeking'. The centripetal force acts perpendicular to the direction of motion of the body at all points so that there is no component in the direction of motion to change its speed. The force, being perpendicular to the circle at all points, *acts along the radius towards the centre*. The centripetal force also varies as its direction changes at each point of the circular path.

The centripetal force is an external force that has to be applied to a body to move it in a circular path.

Examples :

1. When a person swings a stone tied with a thread in a circular path, the thread needs to be continuously pulled inwards. The tension developed in the thread held by the hand provides the centripetal force (Fig. 1.19). If the thread breaks or is released, the stone immediately leaves the circular path and moves along the tangent to the circular path from that particular point. This happens due to the fact that as the tension in the thread vanishes, the centripetal force also vanishes.

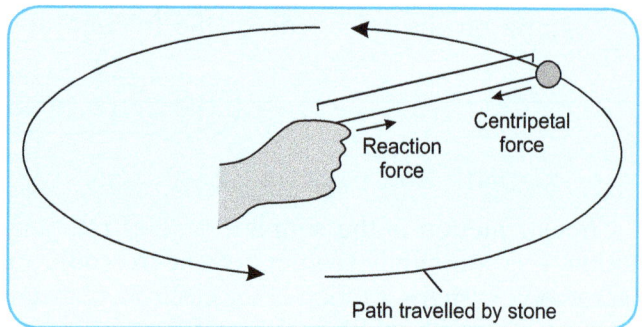

Fig. 1.19 : Centripetal force.

2. The centripetal force required for movement of an electron around the nucleus in an atom is exerted by the electrostatic force of attraction between negatively charged electrons and positively charged nucleus.

3. The planets revolving around the Sun or the satellites revolving around the planets receive centripetal force from the force of gravitational attraction between the two bodies.

4. A car travelling on a road has three forces acting on it. The gravitational force due to the weight of the car that gets balanced by the normal reaction force exerted by the road on the car. The third force is the force of friction that the road exerts on the wheels of a car. When a car makes a turn around a curved road, it is this force of friction acting upon the wheels of the car that provides the centripetal force required for taking a smooth turn.

1.8 CENTRIFUGAL FORCE

While the centripetal force acts towards the centre of a circular path, there is a force that acts in its opposite direction.

The force which appears to act on a body moving in a circular path and is directed away from the centre around which body is moving is known as centrifugal force.

Even though the magnitude of the centrifugal force is same as that of the centripetal force and its direction is opposite to that of the centripetal force, it is not a reaction force to the centripetal force.

In fact, *centrifugal force is not a real force; it is an apparent force or fictitious force or virtual force.* It is an apparent force because it is not a part of an interaction but is a result of rotation. It is not a reaction force and is considered only to understand a particular type of motion (*i.e.* circular motion). This can be illustrated by the following examples.

Examples :

1. When a person inside a car is rounding a curve, it appears to him that all the loose contents of the car are being propelled outwards by some force, whereas to an observer standing outside the car, they are merely continuing in a straight line. This non-existent outward force as seen by an observer in a rotating frame of reference is called centrifugal force.
2. A merry-go-round has a big circular platform that rotates on its own axis. Children sitting on the merry-go-round experience an outward force as it moves along a circular path.

Consider one end of a string tied to a ball and the other end of the string tied at the centre of a merry-go-round.

When the merry-go-round is at stationary, the ball also appears stationary and the string is loose. As the platform of merry-go-round starts rotating, the string becomes tight due to the tension developed in it. If a person is standing on the platform of the merry-go-round, it appears to him that the ball is stationary, whereas to a person who is standing on the ground at some distance from the merry-go-round, it appears that the ball is moving in a circular path (Fig. 1.20).

Explanation :

For the person standing on the platform of the merry-go-round, two forces act on the ball : (a) centripetal force, the tension in the string towards the centre of the circular platform, and (b) the centrifugal force, away from the centre.

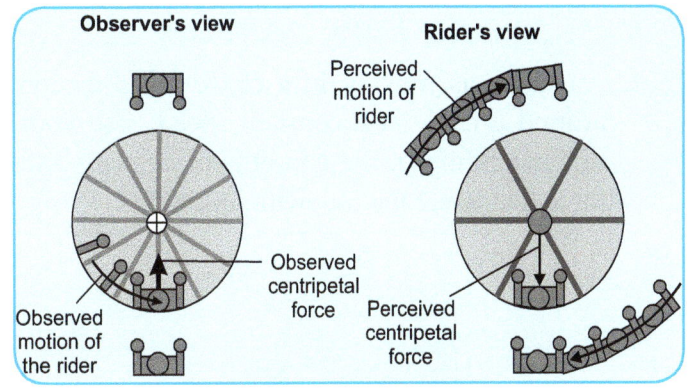

Fig. 1.20 : Centrifugal force.

These two forces are equal and opposite; hence, the net force on the ball is zero and the ball appears stationary.

However, for the person standing on the ground, only one force is visible; which is, the centripetal force due to the tension in the string, and thus to him, the ball appears to be rotating in a circular path.

Now, if the string is cut when the ball is at a particular position, there is no longer a force of tension in the string. To the person standing in the ground, it appears that the ball is moving in a straight-line path; it is a tangent to the point where the ball lies on the circular path. However, to the person standing on the platform, the ball appears to be moving radially away from him but always remains in front of him as his own position changes with the rotation of the platform. For this person, the centripetal force has ceased but the centrifugal force still acts on the ball along the radius of the platform in a direction away from its centre.

1.9 DIFFERENCE BETWEEN CENTRIPETAL AND CENTRIFUGAL FORCE

Centripetal force	Centrifugal force
Centripetal force is a force which acts on a body moving in a circular path and is directed towards the centre around which body is moving.	Centrifugal force is a force which appears to act on a body moving in a circular path and is directed away from the centre around which body is moving.
It is a real force.	It is an imaginary or virtual force.
It is an inward force.	It is an outward force.
Examples of centripetal force are satellite orbiting a planet.	Examples of centrifugal force are : passenger in a turning car feels as if they are pushed outward, riders on a rotating amusement park ride feel pressed to wall.

ILLUSTRATIVE EXAMPLES

1. An object is moving in a clockwise direction around a circle at a constant speed. Use your understanding of the concepts of velocity and force to answer the following questions :

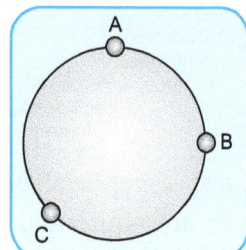

   (a) How will you represent the direction of the force vector when the object is located at point A on the circle?
   (b) How will you represent the direction of the force vector when the object is located at point C on the circle?
   (c) How will you represent the direction of the velocity vector when the object is located at point B on the circle?
   (d) How will you represent the direction of the velocity vector when the object is located at point C on the circle?

   Solution : An object moving in a circle is acted upon by centripetal force that is directed towards the centre and the direction of velocity of the object at any point on the path is given by a tangent drawn at that point.

   (a) The force vector is directed inwards to the circle, which would be downwards when at point A.

   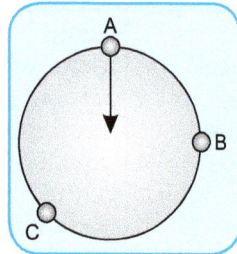

   (b) The force vector is directed inwards, which would be up and to the right when the object is at point C.

   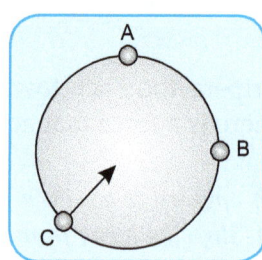

   (c) The velocity vector is directed tangent to the circle, which would be downwards when at point B.

   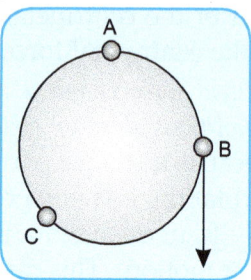

   (d) The velocity is directed tangentially, which would be upwards and leftwards when at point C.

   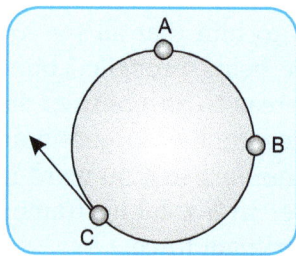

2. Consider a smooth circular table rotating about a fixed vertical axis passing its centre. A person A is sitting at the centre of the disc, holding a string tied with a stone at its other end. Another observer B is standing on the ground at some distance from the table. What will be the observations of (a) person A and (b) person B?

   Solution : (a) To the person A, the stone will appear stationary. The person A will feel two forces acting on the stone : (i) centripetal force, the tension in the string inwards towards the centre of the circular table, and (ii) the centrifugal force, away from the centre. These two forces being equal and opposite, thus, the resultant is zero.

   (b) The person B will observe that the stone is rotating in a circular path due to the centripetal force provided by the tension in the string.

EXERCISE 1(B)

1. What is meant by uniform circular motion? Give example.
2. Why is uniform circular motion an accelerated motion?
3. Which of these remains constant in uniform circular motion : speed, velocity or both?
4. Demonstrate the change of direction of motion of a particle moving in a circular path.

5. With the help of a diagram, show the direction of velocity of a particle moving in a circular path at any instant.
6. How is the uniform circular motion different from uniform linear motion?
7. Is it possible to have an accelerated motion with a constant speed? Explain.
8. Name the force required for uniform circular motion. State its direction.
9. What is meant by centripetal force?
10. What is the source of centripetal force when a piece of stone tied to a string is whirled in a horizontal circle?
11. Explain the motion of a planet around the sun in a circular path.
12. Explain the source of centripetal force for the following :
    (a) Motion of Moon around the Earth.
    (b) Electrons revolving outside the nucleus.
    (c) A car taking a turn on a curved road.
13. What is meant by centrifugal force?
14. State one similarity and one dissimilarity between centripetal and centrifugal force.
15. With reference to their direction of action, how does a centripetal force differ from a centrifugal force?
16. Why is centrifugal force not considered as real force?
17. Explain the concept of centrifugal force with an example.
18. A stone of mass 'm' is rotated in a circular path with a uniform speed by tying a strong string with the help of your hand. Answer the following questions :
    (a) Is the stone moving with a uniform or variable speed ?
    (b) Is the stone moving with a uniform acceleration ? In which direction does the acceleration act ?
    (c) What kind of force acts on the hand and state its direction ?

MULTIPLE CHOICE QUESTIONS

1. Which of these is the cause of uniform circular motion?
   (a) Centripetal force   (b) Centrifugal force
   (c) Both of these   (d) None of these
   Ans : (a)

2. In which of these motions can the speed be constant?
   (a) Linear motion
   (b) Uniform circular motion
   (c) Both of these
   (d) None of these
   Ans : (c)

2

WORK, POWER AND ENERGY

LEARNING OUTCOMES

- Concept of work, expression and units
- Positive, zero and negative works
- Concept of power, expression and units
- Concept of energy, expression and units
- Various forms of energy
- Forms of mechanical energy : kinetic energy and potential energy
- Conservation of energy
- Transformation of energy from one form to another

(A) WORK, POWER AND ENERGY

2.1 WORK

In physics, the term 'work' has a distinct meaning than it does in everyday usage. For example, a layman cannot distinguish the work done by a computer programmer (who is typing on the keyboard) and a mason (who is laying blocks of bricks for a building), because for him it is just 'some' kind of work.

In physics, work is said to be done only when an applied force causes displacement of a body in the direction of the applied force. In the above example, a programmer exerts only a small force on the keys of a keyboard, creating only a small displacement, and thus, a little work is done, whereas a mason exerts a larger force on the concrete bricks and moves them to a significant distance, and hence, relatively more work is done.

However, if a body under the influence of a force produces no motion, then the work done is said to be zero. For example, when a person pushes a wall with all the force, the wall does not get displaced (*i.e.* there is no motion) and hence no work is done. Similarly, when a person holds a heavy bucket of water, the work done is zero because there is no displacement of the bucket. Thus,

Work is said to be done only when a force applied to a body causes displacement in the direction of the applied force (Fig. 2.1).

Example :

Pushing a table, pushing a cart, a player kicking a football, a car moving on a road, walking on the stairs and so on.

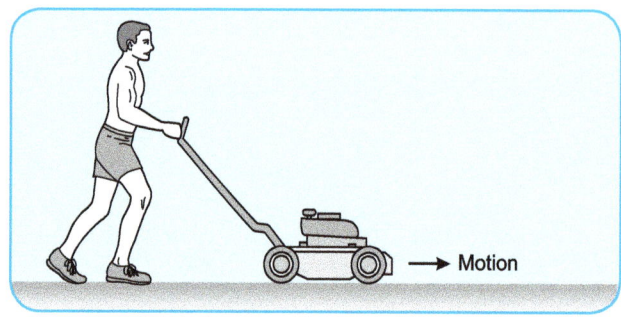

Fig. 2.1 : Work is done while pushing a cart.

Expression for Work Done

The amount of work done by a force depends on the following two factors :

1. The magnitude and direction of the applied force : Work done by a body is directly proportional to the amount of force applied; *i.e.*, greater the applied force, greater is the work done.

WORK, POWER AND ENERGY   31

2. The displacement it produces : Work done by a body is directly proportional to the displacement in the direction of the applied force; *i.e.*, greater the displacement of a body in the direction of the applied force, greater is the work done.

Let there be two forces, say F_A and F_B, such that $F_A > F_B$. Consider these forces when acting on two different bodies produce same amount of displacement; then, the work done by force F_A is greater than the work done by force F_B.

Similarly, if there is a force F that produces displacements S_A and S_B when acting on two different bodies A and B, such that $S_A > S_B$, then the work done by force F on body A is more than that on body B.

The amount of work done by a force is the product of force and the displacement caused by the force in the direction of its application.

Consider a constant force F that is applied on a body when it is at position '*a*', as shown in Fig. 2.2. Due to this force, the body gets displaced to position '*b*' in the direction of the force.

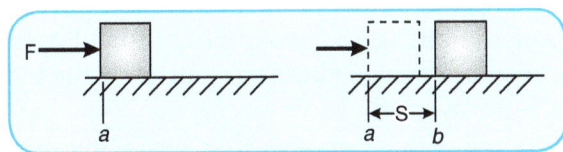

Fig. 2.2 : Work done by a force.

Let this displacement from *a* to *b* be equal to *S*; then, the work done is given by

$$W = F \times S \qquad ....(2.1)$$

In the above equation (2.1) if S = 0, then W = 0; *i.e.*, *if a body does not move under the action of applied force, then no work is done.*

Work is a *scalar* quantity.

Sometimes, the applied force does not cause the displacement of a body in its own direction, but in a direction other than the direction of the force. To determine the amount of work done by force in such a case, either of the two components needs to be considered : (1) the component of displacement of the body in the direction of force or (2) the component of force in the direction of displacement of the body.

1. Component of displacement of the body in the direction of force : Let F be a constant force such that it displaces a body from position A to position B on an inclined surface (Fig. 2.3). The point of application of force moves from A to B along the direction AC. Let the displacement of the body be S from A to B, which is at an angle θ to the direction of force. Let BC be a perpendicular line drawn from point B on AC to find the component of displacement in the direction of the force (*i.e.* AC).

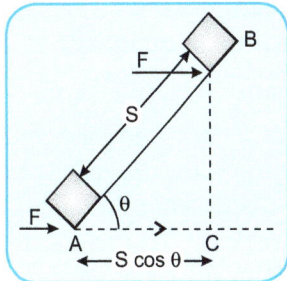

Fig. 2.3 : Work done by a force when the component of displacement of a body is in the direction of force.

Now, in the right/angled triangle ΔACB,

$$\cos \theta = \frac{\text{Base}}{\text{Hypotenuse}} = \frac{AC}{AB} = \frac{AC}{S}$$

or $\qquad AC = S \cos \theta$

We know, work done W = Force F × Component of displacement in the direction of force.

or, $\qquad W = F \times AC$

Hence, $\qquad W = F \times S \cos \theta \qquad ....(2.2)$

2. Component of force in the direction of displacement of the body : Let DA represent the magnitude and direction of force *F* acting on the body that gets displaced from A to B on an inclined surface when the force is applied (Fig. 2.4). The component of force acting in the direction of displacement of the body (*i.e.* AB) is given by EA.

Now, in the right-angled triangle ΔDEA,

$$\cos \theta = \frac{\text{Base}}{\text{Hypotenuse}} = \frac{EA}{DA} = \frac{EA}{F}$$

or, $\qquad EA = F \cos \theta$

Work done W = Component of force in the direction of displacement × Displacement S.

or, $\qquad W = EA \times AB$

Hence, $\qquad W = F \cos \theta \times S \qquad ....(2.3)$

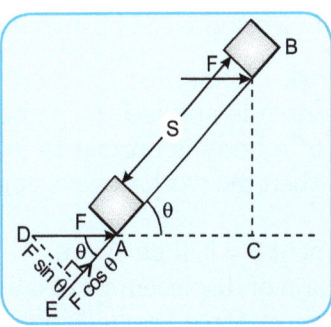

Fig. 2.4 : Work done by a force when the component of force is in the direction of displacement of the body.

Thus, work done W is equal to the product of
1. Magnitude of force F,
2. Magnitude of displacement S and
3. Cosine of angle θ between the directions of force F and displacement S.

Work done is a *scalar* quantity.

Positive, Zero and Negative Work

Work done by a body can be positive, negative or zero, depending upon the angle between the direction of force and the displacement.

1. Positive work : If the displacement of the body is in the direction of the force, or if the angle between the force and the displacement vectors is an acute angle (*i.e.* 0° < θ < 90°), then the work done is positive (Fig. 2.5).

When displacement occurs in the direction of force (*i.e.* θ = 0°), then cos θ = 1

∴   W = F × S

Examples :
(a) When a body of mass *m* falls freely from a height *h* under the force of gravity, then the displacement S of the body is in the direction of the force F, and the work done W by the force is given by
W = FS = *mgh* (as Force = Mass × Acceleration due to gravity)
(b) When a spring is stretched, the stretching force and expansion of spring are in the same direction.
(c) When a coolie or a porter lifts load from the ground, the exerted force, which is against the force of gravity, and the displacement of the load are in the upward direction.

Fig. 2.5 : The force acts in the direction of motion so the work done is positive here.

2. Zero work : If the displacement of a body is zero when a force is applied, or if the direction of displacement of a body is normal to the direction of force applied, then the work done is zero [Fig. 2.6 (a) and 2.6 (b)].

If displacement S = 0, then W = 0

If the direction of displacement of a body is normal to the direction of force applied, then θ = 90° and cos 90° = 0

Hence, W = 0

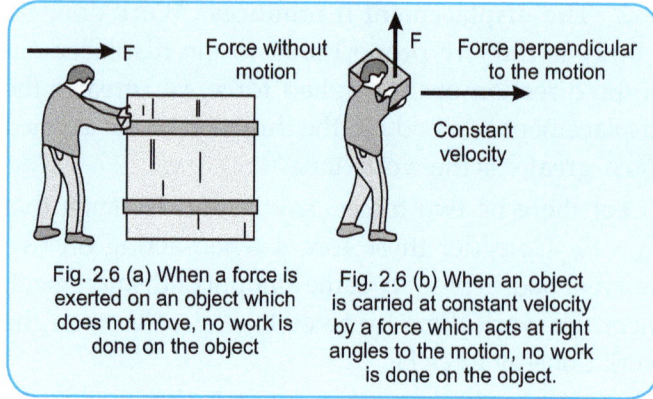

Fig. 2.6 (a) When a force is exerted on an object which does not move, no work is done on the object

Fig. 2.6 (b) When an object is carried at constant velocity by a force which acts at right angles to the motion, no work is done on the object.

Examples :
(a) When a coolie carrying a load on his head walks on a horizontal path, the force due to gravity acts vertically downwards while the displacement of the coolie is in the horizontal direction; *i.e.*, normal to the direction of the force. Thus, the work done is zero.
(b) In an oscillating simple pendulum, the displacement of the bob at any point on the arc is along the tangent drawn at that point, whereas the force due to the tension of the string is along the radius of the arc. Hence, the tension of the string is always perpendicular to the displacement, and the work done by the tension is always zero.
(c) When a body moves in a circular path, the centripetal force is directed towards the centre of the circular path and the displacement at any instant on the path is along the tangent to the path. Thus, the force always acts at right angles to the direction of the displacement of the body, and the work done is zero.

Also, in one complete rotation of the circular path, the total displacement is zero. Hence, the work done is also zero.

Thus, work done by Moon revolving around the Earth or by the Earth revolving around the Sun is zero.

3. Negative work : If the displacement of a body is in the direction opposite to the direction of force, then the work done is negative.

In this case, θ = 180° and cos 180 = –1

Hence,   W = – F × S

This occurs when a force tries to stop a body in motion or it opposes the motion of a body.

Examples :
(a) When a ball with mass *m* is thrown vertically upwards to a height *h*, the displacement of the ball is in the upward direction. It is opposed by the force due to gravity, which acts in the downward direction. Hence, work done is negative and is given by

$$W = -FS = -mgh$$

(b) When a force is applied to push a body on a horizontal surface, the motion of the box is opposed by the force of friction between the body and the surface. The force of friction and the displacement of the body are always in opposite direction, hence, the work done by the frictional force is negative.

(c) When two like charges, say both positives, are moved closer to each other, there occurs an electrostatic force of repulsion between them. The direction of this force is opposite to the direction of displacement of the two charges, and thus, the work done is negative.

2.2 FORCE VERSUS DISPLACEMENT GRAPH

We have, already considered constant force acting on a body. However, if the force is a variable, *i.e.*, if it changes with the displacement, then the work done by a body can be determined by plotting a force displacement graph, where displacement is on the X-axis and force is on the Y-axis. The work done by a body can be calculated by the area enclosed under the graph.

For example, in Fig. 2.7 (a), the area under the graph (*i.e.* the area of the triangle AOB) will give the amount of work done by the body. Similarly, in Fig. 2.7 (b), the total work done by the body can be calculated from the area of the rectangle OABD and the area of the triangle BCD.

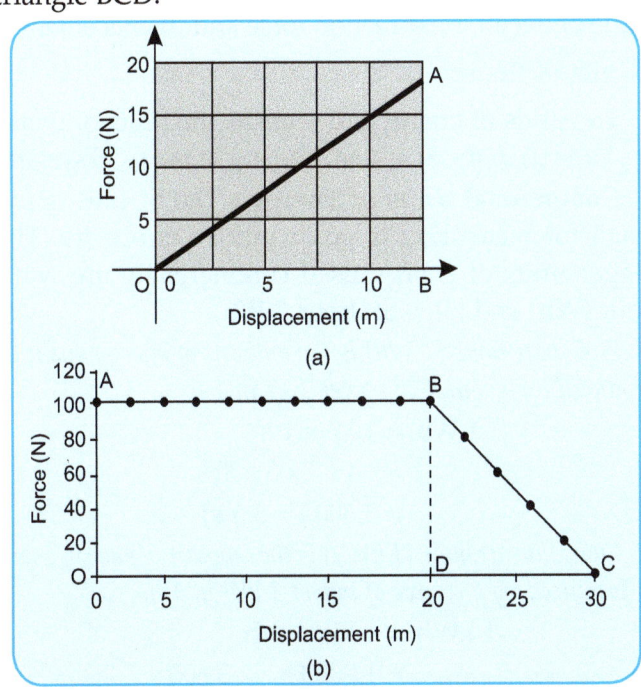

Fig. 2.7 : Force versus displacement graph.

A straight line parallel to the displacement axis implies that the force is constant.

2.3 WORK DONE BY THE FORCE OF GRAVITY AND AGAINST THE FORCE OF GRAVITY

1. When a body is thrown vertically downwards, it is under the influence of force due to gravity. Consider a body of mass *m* thrown vertically downwards from a height *h*. The force due to gravity on the body will be F = *mg* (*g* = acceleration due to gravity), which will act in the downward direction. The displacement S of the body is also in the downward direction; *i. e.*, in the direction of force. It is given as S = *h*.

Work done by the force of gravity
$$W = F \times S$$
or, $$W = mgh \qquad ....(2.4)$$

The work done by the force of gravity is equal for a person walking down the stairs from a certain height or coming down in an elevator from the same height.

2. When a body is thrown vertically upwards, the force of gravity acts against the direction of motion of the body. If the body with mass *m* is thrown vertically upwards through a height *h*, then

Work done by the force of gravity
$$W = -F \times S$$
$$W = -mgh \qquad ....(2.5)$$

The work done against the force of gravity is equal for a person walking up the stairs to a certain height or going up in an elevator to the same height.

NOTE

The work done against the force of gravity is $-mgh$.

Units of Work

We know Work = Force × Displacement
The SI unit of work is *joule* (J).
Thus, 1 joule = 1 newton × 1 metre
When a force of 1 N causes a displacement of 1 m in the direction of its application, the work done is said to be 1 J.

Some bigger units of work are kilojoule (kJ), megajoule (MJ) and gigajoule (GJ).
$$1 \text{ kJ} = 10^3 \text{ J}$$
$$1 \text{ MJ} = 10^6 \text{ J}$$
$$1 \text{ GJ} = 10^9 \text{ J}$$

The CGS unit of work is erg.
$$1 \text{ erg} = 1 \text{ dyne} \times 1 \text{ centimetre}$$
When a force of 1 dyne causes a displacement of 1 cm in the direction of its application, the work done is said to be 1 erg.

Relation between joule and erg

$$1 \text{ J} = 1 \text{ N} \times 1 \text{ m}$$
$$= 10^5 \text{ dyne} \times 10^2 \text{ cm}$$
$$= 10^7 \text{ erg}$$

2.4 POWER

Power is defined as the rate of doing work.

To understand the concept of power, consider two men A and B, each carrying a loaded suitcase from the ground floor to the fifth floor of a building by walking up the stairs. Assume that man A carries the suitcase in 5 min while man B does the same in 10 min. The work done by both men is same, but as man A does it in lesser time than man B, the power of man A is more than that of man B.

Thus, power of a source depends on two factors : (a) the amount of work done by the source and (b) the time taken by the source to do the work.

Expression for Power

If W is the work done in a time interval t, then

$$\text{Power} = \frac{\text{Work done}}{\text{Time taken}}$$

or, $\quad P = \dfrac{W}{t} \quad$ ....(2.6)

or, Power × Time = Work done.

Relation of Power with Force

Let a constant force F be applied on a body. Now, let the body be displaced through a distance S,

Then, we know W = F S

Now power is the rate of doing work. Therefore,

$$P = \frac{W}{t} = \frac{F \times S}{t}$$

∵ $\quad \dfrac{S}{t} = v$ (average velocity)

or $\quad P = F \times v$

Power is a *scalar* quantity.

Units of Power

SI system : Unit of power = Unit of work/Unit of time = J/s = watt

It is represented by the symbol W.

When a work of 1 J is done in 1 s, then the power is said to be 1 W (1 J s⁻¹).

Bigger units of power are kilowatt (kW), megawatt (MW) and gigawatt (GW).

$1 \text{ kW} = 10^3 \text{ W}$
$1 \text{ MW} = 10^6 \text{ W}$
$1 \text{ GW} = 10^9 \text{ W}$

Horse power (hp) : It is another bigger commercial unit of power and is used in auto industries and mechanical engineering.

$1 \text{ hp} = 746 \text{ W} = 0.746 \text{ kW}$

Smaller units of power are milliwatt (mW) and microwatt (μW).

$1 \text{ mW} = 10^{-3} \text{ W}$
$1 \text{ μW} = 10^{-6} \text{ W}$

CGS system : Unit of power = Unit of work/Unit of time = erg/s = erg s⁻¹.

Relation between the two units of power

$1 \text{ W} = 1 \text{ J s}^{-1} = 10^7 \text{ erg s}^{-1}$

2.5 ENERGY

The word 'energy' is commonly used in everyday life. Anybody who does work possesses energy.

Energy is defined as the capacity of a body to do work.

When work is done by a body, its energy decreases, whereas if work is done on a body, its energy increases. Thus, there is always a transfer of energy when work is done.

Example : When a striker hits a stationary carom coin, it sets the carom coin into motion. Here, work is done by the striker on the coin; *i.e.*, energy is transferred from the striker to the coin.

The total amount of work done by a body is numerically equal to its energy.

Energy is a *scalar* quantity.

Relation of Energy with Force

Since energy of a body is the amount of work done by it,

So, E = W = FS cos θ, where F is the force applied on the body, S is the displacement of the body and θ is the angle between the direction force and displacement.

Units of Energy

The units of energy are same as the units of work; *i.e.*, joule (J) in the SI system and erg in the CGS system.

Commercial units of energy : The SI unit is too small for measuring large quantities of energy. The bigger units of energy used commercially are watt-hour (Wh) and kilowatt hour (kWh).

One watt-hour (1 Wh) is the amount of energy spent or produced by a source of power 1 W in 1 h.

$$1 \text{ Wh} = 1 \text{ W} \times 1 \text{ h}$$
$$= 1 \text{ J s}^{-1} \times 3,600 \text{ s}$$
$$= 3,600 \text{ J} = 3.6 \text{ kJ}$$

One kilowatt hour (1 kWh) is the amount of energy spent or produced by a source of power 1 kW in 1 h.

$$1 \text{ kWh} = 1 \text{ kW} \times 1 \text{ h}$$
$$= 1,000 \text{ J s}^{-1} \times 3,600 \text{ s}$$
$$= 3.6 \times 10^6 \text{ J} = 3.6 \text{ MJ}$$

Often, 1 unit of electricity is commonly referred to as 1 kWh.

The commonly used unit of heat energy is calorie (cal).

One calorie (1 cal) is the heat energy required to raise the temperature of 1 g of water by 1 C.

$$1 \text{ cal} = 4.18 \text{ J or } 1 \text{ J} = 0.24 \text{ cal}$$

kilocalorie (kcal) is a bigger unit of heat energy.

$$1 \text{ kcal} = 1,000 \text{ cal} = 4,180 \text{ J}$$

The unit used for energy of atomic particles is electronvolt (eV).

One electronvolt (1 eV) is the energy gained by an electron when it is accelerated through a potential difference of 1 V.

$$1 \text{ eV} = \text{Charge on an electron} \times 1 \text{ V}$$
$$= 1.6 \times 10^{-9} \text{C} \times 1 \text{ V}$$

or $\quad 1 \text{ eV} = 1.6 \times 10^{-9} \text{ J}$

Difference between Work, Power and Energy

Work	Power	Energy
It is the product of force and displacement in the direction of force.	It is the rate of work done by a body.	It is the capacity of a body to do work.
It does not depend on time.	It depends on time.	It does not depend on time.
SI unit is joule (J).	SI unit is watt (W).	SI unit is joule (J).

ILLUSTRATIVE EXAMPLES

1. A work of 600 J is done when a force of 30 N is applied on the pedals of a bicycle. What is the distance through which the bicycle moves ?
   Solution : Given W = 600 J, F = 30 N
   We know W = F × S
   Thus, S = W/F = 600/30 = 20 m
   The bicycle moves through a distance of 20 m.

2. An elevator rises up to a height of 30 m carrying passengers with a total mass of 600 kg. Calculate the work done by the elevator.
   Solution : Given S = h = 30 m, m = 600 kg
   The elevator rises vertically up and work is done against the force of gravity.
   Force required by the elevator to rise up
   $$F = mg = 600 \times 9.8 = 5,880 \text{ N}$$
   Work done W = –F × S
   $\qquad\qquad = -F \times h = -mgh$
   $\qquad\qquad = -5,880 \times 30$
   or $\qquad\qquad = -1,76,400$ J or -176.4 kJ.

   Here, the force due to gravity acts in the direction opposite to the displacement; hence, work done is negative.

3. A lawnmower is pulled with a force of 500 N directed at an angle of 60° with the ground. Calculate the work done by the mower when it is pulled to a distance of 50 m.
   Solution : Given F = 500 N, θ = 60°, S = 50 m
   Work done W = Component of force in the direction of displacement × Displacement
   or, $\quad W = F \cos θ \times S$
   $$W = 500 \times \frac{1}{2} \times 50$$
   $\qquad\qquad\qquad$ [∵ cos 60° = 1/2]
   $\qquad = 12,500$ J or 12.5 kJ
   Work done by the mower is 12.5 kJ.

4. A force of 10 N acting on a body at an angle of 60° with the horizontal direction displaces the body through a distance of 2 m along the surface of a floor. Calculate the work done. Now, let another force acting on the body making an angle of 30° with the horizontal do the same amount of work. What is the value of this force to displace the body through the same distance along the surface of the floor ?
   (Take cos 60° = 1/2, cos 30° = $\frac{\sqrt{3}}{2}$)
   Solution : Given F_1 = 10 N, $θ_1$ = 60°, $θ_2$ = 30°, $S_1 = S_2$ = 2 m
   Work done W = $F_1 \cos θ_1 \times S_1$
   or, W = 10 × cos 60° × 2 = 10 × $\frac{1}{2}$ × 2 = 10 J
   Now, $F_2 \cos θ_2 = W/S_2 = 10/2 = 5$
   or, $F_2 = 5/\cos 30° = 5/0.866 = 5.77$ N

5. A man with a mass of 70 kg runs up a flight of 40 stairs, each 15 cm high in 30 s. Find the power of the man.
   Solution : Given m = 70 kg, Number of stairs = 40, Height of each stair h = 15 cm = (15/100) m = 0.15 m, t = 30 s.
   S = No. of stairs × Height of each stair = 40 × 0.15 = 6 m
   Work done by the man in running up the flight of stairs is against the force of gravity.
   $\qquad$ Force F = mg = 70 × 9.8 = 686 N
   $\qquad\qquad$ W = mg × h = 686 × 6 = 4,116 J
   $$\text{Power P} = \frac{\text{Work done}}{\text{Time taken}}$$
   $$= \frac{4,116}{30} = 137.2 \text{ W}$$

6. A rickshaw-puller pulls the rickshaw by applying a force of 100 N. If the rickshaw moves with a constant velocity of 36 km h^{-1}, find the power of the rickshaw-puller.
   Solution : Given F = 100 N,
   $$v = 36 \text{ km h}^{-1}$$
   $$= \frac{36 \times 1{,}000}{60 \times 60} = 10 \text{ m s}^{-1}$$
   Power P = Force × Velocity
   = 100 × 10 = 1,000 W

7. The heart does a work of 1.2 J in each heartbeat. How many times per minute does it beat if its power is 1.5 W?
   Solution : Given W = 1.2 J, t = 1 min = 60 s, P = 1.5 W
   Total work done by the heart
   = P × t = 1.5 × 60 = 90 J
   No. of heart beats/min
   $$= \frac{\text{Total work done}}{\text{Work done in each beat}}$$
   = 90/1.2 = 75

8. A horse exerts a force of 200 N to pull the cart. If the horse cart system moves with a velocity of 36 km h^{-1} on the level road, then find the power of horse in terms of horsepower (1 h.p. = 746 W).
   Solution : Given F = 200 N,
   $$v = 36 \text{ km h}^{-1} = \frac{36 \times 1{,}000}{60 \times 60} = 10 \text{ m s}^{-1}$$
   Power P = F × v = 200 × 10 = 2,000 W
   Since 746 W = 1 h.p.
   Hence, 2,000 W = 2,000/746 = 2.68 h.p.

   Thus, the power of the horse is 2.68 h.p.

9. Calculate the horse-power of an engine that lifts 10 litre of water from a depth of 50 m in 30 min. (Take g = 10 ms^{-2}, density of water = 1,000 kg m^{-3}, h.p. = 746 W)
   Solution : Given, volume of water = 10 litre = 10 × 10^3 m^3, Density of water = 1,000 kg m^{-3}
   Height h = 50 m, time t = 30 min = 30 × 60 = 1,800 s, g = 10 m s^{-2}
   Mass of water = Volume × Density = 10^4 × 1,000 = 10^7 kg
   Work done by the engine in lifting water = mgh = 10^7 × 10 × 50 = 5 × 10^9 J
   $$\text{Power of the engine} = \frac{\text{Work done}}{\text{Time taken}}$$
   $$= \frac{5 \times 10^9}{1{,}800}$$
   = 2.77 × 10^6 W
   Power of the engine in terms of horse power
   $$= \frac{2.77 \times 10^6}{746} = 3{,}710 \text{ h. p.}$$

10. An electric bulb of 100 W is used for 3 hours per day. Calculate the amount of energy consumed in 5 days.
    Solution : Given P = 100 W, t = 3 hours, No. of days = 5
    Energy consumed in 1 day = Power × Time
    = 100 × 3 = 300 Wh
    1 Wh = 3.6 kJ
    300 Wh = 300 × 3.6 = 1,080 kJ
    Energy consumed in 5 days
    = 5 × 1,080 = 5,400 kJ or 5.4 MJ

EXERCISE 2(A)

1. Define work and state its SI unit. What are the two factors on which the work depends ?
2. How is work done by a force measured when the force :
   (a) is in the direction of displacement.
   (b) is at an angle to the direction of displacement.
3. If force is applied at an angle θ to the direction of displacement of a body, how will you derive the amount of work done?
4. Is work a scalar or a vector quantity? How is it represented?
5. What is the condition for work to be positive?
   Ans : The displacement of the body should be in the direction of force
6. State the two conditions when the work done will be zero.
   Ans : (a) When there is no displacement, (b) When the displacement is normal to the direction of force applied
7. What should be the angle between the direction of force and direction of displacement if (a) work done is zero and (b) work done is negative?
   Ans : (a) 90°, (b) 180°
8. Give one example each of positive work, zero work and negative work.
9. Determine from the below given statements whether work done is positive, zero or negative in each case :
   (a) A weightlifter standing with a heavy weight in his hands for 5 min.

(b) A piece of furniture pushed across the floor.
(c) A stone thrown vertically upwards.
(d) An apple thrown from a height.
(e) A fisherman carrying a basket of fish over his head.
Ans : (a) Zero, (b) Positive, (c) Negative, (d) Positive, (e) Zero.
10. What is the work done by a planet revolving around the Sun?
Ans : Zero.
11. A coolie carrying a load on his head and moving on a frictionless horizontal platform does no work. Explain the reason.
12. Explain briefly why the work done by a fielder when he takes a catch in a cricket match is negative.
13. If the force applied on a body is not constant, how will you determine the amount of work done through the entire displacement ?
14. What will be the nature of force displacement graph if the force applied on a body is constant?
15. What will be the expression for work done when a body is thrown vertically downwards from a certain height?
16. What will the amount of work done when a boy of mass m (a) climbs to a height h through staircases and (b) reaches height h through an elevator ?
Ans : (a) mgh, (b) mgh.
17. What is the relation between SI and CGS unit of work ?
18. Define the term 'power'. State its SI unit.
19. Explain the factors on which power spent by a body depends with the help of an example.
20. State the relation between gigawatt and watt.
21. Define energy. State its SI unit.
22. What is the commercial unit of energy? Define it.
23. What is a kilowatt-hour? State its relation with joule.
24. What is the unit commonly used to measure heat energy? State its relation with joule.
25. What is electron volt (eV)?
26. Differentiate between work, power and energy.
27. Answer the following :
 (a) Name the physical quantity measured in terms of horse power.
 (b) 1 kWh = ... J
Ans : (b) 3.6×10^6

MULTIPLE CHOICE QUESTIONS

1. Work done is zero when :
 (a) force causes displacement in its own direction.
 (b) force causes displacement in opposite direction.
 (c) force causes displacement in a perpendicular direction.
 (d) force causes displacement at an acute angle.
Ans : (c)
2. 1 J is equal to
 (a) 4.18 cal (b) 4.18 erg
 (c) 0.24 cal (d) 0.24 erg
Ans : (c)
3. If a ball is thrown vertically upwards, work done is :
 (a) positive (b) negative
 (c) zero (d) none of these
Ans : (b)
4. eV is the unit of :
 (a) force (b) work
 (c) power (d) energy
Ans : (d)

NUMERICAL PROBLEMS

1. How much force is applied on the body when 150 J of work is done in displacing it through a distance of 10 m in the direction of force?
Ans : 15 N.
2. A block of ice with a mass of 2 kg is sliding across a frozen pond. A force of 12 N is applied in the direction of motion. After the ice block slides 17 m, the force is removed. What is the work done by the applied force?
Ans : 204 J.
3. A 5 kg ball on the end of a string is whirled at a constant speed of 1 m s^{-1} in a horizontal circle of radius 5 m. What is the work done by the centripetal force during one revolution ?
Ans : Zero.
4. An engine does a work of 54,000 J by exerting a force of 6,000 N on it. What is the displacement of the force?
Ans : 9 m.
5. A work of 4,900 J is done when a load of mass 50 kg is lifted to a certain height. Calculate the height through which the load is lifted.
Ans : 10 m.
6. A force of 5 N acting on body at angle of 30° with the horizontal direction displaces it horizontally through a distance of 6 m. Calculate the work done.
Ans : 25.98 J.
7. A body when acted upon by a force of 100 N gets displaced by 2 m. Calculate the work done

by the force when displacement is (a) in the direction of force (b) at an angle of 60° with the force and (c) perpendicular to the force.
Ans : (a) 200 J, (b) 100 J, (c) Zero.

8. Rajan exerts a force of 150 N in pulling a cart at a constant speed of 10 ms^{-1}. Calculate the power exerted.
Ans : 1500 W.

9. An athlete weighing 60 kg runs up a staircase with 10 steps each of 1 m in 30 s. Calculate the (a) force acting on the athlete and (b) power spent by the athlete. (Take $g = 9.8$ m s^{-2})
Ans : (a) 588 N, (b) 196 W.

10. A girl weighing 50 kg runs up a hill at a distance of 10 m in 20 s. Calculate the power spent by the girl. (Take $g = 9.8$ m s^{-2})
Ans : 245 W.

11. A boy weighing 40 kgf climbs up a stair of 30 steps each 20 cm high in 4 minutes and a girl weighing 30 kgf does the same in 3 minutes. Compare :
    (a) the work done by them,
    (b) the power developed by them.
Ans : (a) 4 : 3, (b) 1 : 1

12. Calculate the time taken by a 60 W bulb to consume 3,000 J of energy.
Ans : 50 s

13. An electric iron of power 2 kW is used for 3 h per day. How much energy does it consume in 2 days? Express in joule.
Ans : 2.16 × 10^7 J

14. If the power of a machine is 50 kW, at what speed can it raise a load of 20,000 N?
Ans : 2.5 m s^{-1}

15. Express (a) 7 Wh into joule, (b) 10 J into calorie and (c) 2.5 eV into joule.
Ans : (a) 2.52 × 10^4 J, (b) 2.4 cal, (c) 4 × 10^{-19} J

(B) VARIOUS FORMS OF ENERGY AND CONSERVATION OF ENERGY

Energy exists in various forms, such as mechanical energy, electrical energy, chemical energy, heat energy, light energy, sound energy, nuclear energy and so on. All these energies, under suitable conditions, can change from one form to another.

2.6 MECHANICAL ENERGY

The energy possessed by a body by virtue of its motion or position is called mechanical energy.

The mechanical energy occurs in two forms, namely (a) kinetic energy and (b) potential energy, depending on the cause of the displacement, which could be due to motion of the body on the ground surface or at a higher level above the ground surface.

The sum of kinetic energy and potential energy of a body is its total mechanical energy.

Kinetic Energy

The energy possessed by a body by virtue of its state of motion is called kinetic energy.

It is denoted by the letter K.

Examples :
1. Fast moving wind can turn the blades of a windmill due to the kinetic energy possessed by it.
2. When a hammer hits a nail with a force, it is the kinetic energy of the hammer that helps to drive the nail into the wall.
3. A vehicle in motion, a rolling football, a stone falling from a height, a running horse, a bullet fired from a gun, a shooting arrow and the like possess kinetic energy.

Expression for Kinetic Energy

The kinetic energy possessed by a body depends on its *mass* and *velocity*. It can be understood from the following examples :

Examples :
1. Suppose a 50 g ball and a 200 g ball are thrown with same speed towards a glass window. It will be noticed that the 200 g ball will break the glass while the 50 g ball might not. It is because the ball with a greater mass possesses higher kinetic energy.
2. Take two balls, each of mass 100 g. Now throw these two balls towards the glass window; one ball gently and the other forcefully. It will be noticed that the glass breaks with the ball thrown forcefully but not with the one thrown gently. This is because the ball thrown forcefully has greater velocity and it possesses higher kinetic energy.

Consider a body of mass m moving with a velocity v. Let it cover a distance S when a constant force F is applied on it to bring it to rest. Let a be the uniform retardation produced by the force. The measure of work done will be equal to the kinetic energy of the body.

Kinetic energy of the body = Work done by the retarding force in bringing it to rest.

or, $\qquad K = F \times S \qquad$ ....(i)

For calculating the displacement S, use the equation :
$$v^2 = u^2 - 2aS \qquad ....(ii)$$

Now, initial velocity $u = v$
Final velocity $v = 0$
Acceleration, $a = -a$, as the body is retarding
Substituting the values of u and v in equation (ii),
$$0 = v^2 - 2aS$$
or, $$S = \frac{v^2}{2a} \quad ....(iii)$$
We know, retarding force :
$$F = ma \quad ....(iv)$$
Substituting the values of S and F from equations (iii) and (iv) respectively in equation (i), we get
$$K = ma \times \frac{v^2}{2a}$$
or, $$K = \frac{1}{2}mv^2 \quad ....(2.7)$$
i.e. Kinetic energy = $\frac{1}{2}$ × Mass × (Velocity)^2

From equation (2.7), it can be concluded that
1. Kinetic energy of a body is directly proportional to its mass.
2. Kinetic energy of a body is directly proportional to the square of its velocity.

Relation between kinetic energy and momentum

If a body of mass m is moving with a velocity v, then its,
$$\text{Kinetic energy } K = \frac{1}{2}mv^2 \quad ....(i)$$
$$\text{Momentum } p = mv \quad ....(ii)$$
or, $$v = \frac{p}{m} \quad ....(iii)$$
Substituting the value of v from equation (iii) in equation (i), we have
$$K = \frac{1}{2}m\left(\frac{p}{m}\right)^2$$
or, $$K = p^2/2m \quad ....(iv)$$
or, $$p = \sqrt{2mK} \quad ....(2.8)$$
Thus, kinetic energy is related to momentum as $K = p^2/2m$

And momentum is related to kinetic energy as
$$p = \sqrt{2mK}$$

Work-energy theorem

When a force is applied on a moving body, in the direction of motion of the body, the body accelerates and its kinetic energy increases.

The work-energy theorem states

The increase in kinetic energy of a body is equal to the work done by the force acting on the body.

Consider a body of mass m with an initial velocity u. Let F be a force applied on the body in its direction of motion such that an acceleration a is produced. The velocity of the body changes from u to v when it moves to a distance S.

Work done by the force
$$W = F \times S \quad ....(i)$$
From the equation of motion, $v^2 = u^2 - 2aS$
$$\text{Displacement } S = \frac{v^2 - u^2}{2a}$$
$$\text{Force } F = \text{Mass} \times \text{Acceleration} = ma \quad ...(ii)$$
Substituting the values of S and F from equations (ii) and (iii) in equation (i), we get
$$W = ma \times \left(\frac{v^2 - u^2}{2a}\right)$$
or, $$W = \frac{1}{2}m(v^2 - u^2)$$
or, $$W = \frac{1}{2}mv^2 - \frac{1}{2}mu^2$$
or, $$W = K_f - K_i \quad ....(2.9)$$
$$K_i = \frac{1}{2}mu^2 = \text{Initial kinetic energy}$$
$$K_f = \frac{1}{2}mv^2 = \text{Final kinetic energy}$$

Thus, work done = Increase in kinetic energy.

Forms of Kinetic Energy

Depending on the type of motion of a body, kinetic energy can be categorised into three different forms: (1) translational kinetic energy, (2) rotational kinetic energy and (3) vibrational kinetic energy.

1. Translational kinetic energy : The motion of a body in a straight-line path is called *linear motion* or *translational motion,* and the kinetic energy of the body due to this motion is called *translational kinetic energy.*

Examples : A vehicle moving on a straight road, a freely falling body, a man walking on a straight path, a molecule of monoatomic gas and so on.

2. Rotational kinetic energy : The motion of a body around an axis or a fixed end is called *rotational motion,* and the kinetic energy due to this type of motion is called *rotational kinetic energy.*

Examples : Blades of a moving fan, a spinning top, rotation of Earth around its own axis, electrons spinning around the nucleus of an atom and so on.

The atoms of diatomic and polyatomic molecules, a rolling ball and the wheels of a moving car all possess both translational and rotational kinetic energies.

3. Vibrational kinetic energy : The to and fro motion of a body about its mean position is called the *vibrational motion*. The kinetic energy of the body due to its vibrational motion is called *vibrational kinetic energy.*

Examples : Moving water, a tuning fork struck against a rubber pad, plucking the strings of a guitar, the atoms of a solid, an oscillating pendulum and so on.

A polyatomic molecule has vibrational kinetic energy in addition to the rotational kinetic energy.

Potential Energy

The energy possessed by a body by virtue of its position or configuration is called potential energy.

It is denoted by the letter U.

Examples :
1. Water stored in a tank or dam.
2. A body placed at a height above the ground, such as an aeroplane.
3. A stretched bow, a wound-up watch spring, a stretched rubber band and so on, possess potential energy.

Forms of Potential Energy

There are two forms of potential energy : (1) elastic potential energy and (2) gravitational potential energy.

1. Elastic potential energy : A force when applied on a non-rigid body has the capability to deform it or change its configuration (*i.e.* shape or size). Elasticity is the property by virtue of which a body tends to regain its original configuration when the applied external force is removed.

The potential energy possessed by a body due to its changed configuration or deformed state is called elastic potential energy.

The elastic potential energy of a body is equal to the amount of work done in deforming it.

Examples : Stretched bow, stretched elastic band, wound-up string of a clock and so on.

2. Gravitational potential energy : *The potential energy possessed by a body due to its position with respect to the centre of the Earth is called gravitational potential energy.*

It is negative at finite distance from earth. The gravitational potential energy of a body increases as its distance from the centre of the Earth increases. At infinity, the gravitational potential energy is considered to be zero.

If there is a system consisting of two bodies, then the potential energy possessed by a body is due to the gravitational force of attraction of the other body.

Examples : Water stored at a height, a helicopter in the sky and so on.

Expression for Gravitational Potential Energy

The gravitational potential energy of a body at a height above the ground is measured by the amount of work done in raising the body up to that height against the force of gravity.

Consider a body of mass m, initially at ground level, be raised vertically upwards to a height h. The upward force F required to raise the body is equal to the force of gravity on the body acting downwards.

Force of gravity $F = mg$, where g is the acceleration due to gravity.

Work done in raising the body upwards,
$$W = \text{Force} \times \text{Displacement}.$$
or $\qquad W = mg \times h = mgh$

This work done is stored in the body as gravitational potential energy when it is at a height h.

Thus, $\qquad U = mgh \qquad \qquad ....(2.10)$

As the gravitational potential energy of a body on the ground, *i.e.*, on surface of the Earth, is considered to be zero, the gravitational potential energy of the body is equal to mgh.

However, if the body is raised from a height h_1 to a height h_2 above the ground, there is a gain in its gravitational potential energy.

The gain in potential energy.
= Final potential energy – Initial potential energy
= $mgh_2 - mgh_1 = mg(h_2 - h_1)$

If a body falls from a height h_1 to a height h_2 above the ground, there is a loss in its gravitational potential energy.

The loss in potential energy
= Initial potential energy – Final potential energy
= $mgh_1 - mgh_2 = mg(h_1 - h_2)$

NOTE

The potential energy of a body depends on the vertical height between the initial and final positions of the body and not on the path along which the body is raised. For example, a load of 30 kg can be taken by a staircase or by an elevator to the top of a building. In both cases, the potential energy of the load will be the same.

2.7 CONVERSION OF POTENTIAL ENERGY INTO KINETIC ENERGY

The elastic or gravitational potential energy possessed by a body changes to kinetic energy whenever it is put to use.

The following examples will illustrate this :

1. Consider a bow and an arrow. When the arrow is placed on the string of the bow without pulling it, the system has no energy. Now, if the string is pulled along with the arrow by applying a force in the backward direction, the string gets stretched and the shape of the bow changes. This work done by the force applied is stored in the form of elastic potential energy (Fig. 2.8). When the string is released, the arrow moves forward as the potential energy gets converted to the kinetic energy of the arrow.

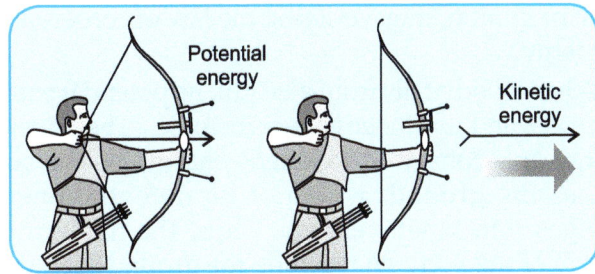

Fig. 2.8 : Conversion of potential energy to kinetic energy in a stretched bow.

2. A watch or a toy that has a spring or key for winding up has potential energy stored in the wound-up state. As the spring or key unwinds, the stored potential energy changes into kinetic energy. This kinetic energy moves the hands of a watch or moves the toy forward.

3. Water stored in a dam at a height possesses gravitational potential energy. When water from the dam is released, the potential energy gets converted into kinetic energy of the flowing water. This kinetic energy of water turns the blades of a turbine to produce electricity.

4. A ball kept at a height above the surface of the ground possesses gravitational potential energy. When it is dropped from this height, its potential energy begins to convert into kinetic energy due to motion and when it reaches the ground, all of its potential energy gets converted into kinetic energy. While falling from a height, if the ball falls on a piece of glass kept on the ground, the glass will break due to the kinetic energy of the ball.

5. A spring in its compressed state possesses elastic potential energy. When it is released, the potential energy changes into kinetic energy. If a ball is placed on a compressed spring and the spring is released, work is done on the ball during the conversion of potential energy of the spring to kinetic energy. The kinetic energy of the spring changes to the kinetic energy of the ball and, as a result, the ball flies away (Fig. 2.9).

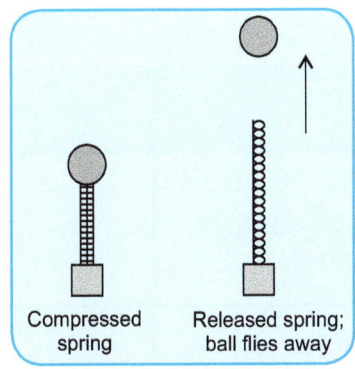

Fig. 2.9 : Conversion of potential energy to kinetic energy in a stretched spring.

2.8 CONSERVATION OF ENERGY

In the universe, the sum of various kinds of energies remains constant. In a given system, one form of energy may get converted into another form, but the total energy always remains the same.

The law of conservation of energy states

Energy can be neither created nor destroyed. It may be transformed from one form to another in a system, but the total energy in a system remains constant.

Conservation of mechanical energy : The total mechanical energy of a system is equal to the sum of its kinetic energy and potential energy.

In a system, whenever there is an interchange between the potential energy and kinetic energy, the sum of the two energies, *i.e.*, the total mechanical energy, remains constant (assuming there are no frictional forces).

$$K + U = \text{Constant}$$

A Theoretical Example to Illustrate the Law of Conservation of Energy

Consider a body of mass m at a height h above the ground. Let the body be released such that it falls freely under the force of gravity. Let us now calculate the sum of kinetic energy and potential energy at positions A, B and C as shown in Fig. 2.10.

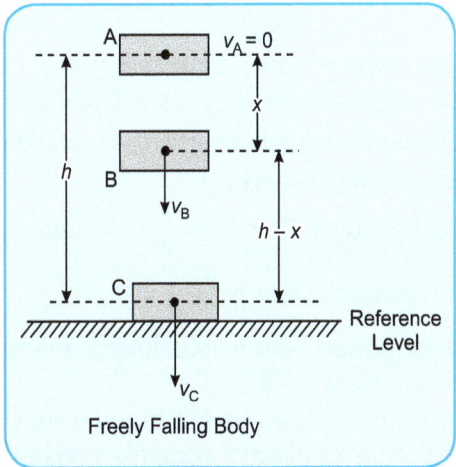

Fig. 2.10 : Conservation of energy in a freely falling body.

1. **At position A, which is at height h above the ground :** At height h, the body is at rest; hence, its velocity v_A is zero.

   We know kinetic energy $K = \frac{1}{2}mv^2$

   As velocity at A, $v_A = 0$, $K = 0$

   Potential energy of the body $U = mgh$

   ∴ Total mechanical energy $= K + U = 0 + mgh = mgh$

2. **At position B, when the body has fallen through a distance x :** Let v_B be the velocity

acquired by the body at point B when it falls through a distance x.

Here, $u = 0$, $S = x$, $a = g$

Using the equation of motion $v^2 = u^2 - 2aS$, we have

$$v_B^2 = 0 + 2gx$$

or, $$v_B^2 = 2gx$$

Kinetic energy, $K = \frac{1}{2} m v_B^2$

$$= \frac{1}{2} m \times (2gx)$$

$$= mgx$$

At position B, height of the body above the ground $= h - x$

So, potential energy $U = mg(h - x)$

∴ Total mechanical energy $= K + U$

$$= mgx + mg(h - x) = mgh$$

3. **At position C, when the body reaches the ground :** When the body reaches point C, let its velocity at C, be v_C.

$u = 0$ (as initially the body was at rest), $S = h$

Using the equation of motion $v^2 = u^2 - 2aS$, we have

$$v_C^2 = 0 + 2gh$$

or, $$v_C^2 = 2gh$$

Kinetic energy, $K = \frac{1}{2} m v_C^2$

$$= \frac{1}{2} m \times (2gh)$$

$$= mgh$$

Potential energy $U = 0$, because $h = 0$

∴ Total mechanical energy $= K + U = mgh + 0 = mgh$

At highest point A (*i.e.* height h), kinetic energy $= 0$ and potential energy $= mgh$

At middle point B, if $x = \frac{1}{2}h$, kinetic energy $= \frac{1}{2}mgh$ and potential energy $= \frac{1}{2}mgh$

At lowest point C (*i.e.* $h = 0$), kinetic energy $= mgh$ and potential energy $= 0$

From the above cases, it can be seen that the total mechanical energy always remains constant at any point of motion, thus verifying the law of conservation of energy.

When a body falls from a height, its potential energy decreases and its kinetic energy increases. The potential energy gets converted to kinetic energy. As the body strikes the ground, whole of its potential energy changes into kinetic energy. Thus, the final kinetic energy of the body on reaching the ground is equal to the initial potential energy at height h.

When a body is thrown vertically upwards from the ground, its initial kinetic energy keeps on decreasing while its potential energy keeps on increasing by the same amount. When the body reaches the maximum height, whole of its kinetic energy gets converted to potential energy and the body comes to rest for a small moment. Due to the effect of force of gravity, the body starts falling down from the highest point and again its potential energy begins to change into kinetic energy.

In deriving the above result, the force of friction between the body and air has been ignored. In actual, force of friction will convert some of the kinetic energy into heat (it is also a form of energy) that will get dissipated in air. Thus, at the ground level, total kinetic energy will be less than mgh.

The conservation of total mechanical energy is valid in vacuum where friction due to air is absent. However, the law of conservation of total energy of all forms remains valid always.

According to law of conservation of energy,

Initial kinetic energy of a body at the ground = Final potential energy of the body at a height

i.e., $\quad \frac{1}{2}mu^2 = mgh$

or, $\quad u = \sqrt{2gh}$ ....(2.11)

Here, u is the initial velocity of the body and h is the height.

Table 2.1 represents the kinetic energy K, potential energy U and total mechanical energy E of a body of mass m at different heights from the ground, when the body is in motion vertically downwards and vertically upwards.

Table 2.1 : Kinetic energy, potential energy and total mechanical energy of a body in vertical motion

Motion of the body	Height of the body from the ground	Kinetic energy (K)	Potential energy (U)	Total mechanical energy (E = K + U)
Vertically downwards	(i) h (highest point)	0	mgh	mgh
	(ii) $\frac{1}{2}h$ (at mid-point)	$\frac{1}{2}mgh$	$\frac{1}{2}mgh$	mgh
	(iii) 0 (on the ground)	mgh	0	mgh
Vertically upwards	(i) 0 (on the ground)	mgh	0	mgh
	(ii) $\frac{1}{2}h$ (at mid-point)	$\frac{1}{2}mgh$	$\frac{1}{2}mgh$	mgh
	(iii) h (highest point)	0	mgh	mgh

2.9 APPLICATION OF LAW OF CONSERVATION OF ENERGY : SIMPLE PENDULUM

A simple pendulum consists of a ball called bob attached to a string from a rigid support. The bob, along with the string, is able to oscillate on both sides.

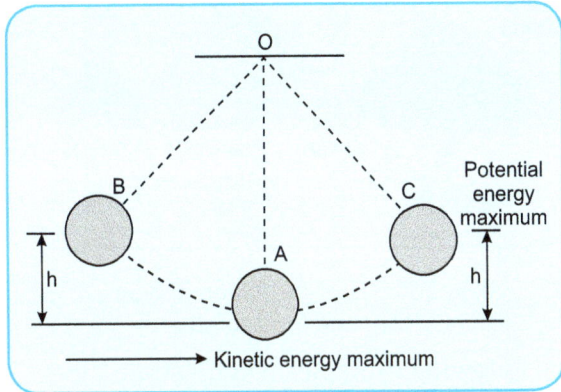

Fig. 2.11 : Conservation of energy in a simple pendulum.

Consider a pendulum with a bob of mass m. The pendulum is at resting position at A, which is known as the *mean position*. When it is displaced towards one side, say side B, and then released, it swings from side B to side C, reaching equal height and covering equal distance on both sides. Positions B and C are its extreme positions. (Fig. 2.11).

At mean position A, in the resting condition, the bob has zero potential energy and maximum kinetic energy. When the pendulum is displaced to position B, the bob gets raised by a vertical height h. At this position, the potential energy increases and is equal to mgh. As the bob is released from B, it reaches back to position A, where its potential energy decreases and becomes zero as the vertical height decreases from h to zero. The potential energy gets converted into kinetic energy. The kinetic energy at point A is equal to the potential energy at point B, i.e. $1/2\ mv^2 = mgh$. As the bob acquires a velocity $v = \sqrt{2gh}$ at position B, it continues to move from position A to position C.

At point C, the bob reaches to a vertical height h, its kinetic energy becomes zero and its potential energy becomes mgh. The bob does not remain at rest at position C, but due to the force of gravity, it moves back from C to A. Again at point A, potential energy decreases and becomes zero and the energy possessed by the bob is the kinetic energy. The bob again swings from position A to position B, and the process continues.

The bob possesses only kinetic energy at the mean or equilibrium position and only potential energy at the two extreme positions.

At intermediate positions, that is between mean position and extreme position (A and B or between A and C), the bob possesses both kinetic and potential energy. The sum of kinetic energy and potential energy remains constant in all positions of the swing, thus following the law of conservation of energy.

NOTE

The above case is true only in a condition of vacuum where there is no opposing force of friction due to air acting on the pendulum.

2.10 VARIOUS FORMS OF ENERGY

Energy exists in various forms in nature such as mechanical energy, sound energy, wind energy, light energy, hydro energy, chemical energy, electrical energy, nuclear energy, solar energy etc. Mechanical energy has been already discussed in the previous section. The other forms of energy are as follows :

1. Heat energy : It is also known as *thermal energy*. The Sun is the direct source of heat energy received by the Earth. Heat energy is released on combustion or burning of certain substances such as wood, coal, gas and oil. When boiling water is converted into steam, it possesses heat energy and can be used to do work. For example, heat energy of steam is used in a steam engine.

At the microscopic level, thermal energy is the energy associated with the random motion of atoms and molecules.

2. Light energy : It is the light energy that makes visible all the objects surrounding us to our eyes. The Sun is the natural source of light energy, and the light received from the solar energy is also known as *radiant energy*. Moon reflects the light of the Sun at night-time. There are other sources that provide light energy, such as a burning candle, fire from woods and artificial electrical devices such as bulb.

At the microscopic level, the light energy is due to small energy particles called *photons*.

3. Chemical energy : It is the form of energy stored in fuels such as coal, petroleum and gas and is released when a reaction takes place. The food that we eat contains chemical energy stored in it. It is the process of photosynthesis through which plants convert the energy absorbed from the Sun into chemical energy of food. Chemical energy gets converted into heat energy when fuels are burnt.

A cell or a battery is a device that contains chemical energy stored in it, and this energy gets converted to electrical energy when a chemical reaction occurs inside it.

At microscopic level, chemical energy is the energy due to certain types of associations or aggregations of atoms in molecules.

4. Electrical energy : Electrical energy is the energy generated due to movement of free electrons from one charged body to another charged body. A body gets charged when it is rubbed with another body due to the force of friction. An electric cell is a source of electrical energy that involves a chemical reaction due to movement of ions towards the electrodes.

5. Nuclear energy : Nuclear energy is the energy released due to reactions such as nuclear fission and nuclear fusion. Nuclear fission is the splitting of nucleus of a heavy atom into a smaller particle with large energy and nuclear fusion involves combining the nuclei of two lighter atoms into a heavier one with large release of energy. In both these processes, there is a loss in mass that gets converted to energy. The energy released in these reactions is used in a nuclear reactor to produce electrical energy and in an atom bomb to produce heat and other forms of energy.

6. Sound energy : It is a form of mechanical vibration perceived by the ears. The vibration produced by a body, such as a stretched string, propagates through a mechanical medium (such as air) and reaches our ears where it produces vibration in the ear - membrane; as a result sound is heard.

2.11 TRANSFORMATION OF ONE FORM OF ENERGY INTO THE OTHER FORM

Energy can neither be created nor be destroyed. It can be converted from one form to another (Fig. 2.12).

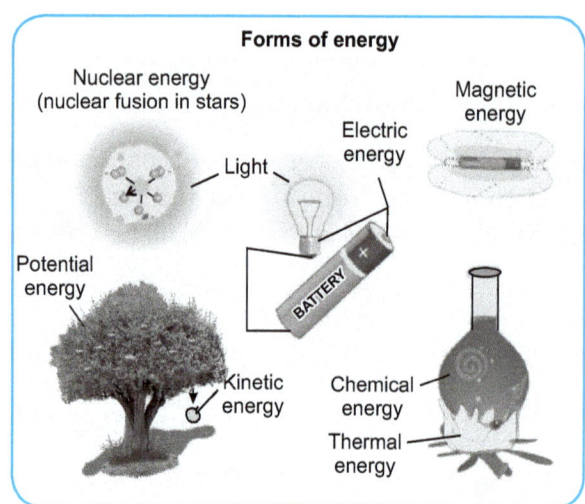

Fig. 2.12 : Transformation of energy from one form to other.

The following examples will illustrate this :

1. Mechanical energy to electrical energy : An electric generator converts mechanical energy into electrical energy.

The water stored in dams at a height has stored potential energy. When water is allowed to fall, the potential energy gets converted into kinetic energy. The kinetic energy possessed by the flowing water can rotate the blades of a turbine kept near the bottom of the dam. The turbine in turn rotates the armature of the generator connected to it, and thus, the kinetic energy gets converted into electrical energy by the generator (Fig. 2.13).

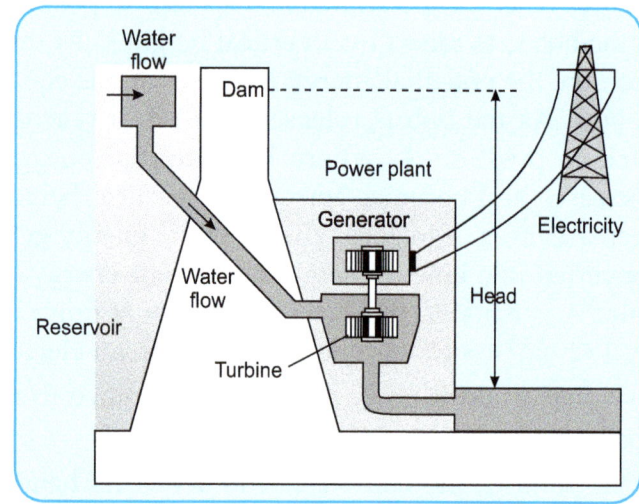

Fig. 2.13 : Mechanical energy to electrical energy.

2. Mechanical energy to heat energy : In the example of water stored in a dam, a part of the kinetic energy of flowing water on striking the ground changes into heat energy due to which the temperature of the water increases.

When brakes of a moving car are applied, the brakes rub against the moving wheels of the car and convert the mechanical energy to heat energy.

When two stones are struck or hands are rubbed against each other, the mechanical energy changes to heat energy.

3. Electrical energy to mechanical energy : The electrical energy on flowing through the coils of an electric motor changes into mechanical energy. The coil is freely suspended in a magnetic field on which a couple acts due to which it rotates. The electric motor is used in many appliances, such as an electric fan, a mixer and a washing machine.

4. Electrical energy to heat energy : In the case of an electric motor, some of the electric energy is also converted into the heat energy, besides the mechanical energy. It is due to this, the coil of a motor gets heated up.

Electric energy is converted to heat energy in many other electrical appliances such as a toaster, geyser, oven and iron.

5. Heat energy to electrical energy : This happens in a thermocouple. A thermocouple consists of two different metals kept at different temperatures; one is the hot junction and the other is the cold junction. Due to the temperature difference at two junctions, an electric potential develops and current begins to flow.

6. Heat energy to mechanical energy : In a steam engine, the heat energy of steam obtained by burning of coal changes into mechanical energy.

7. Electrical energy to chemical energy : When battery is charged, the electrical energy gets converted to chemical energy of the cell.

8. Chemical energy to electrical energy : When a torch is switched on, the chemical energy of the cell is converted to electrical energy.

9. Chemical energy to mechanical energy : In a moving vehicle, the chemical energy of the fuel (petrol or diesel) gets converted to kinetic energy.

10. Chemical energy to light energy : When a fire cracker is exploded, the chemical energy gets converted to light, heat and sound energies.

In an oil lamp or a burning candle, chemical energy gets converted to light and heat energies.

11. Chemical energy to heat energy : In a steam engine, the burning of coal converts the chemical energy to heat energy.

When a matchstick is rubbed against a matchbox, the chemical energy gets converted to heat and light energies.

12. Light energy to chemical energy : During the process of photosynthesis, the light energy absorbed by the chlorophyll pigment of green leaves gets converted to chemical energy of food.

13. Electrical energy to light energy : When an electric bulb is switched on, the electrical energy converts to light energy and thus the bulb glows. A part of electrical energy also gets converted to heat energy and hence a glowing bulb becomes hot.

In a television, the electrical energy gets converted to light energy and sound energy.

14. Light energy to electrical energy : In a solar cell, the light energy received from the Sun gets converted to electrical energy.

In a photovoltaic cell, the light energy gets converted to electrical energy.

15. Electrical energy to sound energy : In an electric bell and a loudspeaker, the electrical energy is converted into sound energy.

In a thunderstorm, the electrical energy gets converted to light and sound energies.

16. Sound energy into electrical energy : A microphone converts sound energy into electrical signals.

17. Electrical energy to magnetic energy : In an electromagnet, an electric current passing through a coil wrapped around a soft iron bar gets converted to magnetic energy and thus the iron bar gets magnetised.

18. Nuclear energy to heat energy : In nuclear fission and fusion reactions, the nuclear energy gets converted to heat and light energies.

ILLUSTRATIVE EXAMPLES

1. Determine the kinetic energy of a roller-coaster car with a mass of 500 kg and moving with a velocity of 15 m s^{-1}.

   Solution : Given $m = 500$ kg, $v = 15$ m s^{-1}
   Kinetic energy,
   $$K = \frac{1}{2}mv^2$$
   or, $$K = \frac{1}{2} \times 500 \times (15)^2$$
   or, $$K = 56{,}250 \text{ J} = 56.25 \text{ kJ}$$
   The kinetic energy of the roller-coaster car is 56.25 kJ.

2. Energy of 6,000 J is spent in raising a suitcase of mass 50 kg to a vertical height. Calculate the vertical height. (Take $g = 10$ m s^{-2})

   Solution : As the suitcase is raised to a height, it has energy stored in it in the form of gravitational potential energy.
   Given, $U = 6{,}000$ J, $m = 50$ kg, $g = 10$ m s^{-2}
   We know $U = mgh$
   $$\therefore \quad h = \frac{U}{mg} = \frac{6{,}000}{50 \times 10} = 12 \text{ m}$$
   Thus, the vertical height to which the suitcase is raised is 12 m.

3. A body of mass 10 kg is taken from a height of 10 m to 20 m. Calculate the increase in its potential energy. (Take $g = 10$ m s^{-2})
   Solution : Given $m = 10$ kg, $h_1 = 10$ m, $h_2 = 20$ m, $g = 10$ m s^{-2}
   Increase in potential energy
   $$= mg(h_2 - h_1)$$
   $$= 10 \times 10 \times (20 - 10)$$
   $$= 1{,}000 \text{ J}$$
   The increase in potential energy of the body is 1,000 J.

4. A body of mass 2 kg falls from a height of 10 m. Calculate the energy possessed by it at any instant of time. (Take $g = 9.8$ m s^{-2})
   Solution : Given $m = 2$ kg, $h = 10$ m, $g = 9.8$ m s^{-2}
   The energy possessed by the body at any instant
   = Initial potential energy of the body
   $= mgh = 2 \times 9.8 \times 10 = 196$ J

5. A body of mass 5 kg is initially at rest. A force of 20 N is applied on it. Calculate the kinetic energy of the body after 10 s.
   Solution : Given $m = 5$ kg, $F = 20$ N, $t = 10$ s, $u = 0$
   We know, $F = ma$
   $\therefore \quad a = \dfrac{F}{m}$
   or $\quad a = \dfrac{20}{5} = 4$ m s^{-2}
   To find the velocity of the body after 10 s, we use the equation :
   $$v = u + at$$
   or $\quad v = 0 + (4 \times 10)$
   or $\quad v = 40$ m s^{-1}
   Now, kinetic energy of the body
   $$K = \tfrac{1}{2} mv^2$$
   $$K = \tfrac{1}{2} \times 5 \times (40)^2$$
   or $\quad K = 4{,}000$ J
   The kinetic energy of the body after 10 s is 4,000 J.

6. A rock is dropped from a height 40 m. Determine the velocity with which it strikes the ground. (Take $g = 10$ m s^{-2})
   Solution : Given $h = 40$ m, $g = 10$ m s^{-2}
   When the rock strikes the ground, its
   Kinetic energy = Potential energy
   $$\tfrac{1}{2} mv^2 = mgh$$
   or $\quad v = \sqrt{2gh}$
   $\quad v = \sqrt{2 \times 10 \times 40}$
   or $\quad v = \sqrt{800}$
   or $\quad v = 28.28$ m s^{-1}
   Thus, the velocity of the rock is 28.28 m s^{-1}.

7. Calculate the work required to be done to slow down a bus with a mass of 2,000 kg moving at a velocity of 60 km h^{-1} to 36 km h^{-1}.
   Solution : Given $m = 2{,}000$ kg
   Initial velocity
   $$u = 60 \text{ km h}^{-1}$$
   $$= \dfrac{60 \times 1{,}000}{3{,}600} = 16.67 \text{ m s}^{-1}$$
   Final velocity $v = 36$ km h^{-1} $= \dfrac{36 \times 1{,}000}{3{,}600} = 10$ m s^{-1}
   Initial kinetic energy
   $$K_i = \tfrac{1}{2} mu^2 = \tfrac{1}{2} \times 2{,}000 \times (16.67)^2$$
   $$= 277.8 \text{ kJ}$$
   Final kinetic energy
   $$K_f = \tfrac{1}{2} mv^2 = \tfrac{1}{2} \times 2{,}000 \times (10)^2$$
   $$= 100 \text{ kJ}$$
   Work done by the force = Change in kinetic energy
   $$= K_f - K_i = 277.8 - 100 = 177.8 \text{ kJ}$$
   Thus, the work required to slow down the bus is 177.8 kJ.

8. A train weighing 5,000 N has a kinetic energy of 10 kJ. Find the velocity of the train. (Take $g = 10$ m s^{-2})
   Solution : Given $W = 5{,}000$ N, $K = 10$ kJ $= 10{,}000$ J, $g = 10$ m s^{-2}
   We know $W = mg$
   $\therefore \quad m = \dfrac{W}{g} = \dfrac{5{,}000}{10} = 500$ kg
   Kinetic energy $K = \tfrac{1}{2} mv^2$
   or $\quad 10{,}000 = \tfrac{1}{2} \times 500 \times v^2$
   or $\quad v^2 = \dfrac{20{,}000}{500} = 40$
   or $\quad v = \sqrt{40} = 6.32$ m s^{-1}
   Thus, the velocity of the train is 6.32 m s^{-1}.

9. How will the kinetic energy of a car change if (a) its mass is tripled, (b) its velocity is doubled and (c) its mass is doubled and velocity is halved ?
   Solution : Kinetic energy $K = \tfrac{1}{2} mv^2$
   i.e., $K \propto m$ and $K \propto v^2$

(a) If mass is tripled and velocity is unchanged, the kinetic energy will also be tripled.
(b) If velocity is doubled and mass is unchanged, the kinetic energy will be increased by four times.
(c) If mass is doubled but velocity is halved, the kinetic energy will be halved.

10. What will be the ratio of kinetic energy of two buses with equal mass moving with different velocities if velocity of bus A is 10 m s^{-1} and velocity of bus B is 12.25 m s^{-1} ?
Solution : Given $v_A = 10$ m s^{-1}, $v_B = 12.25$ m s^{-1}
As kinetic energy K $\propto v^2$
$\therefore \quad \dfrac{K_A}{K_B} = \dfrac{v_A^2}{v_B^2} = \dfrac{(10)^2}{(12.25)^2} = \dfrac{100}{150} = \dfrac{2}{3}$
The ratio of kinetic energy of bus A to bus B is 2 : 3.

11. A body of mass 0.5 kg has a momentum of 30 kg m s^{-1}. Calculate the kinetic energy of the body.
Solution : Given $m = 0.5$ kg, $p = 30$ kg m s^{-1}
Momentum $\quad p = mv$
or $\quad v = \dfrac{p}{m}$
Kinetic energy $= \dfrac{1}{2}mv^2$
or $\quad K = \dfrac{1}{2} \times m \times \left(\dfrac{p}{m}\right)^2$
or $\quad K = \dfrac{p^2}{2m} = \dfrac{(30)^2}{2 \times 0.5} = 900$ J

12. An object of mass 10 kg is raised to a height of 20 m above the ground level. What is its potential energy? If the object is allowed to fall, find its kinetic energy when it is at a height of 5 m above the ground. (Take $g = 9.8$ m s^{-2})
Solution : Given $m = 10$ kg, $h_1 = 20$ m, $g = 9.8$ m s^{-2}, $h_2 = 5$ m
(a) Potential energy at height
$h_1 = mgh_1 = 10 \times 9.8 \times 20 = 1{,}960$ J
(b) Potential energy at height
$h_2 = mgh_2 = 10 \times 9.8 \times 5 = 490$ J
Now, as the total mechanical energy at every point remains the same,
$\therefore$ Kinetic energy + Potential energy = Total mechanical energy.
The total mechanical energy is equal to the potential energy at the highest point.
$\therefore \quad K + U = 1{,}960$
or $\quad K = 1{,}960 - 490 = 1{,}470$ J

13. A bullet of mass 3 g travels with a speed of 600 m s^{-1}. It penetrates a wall that offers a resistive force of 600 N to the motion of the bullet. Find (a) the initial kinetic energy of the bullet, (b) the distance through which the bullet has penetrated before coming to rest and (c) the speed with which the bullet emerges out of the wall if its thickness is 0.7 m.
Solution : Given $m = 3$ g $= 3 \times 10^{-3}$ kg, $v = 600$ ms^{-1}, F = 600 N
(a) Kinetic energy of the bullet =
$\dfrac{1}{2}mv^2 = \dfrac{1}{2} \times 3 \times 10^{-3} \times (600)^2 = 540$ J
(b) The initial kinetic energy of the bullet is equal to the work done against the wall
Work done = Resistive force × Penetration distance
or $\quad 540 = 600 \times S$
or $\quad S = \dfrac{540}{600} = 0.9$ m
The bullet penetrates through a distance of 0.9 m before coming to rest.
(c) The energy spent against the resistive force of wall penetrating through a thickness of 0.7 m
$= 600 \times 0.7 = 420$ J
Kinetic energy left with the bullet on emerging out of the wall $= 540 - 420 = 120$ J
If the speed of bullet is v', then its kinetic energy is $1/2$ mv'^2.
$\dfrac{1}{2}mv'^2 = 120$
or $\quad v'^2 = \dfrac{120 \times 2}{3 \times 10^{-3}}$
or $\quad v' = \sqrt{80 \times 1{,}000}$
or $\quad v' = 282.8$ m s^{-1}
Thus, the speed with which the bullet emerges out of the wall is 282.8 m s^{-1}.

14. A body of mass 2 kg is thrown vertically upwards with an initial velocity of 50 m s^{-1}. Calculate (a) the initial kinetic energy imparted to the body, (b) the maximum height reached if friction due to air is neglected and (c) the maximum height reached if 25 % of the initial energy is lost against air friction. (Take $g = 10$ m s^{-2})
Solution : Given $m = 2$ kg, $u = 50$ m s^{-1}, $g = 10$ m s^{-2}

(a) Initial kinetic energy
$$= \frac{1}{2}mu^2 = \frac{1}{2} \times 2 \times (50)^2 = 2500 \text{ J}$$
(b) In the absence of air friction,
Potential energy at the maximum = Initial kinetic energy
or $\qquad mgh = \frac{1}{2}mu^2$
or $\qquad h = \frac{u^2}{2g} = \frac{(50)^2}{2 \times 10} = 125$ m

(c) If 25% of the initial energy is lost against air friction, then available kinetic energy is
$$\frac{75}{100} \times 2500 = 1875 \text{ J}$$
Now, this available kinetic energy is equal to the potential energy,
i.e., $\qquad mgh = 1875$
or $\qquad h = \frac{1875}{2 \times 10} = 93.75$

15. An oscillating simple pendulum rises to a maximum vertical height of 6 cm at its extreme positions. If the mass of the bob is 300 g, find (a) the velocity of the bob at its resting position and (b) the total energy of the pendulum at any instant while oscillating. (Take $g = 10$ m s^{-2}). Neglect the friction due to air.

Solution : Given $h = 6$ cm $= 0.06$ m,
$\qquad m = 300$ g $= 0.3$ kg, $g = 10$ m s^{-2}

(a) At resting position, the bob possesses kinetic energy
According to the law of conservation,
The kinetic energy at the mean position
= Potential energy at its extreme position
i.e. $\qquad \frac{1}{2}mv^2 = mgh$
or $\qquad v = \sqrt{2gh} = \sqrt{2 \times 10 \times 0.06}$
$\qquad\qquad = 1.09$ m s^{-1}

(b) Total energy of the pendulum = Potential energy at its extreme position
$\qquad = mgh = 0.3 \times 10 \times 0.06 = 0.18$ J

EXERCISE 2(B)

1. What is mechanical energy?
2. Name the two forms of mechanical energy.
   Ans : Kinetic energy and potential energy
3. What is the kind of energy possessed by a moving car?
   Ans : Translational kinetic energy
4. What is the kind of energy possessed by a stretched rubber band?
   Ans : Elastic potential energy
5. What is kinetic energy? Give an example.
6. What is potential energy? Give an example.
7. What are the different forms of kinetic energy? Give one example of each type.
8. What are the different forms of potential energy? Give one example of each type.
9. From the following cases, predict whether the energy possessed is kinetic energy (K) or potential energy (P) :
   (a) A rolling football.
   (b) Water stored in a tank at a height.
   (c) A wound-up watch.
   (d) A stretched bow.
   (e) Water flowing over a turbine.
   (f) The bob of a simple pendulum at its mean position.
   Ans : (a) K, (b) P, (c) P, (d) P, (e) K, (f) K
10. State the two factors that determine the kinetic energy of a body.
    Ans : Mass and velocity
11. State the three factors that determine the potential energy of a body.
    Ans : Mass, acceleration due to gravity and height
12. Give two examples where a body possesses both kinetic and potential energies.
13. Name the form of energy that a body may possess even when it is not in motion?
    Ans : Potential energy
14. Write the expression of kinetic energy of a body. Show its relation with the momentum of the body.
15. State the work energy theorem.
16. What will be the expression for work done on a body of mass m moving with a velocity u when a force applied on it changes its velocity to v?
17. Derive an expression for gravitational potential energy of a body.
18. A ball is placed on a compressed spring. When the spring is released, the ball is observed to fly away.
    (a) What form of energy does the compressed spring possess?
    (b) Why does the ball fly away?
19. State the law of conservation of energy.
20. What is the condition under which the mechanical energy is conserved?
21. Give two examples where the mechanical energy of the system remains constant. State any assumptions if made.

22. When a body is thrown vertically upwards, its velocity becomes zero at the maximum height. What happens to its kinetic energy? What form of energy does it possess upon striking the ground?

23. An apple on a tree falls freely and reaches the ground. State the kind of energy it will possess
    (a) on reaching the ground.
    (b) in air, while falling.
    (c) on top of the tree.
    Ans : (a) Kinetic energy, (b) Kinetic energy + potential energy, (c) Potential energy

24. How will you show that the sum of kinetic energy and potential energy is always conserved in case of a freely falling body under the force of gravity?

25. Draw a diagram to show the energy change in an oscillating simple pendulum. Indicate in your diagram, how the total mechanical energy in it remains constant during the oscillation.

26. Name any five different forms of energy.

27. What is the source of electrical energy?

28. How is nuclear energy obtained?

29. State the energy changes in the following while in use :
    (a) Burning of a candle.
    (b) A microphone.
    (c) A steam engine.
    (d) An electric heater.
    (e) A solar cell.
    (f) Burning of wood.
    (g) A fire cracker.
    (h) An electromagnet.
    (i) A television.
    (j) An electric bulb.
    Ans : (a) Chemical to light and heat, (b) Sound to electrical, (c) Heat to mechanical, (d) Electrical to heat, (e) Solar to electrical, (f) Chemical to heat, (g) Chemical to heat + sound + light, (h) Electrical to magnetic, (i) Electrical to light + sound, (j) Electrical to light + heat

MULTIPLE CHOICE QUESTIONS

1. The energy possessed by the wheels of a moving car is :
   (a) translational kinetic energy
   (b) rotational kinetic energy
   (c) both (a) and (b)
   (d) neither (a) nor (b)
   Ans : (c)

2. An oscillating pendulum at its extreme position possesses :
   (a) kinetic energy   (b) potential energy
   (c) both (a) and (b)   (d) None of these
   Ans : (b)

3. When an electric cell is charged, energy changes from :
   (a) chemical to electrical
   (b) electrical to chemical
   (c) chemical to mechanical
   (d) electrical to mechanical
   Ans : (b)

4. A ball rolls on an inclined plane. On midway through its motion, the ball has
   (a) only kinetic energy
   (b) only potential energy
   (c) both (a) and (b)
   (d) none of the above
   Ans : (c)

5. When the velocity of a particle is doubled, its kinetic energy :
   (a) increases by two times
   (b) increases by four times
   (c) decreases by two times
   (d) decreases by four times
   Ans : (b)

NUMERICAL PROBLEMS

1. A man of mass 50 kg climbs to the top of a building that is 40 m high. What is the potential energy of the man? (Take $g = 9.8$ m s^{-2})
   Ans : 19.6 kJ

2. The kinetic energy of a car is 40 kJ. What is the velocity of the car if its mass is 10,000 kg?
   Ans : 2.8 m s^{-1}

3. A ball of mass 200 g falls from a height of 5 m. What will be its kinetic energy when it just reaches the ground?
   Ans : 9.8 J

4. A force is applied on a body of mass 20 kg moving with a velocity of 40 m s^{-1}. The body attains a velocity of 50 m s^{-1} in 2 s. Calculate the work done on the body.
   Ans : 9,000 J

5. A girl of mass 35 kg climbs up from the first floor of a building at a height 4 m above the ground to the third floor at a height 12 m above the ground. What will be the increase in her gravitational potential energy? (Take $g = 10$ m s^{-2})
   Ans : 2,800 J

6. A body of mass 0.2 kg falls from a height of 10 m to a height of 6 m above the ground. Find the loss in potential energy taking place in the body? (Take $g = 10$ ms^{-2})
   Ans : 8 J

7. When a large box is taken to height of 8 m, the energy spent is 6.4 kJ. What is the mass of the box? (Take $g = 10$ m s^{-2})
   Ans : 80 kg

8. A car and a bus are running at a same speed. If the mass of the bus is five times the mass of the car, what is the ratio of kinetic energy of bus to car?
   Ans : 5 : 1

9. Two bodies A and B with masses 4 kg and 16 kg, respectively, have the same kinetic energy. Calculate the ratio of velocity of A to B.
   Ans : 2 : 1

10. A water reservoir on top of a tower 100 m high contains water of mass 200 kg. Calculate the potential energy stored in the water. (Take $g = 9.8$ m s^{-2})
    Ans : 196 kJ

11. Calculate the work done in stopping a truck of mass 5,000 kg moving with a velocity of 90 km h^{-1}.
    Ans : 1.56 MJ

12. A hammer of mass 1 kg falls freely from a height of 2 m. Calculate (a) the velocity with which it hits the ground and (b) the kinetic energy of the hammer just before it touches the ground.
    Ans : (a) 6.26 m s^{-1}, (b) 19.6 J

13. A bullet of mass 20 g moving with a velocity of 20 m s^{-1} is brought to rest by a wooden plank. Calculate the work done on the bullet before it comes to rest.
    Ans : 4 J

14. Calculate the kinetic energy of a body of mass 0.2 kg and momentum 25 kg m s^{-1}.
    Ans : 1.56 kJ

15. The kinetic energy of a body of mass 0.5 kg is 2,000 J. Calculate its momentum.
    Ans : 44.72 kg m s^{-1}

16. How much work is needed to be done on a ball of mass 20 g to give it a momentum of 10 kg m s^{-1}?
    Ans : 2.5 kJ

17. A body of mass 2 kg is initially at rest. A force of 10 N is applied on it. Calculate the kinetic energy of the body after 5 s.
    Ans : 625 J

18. How fast should a person weighing 1,000 N run so that his kinetic energy is 1,200 J? (Take $g = 10$ m s^{-2})
    Ans : 4.9 m s^{-1}

19. Calculate the work done by the engine if a train weighing 1,000 kgf changes its velocity from 36 km h^{-1} to 72 km h^{-1}. (Take $g = 10$ m s^{-2})
    Ans : 0.15 MJ

20. The momentum of a body is increased by 10 %. What is the % increase in kinetic energy of the body?
    Ans : 21%

21. A ball of mass 5 g falls from a height of 10 m. It rebounds from the ground to 8 m. Find (a) the initial potential energy of the ball, (b) the kinetic energy of the ball just before striking the ground, (c) the kinetic energy of the ball after striking the ground and (d) the loss in kinetic energy on striking the ground. (Take $g = 10$ m s^{-2})
    Ans : (a) 0.5 J, (b) 0.5 J, (c) 0.4 J, (d) 0.1 J

22. A stone of mass 0.3 kg is thrown vertically upwards with an initial velocity of 25 m s^{-1}. Calculate the maximum potential energy gained by the stone.
    Ans : 93.75 J

23. The bob of a simple pendulum is imparted a velocity of 4 m s^{-1} at its mean position. Calculate the maximum vertical height reached by the pendulum in its extreme position (a) if there is no loss of energy due to air friction and (b) if there is a 50% loss of energy due to air friction.
    Ans : (a) 0.8 m, (b) 0.4 m

24. In a hydroelectric power station, water is allowed to fall at a rate of 2,000 kJ s^{-1} on a turbine kept 100 m below the water level. Calculate (a) the potential energy of water falling every 1 s at the highest point, (b) the kinetic energy of this water when it falls through a height of 25 m and (c) the power output in 1 s if 80% of the initial potential energy is converted into electrical energy. (Take $g = 10$ m s^{-2})
    Ans : (a) 2 MJ, (b) 0.5 MJ, (c) 1.6 MW

3

MACHINES

LEARNING OUTCOMES

- Simple machines : Related terms, functions and principle
- Levers : Principles, classification (Class I, II and III), mechanical advantage, velocity ratio and efficiency of different classes
- Pulleys : Types, mechanical advantage, velocity ratio and efficiency of different types

MACHINES, LEVERS AND PULLEYS

3.1 SIMPLE MACHINES

In the modern era, machines have become an indispensable part of our everyday life. We are dependent on machines for almost every task. Thus, the word 'machine' can imply a complex device (or instrument) with complicated mechanism or a simple device with user friendly mechanism depending upon the process involved.

Examples : A scissor, a lemon-squeezer, a food grinder, a nutcracker, a spanner and so on.

The above mentioned examples are simple devices that make our day-to-day work easier. However, in physics, the term 'machine' has a specific meaning *i.e.*, a machine is a device or an object that is employed to do work that cannot be conveniently done without it. Thus,

A machine is a device that helps to overcome resistance due to a large force, or gain speed by applying a small force at a convenient point and in a desired direction.

A machine does not work by itself; it works only when some energy is supplied to it, which is then converted into useful work.

Kinds of Simple Machines

Simple machines can be broadly classified into two classes : (1) lever and (2) inclined plane.

Lever can further be classified as (a) pulley, (b) gear and (c) wheel and axle.

Inclined plane can be classified as (a) wedge and (b) screw.

Some of these machines will be discussed in detail in the following sections.

General Terms Related to Machines

1. Load (L) : The load is the *opposing or resistive force* against which the machine works.

2. Effort (E) : The effort is the *external force* applied on the machine to overcome the load.

3. Mechanical advantage (M.A.) : The mechanical advantage of a machine is the *ratio of the load to the effort.*

$$\text{Mechanical advantage (M.A.)} = \frac{\text{Load (L)}}{\text{Effort (E)}} \quad ...(3.1)$$

This ratio is a measure of the advantage that one obtains by using the machine.

If the effort applied is less than the load, then M.A. > 1.

If the effort applied is greater than the load, then M.A. < 1.

If the effort applied is equal to the load, then M.A. = 1.

M.A. is the ratio of two similar quantities; hence, it has *no unit*.

Examples :
(a) If a load of 50 N is moved by applying an effort of 10 N, then M.A. = 5.
(b) If a load of 20 N is moved by applying an effort of 40 N, then M.A. = 0.5.
(c) If a load of 10 N is moved by applying an effort of 10 N, then M.A. = 1.

4. Velocity ratio (V.R.) : The velocity ratio is the *ratio of the velocity at which the effort is applied on the machine to the velocity at which the load moves.*

$$\text{Velocity ratio (V.R.)} = \frac{\text{Velocity of effort }(V_E)}{\text{Velocity of load }(V_L)}$$

If d_E is the displacement caused by an effort in time t and d_L is the displacement caused by the load in the same time t, then

$$\text{Velocity of effort }(V_E) = \frac{d_E}{t}$$

$$\text{Velocity of load }(V_L) = \frac{d_L}{t}$$

∴ Velocity ratio (V.R.) $= \dfrac{d_E/t}{d_L/t} = \dfrac{d_E}{d_L}$

i.e., $\quad\quad \text{V. R.} = \dfrac{d_E}{d_L} \quad\quad$ ...(3.2)

Thus, *velocity ratio is also defined as the ratio of displacement of effort to the displacement of load.*

♦ If the displacement of effort is more than the displacement of load, then V.R. > 1.
♦ If the displacement of load is more than the displacement of effort, then V.R. < 1.
♦ If the displacement of effort is equal to the displacement of load, then V.R. = 1.

Just like M.A., V.R. is the ratio of two similar quantities; hence, it has *no unit*.

NOTE

The V.R. depends only on the *design* (dimensions) of the machine and is always same or *constant* for a particular machine. However, the M.A. can *vary* for a particular machine as it depends on *friction* (opposing force).

5. Input (W_{input}) : *The work done on the machine or energy supplied to the machine is called the input.* If an effort E causes a displacement d_E in its own direction, then

$$W_{input} = E \times d_E$$

6. Output (W_{output}) : *The work done by the machine on the load is called the output.* If a load L is displaced through a distance d_L, then

$$W_{output} = L \times d_L$$

7. Efficiency (η) : *Efficiency of a machine is the ratio of useful work done by the machine (output) to the work done on the machine (input).* It is represented by Greek symbol η (eta).

$$\text{Efficiency (η)} = \frac{\text{Output }(W_{output})}{\text{Input }(W_{input})} \quad\quad \text{...(3.3)}$$

It is usually expressed as a percentage (%). Thus,

$$\text{Efficiency(η)} = \frac{\text{Output }(W_{output})}{\text{Input }(W_{input})} \times 100\%$$

Efficiency is the ratio of two similar quantities; hence, it has *no unit*.

3.2 FUNCTIONS OF A SIMPLE MACHINE

From the definition of a machine and the general terms discussed above, we can list the functions of a machine as follows :

1. A machine can act as a *force multiplier*, i.e., to do a required work, only a small amount of effort needs to be applied.

Examples : A crowbar or a pulley is used for lifting heavy loads, a spanner or wrench is used to open up a tight nut, a jack is used to lift a car and so on.

In the above examples, effort < load and thus M.A. > 1. Also, V.R. > 1, as the displacement of load is less than the displacement of effort.

2. A machine can act as a *velocity multiplier*, i.e., a small movement of effort causes a large movement of the load.

Examples :
(a) When a large force with small wrist movement is applied on the upper part of a cricket bat, the lower part of the bat moves fast and hits hard on the ball and makes it move through a large distance.
(b) When cutting vegetables using a knife, its handle moves through a small distance while the blade moves through a large distance on the piece of vegetable.

In the above examples, effort > load, thus M. A. < 1. Also V. R. < 1, as the displacement of load is more than the displacement of effort.

3. A machine can act as a *direction changer*, i.e., the direction of effort can be changed to a convenient direction for ease of using a machine.

Example : A pulley can reverse the direction of the force applied. If a pulley is not used when drawing water from a well, then the bucket full of water needs to be pulled upwards using a rope, but if a pulley is used, the same work can be done more conveniently as the effort on the rope needs to be applied in the downward direction.

In this case, M.A. = 1, as effort = load, and V.R. = 1, as the displacement of load is equal to the displacement of effort.

4. A machine can *change the point of application* of effort to a convenient point for ease of doing work.

Example : The rear wheel is connected to the pedals with the help of a chain. Thus, the effort is applied on the pedals and not directly on the rear wheels to rotate it.

NOTE

A machine cannot be used as a *force multiplier* and a *speed multiplier simultaneously*.

3.3 PRINCIPLE OF A MACHINE

The point at which an input energy is applied is called the *effort point*, whereas the point at which output energy is obtained for overcoming the load is called the *load point*.

Example : When a pulley is used to pull a bucket from the well, an effort is applied on one end of the rope while the other end of the rope exerts an upward force on the bucket which overcomes the weight of the load of bucketful of water.

Input energy = Work done at the effort point
= Effort × Displacement of the point of application of effort
Output energy = Work done at the load point
= Load × Displacement of the point of application of load

According to the *law of conservation*, energy can neither be created nor be destroyed. Also output energy can never be greater than input energy. Thus, a machine cannot have an efficiency greater than 100% (or $\eta > 1$).

Ideal machine : A machine in which there is no loss of energy in any way is called an ideal machine. The efficiency of an ideal machine is 100% as the output energy is equal to the input energy.

Practically, an ideal machine does not exist.

Actual machine : A machine in which there occurs a loss of energy such that the output energy is always less than the input energy is called an actual machine. The efficiency of an actual machine is always less than 100% (or $\eta < 1$).

If a machine is 70% efficient, it means that only 70% of the input energy is obtained as useful output energy while the remaining 30% of the supplied energy is lost. The loss of energy can occur due to the following reasons :

1. The parts of a machine are not weightless; a part of input energy is wasted in moving the parts of the machine.

2. The parts of a machine are not frictionless; a part of input energy is wasted in overcoming friction between various parts of the machine.

3. The different parts of a machine do not have perfect rigidity.

3.4 RELATION BETWEEN M.A., V.R. AND η

If an effort E causes a displacement d_E in time t, and a displacement d_L occurs in overcoming a load L in the same time, then

$$\text{Input} = \text{Effort} \times \text{Displacement of effort}$$
$$W_{input} = E \times d_E$$
$$\text{Output} = \text{Load} \times \text{Displacement of load}$$
$$W_{output} = L \times d_L$$
$$\text{Efficiency }(\eta) = \frac{\text{Output }(W_{output})}{\text{Input }(W_{input})}$$

i.e. $\quad \eta = \dfrac{L \times d_L}{E \times d_E} = \dfrac{L}{E} \times \dfrac{d_L}{d_E}$

Since $\dfrac{L}{E} = $ M.A. and $\dfrac{d_E}{d_L} = $ V.R.

$\therefore \quad \eta = \dfrac{\text{M.A.}}{\text{V.R.}}$

i.e. $\quad$ M.A. = V.R. × η ...(3.4)

Thus, *efficiency is the ratio of mechanical advantage to velocity ratio of a machine.*

Only for an ideal machine, $\eta = 1$, where M.A. = V.R. For an actual machine, M.A. < V.R., so $\eta < 1$.

3.5 LEVERS

A lever is the simplest and most common machine used in everyday life.

A lever is a rigid, straight or bent bar capable of rotating around a fixed point or axis called the fulcrum.

A fulcrum (F) does not move but remains fixed when a lever is in use.

Principle of a Lever

A lever works on the *principle of moments*.

According to the principle of moments, in the equilibrium position of the lever,

Moment of load about the fulcrum = Moment of effort about the fulcrum

i.e. Load × Load arm = Effort × Effort arm

$$\frac{\text{Load}}{\text{Effort}} = \frac{\text{Effort arm}}{\text{Load arm}}$$

i.e. $\text{M.A} = \dfrac{\text{Effort arm}}{\text{Load arm}}$ ...(3.5)

This expression is known as the *law of levers*, *i.e.* the M.A. of a lever is equal to the ratio of the length of its effort arm to the length of its load arm.

- If effort arm = load arm, then M.A. = 1.
- If effort arm < load arm, then M.A. < 1.
- If effort arm > load arm, then M.A. > 1.

Thus, to increase the M.A. of a lever, either the effort arm should be increased or the load arm should be decreased.

Classification of Levers

Depending upon the relative positions of the fulcrum, effort and load, the levers can be classified into three classes : (1) Class I levers or levers of the first order, (2) Class II levers or levers of the second order and (3) Class III levers or levers of the third order.

1. Class I levers : A lever in which the load is at one end and effort at the other end with the fulcrum lying in between the two is known as *Class I lever*.

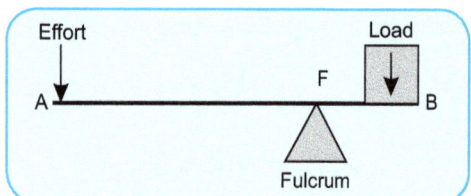

Fig. 3.1 : Class I lever.

In Fig. 3.1, Effort arm = AF and Load arm = BF.

∴ $\text{M.A} = \dfrac{\text{AF}}{\text{BF}}$

Characteristics :

(a) It is not necessary that the fulcrum should lie at the midpoint (centre) of the effort and load arms. It can lie anywhere between the two arms.

(b) The M.A. and V.R. can have any value : > 1, = 1 or < 1.

(c) The M.A. can be increased by moving the fulcrum towards the load, *i.e.* AF > BF.

(d) If the fulcrum is moved towards the load, keeping the load constant, then the effort applied decreases.

Examples :

1. A crowbar (used for lifting stones), shears (used for cutting the thin metal sheets), claw hammer, plier (Fig. 3.2), handle of a common water pump and so on. These levers have a long effort arm. The M.A. and V.R. of these levers are greater than 1, and these types of levers act as a *force multiplier*, *i.e.* a large load can be overcome by applying a small effort.

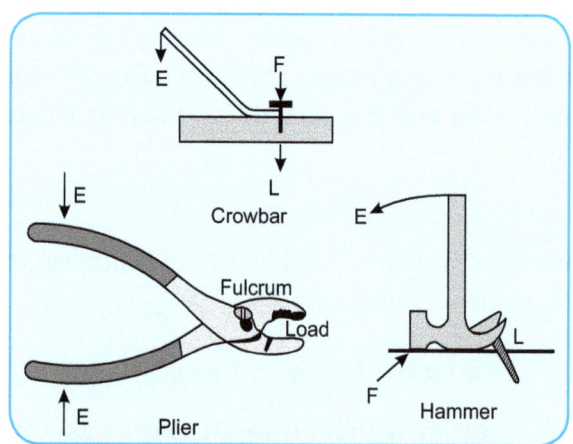

Fig. 3.2. : Crowbar, pliers and hammer.

2. The levers in which the effort arm is shorter than the load arm, the M.A. and V.R. are less than 1. These types of levers, such as a pair of scissors and a long handle oar, act as a velocity multiplier.

Scissors : In scissors, the cutting edge or the blade (load arm) is longer than the handle (effort arm). When the handles are moved through a short distance with an effort, the blades move through longer distance on the cloth (Fig. 3.3).

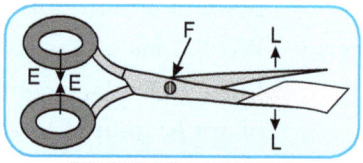

Fig. 3.3 : Scissors

A long-handle oar : It is used by a single person for rowing the boat. Here the fulcrum is the point on the oar at the edge of the boat at which the handle is supported. The effort is applied at one end, keeping the effort arm shorter than the load arm. The longer load arm gives a large movement to the blade of the oar attached to it to push the water back through a longer distance so that the boat can move forward.

Other examples of Class I lever are a see-saw, a beam balance, spade for turning soil, a spoon to open the lid of a tin can and so on.

2. **Class II levers** : A lever in which the load acts in the middle with the effort at one end and fulcrum at the other end is known *as Class II lever* (Fig. 3.4).

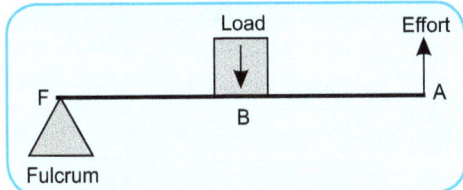

Fig. 3.4 : Class II lever.

Characteristics :

(a) The load and effort are in opposite directions.

(b) The effort arm is always longer than the load arm.

(c) M.A. and V.R. are always < 1.

(d) The M.A. can be increased by moving the load towards the fulcrum.

(e) It always acts as a *force multiplier, i.e.* a less effort is needed to overcome a large load.

Examples : A nut cracker, vegetable cutter (fixed on chopping board), sugarcane cutter, lemon-squeezer, bottle opener, wheel barrow, hinges of a door, lock and key system and so on (Fig. 3.5).

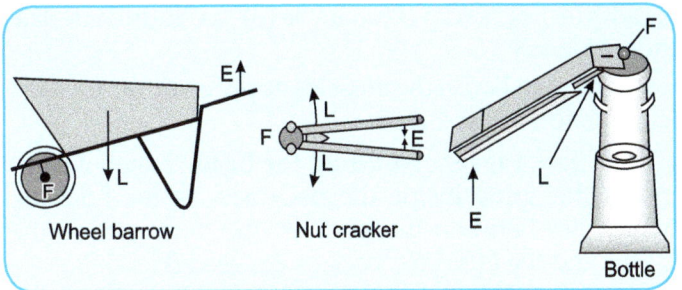

Fig. 3.5 : Examples of Class-II levers.

3. **Class III levers** : A lever in which the effort acts in the middle with the load at one end and fulcrum at the other end is known as Class III lever (Fig. 3.6).

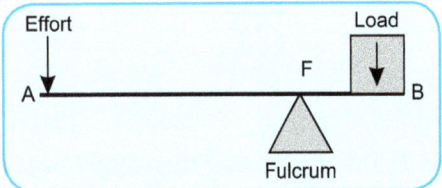

Fig. 3.6 : Class III lever.

Characteristics :

(a) The load and effort are in opposite directions.

(b) The effort arm is always shorter than the load arm.

(c) M.A. and V.R. are always < 1.

(d) It always acts as a *velocity multiplier* as there is a gain in speed.

Examples : Fishing rod, spade, forceps, hair plucker, sugar tongs, fire tongs, knife, a broomstick and so on (Fig. 3.7).

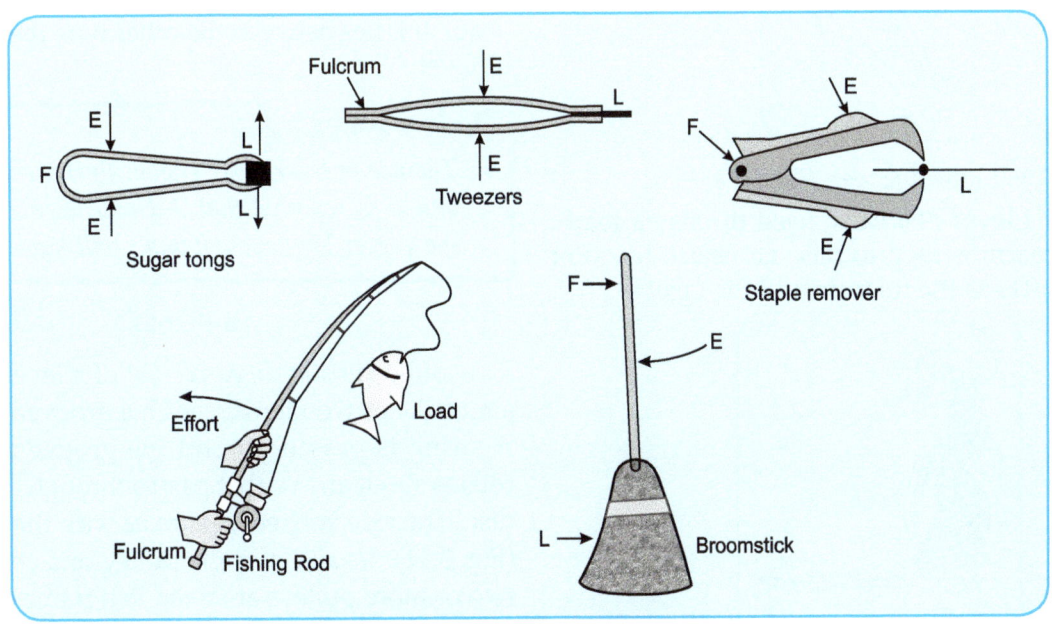

Fig. 3.7 : Examples of Class III levers.

Examples of each class of lever as found in the human body

In human body, the muscles apply an effort by their contraction to lift a load.

1. Class I lever : Nodding the head : When a head nods, the spine inside the neck acts as the fulcrum, which lies between the load (*i.e.* the front part of the head) and the effort (*i.e.* back of the head (Fig. 3.8).

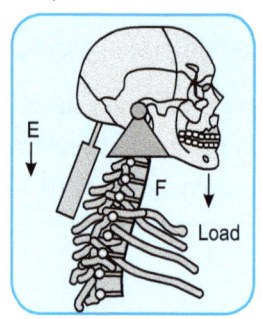

Fig. 3.8 : Nodding of head (Class I lever).

2. Class II lever : Raising the weight of the body on toes : When the toes of the feet are raised, the toes act as the fulcrum. The load is the weight of the body which lies between the fulcrum and the effort, *i.e.* the contraction of the muscles (Fig. 3.9).

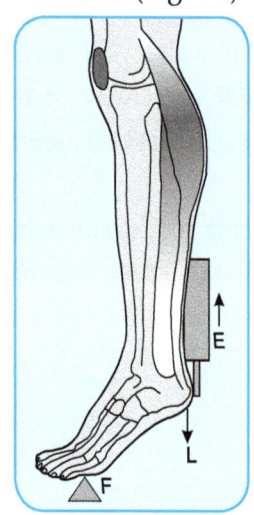

Fig. 3.9 : Lifting the toes (Class II lever).

3. Class III lever : Forearm used to raise a load : When the forearm is used to raise an object, the joint of the elbow acts as the fulcrum and the object

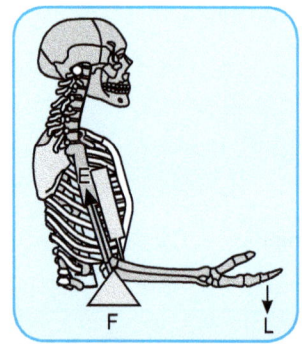

Fig. 3.10 : Raising a forearm (Class III lever).

on the palm acts as the load. The effort is the bicep muscles lying in between the elbow and the palm, *i.e.* in between the fulcrum and the load (Fig. 3.10).

Comparison between the different classes of levers

Class I lever	Class II lever	Class III lever
Fulcrum (F) lies between load (L) and effort (E).	Load(L) lies between fulcrum (F) and effort (E).	Effort (E) lies between fulcrum (F) and load(L).
M.A. can be equal to 1, less than 1 or greater than 1.	M.A. is always greater than 1.	M.A. is always less than 1.
These levers can act as either force multiplier or velocity multiplier.	These levers always act as a force multiplier.	These levers always act as velocity multiplier.
Examples : Scissor, crowbar, nodding of human head and so on.	*Examples :* Nutcracker, bottle opener, raising the weight of human body on toes and so on.	*Examples :* Sugar tongs, spade, raising a load by human forearm etc.

Aid to remember about the three classes of levers :
Learn the word 'FLE' (Fulcrum, Load and Effort).

(a) If F lies between the other two, then it is a Class I lever.

(b) If L lies between the other two, then it is a Class II lever.

(c) If E lies between the other two, then it is a Class III lever.

> **Do You Know ?**
>
> - The use of levers was known to the ancient Greeks, and it is reported that Archimedes once said 'Give me a lever long enough and I will move the world!'

3.6 PULLEY

A pulley is a *modified version* of a lever. A pulley is a metallic or wooden *disc* with a grooved edge or rim. A string is passed around the groove at the rim. It rotates about an *axle* that passes through a centre of the disc. The axle is fixed to a *frame* with the help of nails (Fig. 3.11). *Usually* a single pulley or a combination of two or more pulleys are fixed in a frame called *a block*. A rope or string that is wound around the pulleys in different blocks is called a *tackle*.

A pulley can be either (1) *fixed pulley* if the block is clamped or (2) *movable pulley* if the block is not clamped.

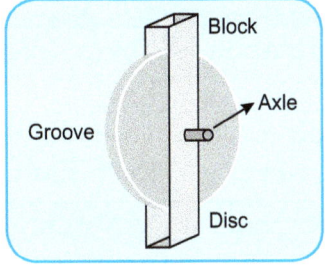

Fig. 3.11 : A pulley.

Single Fixed Pulley

A fixed pulley has its axis of rotation fixed in a position, *i.e.*, its frame is clamped. In this arrangement, the block of the pulley is fixed on a high platform. An extensible string of negligible mass passes through the groove of the pulley. To one end of the string, the load is tied and the effort is applied at the other end (Fig. 3.12). The effort E and load L both act in the downward direction. The tension T of the rope acts on both the sides in the upward direction.

A single fixed pulley can be regarded as a modification of Class I lever where the fulcrum is at the centre and the load and effort arms have the same length.

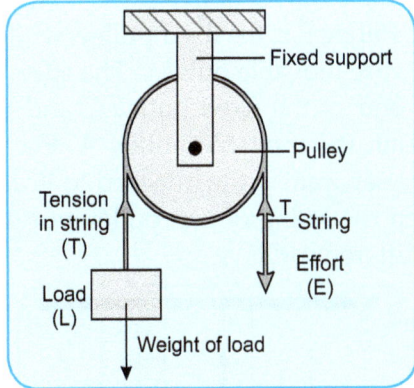

Fig. 3.12 : Single fixed pulley.

M.A., V.R. and η of a single fixed pulley

If the pulley is not rotating and the load due to friction and movable parts is neglected, then both the load and effort are equal to the tension, *i.e.*

$$E = L = T$$

∴ $$\text{M.A.} = \frac{L}{E} = \frac{T}{T} = 1 \qquad \ldots(3.6)$$

In using a single fixed pulley, the effort needed to lift a load is equal to the load, in an ideal condition.

In a single fixed pulley, the distance moved by the load L is same as the distance moved by the effort E, *i.e.*

$$d_E = d_L$$

∴ $$\text{V.R.} = \frac{d_E}{d_L} = 1 \qquad \ldots(3.7)$$

Efficiency, $$\eta = \frac{\text{M.A.}}{\text{V.R.}} = 1 \text{ or } 100\% \quad \ldots(3.8)$$

This holds true for an ideal pulley, *i.e.* if the mass of the string and the friction in the pulley parts are ignored.

However, in practical condition, due to the friction in movable parts of the pulley, the effort required is greater than the load and thus the M.A. is less than 1.

Since both M.A. and V.R. are < 1, there is *no gain* in M.A. or V.R. of the pulley; it acts as neither a *force multiplier* nor a *velocity multiplier*.

A fixed pulley is used only to *change the direction of the force applied* so that the effort can be applied in a convenient direction.

Example : A fixed pulley is used for lifting loads such as a bucket full of water from a well by applying an effort in the downward direction because lifting of loads is more convenient in the direction of gravity. Otherwise, it would require extra effort if applied in the upward direction.

Single Movable Pulley

A movable pulley has an axis of rotation that is not fixed. In this arrangement, the block is not fixed but carries the load. An inextensible string of negligible mass is wound around the groove and its one end is tied with a hook to a fixed support while the other end is kept free to apply the effort E. The load L is suspended from the axle for raising the block. When an effort is applied, the block and the load together move upwards. The tension T acts on the string on both sides of the pulley in the same direction (Fig. 3.13).

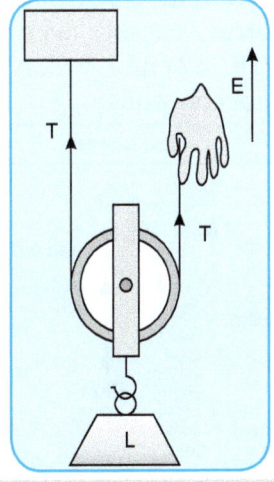

Fig. 3.13 : Single movable pulley.

M.A., V.R. and η of a single movable pulley

In a movable pulley, the string is divided into two segments. The tension acts in the upward direction along the two segments of the string.

Since the effort E at the free end balances the tension T,
∴ E = T

The load L is balanced in the middle by the tension in both the segments.
∴ L = T + T = 2T

Since $\text{M.A.} = \dfrac{\text{Load}}{\text{Effort}}$

∴ $\text{M.A.} = \dfrac{2T}{T} = 2$ ...(3.9)

Since M.A. = 2 (i.e. M.A. > 1), a single movable pulley acts as a *force multiplier*, i.e. to lift a load, an effort equal to half the load needs to be applied.

If the effort at the free end of the string moves by a distance d, then the load is pulled up by a distance $d/2$.

$d_E = d, \; d_L = \dfrac{d}{2}$

$\text{V.R.} = \dfrac{d_E}{d_L} = \dfrac{d}{d/2} = 2$ ...(3.10)

Efficiency, $\eta = \dfrac{\text{M.A.}}{\text{V.R.}} = \dfrac{2}{2} = 1$ or 100% ...(3.11)

This is valid for an ideal pulley, i.e., if the weight of the pulley is negligible as compared to the load L.

However, in an actual movable pulley, due to friction between the parts and due to the weight of the pulley and string, the M.A. < 2 and η < 100%, but the V.R. will always remain 2.

Use of a Fixed Pulley along with a Movable Pulley to Change the Direction of Effort

It is inconvenient to use a single movable pulley as it is difficult to apply effort in an upward direction. A single movable pulley is always used along with a fixed pulley so that the effort may be applied in a downward direction. In this combination, the load is attached to the axle of the movable pulley, whereas the effort is applied in the downward direction at the free end of the string passing over the fixed pulley (Fig. 3.14). The V. R. = 2 and 1 < M. A. < 2, i.e. same as that of a single movable pulley.

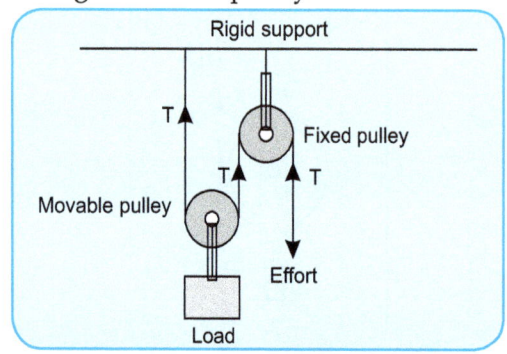

Fig. 3.14 : Single movable pulley with a fixed pulley.

Difference between single fixed and single movable pulley

Single fixed pulley	Single movable pulley
The axis of rotation is fixed.	The axis of rotation is not fixed.
Load and effort move in opposite direction.	Load and effort move in same direction.
M.A. = 1 in ideal condition.	M.A. = 2 in ideal condition.
V. R. = 1.	V.R. = 2.
It is used to change the direction of effort in a convenient direction, i.e. from upward to downward.	It is used to multiply the force.

3.7 COMBINATION OF PULLEYS

To lift a heavy load, a pulley system with M.A. > 2 is required. To achieve this, a combination of several pulleys is used. This combination can be of two types : (1) one fixed pulley with several movable pulleys and (2) several pulleys in two blocks, known as *block and tackle system*.

1. One fixed pulley with several movable pulleys

In Fig. 3.15, a system of five pulleys A, B, C, D and E is shown. Pulley E is the fixed pulley, while the other four pulleys are movable pulleys. The effort is applied at the free end of the fixed pulley E and the load is lifted through the movable pulley A. Each movable pulley has a separate string attached to it. The tension T is same in the string of one pulley but different in strings of different pulleys.

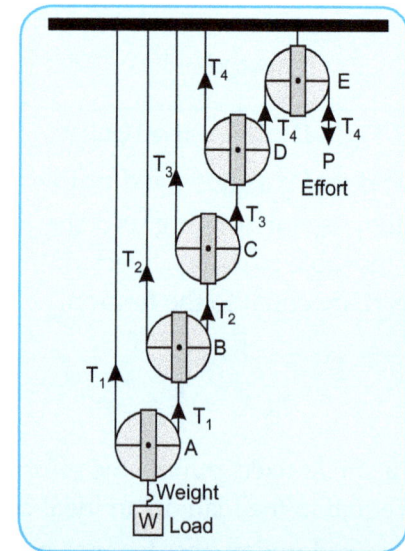

Fig. 3.15 : One fixed pulley with four movable pulleys.

Mechanical advantage : Load L is supported by the two segments of the string passing over pulley A. Tension T_1 in the string is given as

$$2T_1 = L \text{ or } T_1 = \frac{L}{2}.$$

Now, two segments of the string passing over pulley B support the tension T_1 and so tension T_2 is given as

$$2T_2 = T_1 \text{ or } T_2 = \frac{T_1}{2} = \frac{L}{2^2}$$

Similarly, the tension T_3 in the two segments of the string passing over the pulley C is given as

$$2T_3 = T_2 \text{ or } T_3 = \frac{T_2}{2} = \frac{L}{2^3}$$

And the tension T_4 in the two segments of the string passing over the pulley D is given as

$$2T_4 = T_3 \text{ or } T_4 = \frac{T_3}{2} = \frac{L}{2^4}$$

In an equilibrium condition, the effort applied by the string of pulley E is equal to the tension in the string passing over pulley D, i.e.

$$E = T_4$$

i.e. $$E = \frac{L}{2^4}$$

Since $$\text{M.A.} = \frac{L}{E}$$

∴ $$\text{M.A.} = \frac{L}{L/2^4} = 2^4$$

If in a system, there are n numbers of movable pulleys with one fixed pulley, then the M.A. is given as

$$\text{M.A.} = 2^n \qquad ...(3.12)$$

Velocity ratio : In this arrangement of combination of pulleys, one end of each string passing over a movable pulley is fixed and the other end of the string moves up twice the distance moved by the preceding pulley.

Suppose the load L attached to the pulley A moves by a distance d, then the string attached to the axle of pulley B moves up by a distance $2d$. The string attached to the axle of pulley C moves up by a distance $2 \times 2d = 2^2 d$. Similarly, the string passing over the pulley D will move up by a distance $2 \times 2^2 d = 2^3 d$ and the end of the string passing over the fixed pulley E will move by a distance $2 \times 2^3 d = 2^4 d$ or $d_E = 2^4 d$.

Since $$\text{V.R.} = \frac{d_E}{d_L}$$

∴ $$\text{V.R.} = \frac{2^4 d}{d} = 2^4$$

If a system consists of n numbers of movable pulleys connected to one fixed pulley, then velocity ratio is given as

$$\text{V.R.} = 2^n \qquad ...(3.13)$$

Efficiency, $$\eta = \frac{\text{M.A.}}{\text{V.R.}} = \frac{2^n}{2^n}$$

$$= 1 \text{ or } 100\% \qquad ...(3.14)$$

Again, this is valid only in an ideal pulley system. In actual system, due to the weight of the pulleys and the string and due to friction between the parts, the efficiency is always less than 1.

2. Several pulleys in two blocks or block and tackle system

This system consists of two sets of pulleys. The upper set consisting of several pulleys is attached to a rigid support at the top and is called the *block*. The lower set consisting of several pulleys is movable, carries the load L and is called the *tackle*.

An inextensible string of negligible mass passes over the rim of all the pulleys. One end of the string is free where the effort E is applied. The other end of the string is attached to the hook of the upper or lower block, depending on the number of pulleys in each block.

The number of pulleys in the upper block is equal to or one more than the number of pulleys in the lower block.

If the number of pulleys in the upper block is more than in the lower block then the end of the string is attached to the hook of the lower block. In Fig. 3.16, the upper block consists of three pulleys while the lower block consists of two pulleys. The end of the string can be seen attached to the hook of the lower block.

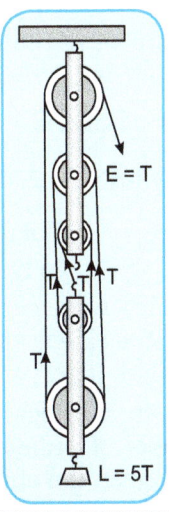

Fig. 3.16 : Block and tackle for five pulleys.

However, if the number of pulleys is same in both the blocks then the end of the string is attached to the hook of the upper block so that the effort is applied in the downward direction for convenience. In Fig. 3.17, both the upper and the lower block consist of two pulleys. In this case, the end of the string is attached to the hook of the upper block.

The tension T is same along the entire length of the string.

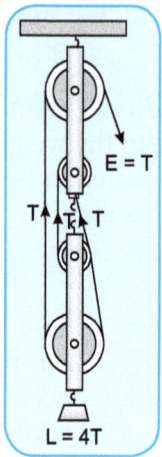

Fig. 3.17 : Block and tackle for four pulleys.

Mechanical advantage : In Fig. 3.16, showing *five* pulleys (three in the upper block and two in the lower block), the load L is supported by the tension in all five segments of the string and the effort is supported by the tension in the last segment.

∴ L = 5T and E = T

Since M.A. = $\frac{\text{Load}}{\text{Effort}}$

∴ M.A. = $\frac{5T}{T}$ = 5

Similarly, in the system of *four* pulleys,

L = 4T and E = T

∴ M.A. = $\frac{4T}{T}$ = 4

If n is the total number of pulleys used in both the blocks, then

L = nT and E = T   ...(3.15)

∴ M.A. = $\frac{nT}{T} = n$ ...(3.16)

= Total number of pulleys in both the blocks

From equation (3.15), E = L/n, more the number of pulleys in a block and tackle system, less is the effort that needs to be applied. It acts as a *force multiplier*.

Velocity ratio : In a block and tackle system composed of n number of pulleys, if the load moves through a distance d, then the effort moves through a distance nd, *i.e.*, $d_L = d$ and $d_E = nd$.

Since V.R. = $\frac{d_E}{d_L}$

∴ V.R. = $\frac{nd}{d} = n$ ...(3.17)

The velocity ratio is always equal to the number of string segments supporting the load.

Efficiency (η) = $\frac{\text{M.A.}}{\text{V.R.}} = \frac{n}{n}$ = 1 or 100%   ...(3.18)

This is valid only in an ideal system.

In an actual system, the M.A. and the η decrease due to weight of the pulleys and the string and due to friction between the moving parts.

Effect of weight of pulleys on M.A., V.R. and η : Let there be n pulleys in a system and let the weight of the lower block along with the pulleys be w.

In an equilibrium position,

E = T and L + w = nT

i.e. L = nT − w = nE − w

Since M.A. = $\frac{\text{Load}}{\text{Effort}}$

∴ M.A. = $\frac{nE - w}{E} = n - \frac{w}{E}$ ...(3.19)

i.e., M.A. < n

The velocity ratio remains unchanged, *i.e.*

V. R. = n ...(3.20)

Efficiency (η) = $\frac{\text{M. A.}}{\text{V. R.}} = \frac{n - w/E}{n}$

= $1 - \frac{w}{nE}$ ...(3.21)

Due to the weight of the lower block of the pulleys, the efficiency gets reduced. Thus, for greater efficiency, the weight in the lower block should be light and the friction in the pulley parts should be minimised by applying lubricants.

ILLUSTRATIVE EXAMPLES

1. A machine has a mechanical advantage equal to 4. It raises a load of 20 N. Calculate the minimum effort that has been applied to it.

   Solution : Given,

   M.A. = 4, L = 20 N

   Effort (E) = $\frac{L}{M. A.} = \frac{20}{4} = 5 N$

   The effort applied to the machine is 5 N.

2. An effort of 8 kgf is applied on a machine through a distance of 60 cm when a load of 80 kgf moves through a distance of 4 cm. Calculate the (a) velocity ratio, (b) mechanical advantage and (c) % efficiency of machine.

   Solution : Given, E = 8 kgf, d_E = 60 cm, L = 80 kgf, d_L = 4 cm

   (a) Velocity ratio (V.R.) = $\frac{d_E}{d_L} = \frac{60}{4} = 15$

   (b) Mechanical advantage (M.A.) = $\frac{L}{E} = \frac{80}{8} = 10$

   (c) % Efficiency (η) = $\frac{M.A.}{V.R.} \times 100 = \frac{10}{15} \times 100$

   = 66.66%

3. Draw a simple diagram of (a) a wheel barrow and (b) a plier and mark on it the fulcrum and

points of load and effort. To which class of levers does each of these belong ?

Solution :

(a)

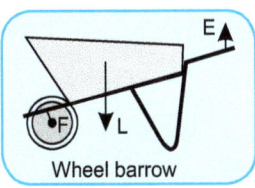

It belongs to the Class II type of lever.

(b)

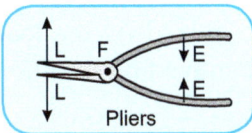

It belongs to the Class I type of lever.

4. A crowbar of length 150 cm has its fulcrum at a distance of 25 cm from the load. Calculate the mechanical advantage of this crowbar.

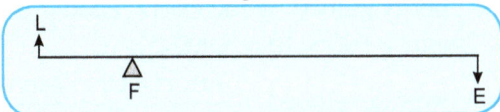

Solution : Given, Total length of the bar = 150 cm, Load arm = 25 cm.
So, Effort arm = 150 − 25 = 125 cm
M.A. = Effort arm/Load arm = 125/25 = 5.

5. To lift a piece of burning coal of mass 200 g, a cook uses a fire tong of length 25 cm. He applies the effort at a distance of 8 cm from its fulcrum. Find the effort applied by the cook. (Take $g = 10$ m s^{-2})

Solution : Given, m = 200 g = 0.2 kg, Load arm = 25 cm = 0.25 m, Effort arm = 8 cm = 0.08 m, g = 10 m s^{-2}
Load, L = $m \times g$ = 0.2 × 10 = 2 N
Applying the principle of moments,
Load × Load arm = Effort × Effort arm
∴ Effort = Load × $\dfrac{\text{Load arm}}{\text{Effort arm}}$
= $2 \times \dfrac{0.25}{0.08}$ = 6.25 N

6. The length of a nutcracker is 30 cm. A nut is kept 6 cm away from the fulcrum and an effort of 30 N is applied at the other end of the nutcracker. Calculate the (a) resistance offered by the nutcracker and (b) find the mechanical advantage.

Solution : A nutcracker belongs to the Class II type of lever, i.e. the load lies between the effort and the fulcrum.

Given, Length of the nutcracker = Effort arm = 30 cm = 0.30 m, Load arm = 6 cm = 0.06 m, Effort E = 30 N

(a) Resistance offered by the nutcracker is equal to its load.
Applying the principle of moments,
Load × Load arm = Effort × Effort arm
∴ Load = Effort × $\dfrac{\text{Effort arm}}{\text{Load arm}}$
= $30 \times \dfrac{0.30}{0.06}$ = 150 N

(b) M.A. = $\dfrac{\text{Effort arm}}{\text{Load arm}} = \dfrac{0.30}{0.06} = 5$

7. The given diagram shows a lever in use. (a) To which class of lever does it belong ? (b) If FA = 40 cm, AB = 60 cm, find the mechanical advantage of the lever.

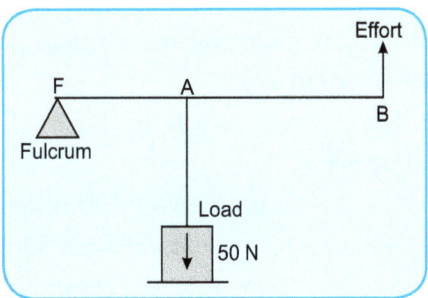

Solution :

(a) Since the load lies in between the fulcrum and the effort, it is a Class II lever.

(b) Given FA = 40 cm = Load arm, AB = 60 cm, Load, L = 50 N
Effort arm = FA + AB
= 40 + 60 = 100 cm
M.A. = $\dfrac{\text{Effort arm}}{\text{Load arm}} = \dfrac{100}{40} = 2.5$

8. A mass of 200 kg drives a machine when it falls to a distance of 10 m in 5 s. The machine lifts a load of mass 800 kg vertically upwards. Calculate (a) the work done by the falling mass in its displacement, (b) the power input provided to the machine, (c) the power output of the machine if its efficiency is 70% and (d) the work done by the machine in 5 s. (Take $g = 10$ m s^{-2})

Solution : Given, m = 200 kg, S = 10 m, t = 5 s, L = 800 kg, g = 10 m s^{-2}, η = 70%

(a) Force exerted by the falling mass
= $m \times g$ = 200 × 10
= 2,000 N

Work done by the falling mass
$$= F \times S = 2{,}000 \times 10$$
$$= 20{,}000 \text{ J}$$

(b) Power input $= \dfrac{\text{Work done on machine}}{\text{Time taken}}$

$$= \dfrac{20{,}000}{5} = 4{,}000 \text{ W}$$

(c) Efficiency $= \dfrac{\text{Power output}}{\text{Power input}}$

∴ Power output = Efficiency × Power input

$$= \dfrac{70}{100} \times 4{,}000 = 2{,}800 \text{ W}$$

(d) Work done by the machine
$$= \text{Power output} \times \text{Time}$$
$$= 2{,}800 \times 5 = 14{,}000 \text{ J}$$

9. A woman draws water from a well using a fixed pulley. The mass of the bucket and water together is 6 kg. The force applied by the woman is 70 N. Calculate the mechanical advantage. (Take $g = 10$ m s^{-2})

Solution : Given, $m = 6$ kg, Effort (E) = 70 N, $g = 10$ m s^{-2}

Load = Weight of bucket and Water
$$= m \times g = 6 \times 10 = 60 \text{ N}$$
M.A. = Load/Effort
$$= 60/70 = 0.857$$

10. A combination of a movable pulley P_1 with a fixed pulley P_2 is used for lifting up a load of 20 kgf. Calculate the effort applied at the free end of the string, neglecting the weight of the pulley P_1 and friction.

Solution : Given, load = 20 kgf
Let the effort move by a distance d.
Then the load will move by a distance $d/2$
From the principle of moments,
Load × Load arm = Effort × Effort arm
i.e., $20 \times d/2 = \text{Effort} \times d$
∴ Effort = 20/2
$$= 10 \text{ kgf} = 10 \times 9.8 = 98 \text{ N}$$

11. In the given figure, a load of 500 N is lifted by a man with the help of a fixed pulley through a height of 10 m in 20 s. The effort applied at the free end is 600 N. (a) Calculate the velocity ratio of the pulley, (b) the mechanical advantage, (c) the efficiency of the pulley, (d) the energy gained by the load and (e) the power developed by the man.

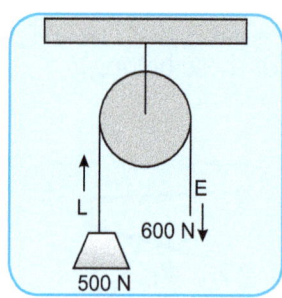

Solution : Given, L = 500 N, S = 10 m, t = 20 s, E = 600 N

(a) The velocity ratio of a fixed pulley is 1 as the distance moved by the load is equal to the distance moved by the effort.

(b) M.A. $= \dfrac{L}{E} = \dfrac{500}{600} = 0.833$

(c) Efficiency $(\eta) = \dfrac{\text{M.A.}}{\text{V.R.}} \times 100\%$

$$= \dfrac{0.833}{1} \times 100 = 83.3\%$$

(d) Energy gained by the load = Load × Displacement = 500 × 10 = 5,000 J

(e) Power developed $= \dfrac{\text{Effort} \times \text{Displacement}}{\text{Time}}$

$$= \dfrac{600 \times 10}{20} = 300 \text{ W}$$

12. A system of pulleys with a velocity ratio of 4 is used to lift a load of 200 kgf through a vertical height of 15 m. The effort required is 80 kgf in the downward direction. Calculate (a) the number of pulleys in the system, (b) the distance moved by the effort, (c) mechanical advantage and (d) efficiency of the pulley system.

Solution : Given, V.R. = 4, L = 200 kgf, $d_L = 15$ m, E = 80 kgf

(a) No. of pulleys = V.R. of the system = 4

(b) V.R. $= \dfrac{d_E}{d_L}$

∴ $d_E = $ V.R. $\times d_L = 4 \times 15 = 60$ m

(c) M.A. $= \dfrac{L}{E} = \dfrac{200}{80} = 2.5$

(d) Efficiency $(\eta) = \dfrac{\text{M.A.}}{\text{V.R.}} \times 100 = \dfrac{2.5}{4} \times 100 = 62.5\%$

13. A block and tackle system consisting of five pulleys has three pulleys in the upper block and two pulleys in the lower block. If the load is raised by 1 m, through what distance will the effort move ?

Solution : As there are five pulleys in the system, V.R. = 5, given $d_L = 1$ m

Since V.R. $= \dfrac{d_E}{d_L}$

∴ $d_E = $ V.R. $\times d_L = 5 \times 1 = 5$ m

EXERCISE

1. What do you understand by a simple machine?
2. Name any two simple machines used in everyday life.
   Ans : Scissors and nutcracker.
3. What is mechanical advantage? State its unit.
4. What is velocity ratio? Does it have any unit?
5. What is the condition for mechanical advantage to be less than 1 and velocity ratio to be greater than 1?
6. With reference to the terms mechanical advantage, velocity ratio and efficiency of a machine, name and define the term that will not change for a machine of a given design.
7. What is efficiency of a machine?
8. State the different functions of a machine?
9. Name a machine that can be used to (a) multiply force and (b) change the direction of force applied.
   Ans : (a) Lever, (b) A single fixed pulley.
10. State the mechanical advantage if a machine should act as a (a) force multiplier and (b) direction changer.
    Ans : (a) M.A. > 1, (b) M.A. = 1
11. If mechanical advantage and velocity ratio are less than 1, will a machine be velocity multiplier or force multiplier?
    Ans : Velocity multiplier.
12. A scissor is a .... multiplier.
    Ans : Force
13. Give one example of a machine for the use of (a) changing the direction of force and (b) changing the point of application of force.
    Ans : (a) Pulley, (b) Bicycle.
14. What is meant by an ideal machine?
15. In what ways an ideal machine differs from a practical machine?
    Ans : An ideal machine is 100% efficient unlike a practical machine.
16. Can a machine act as a force multiplier and a speed multiplier at the same time?
    Ans : No
17. Why is a machine not 100% efficient?
18. Write a relation between the mechanical advantage (M.A.) and velocity ratio (V.R.) of an ideal machine.
    Ans : M.A. = V.R.
19. Derive the relation between mechanical advantage, velocity ratio and efficiency of a machine.
20. What is the magnitude of mechanical advantage and velocity ratio of an actual machine?
21. What is a lever? What is the principle of its working?
22. Write an expression for the mechanical advantage of a lever.
23. How are levers classified? Give two examples of each type.
24. State the characteristics of a Class I lever. Give one example of a Class I lever where mechanical advantage is equal to one.
25. Give two examples each of Class I lever where mechanical advantage is (a) less than 1 and (b) more than 1.
26. Draw a labelled sketch of a Class II lever and state its characteristics. Give two examples of such a lever.
27. What is the mechanical advantage and velocity ratio of a Class II lever?
    Ans : M.A. > 1, V.R. > 1
28. Where are the load, effort and fulcrum of a Class III lever located? Give two examples of Class III lever.
29. The following are the examples of levers. State the class of lever to which each one belongs, giving the relative position of load (L), effort (E) and fulcrum (F).
    (a) Scissors
    (b) Sugar tongs
    (c) Nut cracker
    (d) Pliers
    (e) Wheel barrow
30. Explain why scissors for cutting cloth may have blades much longer than the handles but shears for cutting metal have short blades and long handles?
31. State the use of a lever that has a mechanical advantage less than 1. Give a suitable example.

32. Which class of levers has a mechanical advantage always greater than 1? What change can be brought about in this lever to increase its mechanical advantage?

33. The figure given below shows a crowbar. Mark the position of fulcrum, load and effort. To which class of lever does it belong?

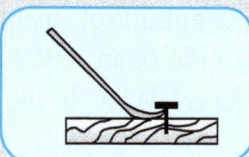

34. The figure given below is of a nutcracker. Mark the position of fulcrum, load and effort. To which class of lever does it belong?

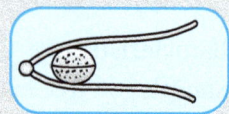

35. Why is the mechanical advantage of a Class II lever always greater than 1, whereas that of a Class III lever is always less than 1?

36. What type of lever is formed by the human body while (a) nodding the head and (b) raising the toes of the feet?

37. Indicate the position of the fulcrum, load and effort in case of a human forearm.

38. Draw a simplified diagram of a lemon crusher, indicating direction of load and effort.

39. State the class of levers and the relative positions of load (L), effort (E) and fulcrum (F) in the following cases : (a) bottle opener and (b) sugar tongs.

    Ans : (a) Bottle opener : Class II lever, L lies between F and E, (b) Sugar tongs : Class III lever, E lies between F and L.

40. Draw diagrams and mark the positions of load (L), effort (E) and fulcrum (F) in the following cases : (a) see-saw, (b) claw hammer and (c) forceps.

41. What is a pulley?

42. What are the two different types of pulley? How do they differ from each other?

43. What is a single fixed pulley? State its use.

44. What is the mechanical advantage of an ideal single fixed pulley? Is it same for an actual pulley?

45. Can a single fixed pulley act as a speed multiplier?
    Ans : No.

46. What is the velocity ratio of a single fixed pulley?
    Ans : V.R. = 1

47. What is a single movable pulley? State its mechanical advantage in the ideal situation.

48. Draw a diagram of a single movable pulley. How does it act as a force multiplier?

49. What is the velocity ratio of an ideal single movable pulley? Does it differ in an actual case?

50. Give two reasons why the efficiency of a single movable pulley is not 100%.

51. Why is a fixed pulley used along with a movable pulley?

52. Draw a diagram showing a single fixed pulley along with a single movable pulley.

53. If d is the distance moved by the effort in a single movable pulley, by what distance will the load get raised?

54. The given diagram shows a system of two pulleys. (a) Which of these is a fixed pulley? (b) What does A and B represent in the figure? (c) Mark the direction of tension on each strand of the string. (d) What is the velocity ratio and mechanical advantage of the system, assuming it to be an ideal system?

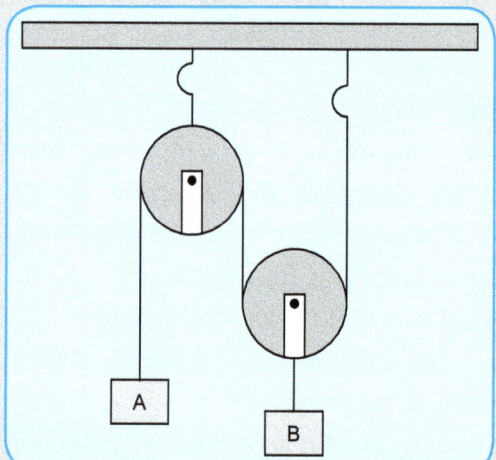

55. The given diagram shows a system of three pulleys with a load of 100 N. (a) Mark the effort in the diagram. (b) What will be the magnitude of the effort? (c) Mark the tension in each segment of the string of the system. (d) What will be the mechanical advantage and velocity ratio of the system?

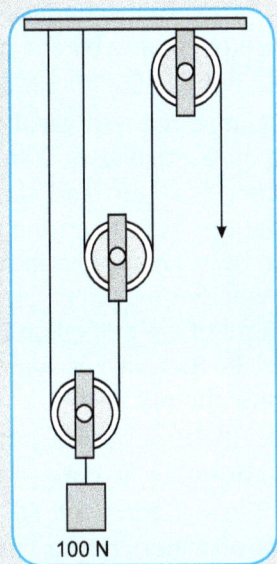

56. Draw a diagram of combination of four movable pulleys and one fixed pulley showing the direction of load, effort and tension in each strand of the string. State its mechanical advantage and velocity ratio.
57. Why is a combination of pulleys used instead of a single one?
58. What is a block and tackle system?
59. Draw a diagram of a block and tackle system with two pulleys in each of the upper and lower block. Mark the effort, load and tension in each strand of the system. What will be its velocity ratio?
60. How will you obtain a velocity ratio of 5 in a block and tackle system?
61. How can you increase the mechanical advantage of a block and tackle system of pulleys?
62. State the effect of weight of pulleys on the mechanical advantage of block and tackle system. Write an expression for it.
63. Why should the weight of lower block of block and tackle system of pulleys be negligible?

MULTIPLE CHOICE QUESTIONS

1. In the lever of Class III :
    (a) the load lies in the middle of F and E
    (b) the fulcrum lies in the middle of E and L
    (c) the effort lies in the middle of F and L
    (d) None of the above
    Ans : (c)
2. A spade is an example of :
    (a) lever of Class I   (b) lever of Class II
    (c) lever of Class III   (d) Both (a) and (b)
    Ans : (c)
3. A fixed pulley is a simple machine to
    (a) multiply force
    (b) apply a force in a convenient direction
    (c) apply a force at a convenient point
    (d) None of these
    Ans : (b)
4. Efficiency of a machine is :
    (a) output + input   (b) output – input
    (c) output/input   (d) output × input
    Ans : (c)
5. For Class I lever :
    (a) M.A. = 1   (b) M.A. > 1
    (c) M.A. < 1   (d) All of these
    Ans : (d)
6. Efficiency of a machine is :
    (a) M.A./V.R.   (b) V.R./M.A.
    (c) M.A. × V.R.   (d) not related to these
    Ans : (a)
7. The mechanical advantage of a combination of single fixed pulley and a single movable pulley in an actual situation is :
    (a) 1   (b) 2
    (c) less than 1   (d) less than 2
    Ans : (d)

NUMERICAL PROBLEMS

1. The mechanical advantage of a machine is 4. Its velocity ratio is 5.5. Calculate the % efficiency of the machine.
    Ans : 72.72%
2. A pair of scissors has a 20 cm long blade and an 8 cm long handle. What is its mechanical advantage?
    Ans : 0.4
3. A crowbar of length 150 cm has its fulcrum situated at a distance of 30 cm from the load. Calculate the mechanical advantage of the crowbar.
    Ans : 4
4. A man can open a nut by applying a force of 150 N by using a lever handle of length 0.4 m. What should be the length of the handle if he is able to open it by applying a force of 60 N?
    Ans : 1 m
5. The diagram below shows the use of a lever. (a) State the principle of moments as applied to the above lever. (b) Give an example of this

lever. (c) If FA = 10 cm, AB = 50 cm, calculate the minimum effort required to lift the load.

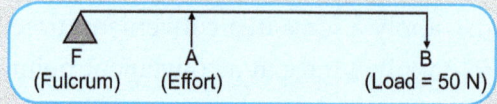

Ans : (c) 300 N

6. In operating a water pump, a resistance of 450 N is overcome by an effort of 75 N. If the distance of fulcrum from the point where resistance acts is 20 cm, find the distance from the fulcrum, where the load is applied.

   Ans : 1.2 m

7. The efficiency of a machine with mechanical advantage 5 is 80%. If the displacement of the effort in lifting a load using the machine is 20 cm, find the displacement of the load.

   Ans : 3.2 cm

8. A cook uses a 'fire tong' of length 28 cm to lift a piece of burning coal of mass 250 g. If he applies his effort at a distance 7 cm from the fulcrum, what is the effort in SI unit? (Take $g = 10$ m s^{-2})

   Ans : 10 N

9. The load arm and effort arm of a lever are 10 cm and 50 cm, respectively. The load and effort are applied on the opposite sides of the fulcrum. (a) Identify the class of the lever. (b) Find its mechanical advantage. If the effort applied is 10 N, (c) how much load can be raised by it?

   Ans : (a) Class I lever, (b) 5, (c) 50 N

10. The given figure shows a wheel barrow of weight 15 kgf which holds sand of 60 kgf. Calculate the minimum force required to keep the leg off the ground.

    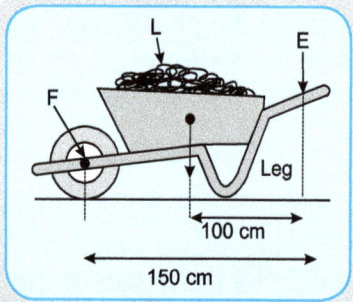

    Ans : 25 kgf

11. An effort of 500 N is applied through a distance of 0.5 m on a machine whose efficiency is 90% such that the resistance is overcome through a distance of 0.04 m. Calculate the (a) velocity ratio, (b) mechanical advantage and (c) resistance overcome by the machine.

    Ans : (a) 12.5, (b) 11.25, (c) 5,625 N

12. The maximum force that can be borne by the nut placed in a cracker is 200 N. The length of the cracker is 20 cm and the nut is placed at a distance of 15 cm from the free end of the cracker. If a boy can apply a maximum force of 25 N, find whether he can crack the nut? If not, find the length of the extension rod that should be attached to the cracker handle so that the boy can crack the nut.

    Ans : No, the boy cannot crack the nut, extension required = 20 cm.

13. A man applies a force of 80 N to draw a 5 kg bucket of water from a well. He is using a single fixed pulley. Calculate the mechanical advantage and efficiency of the pulley. (Take $g = 10$ m s^{-2})

    Ans : (a) 0.625, (b) 62.5%

14. A pulley system has a velocity ratio of 2 and an efficiency of 85%. Calculate the mechanical advantage and the effort required to raise a load of 250 N.

    Ans : (a) 1.7, (b) 147 N

15. A fixed pulley is driven by a mass of 80 kg falling at a rate of 6 m in 3 s. It lifts a load of 400 kgf. (a) Calculate the power input to the pulley. (b) If the efficiency of the pulley is 80%, find the work done by the pulley in 3 s. (Take $g = 10$ m s^{-2})

    Ans : (a) 1,600 W, (b) 3,840 J.

16. In the given figure, a load of 200 N is lifted by a girl with the help of a fixed pulley through a height of 8 m in 10 s. The effort applied at the free end is 320 N. (a) Calculate the velocity ratio of the pulley, (b) the mechanical advantage, (c) the efficiency of the pulley, (d) the energy gained by the load and (e) the power developed by the girl.

    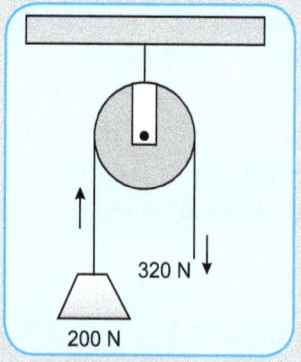

    Ans : (a) 1, (b) 0.625, (c) 62.5%, (d) 1,600 J, (e) 256 W.

17. A pulley system has three pulleys. A load of 120 N is overcome by applying an effort of 50 N. Calculate the mechanical advantage and efficiency of this system.
    Ans : 2.4, 80%

18. The given figure shows a combination of a fixed and a movable pulley. The tension in the string is 50 N. (a) Mark the direction of the tension in all the strands of the string. (b) What is the magnitude of effort? (c) What is the magnitude of load that can be lifted upwards?
    (Assume it to be an ideal situation)

    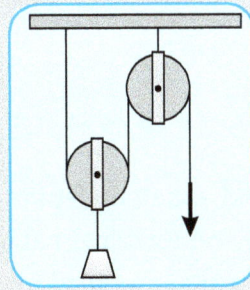

    Ans : (a) The tension will be in the upward direction in all strands, (b) 50 N, (c) 100 N

19. A system of pulley consists of one fixed and five movable pulleys. (a) What will be the velocity ratio of the system? (b) If the weight of the parts and friction between them is considered, what will be the mechanical advantage of the system?
    Ans : (a) $2^5 = 32$, (b) M.A. will be less than 32

20. A pulley system with a velocity ratio of 5 is used to lift a load of 200 kgf through a vertical height of 10 m. The effort required is 50 kgf in the downward direction. Calculate the (a) distance moved by the effort, (b) the work done by the effort, (c) the mechanical advantage and (d) the efficiency of the system. (Take $g = 10$ m s^{-2})
    Ans : (a) 50 m, (b) 25,000 J, (c) 4, (d) 80%

21. A block and tackle system has a velocity ratio of 4. Draw a labelled diagram of the system indicating the points of application and directions of load and effort. If a force of 400 kgf is exerted, what is the mechanical advantage of the system and the maximum load that can be raised with the system if its efficiency is 75%? (Take $g = 10$ ms^{-2})
    Ans : (a) 3, (b) 12,000 N

22. A block and tackle system has V.R. = 5.
    (a) Draw a neat labelled diagram of a system indicating the direction of its load and effort.
    (b) Rohan exerts a pull of 150 kgf. What is the maximum load he can raise with this pulley system if its efficiency = 75%?
    Ans : (b) 562.5 kgf.

23. The figure shows a block and tackle system of pulleys used to lift a load. (a) Mark the direction of point of application of load and effort. (b) How many strands of the tackle are supporting the load? (c) Indicate the direction of the tension in each strand. (d) What is the velocity ratio of the system? (e) When the load is pulled up by a distance of 2 m, how far does the effort end move?

    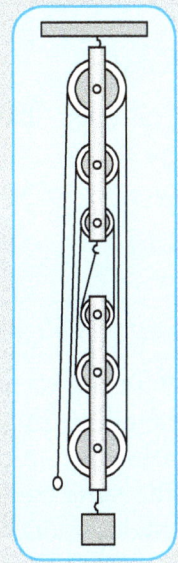

    Ans : (b) 6, (d) 6, (e) 12 m.

24. From the diagram given below, answer the questions that follow :

    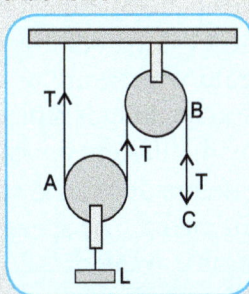

    (a) What kind of pulleys are A and B?
    (b) State the purpose of pulley B.
    (c) What effort has to be applied at C to just raise the load L = 20 kgf? (Neglect the weight of pulley A and friction)
    Ans : (c) 10 kgf

4

REFRACTION OF LIGHT AT PLANE SURFACES

LEARNING OUTCOMES
- Refraction : Concepts, laws of refraction, refraction through a glass block and a prism and angle of deviation
- Real depth and apparent depth
- Critical angle and total internal reflection
- Effects of refraction and total internal reflection

(A) REFRACTION

4.1 REFRACTION OF LIGHT

We are familiar with the rectilinear propagation of light, *i.e.* light travelling in straight lines. This rectilinear propagation is valid only if (a) light propagates through the same medium and (b) optical density of the medium does not change.

If any of these above two conditions are violated, when the light is travelling obliquely in a medium, then it deviates from its path. This implies that light will deviate from its path (a) if the density of medium through which light is travelling changes due to change in temperature, pressure or any other factor and (b) if one optical medium is replaced with another optical medium (with different optical density).

This deviation occurs due to the variation in speed of light in different media. The speed of light in air is 3×10^8 m s^{-1}, whereas in water, it is 2.25×10^8 m s^{-1} and in glass, it is 2×10^8 m s^{-1}. The speed of light decreases in an optically denser medium and increases in an optically rarer medium. Thus, water and glass are optically denser than air.

NOTE

Optical density is different from density of a medium. While density of a medium depends on the packing of its molecules, the optical density of a medium depends on the speed of light in that medium. A medium with less density than some other medium might be optically denser than that medium. For example, mustard oil and water *i.e.* mustard oil is optically denser than water but water is denser than mustard oil.

Example : Kerosene is less dense than water but its optical density is more than water. The speed of light in water is 2.25×10^8 m s^{-1}, whereas the speed of light in kerosene is 2.08×10^8 m s^{-1}.

When light rays travels from one medium to another medium, the rays bend or change their direction at the boundary. This phenomenon is known as *refraction of light*.

The phenomenon that causes a change in direction of a ray of light when it travels from one transparent medium (or optical medium) to another transparent medium is called refraction.

When a ray of light travelling in one optical medium strikes obliquely at the surface of another transparent medium, a part of the light gets reflected and returns to the same medium. The remaining part of the light that enters the other medium gets deviated from its original path and undergoes refraction.

Thus, the *change of medium* causes a *partial reflection* and *partial refraction of light* at the boundary separating the two media.

Cause of refraction : It is the change in speed of light when it passes from one medium to another that causes the bending or change in path of light.

4.2 TERMS RELATED TO REFRACTION

1. **Incident ray** : A ray of light travelling from one optical medium towards another optical medium is called *incident ray*. In Fig. 4.1, AO is the incident ray.

2. **Point of incidence** : The point on the boundary separating the two media where an incident ray strikes is called the *point of incidence*. In Fig. 4.1, O is the point of incidence.

3. **Normal** : A perpendicular drawn at the point of incidence is called the *normal*. NN' is the normal as shown in Fig. 4.1.

4. **Angle of incidence i** : The angle which the incident ray makes with the normal is called the *angle of incidence*. ∠AON is the angle of incidence in Fig. 4.1.

5. **Angle of refraction r** : The angle which the refracted ray makes with the normal is called the *angle of refraction*. ∠BON' is the angle of refraction in Fig. 4.1.

6. **Refracted ray** : A ray of light which deviates from its straight path and gets bent while travelling from one optical medium to another is called the *refracted ray*. OB is the refracted ray in Fig. 4.1.

7. **Angle of deviation δ** : The angle between the refracted ray and the direction of incident ray is called the *angle of deviation*. In Fig. 4.1, ∠BOD is the *angle of deviation*.

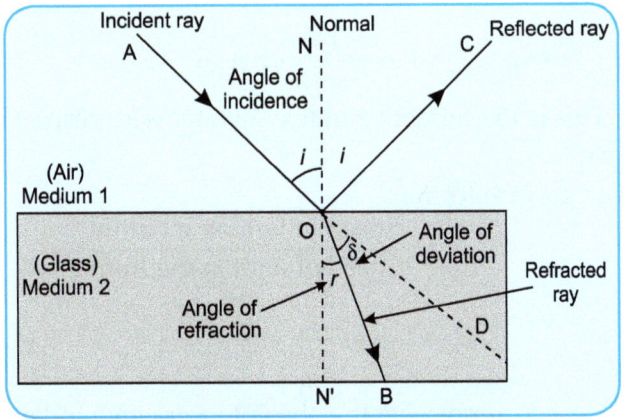

Fig. 4.1 : Refraction of light.

Consider a rectangular glass slab as shown in Fig. 4.1. There are two media, one medium is air and the other is glass. When a ray of light AO travelling in air falls on the upper surface of the glass slab, a part of it gets reflected as ray OC back into the air and the rest of it enters into the glass slab. The direction of ray AO changes as it enters the glass and goes along the ray OB inside it. The rays AO and OB are not in the same straight path; the light ray gets refracted at point O, *i.e.* at the boundary separating the two media.

The angle of refraction r is not equal to the angle of incidence i.

The following cases can occur when a ray of light travels from one medium to another :

1. **When a ray of light travels obliquely from an optically rarer medium to an optically denser medium :** When a ray of light travels from an optically rarer medium, such as air, to an optically denser medium, such as glass or water, it *bends towards the normal*, which implies that the angle of incidence is always greater than the angle of refraction, *i.e.* ∠i > ∠r and deviation angle $\delta = i - r$ (Fig. 4.2).

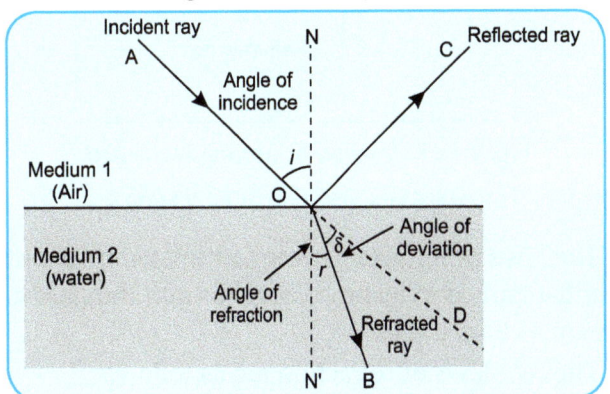

Fig. 4.2 : Refraction of light from a rarer to denser medium.

2. **When a ray of light travels obliquely from an optically denser medium to an optically rarer medium :** When a ray of light travels from an optically denser medium, such as glass or water, to an optically rarer medium, such as air, it *bends away from the normal*, which implies that the angle of incidence is always smaller than the angle of refraction, *i. e.* ∠i < ∠r and deviation angle $\delta = r - i$ (Fig. 4.3).

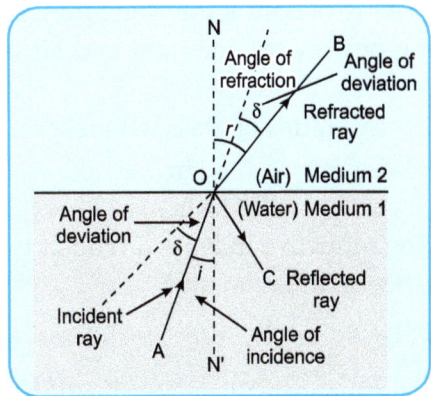

Fig. 4.3 : Refraction of light from a denser to rarer medium.

3. When a ray of light travels from one optical medium to another optical medium being incident normally on the boundary of two media : When a ray of light strikes normally at the point of incidence, the angle of incidence is zero. In this case, the light does not deviate from its path and thus, the angle of refraction is also zero (Fig. 4.4). Thus, the angle of refraction is equal to the angle of incidence, i.e. $\angle i = \angle r = 0$. The deviation angle is also zero, $\delta = 0$.

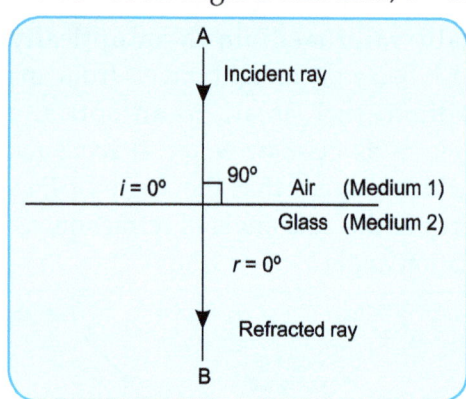

Fig. 4.4 : Refraction at normal incidence.

4.3 LAWS OF REFRACTION

The laws of refraction were formulated by a Dutch scientist named Willebrord Snellius and thus are also known as *Snell's laws*.

The two laws of refraction are as follows :
1. *The incident ray, the refracted ray and the normal at the point of incidence lie in the same plane.*
2. *The ratio of the sine of angle of incidence to the sine of angle of refraction for two given optical media is a constant quantity.*

This ratio is called the *refractive index of the second medium with respect to the first medium*. It is denoted by the Greek letter μ (mew) or English letter n.

$$\frac{\sin i}{\sin r} = {}^1\mu_2 \qquad ...(4.1)$$

Suppose a ray of light is travelling from air to glass, then glass is the second medium and air is the first medium.

The refractive index of glass with respect to air is

$${}^a\mu_g = \frac{\sin i}{\sin r}$$

Unit : The refractive index is a ratio of two similar quantities; hence, it has no unit.

4.4 RELATION BETWEEN REFRACTIVE INDEX AND SPEED OF LIGHT ($\mu = c/v$)

The speed of light in vacuum is 3×10^8 m s^{-1} and is constant for light of all colours and wavelengths. The speed of light changes very slightly while travelling from vacuum to air and so the speed of light in vacuum and air is considered to be same. It is denoted by letter c. The speed of light is maximum in air and decreases in any other medium.

The refractive index of a medium is defined with respect to vacuum or air and is called the *absolute refractive index*.

The ratio of speed of light in vacuum or air to the speed of light in a medium is known as the absolute refractive index of that medium.

$$\mu \text{ or } n = \frac{\text{Speed of light in vaccum or air }(c)}{\text{Speed of light in a medium }(v)} \quad ....(4.2)$$

Since the speed of light is maximum in vacuum and is less in any other medium, the absolute refractive index of a medium is always greater than 1 ($\mu > 1$).

Example : The speed of light in air is 3×10^8 m s^{-1} and in water is 2.25×10^8 m s^{-1}. The refractive index of water is

$$\mu_{water} = \frac{3 \times 10^8}{2.25 \times 10^8} = 1.33$$

In general, the ratio of speed of light in first medium to the speed of light in second medium will give the refractive index of second medium with respect to the first medium.

Suppose v_g is the speed of light in glass and v_w is the speed of light in water, then

$${}^{glass}\mu_{water} = \frac{v_g}{v_w}$$

This represents the refractive index of water with respect to glass.

$v_g = 2 \times 10^8$ m s^{-1}, $v_w = 2.25 \times 10^8$ m s^{-1}

$${}^{glass}\mu_{water} = \frac{2 \times 10^8}{2.25 \times 10^8} = 0.89$$

This is the refractive index of water with respect to glass.

In general form,

$${}^1\mu_2 = \frac{\text{Speed of light in medium 1}}{\text{Speed of light in medium 2}}$$

i.e., $\quad {}^1\mu_2 = \dfrac{v_1}{v_2} = \dfrac{c/\mu_1}{c/\mu_2} = \dfrac{\mu_2}{\mu_1} \quad ....(4.3)$

Here μ_1 represents the absolute refractive index of medium 1 and μ_2 represents the absolute refractive index of medium 2.

Example : The absolute refractive index of glass is 1.5 and the absolute refractive index of water is 1.33

$$\therefore {}^{glass}\mu_{water} = \frac{\mu_{water}}{\mu_{glass}} = \frac{1.33}{1.5} = 0.89$$

This is same as derived above.

If the refractive indices of two media are same, then the speed of light will be same in both media and hence a ray of light passing from one such medium to another will not undergo any change in its path even if the angle of incidence is not zero.

Thus, there are *two* conditions under which a ray of light remains *undeviated* while travelling from one medium to another:

1. When the angle of incidence *i* is zero at the boundary separating the two media.
2. When the refractive indices of two media are same.

Table 4.1 shows the value of refractive index of some common substances.

Table 4.1 : Refractive index of some common substances

Substance	Value of μ
Vacuum	1.00
Air	1.0003
Ice	1.31
Water	1.33
Ethanol	1.36
Acetone	1.36
Human lens	1.38
Kerosene	1.44
Sulphuric acid	1.43
Fused silica	1.46
Glycerol	1.47
Turpentine oil	1.47
Benzene	1.50
Ordinary glass	1.50
Rock salt	1.51
Crown glass	1.52
Amber	1.55
Flint glass	1.62
Carbon disulphide	1.63
Sapphire	1.76
Ruby	1.77
Diamond	2.42
Silicon	3.48
Germanium	4.05

Factors Affecting Refractive Index of a Medium

1. Optical density : The refractive index of air is considered as 1. As the speed of light decreases in a medium relative to air, the refractive index of the medium is higher than that of air. When two transparent media are compared, the optically denser medium will have a higher refractive index while the optically rarer medium will have a lower refractive index.

2. Temperature : The speed of light in a medium increases with increase in temperature and thus, the refractive index of the medium decreases.

3. Wavelength of light : The speed of light is same for all wavelengths or colours in air but varies in any other medium. The refractive index of a medium increases with decrease in wavelength of light. The wavelength of violet light is shortest while that of red light is longest. In a given medium, the speed of violet light is slower than the speed of red light and thus, the refractive index of violet light is more than that of red light ($\mu_V > \mu_R$).

The *frequency of light* is a characteristic of the source of light and does not change due to refraction.

If a ray of light of wavelength λ and frequency ν travels from air (speed of light = c) to another medium in which the speed of light is v, then the frequency of light remains the same, but the wavelength of light changes. Let the new wavelength be λ'.

Then, $c = \nu\lambda$ and $v = \nu\lambda'$

$$\therefore \quad \frac{c}{v} = \frac{\nu\lambda}{\nu\lambda'}$$

i.e. $\quad \lambda' = \frac{v}{c}\lambda$

Since $\frac{c}{v} = \mu$ (refractive index)

$$\therefore \quad \lambda' = \frac{\lambda}{\mu} \qquad \ldots(4.4)$$

When light passes from a denser to a rarer medium, its wavelength increases, *i.e.* $\lambda' > \lambda$ whereas if light passes from a rarer to a denser medium, its wavelength decreases, *i.e.* $\lambda' < \lambda$.

4.5 EXPERIMENTAL VERIFICATION OF LAWS OF REFRACTION

Procedure :

1. Fix a white sheet of paper on a drawing board with the help of drawing pins.

2. Place a rectangular glass slab ABCD on a white sheet of paper fixed on a drawing board and trace its boundary using a pencil.

3. Remove the glass slab and draw a normal N_1N_2 passing through a point O which lies on the boundary line AB of the glass slab (Fig. 4.5).

4. Draw a straight line IO inclined at an angle, say 30° to the normal. IO is the incident ray.

5. Fix two drawing pins P and Q vertically on the line IO, such that the distance between the pins is about 4 cm.

6. Place the glass slab exactly on its boundary ABCD.

7. Now fix two other pins R and S, looking from the other side of the glass slab, i.e. from side CD, such that the base of all four pins P, Q, R and S appears to lie on the same straight line.

8. Remove the four pins one by one and mark the position of all pin points P, Q, R and S with a fine pencil dot.

9. Join the pin points R and S and draw a line O'E, producing it backwards to join with point O. The ray OO' is the refracted ray and O'E is the emergent ray.

10. $\angle ION_1$ is the angle of incidence i and $\angle O'ON_2$ is the angle of refraction r. Measure the angles i and r. Find the values of sin i and sin r and calculate the ratio sin i/sin r which will give the refractive index of glass with respect to air.

11. Repeat the procedure with different angles of incidence and record the values of sin i and sin r in the observation table as shown below. Calculate the value of refractive index for each observation.

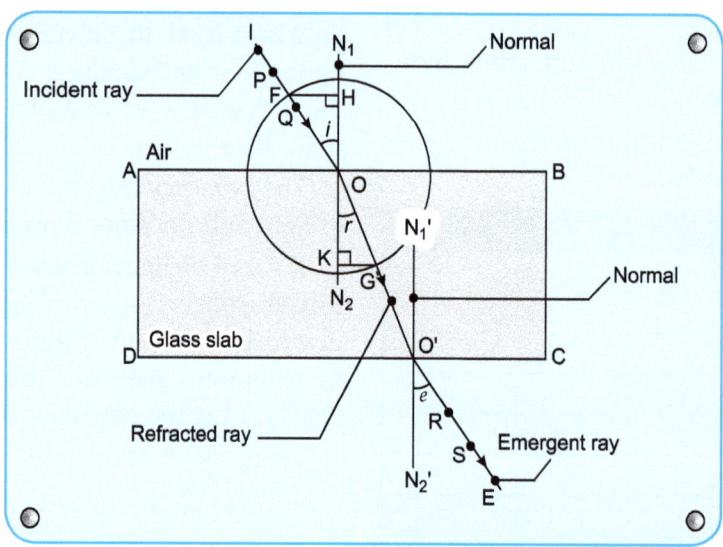

Fig. 4.5 : Experimental verification of laws of refraction

Alternate method

To find the value of refractive index of glass without measuring the values of i and r :

1. Keeping point O as the centre, using a protractor, draw a circle of a convenient radius in such a way that it cuts the incident ray at point F and the refracted ray at point G.

2. Draw two perpendiculars, one is FH from point F and the other is GK from point G, on the normal N_1N_2.

3. Measure the length of these perpendiculars FH and GK and find the value of FH/GK. This ratio gives the refractive index since

$$\mu = \frac{\sin i}{\sin r} = \frac{FH/OF}{GK/OG}$$

(sin θ = perpendicular/hypotenuse). OF and OG are the radii of same circle; hence, μ = FH/GK.

4. Repeat the procedure with different angles of incidence and, in each case, find the ratio FH/GK. Record the values in the observation table as shown below and calculate the value of refractive index in each case.

Angle i	Angle r	sin i	sin r	μ = sin i/sin r or FH/GK
30°				
40°				
50°				
60°				
70°				

Since the incident ray, the refracted ray and the normal are lying in the same plane, i.e. the plane of the paper, this verifies the first law of refraction.

Also, the ratio FH/GK or sin i/sin r is found to be a constant value for each angle of incidence, thus verifying the second law of refraction. The value of μ obtained gives the refractive index of glass.

4.6 PRINCIPLE OF REVERSIBILITY OF PATH OF LIGHT

According to the principle of reversibility, *if a ray of light travels from medium 1 to medium 2 along a certain path, then it will follow exactly the same path while travelling from medium 2 to medium 1.* This implies that the path of light is reversible.

Fig. 4.6 shows a ray of light IO incident at an angle i on a plane surface separating two media 1 and 2. The ray IO gets refracted along OR at an angle of refraction r.

∠ION is the angle of incidence and ∠RON' is the angle of refraction.

The refractive index of medium 2 with respect to medium 1 is

$$^1\mu_2 = \frac{\mu_2}{\mu_1} = \frac{\sin i}{\sin r} \qquad ...(i)$$

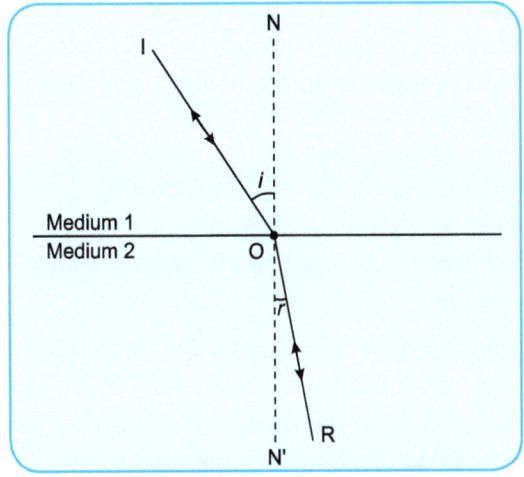

Fig. 4.6 : Principle of reversibility.

If a plane mirror is kept at right angles to the path of refracted ray OR, it is found that the light retraces its path if it is made to travel from medium 2 to medium 1. Now, the ray RO acts as the incident ray and ray OI acts as the refracted ray. ∠RON' is the angle of incidence and ∠ION is the angle of refraction.

Now, the refractive index of medium 1 with respect to medium 2 will be

$$^2\mu_1 = \frac{\mu_1}{\mu_2} = \frac{\sin r}{\sin i} \qquad ...(ii)$$

From equations (i) and (ii),

$$^1\mu_2 \times {}^2\mu_1 = \frac{\sin i}{\sin r} \times \frac{\sin r}{\sin i} = 1$$

i.e. $\quad ^1\mu_2 = \dfrac{1}{^2\mu_1}$ and $^2\mu_1 = \dfrac{1}{^1\mu_2}$ ...(4.5)

Thus, if refractive index of water with respect to air ($^a\mu_w$) is 4/3, then the refractive index of air with respect to water ($^w\mu_a$) will be 3/4.

4.7 REFRACTION OF LIGHT THROUGH A RECTANGULAR GLASS SLAB

Emergent Ray is Parallel to Incident Ray

Consider a rectangular slab ABCD (Fig. 4.7). A ray of light PO incident at point O falls on the surface AB of the slab. NN' is a normal at the point of incidence on the surface AB. Since the ray PO enters from air to glass, *i.e. from a rarer medium to a denser medium*, it *bends towards the normal* NN' and travels as ray OQ inside the glass slab in a straight path. On the lower surface, CD of the glass slab, the ray OQ undergoes another refraction. N_1N_2 is the normal to the surface CD at the point of incidence Q. The ray OQ now travels from glass to air, *i.e. from a denser to a rarer medium*, and so it *bends away from the normal* N_1N_2 and travels along ray QR.

The ray PO is the incident ray, ray OQ is the refracted ray and ray QR is the emergent ray. ∠PON is the angle of incidence i, ∠QON' is the angle of refraction r and ∠RQN_2 is the angle of emergence e. The angle of emergence e is always found to be equal to angle of incidence i. Thus, the emergent ray QR is parallel to the incident ray PO.

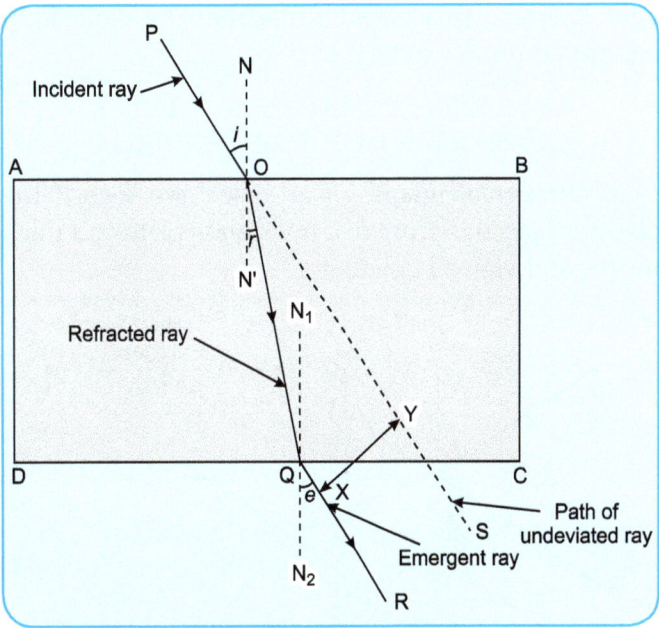

Fig. 4.7 : Refraction through a rectangular glass block

Lateral displacement

In the phenomenon of refraction through a rectangular glass slab, it is seen that the emergent ray is parallel to incident ray as the angle of emergence is equal to the angle of incidence. The incident ray and emergent ray are parallel in the same direction but do not lie on the same line. The emergent ray gets laterally displaced from the path of incident ray. The dotted line in Fig. 4.7 shows the path of light if it remains undeviated in the absence of glass slab. The perpendicular distance XY as shown in Fig. 4.7 between the emergent ray and the direction of incident ray is called the *lateral displacement*.

Factors affecting lateral displacement are as follows :

1. Thickness of glass slab : Lateral displacement is directly proportional to the thickness of glass slab, *i.e.* the perpendicular shift between the emergent ray and path of incident ray increases with the increase in thickness of the slab (or medium).

2. Refractive index of the glass : Lateral displacement is directly proportional to the refractive index of the glass (or optical material). Lateral displacement increases with increase in refractive index of the medium.

3. Angle of incidence : Lateral displacement is directly proportional to the angle of incidence, *i.e.* it increases with the increase in angle of incidence.

4. Wavelength of light : Lateral displacement is inversely proportional to the wavelength of light used, *i.e.* it increases with the decrease in the wavelength of light. Lateral displacement is maximum for violet light and minimum for red light.

4.8 MULTIPLE IMAGES IN A THICK GLASS PLANE OR THICK MIRROR

A number of images of an object are seen if the object is placed in front of a thick glass plate or a thick mirror and viewed obliquely.

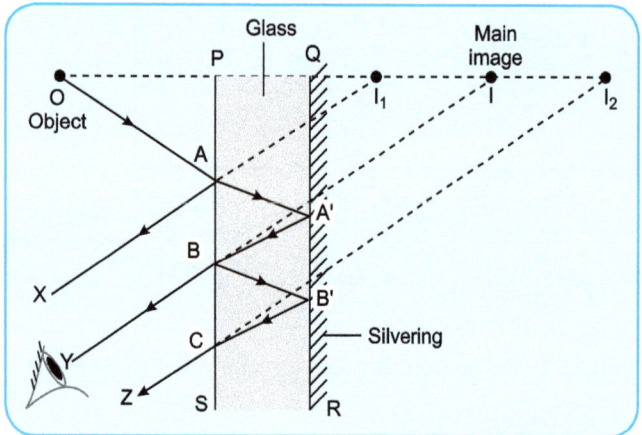

Fig. 4.8 : Multiple reflections in a thick plane mirror.

Let PQRS be a thick plane mirror. The surface QR is the silvered surface of the mirror. An object O is placed in front of the mirror. Let one ray of light be incident normally on the mirror. When another ray of light OA falls on the surface PS of the mirror, a small part of it gets reflected as ray AX (Fig. 4.8). Due to this reflection, a faint virtual image is formed at I_1 behind the mirror. However, a large part of the incident light entering from air to mirror undergoes refraction. AA' is the refracted ray inside the mirror. The ray AA' now strikes the silvered surface QR of the mirror and gets strongly reflected back as ray A'B inside the mirror. The ray A'B then undergoes partial refraction and partial reflection. The ray BY is the refracted ray while moving from mirror to air and ray BB' is the partially reflected ray inside the mirror. The ray BY forms a virtual image I_2. The reflected ray BB' further undergoes multiple reflections and refractions, giving rise to multiple images.

Out of all the images formed, the *second image* is the *brightest image* as the ray of light suffers the first strong reflection at the silvered surface QR of the mirror. In the subsequent images formed, the *brightness gradually diminishes* as some amount of light gets absorbed at each reflection.

4.9 PRISM

A prism is a piece of glass or any other transparent refracting medium bounded by five plane surfaces inclined at some angles.

A prism has five sides whose two opposite surfaces are two identical triangles, ΔABC and ΔPQR, as shown in Fig. 4.9, and the other three surfaces are rectangular. The two opposite rectangular surfaces are the *refracting surfaces*, shown as ABQP and ACRP in Fig. 4.9. The angle between the two refracting rectangular surfaces is called *refracting angle or angle of prism*, shown by ∠ BAC. The angle of prism is denoted by letter *A*. The line along which the two refracting surfaces meet is called the *refracting edge*. The line AP represents the refracting edge. The third rectangular surface BCRQ is the *base* of the prism. Any section of the prism perpendicular to the refracting edge is called the *principal section of prism*. ABC is the principal section of the prism.

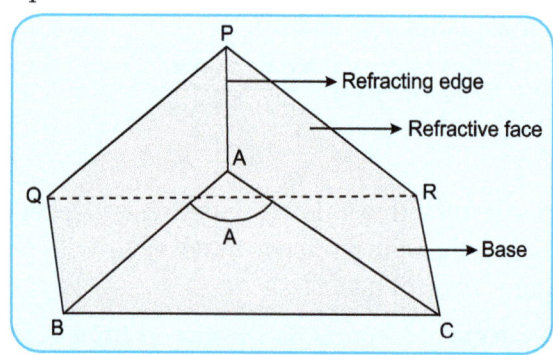

Fig. 4.9 : Prism.

NOTE

For drawing ray diagrams, only the principal section ABC of a prism is used.

4.10 REFRACTION OF LIGHT THROUGH A PRISM

Fig. 4.10 shows the principal section ABC of a prism. BAC is the angle of prism (A). EF is an incident ray entering from a monochromatic source of light (*i.e.* a ray of light of single colour). It strikes the refracting surface AB of the prism at point F such that EFN_1 is the angle of incidence i_1. As the ray is travelling from a rarer medium (air) to a denser medium (glass), it bends towards the normal NN_1 and travels as ray FG inside the glass. ∠NFG is the angle of refraction r_1 on the refracting face AB. The refracted ray FG strikes the refracting face AC of the prism such that the angle of incidence is ∠FGN = r_2. Now, this ray suffers refraction from glass to air, *i.e.* from a denser medium to a rarer medium, and emerges as ray GH away from the normal NN_2. The ray GH is the emergent ray and $N_2GH = i_2$ is the angle of emergence.

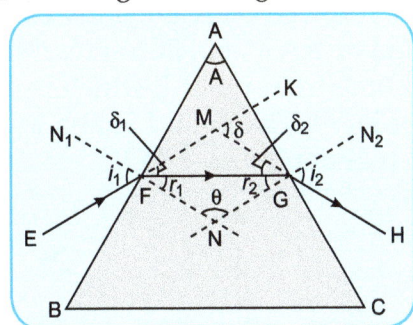

Fig. 4.10 : Refraction through a prism.

Thus, a ray of light suffers refraction at two faces of the prism, *i.e.* AB and AC. At the face AB, the ray EF bends as ray FG towards the normal instead of going along ray EFK and thus there occurs a deviation by ∠MFG = δ_1. Now, the ray FG bends and emerges as ray GH on the face AC of the prism and appears to come along MGH. There occurs a deviation by ∠MGF = δ_2.

If there was no prism, then the ray of light EF would travel along straight path EFK as there would not be any refraction. The emergent ray GH leaving the prism appears to be coming along ray MGH. Thus, a deviation by ∠KMG is produced by the prism. This angle is called the *angle of deviation* δ. It is the angle between incident ray EF and emergent ray GH.

From Fig. 4.10, ∠KMG = ∠MFG + ∠MGF (since exterior angle = sum of interior opposite angles).
 i.e. $\delta = \delta_1 + \delta_2$.
Now, angle of deviation is the difference between angle of incidence and angle of refraction.
 i.e. $\delta_1 = (i_1 - r_1)$ and $\delta_2 = (i_2 - r_2)$
Thus, $\delta = (i_1 - r_1) + (i_2 - r_2)$
∴ $\delta = (i_1 + i_2) - (r_1 + r_2)$

Now, ∠AFN = ∠AGN = 90° (since N_1N and N_2N are normals at point F and G, respectively).

Consider the quadrilateral AFNG.
∠AFN = ∠AGN = 90° (already shown)
So, ∠FAG + ∠FNG = 180°
Since ∠FAG = A (angle of prism)
∴ ∠FNG = 180° − A
Also, from ΔFNG, ∠FNG = 180° − ($r_1 + r_2$)
∴ 180° − A = 180° − ($r_1 + r_2$)
i.e. A = ($r_1 + r_2$)
Thus, $\delta = (i_1 + i_2) - A$
∴ $i_1 + i_2 = A + \delta$ ...(4.6)

NOTE

The angle of emergence is denoted as *e* and angle of incidence as *i*; thus, $i + e = A + \delta$.

Factors Affecting the Angle of Deviation

The value of angle of deviation produced by the prism depends on the following factors : (1) Angle of incidence (*i*), (2) Refractive index of prism material (μ), (3) Angle of prism (A) and (4) Colour or wavelength of incident light (λ).

1. Dependence of angle of deviation on the angle of incidence; *i*-δ graph : It has been experimentally observed that at first the angle of deviation decreases with increase in angle of incidence. There is a particular stage when for a given angle of incidence, the angle of deviation is minimum. This position is called *minimum deviation position of prism*. If the angle of incidence is further increased, the angle of deviation also increases.

The graph called the *i*-δ curve in Fig. 4.11 shows the variation in the angle of deviation (δ) with the angle of incidence (*i*). δ_m in the graph represents the minimum angle of deviation (δ_{min}).

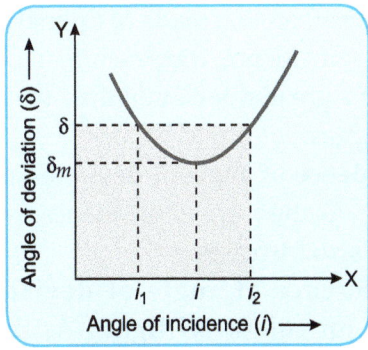

Fig. 4.11 : *i*-δ curve.

It has been found experimentally that in the minimum deviation position,

(a) Angle of incidence is equal to angle of emergence, *i.e.* $i_1 = i_2$ and

(b) Angle of refraction r_1 on the face AB of the prism is equal to the angle r_2 on the face AC of the prism, i.e. $r_1 = r_2$.

In the position of minimum deviation, $\delta = \delta_{min}$,
$i_1 = i_2 = i$
We know that, $i_1 + i_2 = A + \delta$
Hence, $i + i = A + \delta_{min}$
i.e. $\delta_{min} = 2i - A$ ...(4.7)

The value of δ_{min} is unique for a given prism and given colour of light.

NOTE

If the principal section of a prism is an *isosceles triangle*, then the refracted ray inside the prism will *travel parallel* to its base in the position of minimum deviation.

Example : If a prism made of glass with its angle $A = 60°$ is chosen, the values of different angles of deviation can be calculated by varying the angle of incidence and measuring the angle of emergence in each case.

If angle of incidence $i_1 = 30°$, then angle of emergence $i_2 = 77°$

∴ $30° + 77° = 60° + \delta$
i.e. $\delta = 47°$

The value of δ is minimum when the angle of incidence is 48°.

When $i_1 = 48°$, $i_2 = 48°$
$\delta_{min} = 2i - A = 2 \times 48° - 60° = 36°$

Thus, minimum angle of deviation is 36°.

2. Dependence of angle of deviation on refractive index (μ) of the prism : As the refractive index of a given material increases, the angle of deviation also increases. A prism made of flint glass has a higher refractive index than that made of ordinary glass. For a given angle of incidence, the prism made of flint glass will produce a greater deviation than the prism made of ordinary glass.

3. Dependence of angle of deviation on the angle of prism (A) : As the angle of prism increases, the angle of deviation also increases.

4. Dependence of angle of deviation on the wavelength (or colour) of light : As the refractive index of a medium is maximum for violet light (smallest wavelength), the angle of deviation is also maximum for violet light for a given angle of incidence and least for red light (longest wavelength), i.e. $\delta_V > \delta_R$.

4.11 REAL AND APPARENT DEPTHS

Due to the phenomenon of refraction of light, an object placed in a denser medium appears to be at a depth less than the real depth when viewed from a rarer medium. This depth at which the object appears is known as *apparent depth*.

Consider a point object O placed at the bottom of an optically dense medium such as glass or water. The boundary surface separating the medium from air is represented by XY in Fig. 4.12. A number of rays starting from the object travel in all directions. Let OA be one ray of light which is incident normally on the surface XY. It passes out undeviated along the path AA' in the air. Another ray OB starting from the object, on striking the boundary surface, suffers refraction and bends away from the normal N'BN (as it is travelling from a denser to a rarer medium) at the point of incidence B. It then travels along ray BC in the air. The refracted rays AA' and BC on reaching the eye appear to come from point I, which is the virtual image of point O. The point I is at a lesser depth than the actual depth (AI < AO).

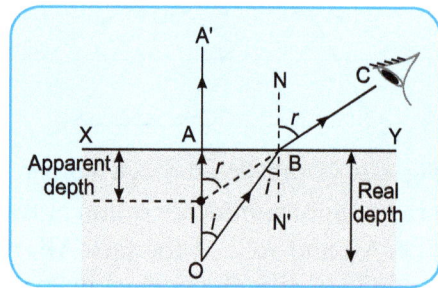

Fig. 4.12 : Real and apparent depths.

It can be proved that refractive index of a medium 2 with respect to medium 1 is equal to the ratio between the real depth and apparent depth as follows :

From Fig. 4.12, we have the incident ray OB, angle of incidence $i = \angle OBN'$ and angle of refraction $r = \angle CBN$.

Since AO and BN' are parallel lines with OB as a transversal line,
$\angle AOB = \angle OBN' = i$
Similarly, $\angle AIB = \angle CBN = r$

As light is travelling from medium 2 (glass or water) to medium 1 (air),

∴ $^2\mu_1 = \dfrac{\sin i}{\sin r}$

i.e. $^2\mu_1 = \dfrac{\sin \angle AOB}{\sin \angle AIB}$

Now in $\triangle AOB$, $\sin \angle AOB = BA/OB$ and from $\triangle AIB$, $\sin \angle AIB = BA/IB$

$$\therefore \quad {}^2\mu_1 = \frac{BA/OB}{BA/IB} = \frac{IB}{OB}$$

Now, the points A and B are very close, *i.e.* the object is viewed from a point vertically above the object.

Hence, IB = IA and OB = OA

$$\therefore \quad {}^2\mu_1 = \frac{IA}{OA}$$

By the principle of reversibility,

$${}^1\mu_2 = \frac{1}{{}^2\mu_1}$$

$$\therefore \quad {}^1\mu_2 = \frac{1}{IA/OA}$$

$$= \frac{OA}{IA} = \frac{\text{Real depth}}{\text{Apparent depth}}$$

i.e. Apparent depth = $\dfrac{\text{Real depth}}{{}^1\mu_2}$ ...(4.8)

Example : The refractive index of water with respect to air is 4/3. This means that the depth of a water body such as a lake or pond appears three-fourth of its real depth on viewing it from vertically above in the air. It is due to this reason that a fish in a pond appears to be nearer to the surface of water than the actual depth when seen from outside the pond.

Now, the shift in the depth = OI = Real depth – Apparent depth

or,   Shift = Real depth $\left(1 - \dfrac{1}{{}^1\mu_2}\right)$ ...(4.9)

This shift by which the object appears to be raised depends on the following factors :

1. Refractive index of the medium : The shift increases with increase in refractive index of the medium.

2. Thickness of the denser medium : The shift increases with increase in thickness of the denser medium.

3. Wavelength or colour of incident light : The shift decreases with the increase in wavelength of light used. The shift is more for violet light than for the red light in a given medium.

NOTE

If an object lying in a denser medium is viewed vertically above from a rarer medium, then the apparent depth of the object will always be less than the real depth for all angles of observation.

4.12 SIMPLE EFFECTS OF REFRACTION

1. Apparent bending of a stick under water : When a stick is immersed obliquely in water, it appears bent and thus short.

Consider a stick AC immersed obliquely in water such that part AB of the stick lies in water and part BC lies above the water, *i.e.* in air (Fig. 4.13). A ray of light after starting from point A on tip of the stick will suffer refraction at the boundary surface separating water and air and will *bend away from the normal* (as light is travelling from a denser to a rarer medium). When this refracted beam reaches the eye, it appears to come from point A' as the eye retraces a straight-line path. This point A' is the virtual image of point A. Similarly, a virtual image for every point of the stick under water is formed and the part AB of the stick appears raised as A'B. Thus, the stick appears bent at point B on the boundary surface separating water and air.

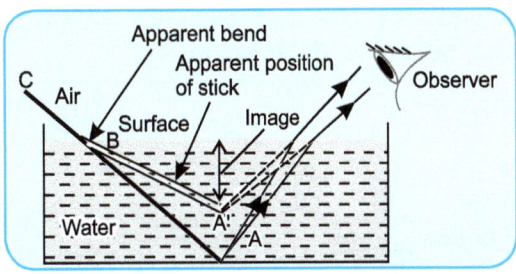

Fig. 4.13 : Bending of stick due to refraction

2. A coin placed in a beaker filled with water appears to be raised : Place a coin at the bottom of an empty beaker. It is not visible when viewed below the edge of the beaker from a certain distance. Now gently pour water in the beaker and fill it completely to the top. The coin becomes visible from the same position because rays of light diverging from the coin on emerging out of water suffer refraction and hence bend away from the normal. When these refracted rays reach the eye, they appear to come from a point above the point where the coin is placed. Thus, the coin appears to be raised when the beaker is filled with water.

3. Apparent position and twinkling of stars : The atmosphere is made up of a number of parallel layers of air of varying densities. The layer of air nearest to the surface of the Earth is the most dense, whereas the layer farthest from the surface of the Earth is the least dense. These layers of air are not stationary but continuously intermingle, thereby changing the density of one or more layers of air.

When rays of light entering from a star up in the horizon pass through the atmosphere, they bend towards the normal, *i.e.* towards the Earth. When the refracted rays of light reach the eye, the eye traces a straight-line path and the rays appear to come from a *point which is high up* than the original position of the star. This point gives the apparent position of the star.

As the air layers of different densities mix, they change the apparent position of the star. When the star is within the line of sight, it is visible, but when it falls out of sight, it becomes invisible. The collective effect of this change shifts the apparent position of the star and it appears to twinkle.

4. The Sun is seen a few minutes before it rises above the horizon in the morning and few minutes longer after it sets in the evening : As the light from the Sun enters the Earth's atmosphere, it bends towards the surface of the Earth due to refraction. When the Sun is below the horizon before rising, its apparent position is higher up the horizon due to refraction and thus it is visible a few minutes before its actual rising.

Similarly, when the Sun is low in the sky, it appears to be at a higher position due to refraction. When it looks like the Sun is about to drop below the horizon, it has already set. Thus, it is seen few minutes longer after it has set below the horizon.

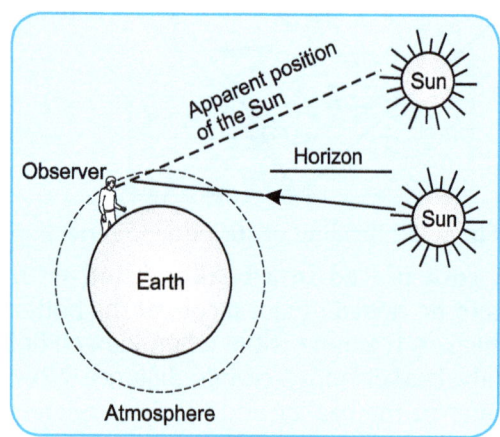

Fig. 4.14 : Atmospheric refraction effects at sunrise and sunset

5. A tank or a pond appears shallow than its actual depth.

6. The legs of a person standing in a swimming pool will appear shorter than the actual length.

7. If a glass block is placed on a sheet of printed paper, the print will appear raised and magnified.

Do You Know ?

- *Planets are much closer to the Earth than stars and appear like discs, while the stars appear like points when viewed through a telescope. The light from star gets refracted in different directions in the layers of atmosphere, whereas due to the finite size of the planet and its closeness to Earth, it averages out the turbulent effects of the atmosphere, resulting in a stable image being formed. The result is planets do not twinkle while stars do.*

4.13 APPLICATIONS OF REFRACTION OF LIGHT

1. Refraction is responsible for image formed by lenses, which are commonly used in binocular and telescopes, allowing to view distant objects clearly, or in magnifying glasses and microscopes to view small objects, such as microorganisms which are not seen with naked eye.

2. Spear fisherman use a strange trick to catch their fishes or other animals. They aim at a point slightly below where the fish seems to be. The reason is that light changes direction when it moves from one transparent substance, such as water to another different density such as air. This change of direction is called refraction.

ILLUSTRATIVE EXAMPLES

1. "The absolute refractive index of glass is 1.5'. Explain the statement.
   Solution : The absolute refractive index of a medium is the ratio of speed of light in air to the speed of light in the given medium. The given statement enumerates that the speed of light in air is 1.5 times the speed of light in glass.

2. The absolute refractive index of alcohol is 1.37. Calculate the speed of light in alcohol.
   Solution : Absolute refractive index of alcohol
   $$= \frac{\text{Speed of light in air or vacuum}}{\text{Speed of light in alcohol}}$$
   ∴ Speed of light in alcohol
   $$= \frac{\text{Speed of light in air}}{\text{Refractive index of alcohol}}$$
   $$= \frac{3 \times 10^8}{1.37} = 2.19 \times 10^8 \text{ m s}^{-1}$$

3. The refractive index of glass is 1.5 and that of water is 1.33. What is the refractive index of glass with respect to water ?
   Solution : Given $^a\mu_g = 1.5$ and $^a\mu_w = 1.33$
   Refractive index of glass with respect to water
   $$^w\mu_g = \frac{\text{Refractive index of glass}}{\text{Refractive index of water}}$$
   $$^w\mu_g = \frac{^a\mu_g}{^a\mu_w} = \frac{1.5}{1.33} = 1.127$$

4. A red light of wavelength 780 nm travelling in air enters a glass block and gets refracted. The wavelength of red light changes inside the glass and becomes green light. If the refractive index of glass is 1.5 and speed of light in air is 3×10^8 m s^{-1}, find the (a) frequency of light in air and (b) the wavelength of green light inside the glass block.

Solution : Given λ_{air} = 780 nm = 780 × 10⁻⁹ m, μ = 1.5, c = 3 × 10⁸ m s⁻¹
(a) Using the equation,
$$c = \nu\lambda \text{ (in air)}$$
$$\nu = \frac{c}{\lambda_{air}} = \frac{3 \times 10^8}{780 \times 10^{-9}} = 3.84 \times 10^{14} \text{Hz}$$
The frequency of light in air is 3.84 × 10¹⁴ Hz.
(b) Wavelength of green light in glass block = λ'
$$\lambda' = \frac{\lambda}{\mu} = \frac{780 \times 10^{-9}}{1.5}$$
$$= 520 \times 10^{-9} \text{ m or 520 nm}$$
The wavelength of green light inside the glass block is 520 nm.

5. In the figure below, a glass slab is hanging in air. A ray of light travelling in air strikes the glass slab and on refraction moves out of glass to air. Draw the path of light and label all relevant angles.

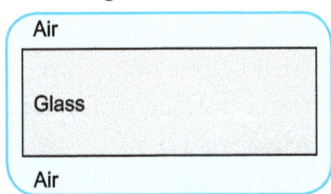

Solution : A ray of light AB is incident on the surface of glass slab. It moves from rarer (air) to denser (glass) medium, hence bends towards the normal N_1N_2 refraction $\angle ABN_1$ is the angle

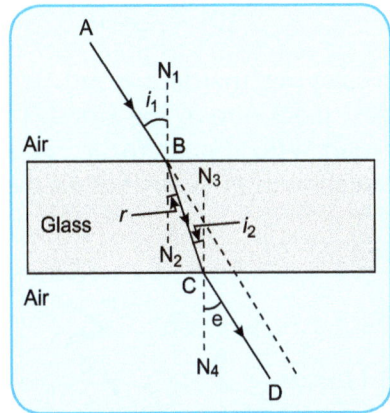

of incidence i_1 and $\angle N_2BC$ is the angle of refraction r. At point C, the ray of light suffers another refraction. Since it moves from glass to air, *i.e.* from denser to rarer medium, it bends away from the normal N_3N_4. $\angle BCN_3$ is the angle of incidence i_2 and angle $\angle N_4CD$ is the angle of emergence e.

6. The given figure shows a ray of light OP incident on a rectangular glass slab ABCD which is silvered at the surface CD. The ray gets partly refracted and partly reflected. Trace the path of refracted and reflected rays and show four rays emerging from the surface AB after reflection from silvered surface.

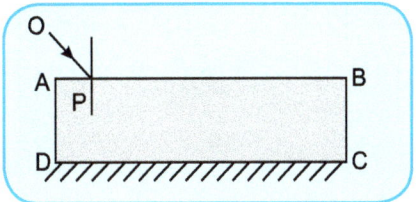

Solution : When the incident ray OP strikes the surface AB of the glass slab, a part of it gets reflected as ray PQ and a part of it gets refracted as ray PR. The ray PR on striking the silvered surface CD gets reflected and on striking the

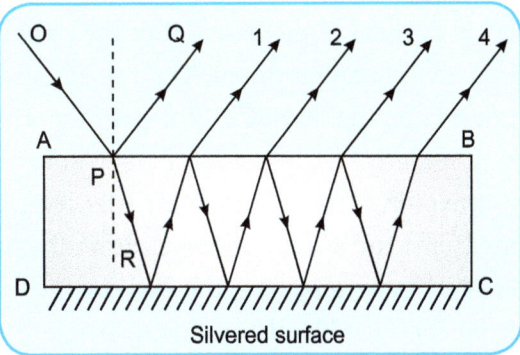

surface AB gets refracted as ray 1. Thus, multiple reflections and refractions occur inside the glass slab.

The four rays emerging from the surface AB after reflection from silvered surface CD and after refraction are labelled as 1, 2, 3 and 4.

7. The figure below shows an equilateral prism ABC. A ray of light EF is incident on the face AC of the prism as shown. Complete the diagram and show the refracted and emergent rays. Label all the relevant angles. Explain the diagram.

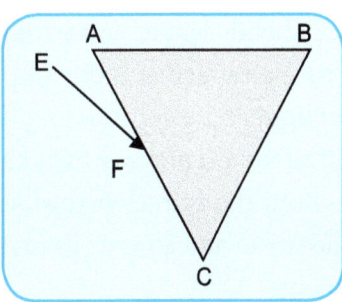

Solution : The completed diagram is given below. EF is the incident ray, FG is the refracted ray and GH is the emergent ray.

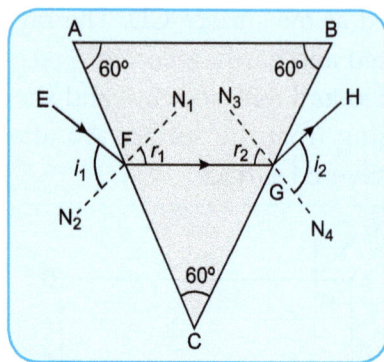

Explanation : The ray EF is incident on the face AC of the prism at point F at an angle of incidence equal to i_1. This ray suffers refraction on going from air to glass (rarer to denser medium) and bends towards the normal N_1N_2. The angle of refraction is r_1. The refracted ray FG is parallel to the base AB of the prism since it is an equilateral prism. The ray FG strikes at point G on the face BC of the prism at an angle r_2. It undergoes another refraction. Now, the ray is travelling from glass to air (denser to rarer medium) and so it bends away from the normal N_3N_4. Upon refraction, the ray emerges as GH from the face BC of the prism. Angle i_2 is the angle of emergence.

8. Assume a ray of light EF which is of red colour and a ray of light PQ which is of violet colour which strike the face of a prism. Show with the help of a diagram, how these rays will emerge. In which case will the angle of deviation be greater?

   Solution : The completed diagram is shown below.

   Rays EF and PQ strike the face AB of the prism and undergo refraction. These rays bend towards the normal on travelling from air to glass. The red ray EF bends less as compared to the violet ray PQ as the refractive index of prism is more for violet light and less for red light. Ray EF gets refracted as ray FG and ray PQ gets refracted as ray QR. Both the refracted rays strike the face AC of the prism and emerge as rays GH and RS, respectively.

   From the figure, it can be seen that the angle of deviation HLM for red light (δ_R) is less than the angle of deviation STU for violet light (δ_V).

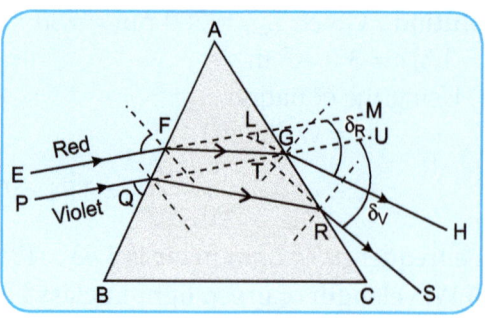

9. A swimming pool appears to be 2 m deep. How deep is it actually? Refractive index of water is 1.33.

   Solution : Given, Apparent depth = 2 m, $\mu = 1.33$

   $$\mu = \frac{\text{Real depth}}{\text{Apparent depth}}$$

   $\therefore$ Real depth = $\mu \times$ Apparent depth

   $= 1.33 \times 2$ m $= 2.66$ m

10. A small pin fixed on a tabletop is viewed vertically above from a distance of 30 cm. By what distance would the pin appear to be raised if it is viewed from the same point through a 10 cm thick glass slab held parallel to the table? Refractive index of the glass is 1.5.

    Solution : Given, Real depth = 10 cm, $\mu = 1.5$

    Shift in the depth (or thickness) $= \text{Real depth}\left(1 - \frac{1}{\mu}\right)$

    $= 10\left(1 - \frac{1}{1.5}\right)$

    $= 10\left(\frac{1.5 - 1}{1.5}\right) = 3.33$ cm

11. A fish is lying inside a pond. If viewed by a person from above the pond, the position of the fish will appear to be raised. Draw a diagram showing the position of the fish to the observer.

    Solution :

    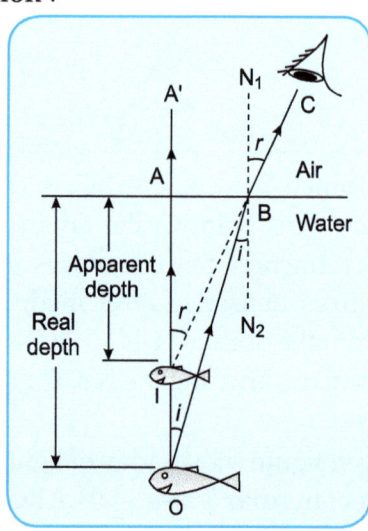

The completed diagram is shown in the above figure. Two incident rays OA and OB are shown in the figure. Ray OA being incident normally remains undeviated as ray AA', whereas ray OB on striking the surface of the pond undergoes refraction and bends away from the normal as refracted ray BC. When an observer views from the top, it appears to him as if the ray BC is coming from point I which is the virtual image of the fish. The actual position of the fish is at a depth AO, whereas the apparent position is at a depth AI which is lesser than the real depth.

EXERCISE 4(A)

1. What do you understand by the term 'refraction of light'?
2. State the two conditions under which the path of a ray of light will deviate?
3. In which medium will the speed of light be greater–denser or rarer?
   Ans : Rarer
4. Define the following terms : (a) point of incidence, (b) angle of refraction and (c) angle of deviation.
5. A boundary separates two media : air and glass. A ray of light incident on this boundary suffers reflection and refraction on passing from air to glass. Draw a labelled diagram to show this.
6. Draw diagrams to show the refraction of light from (a) air to water and (b) water to air. Label the relevant rays and angles.
7. A ray of light moves from a rarer medium to a denser medium as shown in the diagram. Out of the three rays shown, which ray represents the partially reflected ray?
   Ans : Ray 2

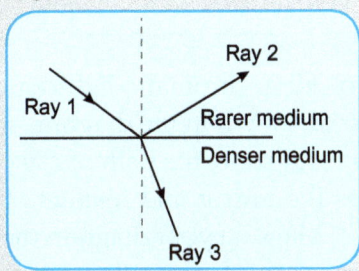

8. Complete the following diagrams :

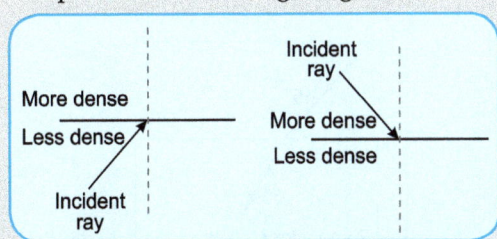

9. State the laws of refraction of light.
10. What is refractive index? Which medium has the lowest value of refractive index?
11. State the relation of refractive index with the speed of light of a medium.
12. In the given figures, trace the path of refracted ray.

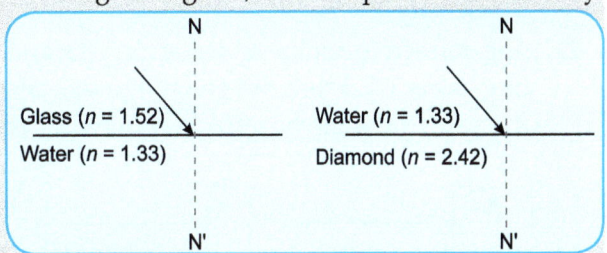

13. Name the subjective property of light related to its wavelength.
14. Define the term 'refractive index' of a medium in terms of velocity of light.
15. 'The refractive index of diamond is 2.42. What is the meaning of this statement?
16. How does the speed of light change when it (a) passes from air to glass and (b) glass to water.
    Ans : (a) The speed decreases, (b) The speed increases
17. The refractive indices of three media A, B and C are 2.55, 1.75 and 2.15, which medium has (a) the highest optical density and (b) lowest optical density?
    Ans : (a) A, (b) B
18. The refractive index of medium A is 1.5, medium B is 1.7 and medium C is 1.31. In which of these media will light travel the fastest?
    Ans : C
19. The given diagram shows the refraction of light from air to a medium X. From the figure, (a) write the value of angle of incidence, (b) write the value of angle of refraction and (c) find the refractive index of the medium X with respect to air.

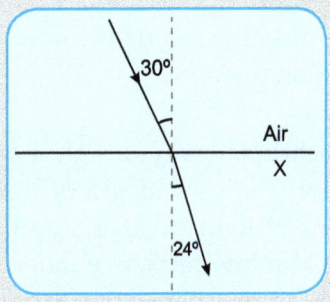

Ans : (a) 30°, (b) 24°, (c) 1.25

20. (a) Write a relationship between angle of incidence and angle of refraction for a given pair of media.
    (b) When a ray of light enters from one medium to another having different optical densities it bends. Why does this phenomenon occur?
    (c) Write one condition where it does not bend when entering a medium of different optical density.
21. The refractive index of water is 1.33 and that of glass is 1.5. From the given figures, calculate the value of angle of refraction in each case.

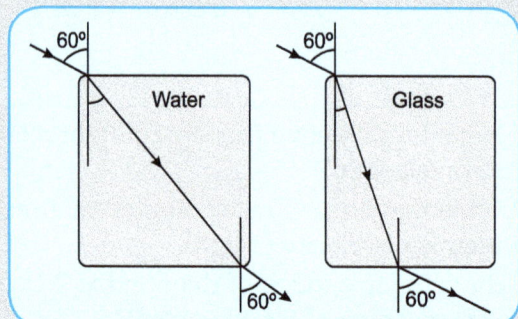

22. Name any two factors on which the refractive index of a medium depends. How does it vary with variation in these stated factors?
23. Out of violet colour and red colour light, which one has a slower speed and smaller refractive index for a given medium?
24. Does the frequency of a ray of light change upon refraction?
25. A ray of light is incident as a normal ray on the surface of separation of two different media. What is the value of the angle of incidence in this case?
26. A boy uses blue colour of light to find the refractive index of glass. He then repeats the experiment using red colour of light. Will the refractive index be the same or different in the two cases? Give a reason to support your answer.
27. Can the absolute refractive index of a medium be less than one?
    Ans : No
28. A monochromatic ray of light passes from air to alochol. The wavelength of light in air is λ, the speed of light in air is c and in alcohol is v. If the absolute refractive index of alcohol is 1.36, (a) Write the relation between c and v. (b) What is the wavelength of light in alcohol?

29. A ray of light is moving from a rarer medium to a denser medium and strikes a plane mirror placed at 90° to the direction of ray as shown in the diagram. (a) Copy the diagram and mark arrows to show the path of the ray of light after it is reflected from the mirror. (b) Name the principle you have used to mark the arrows to show the direction of the ray.

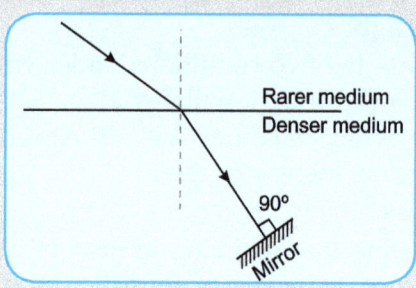

30. In the given diagram, PQ is a ray of light incident on a rectangular glass block. (a) Copy the diagram and complete the path of the ray of light through the glass block. Mark the angle of incidence by letter i and angle of emergence by letter e. (b) How are the angles i and e related to each other?

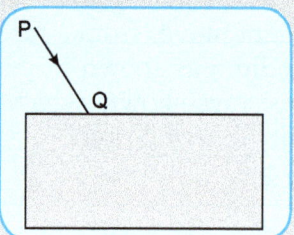

31. A ray of monochromatic light enters a liquid from air as shown in the diagram. (a) Copy the diagram and show the path of ray of light after it strikes the mirror and re-enters the medium of air. (b) Mark on your diagram the two angles on the surface of separation when the ray of light moves out from the liquid to air.

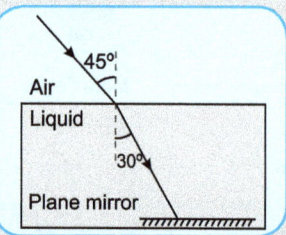

32. A ray of monochromatic light with a frequency of 5.09×10^{14} Hz is incident on an interface of air and corn oil at an angle of 35° as shown. The ray is transmitted through parallel layers of corn oil and glycerol and is then reflected

from the surface of a plane mirror, located below and parallel to the glycerol layer. The ray then emerges from the corn oil back into the air at point P. (a) State whether the angle of refraction will be greater or less than 35°. (b) Why does the ray of light remain undeviated on passing from corn oil to glycerol ? (c) Show how will the ray P emerge from corn oil to air. (d) If the plane mirror is removed from below, how will the ray of light emerge ?

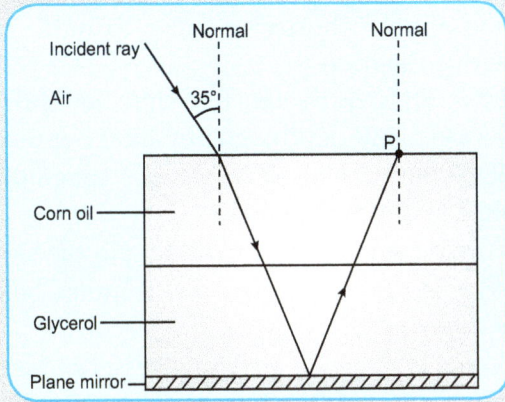

33. State the principle of reversibility of path of light.
34. What is lateral displacement? What are the factors affecting it?
35. For which colour of light is the lateral displacement minimum?
36. When an object is held in front of a thick plane glass mirror, what are the number of images obtained? Which image is the brightest one? Explain.
37. What is a prism?
38. Draw a diagram of a prism and label its different parts.
39. Define the term 'angle of deviation'.
40. Complete the path of a given ray of light through a prism.

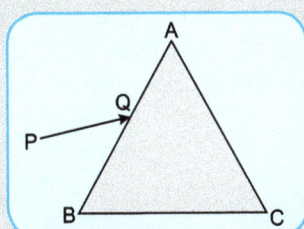

41. What is the reason for deviation produced by a prism?
42. State the factors on which the angle of deviation depends.
43. State the dependence of angle of deviation :
    (a) On the refractive index of the material of the prism.
    (b) On the wavelength of light.
44. Draw a curve showing the variation in angle of deviation with the angle of incidence at the surface of a prism.
45. Derive a relation between angle of incidence (*i*), angle of emergence (*e*), angle of prism (A) and angle of deviation (δ) for a ray of light passing through a prism.
46. What do you understand by minimum deviation?
47. How does the angle of minimum deviation produced by a prism change with (a) decrease in wavelength of light and (b) increase in refracting angle of prism?
48. Write a relation between the angle of incidence (*i*), angle of emergence (*e*), angle of prism (A) and angle of deviation (δ) for a ray of light passing through an equilateral prism.
49. Which coloured light–red or blue–will deviate more on passing through a prism ?
50. An object O is viewed by an observer through a prism ABC. Complete the diagram to show the image formed by the prism and as seen by the observer.

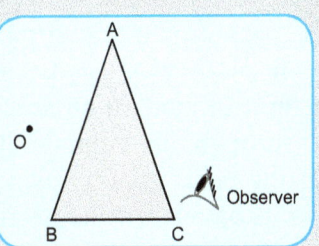

51. A monochromatic ray of light is incident on an equilateral glass prism at an angle of incidence equal to 45° and suffers minimum deviation by an angle of 30°. (a) What is the angle of emergence? (b) If the angle of incidence is changed to (i) 25° and (ii) 50°, will the angle of deviation will be more or less than 30° ?
52. In the figures given below, a ray of light of red colour is incident normally on the two prisms. Draw the path of the ray of light as it enters and emerges from the prism in each case. Mark the necessary angles.

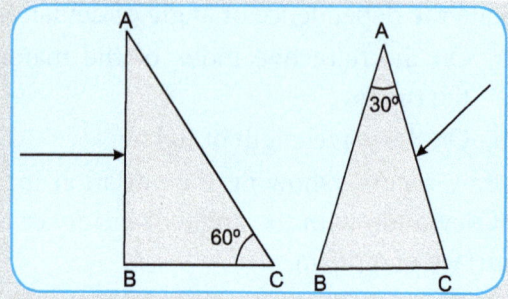

53. A ray of light is incident on a prism ABC as shown. The prism is kept over a plane mirror. Show the approximate path of emergence of the ray of light.

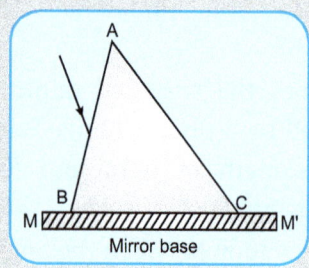

54. Two prisms, ABC and XYZ, are kept with their faces parallel to each other. A monochromatic ray of light is incident on the face AC of the prism. Complete the diagram to show the path of the ray as it emerges from the prism XYZ.

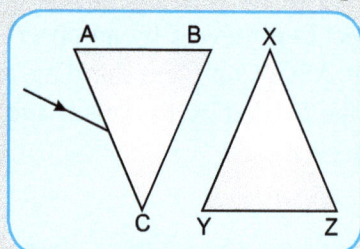

55. A ray of light incident at an angle of incidence i passes through an equilateral glass prism such that the refracted ray inside the prism is parallel to its base and emerges from the prism at an angle of emergence e. (a) How is the angle of emergence e related to the angle of incidence i ? (b) What can you say about the value of angle of deviation in such a situation ?
56. What do you understand by real depth and apparent depth?
57. How is the refractive index of a medium related to its real depth and apparent depth?
58. Does the depth of a tank of water appear to change or remain the same when viewed normally from above?
59. Why does the depth of water in a pond appear only three-fourth of its original depth? Explain with the help of a diagram.
60. Jatin puts a pencil into a glass container having water and is surprised to see the pencil in a different state.
    (a) What change is observed in the appearance of the pencil ?
    (b) Name the phenomenon responsible for the change.
    (c) Draw a ray diagram showing how the eye sees the pencil.
61. A person swimming in a pool observes a tree outside from the bottom of the pool. Will the tree appear shorter or taller to him? Explain with a diagram.
62. Give an expression for shift or difference between real depth and apparent depth.
63. State the factors on which the magnitude of shift of depth depends.
64. Why do stars appear twinkling in the sky?
65. Why is the Sun seen a few minutes before it actually rises?
66. A coin is placed in an empty vessel and is out of line of sight for a person standing at a distance. When water is poured in this vessel, the coin becomes visible. How will you explain this?

MULTIPLE CHOICE QUESTIONS

1. A ray of light while travelling from an optically denser medium to a rarer medium will ;
   (a) bend towards the normal
   (b) bend away from the normal
   (c) travel along the normal
   (d) None of the above
   Ans : (b)
2. A ray of light while travelling from medium A to medium B deviates away from the normal. The speed of light in medium :
   (a) A is more than B   (b) B is more than A
   (c) A is same as B   (d) None of these
   Ans : (b)
3. Four optical media A, B, C and D have refractive indices as 1.50, 1.00, 1.250 and 1.70, respectively. The light will travel fastest in medium :
   (a) A   (b) B
   (c) C   (d) D
   Ans : (b)
4. Which of these media has highest refractive index?
   (a) Glass   (b) Air
   (c) Diamond   (d) Water
   Ans : (c)

5. In an equilateral prism, the angle of incidence is 45° and the angle of emergence is 55°. The angle of deviation of the ray of light is :
   (a) 45°   (b) 40°
   (c) 35°   (d) 50°
   Ans : (b)

6. The angle of deviation is maximum for light of colour :
   (a) red   (b) blue
   (c) violet   (d) green
   Ans : (c)

NUMERICAL PROBLEMS

1. A beam of light passes from air to a medium X. If the angle of incidence is 45° and angle of refraction is 30°, calculate the refractive index of X.
   Ans : 1.414

2. The refractive index of glass with respect to air is 1.5. What will be the refractive index of air with respect to glass?
   Ans : 0.667

3. The speed of light in glass is 2×10^5 km/s. What is the refractive index of glass?
   Ans : 1.5

4. Light enters from air to dense flint glass with refractive index 1.65. What will be the speed of light in flint glass?
   Ans : 1.81×10^8 m s^{-1}

5. The absolute refractive index of flint glass is 1.65 and that of alcohol is 1.36. What is the refractive index of flint glass with respect to alcohol?
   Ans : 1.21

6. Light of wavelength 600 nm enters glass which has a refractive index of 1.5. What will be the frequency of the light ray inside glass?
   Ans : 5×10^{14} Hz.

7. A ray of light of frequency 5×10^{14} Hz passes through a liquid. The wavelength of light measured inside the liquid is found to be 450 nm. Calculate the refractive index of the liquid.
   Ans : 1.33

8. A prism of refracting angle 60° has angle of minimum deviation equal to 36°. What is the angle of incidence?
   Ans : 48°

9. If a fish is 40 cm below the surface of a pond, how deep does it appear to an observer directly above? The refractive index of water is 1.33.
   Ans : 30.1 cm

10. The apparent depth of an object at the bottom of a tank filled with a liquid of refractive index 1.3 is 7.7 cm. What is the actual depth of the liquid in the tank?
    Ans : 10.01 cm

11. A coin placed at the bottom of a beaker appears to be raised by 4 cm. If the refractive index of water is 4/3, find the depth of water in the beaker.
    Ans : 16 cm

12. The speed of light in glass is 2×10^8 m s^{-1} and in air is 3×10^8 m s^{-1}. An ink dot is covered by a glass plate of 6 cm thickness. Calculate the shift in the ink dot where it appears to be raised from the original position.
    Ans : 2 cm

13. A tank is filled with water to a height of 12.5 cm. The apparent depth of a pin lying at the bottom of the tank as measured by a microscope is found to be 9.4 cm. (a) What is the refractive index of water? (b) If water is replaced by a liquid of refractive index 1.63 up to the same height, by what distance would the microscope have to be moved to focus on the pin again?
    Ans : (a) 1.33, (b) 1.73 cm

(B) CRITICAL ANGLE AND TOTAL INTERNAL REFLECTION

4.14 TRANSMISSION OF LIGHT FROM A DENSER MEDIUM TO A RARER MEDIUM AT DIFFERENT ANGLES OF INCIDENCE

When a ray of light travelling in a denser medium, such as glass or water, falls on the surface of a rarer medium, such as air, a part of it gets reflected into the denser medium and part of it gets refracted into the rarer medium. The refracted ray bends away from the normal at the point of incidence. The ray of light can be incident on the boundary surface separating the two media at different angles of incidence. With different angles of incidence, the angles of refraction also vary, though the angle of reflection is always equal to the angle of incidence (law of reflection). At a particular angle of incidence, when the angle of refraction is equal to 90°, it is known as *critical angle*.

Case 1 : When the angle of incidence is small ($i < i_c$)

In Fig. 4.15, XY is a boundary surface separating two media : one is denser (glass or water) and the other is rarer (air). Let AO be a ray of light travelling from a denser to a rarer medium. It is incident at the boundary surface separating the two media at a small angle of incidence i. A part of this ray gets reflected as ray OB into the denser medium and a part of it gets refracted as ray OC. The ray OC bends away from the normal in the rarer medium and the angle of refraction r is greater than the angle of incidence i.

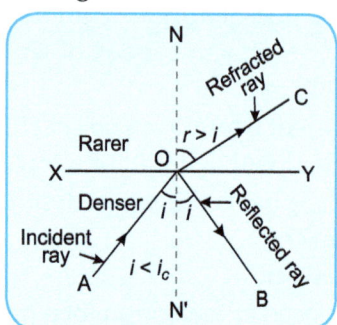

Fig. 4.15 : Refraction from a rarer to a denser medium when $i < i_c$.

Case 2 : When the angle of incidence is equal to the critical angle ($i = i_c$)

If the angle of incidence is increased, the angle of refraction also increases correspondingly. The angle of refraction reaches its highest value of 90° at a certain angle of incidence i called *critical angle i_c*, but the intensity of the refracted ray keeps on decreasing and the intensity of reflected ray increases.

In Fig. 4.16, AO is the incident ray, OB is the reflected ray and OC is the refracted ray which makes an angle of 90° with the normal NN'.

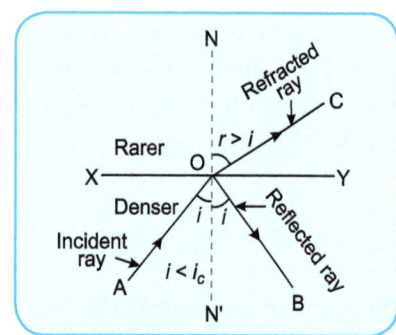

Fig. 4.16 : Refraction from a rarer to a denser medium when i = i$_c$.

Case 3 : When the angle of incidence is greater than the critical angle ($i > i_c$)

If the angle of incidence is further increased beyond the critical angle, then the incident ray gets totally reflected and no refraction occurs.

In Fig. 4.17, ray OA is incident at angle $i > i_c$. No refraction occurs at this angle and thus no refracted ray is obtained. The incident ray gets totally reflected as ray OC.

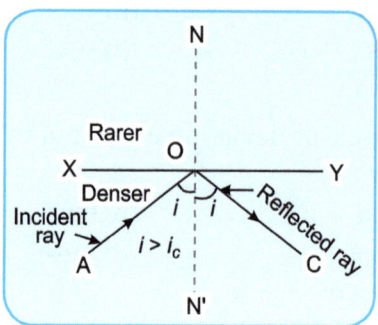

Fig. 4.17 : Refraction from a rarer to a denser medium when $i > i_c$.

Critical angle : *The angle of incidence in a denser medium corresponding to which the angle of refraction in the rarer medium is 90 is called the critical angle.*

4.15 RELATION BETWEEN THE CRITICAL ANGLE AND THE REFRACTIVE INDEX $\left(\mu = \dfrac{1}{\sin i_c}\right)$

When the angle of incidence is equal to critical angle i_c, the angle of refraction is 90°.

From Snell's law of refraction,

The refractive index of rarer medium, such as air, with respect to denser medium, say glass, will be

$$^g\mu_a = \frac{\sin i_c}{\sin 90°}$$

Since sin 90° = 1

∴ $\qquad ^g\mu_a = \sin i_c.$

From the principle of reversibility, the refractive index of glass with respect to air will be

$$^a\mu_g = \frac{1}{^g\mu_a} = \frac{1}{\sin i_c} \text{ or cosec } i_c \quad ...(4.10)$$

Thus, if the refractive index of the denser medium with respect to the rarer medium is known, the critical angle for that pair of media can be calculated from the above relation.

Examples :

(a) The refractive index of water with respect to air is $^a\mu_w = 1.33$.

∴ $\qquad \sin i_c = \dfrac{1}{^a\mu_w} = \dfrac{1}{1.33} = 0.752$

i.e. $\qquad i_c = 49°$

(b) The refractive index of diamond with respect to air is $^a\mu_d = 2.42$.

∴ $\qquad \sin i_c = \dfrac{1}{^a\mu_d} = \dfrac{1}{2.42} = 0.413$

i. e. $\qquad i_c = 25°$

Table 4.2 gives the values of critical angle for some substances with respect to air.

Table 4.2 : Critical angles for some common substances

Substance	Refractive index (μ)	Critical angle i_c = $\sin^{-1}\left(\frac{1}{\mu}\right)$
Water	1.33	49°
Alcohol	1.36	47°
Kerosene	1.44	44°
Turpentine oil	1.47	43°
Glass	1.50	42°
Sapphire	1.76	34°
Diamond	2.42	25°

Factors Affecting the Critical Angle

For a given pair of media, the critical angle is affected by the following two factors :

1. Wavelength or colour of light : The refractive index of a medium is higher for shorter wavelength of light, *i.e.* violet colour, and is lower for longer wavelength of light, *i.e.* red colour. The critical angle is inversely proportional to the refractive index of a given medium. Hence, the critical angle *increases with increase in wavelength of the light*. It is longer for red colour and shorter for violet colour.

2. Temperature : With increase in temperature, the refractive index of a medium decreases and so the *critical angle for that pair of media increases*.

4.16 TOTAL INTERNAL REFLECTION

We know that when light travels from a denser medium to a rarer medium, with angle of incidence greater than the critical angle, refraction does not occur. The entire light undergoes reflection in the same direction. In Fig. 4.18, a ray AO is incident on the surface separating two media at an angle greater than critical angle i_c. It can be seen that there is no refraction and hence no refracted ray. The whole of light undergoes reflection, and ray OC represents the reflected ray in the same medium.

The phenomenon due to which a ray of light, while travelling from a denser medium to a rarer medium at an angle of incidence greater than the critical angle, gets reflected into the denser medium is called the *total internal reflection*.

The two conditions essential for the total internal reflection are as follows :
1. The rays of light must travel from the optically denser medium to the optically rarer medium.
2. The angle of incidence at the surface separating the two media must be greater than the critical angle.

Refraction and Total Internal Reflection of Light at Different Angles of Incidence

The phenomenon of refraction and total internal reflection by varying the angle of incidence can be demonstrated with the help of a beam of laser light (Fig. 4.19).

Let O be a point source of light kept in a denser medium. We know that rays of light travel from a denser medium to a rarer medium at increasing angles of incidence.

1. For ray OA, the angle of incidence is zero, a part of it is reflected as AO and part of it is refracted as ray AB.
2. The angle of incidence is less than the critical angle ($i < i_c$) for rays OA_1 and OA_2. A part of these rays gets reflected as A_1A_1' and A_2A_2', respectively, and a part of these gets refracted as rays A_1B_1 and A_2B_2, respectively.
3. The angle of incidence is equal to the critical angle ($i = i_c$) for the ray OA_3. A part of it gets reflected as A_3A_3' and part of it gets refracted as A_3B_3 at an angle of refraction equal to 90°.
4. The angle of incidence is greater than the critical angle ($i > i_c$) for ray OA_4. No refraction occurs and it gets totally reflected as ray A_4B_4.

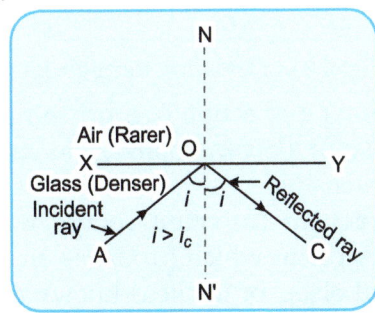

Fig. 4.18 : Total internal reflection.

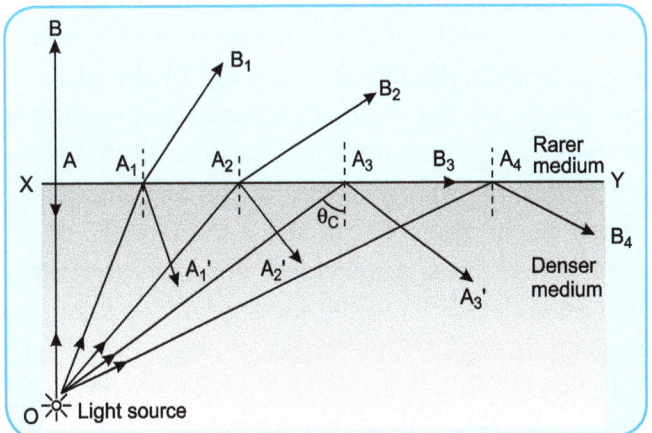

Fig. 4.19 : Refraction and total internal reflection.

> **NOTE**
>
> In the process of total internal reflection, 100% intensity of light is reflected back, unlike a plane mirror where some part of the light gets refracted or absorbed.

4.17 TOTAL INTERNAL REFLECTION IN A PRISM

Prisms can be of three different types depending on the angles they make up with its principal section. (1) *Right-angled isosceles prism* : The three angles are 45°, 90° and 45°, (2) *Equilateral prism* : The three angles are 60°, 60° and 60°, (3) *Right-angled prism* : The three angles are 30°, 90° and 60°.

1. Total internal reflection through a right-angled isosceles prism (45°, 90°, 45°)

A right-angled isosceles prism is a totally reflecting prism. It has an angle of 90° between its two refracting surfaces, and the other two angles are 45° each. A ray of light incident normally on any of its faces suffers total internal reflection inside the prism.

Whenever a ray of light travelling through this prism strikes the glass-air interface at an angle greater than 42° (the critical angle), it undergoes total internal reflection.

This type of prism can be used to (a) deviate rays of light through 90°, (b) deviate rays of light through 180° and (c) erect an inverted image without any deviation in its path.

(a) To deviate a ray of light through 90° : Fig. 4.20 shows the principal section ABC of a totally reflecting prism. The path of two rays of light EF and GH is shown in Fig. 4.20. These rays are incident normally on the face AB of the prism and so pass undeviated into the prism where these strike the face AC of the prism at an angle of incidence equal to 45°, which is greater than the critical angle 42° of the glass-air interface. Since the angle of incidence is greater than the critical angle, no refraction occurs and these rays suffer total internal reflection at the face AC. Upon reflection, the rays of light strike the face BC of the prism where these are incident normally and hence pass undeviated. Thus, the incident ray of light gets deviated through 90° on passing through the prism.

If the rays of light are incident on the face BC of the prism, then these will deviate through 90° and emerge from face AB after total internal reflection.

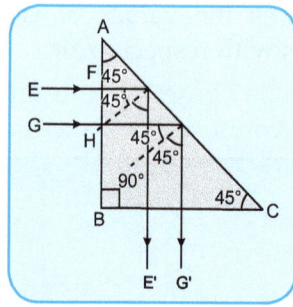

Fig. 4.20 : Deviation through 90°

Use : Since 100% intensity of light gets reflected in the phenomenon of total internal reflection, a totally reflecting prism is thus preferred in a *periscope* instead of a plane mirror in which there is loss of intensity of light due to refraction and absorption of some part of light.

(b) To deviate a ray of light through 180° : Consider an object EF, from which parallel rays of light emerge and are incident normally on the face AC of the prism (Fig. 4.21). As the angle of incidence is zero, these rays remain undeviated inside the prism. The rays of light strike the face AB of the prism at an angle 45°, which is greater than the critical angle (42°) for glass-air interface. The rays of light suffer total internal reflection and strike the face BC of the prism where these are again incident at an angle of 45°, *i.e.* greater than critical angle. They again suffer total internal reflection for the second time and now strike the face AC of the prism normally. These rays remain undeviated and emerge from the face AC, forming an image E'F' of the object EF which is turned by 180°. Thus, a beam of light gets deviated by 180°.

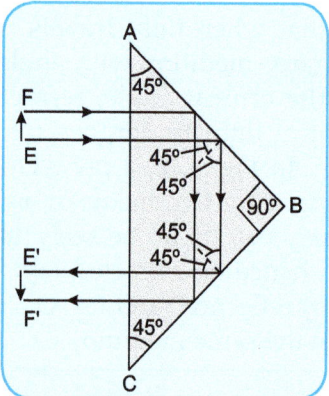

Fig. 4.21 : Deviation through 180°

Use : This type of action of a prism finds use in a prism *binocular* or a *camera* to invert an image without any loss of intensity.

(c) To erect an inverted image without any deviation : A prism which produces an erect image of an inverted object or image is known as an *erecting prism*.

To produce an erect image, the rays of light should be parallel to the hypotenuse, on striking the base of the right-angled isosceles prism.

Consider an object EF, from which rays of light parallel to the face AC (hypotenuse) of the prism emerge. These rays strike the face AB (base) of the prism. These rays suffer refraction on entering the prism from air and bend towards the normal. The refracted rays strike the face AC of the prism such that the angle of incidence is greater than the critical angle (42°) of glass-air interface (Fig. 4.22).

The rays suffer total internal reflection at the face AC, and the reflected rays strike the face BC of the prism. The angle of incidence striking the face BC is less than the critical angle and so the rays suffer refraction. On moving from glass to air, the rays bend away from the normal and emerge from the face BC of the prism. The emergent rays are parallel to the face AC of the prism and are inverted. For an inverted object EF, an erect image E'F' is thus obtained.

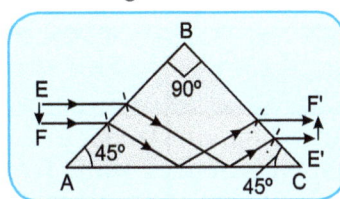

Fig. 4.22 : Erecting prism.

Use : An erecting prism is used in a *slide projector*.

2. Total internal reflection through an equilateral prism (60°, 60°, 60°)

The principal section of an equilateral prism has all the angles equal to 60°. This prism can be used to deviate a ray of light through 60° by total internal reflection. In Fig. 4.23, a ray of light EF is incident normally on the face AB of the prism and hence it remains undeviated as ray FG inside the prism. This ray FG strikes the face AC of the prism such that the angle of incidence is equal to 60°. Since this angle being greater than the critical angle (42°), the ray suffers total internal reflection at the face AC of the prism separating air. From the law of reflection, angle of incidence is equal to angle of reflection, *i.e.* 60°. The total angle EGH is thus equal to 120°. The reflected ray GH obtained after total internal reflection strikes the face BC of the prism normally and hence remains undeviated. It emerges from the prism as ray HI. If the incident ray is produced backwards, it can be noticed that the incident ray EF has deviated through an angle of 60° from its initial direction towards the base of the prism.

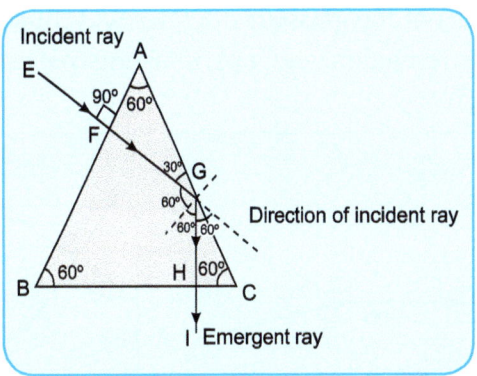

Fig. 4.23 : Deviation by an equilateral prism.

3. Action of a right-angled prism (30°, 90°, 60°)

(a) Deviation of a ray of light by an angle less than 60° by total internal reflection : Consider a ray of light EF incident normally on the face BC (base) of the prism. It remains undeviated as ray FG inside the prism and strikes the face AC (hypotenuse) of the prism such that the angle of incidence is 60° at point G. Since this angle of incidence being greater than the critical angle (42°), the ray FG suffers total internal reflection at the glass-air interface. The reflected ray GH strikes the face AB (perpendicular) of the prism at an angle of 30°. Since this angle being less than the critical angle, the ray GH gets refracted as ray HI and bends away from the normal in air. The angle of refraction is greater than the angle of incidence but less than 60°. Thus, the incident ray EF emerges from the prism as ray HI and deviates through an angle which is less than 60° (Fig. 4.24).

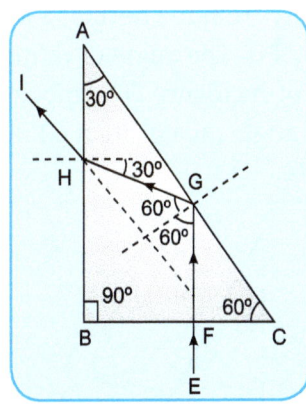

Fig. 4.24 : Deviation through a right-angled prism

(b) Refraction but no total internal reflection : If a ray of light EF is incident normally on the face AB (perpendicular) or face AC (hypotenuse) of the right-angled prism ABC, it enters undeviated as ray FG inside the prism and strikes the opposite face AC or AB, respectively, such that the angle of incidence at point G is 30°. This angle is less than the critical angle (42°) of the glass-air interface and thus the rays undergo refraction and not total internal reflection (Fig. 4.25).

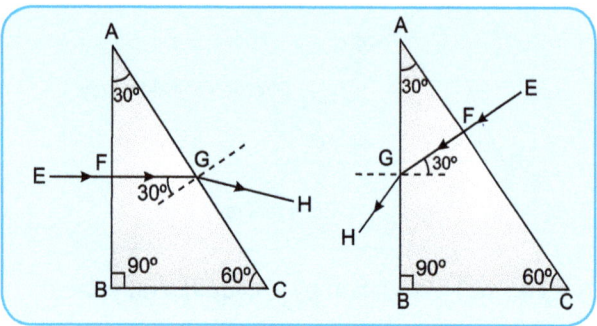

Fig. 4.25 : No total internal reflection through a right-angled prism.

Exceptional case : There is one exceptional condition when total internal reflection can occur through a ray of light incident on the face AC (hypotenuse) of the prism.

From the point B of the prism, draw a perpendicular BD on the face AC of the prism. Now, if a ray of light EF is incident normally on the portion DC of the face AC of the prism, it remains undeviated and travels as ray FG inside the prism. This ray FG strikes the face BC of the prism at point G, such that the angle of incidence is 60°, which is greater than the critical angle (42°), and so the ray FG suffers total internal reflection. The reflected ray GH strikes the face AB of the prism at an angle of incidence 30°. This angle is less than the critical angle and so the ray GH suffers refraction from glass to air. It bends away from the normal and emerges from the prism as ray HI. The angle of refraction is greater than the angle of incidence. The incident ray EF gets deviated by an angle greater than 60° and emerges as ray HI (Fig. 4.26).

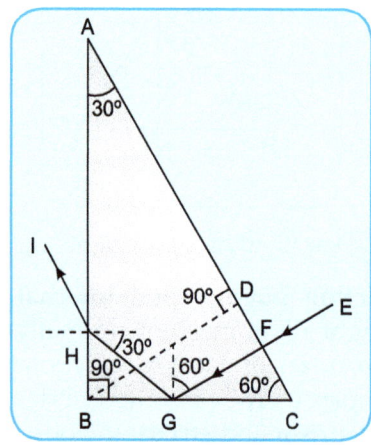

Fig. 4.26 : Total internal reflection through a right-angled prism.

4.18 TOTALLY REFLECTING PRISM VERSUS PLANE MIRROR

In the phenomenon of total internal reflection occurring in a prism, the entire incident light, i.e. 100% of it, gets reflected into the denser medium, whereas in ordinary reflection occurring from a plane mirror, some amount of the light gets absorbed and some amount gets refracted. Thus, only partial reflection takes place.

Thus, a totally reflecting prism is preferred over a plane mirror in construction of a periscope to deviate light rays by 90° in binocular and camera to deviate rays of light by 180°. The image obtained by the use of such a prism is much brighter than that obtained by a plane mirror. Also, the intensity of image formed by such a prism remains unaltered, whereas the intensity of image formed by a plane mirror decreases with time, due to deterioration of silvered surface of the plane mirror with long use.

Differences between reflection from a plane mirror and total internal reflection

Reflection from a plane mirror	Total internal reflection
It can occur when an incident light travels from any medium at any angle of incidence.	It occurs only when a light from a denser medium travels to a rarer medium at an angle of incidence greater than the critical angle for the given pair of media.
Only partial reflection occurs. A part of light gets refracted and absorbed.	The entire (100%) light gets reflected. No refraction or absorption occurs.
The energy of reflected ray is less than the energy of incident ray, i.e. there is a loss of energy.	The energy of reflected ray is same as that of the incident ray, i.e. there is no loss of energy.
The image obtained is less bright.	The image obtained is much brighter.
The intensity of image decreases with time due to wear and tear of silvering on the mirror.	The intensity of the image remains unchanged even after a long usage.

4.19 SIMPLE EFFECTS OF TOTAL INTERNAL REFLECTION

Some of the common effects or consequences of total internal reflection are as follows :

1. Formation of mirage : Mirage is an optical illusion, which is usually seen in deserts on hot summer days.

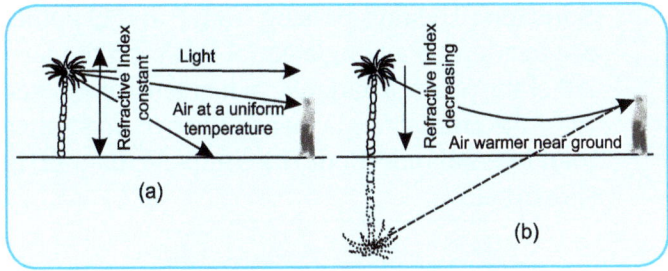

Fig. 4.27 : Formation of Mirage

The temperature of air near the surface of the sand is maximum and hence is rarer or lighter. The upper layers of air, which are relatively cooler, are denser. When rays of light from a distant object, such as the top of a tree, travel towards the ground, they move from a denser to a rarer medium and bend away from the normal. At a particular layer, when the angle of incidence becomes greater than the critical angle in the denser layer of air, the total internal reflection occurs. To an observer who is standing far away, the rays appear to be coming from the mirror image of the tree, and this creates an optical illusion of reflection from a pond of water, though in reality there is no water around.

2. The upper surface of water held in a beaker appears silvery : The rays of light entering in water from below suffer refraction at the water-air interface. The critical angle for this interface is 49°. When the rays of light strike the surface of water at an angle of incidence greater than this critical angle, they suffer total internal reflection. When these reflected rays emerge from the water, they appear to come from the upper surface of water which appears silvery.

Similarly, an empty test tube when held obliquely in water and viewed from top appears silvery. A crack in a glass windowpane appears silvery due to the presence of air in the crack.

3. Sparkling of diamonds : Diamonds are cut at very sharp angles, creating a number of refractive surfaces. The critical angle for diamond is 25°. When a ray of light enters a diamond, it suffers a series of total internal reflections as the critical angle is very small. The ray of light gets trapped within the diamond for some time. Due to this trapped light energy, a diamond sparkles.

4. Looming : Similar to mirage, looming is also an optical illusion that takes place in polar regions. In this case, the lower layers of air are denser and the optical density of air layers decreases with height. Thus, an image of a distant object such as a ship in water appears in the air when total internal reflection takes place.

5. Optical fibres : Optical fibres are made of a very fine quality of glass or quartz. They are coated with a thin layer of material of lower refractive index than that of the fibre. The thickness of the strand is equivalent to that of a human hair. The optical fibre works on the principle of total internal reflection. If a beam of light is passed through a thin glass rod, total internal reflection traps the light inside the rod. This phenomenon enables doctors to inspect many internal body sites through an instrument called *endoscope*. A bundle of fibres transmit an image that can be inspected visually outside the body. Optical fibres are also used in the field of telecommunication for transmitting and receiving signals converted into light pulses.

4.20 APPLICATIONS OF TOTAL INTERNAL REFLECTION

1. Total internal reflection is the operating principle of optical fibres which are used in the endoscopes, tele-communications, internet wires etc.
2. Total internal reflection principle used in the automotive rain sensors.
3. Prism in the binoculars.
4. Diamonds shine brightly due to total internal reflection.

ILLUSTRATIVE EXAMPLES

1. Three rays of light red (R), green (G) and blue (B) are incident on the face AB of a right-angled prism ABC as shown in the figure. The refractive indices of the material of the prism of red, green and blue wavelengths are 1.39, 1.44 and 1.47, respectively. Trace the path of the rays through the prism.

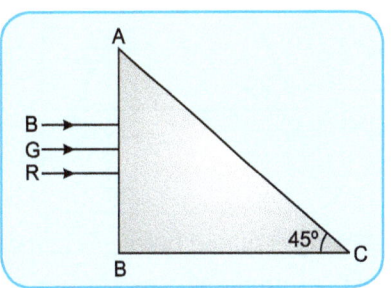

Solution : From the relation, $\mu = \dfrac{1}{\sin C}$

Critical angle for red light $C_R = \sin^{-1}\left(\dfrac{1}{1.39}\right) = 46°$

Critical angle for green light $C_G = \sin^{-1}\left(\dfrac{1}{1.44}\right) = 44°$

Critical angle for blue light $C_B = \sin^{-1}\left(\dfrac{1}{1.47}\right) = 42.9°$

The three rays are incident normally on the face AB of the prism and hence enter the prism undeviated. The rays strike the face AC of the prism at an angle of 45° which is greater than the critical angle for blue and green rays. Hence, these two rays suffer total internal reflection. The critical angle of red light being more than the angle of incidence, it suffers refraction and emerges from the prism face AC, bending away from the normal.

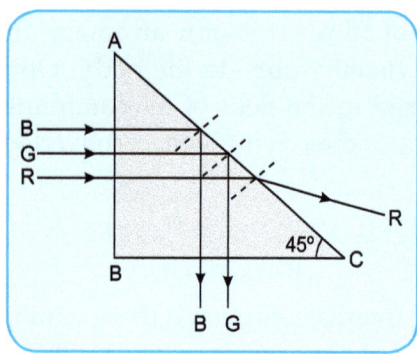

2. In the above example, if the three rays of light are incident normally on one of the faces of an equilateral prism, how will the rays emerge?

Solution : If the three rays are incident normally on one of the faces, say face AB of an equilateral prism, these rays will enter the prism and strike the face AC at an angle of incidence equal to 60°. This angle of incidence is greater than the critical angle for all the three rays and thus all of them suffer total internal reflection. These rays emerge from the face BC of the prism.

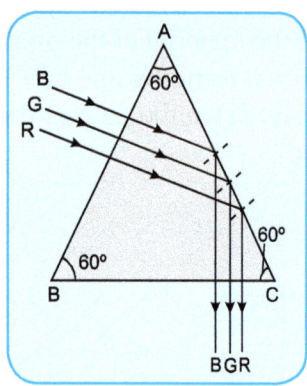

3. An object PQ is placed before a right-angled prism with critical angle 41°, as shown in the figure. Trace the path of the ray from P and Q passing through the prism and show the image formed.

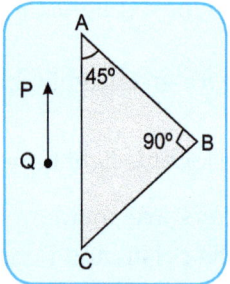

Solution : The rays passing from P and Q points are incident at an angle equal to 45° on the face AB of the prism. This angle of incidence is greater than the critical angle; hence, the two rays suffer total internal reflection. The complete diagram is shown below.

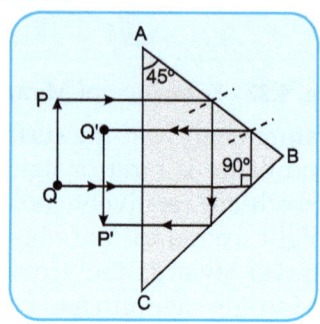

From the diagram, it can be seen that the image P'Q' of the object PQ is inverted, *i.e.* it suffers 180° deviation.

4. Three rays of light A, B and C are incident at the point O which is the centre of a semicircular glass block at different angles of incidence such that angle of incidence for ray A < B < C. If angle BON' is the critical angle, then draw the paths of all the three rays when they strike the edge XY at point O.

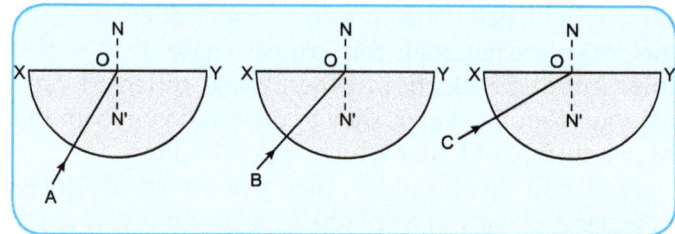

Solution : Angle of incidence for ray A is smaller than critical angle, so it will undergo refraction. The refracted ray OA' will bend away from the normal NN'.

Since angle BON' is the critical angle, the angle of refraction N'OY will be 90°. The refracted ray OB' will pass along the edge XY.

Angle of incidence for ray B is greater than critical angle, so it will suffer total internal reflection as shown by reflected ray OC'.

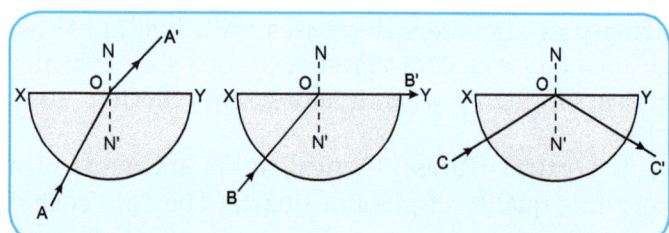

REFRACTION OF LIGHT AT PLANE SURFACES

EXERCISE 4(B)

1. What is meant by the term 'critical angle'?
2. Explain critical angle with the help of a diagram.
3. What is the relation between critical angle and refractive index of a medium?
4. What is the magnitude of critical angle for (a) water-air interface and (b) glass-air interface?
   Ans : (a) 49°, (b) 42°
5. If the critical angle for diamond is 25°, what is the refractive index of diamond?
   Ans : 2.36
6. What are the two factors affecting the critical angle for a pair of media?
7. If the critical angle for blue light is $x°$ for a certain pair of media, what will be the critical angle for red light and violet light for the same pair of media-more than, less than or equal to $x°$?
   Ans : More than $x°$ for red light and less than $x°$ for violet light
8. If the angle of incidence is equal to critical angle for a glass–air interface, what will be the angle of refraction?
9. If the angle of incidence i is greater than the critical angle for a glass-air interface, what will be the angle of refraction?
   Ans : i
10. What is total internal reflection? Explain with a diagram.
11. State the two conditions essential for total internal reflection to occur.
12. Three rays A, B and C start from a point source O inside a glass block. The critical angle for glass-air interface is 48° as shown by angle OBN'. (a) Show the path of the three rays after these strikes the boundary XY of glass-air interface. (b) Name the phenomenon exhibited by each ray.

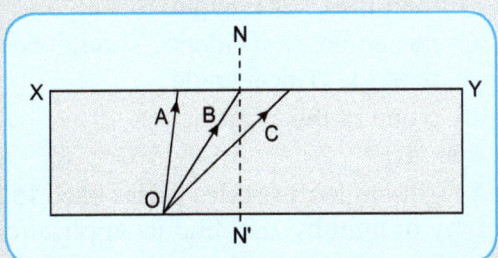

13. The critical angle for diamond is 24°. Since this angle is small, a number of total internal reflections take place inside it before a ray of light emerges from it. In the figure given below, trace the path of an incident light as it emerges after suffering total internal reflection through the four given points.

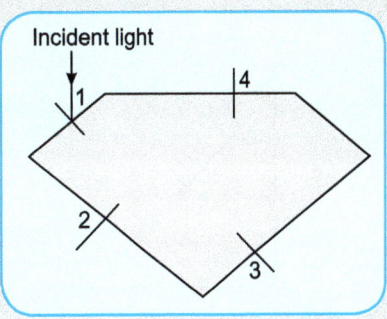

14. The refractive index of water is 1.33. From a point source O inside a vessel containing water, draw three rays OA, OB and OC incident on the water-air surface at an angle of incidence equal to 30°, 48° and 60°, respectively. Show the direction of these rays as they emerge from the water.
15. Which type of prism is a totally reflecting prism? What are the different actions that it can produce?
16. Show with the help of a diagram, how a totally reflecting prism can be used to deviate a ray of light by 90°. What is the application of such a prism?
17. A ray of light EF passes through a right-angled glass prism as shown in the diagram. (a) What are the angles of incidence at the faces AB, AC and BC? (b) What is the phenomenon that the ray suffers at the face AC? If the refractive index of the prism material is decreased and made equal to that of water, then how will the path of ray EF gets affected?

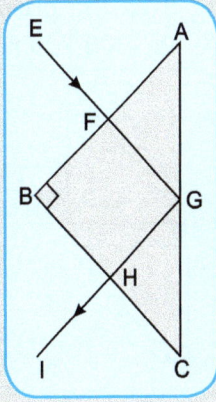

18. A ray of light PQ is incident normally on the hypotenuse of an isosceles right-angled prism ABC as shown in the diagram. (a) Copy the diagram and complete the path of the ray PQ till it emerges from the prism. (b) What is the value of angle of deviation of the ray? (c) Name an instrument where this action of the prism is used?

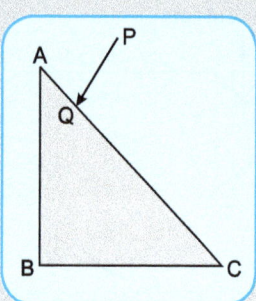

19. If a ray of light needs to be deviated by 60°, which type of prism will be suitable for this purpose? Explain how this can be achieved with a suitable diagram.

20. Copy the diagram given below and complete the path of light ray till it emerges out of the prism. The critical angle of glass is 42°. In your diagram mark the angles wherever necessary.

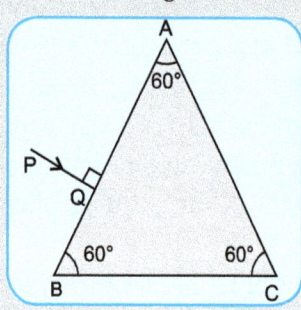

21. What are the conditions under which a right-angled prism with the three angles equal to 30°, 90° and 60° does not suffer total internal reflection?

22. The figure below shows two isosceles right-angled prisms X and Y. Two parallel rays of light are incident on one of the faces of prism X. Complete the diagram to show the rays emerging from the prism Y. Explain the principle used for completing the diagram.

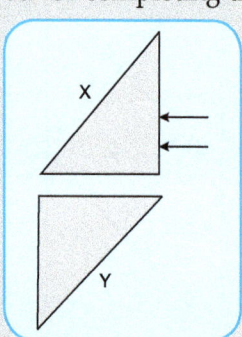

23. The figure below shows two isosceles right-angled prisms X and Y. A monochromatic ray of light is incident on the prism Y as shown. Complete the path of this ray of light as it emerges from the prism X.

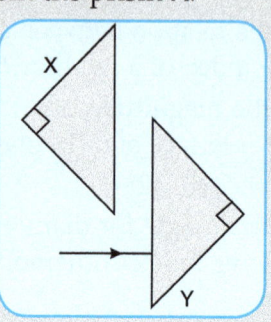

24. Name the type of prism used instead of a plane mirror to turn a ray of light through 180°. Explain with a diagram how this deviation can be obtained. Name the instrument in which it is used.

25. What is the advantage of using a totally reflecting prism instead of a plane mirror as a reflector?

26. What are the differences between reflection of light from a plane mirror and total internal reflection of light from a prism?

27. What is mirage? Explain with a simple diagram.

28. Explain the following :
    (a) sparkling of diamonds
    (b) looming
    (c) silvery appearance of the surface of water held in a beaker

MULTIPLE CHOICE QUESTIONS

1. The critical angle for glass-air interface is generally taken as :
    (a) 40°   (b) 42°
    (c) 45°   (d) 48°
    Ans : (b)

2. For total internal reflection to occur :
    (a) the angle of incidence should be equal to the critical angle
    (b) the angle of incidence should be smaller than the critical angle
    (c) the angle of incidence should be greater than the critical angle
    (d) None of the above
    Ans : (c)

3. A right-angled isosceles prism used to deviate a ray of light by 180° find its application in a :
    (a) binocular   (b) periscope
    (c) microscope   (d) projector
    Ans : (a)

5

REFRACTION OF LIGHT THROUGH A LENS

LEARNING OUTCOMES

- Lens and its types
- Refraction of light through lenses
- Image formation by a lens : Types of images, ray diagram determination and characteristics of various types of images formed
- Sign convention rule for spherical lenses
- Lens formula
- Linear magnification
- Power of a lens
- Magnifying glass or a simple microscope : Its principle and working
- Differentiation between a concave and a convex lens

(A) LENS AND REFRACTION

5.1 LENS AND ITS TYPES

A *lens* is a piece of transparent optical medium bounded by two curved surfaces which are generally spherical.

A lens is generally made of *glass* or *transparent polycarbonate* or *transparent plastic material*.

A lens can have either one spherical surface and one plane surface or two spherical surfaces. If a lens has one plane surface, it can be considered as a spherical surface of infinite radius of curvature.

Lenses are divided into two broad classes : (1) Convex or converging lens and (2) Concave or diverging lens.

Convex or Converging Lens

A convex lens has one or two spherical surfaces such that it is thicker in the middle and tapering or thinner at the edges.

A beam of light *converges* on passing through a convex lens; hence, it is also called a *converging lens*.

Subtypes of Convex Lens

Depending on its shape, a convex lens can be further classified into following three types (Fig. 5.1):

(a) Biconvex or double convex lens or equi-convex lens : Both the surfaces of this type of lens are convex.

(b) Plano-convex lens : It has one surface plane and the other surface convex.

(c) Concavo-convex lens : It has one surface convex and the other surface concave such that it is thicker in the middle compared to its edges.

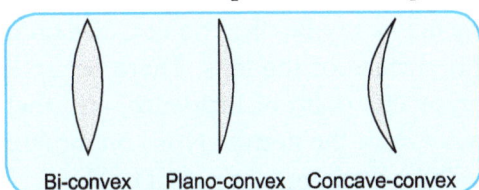

Fig. 5.1 : Types of convex lenses.

Concave or Diverging Lens

A concave lens has one or two spherical surfaces such that it is tapering or thinner in the middle and thicker at its edges.

A beam of light *diverges* on passing through a concave lens; hence, it is also called a *diverging lens*.

Subtypes of Concave Lens

A concave lens can be further classified into following three types (Fig. 5.2):

(a) Biconcave or double concave lens or equi-concave lens : Both the surfaces of this type of lens are concave.

(b) Plano-concave lens : It has one surface plane and the other surface concave.

(c) Convexo-concave lens : It has one surface concave and the other surface convex such that it is thinner in the middle compared to its edges.

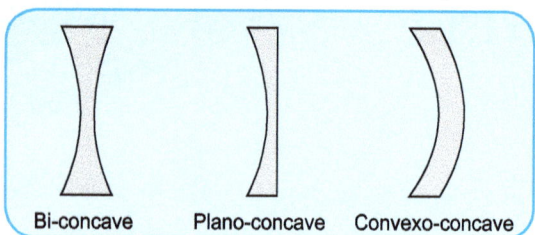

Fig. 5.2 : Types of concave lenses.

NOTE

Both concavo-convex lens and convexo-concave lens are made of one convex and one concave surface, but they differ in their shapes and actions. A concavo-convex lens is thicker in the middle, whereas a convexo-concave lens is thinner in the middle. A concavo-convex lens has a converging action on a beam of light, whereas a convexo-concave lens has a diverging action on a beam of light.

5.2 REFRACTION OF LIGHT THROUGH BICONVEX AND BICONCAVE LENS

Fig. 5.3 shows refraction of a ray of light through a biconvex and biconcave lens.

A ray of light AB is incident on the left surface of both the lenses. It enters the lens and suffers refraction on travelling from air to glass. The ray AB bends towards the normal NN′ inside the lens and gets refracted as ray BC. The point C lies on the right or second surface of the lens. There occurs another refraction at this point of incidence, and the ray BC bends away from the normal N_1N_2 on moving out of the lens. Thus, it emerges as ray CD.

From Fig. 5.3, it can be seen that a ray of light suffers two refractions on passing through either of the lenses and bends at both surfaces of a lens in the same direction. The deviation produced by both the surfaces of a lens gets added up. It can also be seen from Fig. 5.3 that the ray of light bends towards the middle of a convex lens, i.e. a convex lens converges the light, whereas the ray of light bends towards the periphery or edges of a concave lens, i.e. a concave lens diverges the light.

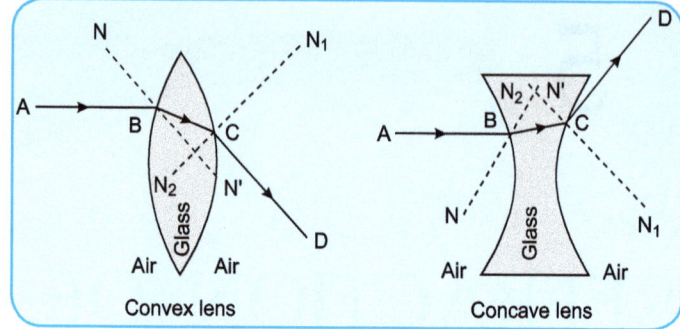

Fig. 5.3 : Refraction through a lens.

5.3 ACTION OF A LENS AS A SET OF PRISMS

A lens may be considered to be made up of a set of prisms as shown in Fig. 5.4.

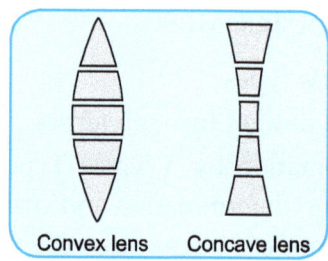

Fig. 5.4 : A lens as a set of prisms.

The prisms in the central portion of the lens can be combined and considered as one rectangular block so that a lens can be considered to be made up of a rectangular block in the centre with two prisms on either of its sides, as shown in Fig. 5.5.

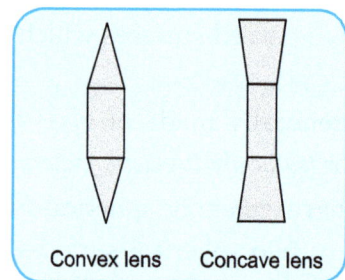

Fig. 5.5 : A lens being made of a rectangular block in the middle with prisms on either side.

In Fig. 5.5, the prism in the upper part of a convex lens has its base downwards and the prism in its lower part has its base upwards. This is opposite in the case of a concave lens. In a concave lens, the prism in the upper part has its base upwards, whereas the prism in the lower part has its base downwards.

Convergent Action of a Convex Lens

Fig. 5.6 shows three parallel rays A, B and C incident on the upper part, central part and lower part of a convex lens, respectively. We know that when a ray of light passes through a prism, after refraction, it always bends towards the base of the prism. Also, it is known that greater the refracting angle of the prism, greater is the deviation produced. The ray A is incident on the prism at upper part of the lens that has its base downwards. Hence, the ray A after refraction bends towards the downward direction. The ray B is incident in the central rectangular block in a normal direction and hence passes undeviated. The ray C is incident on the prism at lower part of the lens that has its base upwards. Hence, the ray C after refraction bends towards the upward direction. Thus, the parallel rays of light on passing through a convex lens converge at a point F.

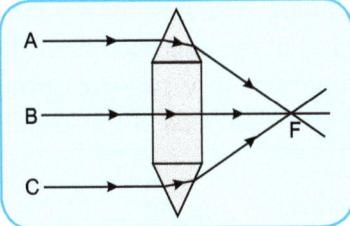

Fig. 5.6 : Convergent action of a concave lens.

Divergent Action of a Concave Lens

Fig. 5.7 shows three parallel rays A, B and C incident on the upper part, central part and lower part of a concave lens, respectively. The ray A is incident on the prism of upper part of the lens that has its base upwards. Hence, the ray A after refraction bends towards the upward direction. The ray B is incident in the central rectangular block in a normal direction and hence passes undeviated. The ray C is incident on the prism of lower part of the lens that has its base downwards. Hence, the ray C after refraction bends towards the downward direction. Thus, the parallel rays of light on passing through a concave lens diverge and appear to come from a point F lying on the side of incident rays.

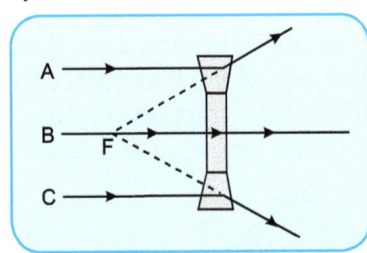

Fig. 5.7 : Divergent action of a concave lens.

5.4 IMPORTANT TERMS RELATED TO A LENS

1. Centre of curvature : The *centre of curvature* of a spherical lens is the centre of the sphere of glass of which the lens is a part. A lens has two centres of curvature.

C_1 and C_2 are the two centres of curvature for the surfaces 1 and 2 of a lens.

For a convex lens, C_1 lies to the right of surface 1 and C_1 lies to the left of surface 2 (Fig. 5.8).

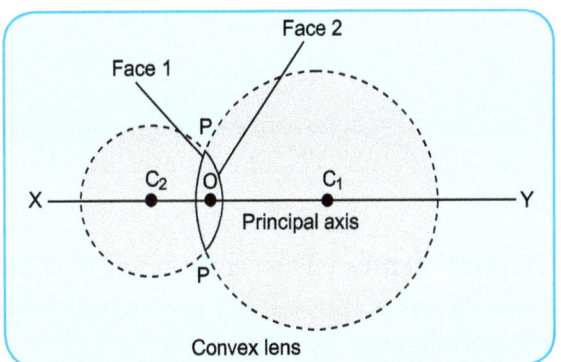

Fig. 5.8 : Centre of curvature, optical centre and principal axis of a convex lens.

For a concave lens, C_1 lies to the left of surface 1 and C_2 lies to the right of surface 2 (Fig. 5.9).

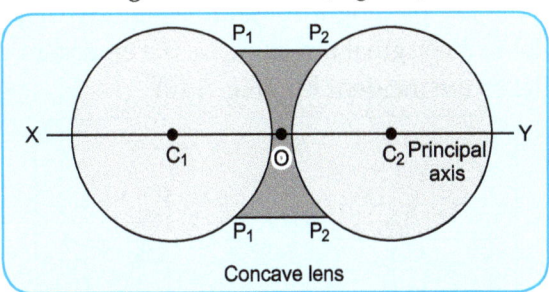

Fig. 5.9 : Centre of curvature, optical centre and principal axis of a concave lens.

2. Principal axis : An imaginary line joining the centres of curvature C_1 and C_2 of two spherical surfaces of the lens is called the *principal axis*. In Figs. 5.8 and 5.9, XY is the principal axis passing through C_1 and C_2 and extending on either side of the lens.

3. Radius of curvature : The *radius of curvature* of a surface of lens is the radius of the sphere of which the lens surface is a part.

Convex lens : If P is taken as a point where the two spheres intersect, then PC_1 is the radius of curvature of surface 1 and PC_2 is the radius of curvature of surface 2 of the convex lens, as shown in Fig. 5.8.

If a convex lens is thin, then $PC_1 = OC_1$ and $PC_2 = OC_2$, where O is the centre of the lens.

Concave lens : Let P_1 be a point on the left edge on both upper and lower part of the concave lens and P_2 a point on the right edge on both upper and lower part of the concave lens such that P_1 and P_2 lie on the circumference of the spheres of which the surfaces 1 and 2 of the lens are a part.

P_1C_1 is the radius of curvature of surface 1 and P_2C_2 is the radius of curvature of surface 2 of the concave lens, as shown in Fig. 5.9.

If a concave lens is thin, then $P_1C_1 = OC_1$ and $P_2C_2 = OC_2$, where O is the centre of the lens.

NOTE

In the case of an equi-convex or equi-concave lens, the radii of curvature of both surfaces of a lens are equal.

4. Optical centre : The centre point of a lens is known as its *optical centre*. It lies on the principal axis of a lens and denoted by 'O'.

The property of optical centre is that any ray of light passing through it emerges parallel to the direction of incidence ray. Since the central portion of a thick lens can be treated as a rectangular glass slab with parallel sides, the ray passing through it is slightly displaced parallel to its original direction, *i.e.* the emergent ray is parallel to the incident ray (Fig. 5.10).

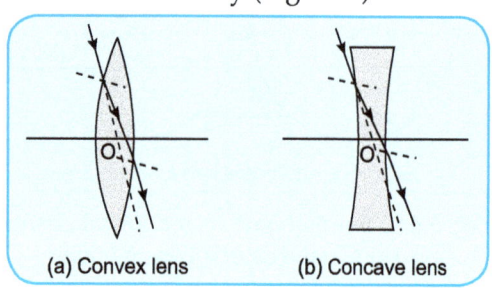

Fig. 5.10 : Optical centre of a convex and concave lens.

However, generally the lens is very thin and the lateral displacement being very small is thus ignored. The ray of light is therefore, assumed to travel straight through the optical centre and hence passes undeviated without suffering any refraction (Fig. 5.11).

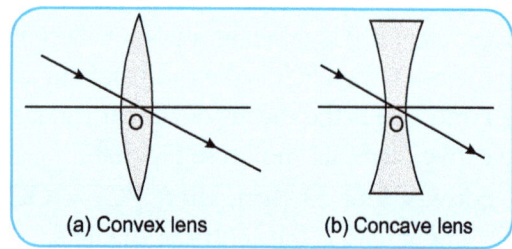

Fig. 5.11 : Optical centre of a thin lens.

The optical centre of a thin lens is a point on the principal axis of the lens through which an incident ray of light emerges undeviated.

NOTE

In ray diagrams, a lens is considered to be thin and so a ray of light passing through the optical centre is drawn as a straight line without any deviation.

5. Principal foci : Considering that the medium on both sides of a lens is same, there *are two principal foci* for a lens, as a ray of light can pass through a lens from either of the directions.

The two foci are located at equal distance from the optical centre, on either side of the lens. The two principal foci are known as *first focus* or *first focal point* (F_1) and *second focus* or *second focal point* (F_2).

Convex Lens

First focal point : The first focal point is a point on the principal axis of the lens such that, after refraction, the rays starting from it or passing through it become parallel to the principal axis of the lens (Fig. 5.12).

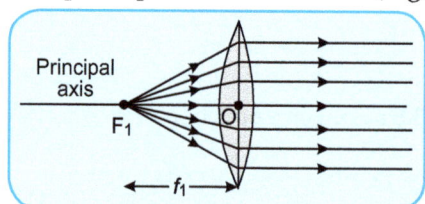

Fig. 5.12 : First focus of a convex lens.

Second focal point : The second focal point is a point on the principal axis of the lens such that the rays of light incident parallel to the principal axis, after refraction through the lens, pass through it (Fig. 5.13).

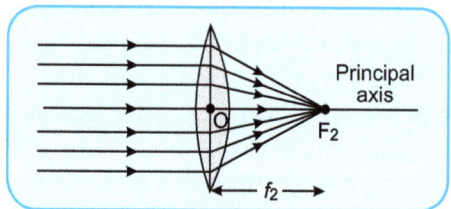

Fig. 5.13 : Second focus of a convex lens.

Concave Lens

First focal point : The first focal point is a point on the principal axis of the lens such that the incident rays of light that after refraction become parallel to the principal axis of the lens appear to meet at this point (Fig. 5.14).

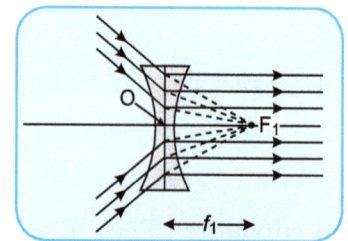

Fig. 5.14 : First focus of a concave lens.

Second focal point : The second focal point is a point on the principal axis of the lens such that the rays of light incident parallel to the principal axis, after refraction through the lens, appear to diverge from this point (Fig. 5.15).

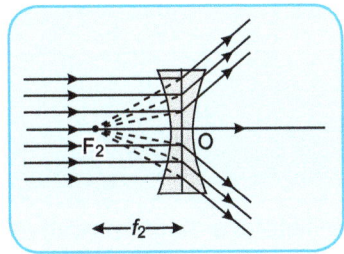

Fig. 5.15 : Second focus of a concave lens.

6. **First focal length** : It is the distance from the optical centre O to the first focal point F_1 of the lens.

In Figs. 5.12 and 5.14, f_1 is the first focal length, *i.e.* $OF_1 = f_1$.

Second focal length : It is the distance from the optical centre O to the second focal point F_2 of the lens.

In Figs. 5.13 and 5.15, f_2 is the second focal length, *i.e.* $OF_2 = f_2$.

The focal length of a lens depends on two factors :

(a) *Refractive index* of the material of the lens with respect to its surrounding medium. The focal length of a lens made of glass will be less in air but more if placed in water.

(b) The *radii of curvature* of the two surfaces of a lens. The focal length of a thick lens is less than the focal length of a thin lens made of a same material.

7. **First focal plane** : It is a plane passing through the first focal point and normal to the principal axis of the lens.

Second focal plane : It is a plane passing through the second focal point and normal to the principal axis of the lens.

Important Points to be Noted

- The magnitudes of first and second focal lengths are equal ($f_1 = f_2$) when the medium on both sides of the lens is same.
- When simply a focus of a lens is said, it implies the second focal point and so the focal length is also the second focal length of the lens.
- The focus of a convex lens is a *real focus* as the parallel rays of light incident on a convex lens actually pass through this point. However, the focus of a concave lens is a *virtual focus* as the parallel rays of light incident on a concave lens appear to diverge from this point and do not actually meet.

- If parallel rays of light are incident obliquely on a convex lens and are not parallel to the principal axis, then these rays after refraction do not converge at the focus (F_2) but at a point B that lies in the second focal plane of the lens. This point B is therefore, a point on the second focal plane where the incident ray AO passing through the optical centre of the lens meets the focal plane (Fig. 5.16).

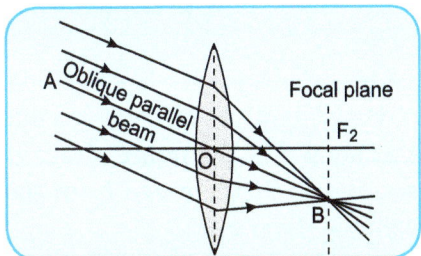

Fig. 5.16 : Refraction of an oblique parallel beam of light through a convex lens.

If parallel rays of light are incident obliquely on a concave lens and are not parallel to the principal axis, then these rays, after refraction, appear to diverge from a point B that lies in the second focal plane of the lens (Fig. 5.17).

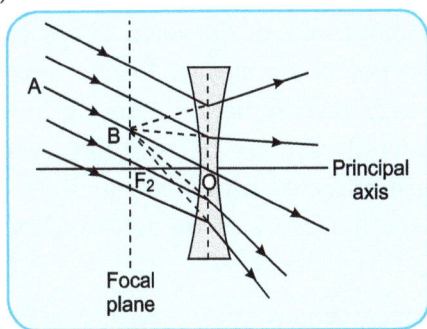

Fig. 5.17 : Refraction of an oblique parallel beam of light through a concave lens.

The focal length of a lens remains unchanged when a part of it is covered, and due to this, the position, size and nature of the image formed by it remain unchanged. As, the amount of light entering the lens will decrease and thus, the intensity of the image formed will decrease.

ILLUSTRATIVE EXAMPLES

1. Show with the help of a diagram, how an incident ray will emerge from a thick convex lens and a thin convex lens when it passes through the optical centre?

   Solution : The diagram is given below, in a thick convex lens, due to refraction inside the lens, the emergent ray will be laterally displaced and parallel to the path of incident ray.

In the case of a thin lens, the lateral displacement is almost negligible and is ignored; hence, the incident ray passes undeviated through it.

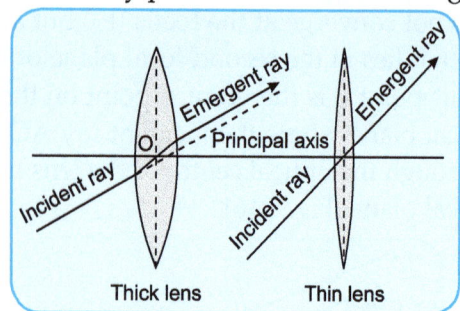

Thick lens   Thin lens

2. Two rays of light are incident on a thick concave lens as shown in the figure. Trace the path of these rays as they emerge from the lens and explain the diagram.

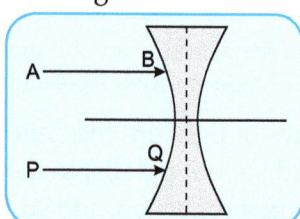

Solution : The diagram is given below. Two incident rays AB and PQ are parallel to the principal axis of the lens. These rays suffer refraction on the surface 1 of the lens and bend towards the normal on entering the lens. The refracted rays are BC and QR, respectively. These refracted rays suffer another refraction on the surface 2 of the lens and bend away from the normal on emerging from the lens. The emergent rays are CD and RS, respectively.

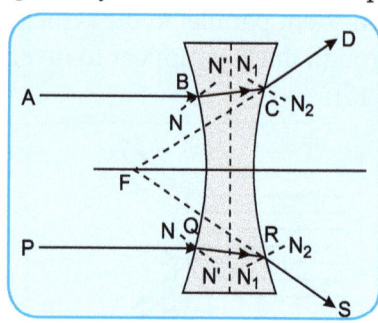

3. With the help of a diagram, show the converging action of a convex lens, considering it to be made up of a number of prisms. Which rays will deviate the most ?

Solution : The completed diagram is shown below. Since the deviation of an incident ray depends on the refracting angle of a prism, the rays of light incident on the upper and lower part of a lens will deviate the most due to greater refracting angle of the prism making the upper and lower portion of the lens.

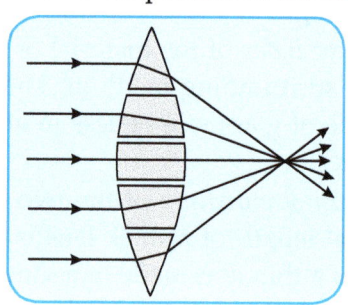

EXERCISE 5(A)

1. What is a lens?
2. What are the two basic types of lenses?
   Ans : Concave and convex.
3. Which lens is also called a diverging lens?
   Ans : Concave.
4. Out of a biconcave and a biconvex lens, which lens will have a convergent action on a beam of light?
   Ans : Biconvex
5. What are the different subtypes of concave and convex lens? Draw diagrams to illustrate them.
6. How will you represent the refraction of two light rays incident parallel to the principal axis of a convex lens if the convex lens is considered as a combination of a glass block and two triangular glass prisms?
7. How will you represent the refraction of two light rays incident parallel to the principal axis of a concave lens if the concave lens is considered as a combination of a glass block and two triangular glass prisms?
8. Show the convergent action of a convex lens if a parallel beam of light is incident on it.
9. Show the divergent action of a concave lens if a parallel beam of light is incident on it.
10. What is centre of curvature of a lens?
11. Where are the centres of curvature of a concave lens located? Show with the help of a diagram.
12. Define the term 'principal axis of a lens'.
13. What is optical centre of a lens? Illustrate with the help of diagrams.
14. When does a ray of light falling on a lens pass through it undeviated?
    Ans : When the ray of light falls on the optical centre of the lens, it passes undeviated through the lens.

15. The given figure is a thin convex lens. Trace the path of the three incident rays.

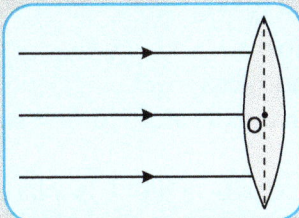

16. The given figure is a thick convex lens. Trace the path of the two incident rays.

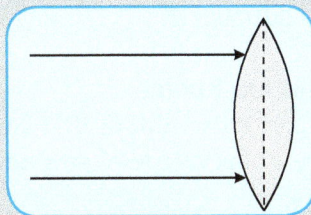

17. In which type of lens are the radii of curvature equal?
    Ans : Equi-convex and equi-concave lens.
18. State the condition under which there are two principal foci of a lens.
    Ans : When the medium on both sides of the lens is same.
19. Define the term 'first focal point of a concave and a convex lens' and illustrate with the help of proper diagrams.
20. What is meant by first focal length of a lens?
21. Draw a diagram to represent the second focus and second focal length of a convex lens.
22. Draw a diagram to represent the second focus and second focal length of a concave lens.
23. What do you understand by the term 'focal plane of a lens'?
24. A ray of light is incident on a lens as shown in the figure. (a) Which lens is shown in the diagram ? (b) Draw the principal axis of this lens. (c) Trace the path of this incident ray through the lens. (d) At which point does the emergent ray meet the principal axis?

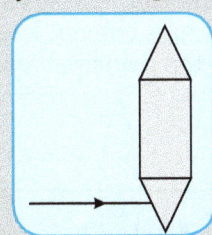

25. A ray of light is incident on a lens as shown in the figure. (a) Which lens does it represent? (b) What is the line XY called? (c) Trace the path of this incident ray through the lens. (d) Will the final emergent ray meet the line XY? (e) Mark the focus of the lens.

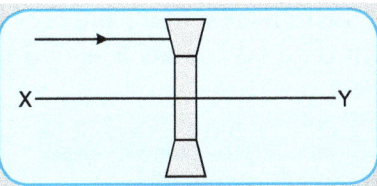

26. What are the two factors on which the focal length of a lens depends?
    Ans : Refractive index of the material of the lens and the radii of curvature of the two surfaces of lens.
27. Two rays of light, after refraction through a convex lens, emerge parallel to the principal axis. (a) Draw a ray diagram to show the incident and emergent rays. (b) Name the point from which these rays start.
28. Two rays of light, after refraction through a concave lens, emerge parallel to the principal axis. (a) Draw a ray diagram to show the incident and emergent rays. (b) Name the point where the incident rays meet the principal axis when produced.
29. A beam of light parallel to the principal axis of a convex lens is incident on it. (a) How will the rays emerge after refraction? (b) Draw a ray diagram to illustrate this. (c) Name the point where these rays will meet?
30. A beam of light parallel to the principal axis of a concave lens is incident on it. (a) How will the rays emerge after refraction? (b) Draw a ray diagram to illustrate this. (c) Name the point where these rays appear to come from.
31. In the given figure, F_1 and F_2 are the two foci of a thin concave lens. A ray of light AB is incident on the lens as shown in the two figures. Trace the path of this ray as it emerges from the lens in each case.

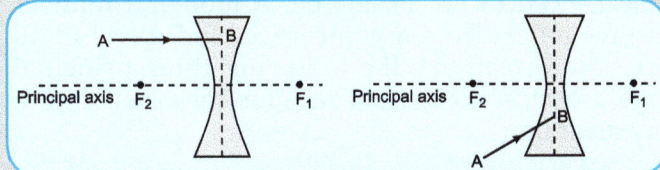

32. In the given figure, F_1 and F_2 are the two foci of a thin convex lens. A ray of light AB is incident on the lens as shown in the two figures. Trace the path of this ray as it emerges from the lens in each case.

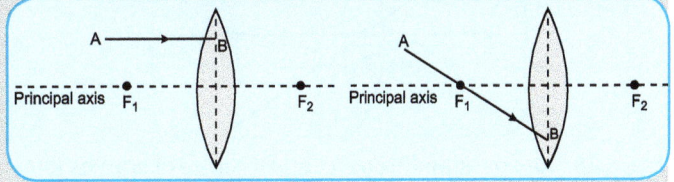

33. Show the refraction of a parallel oblique beam of light on a (a) convex lens and (b) concave lens.

MULTIPLE CHOICE QUESTIONS

1. A convexo-concave lens is :
   (a) thicker in the middle and thinner at the edges
   (b) thinner in the middle and thicker at the edges
   (c) thicker in the middle with one plane surface
   (d) thinner in the middle with one plane surface
   Ans : (b)

2. A ray of light incident obliquely on a lens does not suffer refraction. The ray is passing through the :
   (a) centre of curvature of lens
   (b) optical centre of lens
   (c) first focus of lens
   (d) second focus of lens
   Ans : (b)

3. A parallel beam of light on passing through a concave lens appears to meet at a point on the principle axis of the lens. The point is called :
   (a) optical centre
   (b) first focus
   (c) second focus
   (d) centre of curvature of first surface
   Ans : (c)

4. A point source of light is placed in front of a convex lens such that a divergent beam starting from it on passing through the lens is parallel to the principal axis. The point source of light is situated at :
   (a) first focal point
   (b) second focal point
   (c) centre of curvature of first surface
   (d) centre of curvature of second surface
   Ans : (a)

5. A small bulb is placed at the focal point of a convex lens. When the bulb is switched on, the lens produces :
   (a) a convergent beam of light
   (b) a divergent beam of light
   (c) a parallel beam of light
   (d) a patch of coloured light
   Ans : (c)

(B) IMAGE FORMATION BY A LENS : POWER AND MAGNIFICATION

5.5 PRINCIPAL RAYS FOR CONSTRUCTION OF RAY DIAGRAMS

The position, nature and size of an image formed by a mirror can be determined by construction of ray diagrams. Similarly, ray diagrams can also be used for image formation of an object by a lens. For any ray diagram, at least two rays, starting from a point object, need to be considered. Although a number of rays reflect from a point object and travel in all possible directions, the following three principal rays are most convenient rays for construction of a ray diagram.

For Convex Lens

1. A ray of light that passes through the optical centre of a convex lens does not suffer any refraction, that is, it passes through the lens without any deviation (Fig. 5.18).

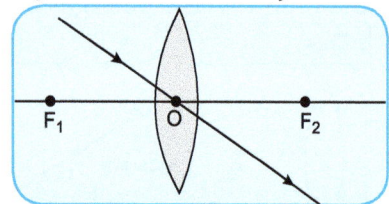

Fig. 5.18 : Ray passing through optical centre of convex lens.

2. A ray of light travelling parallel to the principal axis, after refraction through a convex lens, passes through the second focus (F_2) (Fig. 5.19).

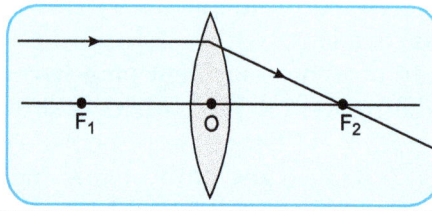

Fig. 5.19 : Ray parallel to principal axis of convex lens.

3. A ray of light that passes through the first principal focus (F_1) of a convex lens, after refraction, emerges parallel to the principal axis (Fig. 5.20).

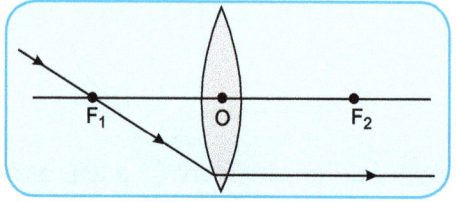

Fig. 5.20 : Ray passing through principal focus of convex lens.

For Concave Lens

1. A ray of light that passes through the optical

centre of a concave lens does not suffer any refraction, that is, it passes through the lens without any deviation (Fig. 5.21).

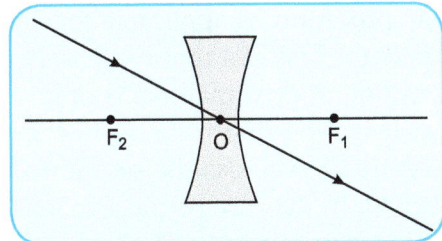

Fig. 5.21 : Ray passing through optical centre of concave lens.

2. A ray of light travelling parallel to the principal axis, after refraction through a concave lens, appears to pass through the second focus (F_2) (Fig. 5.22).

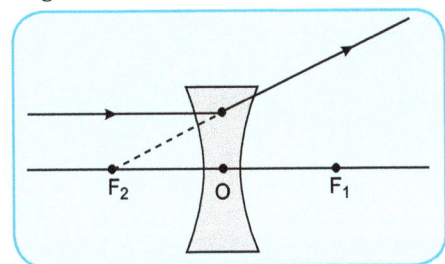

Fig. 5.22 : Ray parallel to principal axis of concave lens.

3. A ray of light travelling along the direction of first principal focus (F_1) of a concave lens, after refraction, emerges parallel to the principal axis (Fig. 5.23).

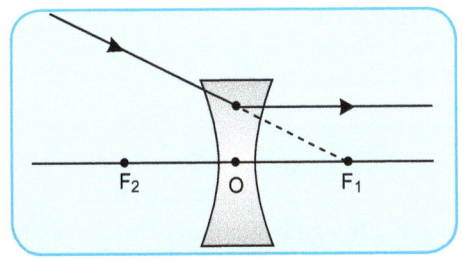

Fig. 5.23 : Ray passing through principal focus of concave lens.

An object may be considered to be made up of a number of point objects. Among the three principal rays discussed above, any two convenient rays emerging from a point on the object are chosen and the point where these rays meet or appear to meet after refraction from a convex or concave lens gives the image of that point of the object. The image obtained for each point of the object together gives the full image of the given object.

5.6 TYPES OF IMAGES

There are two types of images formed by a lens : (1) real image and (2) virtual image.

1. Real image : A real image is formed when rays emerging from the lens after refraction *actually meet* at a point. A real image can be obtained on a screen if placed in front of this point. A real image is formed by a *convex lens*.

2. Virtual image : A virtual image is formed when rays emerging from the lens after refraction do not actually meet at a point but *appear to diverge* from this point. It is formed by a *concave lens*. A virtual image cannot be obtained on a screen, but it can be seen through eyes as the lens of the eye is a convex lens that converges the divergent rays to form an image of the object on the retina of the eye.

5.7 RAY DIAGRAMS TO LOCATE THE IMAGE OF A SMALL LINEAR OBJECT FORMED BY A LENS

The step-by-step method for drawing a ray diagram to locate the position of an image formed by a thin convex lens is as follows :

1. Draw a principal axis, *i.e.,* draw a straight horizontal line on the paper and label it as XY.

2. In the middle of the line XY, mark a point O. This is the optical centre of the lens. Now, draw a thin convex lens around the point O, *i.e.* draw a dotted vertical line passing through O, and then draw the two curved surfaces around this line. In a thin lens, a ray of light will bend around this vertical line as this represents the principal section of the lens.

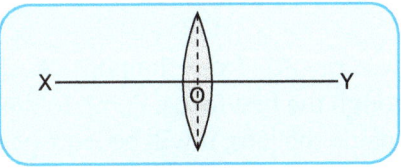

Fig. 5.24

3. Mark two points F_1 and F_2, which represent the two principal foci on the principal axis XY. Point F_1 will be on the left side of O and point F_2 will be on the right side of O. The scale chosen should be such that distance $OF_1 = OF_2$, because the medium (air) is same on both sides of the lens.

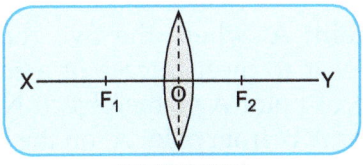

Fig. 5.25

4. Now draw the object of given height and at a given position on the principal axis by choosing a convenient scale and mark it as AB.

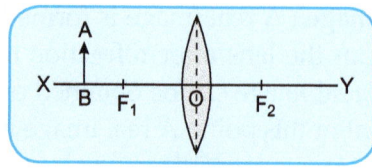

Fig. 5.26

5. From the top point A of the object, draw a ray of light passing straight through the point O (optical centre) of the lens without any refraction. Mark the emergent ray as OA'.

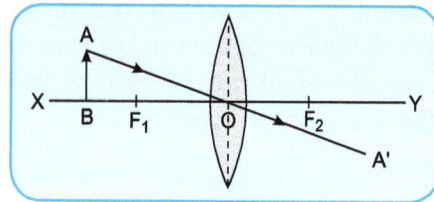

Fig. 5.27

6. Draw a second ray of light; it can be chosen from any of the other two convenient rays discussed above.

(a) Draw a ray AD from the point A of the object parallel to the principal axis XY up to the lens. Inside the lens, it will suffer refraction. The ray will bend and will pass through the second focus, F_2, of the lens as emergent ray DA'.

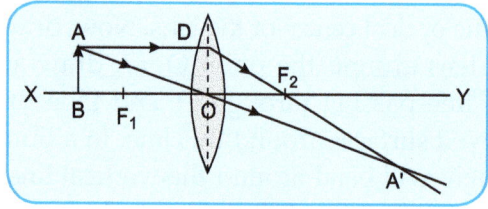

Fig. 5.28

OR

(b) Draw a ray AD from the point A of the object passing through the first focus, F_1, up to the lens. After refraction inside the lens, it will become parallel to the principal axis XY and will emerge as ray DA'.

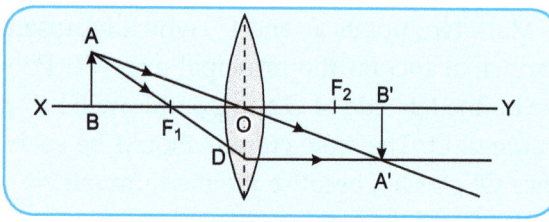

Fig. 5.29

7. The point A' where the two refracted rays meet (or appear to meet in case of a concave lens) is the image of point A of the object. Now, draw a perpendicular A'B' from point A' on the line XY. A'B' is the image of the object AB.

8. Measure the height of image A'B' and the distance OB' of the image from the lens and convert it into the actual scale to get the actual height and position of the image formed.

9. The same steps can be used to obtain the image of any point of the object lying in between the points A and B of the object.

The same procedure is applicable for drawing the ray diagram in the case of a concave lens. In a concave lens, the position of principal foci is opposite to that of a convex lens. The first focus F_1 lies on the right of optical centre O, whereas the second focus F_2 lies on the left of O. In the case of concave lens, the rays after refraction do not meet at a point but appear to meet when the rays are produced. This point where the refracted rays appear to meet say a A' then draw a perpendicular on principal axis as A'B' which gives the image A'B' of the object AB (Fig. 5.30).

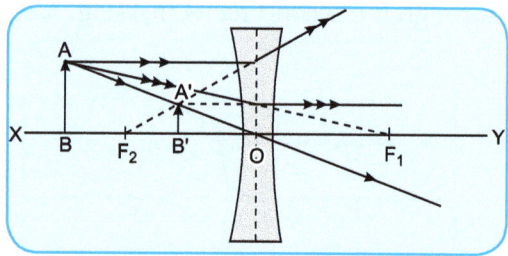

Fig. 5.30 : Three principal rays in a concave lens.

5.8 CHARACTERISTICS OF IMAGES FORMED BY A CONVEX LENS FOR DIFFERENT POSITIONS OF THE OBJECT

Case 1 : When the object is at infinity.

(a) The rays emerging from the object are parallel to the principal axis.

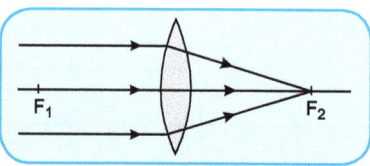

Fig. 5.31 : Image formation by a convex lens when the object is at infinity

When an object is at infinity, due to finite size of the object and infinite distance, the rays emerging from it are parallel to the principal axis. These rays on refraction through the convex lens pass through the second focus F_2 of the lens. Thus, a point image is formed at the second focus (Fig. 5.31).

Characteristics of the image formed :

(a) Image is real.
(b) Image is inverted.
(c) Image is diminished to a point.
(d) Image is formed at the second focus F_2 on the principal axis.

Use : Due to the above property, a convex lens can be used as a *burning glass*. The rays emerging from the

Sun (being at an infinite distance) are parallel rays that on passing through a convex lens get concentrated at the second focus of the lens. If a piece of paper is kept at this point, due to the concentrated heat radiations, the temperature of paper rises to ignition point and catches fire.

(b) The rays emerging from the object are not parallel to the principal axis.

If an object AB is at a far distance and the parallel rays of light emerging from a point of the object are not parallel to the principal axis but incident obliquely on the convex lens, then the image of the object is formed in the focal plane of the lens.

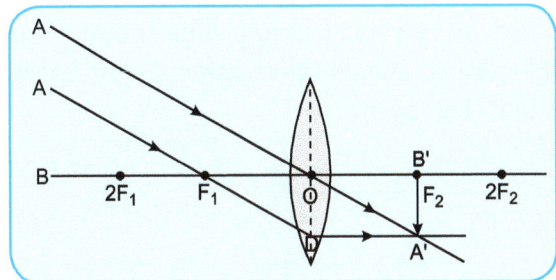

Fig. 5.32 : Image formation for an object at infinity when rays of light are not parallel to the principal axis.

In Fig. 5.32, two parallel oblique rays are shown. A ray emerging from top point A of the object and incident on the optical centre O of the lens passes undeviated through it as ray OA'. Another ray appearing from the same point of the object is incident on the lens after passing through the first focus F_1. It suffers refraction and emerges as ray DA', parallel to the principal axis. The two refracted rays OA' and DA' meet at point A', which is the real image of point A of the object. The image B' of bottom point B of the object will be formed at F_2. Thus, B'A' is the highly diminished image of the object AB formed on the focal plane of the lens.

Characteristics of the image formed :
(a) Image is real.
(b) Image is inverted.
(c) Image is highly diminished.
(d) Image is formed in the focal plane on the side of second focal point of the lens.

Use : A convex lens can be used as an *objective lens* of a telescope. In this case, the object lies very far from the lens and a small, inverted image of the far-off object is formed in the focal plane of telescope.

Case 2 : When the object is beyond $2F_1$ but not at infinity.

Consider an object AB situated on the principal axis of a convex lens at a distance beyond $2F_1$. A ray of light emerging from top point A of the object and incident on the optical centre O of the lens passes undeviated through it as ray OA'. Another ray AD, starting from the same point of the object and moving parallel to the principal axis, after refraction from the lens passes

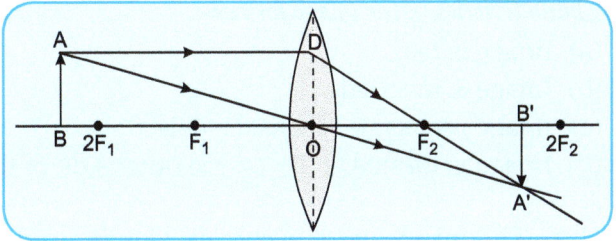

Fig. 5.33 : Image formation by a convex lens when the object is beyond $2F_1$.

through the second focus F_2 as ray DA'. The two refracted rays OA' and DA' meet at point A', which is the real image of point A of the object. By drawing a perpendicular A'B' from the point A' on the principal axis, the image A'B' of the object AB is obtained, which is real, inverted and diminished (Fig. 5.33).

Characteristics of the image formed :
(a) Image is real.
(b) Image is inverted.
(c) Image is diminished.
(d) Image is formed between the F_2 and $2F_2$ on the other side of the lens.

Use : A convex lens can be used as a *photographic camera lens*. When the object to be photographed lies at a distance that is not very far, a small inverted image of the object is formed on the camera film placed between F_1 and $2F_1$ of the lens.

Case 3 : When the object is at $2F_1$.

Consider an object AB situated on the principal axis of a convex lens at a distance twice the focal length of

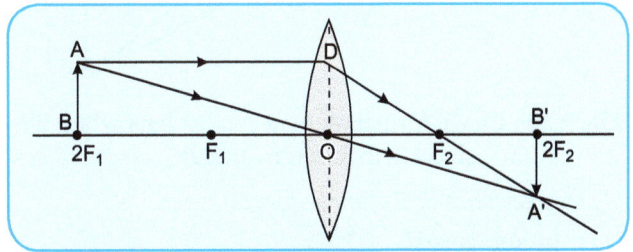

Fig. 5.34 : Image formation by a convex lens when the object is at $2F_1$.

the lens, *i.e.* at $2F_1$. A ray of light emerging from top point A of the object and incident on the optical centre O of the lens passes undeviated through it as ray OA'. Another ray AD, starting from the same point of the object and moving parallel to the principal axis, after refraction from the lens passes through the second focus F_2 as ray DA'. The two refracted rays OA' and

DA' meet at point A', which is the real image of point A of the object. By drawing a perpendicular A'B' from the point A' on the principal axis, the image A'B' of the object AB is obtained, which is real, inverted and same size as the object (Fig. 5.34).

Characteristics of the image formed :
(a) Image is real.
(b) Image is inverted.
(c) Image is of same size as the object.
(d) Image is formed at $2F_2$ on the other side of the lens.

Use : This property of a convex lens is used in a *terrestrial telescope* for erecting an inverted image formed by the objective lens of a telescope. It is also used in a photocopy machine.

Case 4 : When the object is between F_1 and $2F_1$.

Consider an object AB situated on the principal axis of a convex lens at a distance between F_1 and $2F_1$. A ray of light coming from top point A of the object and incident on the optical centre O of the lens passes undeviated through it as ray OA'. Another ray AD, starting from the same point of the object and moving parallel to the principal axis, after refraction from the lens passes through the second focus F_2 as ray DA'. The two refracted rays OA' and DA' meet at point A', which is the real image of point A of the object. By drawing a perpendicular A'B' from the point A' on the principal axis, the image A'B' of the object AB is obtained, which is real, inverted and magnified (Fig. 5.35).

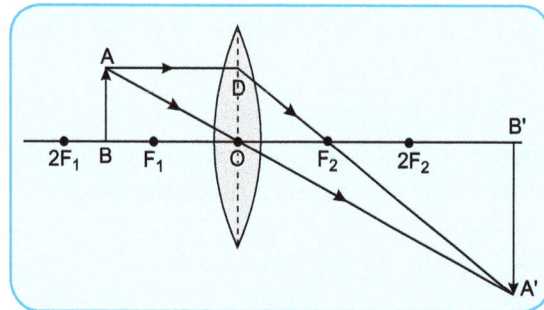

Fig. 5.35 : Image formation by a convex lens when the object is between F_1 and $2F_1$.

Characteristics of the image formed :
(a) Image is real.
(b) Image is inverted.
(c) Image is enlarged or magnified.
(d) Image is formed beyond $2F_2$ on the other side of the lens.

Use : This property of a convex lens is used in an *optical projector* or a *slide projector* when a magnified image is formed on the screen placed on the other side of the lens.

To obtain an erect image on the screen, the slide or film is placed in front of the lens just beyond the focus in an inverted position.

Case 5 : When the object is at F_1.

Consider an object AB situated on the principal axis of a convex lens at the first focus F_1. A ray of light emerging from top point A of the object and incident on the optical centre O of the lens passes undeviated through it as ray OA'. Another ray AD, starting from the same point of the object and moving parallel to the principal axis, after refraction from the lens passes through the second focus F_2 as ray DF_2. The two refracted rays OA' and DF_2 are parallel to each other and do not meet at any finite point. Thus, an image is formed at an infinite distance, which is highly magnified (Fig. 5.36).

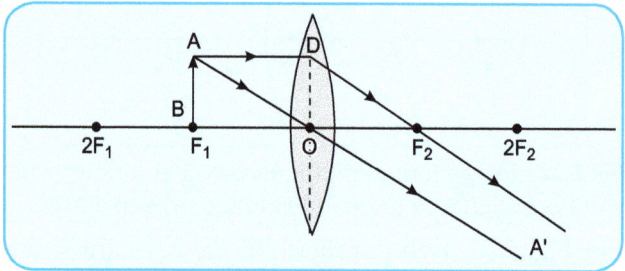

Fig. 5.36 : Image formation by a convex lens when the object is at F_1.

Characteristics of the image formed :
(a) Image is real.
(b) Image is inverted.
(c) Image is highly magnified or highly enlarged.
(d) Image is formed at infinity, at a very large distance on the other side of the lens.

Use : This property of a convex lens is used in *searchlights* and in a *spectrometer*. A powerful source of light is placed at the focus of a convex lens so as to obtain a powerful parallel beam of light.

Case 6 : When the object is located between the optical centre (O) and the first focus (F_1).

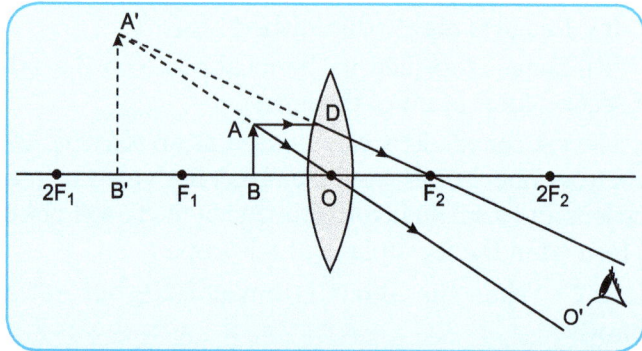

Fig. 5.37 : Image formation by a convex lens when the object is between the optical centre and the focus

Consider an object AB situated on the principal axis of a convex lens between the optical centre O and the first focus F_1. A ray of light emerging from the top point A of the object and incident on the optical centre O of the lens passes undeviated through it as ray OO'. Another ray AD, starting from the same point of the object and moving parallel to the principal axis, after refraction from the lens passes through the second focus F_2 as ray DF_2. The two refracted rays OO' and DF_2 do not meet each other, but appear to diverge from a point A' when the rays are produced backwards. The point A' is the *virtual image* of the point A of the object. Similarly, B' is the virtual image for point B of the object. For the object AB, a magnified virtual image A'B' is formed behind the object on the same side of the lens. The lens of the eyes converges the divergent rays when placed between them and a real image is formed by the lens on the retina of the eye (Fig. 5.37).

Characteristics of the image formed :

(a) Image is virtual.

(b) Image is erect.

(c) Image is magnified or enlarged.

(d) Image is formed behind the object on the same side of the lens.

Use : In this case, the convex lens acts as a *magnifying glass* or a *simple microscope* and can be used for the following applications :

1. Reading tiny prints or small letters of a book.

2. Studying biological specimens such as parts of a flower.

3. Viewing clearly the fine lines of a hand.

Table 5.1 : Summary of Formation of Different Types of Images by a Convex Lens

Position of the object	Position of the image	Size of the image	Nature of the image	Use of the lens
At infinity	At F_2	Highly diminished to a point	Real and inverted	Burning glass
Beyond $2F_1$	Between F_2 and $2F_2$	Diminished	Real and inverted	Camera lens
At $2F_1$	At $2F_2$	Same size	Real and inverted	Telescope, photocopy machine
Between F_1 and $2F_1$	Beyond $2F_2$	Magnified	Real and inverted	Slide projector
At F_1	At infinity	Highly magnified	Real and inverted	Searchlight, spectrometer
Between O and F_1	Behind the object	Magnified	Virtual and erect	Magnifying glass or simple microscope

5.9 CHARACTERISTICS OF IMAGES FORMED BY A CONCAVE LENS FOR DIFFERENT POSITIONS OF THE OBJECT

Case 1 : When the object is at infinity.

(a) **The rays coming from the object are parallel to the principal axis.**

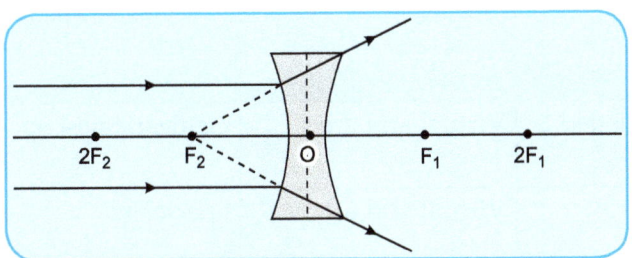

Fig. 5.38 : Image formation by a concave lens when the object is at infinity.

When an object is at infinity, the rays of light emerging from it are parallel to the principal axis of the concave lens. These rays on refraction through the concave lens appear to diverge through the second focus F_2 of the lens. Thus, a virtual, erect and point image is formed at the second focus on the same side of the object (Fig. 5.38).

Characteristics of the image formed :

(a) Image is virtual.

(b) Image is erect.

(c) Image is diminished to a point.

(d) Image is formed at the second focus F_2 on the principal axis.

(b) The rays emerging from the object are not parallel to the principal axis.

If an object AB is at a far distance and the parallel rays of light coming from a point of the object are not parallel to the principal axis but incident obliquely on the concave lens, then the image of the object is formed on the second focus of the lens.

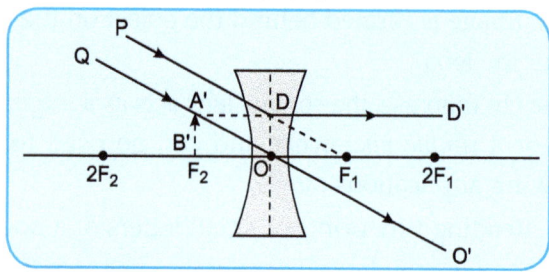

Fig. 5.39 : Image formation by a concave lens when the object is at infinity but the rays emerging from the object are not parallel to the principal axis.

In Fig. 5.39, two parallel oblique rays are shown. A ray QO emerging from top point A of the object and incident on the optical centre O of the lens passes undeviated through it as ray OO′. Another ray PD, appearing from the same point of the object and incident towards the first focus F_1 of the lens, after refraction from the lens emerges as ray DD′, parallel to the principal axis. The refracted ray DD′ when produced backwards appears to meet the ray QO′ at A′ which lies on the second focal plane of the lens, which is the virtual image of point A of the object. Similarly, a virtual image B′ of the point B of the object is formed at point F_2. Thus, a virtual, erect and highly diminished image A′B′ of the object AB is formed on the second focus F_2.

Characteristics of the image formed :
(a) Image is virtual.
(b) Image is erect.
(c) Image is highly diminished.
(d) Image is formed at the second focal point of the lens on the side of the object.

Use : It is used in a *Galilean telescope* where the concave lens acts as an eye lens.

Case 2 : When the object is anywhere between optical centre of the lens and infinity.

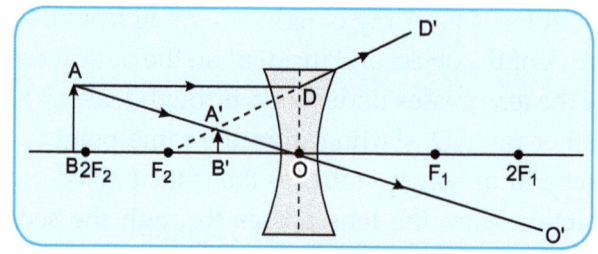

Fig. 5.40 : Image formation by a concave lens when the object is between optical centre and infinity.

Consider an object AB situated on the principal axis of a concave lens at a point between optical centre O and infinity, *i.e.* at a finite distance. A ray of light emerging from top point A of the object and incident on the optical centre O of the lens passes undeviated through it as ray OO′. Another ray AD, starting from the same point of the object and moving parallel to the principal axis, after refraction from the lens emerges as ray DD′. It appears to be emerging from the second focus F_2 of the concave lens. The refracted ray DD′ when produced backwards and the ray AO′ do not meet each other actually, but appear to meet at a point A′ when produced backwards. The point A′ is the *virtual image* of the point A of the object. Similarly, B′ is the virtual image for point B of the object. For the object AB, a diminished, erect and virtual image A′B′ is formed between the optical centre and second focus F_2 of the lens on the side of the object (Fig. 5.40).

Characteristics of the image formed :
(a) Image is virtual.
(b) Image is erect.
(c) Image is diminished.
(d) Image is formed between the lens and second focus on the side of the object.

Use : This property of concave lens is used in making *spectacles* for short-sighted persons.

Table 5.2 : Summary of Formation of Different types of Images by a Concave Lens

Position of the object	Position of the image	Size of the image	Nature of the image	Use of the lens
At infinity	At F_2, on the same side of lens as the object	Highly diminished to a point	Virtual and erect	Galilean telescope
Between infinity and optical centre	Between focus F_2 and optical centre, on the same side of the lens as the object	Diminished	Virtual and erect	Spectacles

5.10 SIGN CONVENTION FOR SPHERICAL LENSES

These days New Cartesian sign convention is used for measuring the various distances like image distance, object distance in the ray diagrams of spherical lenses (concave lenses and convex lenses). According to New Cartesian sign convention :

1. All the distances are measured from the *optical centre* of the lens.
2. The distances measured in the same direction as that of incident ray are taken as positive while the distances measured in the opposite direction of incident ray are taken as negative.
3. The distances measured upward and perpendicular to the principal axis are taken as positive on the other hand the distances measured downward and perpendicular to the principal axis are taken as negative.
4. The object is placed on the left side of the lens.

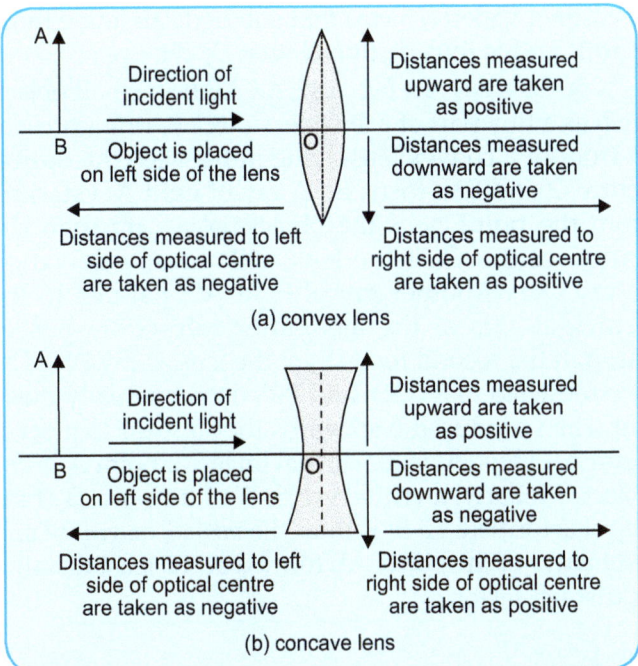

Fig. 5.41 : Sign convention for spherical lenses.

Fig. 5.41 shows New Cartesian sign convention for spherical lenses. In this, object is always taken on the left side of the lens. Hence, direction of incident ray is from left side to right side. Thus, all the distances measured from the optical centre to left side of the lens are taken as negative whereas all the distances measured from the optical centre to right side of the lens are taken as negative.

The distance of the object from the lens is always negative as object is placed on the left side of the lens.

By sign convention the focal length of the convex lens is positive and focal length of the concave lens is negative.

5.11 LENS FORMULA

A formula which gives the relationship between object distance (u), image distance (v) and focal length (f) of a lens is called *lens formula* which can be written as

$$\frac{1}{v} - \frac{1}{u} = \frac{1}{f}$$

The lens formula is applicable for both convex and concave lenses.

5.12 LINEAR MAGNIFICATION

The size of the image formed by a lens depends on the position of the object from the lens. When the position of the object changes, the position as well as the size of the image change. The size of the image relative to the size of the object is given by the linear magnification. *The ratio of the height of the image to the height of the object is called linear magnification,* i.e.,

$$\text{Magnification} = \frac{\text{Height of image}}{\text{Height of object}}$$

or

$$m = \frac{h_2}{h_1}$$

Linear magnification can also be given in terms of the image distance and object distance.

The linear magnification produced by a lens is equal to the ratio of image distance to the object distance, i.e.,

$$\text{Magnification} = \frac{\text{Image distance}}{\text{Object distance}}$$

or

$$m = \frac{v}{u}$$

If the magnification m has a negative value then the image formed will be real and inverted. On the other hand if magnification m has a positive value the image is virtual and erect. We know that a concave lens forms only virtual images so the magnification produced by a concave lens is always positive. Also, a concave lens always forms images which are smaller than the object so the magnification produced by a concave lens is always less than 1. On the other hand a convex lens can form virtual as well as real images therefore, the magnification produced by a convex lens can be either positive or negative. Also image formed by convex lens can be smaller than the object, equal to the object or bigger than the object so magnification produced by convex lens can be less than 1, equal to 1 or greater than 1.

5.13 POWER OF A LENS

The power of a lens is a measure of deviation of a beam of light produced by it. Due to refraction of light through a lens, the rays deviate. A lens that produces more deviation is considered to have more power.

A lens that has a short focal length (or more curvature) will deviate the rays of light more than a lens that has a large focal length (or less curvature).

The reciprocal of focal length of a lens (in metres) is called the power of a lens.

The unit of power of a lens is *dioptre* (D).

A lens is said to have a power of 1 dioptre if its focal length is 1 m.

$$\text{Power of a lens (in dioptre)} = \frac{1}{\text{Focal length of the lens (in metres)}}$$

$$P \text{ (in D)} = \frac{1}{f \text{ (in m)}} \quad ...(5.1)$$

If the focal length is given in centimetres, then the above formula is modified as :

$$P = \frac{1}{\frac{f \text{ (in cm)}}{100}}$$

i.e.
$$P = \frac{100}{f \text{ (in cm)}} \quad ...(5.2)$$

The power of a lens can be positive or negative. It depends on the direction in which a ray of light is deviated. A *convex lens* deviates a ray towards its centre and its power is considered *positive* (+D), while a *concave lens* deviates a ray away from its centre and its power is considered *negative* (–D).

Thus, the power of a convex lens of focal length 10 cm is +10.0 D, while the power of a concave lens of same focal length is –10.0 D.

In optical instruments, a number of lenses are combined so as to increase the magnification or sharpness of the image. The net power of these lenses placed in contact with one another is the algebraic sum of the individual powers of the lenses.

If a convex lens and a concave lens of same focal length are placed in contact with each other, then power of the their combination is zero (as it is positive for convex lens and negative for concave lens). This combination will behave like a glass plate.

5.14 MAGNIFYING GLASS (OR A SIMPLE MICROSCOPE)

A magnifying glass is a simple device made up of a biconvex lens of very short focal length mounted on a frame with a holder.

Principle and working : To view any object, with naked eye even though it is tiny, it should be placed at a minimum distance of 25 cm (or 0.25 m) from the eye. This distance is known as the *least distance of distinct vision (D)* for a normal eye and is a standard value for a normal adult. This distance enables an eye to see an object distinctly and in maximum size. It varies with age and increases for an older person.

The size of the image seen through a magnifying glass depends on the angle subtended by the object at the eye. If the angle subtended by the object at the eye is small, the size of the image formed on the retina of the eye will also be small. If the angle subtended by an object is less than 1'(1/60°) on the eye, then the eye will not be able to see the object distinctly. To observe such a small object that subtends an angle less than 1' when placed at the least distance of distinct vision, a magnifying glass is used. The convex lens of the magnifying glass is held near to the object to be magnified, such that the object lies between the optical centre and principal focus, or closer to the principal focus of the lens. The eye is kept close to the lens on the other side of the object. A virtual, erect and magnified image of the object is then formed at the least distance of distinct vision (25 cm) that subtends an angle more than 1' and is thus distinctly seen by the eye.

Ray diagram : In Fig. 5.42, let AB be a small object, such as a tiny part of a jewellery piece (a ring), present in front of a convex lens, lying in between the optical centre O and first focus F_1. A ray of light AO starting from the point A of the object passes through the optical centre O of the lens without any deviation as ray OO'. Another ray of light AP, parallel to the principal axis of the lens, after refraction, passes through the second focus F_2 of the lens as ray PP'. The two refracted rays, OO' and PP', do not actually meet, but when produced backwards they appear to meet at point A'. Thus, A' is the virtual image of point A of the object. Similarly, a virtual image B' of the point B of the object is formed. A' B' is thus, the *virtual, magnified and erect image* of the object AB formed at the least distance of distinct vision.

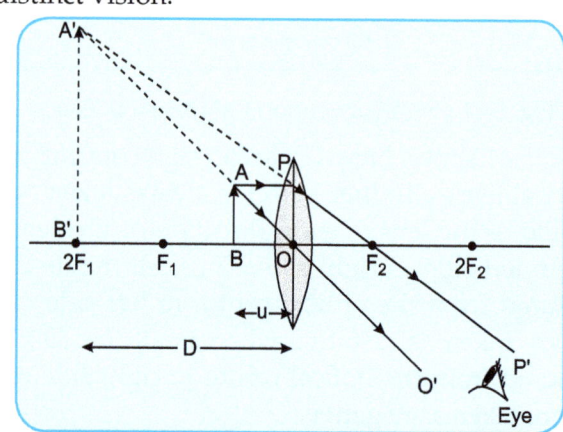

Fig. 5.42 : Ray diagram for location of image by a magnifying glass.

To observe the image, the eye is kept very close to the lens on the other side of the object, as shown in Fig. 5.42.

Magnifying power : The magnifying power of a microscope is $m = 1 + (D/f)$, where D is 25 cm or 0.25 m (least distance of distinct vision) and f is the focal length of the lens.

Thus, for a simple microscope, magnifying power is given as

$$m = 1 + \frac{0.25}{f} \qquad ...(5.3)$$

The shorter the focal length of a magnifying glass, the larger is the magnifying power.

Example : If the focal length of a magnifying glass is 1 m (or 100 cm), its magnifying power is 1.25, whereas if the focal length is 0.1 m (or 10 cm), its magnifying power is 3.5.

Thus, the magnifying power of a simple microscope can be increased by using the lens of a short focal length.

Uses : The highest magnification that can be obtained from a simple microscope is about 10 and is commonly used by watchmakers and jewellers to see small parts of a watch or jewel stones. A simple microscope is also used for reading fine prints or small letters, for viewing fine texture of threads and fibres, size of soil particles and so on.

It is used in optical instruments such as a compound microscope, telescope and spectrometer in combination with other image-forming lens system. In some cases, a magnifying glass is provided above the vernier scale to read the readings accurately and is called a *reading lens*.

5.15 APPLICATION OF LENSES

Some of the common applications of lenses are as follows :

1. A convex lens is used in a photographic camera, slide projector and so on to obtain a real and inverted image of the given object.

2. A magnifying glass is also a convex lens of short focal length to observe a magnified image of small objects.

3. A combination of convex lenses is used in a compound microscope and astronomical telescope.

4. Convex lenses are used to obtain a pure spectrum in a spectroscope.

5. A concave lens is used as an eye lens in a Galilean telescope to obtain an erect image of the object.

6. Human eye lens is also a convex lens. With age, the eyesight becomes poor. In such cases, spectacles having concave and convex lenses are used to see the objects clearly.

5.16 TO DIFFERENTIATE BETWEEN A CONCAVE LENS AND A CONVEX LENS

One can differentiate between a concave lens and a convex lens by the following two methods :

1. By touching : A lens can be recognised by its shape. If on touching, a lens is thick in the middle and thin at the periphery, then it is a convex lens, but if a lens is thin in the middle and thick at the periphery, then it is a concave lens.

2. By observing the image :

(a) Look for an image of a distant object through a given lens. If the image appears inverted, then the lens is convex, but if the image appears erect or upright, then the lens is concave.

(b) Keep a given lens near a printed paper. If the letters appear magnified, then it is a convex lens, but if the letters appear diminished, then it is a concave lens.

Difference between a Convex Lens and a Concave Lens

Convex Lens	Concave Lens
It is thick in the middle and thin at the edges.	It is thin in the middle and thick at the edges.
It is also known as a converging lens as it converges the parallel rays of light incident on it towards the principal axis.	It is also known as a diverging lens as it diverges the parallel rays of light incident on it away from the principal axis.
It has a real focus.	It has a virtual focus.
The image formed can be real or virtual, magnified or diminished, inverted or erect, depending on the position of the object.	The image formed is always virtual, diminished and erect.
It has a positive focal length.	It has a negative focal length.

ILLUSTRATIVE EXAMPLES

1. The figure given below shows a refracted ray PQ from a convex lens. Draw the corresponding incident ray and complete the diagram.

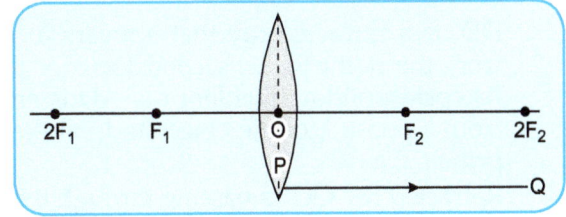

Solution : Since the refracted ray is parallel to the principal axis of the lens, the incident ray will pass through the first focus F_1 of the lens. It is shown as ray AP in the completed diagram.

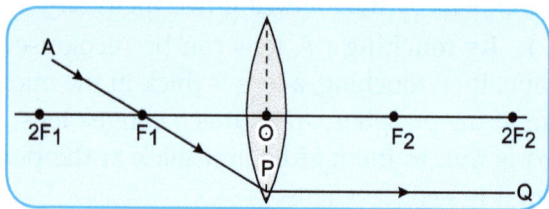

2. The figure given below shows a refracted ray DD' from a concave lens. Draw the corresponding incident ray and complete the diagram.

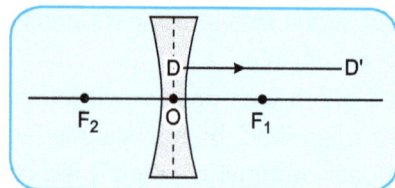

Solution : Since the refracted ray DD' is parallel to the principal axis, the incident ray shown as AD in the diagram is incident on the lens in such a way that it appears to pass through the first focus when produced backwards. The complete diagram is given below.

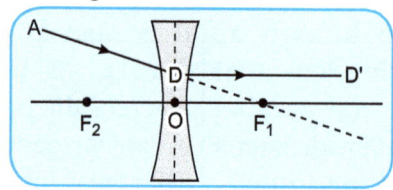

3. The figure given below shows two refracted rays DD' and OO' through a concave lens. Complete the diagram showing the corresponding incident rays emerging from a point of an object placed on the principal axis. Where will the image of the object form?

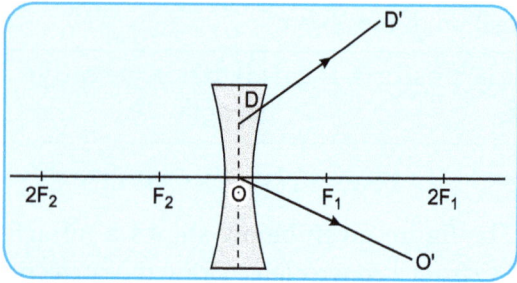

Solution : The completed diagram is shown below.

DD' is a refracted ray that appears to diverge from the point F_2, i.e. second focus of the lens. Its corresponding incident ray AD is emerging from a point A of the object and parallel to the principal axis.

Refracted ray OO' is passing through the optical centre of the lens; hence, its corresponding incident ray is AO coming from point A of the object.

The image of the object AB will form between the focus and the optical centre of the lens on the same side of the object where the two refracted rays appear to meet when produced backwards.

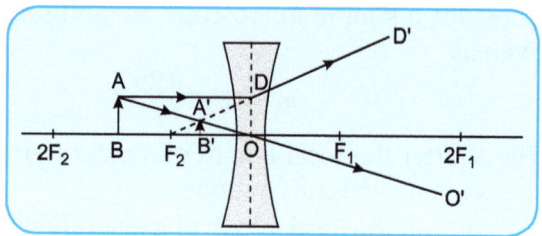

4. The figure given below shows an object BA placed in front of a convex lens on the principal axis. (a) Draw the three principal rays to show the formation of image of the object. (b) What are the characteristics of the image formed? (c) If the object is moved a little distance away from its original position such that it lies at $2F_1$, then where will the image be formed and what will be the size of this image?

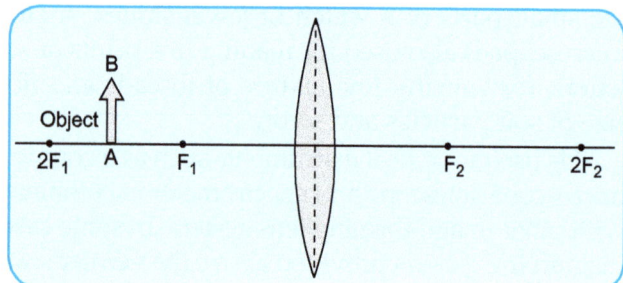

Solution :
(a) The three principal rays are shown as BX, BO and BY incident on the convex lens, emerging from the point B of the object. These rays after refraction meet at a point B', which is the image of point B of the object. A'B' is the image of the object AB.

(b) The image formed is real, inverted and magnified.

(c) If the object is moved to position $2F_1$, the image will be formed at position $2F_2$. The size of the image will be same as the size of the object.

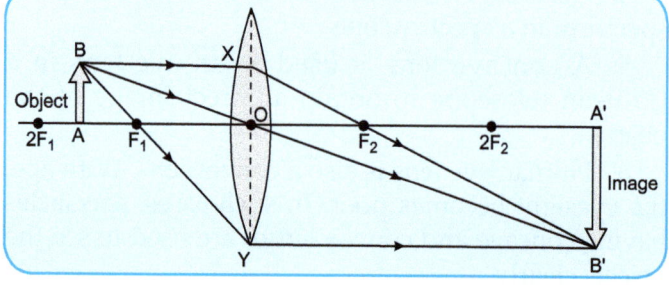

5. The figure given below shows an object AB and its image A'B' formed by a lens. (a) State the type of lens that will form this image. (b) Complete the ray diagram to show the formation of the image. (c) State the characteristics of the image.

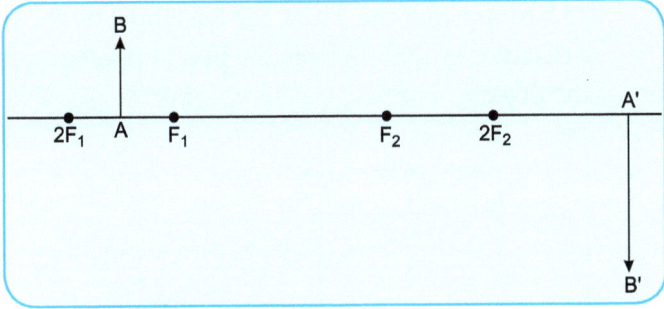

Solution:
(a) Since the image is inverted, the lens forming it is a convex lens.
(b) The completed ray diagram is shown below.

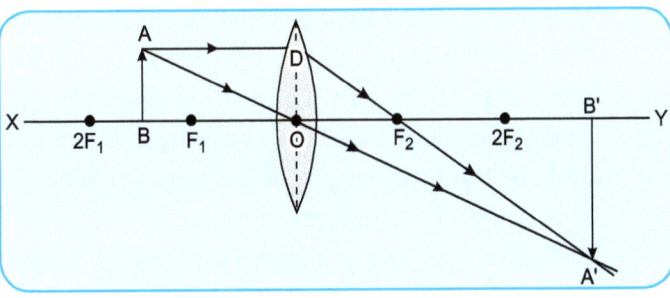

(c) Characteristics of the image : real, inverted and magnified.

6. The given figure shows an object AB and an image A'B' formed by a lens. (a) Locate the lens and mark the focus of the lens. What type of lens will produce this type of image ? (b) Complete the ray diagram.

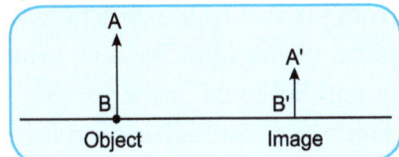

Solution:
(a) Since the image is virtual and erect, the type of lens forming it should be a concave lens. The lens is drawn with its optical centre O and the focus is marked as F_2.

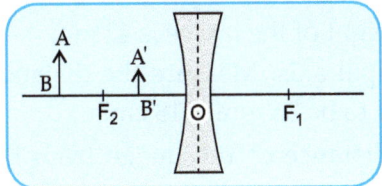

(b) To complete the diagram, two principal rays are used. A ray of light emerging from top point A of the object and incident on the optical centre O of the lens passes undeviated through it as ray OO'. Another ray AD, starting from the same point of the object and moving parallel to the principal axis, after refraction from the lens emerges as ray DD'. It appears to be emerging from the second focus F_2 of the concave lens. The two refracted rays OO' and DD' do not meet each other actually, but appear to meet at a point A' when produced backwards. The point A' is the *virtual image* of the point A of the object. Similarly, B' is the virtual image for point B of the object. For the object AB, a diminished, erect and virtual image A'B' is formed between the optical centre and second focus F_2 of the lens on the side of the object.

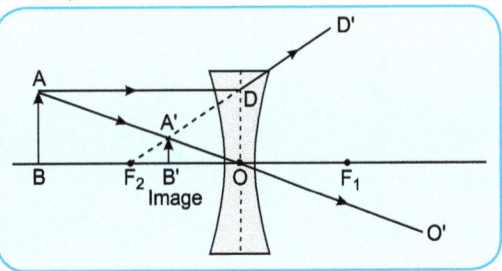

7. A convex lens can act as a burning glass. Draw a ray diagram showing how it can be achieved.

Solution:
When parallel rays of light emerging from the Sun are incident on a convex lens, these rays, after refraction, meet at the focus of the lens. When a piece of paper is placed on the focal plane of the lens, the concentrated rays of the Sun ignite the paper, which in turn burns the paper.

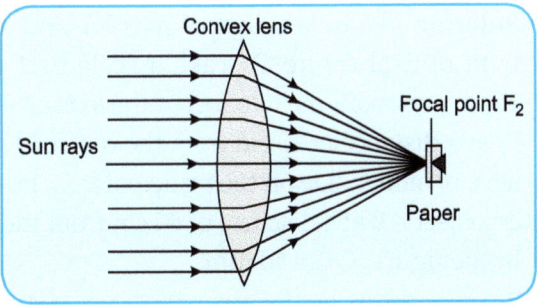

8. An object of length 13 cm stands vertically on the principal axis of a convex lens of focal length 20 cm, at a distance of 30 cm from the lens.

Complete the ray diagram to find the position, size and nature of the image.

Solution : Draw a principal axis XY and a lens with optical centre O. Take a scale of 1 cm = 1 mm and mark the two foci of the lens as F_1 and F_2 at a distance of 20 cm from the centre O of the lens, on either side on the principal axis. Position of an object AB of size 13 cm (in the figure = 13 mm) at a distance of 30 cm from the lens. In the figure, OB = 30 mm.

For completing the ray diagram, take two incident rays AD and AO from the point A of the object. The ray AO incident on the optical centre of the lens passes undeviated as ray OA'. The ray AD parallel to the principal axis, after refraction from the lens, passes through the second focus F_2 of the lens. The two refracted rays meet at point A' where an inverted image B'A' of the object is formed.

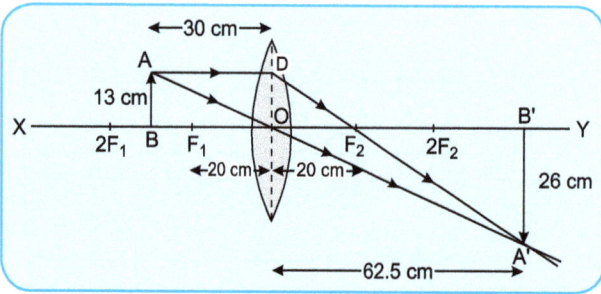

Measure the distance OA'. It is found to be 62.5 mm = 62.5 cm. Measure the length B'A'. It is found to be 26 mm = 26 cm. The image formed is a magnified image.

9. A camera lens has a focal length of 10 cm. An object is located at a distance of 40 cm from the lens. Draw a ray diagram and find out how far the lens must be set away from the film to photograph the given object.

Solution : Draw a principal axis XY and a lens with optical centre O. Take a scale of 1 cm = 1 mm and mark the two foci of the lens as F_1 and F_2 at a distance of 10 cm from the centre O of the lens, on either side on the principal axis. Position an object AB at a distance of 40 cm from the lens. In the figure, OB = 40 mm.

For completing the ray diagram, take two incident rays AD and AO from the point A of the object. The ray AO incident on the optical centre of the lens passes undeviated as ray OA'. The ray AD parallel to the principal axis, after refraction from the lens, passes through the second focus F_2 of the lens. The two refracted rays meet at point A' where an inverted image B'A' of the object is formed.

Measure the distance OA'. It is found to be 13.5 mm = 13.5 cm. Thus, the lens must be set at a distance of 13.5 cm from the film to photograph the object.

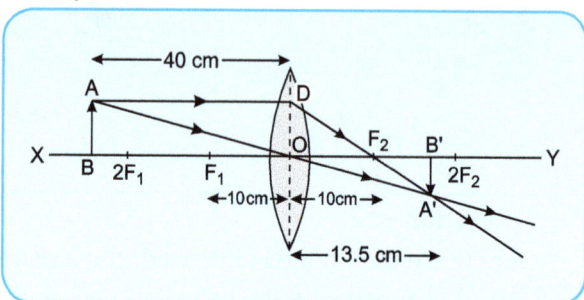

10. A convex lens forms an image 42 cm long of an object 11 cm long kept at a distance of 5 cm from the lens. The object and image are located on the same side of the lens. Draw a ray diagram and find (a) the distance of the image from the object and (b) the focal length of the lens. (c) What is the nature of the image?

Solution : (a) Draw a principal axis XY and a lens with optical centre O. For the distance of the object and image from the lens, take scale of 1 cm = 2 mm, and for length of the object and image, take scale of 1 cm = 1 mm.

Mark the object AB in front of the lens at a distance of 10 mm (5 cm). Let the height of the object AB be 11 mm (11 cm). Draw a ray of light from point A of the object passing through the optical centre O of the lens draw other ray from A parallel to the principal axis which after refraction passes through second focus of convex lens. These two rays do not meet but when we produce backwards these two rays meets at A'. Hence A' is the virtual image of A. Now draw perpendicular A'B' on principal axis from A. Thus A'B' is the virtual image of AB. Mark the image A'B' from a point of this ray such that the height of the image is 42 mm = 42 cm on the principal axis. Measure the distance OB'. It is found to be 36 mm = 18 cm.

The distance of the image from the object is 18 cm.

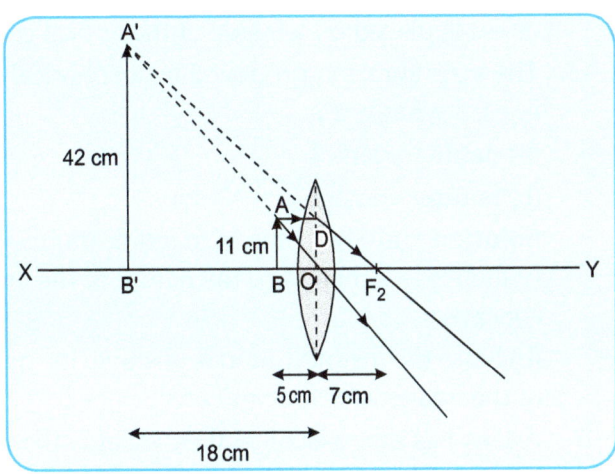

(b) Measure the distance OF_2. It is found to be 14 mm = 7 cm.
Thus, focal length of the lens is 7 cm.
(c) The image formed is virtual, upright and magnified.

11. A convex lens of focal length 5 cm is placed at a distance of 6 cm from a wall. How far from the lens should an object be placed so as to form its real image on the wall?

Solution: Since the image formed is real on the wall at a distance of 6 cm from the convex lens. Hence distance of the image from the wall is 6 cm i.e., image distance $v = 6$ cm.
Now, image formed is real and on the right side of the lens, so the image distance will be positive, since the lens is convex so focal length will be positive.
Here, image distance, $v = +6$ cm
Focal length, $f = +5$ cm
Object distance, $u = ?$
Now, by lens formula :

$$\frac{1}{v} - \frac{1}{u} = \frac{1}{f}$$

$$\frac{1}{6} - \frac{1}{u} = \frac{1}{5}$$

$$\frac{1}{u} = \frac{1}{6} - \frac{1}{5}$$

$$\frac{1}{u} = \frac{5-6}{30}$$

$$\frac{1}{u} = -\frac{1}{30}$$

$$u = -30 \text{ cm}$$

Thus, the object should be placed at a distance of 30 cm in front of the convex lens. The minus sign shows that object is placed on the left side of the lens.

12. An object is placed perpendicular to the principal axis of a convex lens of focal length 6 cm. The distance of the object from the lens is 8 cm. Find the distance of image from the lens.

Solution: Here the lens is convex so focal length will be positive.
Now, object distance, $u = -8$ cm
Focal length, $f = 6$ cm
Image distance, $v = ?$
By lens formula

$$\frac{1}{v} - \frac{1}{u} = \frac{1}{f}$$

$$\frac{1}{v} - \frac{1}{-8} = \frac{1}{6}$$

$$\frac{1}{v} + \frac{1}{8} = \frac{1}{6}$$

$$\frac{1}{v} = \frac{1}{6} - \frac{1}{8}$$

$$\frac{1}{v} = \frac{4-3}{24}$$

$$\frac{1}{v} = \frac{1}{24}$$

$$v = +24 \text{ cm}$$

The positive sign of v shows that the image is formed at a distance of 24 cm on the right side of the optical centre.

13. A concave lens forms the image of an object kept at a distance of 20 cm in front of it, at a distance of 10 cm on the side of the object. Find the nature of the image and focal length of the lens.

Solution: Since the image is formed on the same side of the object so both object distance and image distance will be taken as negative.
Here, image distance, $v = -10$ cm.
Object distance, $u = -20$ cm
Focal length, $f = ?$
From lens formula

$$\frac{1}{v} - \frac{1}{u} = \frac{1}{f}$$

$$\frac{1}{-10} - \frac{1}{-20} = \frac{1}{f}$$

$$-\frac{1}{10} + \frac{1}{20} = \frac{1}{f}$$

$$\frac{-2+1}{20} = \frac{1}{f}$$

$$-\frac{1}{20} = \frac{1}{f}$$

$$f = -20 \text{ cm}$$

The nature of the image is virtual and erect. Since the image is formed by concave lens.

14. A concave lens has focal length 18 cm. At what distance should the object from the lens be placed so that it forms an image at 12 cm from the lens.

Solution : We know that a concave lens always forms a virtual and erect image on the same side of the object so image distance is negative. Also the lens is concave so the focal length is also negative.

Here, image distance, $v = -12$ cm

Focal length, $f = -18$ cm

Object distance, $u = ?$

By lens formula

$$\frac{1}{v} - \frac{1}{u} = \frac{1}{f}$$

$$\frac{1}{-12} - \frac{1}{u} = \frac{-1}{18}$$

$$-\frac{1}{u} = -\frac{1}{18} + \frac{1}{12}$$

$$-\frac{1}{u} = \frac{-2+3}{36}$$

$$-\frac{1}{u} = \frac{1}{36}$$

$$u = -36 \text{ cm}$$

Hence, the object is placed at a distance of 36 cm from the lens and negative sign shows that the object is placed on left side of the optical centre.

15. The magnification produced by a spherical lens is + 0.5 what is the
    (a) nature of lens ?
    (b) nature of image ?

Solution : (a) The value of magnification is +0.5 (which is less than 1) so the nature of the lens is concave.

(b) Since the magnification is positive, the nature of the image is virtual and erect.

16. A lens has a power of +2.0 D. What is the focal length and nature of the lens ?

Solution : The power of given lens has a positive sign so it is a convex lens.

Also Power $= \dfrac{1}{f \text{ (in metre)}}$

$$2 = \frac{1}{f}$$

$$f = \frac{1}{2}$$

$$f = 0.5 \text{ m}$$

EXERCISE 5(B)

1. State the three principal rays that are drawn to construct a ray diagram for an image formed by a lens. Explain with diagrams.

2. The two figures below show two incident rays with their corresponding refracted rays. In both the figures, (a) mark the incident and refracted rays. (b) What is the point in these figures called where the two refracted rays meet or appear to meet? Mark this point in the figures.

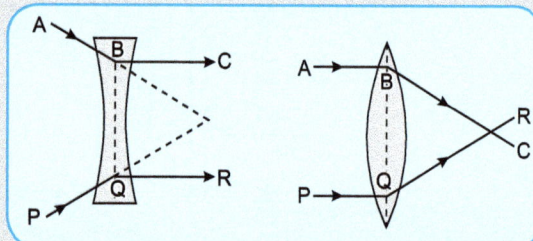

3. In the figures given below, a refracted ray is shown emerging from a convex lens and a concave lens. F_1 and F_2 are the two principal foci of each lens. Complete the diagram by showing their corresponding incident rays.

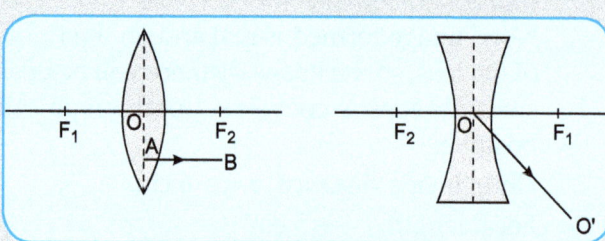

4. In the diagrams given below, two rays incident on a convex and a concave lens are shown. Complete the path of both the rays in each diagram as they emerge from the lens after refraction.

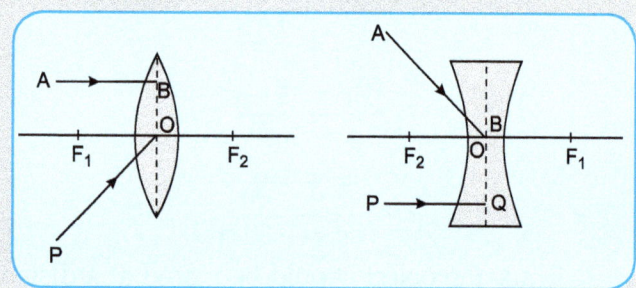

5. What are the differences between a real image and a virtual image ?

6. From the diagram given below, (a) name the lens L_1L_2. (b) What are the points X and

X' called? (c) Complete the ray diagram to show the formation of image of the object AB. (d) State the characteristics of the image. (e) In which device is this type of action of lens is used?

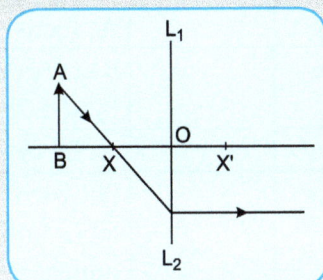

7. From the diagram given below, (a) name the lens L_1L_2. (b) What are the points X and X' called? (c) Complete the ray diagram to show the formation of image of the object AB. (d) State the characteristics of the image.

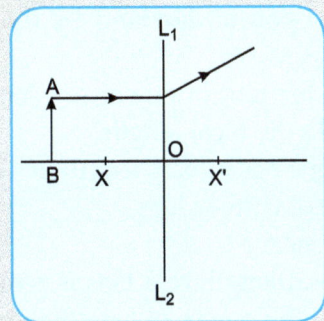

8. An object AB is placed between $2F_1$ and F_1 on the principal axis of a convex lens as shown in the diagram below :

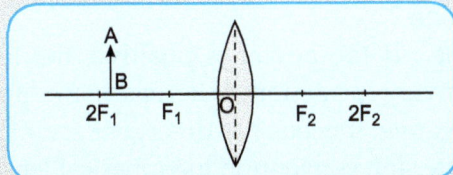

Copy the diagram, and using three rays starting from point A, obtain the image of the object formed by the lens.

9. (a) Where should an object be placed so that a real and inverted image of the same size as the object is obtained using a convex lens ?
   (b) Draw a ray diagram to show the formation of the image as specified in the part (a).

10. An object AB is placed on the focus of a convex lens as shown. (a) Complete the ray diagram to show the formation of the image. (b) Where is the image formed? (c) What are the characteristics of the image formed? (d) Name a device where this action of the lens is used.

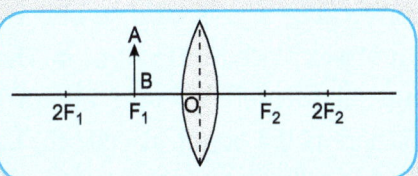

11. An object AB is placed between the optical centre and focus of a convex lens as shown. (a) Complete the ray diagram to show the formation of the image. (b) Where is the image formed ? (c) What are the characteristics of the image formed ? (d) Name a device where this action of the lens is used.

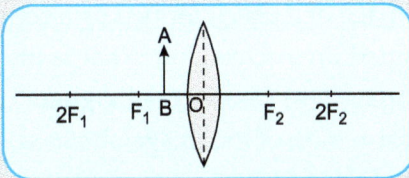

12. An object AB is placed between F_2 and $2F_2$ of a concave lens as shown. (a) Complete the ray diagram to show the formation of the image. (b) Where is the image formed ? (c) What are the characteristics of the image formed ? (d) Name a device where this action of the lens is used.

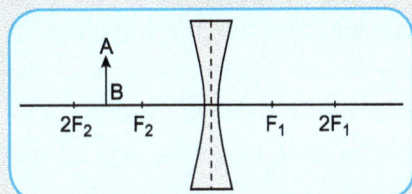

13. A converging lens is used to obtain an image of an object placed in front of it. The inverted image is formed between F_2 and $2F_1$ of the lens. (a) Where is the object placed? (b) Draw a ray diagram to illustrate the formation of the image obtained.

14. An object is placed in front of a lens between its optical centre and the focus and forms a virtual, erect and diminished image. (a) Name the lens which formed this image. (b) Draw a ray diagram to show the formation of the image with the above-stated characteristics.

15. Which lens can produce a real and inverted image of an object?
    Ans : Convex lens

16. A lens produces a virtual image between the object and the lens.
    (a) Name the lens.
    (b) Draw a ray diagram to show the formation of this image.

17. A converging lens is used to obtain an image of an object placed in front of it. The inverted image is formed beyond $2F_2$ of the lens. (a) Where is the object placed? (b) Draw a ray diagram to illustrate the formation of the image obtained. (c) State the other two characteristics of the image. (d) Name a device where this application of a lens is used.
18. Draw a ray diagram to show how a converging lens can form a real, inverted and diminished image of an object.
19. An image of a pencil formed by a convex lens is obtained on a screen. (a) What is the nature of the image? (b) Draw a ray diagram to illustrate the formation of the image obtained.
20. An object is placed on the focus of a concave lens. (a) Where will the image be formed? (b) Draw a ray diagram to illustrate the formation of the image obtained. (c) State the characteristics of the image.
21. Draw a ray diagram to show the action of a convex lens as a magnifying glass.
22. Which lens always forms a virtual image? What is the size of the image formed?
    Ans : Concave lens. The size of the image is diminished.
23. A lens forms a virtual and magnified image of an object. (a) Name the lens. (b) What is the nature of the image?
    Ans : (a) Convex, (b) Erect.
24. State two characteristics of an image formed by a convex lens.
25. State two characteristics of an image formed by a concave lens.
26. In the following cases, where will the image of an object be formed if the object is (a) at infinity, (b) same size as that of the image, (c) at F and (d) beyond 2F in case of a convex lens?
    Ans : (a) at F, (b) at 2F, (c) at infinity, (d) between F and 2F
27. If an object is brought from $2F_2$ to F_2 in front of a convex lens, state the changes in position, size and nature of the image. Illustrate with the help of ray diagrams.
28. Complete the following table :

Types of lens	Position of the object	Position of the image	Nature and size of the image
Convex		At focus	
Convex		Between F_2 and $2F_2$	
Concave		At focus	
Concave		Between focus and optical centre	

29. If an object is brought from infinity to focus in front of a concave lens, state the changes in position, size and nature of the image. Illustrate with the help of ray diagrams.
30. What do you understand by the power of a lens?
31. What is the unit of power of a lens? How is it related to the focal length?
32. A thin lens has a focal length of –10 cm. Is it a concave or convex lens ?
    Ans : Concave
33. If the focal length of a lens is reduced to half, how will the power of lens change ?
    Ans : The power will get doubled.
34. How is the positive or negative sign of power of a lens related to its convergent or divergent action ?
    Ans : If the power is positive, the lens has convergent action, whereas if the power is negative, the lens has divergent action.
35. State sign convention for spherical lenses.
36. What is lens formula ?
37. What is a magnifying glass? What are its uses?
38. What is meant by least distance of distinct vision?
39. What is the magnitude of smallest angle subtended by an object on the eye to see it distinctly?
    Ans : 1' (1/60°)
40. In the case of a magnifying glass, where is the object placed in reference to its principal focus? Where is the image formed ?
    Ans : The object is placed between the optical centre and principal focus. The image is formed behind the object, on the same side.

41. Draw a ray diagram to show the formation of image by a magnifying glass. State the characteristics of the image formed.
42. Define magnifying power of a simple microscope. Give an expression to determine it in terms of the focal length.
43. How can the magnifying power of a simple microscope be increased?
    Ans : By using the lens of a short focal length.
44. State a few applications of concave and convex lenses.
45. How will you differentiate between a concave and a convex lens by simply touching it ?
46. An image of a distant object when viewed through a lens appears erect. Is it a concave or a convex lens ?
    Ans : Concave
47. You are provided with a printed piece of paper. Using this paper, how will you differentiate between a convex lens and a concave lens ?
    Ans : The lens is held close to the printed piece of paper. If the image of the letters appears enlarged and erect, then it is a convex lens, whereas if the image of the letters appears diminished and erect, then it is a concave lens.
48. State few differences between a concave and a convex lens.

MULTIPLE CHOICE QUESTION

1. A ray of light travelling parallel to the principal axis of a convex lens, after refraction :
   (a) passes through F_1
   (b) passes through F_2
   (c) appears to pass through F_1
   (d) appears to pass through F_2
   Ans : (b)

2. When an image is formed at $2F_2$ of a convex lens, the object is at :
   (a) F_2 (b) between F_2 and $2F_2$
   (c) $2F_1$ (d) between F_1 and $2F_1$
   Ans : (c)

3. When an object is placed at a distance of 10 cm in front of a convex lens, its image is formed at a distance of 10 cm behind the lens. The focal length of the lens is :
   (a) 5 cm   (b) 10 cm
   (c) 15 cm   (d) 20 cm
   Ans : (a)

4. The characteristics of an image formed by a concave lens are :
   (a) real, inverted and magnified
   (b) real, erect and diminished
   (c) virtual, erect and diminished
   (d) virtual, erect and magnified
   Ans : (c)

5. On increasing the focal length of a lens, its power :
   (a) increases
   (b) decreases
   (c) remains unchanged
   (d) first decreases and then increases
   Ans : (b)

6. When a convex lens is used as a magnifying glass, the position of the object is :
   (a) between optical centre and F_1
   (b) F_1
   (c) between F_1 and $2F_1$
   (d) at infinity
   Ans : (a)

7. The least distance for distinct vision of a human eye is :
   (a) 2.5 mm   (b) 25 mm
   (c) 2.5 cm   (d) 25 cm
   Ans : (d)

NUMERICAL PROBLEMS

1. The focal length of a concave lens is 50 cm. Find the power of the lens.
   Ans : –2.0 D.

2. The power of a lens is +4.0 D. Find its focal length and state the kind of the lens.
   Ans : 25 cm, convex lens.

3. The focal length of a magnifying glass is 25 cm. What is its magnifying power ?
   Ans : 4.

4. The magnifying power of a simple microscope is 6. What is the focal length of its lens ?
   Ans : 16.67 cm.

5. Calculate the focal length of a convex lens which produces a virtual image at a distance of 50 cm of an object placed 20 cm in front of it.
   Ans : 33.3 cm.

6. An object 5 cm in length is held 25 cm away from a converging lens of focal length 10 cm.

Draw the ray diagram and find the position, size and nature of the image formed.

Ans : + 16.67 cm, 3.3 cm.

7. An object of height 4.0 cm is placed at a distance 24 cm in front of a convex lens of focal length 8 cm. Find the position, size and nature of the image.

   Ans : 12 cm, 2 cm, real, inverted and diminished.

8. An object is placed at a distance of 10 cm from a convex lens of focal length 15 cm. Find the position and nature of the image.

   Ans : – 30 cm, virtual and erect.

9. The magnification produced by spherical lens is + 0.25, what is the nature of image and nature of lens ?

   Ans : Virtual and erect, concave lens.

10. An object placed 50 cm from a lens produces a virtual image at a distance of 10 cm in front of the lens. Draw a diagram to show the formation of image. Calculate the focal length of the lens and magnification produced.

    Ans : – 12.5 cm, + 0.2.

11. Find the position of the virtual image formed when an object 2 cm tall is placed 20 cm from :
    (a) a converging lens of focal length 40 cm.
    (b) a diverging lens of focal length 40 cm.

    Ans : (a) – 40 cm, (b) – 13.3 cm.

6

THE ELECTROMAGNETIC SPECTRUM

LEARNING OUTCOMES

- Electromagnetic spectrum : Classification, properties and characteristics of different radiations
- Deviation of light by a prism
- Dispersion and spectrum
- Scattering of light and its simple effects

(A) ELECTROMAGNETIC SPECTRUM AND ITS CLASSIFICATION

6.1 ELECTROMAGNETIC SPECTRUM

In 1864, James Clerk Maxwell predicted that light, radiant heat and other radiations if any, propagate in the free space at a speed of 3×10^8 m s^{-1} in the form of electromagnetic waves. This theory was formally accepted in 1865. Therefore, an *electromagnetic wave* is a wave that is capable of transmitting its energy through vacuum (empty space). For instance, the electromagnetic waves that are produced on the Sun subsequently travel to Earth through the vacuum of outer space. These waves are produced by the vibration of charged particles. They consist of both electric and magnetic components.

Electromagnetic waves exist in an enormous range of frequencies. This continuous range of frequencies is known as the *electromagnetic spectrum*.

The relationship between speed (*c*), frequency (ν) and wavelength (λ) of the electromagnetic waves is given by the equation,

$$c = \nu \lambda \qquad \ldots(6.1)$$

Based on the increasing order of their wavelengths or decreasing order of their frequencies, the electromagnetic spectrum is divided as follows :

(1) Gamma rays, (2) X-rays, (3) Ultraviolet (UV) rays, (4) Visible light, (5) Infrared radiations, (6) Microwaves and (7) Radio waves.

Fig. 6.1 shows the order of electromagnetic waves of the spectrum in increasing order of their wavelengths. However, it is to be noted that the above-stated regions do not have sharp boundaries of frequency or wavelength, but they overlap.

The approximate range of wavelengths of different electromagnetic waves is given as follows :

1. **Gamma rays :** Wavelength less than 1 pm (10^{-12} m).
2. **X-rays :** Wavelengths ranging from 1 pm to 100 Å (10^{-11} m or 0.01 nm to 10^{-8} m or 10 nm).
3. **Ultraviolet rays :** Wavelengths ranging from 100 Å to 4,000 Å (10^{-8} m or 10 nm to 4×10^{-7} m or 400 nm).
4. **Visible light :** Wavelengths ranging from 4,000 Å to 8,000 Å (4×10^{-7} m or 400 nm to 8×10^{-7} m or 800 nm).
5. **Infrared radiations :** Wavelengths ranging from 8,000 Å to 10^7 Å (8×10^{-7} m or 800 nm to 10^{-3} m or 1 mm).
6. **Microwaves :** Wavelengths ranging from 10^7 Å to 3×10^{10} Å (10^{-3} m or 1 mm to 3 m).
7. **Radio waves :** Wavelengths ranging from 3×10^{10} Å to 10^{15} Å (3 m to 10^5 m or 100 km) or more.

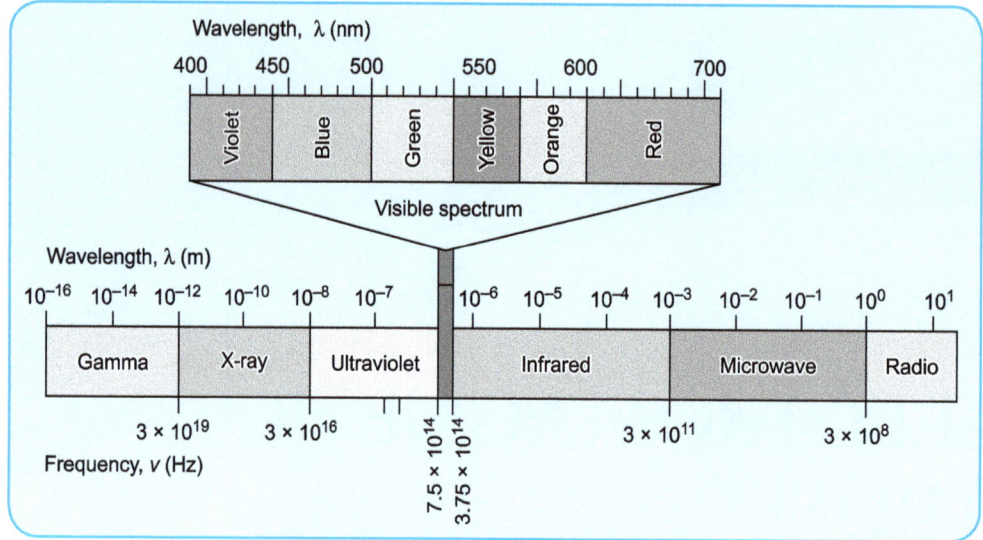

Fig. 6.1 : Electromagnetic spectrum.

6.2 COMMON PROPERTIES OF ELECTROMAGNETIC WAVES

1. Electromagnetic waves are transverse waves or non-mechanical waves.
2. These waves can propagate through vacuum and thus do not require any material medium for propagation.
3. All the waves of the electromagnetic spectrum travel at a speed that is same as the speed of light, i.e. 3×10^8 ms^{-1}, in vacuum.
4. Electromagnetic waves carry energy that can be transferred to objects placed in their paths. The energy carried by these waves is distributed equally between the electric and magnetic fields.
5. Electromagnetic waves are not affected by external electric or magnetic fields.
6. These waves exhibit the phenomenon of reflection and refraction. The frequency of these waves remains unchanged while travelling from one medium to another the speed and wavelength of these waves change during refraction.

6.3 CHARACTERISTICS OF DIFFERENT ELECTROMAGNETIC RADIATIONS

1. Gamma rays : These waves were discovered by Henri Becquerel. These are electromagnetic radiation with high energy, high frequency and short wavelength. These rays have a frequency higher than 10 EHz (> 10^{19} Hz), wavelength less than 1 pm and energy greater than 100 keV.

Sources : The natural sources of gamma rays are decay of radioactive elements such as uranium, radium and caesium, as they undergo a transition from a high energy state to a low energy state or from fusion and fission reactions of these elements along with the release of energy. Gamma rays are also present in cosmic radiations and lightning strikes.

Properties : Gamma rays have a high penetration power. They can penetrate through several centimetres in thick metals such as iron and steel, human tissues and several metres in air. These rays are biologically hazardous and cause damage to tissues. These rays have no mass and no charge. These rays produce fluorescence upon striking materials such as zinc sulphide.

Uses :

- Gamma radiations are used in industries such as refining, mining, chemical, soaps and detergents for measurement of density and thickness.
- These are used for sterilization of medical equipments, for killing cancerous cells and for diagnostic purposes.
- Gamma rays are also used for destructive purposes, such as their important role in development of the atomic bomb.

2. X-rays : X-rays were discovered by Wilhelm Rontgen. The wavelengths of X-rays are shorter than UV rays and longer than gamma rays. X-rays have a wavelength in the range of 0.01–10 nm, corresponding to frequencies in the range of 30 PHz to 30 EHz (3×10^{16} – 3×10^{19} Hz) and energies in the range of 100 eV to 100 keV.

Sources : X-rays are emitted by electrons. They can be generated by a vacuum tube that uses a high voltage to accelerate the electrons released by a hot cathode to a high velocity. The high velocity electrons collide with a metal target called the *anode* (e.g. tungsten, cobalt) and create the X-rays.

Properties : X-ray photons carry high energy that can ionize atoms and disrupt molecular bonds. These rays can penetrate through human tissues and are harmful. These rays can easily traverse through thick objects without being absorbed much or scattered. These rays strongly affect photographic plates and can be viewed only through photographic films. These rays cause fluorescence by knocking out electrons from inner shells of certain metallic atoms.

Uses :
- X-rays with longer wavelengths are called *soft X-rays* and are used for detection of breakage in human bones and teeth (radiography). These rays can penetrate most of the body tissues, such as skin and flesh, but are slow to penetrate the bones and teeth since the calcium present in them absorb most of X-rays and thus are used to detect bone fractures and oral cavities.
- These rays are used in medical diagnosis (CAT scan) and in treatment of cancer.
- X-rays are used as scanners to scan objects such as luggage at airport terminals.
- These are used in industries for inspection of welds.
- X-rays of shorter wavelength are called *hard X-rays* and are used for studying patterns of atomic arrangement in crystals.

3. Ultraviolet (UV) radiations : 'Ultraviolet' means 'beyond violet'. Since violet is the colour of the highest frequencies of visible light, ultraviolet light has a higher frequency than violet light. UV radiations have wavelengths shorter than visible light but longer than X-rays (in the range of 10–400 nm in wavelength). These rays were discovered by a German physicist J.W. Ritter. He discovered that when a silver chloride paper was placed beyond a violet region, it first turned to violet, then dark brown and then black. The ray that produced strong chemical effect in silver chloride paper was named *chemical ray* or *actinic ray*. Later, these rays were named *ultraviolet rays*. These radiations are absorbed by glass but can pass through quartz. For this reason, a quartz prism, instead of a glass prism, is used to obtain these radiations.

Sources : UV radiation is present in sunlight and is produced by electric arcs and specialized lights such as mercury vapour lamps, tanning lamps and black lights. Most of the UV radiation from the Sun is absorbed by the 'ozone' layer of the atmosphere.

Properties : UV spectrum is divided into three parts. These parts are divided on the basis of the energy of the UV rays. The three categories are the (a) *near UV region*, (b) *far UV region* and (c) *extreme UV region* in ascending order of the energy spectrum. The energy of the UV rays varies from 3 eV to 124 eV. The near UV region is near to the visible light in the electromagnetic spectrum, whereas the extreme UV region falls close to the X-ray spectrum.

Extreme UV rays that have highest energy are capable of ionizing particles. Far UV rays do not have the capability to ionize the particles but can break the chemical bonds. About 7% of the radiation from the Sun is near UV and this part of sunlight is responsible for sunburns and suntans.

UV rays strongly affect photographic plates and produce fluorescence when incident on substances such as zinc sulphide and quinine sulphate solution. These rays have both harmful and beneficial effects on human health.

Uses :
- UV rays produce vitamin D in plants and animals.
- These are used for purification of water and for sterilization of surgical instruments.
- These are used for killing germs and bacteria.
- UV rays are used as optical sensors in certain instruments and as an investigative tool in forensics.
- These are used for detection of fire, original gems from fake ones, certain compounds and forgery of documents.
- These are also used to attract flies and bugs towards electric grids.

4. Visible light : The wavelength of visible light ranges from 400 nm to 800 nm. It is this portion of the electromagnetic spectrum that is visible to the human eyes and thus objects can be observed. When visible light is passed through a prism, various colours are produced based on their wavelength. This spectrum of visible light is called by the acronym VIBGYOR, indicating the colours violet, indigo, blue, green, yellow, orange and red. The violet light is the shortest wavelength visible light, whereas the red light is the longest wavelength visible light. This dispersion of white light into colours was discovered by Newton.

Sources : The Sun is the natural source of visible light. Other artificial sources are electric bulb, flame from candle, oil lamp and other hot sources.

Properties : Visible light travels in a straight-line path at a speed of 3×10^8 m s^{-1}. It has both particle and wave natures. It undergoes the phenomena of reflection, refraction, absorption, diffraction and so on.

Uses :
- It is the visible light that makes it possible to see objects around us.
- The light from Sun is used in photosynthesis.
- It is used in photography, spectral analysis and fibre optics.

5. Infrared radiations : The infrared radiations lie beyond the red region and have a wavelength varying from 800 nm to 1 mm. These radiations were discovered by Sir William Herschel in 1800. He discovered a type of invisible radiation beyond the red light of visible spectrum by means of its effect on a thermometer. When a thermometer with a blackened bulb was moved from violet region to red region, there was a sudden rise in temperature beyond the red region. This strong heating effect that is not visible is produced by the infrared radiations. A thermopile is also used for detection of infrared radiations. If infrared radiations are present, the galvanometer connected with the thermopile shows deflection. A glass prism absorbs infrared radiations. Hence, a prism made of rock salt is used to detect these radiations.

Sources : The Sun is the natural source of infrared radiations. Other sources are hot bodies such as flame, fire, lamp and burning gases. Any substance that radiates heat is a source of infrared radiations.

Properties : These rays travel in straight line similar to the visible light with the same speed. They undergo reflection and refraction and are focussed by parabolic mirrors and lenses that can burn a paper when kept at the focus of these mirrors or lenses. However, these rays do not affect photographic plates. A blackened bulb thermometer and a thermopile can be used to detect these radiations. These rays are less scattered by fog and mist in the atmosphere due to their long wavelength. A high dose of these rays can cause damage to skin due to burns and are harmful for eyes.

The infrared radiations are subdivided into five categories based on the wavelength : (a) *near infrared* (it is nearer to the visible region), (b) *short-wavelength infrared*, (c) *mid-wavelength infrared*, (d) *long-wavelength infrared* and (e) *far infrared* (it is nearer to the microwaves).

Uses :
- These rays do not affect photographic plates; hence, infrared lamps are used in dark rooms to develop the photographs.
- These rays can penetrate in mist and fog without much scattering; hence, these are used in photography during fog and also at night-time.
- These radiations are used for therapeutic purposes. Due to the heating effect, these are used to relieve pains from muscles and swollen joints.
- These radiations are used in night-vision devices (*e.g.* goggles) to see objects in dark.
- These radiations are used as signals through missiles in wars. A sensor of infrared radiation present in the missile detects the heat trail left behind by the enemy plane and sends a signal to the computer that guides the missile towards the target.
- These are used in long-distance telecommunication and in electronic equipments such as remote control and mobile phones.
- These rays are used in household appliances like toasters and heat lamps. In industries, they are used for welding and drying.
- These are used in astronomical study of stars and galaxies.

6. Microwaves : In 1888, Heinrich Hertz was the first to discover the microwaves. These radiations have wavelength ranging from 1 mm to 1 m or frequency ranging from 300 MHz (or 0.3 GHz) to 300 GHz.

Sources : The Sun emits very low levels of microwave radiations. Microwave sources are specialised vacuum tubes in which electric or magnetic fields are used.

Properties : Microwave radiations have good penetration power and can penetrate haze, light rain, snow, clouds and smoke.

Uses :

Microwaves are used for remote sensing, satellite communication and in houses for cooking in microwave ovens.

7. Radio waves : These waves have the longest wavelength in the electromagnetic spectrum, ranging from 1 m to 100 km or frequency corresponding to 300 MHz to 3 kHz or less. These were discovered by G. Marconi in 1907.

Sources : Lightning and astronomical objects are the natural sources of radio waves. The artificial sources are radio towers, satellites, cell phones, radars and other navigation systems.

Properties : These waves exhibit all the common properties of other electromagnetic radiations and can be subdivided into several categories based on the wavelength range.

Uses :
- The radio waves are used in communication systems such as TV broadcasting, radio broadcasting and mobile communication.
- These are used in navigation of ships and aircraft.
- These waves are also used by humans to communicate with each other.

> **Do You Know ?**
> Microwaves warm up food by making the molecules in the food vibrate at incredible speed. Microwaves turn into heat as soon as they are absorbed by the food.

Table 6.1 summarises the characteristics of the different waves of electromagnetic spectrum.

Table 6.1 : Characteristics of Electromagnetic Spectrum

Electromagnetic region	Wavelength	Frequency (in hertz)	Source	Detector	Application
Gamma rays	< 0.01 nm	> 3×10^{19}	Cosmic rays, decay of radioactive substances, nuclear fusion and fission reactions	Spectrometer	For killing cancerous cells, for checking welds in industries
X-rays	0.01–10 nm	3×10^{16} – 3×10^{19}	When high-velocity electrons collide with a heavy metal target	Photographic plate, fluorescent screen	Medical radiography, crystallography, for scanning objects
Ultraviolet radiation	10–400 nm	7.5×10^{14} – 3×10^{16}	Sun, mercury vapour lamp, arc lamp	Photographic plate, fluorescence, chemical effect on dyes	Sterilisation of surgical instruments, vitamin D production, detection of fake gems, forgery
Visible light	400–800 nm	3.75×10^{14} – 7.5×10^{14}	Sun, electric bulb, flame, hot bodies	Eyes, photographic film	Observing objects, fibre optics
Infrared radiation	800 nm to 1 mm	3×10^{11} – 3.75×10^{14}	Sun, hot bodies such as fire, burning gases	Blackened bulb thermometer, thermopile	Night-vision devices, developing photographs, sensor in missiles
Microwaves	1–10 m	3×10^{8} – 3×10^{11}	Electronic currents in special vacuum tubes	Electronic circuits	Radar, television, microwave ovens, cell phones
Radio waves	> 10 m	– 3×10^{8} 3×10^{3}	Electronic circuits and radio transmitters	Aerials of radio and television receiver	TV and radio broadcasting, navigation

ILLUSTRATIVE EXAMPLES

1. An electromagnetic wave has a wavelength of 800 nm. Calculate its frequency.
   Solution : Given, $\lambda = 800$ nm $= 800 \times 10^{-9}$ m
   Speed of electromagnetic wave, $c = 3 \times 10^8$ ms^{-1}
   Using the equation,
   $$c = \nu \lambda$$
   or
   $$\nu = \frac{c}{\lambda} = \frac{3 \times 10^8}{800 \times 10^{-9}}$$
   $$= 3.75 \times 10^{14} \text{ Hz}$$

2. The frequency of infrared radiations is 3×10^{11} Hz. Calculate the wavelength of these radiations.

Solution : Given, $\nu = 3 \times 10^{11}$ Hz.

Speed of infrared radiations $c = 3 \times 10^8$ ms^{-1}
Using the equation, $c = \nu\lambda$

i.e., $\lambda = \dfrac{c}{\nu} = \dfrac{3 \times 10^8}{3 \times 10^{11}}$

$= 10^{-3}$ m or 1 mm

EXERCISE 6(A)

1. What is meant by electromagnetic spectrum?
2. Name the radiations that are part of the electromagnetic spectrum.
3. State the relation between speed, frequency and wavelength of an electromagnetic wave.
   Ans : $c = \nu\lambda$, where c is the speed, ν is the frequency and λ is the wavelength of the electromagnetic wave.
4. State any three properties common to all electromagnetic waves.
5. Name any four regions of the electromagnetic spectrum in increasing order of frequency.
   Ans : Radio waves < Microwaves < Infrared radiations < Visible light.
6. Arrange the following radiations in the order of decreasing wavelength : gamma rays, ultraviolet rays, X-rays, radio waves and infrared rays.
   Ans : Infrared radiations > Ultraviolet rays > X-rays > Gamma rays.
7. Among the radiations of electromagnetic spectrum, which one has the highest penetrating power?
   Ans : Gamma rays.
8. What is the wavelength range of gamma rays? What are its sources?
9. State any two uses of gamma rays.
10. A wave has a wavelength less than 10 nm. Name the radiation and state one of its uses.
11. What is the frequency range of ultraviolet rays? How were these rays discovered?
12. State one harmful and one beneficial use of UV radiations.
13. Name the region that lies between the ultraviolet and infrared regions.
    Ans : Visible light
14. What is the range of wavelength of electromagnetic waves that are visible to us?
    Ans : 400–800 nm
15. Name the radiations that are absorbed by glass prism.
    Ans : UV radiations
16. What are infrared radiations? State its properties.
17. Draw a comparison between UV rays and microwaves.
18. Name the region just beyond (a) the violet end of visible spectrum and (b) the red end of visible spectrum.
    Ans : (a) UV region, (b) Infrared region.
19. Name two electromagnetic waves of wavelength greater than the infrared radiations and state one use of each.
20. State two sources of (a) ultraviolet rays, (b) infrared rays and (c) visible light.
21. A wave has a frequency range of 300 MHz to 300 GHz. Name the wave.
    Ans : Microwave.
22. Two waves X and Y have wavelength of 10 nm and 400 nm, respectively. (a) Name the two waves. (b) State one source of each of these waves. (c) What will be the ratio of their speeds in vacuum?
23. Suggest one way in each case by which we can detect the presence of (a) infrared radiations and (b) ultraviolet radiations.
24. Give one use of infrared radiations.
    Ans : For photography during night.
25. Name the radiations :
    (a) that are used for photography at night.
    (b) used for detection of fracture in bones.
    (c) whose wavelength range is 100–4,000 Å.
    Ans : (a) Infrared radiations, (b) X-rays, (c) UV rays.
26. (a) Name the high energetic invisible electromagnetic waves which help in the study of the structure of crystals.
    (b) State an additional use of the waves mentioned in part (a).
    Ans : (a) X-rays, (b) For the detection of fracture in bones.
27. Explain the following :
    (a) X-rays are used for detection of bone fractures.
    (b) A blackened bulb thermometer is used to detect infrared radiations.

(c) Photographs are developed in dark rooms in presence of infrared lamps.

(d) A quartz prism is used to obtain the ultraviolet radiations.

28. Name the radiation for the following purpose :
    (a) Vitamin D production
    (b) Satellite communication
    (c) Navigation systems
    (d) For CAT scan
    (e) For killing cancerous cells
    Ans : (a) UV rays, (b) Microwaves, (c) Radio waves, (d) X-rays, (e) Gamma rays

MULTIPLE CHOICE QUESTIONS

1. Which of these rays has the highest penetration power?
   (a) X-rays   (b) microwaves
   (c) UV rays   (d) gamma rays
   Ans : (d)

2. A thermopile is used for detection of :
   (a) infrared rays   (b) visible light
   (c) X-rays   (d) radio waves
   Ans : (a)

3. Ultraviolet rays are not used for :
   (a) purification of water
   (b) detection of fake gems
   (c) photography at night
   (d) killing germs
   Ans : (c)

4. Microwaves are used in :
   (a) sterilization of surgical instruments
   (b) producing fluorescence
   (c) satellite communication
   (d) developing photographs
   Ans : (c)

5. The frequency of radio waves lies in the range of :
   (a) 30 kHz–300 MHz   (b) 3 kHz–300 GHz
   (c) 3 kHz–30 MHz   (d) 30 kHz–30 GHz
   Ans : (b)

NUMERICAL PROBLEMS

1. The wavelength of blue light is 500 nm. Calculate its frequency.
   Ans : 6×10^{14} Hz

2. The frequency of microwaves is 300 MHz. What will be its wavelength?
   Ans : 1 m

3. What will be the wavelength of yellow light if its frequency range is 5×10^8 MHz?
   Ans : 600 nm

(B) DEVIATION, DISPERSION AND SCATTERING OF LIGHT

6.4 DEVIATION PRODUCED BY A PRISM

The speed of light varies from medium to medium. Due to the difference in speed of light in different media, a ray of light travelling from one medium to another gets deviated from its path. This deviation in path of light occurs at the boundary separating the two media.

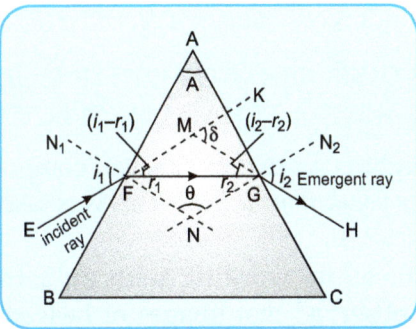

Fig. 6.2 : Deviation of light by a prism.

Fig. 6.2 shows deviation of light produced by a triangular prism. ABC is the principal section of the prism and ∠BAC is the angle of prism (A). EF is an incident ray entering from a monochromatic source of light (i.e. a ray of light of single colour). It strikes the refracting surface AB of the prism at point F. As the ray is travelling from a rarer medium (air) to a denser medium (glass), it bends towards the normal NN_1 and travels as ray FG inside the glass. The refracted ray FG strikes the refracting face AC of the prism and suffers refraction from glass to air, i.e. from a denser medium to a rarer medium and it emerges as ray GH away from the normal NN_2. The ray GH is the emergent ray.

Thus, a ray of light suffers refraction at two faces of the prism, i.e. AB and AC. At the face AB, the ray EF bends as ray FG towards the normal instead of going along ray EFK and thus there occurs a deviation by ∠MFG = δ_1. Now, the ray FG bends and emerges as ray GH on the face AC of the prism and appears to come along MGH. There occurs a deviation by ∠MGF = δ_2.

If there was no prism, then the ray of light EF would travel along straight path EFK as there would not be any refraction. The emergent ray GH entering out of the prism appears to be coming along ray MGH. Thus, a deviation by ∠KMG is produced by the prism. This angle is called the *angle of deviation* δ. It is the angle between *incident ray EF* and *emergent ray GH*.

From Fig. 6.2, ∠KMG = ∠MFG + ∠MGF ...(6.2)
i.e. $\delta = \delta_1 + \delta_2$

Factors Affecting the Angle of Deviation

The value of angle of deviation produced by the prism depends on the following factors :

1. Angle of incidence (*i*),
2. Refractive index of prism material (*μ*),
3. Angle of prism (A) and
4. Colour or wavelength of incident light (λ).

Dependence of Deviation on Colour or Wavelength of Incident Light

When a beam of light entering a prism is not monochromatic, but a mixture of several colours, then the emergent beam also has several colours arranged in a specific order. Since the speed of light decreases with the decrease in wavelength of light, the refractive index of prism is more for shorter wavelength and less for longer wavelength of light. As the refractive index of a material increases, the angle of deviation also increases. Thus, deviation produced by a prism increases with the decrease in wavelength of light.

In the *visible light*, the *violet colour* with the *shortest wavelength* (400 nm) has the *minimum speed* and undergoes *maximum deviation*, whereas the *red colour* with the *longest wavelength* (700 nm) has the *maximum speed* and undergoes *minimum deviation* ($\delta_V > \delta_R$).

6.5 DISPERSION OF WHITE LIGHT THROUGH A PRISM AND SPECTRUM

White light is a mixture of seven components and is known as *polychromatic light*. This was discovered by Sir Isaac Newton.

Newton, while working with an astronomical telescope, observed that images of heavenly bodies, such as stars, were coloured near the fringes. He thought that it was a defect of the telescopic lens. Thus, he repeated his experiment with polished lenses, but found the same observation. The colour still persisted on the images. From this observation, he suggested that the fault is not with the lenses but there is something in the nature of light itself. To confirm this conclusion, he conducted an experiment.

Newton's Experiment : In his experiment, Newton allowed a beam of sunlight to enter through a small opening in the window of a dark room. An equilateral prism was placed in the path of the beam of light and a white screen was placed on the other side of the prism to receive the rays of light emerging from the prism after refraction (Fig 6.3).

Newton observed that the light obtained on the white screen was a band of seven colours, resembling those of the rainbow formed after a rain. The order of colours from the base of the prism was *violet, indigo, blue, green, yellow, orange* and *red* (*VIBGYOR*). Each colour corresponds to a small range of wavelength.

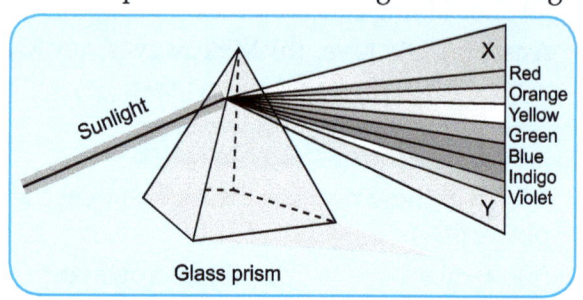

Fig. 6.3 : Dispersion of white light through a prism.

The band of colours obtained is termed as *spectrum* and the phenomenon of splitting of white light is called *dispersion*.

Dispersion : The phenomenon of splitting of white (or polychromatic) light into its component colours, on passing through a prism, is known as *dispersion*.

Spectrum : The band of different colours obtained on a screen when a white (or polychromatic) light splits into its component colours, on passing through a prism, is known as *spectrum*.

Explanation of dispersion : The angle of deviation is different for different wavelengths of light. It is *minimum for red light* (long wavelength) and *maximum for violet light* (short wavelength). When a white light is incident on the first face of a prism, the light rays of different colours deviate through different angles due to difference in their speeds inside the glass prism. Due to different deviation angles, the white light gets dispersed or separated. These dispersed rays on striking the second or opposite face of the prism suffer only refraction and no dispersion. These different rays deviate through different angles and get further separated. These rays then emerge as a band of different colours called the *spectrum*.

The *rainbow* is the classic example of spectrum formed due to the dispersion of light in nature. The tiny droplets of water suspended in air just after a rain act as small innumerable prisms. When sunlight passes through these droplets, it gets dispersed to form a band of seven colours, with red colour appearing on the upper arc and violet colour appearing on the lower arc of the rainbow.

Prism itself does not produce colour

One might argue that the light by itself is white and it is the prism that colours the white light. To disprove this, Newton conducted another experiment.

Experiment : White light entering from a slit S was made to fall on an equilateral prism P kept in a darkened room (Fig. 6.4). The dispersed light was received on a screen XY with a narrow hole H to allow light rays of only a particular colour to pass through it. The light passing out of the hole of the screen, say yellow light, was made to fall on prism Q, placed in an inverted position with its base upwards, and screen X'Y' was placed on the other side of this prism.

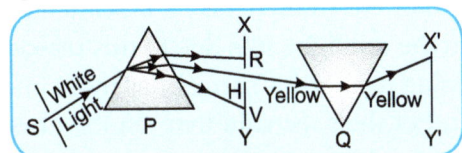

Fig. 6.4 : Experiment to show that a prism itself does not produce colour.

It was observed that the emergent light obtained on the screen X'Y' was of same colour, *i.e.* yellow, as that of the light incident on the prism Q through the hole H.

By moving the screen XY up or down, the experiment can be conducted for any colour of light. It has been found that in each case, only refraction takes place and the colour of light obtained is same as that of the light incident on prism Q.

This proves that prism itself does not produce any colour and the white light gets dispersed at the first face of the prism only.

NOTE

If the prism Q is kept with its base downwards, rather than as shown in Fig. 6.4, the yellow ray of light will get deviated in downward direction (see Fig. 6.5).

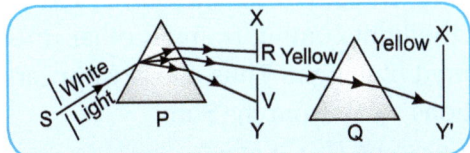

Fig. 6.5 : A prism does not produce colour.

Recombination of colours using two prisms

The colours of spectrum of white light can recombine to reproduce white light. This can be demonstrated by the following experiment.

Experiment : Take two exactly similar prisms A and B, made of same material and same refracting angle. Place the two prisms with their base inverted relative to each other (Fig. 6.6). Now pass white light through a narrow slit and allow it to fall on prism A, which has its base downwards. Due to dispersion, the rays of light emerge from the prism A as a spectrum (VIBGYOR) and the deviation of light rays takes places downwards, *i.e.* towards the base of the prism A. This can be verified by placing a white screen between the two prisms.

Now let the dispersed light fall on the prism B, which has its base upwards. This prism deviates the light rays upwards, *i.e.* in a direction opposite to the deviation caused by prism A.

It is observed that the light emerging from the prism B, when made to fall on a white screen, is white and in a direction parallel to the incident rays on the prism A.

The reason for this observation is that the prism B turns the dispersed colours towards its base through different angles of deviation, such that all the light rays are incident at the same point, before emerging from prism B. Therefore, all the colours recombine to form white light.

The prism A is called the *dispersing prism*, as it disperses the white light, whereas the prism B is called the *recombination prism*, as it recombines the dispersed light. The two prisms collectively act as a *glass slab* with parallel sides.

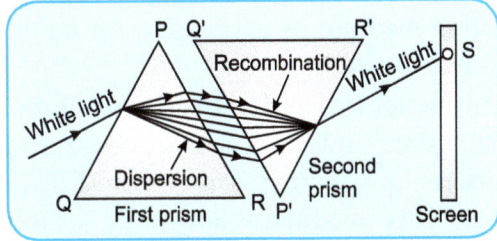

Fig. 6.6 : Recombination of colours.

6.6 WAVELENGTH AND FREQUENCY RANGE OF COLOURS IN WHITE LIGHT

White light is polychromatic in nature, *i.e.* composed of lights of different wavelengths that produce the sensation of different colours on exciting the retina of our eyes. The wavelength is the characteristic of colour, whatever may be the source. There are seven prominent colours in the white light. These are violet, indigo, blue, green, yellow, orange and red.

If an electromagnetic wave of 8,000 Å excites our retina, our brain perceives it as a colour of bright red. If the wavelength decreases to 7,000 Å, the perception of colour is still red, until the wavelength is decreased to 6,200 Å, when the perception changes to orange.

The perception of colour changes with decrease in wavelength, and at 4,000 Å, the colour perceived is dark violet. If the wavelength is further decreased, the retina does not get excited. The red light has the longest wavelength or lowest frequency, while the violet light has the shortest wavelength or highest frequency.

Table 6.2 gives the range of wavelength and frequency for different colours of the white light.

Table 6.2 : Range of Frequency and Wavelength

Colour	Approximate wavelength range (in Å)	Frequency range (in 10^{14} Hz)
Violet	4,000–4,460	7.5–6.73
Indigo	4,460–4,640	6.73–6.47
Blue	4,640–5,000	6.47–6.01
Green	5,000–5,780	6.01–5.19
Yellow	5,780–5,920	5.19–5.07
Orange	5,920–6,200	5.07–4.84
Red	6,200–8,000	4.84–3.75

In Table 6.2, the wavelength has been expressed in unit angstrom, 1 Å = 10^{-10} m.

6.7 SCATTERING OF LIGHT

Scattering is the process of deflection of a ray of light from its straight path by irregularities in the propagation medium or particles, or in the interface between two media.

When the light passes through a medium, a part of it is absorbed and the rest is scattered away. The basic process in scattering is *absorption of light* by the molecules of the medium followed by *re-radiation* in different directions. The strength of scattering can be measured by the loss of energy in the light beam as it passes through the medium. The strength of scattering depends on the size of the particle causing the scattering and the wavelength of light.

When the light from the Sun enters the Earth's atmosphere, it gets scattered by the air and dust particles of the atmosphere. This phenomenon of scattering of light by the molecules of air was first studied by a scientist Rayleigh and is called *Rayleigh scattering*.

In Rayleigh scattering, the intensity of scattered light has a strong dependence on the size of the particles. It is also known as *coherent scattering*. In coherent scattering, there is no change in the wavelength of light, *i.e.* scattered light has the same wavelength as that of the incident light. This happens when the air molecules have a size smaller than the wavelength of incident light. These molecules absorb the energy of incident light and re-emit it without any loss of energy. The intensity of scattered light is inversely proportional to the fourth power of the wavelength of light,

$$I \propto \frac{1}{\lambda^4} \quad \ldots(6.3)$$

This means that the shorter wavelength in the visible light is scattered more than the longer wavelength. The violet light has a wavelength of 4,000 Å while the red light is 8,000 Å in the visible spectrum. Thus, *the violet light is scattered the most while the red light is scattered the least.* The wavelength of violet light is half of the wavelength of red light; hence, it is scattered 16 times more than the red light. It is due to this reason that the light reaching the Earth's surface has more intensity on the red end of the spectrum than on the violet end of the spectrum.

If the air molecules have a size bigger than the wavelength of incident light, then the intensity of scattered light is same for all wavelengths of light.

Effects of Scattering

The following are some of the effects of scattering of sunlight by the Earth's atmosphere :

1. Red colour during sunrise and sunset : During sunrise and sunset, the light has to travel a longer path through the atmosphere. The violet and blue lights, due to their short wavelengths, get scattered away from the Sun, while the red light, being of long wavelength, gets least scattered. Thus, to an observer, the light coming from the Sun is deprived of blue colour and it appears red.

2. Blue colour of the sky : Among the short wavelengths of light, blue light is present in larger proportion in the sunlight. The blue light due to its short wavelength gets scattered the most by the air molecules of the Earth's atmosphere in comparison to the red light of longer wavelength. Due to this, the light coming directly from the Sun is red in colour, whereas the light coming from all other directions is the scattered blue light. Thus, the sky appears blue in all directions away from the Sun.

3. White colour of sky at noontime : At noontime, the position of the Sun is directly overhead and thus light rays have to travel a comparatively short distance through the atmosphere to reach the Earth. As a result, there is not much scattering of sunlight and hence the sky appears white in colour.

4. White colour of clouds : The size of water vapour and dust molecules present inside the clouds is bigger than the wavelength of visible light. Also, the distance of clouds from the Earth's surface is less as compared to Sun. Thus, all the colours of white light coming from the Sun, when incident on the clouds, get equally scattered. Since the intensity of scattered light is equal, the clouds appear white. It is also known as *Mie scattering*.

5. Red light used as a danger signal : In the visible light, the red light, which has longest wavelength, gets least scattered by the air molecules of the atmosphere. As a result, it can deeply penetrate and is visible from far distance as compared to lights of shorter wavelengths. Hence, it is used as a danger signal so that it is visible from far distance even when the atmosphere is foggy or misty.

> **Do You Know ?**
>
> *There is no atmosphere on the Moon and therefore no scattered light from the Sun reaches the Moon. To an observer on the Moon, the sky appears black in the directions away from the Sun.*

ILLUSTRATIVE EXAMPLES

1. A light composed of red and blue colours is incident on (a) a single prism, (b) a glass slab, (c) on prism A kept near another inverted prism B, as shown in the figure. Complete the diagrams by showing the emergent rays in each case.

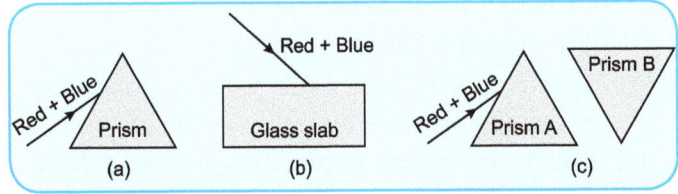

Solution :

(a) A prism causes dispersion of incident light into its components with different angles of deviation. Upon refraction, at the two inclined faces of the prism, the incident light will disperse into red and blue lights. Since the wavelength of red light is longer than the wavelength of blue light, the red light gets deviated by a smaller angle than the blue light, on passing through a prism.

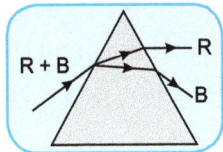

(b) In the case of a glass slab, the two faces are parallel to each other. The incident ray, upon refraction through the first face, gets dispersed into its component colours. Each component ray, when incident on the second face of the slab, gets refracted and emerges parallel to the incident ray. There is no further separation of colours. The emergent coloured rays are close and parallel to each other and are difficult to distinguish.

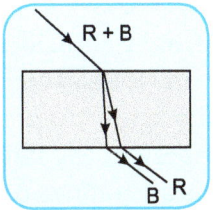

(c) A ray of light made of blue and red colours when incident on a prism gets dispersed into its two component colours upon refraction through the two faces of a prism. When another inverted prism is kept next to this prism, the emergent red and blue rays strike the first face of this prism. The rays get refracted towards the base of the prism and are incident at the same point on the second face of this prism. Thus, these rays recombine and emerge together as a ray of single colour.

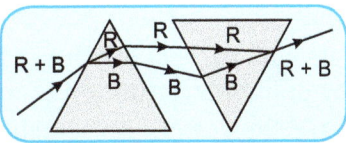

2. A beam of white light is incident on a prism A, such that a spectrum is obtained upon dispersion through it on a screen PQ kept on the other side of the prism. The screen has a narrow aperture so as to allow only yellow light to pass through it. Prism B (same orientation as A) and a screen P'Q' are placed near the screen PQ. Draw a diagram to illustrate this.

Solution : White light from a source is incident on prism A. It gets dispersed into a spectrum of seven colours from red to violet. The red light(R) deviates the least while the violet light(V) deviates the most. The yellow light(Y) has an angle of deviation somewhere between the angles of these two colours, as shown in the

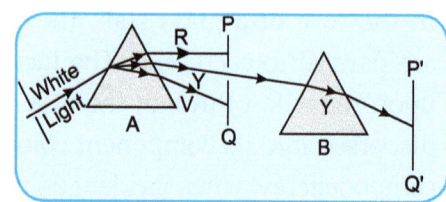

figure. The screen PQ has an aperture to pass only yellow light. Yellow light passes through it and is incident on prism B. Upon refraction through the prism B, it bends towards its base and emerges as a single yellow light as obtained on the screen P'Q'.

3. A beam of light is incident normally on the face AB of an isosceles right-angled triangle as shown in the figure. Complete the diagram and show the emergent ray if the light is composed of (a) yellow and orange colours and (b) yellow and green colours. Consider the critical angle for glass-air interface for yellow light to be 45°.

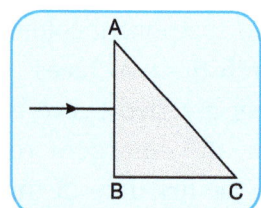

Solution : When a beam of light is incident normally on the face of a prism, it passes without deviation and thus there is no dispersion of light into its component colours.

The refracted beam inside the prism strikes the face AC of the prism at an angle of 45°. The critical angle for yellow colour is given as 45°, so the angle of refraction will be 90° for yellow light. It suffers refraction and emerges along the face AC of the prism. Now, the orange colour has greater wavelength than the yellow colour and thus the critical angle will be more than 45°. Since the light is incident at an angle of 45° on the face AC, which is less than the crtitical angle of orange light, it suffers refraction and emerges from the prism, bending away from the normal (denser to rarer medium). However, the wavelength of green light is shorter than the wavelength of yellow light; hence, the critical angle for green light is smaller than 45°. Since light is incident at an angle of 45° on the face AC, which is more than the crtitical angle of green light, it suffers total internal reflection and strikes normally on the face BC of the prism and emerges without any deviation.

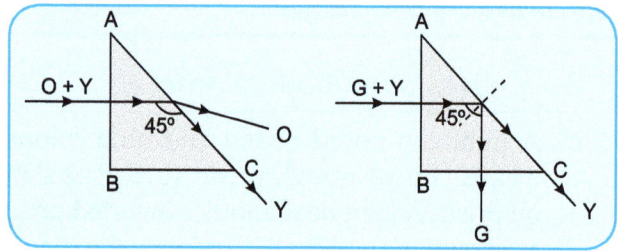

EXERCISE 6(B)

1. Illustrate with the help of a diagram the deviation of a ray of light on striking a triangular prism.
2. What are the factors on which the deviation produced by a prism depends on?
   Ans : The angle of incidence, the angle of prism and the refractive index of the material.
3. How is deviation produced by a triangular prism dependent on wavelength of light incident on it?
   Ans : The deviation increases with decrease in wavelength of light.
4. Which colour of light deviates the most and which colour deviates the least among the visible light?
   Ans : Violet light deviated the most while red light deviates the least.
5. What is meant by polychromatic light?
6. What is meant by dispersion of light?
7. What is the cause of dispersion of white light through a prism?
8. What is a spectrum?
9. Illustrate with the help of a diagram the dispersion of white light by a prism.
10. The figure below shows three rays of light, A, B and C, after dispersion through a prism. Differentiate them as red, yellow and blue colours.

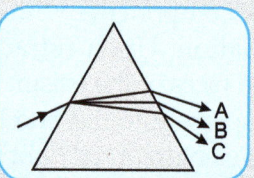

11. A beam of white light is incident on a prism. It gets dispersed into its constituent colours upon refraction through it. The figure shows the emergence of violet light. Show the deviation and emergence of green and red light in the figure.

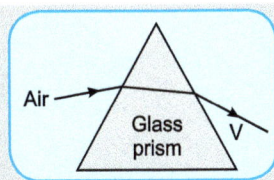

12. Among red and blue light, which coloured light will travel faster in a prism?
    Ans : Red light.
13. In the figure given, a thin beam of white light is incident on a prism. Complete the diagram to show the effect of prism on the beam and show what is obtained on a white screen placed on the other side of the prism.

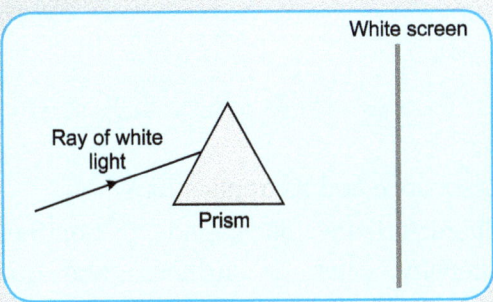

14. In the above case, if a slit is made in the screen, such that it allows only blue light to pass through it, then what will be observed on another screen kept parallel to the first screen?
15. If a monochromatic beam of light is incident on an equilateral prism, such that it undergoes minimum deviation, then how will the beam pass through the prism with respect to its base?
16. Name the seven colours of the spectrum of white light as obtained on a screen after dispersion through a prism.
17. How will you experimentally prove that a prism itself does not produce any colour?
18. Draw a diagram to show how different colours of white light can recombine to produce white light.
19. Complete the diagram given below and show what is obtained on the screen.

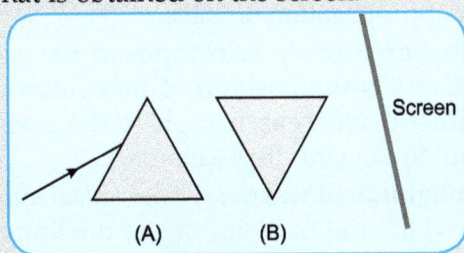

20. Which of the colours in the visible spectrum have frequency more than the green light?
    Ans : Blue, indigo and violet.
21. What is the approximate wavelength range for (a) violet light and (b) red light?
    Ans : (a) 400 nm, (b) 800 nm.
22. Which colours of the spectrum of white light have wavelengths longer than yellow light?
    Ans : Orange and red.
23. What do you understand by the term 'Scattering of light'? Which colour of white light is scattered the least and why?
24. What is Rayleigh scattering?
25. How does the intensity of scattered light depend on the wavelength of incident light?
26. Under what condition is the intensity of scattered light same for all wavelengths of light?
    Ans : If the size of air molecules is bigger than the wavelength of incident light.
27. Which characteristic property of light is responsible for blue colour of the sky?
    Ans : Scattering.
28. Why does the Sun appear red at sunrise?
29. What is the reason for blue colour of the sky when viewed in any direction away from the Sun?
30. When does the sky appear white and why?
31. Why do the clouds appear white?

MULTIPLE CHOICE QUESTIONS

1. When a spectrum is obtained on dispersion of white light through a prism, which of these colours is nearest to the base of the prism?
   (a) violet   (b) green
   (c) yellow   (d) red
   Ans : (a)
2. Rainbow is formed due to :
   (a) scattering of light   (b) dispersion of light
   (c) refraction of light   (d) reflection of light
   Ans : (a)
3. The colour which deviates the most during dispersion of white light is :
   (a) red   (b) blue
   (c) orange   (d) violet
   Ans : (d)
4. The intensity of scattered violet light is 16 times the intensity of scattered :
   (a) green light   (b) red light
   (c) yellow light   (d) blue light
   Ans : (b)
5. Which of these colours of the sunlight is least scattered?
   (a) blue   (b) green
   (c) red   (d) yellow
   Ans : (c)

7

SOUND

LEARNING OUTCOMES

- Sound waves and its characteristics
- Reflection of sound waves : Echo and its applications
- Free vibrations, damped vibrations and forced vibrations with examples
- Resonance and its applications
- Characteristics of sound : Loudness and intensity, pitch or shrillness and quality or timbre
- Distinction between music and noise and noise pollution

(A) SOUND WAVES, VIBRATIONS AND RESONANCE

7.1 WAVES

A disturbance or vibration that transfers energy progressively from one point to another in a medium without there being a direct contact between the two points is called a wave.

A wave is produced by the vibrations of the particles of the medium through which it passes. When a wave passes through a medium, the medium itself does not move along the direction of the wave, only the particles of the medium vibrate about their fixed positions.

Types of Waves

Waves can be broadly classified into two types based on their ability or inability to propagate through vacuum.

1. Mechanical waves : *Mechanical waves* are those waves that require a material medium for their propagation. These are also called *elastic waves*.

Examples : Sound waves, water waves, waves on a stretched spring and so on.

2. Non-mechanical waves : *Non-mechanical waves* are those waves that do not require any material medium for their propagation. They can even *travel through vacuum*.

Examples : All electromagnetic waves such as light waves, radio waves, X-rays and so on.

Mechanical waves can further be classified into following two types (Fig. 7.1).

(a) Transverse waves : *A transverse wave* is that wave in which the particles of the medium vibrate about their mean positions at right angles to the direction of propagation of wave.

A transverse wave is composed of *crests* and *troughs*. Crest is the position of maximum upward displacement, whereas trough is the position of maximum downward displacement.

(b) Longitudinal waves : *A longitudinal wave* is that wave in which the particles of the medium vibrate about their mean positions along the line of direction of propagation of wave.

A longitudinal wave is composed of *compressions* and *rarefactions*. Compression is a region of high pressure and low volume, whereas rarefaction is a region of low pressure and high volume.

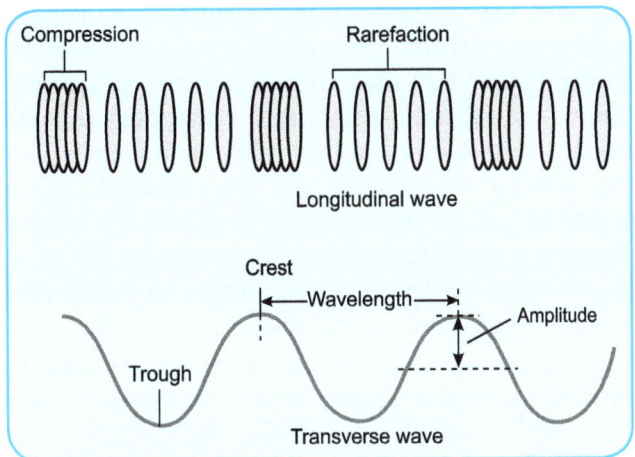

Fig. 7.1 : Longitudinal and transverse waves.

Solids can transmit both transverse and longitudinal waves because their rigidity makes it possible to restore forces in all directions. However, liquids and gases transmit only longitudinal waves because they cannot restore all forces. The liquid can transmit transverse waves from its surface only and not from inside.

Terms Related to Wave Motion

1. **Amplitude (*a*) :** Amplitude of a wave is the maximum displacement of the particle of a medium on either side of its mean position.

2. **Time period (T) :** It is the time taken by a particle of the medium to complete one oscillation or vibration.

3. **Frequency (ν) :** It is the number of oscillations completed by a particle in one second.

4. **Wavelength (λ) :** It is the distance measured in the direction of propagation of a wave, between two successive points in the wave that are characterized by the same phase of oscillation.

5. **Wave velocity (*v*) :** It is the distance travelled by a wave in one second.

The relation between time period and frequency is ν = 1/T and the relation between wavelength, frequency and wave velocity is $v = \nu\lambda$.

7.2 CHARACTERISTICS OF WAVES

1. When energy is transferred to any part of the medium, then disturbance is produced in it by the *periodic motion* of the particles about their mean position.
2. The energy moves forward in the form of *waves* while particles of the medium *oscillate* about their mean position.
3. The *velocity of wave* is different from the velocity with which the particles oscillate about their mean positions.
4. Energy is transferred from one particle of a medium to the next particle in a fixed time, *i.e.* energy is transferred at a *constant speed* from one place of a medium to another place. There is a *constant phase difference* between two consecutive particles.

7.3 SOUND WAVES

Sound is a type of energy in the form of mechanical waves that produces a sensation of hearing in our ears.

Sound is produced by vibration of a body and requires a material medium for its propagation.

A sound wave is the pattern of disturbance caused by the movement of energy travelling through a medium as it propagates away from the source of sound.

Sound waves are longitudinal waves in solid, inside a liquid and in gas (air). Sound waves can propagate as transverse waves only in a solid and on the surface of a liquid.

Sound travels with a finite speed in a medium and takes some time to reach our ears from its source of production.

The speed of a longitudinal wave depends on two factors : (a) the *elasticity* E of the medium and (b) the *density* ρ of the medium.

The speed of sound in a medium is related to these factors as

$$v = \sqrt{E/\rho} \qquad ...(7.1)$$

Elasticity is related to the tendency of a material to maintain its shape and not deform whenever a force or stress is applied on it. In general, solids have the strongest elasticity, followed by liquids and then gases. For this reason, longitudinal sound waves travel faster in solids than they do in liquids and in gases, *i.e.*

$$v_{\text{solids}} > v_{\text{liquids}} > v_{\text{gases}}$$

The speed of sound is nearly 5,100 ms^{-1} in steel, 1,450 m s^{-1} in water and 330 ms^{-1} in air at 0°C.

The speed of sound is inversely proportional to the square root of density of the gas,

$$v \propto 1/\sqrt{\rho} \qquad ...(7.2)$$

Lighter the gas through which the sound passes, greater will be the speed of sound. The speed of sound in a gas *increases with the increase in temperature* of the gas. This happens because with increase in temperature, the density of a gas decreases. The speed of sound also *increases with increase in humidity* in air. However, speed of sound in a gas is *independent of pressure, wavelength, frequency and amplitude.*

Sound waves differ from the electromagnetic waves (such as gamma rays, X-rays, UV rays, light rays, etc.)

in a number of ways. Sound waves require a material medium for propagation, whereas electromagnetic waves do not require a material medium. They can even travel in vacuum. In the case of sound waves, the energy transfer is through the vibrations of the particles of the medium about their mean positions, whereas in electromagnetic waves, the transfer of energy is in the form of photons. The speed of electromagnetic waves in air (or vacuum) is much higher (3×10^8 m s^{-1}) than the speed of sound in air (330 m s^{-1}).

Difference between light waves and sound waves

Light waves	Sound waves
These are electromagnetic waves, *i.e.* non-mechanical in nature.	These are mechanical or elastic waves.
These can travel in vacuum.	These cannot travel in vacuum; require a material medium for propagation.
These are transverse waves.	These can be transverse as well as longitudinal waves.
The speed of light waves in air is 3×10^8 m s^{-1}.	The speed of sound waves in air is 330 m s^{-1}.
The frequency of visible light waves is in the range of $3.75 \times 10^{14} - 7.5 \times 10^{14}$ Hz.	The frequency of audible sound waves is in the range of 20–20,000 Hz.

Propagation of Sound Waves

In air, sound waves propagate as longitudinal waves that comprises compressions and rarefactions.

A *compression* is that part of a longitudinal wave in which the particles of the medium are closer to one another than they normally are and there is a momentary reduction in volume of the medium or a temporary increase in density of the medium. Compression is a region of *high pressure*.

A *rarefaction* is that part of a longitudinal wave in which the particles of the medium are farther apart than normal, and there is a momentary increase in the volume of the medium or a temporary decrease in the density of the medium. Rarefaction is a region of *low pressure*.

The compressions and rarefactions carry the disturbance with a definite velocity, depending on the nature of the medium.

7.4 REFLECTION OF SOUND WAVES

Reflection of a wave is the change in direction of path of a wave at an interface between two different media so that the wave returns along a different path to the medium from which it originated.

Sound waves also undergo reflection. When a sound wave travelling in a medium strikes the surface separating any two media (such as wall, metal sheet, hard wood), a part of incident wave gets reflected into the initial medium, obeying ordinary laws of reflection, *i.e.* the incident ray, the reflected ray and the normal, all lie in the same plane and the angle of reflection is equal to the angle of incidence. The rest of the wave gets partly absorbed and partly refracted or transmitted into the second medium.

For reflection of longitudinal sound waves, the size of the reflective surface should be bigger than the wavelength of sound wave. Unlike light waves, sound waves do not require a highly polished or shining surface for reflection. They can get reflected from any smooth or rough surface, provided the dimension of the surface is large enough.

Example : The rolling sound of thunder is due to successive reflections from clouds and land surfaces.

The phenomenon of reflection of sound waves is utilised in megaphone, hearing aid, soundboards and so on.

NOTE

The sound audible to us has a very wide frequency range (from 20 Hz to 20,000 Hz), and thus a very wide range of wavelength. As a result, the overall nature of the reflection varies according to the texture and structure of the surface on which the sound wave of a particular frequency is incident.

7.5 ECHO

We have often experienced that if a person standing on a hilltop, or any empty room surrounded by walls, shouts loudly, two sounds are heard. One is the sharp original sound of the person heard instantly, while the other is the faint sound heard after some time. This sound is heard after reflection from hills or walls and is called echo.

The sound heard after reflection from a distant object (high building, a cliff, mountain, etc.) after the original sound from a given source dies off is called an echo.

Conditions for Formation of an Echo

The formation of an echo depends on two factors : (1) minimum time and (2) minimum distance.

1. Minimum time : It has been found that the sensation of any sound persists for 0.1 s in our ears after the original sound from the source dies off. This time is called *persistence of audibility*. If any sound after reflection reaches the ear in less than 0.1 s, it cannot be distinguished from the original sound and so an echo cannot be heard. Thus, the condition for formation of an echo is that the reflected sound should reach at least 0.1 s after the original sound ceases.

2. Minimum distance : Let d be the distance between the source of sound and the reflecting surface, t be the time after which an echo is heard and v be the speed of sound. The total distance travelled by sound to reach an observer standing near the source of sound is $2d$ in time t.

Since, Speed = Distance travelled in 1 s,

$$\therefore \quad v = \frac{2d}{t}$$

i.e. $$d = \frac{vt}{2} \quad ...(7.3)$$

Speed of sound in air is 340 m s^{-1}, t = 0.1 s,

$$\therefore \quad d = \frac{340 \times 0.1}{2} = 17 \text{ m}$$

Thus, the minimum distance required between the source of sound and the reflecting surface to hear an echo distinctly is 17 m in air.

If the distance between the source of sound and the reflecting surface is less than 17 m, an echo will not be heard because the reflected sound wave will reach the ears of the observer simultaneously with the original sound.

Conditions for Hearing an Echo Distinctly
1. The minimum distance between the source of sound and the reflecting surface should be 17 m in air.
2. The wavelength of sound should be less than the size of the reflecting body.
3. The intensity of sound should be sufficient so as to hear the reflected sound.

Reverberation : When a series of repeated reflections fall on the ear from various reflectors, one after another, the sound gets prolonged and a continuous rolling sound can be heard. This is known as *reverberation*.

This effect occurs only when the distance between the reflector and the source of sound is less than 17 m and no echo is formed.

Example : Reverberation occurs if a person speaks in a large empty room or in large monuments such as the Taj Mahal.

7.6 USE OF ECHO TO DETERMINE THE SPEED OF SOUND IN AIR

A method for determining the speed of sound is to find out the time interval for hearing an echo on a hilltop or a cliff.

A person stands at a known distance d (say 100 m) from a cliff and fires a pistol or a powerful cracker to produce sound. Simultaneously, while firing, he starts a stopwatch. The stopwatch is stopped as soon as the echo is heard. Let the time interval noted be t. The distance travelled by the sound during this time is twice the distance, i.e. $2d$, after reflection. The speed of sound is then calculated as

$$\frac{\text{Distance travelled}}{\text{Time taken}} = \frac{2d}{t} \quad ...(7.4)$$

By repeating the experiment a few number of times, the average velocity of sound can be calculated.

7.7 APPLICATIONS OF ECHO

1. SONAR (Sound Navigation And Ranging): It is a technique of using *ultrasonic* sound waves (frequency > 20,000 Hz) to locate underwater objects. It is used by warships or sailing ships to locate under water submarines or depth of the ocean bed and so on, as ultrasonic waves can travel undeviated underwater for many kilometres and are not easily absorbed by the medium, unlike sounds in the audible range.

To find the depth of an ocean, a ship sends ultrasonic waves downwards in the water through a transmitter. When these sound waves reach the ocean floor, they are reflected to the ship and are received by a suitable receiver placed close to the sound source. The time taken by the sound to travel from the source to the receiver is recorded. Since the velocity of sound in water is known, the distance of the ocean floor from the ship can be calculated as $d = vt/2$.

Similarly, this method is used to locate any enemy submarine or any other obstacle present inside the water. Ultrasonic waves will hit the obstacle and reach back to the receiver after reflection.

This method of use of echo in SONAR is known as *echo depth sounding*.

2. RADAR (Radio Detection And Ranging) : In this technique, instead of sound waves, electromagnetic waves of long wavelength, such as radio waves, are used to locate an enemy aircraft or ship. Radio waves are sent in all directions in space. The radio waves on striking an aircraft get reflected, which are in turn received by a receiver on the radar device itself. On receiving the radio waves, the position of the enemy aircraft can be located.

3. Use of echoes by fishermen or trawlers : Similar to sonar, a trawler sends a beam of ultrasonic waves from a source into the sea. The waves on striking a shoal of fish reflect to the source and are received by a detector. The distance of the fish can be calculated by noting the time taken by the waves to reach back to the receiver ($d = vt/2$).

4. Use of echoes by animals such as bats and dolphins : bats can produce and detect high frequency sound waves of about 100 kHz that does not lie in human audible range. These waves are used to locate obstacles at night. These sound waves strike any obstacle in their path and are reflected as echoes to the bat's ear. These echoes guide the bats to fly safely in air avoiding collision with any obstacle. This method is known as echolocation or *sound ranging*.

Dolphins use both high frequency and low frequency sound for echolocation. The low frequency sound travels the farthest distance and is used by a dolphin to detect any object. The dolphin then switches to a high frequency sound to obtain a more accurate picture of the object. They also use echolocation system for communication with other dolphins to locate their prey or to avoid predators.

5. Use of echoes in medical science : The echo method of ultrasound wave is used by doctors to observe images of soft tissue in the human body such as liver, gall bladder, stomach and uterus. It is known as *ultrasonography*. The ultrasonic waves reflect off from the soft tissues and a computer transforms the reflected waves into an image on a computer screen. The picture obtained is called a *sonogram*. The process of obtaining the image of heart by this procedure is called *echocardiography*.

6. Echoes are also used by geologists for mineral inspection and by military men to locate gun positions of enemy army.

7.8 VIBRATIONS

Vibration is a mechanical phenomenon in which oscillations occur about an equilibrium point if a disturbance is caused in a body.

The oscillations may be random or periodic.

Sound waves are generated by vibrating objects, such as the vocal cords that vibrate to produce our voice.

Vibrations can be of three types : (1) free or natural, (2) damped, and (3) forced.

(1) Free or Natural Vibrations

Free vibrations occur when a mechanical system is set off with an initial input and then allowed to oscillate freely. For example, consider a child sitting on a swing. When the swing is pulled back and then let go, it moves backward and forward freely. These are natural vibrations.

The vibrations produced in a body on being slightly disturbed and which remain sustained in absence of any external force are known as free or natural vibrations.

Bodies with free vibrations have a definite frequency and time period, depending on their shape, size and structure. The frequency of a freely vibrating body is called its natural frequency.

NOTE

In free vibrations, the amplitude and frequency remain constant, in absence of any resistance. Theoretically, free vibrations are possible only in vacuum. The presence of medium (such as air) offers resistance due to which the energy of the body and its amplitude of vibration do not remain constant but gradually decrease with time. An ideal free vibration cannot be realised in practice.

Fig. 7.2 shows the displacement-time graph for free vibrations of a body in an ideal condition (*i.e.* in vacuum).

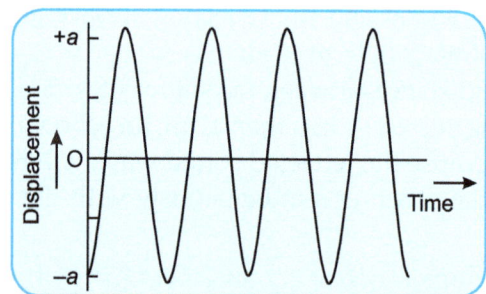

Fig. 7.2 : Displacement-time graph for free vibration (in vacuum).

Examples :

1. A simple pendulum : A simple pendulum vibrates to and fro, about its mean position, if the bob of the pendulum is slightly disturbed from its mean position. The frequency of vibration of a simple pendulum depends on its length (l) and acceleration due to gravity (g) at that place. At a given place, different pendulums with different lengths will vibrate with different frequencies. The frequency of a simple pendulum is given by the following equation,

$$\nu = \frac{1}{2\pi}\sqrt{\frac{g}{l}} \qquad \text{...(7.5)}$$

The smaller the length of a pendulum, higher will be its frequency. Thus, if at a place on the Earth's surface where $g = 9.8$ m s^{-2} and the length of the pendulum is 0.25 m, then its natural frequency will be 1 Hz.

2. Musical Instruments :

(a) Stringed Instruments : When the strings of a guitar, sitar or violin are plucked, they begin to vibrate with a natural frequency. The frequency of these vibrations depends on the length (l), radius (r) and tension (T) of the string. The frequency of these strings is given by the equation,

$$v = \frac{1}{2l}\sqrt{\frac{T}{\pi r^2 d}} \quad ...(7.6)$$

Here, d is the density of the material of which the string is made up of. The material of string is constant for a given instrument and thus the density. $\pi r^2 d$ represents the mass of unit length of the string. From Equation (7.6), the frequency is inversely proportional to the length $\left(v \propto \frac{1}{l}\right)$ and square root of radius of the string $\left(v \propto \frac{1}{\sqrt{r^2}}\right)$ but directly proportional to the square root of tension in the string, $(v \propto \sqrt{T})$. The smaller the length and radius of the string or more the tension in the string, higher is the frequency produced.

(b) Piano : When the keys of a piano are pressed, various strings begin to vibrate with their natural frequencies.

(c) Flute or organ pipe : An organ pipe is a simple instrument with holes that vibrate when air passes through a narrow slit at its top. The natural frequency of its vibration is inversely proportional to the length of column of air passing through it $(v \propto 1/l)$. The frequency can be changed by changing the length of air column. Thus, by opening one or more holes present on it, its frequency can be increased.

3. Stretched string : A string, when fixed at both ends, can vibrate when plucked at any point between its ends. It can vibrate in different modes, depending on the point where it is plucked. The different modes

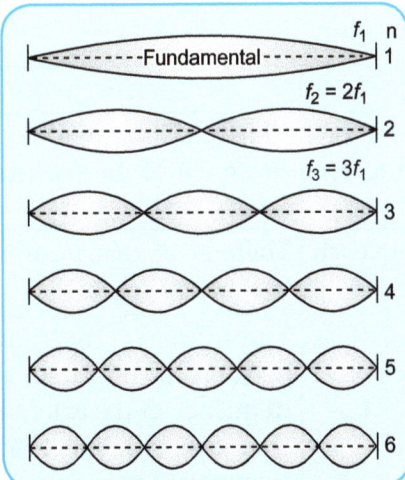

Fig. 7.3 : Different modes of vibration in a string.

of vibration in a string are of frequencies in ratio 1 : 2 : 3 : 4 ... and so on. For example, if it is plucked at half the length of string from one end (*i.e.* in the middle), it will vibrate in one loop with frequency v or f known as *principal note* or *fundamental/first harmonic*. The frequency will vary depending on the number of loops of vibration, which in turn depends on the point on the string where it is plucked. If the string is plucked at one-fourth length of string from any end, it will vibrate in two loops with frequency $2f$ (Fig. 7.3). It is called the *first subsidiary vibration* or *second harmonic*. If it vibrates in three loops, which happens when it is plucked at one-sixth length of the string from one end, then the frequency is $3f$ and is called *second subsidiary vibration* or *third harmonic* and so on.

4. Spring : When a spring, with a load suspended from it, is stretched (or compressed) and then released, it begins to vibrate. Its frequency depends on the mass of the suspended load (m) and hardness of the spring (k). If the mass is decreased, the frequency will increase $\left(v \propto \sqrt{k/m}\right)$ and vice versa. Thus, the frequency will be different for a spring with different loads and also for same load in different springs.

5. A tuning fork : When a tuning fork is struck against a rubber pad, it begins to vibrate with its natural frequency and produces a sensation of sound to our ears. The vibration produced is of single frequency and is called a *pure note*.

6. A metal blade : When a metal blade clamped at one of its ends is gently disturbed, it begins to vibrate. The frequency of the blade can be increased or decreased by changing its length as frequency is inversely proportional to the length.

(2) Damped Vibrations

The amplitude of any freely vibrating body decreases with time due to the resisting force exerted by the surrounding medium and the body stops vibrating after sometime. However, the time period or frequency of vibration remains the same, *i.e.* the motion is periodic in nature.

The periodic vibrations of continuously decreasing amplitude due to the presence of resisting forces are called damped vibrations.

It has been found that the resisting or frictional force is proportional to the velocity of the body and the nature of surrounding medium such as density and viscosity. Under the influence of frictional force, the vibrating body continuously loses its energy and thus its amplitude also decreases gradually, until it comes to rest. The energy from the vibrating body is lost in the form of heat energy and gets dissipated to the surrounding medium.

Fig. 7.4 shows the displacement–time graph for damped vibrations of a body.

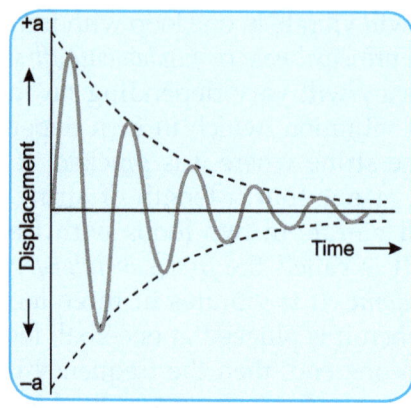

Fig. 7.4 : Displacement–time graph for damped vibrations.

Examples :
1. Vibrations of a simple pendulum in air.
2. Vibrations of a tuning fork in air.
3. Vibrations of musical instruments in air.
4. Vibrations of a swing in air.

(3) Forced Vibrations

Due to the resisting force of surrounding medium (damping), a freely vibrating body cannot maintain constant amplitude of vibration. In order to maintain constant amplitude of vibration in a body, an external periodic force needs to be applied, which can compensate for the loss of energy in each vibration caused by the damping forces. This external periodic force is called the *driving force* and the vibrations produced by the driving force are called *forced vibrations*.

The vibrations that take place in a body under the influence of an external periodic force are called forced vibrations.

Characteristics of forced vibrations :
1. Under the influence of external periodic force, a body does not vibrate with its natural frequency but acquires the frequency of the external periodic force.
2. The magnitude of amplitude of vibration depends on the frequency of the driving force, although it remains constant with time.
3. The amplitude of oscillations is very small if the frequency of external force is different from the natural frequency of the body.
4. The amplitude of oscillations is very large if the frequency of external force is same as that of the natural frequency of the body.

Examples :
1. Musical instruments, such as sitar, guitar and violin, consist of a set of stretched strings mounted on a *hollow soundbox* containing air. When the strings of these instruments are set into vibration by either strumming or plucking, these vibrations get transferred to the air in the hollow soundbox of the instrument. The vibrations produced in the air are the forced vibrations. Due to the large volume of air present in the soundbox, the forced vibrations have more energy. This causes an increase in the amplitude and thus a loud sound is produced.
2. When the stem of a vibrating tuning fork is pressed against a tabletop or a large hollow box, the tabletop or the box is forced to vibrate with the frequency of the tuning fork. Due to the large surface area of the table or air in the box, the forced vibrations have a much greater energy than the vibrations of tuning fork. As a result, a loud sound is heard.
3. In loudspeakers, headphones and microphones, a thin, semi-rigid membrane called the diaphragm is attached to the voice coil. This coil moves in a magnetic field, forcing the diaphragm to vibrate, thereby producing sound.

Comparison of Types of Vibration

Free vibrations	Damped vibrations	Forced vibrations
These vibrations occur in the absence of any resisting force.	These vibrations occur when there is a resisting force opposing the free vibrations.	These vibrations occur in the presence of an external periodic force.
The energy of these vibrations remains constant.	There is some loss of energy in each vibration, in the form of heat.	There is an increase in energy due to these vibrations.
The frequency of vibration is equal to the natural frequency and remains constant.	The frequency of vibration is less than the natural frequency and remains constant.	The frequency of vibration may be more or less than the natural frequency of the external force and changes with the change in the frequency of driving force.
The amplitude of vibration remains constant.	The amplitude of vibration decreases gradually with time.	The amplitude of vibration may be small or large, depending on the frequency of the driving force.

7.9 RESONANCE

Resonance is a special type of *forced vibrations* that occurs when the frequency of the applied external periodic force is equal to the integral multiple of the natural frequency of the body. The amplitude of these vibrations is very large and results in a large sound. These vibrations are known as *resonant vibrations*.

Resonance can be defined as a phenomenon in which the frequency of an external (or driving) force is equal to the natural frequency of the body on which the force acts, thereby leading to vibrations with an increased amplitude.

It can also be defined as, "a phenomenon in which a vibrating system or external force drives another system to oscillate with greater amplitude at a specific preferential frequency."

Experiments to Demonstrate Resonance

1. Resonance with tuning forks : Take two identical tuning forks X and Y, each of same frequency, and mount them on two separate soundboxes. Place the boxes in such a way that their open ends face each other, as shown in Fig. 7.5. Strike one of the prongs of a tuning fork, say X, with a rubber pad so that it starts vibrating.

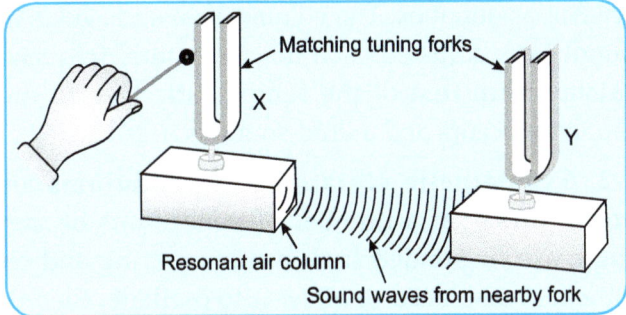

Fig. 7.5 : Resonance with tuning forks.

It is observed that the other tuning fork, *i.e.* fork Y, also starts to vibrate and produces a loud sound.

Explanation : On striking the prong of tuning fork X, the vibrations produced are transferred to its soundbox. Due to a large surface area of air in the box, the forced vibrations have large amplitude. These vibrations in turn transfer the energy to the soundbox of tuning fork Y. This results in vibration of air present inside it with the same frequency as that of tuning fork X. The frequency of these vibrations is exactly same as that of tuning fork Y and thus picks up these vibrations and starts vibrating due to resonance.

2. Resonance with simple pendulum : Take a thin stretched wire or a string between any two points. Suspend four pendulums A, B, C and D from this wire such that the length of pendulums A and C is equal, the length of pendulum B is longer and the length of pendulum D is smaller, as shown in Fig. 7.6. The natural frequencies of pendulums A and C will be same, pendulum B will be less than A or C due to longer length and pendulum D will be more due to shorter length.

Now, displace the pendulum A on one side, normal to its length, so that it starts oscillating with its natural frequency.

It is observed that all the pendulums start oscillating in a few moments. However, the pendulums A and C oscillate with equal and greater amplitude and are in same phase, that is, they reach their extreme positions simultaneously, whereas pendulums B and D oscillate with smaller amplitude and are not in same phase as that of A or C.

Explanation : When pendulum A is made to oscillate, its vibrations are transferred to the other three pendulums through the wire. The pendulums B and D oscillate with smaller amplitude due to forced vibrations as their natural requencies do not match (different lengths), whereas the pendulum C comes in a state of resonance due to the same frequency as that of A (same lengths). Due to resonance, the amplitude of vibration is large in pendulums A and C.

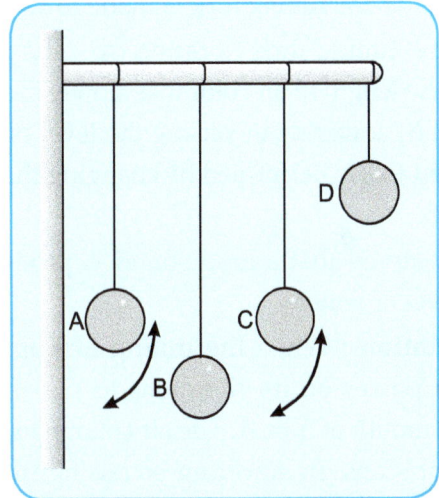

Fig. 7.6 : Forced and resonant vibrations of simple pendulums.

3. Resonance in air column : A *resonance tube* is used for studying resonance in air column. It consists of a long narrow cylindrical glass tube A fixed on a clamp stand. This glass tube is connected at its lower end to a vessel B through rubber tube. The vessel B is movable, that is, it can be clamped to a desirable height and is known as *reservoir*. Both the tube and vessel are filled partially with water. A tuning fork is held above the tube A, close to its mouth, such that its tube works as a *closed-end air pipe* (Fig. 7.7). An air column is formed in this tube between the surface of water and its mouth. When the tuning fork is made to vibrate by striking it with a rubber pad, the air column formed in the tube is forced to vibrate with its natural frequency. This frequency depends on the length of the air column. The length of the air column in tube A can be increased (or decreased) by moving up (or down) the reservoir vessel B.

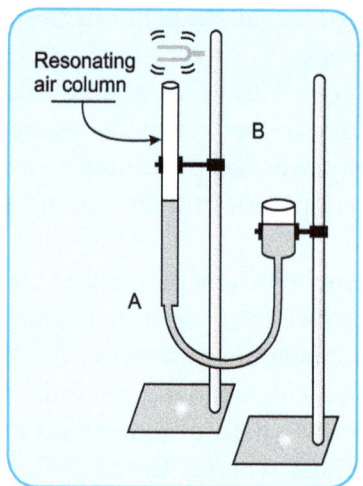

Fig. 7.7 : Resonance in air column with one end closed.

In the beginning, the tube A is filled with water up to the top and the tuning fork is made to vibrate.

With the tuning fork vibrating over the mouth of the tube, the length of air column is slowly increased or decreased by lowering or raising the level of water in tube A, and this is performed by changing the position of vessel B.

It is observed that a loud sound is produced at a certain level of water.

Explanation : When the tuning fork is made to vibrate, it passes on its vibrations to the air column inside the mouth of tube A. The air column experiences forced vibrations. By lowering or raising the level of water in the tube, the length of air column is increased or decreased. This changes the frequency of air column. At a certain length of air column, a loud sound is heard. This is the level at which the natural frequency of air column equals the frequency of the tuning fork and thus resonance occurs.

From this experiment, it can be concluded that for a resonance to occur, the natural frequency of a given body must be equal to the integral multiple of the frequency of the vibrating body.

Difference between Forced and Resonant Vibrations

Forced vibrations	Resonant vibrations
These vibrations of a body are produced by an external periodic force that has a frequency different from the natural frequency of the body.	These vibrations of a body are produced by an external periodic force that has a frequency exactly equal to the natural frequency of the body.
The amplitude of vibration is usually small.	The amplitude of vibration is very large.
The vibrations produced in the body are out of phase with the external periodic force.	The vibrations produced in the body are in phase with the external periodic force.
Once the external periodic force ceases to act, these vibrations last for a very small time.	These vibrations last for a long time even after the external periodic force has ceased to act.

Examples of resonance :

1. Resonance in air column and tuning fork : A tuning fork is often mounted on a hollow box that serves as a soundbox. The volume of air enclosed in the soundbox is adjusted such that its natural frequency matches with that of the tuning fork. Due to this, resonance occurs and a loud sound is heard.

2. Sympathetic vibrations of pendulums and tuning forks : If a number of pendulums of same length are suspended from a rubber string and one of them is displaced to allow it to oscillate, then the other pendulums also start vibrating as their natural frequencies match the oscillating pendulum. They

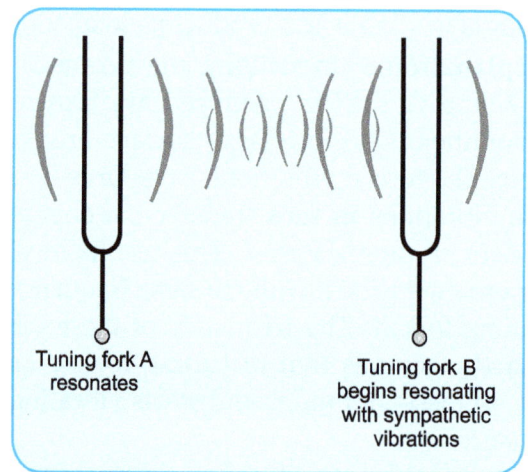

Fig. 7.8 : Sympathetic vibrations of tuning fork.

vibrate with large amplitude due to resonance and also are in phase, *i.e.* they oscillate in the same direction.

These vibrations that occur in the other pendulums without being displaced or touched are known as *sympathetic vibrations*. Sympathetic vibrations are also observed in two similar tuning forks placed at a distance when one of them is made to vibrate (Fig. 7.8).

3. Vehicles : Resonance is common in vehicles and parts of machines. When a vehicle such as a motorcycle, car or train is driven, the piston of the engine vibrates, whose frequency is dependent on the speed of the vehicle. The vibrations of the engine piston are forced on to other parts of the vehicle. The frequency of these vibrations of the engine might match the natural frequency of other parts of the vehicle, such as the frame of a motorcycle at a particular speed. This occurs at some particular speed of the vehicle and results in resonance. Due to resonance, a loud sound is then heard.

If any of the parts of a vehicle in which resonant vibrations are produced are not fixed tightly, then these parts may drop down due to the force of these high-energy vibrations. When resonant vibrations occur, the speed of the vehicle is often changed to avoid loud sound and damage to any of the parts of the machine.

Similarly, loud sound due to resonance is heard in different types of machines.

4. Musical instruments : The strings of musical instruments by themselves produce a feeble sound that cannot be heard from a far distance. Thus, most musical instruments are provided with a hollow chamber called the soundbox, which serves as a reservoir of air. It is the natural frequency of air column in this box that matches the frequency of vibrating strings of instruments.

Similarly, brass instruments such as a saxophone involve blowing of air into a mouthpiece. The vibrations of the air in the lips against the mouthpiece produce a range of frequencies. One of the frequencies in the range of frequencies matches the natural frequency of the air column inside of the brass instrument. This forces the air inside of the column into resonance vibrations.

The result of resonance is always a big vibration, which results in a loud sound.

5. Dancing glasses : It is often observed that when a particular note is struck on playing any musical instrument, old glasses or other cutlery pieces nearby begin to vibrate as their natural frequency matches the frequency of the particular note. Due to the phenomenon of resonance, the vibrations in these glasses are so large that they might even break.

6. Suspension bridge : When a troop of soldiers cross a suspension bridge, they are often asked to break their steps. This is because when the soldiers march together in steps, then their vibrations are in phase, resulting in forced vibration in the bridge. The frequency of these forced vibrations might match the frequency of the steps of soldiers, resulting in resonance. The vibrations due to resonance will be of large amplitude and might result in bridge collapsing. To avoid this collapse, the soldiers break their steps.

7. Resonance in electromagnetic waves : The phenomenon of resonance is not only confined to sound waves but also to electromagnetic waves such as radio waves and microwaves, which are used in television broadcasting and satellite communication. When a radio station broadcasts at a certain frequency, these vibrations are transferred to the antenna and produces forced vibrations. When a person tunes a radio, he merely changes the frequency of his radio set. When the frequency of a radio set matches the frequency of a broadcasting station, resonance occurs. The energy of the signal received from the waves due to resonant vibrations is then amplified, resulting in sound.

7.10 APPLICATIONS OF NATURAL, DAMPED, FORCED VIBRATIONS AND RESONANCE

1. Natural Vibrations : These are used in musical instruments such as piano, flute, guitar etc.

2. Damped Vibrations : Such vibrations are observed in doors with some automatic closing arrangement and vibrations of rigid body.

3. Forced Vibrations : Such vibrations are observed in loudspeakers, headphone and microphones.

4. Resonance : It is used in time keeping mechanisms of modern clocks and watches. Resonance is also used, in the building of bridges over the river magnetic resonance imaging, microwave cooking.

ILLUSTRATIVE EXAMPLES

1. The wavelength and frequency of a sound wave in a certain medium is 25 cm and 1,500 Hz. Keeping the same medium, if the wavelength is changed to 30 cm, calculate the (a) velocity of sound and (b) new frequency.

   Solution :
   (a) Given : $\lambda = 25$ cm $= 0.25$ m, $\nu = 1,500$ Hz
   Using the relation, $v = \nu\lambda$,
   $\therefore \quad v = 1,500 \times 0.25 = 375$ m s^{-1}
   (b) Given : $\lambda = 30$ cm $= 0.30$ m, $v = 375$ m s^{-1}
   From the relation, $v = \nu\lambda$
   $\nu = v/\lambda = 375/0.30 = 1,250$ Hz

2. A sound wave has a frequency of 3 kHz and a wavelength of 50 cm. How long will it take for the wave to travel a distance of 2 km?
Solution : Given : v = 3 kHz = 3,000 Hz, λ = 50 cm = 0.50 m, d = 2 km = 2,000 m
Using the relation, $v = \nu\lambda$,
$$v = 3,000 \times 0.50$$
$$= 1,500 \text{ m s}^{-1}$$
Time required for the wave to travel
$$= \frac{d}{v} = \frac{2000}{1500} = 1.33 \text{ s}$$

3. An echo is heard in 3 s after the emission of sound. If the speed of sound in air is 340 m s^{-1}, what is the distance of the reflecting surface from the source?
Solution : Given : t = 3 s, v = 340 m s^{-1}
If d is the distance of the reflecting surface from the source, then the total distance travelled to and fro by sound is $2d$.
$$\text{Speed} = \frac{\text{Total distance travelled}}{\text{Total time taken}}$$
i.e. $$v = \frac{2d}{t}$$
i.e. $$d = \frac{v \times t}{2}$$
i.e. $$d = \frac{340 \times 3}{2} = 510 \text{ m}$$

4. A man stands 70 m in front of a large wall and claps about 31 times after each successive echo. If the total time taken for these numbers of claps is 12.5 s, calculate the speed of sound.
Solution : Given : d = 70 m, t = 12.5 s
Time interval between 1st and 31st clap = 12.5 s
Thus, time interval between any two successive claps = $\frac{12.5}{30}$. This is the time taken to hear the echo.
$$\text{Speed} = \frac{\text{Total distance travelled}}{\text{Total time taken}}$$
i.e. $$v = \frac{2d}{t}$$
i.e. $$v = \frac{2 \times 70}{12.5/30} = 336 \text{ m s}^{-1}$$

5. A boy stands between two parallel cliffs and fires a gun. He hears two successive echoes, one after 2 s and the other after 4 s. Calculate the distance between the two cliffs. Take speed of sound in air as 330 m s^{-1}.
Solution : Given : t_1 = 2 s, t_2 = 4 s, v = 330 m s^{-1}
Distance of body from nearer cliff,
$$d_1 = \frac{v \times t_1}{2} = \frac{330 \times 2}{2} = 330 \text{ m}$$
Distance of boy from the farther cliff,
$$d_2 = \frac{v \times t_2}{2} = \frac{330 \times 4}{2} = 660 \text{ m}$$
Total distance between the two cliffs
$$d_1 + d_2 = 330 + 660 = 990 \text{ m}$$

6. A person is standing between two parallel cliffs that are separated by a distance of 1,000 m. He claps his hands and hears the first echo after 2 s. If the speed of sound is 330 m s^{-1}, after how much time will he hear the second echo?
Solution : Given : Total distance between the two cliffs = 1,000 m, t_1 = 2 s, v = 330 m s^{-1}.
Let the distance of the person from the nearer cliff be x m, i.e. $d_1 = x$ m.
Then, the distance of the person from the farther cliff, $d_2 = (1,000 - x)$ m
$$\text{Speed} = \frac{\text{Total distance travelled}}{\text{Total time taken}}$$
∵ $$v = \frac{2d}{t}$$
i.e. $$d = \frac{v \times t}{2}$$
i.e. $$d_1 = \frac{v \times t_1}{2} = \frac{330 \times 2}{2} = 330 \text{ m}$$
i.e. $$x = 330 \text{ m}$$
Now, $d_2 = (1,000 - x) = (1,000 - 330) = 670$ m
$$t_2 = \frac{2d_2}{v} = \frac{2 \times 670}{330} = 4.06 \text{ s}$$

7. A man standing in front of a cliff fires a gun. An echo is heard after 5 s. On moving 85 m closer to the cliff, he again fires a gun and hears an echo after 4.5 s. Calculate (a) the distance of man from the cliff to his initial position and (b) the speed of sound.
Solution : Let the position of man be x m from the cliff, i.e. $d_1 = x$ m and v be the speed of sound.
Given t_1 = 5 s
$$\text{Speed} = \frac{\text{Total distance travelled}}{\text{Total time taken}}$$
i.e. $$v = \frac{2 \times x}{5} = \frac{2x}{5} \quad ...(i)$$
Given t_2 = 4.5 s
The man moves 85 m closer to the cliff, so $d_2 = (x - 85)$ m
∴ $$v = \frac{2(x-85)}{4.5} = \frac{2x - 170}{4.5} \quad ...(ii)$$
Comparing equation (i) and (ii),

$$\frac{2x}{5} = \frac{2x-170}{4.5}$$

i.e. $\quad 9x = 10x - 850$

i.e. $\quad x = 850$ m

The distance of man from the cliff to his initial position is 850 m.

Substituting the value of x in equation (i), we get

$$v = \frac{2x}{5} = \frac{2 \times 850}{5} = 340 \text{ m s}^{-1}$$

8. A sonar device on a submarine sends out a signal and receives an echo about 3 s later. If the speed of ultrasonic waves in water is 1,450 m s^{-1}, find the distance between the submarine and the reflecting object.

   Solution : Given : $t = 3$ s, $v = 1,450$ m s^{-1}.
   Total distance travelled by the ultrasonic waves is $2d$.
   Since Distance = Speed × Time
   ∴ $\quad 2d = 1450 \times 3$
   i.e. $\quad d = \frac{4350}{2} = 2175$ m

9. The stem of a vibrating tuning fork is pressed against a hollow matchbox and a hollow shoebox. (a) Name the type of vibrations that the tuning fork sets these boxes to. (b) In which box will the sound be louder? (c) If an exactly similar vibrating tuning fork is brought close to this fork, what will be the effect?

   Solution :
   (a) The vibrations that the tuning fork sets to these boxes are known as forced vibrations.
   (b) The sound produced by pressing the tuning fork on the shoebox will be louder because its size is large and the volume of air contained in it is more than that contained in a matchbox. The more the volume of air that can be set into vibration, louder is the sound produced.
   (c) If an exactly similar vibrating tuning fork is brought close to the original fork, the natural frequencies of the two forks will be same, resulting in resonance. Due to resonance, a loud sound of very large amplitude will be produced.

10. The figure given below shows different modes of vibration of a stretched string.

    (a) Which figure represents the frequency of a principal note?

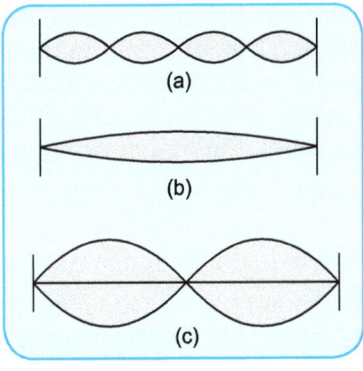

    (b) Which of these vibrations has the largest amplitude?
    (c) What is the ratio of wavelength between vibration (a) and (b)?

    Solution : (a) Figure (b) represents the frequency of a principal note, as it vibrates in a single loop.
    (b) The vibrations in Figure (c) is of largest amplitude.
    (c) If f is the frequency of the principal note in Figure (b), then the frequency of note in Figure (a) will be $4f$. It represents a third subsidiary of principal note.
    Ratio of frequency of vibration (a) to vibration (b) will be $4f : f = 4 : 1$.
    Since wavelength $\lambda = v/\nu$, i.e. an inverse relation with frequency.
    Thus, the ratio of wavelengths of vibration (a) : (b) = 1 : 4.

11. A tuning fork vibrates with a natural frequency of 512 Hz. If two strings, one of frequency 256 Hz and the other of frequency 512 Hz, are brought in the vicinity of this tuning fork, what would be the effect in each case?

    Solution : The tuning fork will cause forced vibrations in each string. The amplitude of vibrations in the string of frequency 256 Hz would be very small, whereas the amplitude of vibrations in the string of 512 Hz would be very large due to the phenomenon of resonance. Since the natural frequency of tuning fork and second string being exactly same, they will result in resonance.

12. A vibrating tuning fork is placed over a mouth of a burette that is fully filled with water. Its stopcock is opened and water is allowed to fall gradually. What would be the possible observation?

    Solution : When the water level begins to fall due to opening of stopcock, the length of air column inside the burette begins to increase. At a particular water level, the length of air column would be such that its natural frequency would match the natural frequency of the vibrating tuning fork. This will result in the phenomenon of resonance, giving rise to a loud sound.

As the water level is allowed to fall further, at a certain level, the length of air column inside the burette would be three times the previous length. At this stage too, the natural frequency of air would be equal to the natural frequency of the vibrating tuning fork and thus resonance will occur again.

EXERCISE 7(A)

1. Define a wave. What are the two broad types of waves?
2. What is meant by a transverse wave? Draw a diagram.
3. Draw a diagram of a longitudinal wave.
4. Define the following terms in relation to a wave :
   (a) amplitude, (b) frequency, (c) wavelength and (d) wave velocity.
5. State any three characteristics of a wave.
6. What is the relation between frequency, wavelength and wave velocity of a wave?
   Ans : $v = \nu\lambda$, where v is the wave velocity, ν is the frequency and λ is the wavelength of a wave.
7. State the two factors on which the speed of a sound wave travelling in a medium depends on?
   Ans : Elasticity and density of the medium.
8. State any three differences between light waves and sound waves.
9. What is meant by reflection of sound waves?
10. (a) What is an echo ?
    (b) State two conditions for an echo to take place.
11. Why will an echo not be heard when the distance between the source of sound and the reflecting surface is 10 m?
12. What is meant by reverberation? How is it different from an echo?
13. Explain how can the method of echo be used to determine the speed of sound in air?
14. State any two applications of an echo.
15. What is the principle on which SONAR is based?
16. (a) Name the waves used for echo depth sounding.
    (b) Give one reason for their use for the above purpose.
    (c) Why are the waves mentioned by you not audible to us ?
17. Name the type of waves that are used in sound ranging. Why are these waves not audible to us? Give one use of sound ranging.
18. State the use of echo by animals such as bat and dolphin.
19. How is the echo useful to fishermen?
20. What is the use of echo in medical science?
21. What is the principle of radar?
22. What is meant by free vibrations of a body? Give an example.
23. Name the quantities that remain constant in free vibrations.
    Ans : Amplitude and frequency
24. What is the condition essential for free vibrations of a body?
    Ans : It occurs only in vacuum.
25. Why is it not possible to have an ideal free vibration in actual practice?
26. (a) Draw a graph between displacement and the time for a body executing free vibrations.
    (b) Where can a body execute free vibrations ?
27. What is meant by natural frequency? State the factors on which it depends.
28. State the factors on which the frequency of a simple pendulum depends?
    Ans : Length of the pendulum and acceleration due to gravity
29. If the length of a simple pendulum is four times the original length, what will be the effect on its frequency?
    Ans : The frequency will get halved
30. State the factors on which the frequency of stringed instruments depend?
    Ans : Length, radius and tension of the string
31. Name one factor that affects the frequency of sound emitted due to vibrations in an air column.
    Ans : Length of air column
32. State two ways by which the frequency of transverse vibrations of a stretched string can be increased.
33. State one way by which the frequency of a note produced by a flute can be increased.
    Ans : By opening one or more holes of the flute
34. The figure below shows different modes of vibration of a string. (a) Which of these represents a principal note? (b) Which of these represents second harmonic? (c) If the frequency of principal note is f, what will be the frequency of vibration in mode (d)? (d) What is the ratio of wavelengths of note (b) and note (d)?

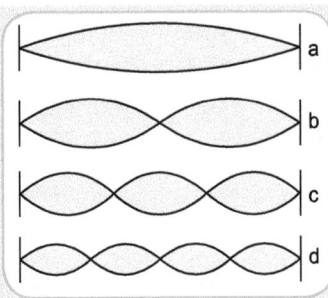

35. What is the purpose of strings of different thickness in a stringed instrument?
36. A metal blade, fixed at one end, is made to vibrate by gently pressing it. How can the frequency of these vibrations be increased?
    Ans : By decreasing the length of the blade
37. How can the frequency of a vibrating spring with a suspended load be decreased?
38. What are damped vibrations? Give an example.
39. What are the differences between free vibrations and damped vibrations?
40. The given diagram shows the displacement-time graph for a vibrating body. (a) Name the type of vibrations produced by the vibrating body. (b) Give one example of a body producing such vibrations. (c) Why is the amplitude of the wave gradually decreasing? (d) What will happen to the vibrations of the body after sometime?

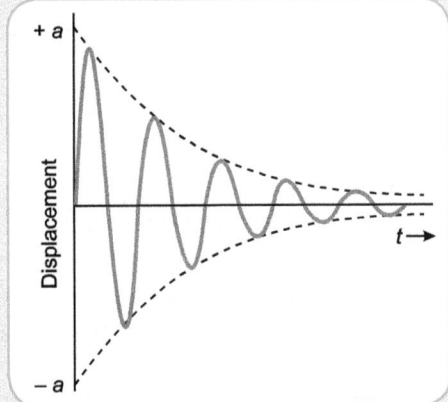

41. What are forced vibrations? Explain with an example.
42. State the characteristics of forced vibrations.
43. When a vibrating tuning fork is pressed against a tabletop, the table also begins to vibrate. Name the type of vibrations executed by the table.
44. What are the differences between free vibrations and forced vibrations?
45. What is meant by resonance? Explain with the help of a simple experiment.
46. What is the condition necessary for resonance to take place?
47. When acoustic resonance takes place, a loud sound is heard. Explain why does this happen?
48. Which of the following frequencies does a tuning fork of 256 Hz resonate : 288 Hz, 314 Hz, 333 Hz and 512 Hz?
49. State two ways in which resonance differs from forced vibrations.
50. The figure below shows three tuning forks A, B and C, each mounted on a hollow soundbox, with open ends of box A facing box B in one case and facing box C in the second case. (a) If the fork A is set into vibration, what will be your observations in each case? (b) In which case will the amplitude of forced vibrations be large? (c) Will resonance take place in any of the two cases?

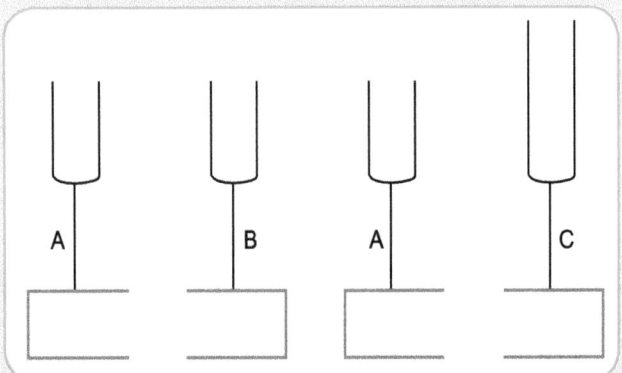

51. In the diagram given below, A, B, C, D are four pendulums suspended from the same elastic string PQ. The length of A and C are equal to each other while the length of pendulum B is smaller than that of D. Pendulum A is set into a mode of vibrations.

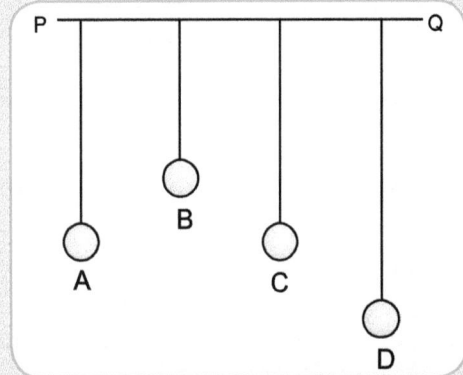

(a) Name the type of vibrations taking place in pendulums B and D ?
(b) What is the state of pendulum C ?
(c) State the reason for the type of vibrations in pendulums B and C ?

52. A vibrating tuning fork is placed over the mouth of a burette filled with water. The tap of the

burette is opened and the water level gradually starts falling. It is found that the sound from the tuning fork becomes very loud for particular length of the water column. (a) Name the phenomenon taking place when this happens. (b) Why does the sound become very loud for this length of the water column?

53. Why does the phenomenon of resonance occur multiple times when the level of water in a resonance tube with a vibrating tuning fork close to its mouth is gradually decreased?

54. Explain the following :
    (a) Stringed musical instruments, such as the guitar, are provided with a hollow box.
    (b) Soldiers often break their steps when their troop passes over a suspension bridge.
    (c) A rattling sound is often heard when a vehicle is driven at a particular speed.
    (d) Old glasses often break when some kind of music is played near them.

55. (a) Name the phenomenon involved in tuning a radio set to a particular station.
    (b) Define the phenomenon named by you in part 9 (a) above.
    (c) What do you understand by loudness of sound ?
    (d) In which units is the loudness of sound measured ?

MULTIPLE CHOICE QUESTIONS

1. The minimum time for reflected sound to reach after the original sound is heard to hear an echo is :
   (a) 0.2 s (b) 0.1 s
   (c) 0.4 s (d) 0.3 s
   Ans : (b)

2. The waves used in radar are :
   (a) infrasonic waves (b) ultrasonic waves
   (c) radio waves (d) light waves
   Ans : (c)

3. A simple pendulum oscillating with a certain frequency ceases to oscillate after some time. The vibrations executed are :
   (a) free vibrations (b) damped vibrations
   (c) forced vibrations (d) resonant vibrations
   Ans : (b)

4. Resonance is a special case of :
   (a) free vibrations (b) damped vibrations
   (c) forced vibrations (d) none of these
   Ans : (c)

5. A guitar of frequency 400 Hz will resonate with another guitar of frequency :
   (a) 100 Hz (b) 200 Hz
   (c) 400 Hz (d) 800 Hz
   Ans : (c)

NUMERICAL PROBLEMS

1. Calculate the wavelength of a sound whose frequency is 220 Hz and speed is 440 m s^{-1} in a given medium.
   Ans : 2 m

2. The maximum limit of sound that can be heard by a human ear has a frequency of 20,000 Hz. Calculate its corresponding wavelength, if the speed of sound in air is 330 m s^{-1}.
   Ans : 16.5 mm

3. An echo is heard in 6 s. What is the distance of reflecting surface from the source of sound if the speed of sound is 340 m s^{-1}?
   Ans : 1,020 m

4. Calculate the minimum distance required between the source of sound and the reflecting surface to hear an echo underwater, if the speed of sound in water is 1,450 m s^{-1}.
   Ans : 72.5 m

5. A man standing 25 m away from a wall produces a sound and receives the reflected sound. (a) Calculate the time after which he receives the reflected sound if the speed of sound in air is 350 m s^{-1}. (b) Will the man be able to hear a distinct echo? Give reason.
   Ans : (a) 0.143 s, (b) Yes

6. A sonar device on a submarine sends out a signal and receives an echo about 5 s later. Calculate the speed of sound in water if the distance of the object from the submarine is 3,625 m.
   Ans : 1,450 m s^{-1}

7. A sound made on the surface of a lake takes 3 s to reach a boatman. How much time will it take to reach a diver inside the water at the same depth? Velocity of sound in air is 330 m s^{-1}, velocity of sound in water is 1,450 m s^{-1}.
   Ans : 0.68 s

8. An observer stands at a certain distance away from a cliff and produces a loud sound. He hears the echo of the sound after 1.8 s. Calculate the distance between the cliff and the observer if the velocity of sound in air is 340 m s^{-1}.
   Ans : 306 m

9. A person standing between two vertical cliffs and 480 m from the nearest cliff shouts. He hears the first echo after 3 s and the second echo 2 s later. Calculate :
   (a) The speed of sound.
   (b) The distance of the other cliff from the person.
   Ans : (a) 320 m s^{-1}, (b) 800 m.

10. A man standing in front of a cliff fires a gun. An echo is heard after 3 s. On moving 80 m closer to the cliff, he again fires a gun and hears an echo after 2.5 s. Calculate (a) the distance of man from the cliff to his initial position and (b) the speed of sound.
    Ans : (a) 480 m, (b) 320 m s^{-1}

11. A simple pendulum has a frequency of 6 vibrations per second. An observer displaces the pendulum at rest and simultaneously fires a gun. He hears an echo from a wall when the pendulum completes 10 vibrations. Find the distance between the wall and the observer if the speed of sound is 330 m s^{-1} in air.
    Ans : 275 m

12. A ship sends ultrasonic waves to the bottom of the sea to locate a sunken ship. It takes 2.5 s to receive back the waves sent. If the velocity of these waves in seawater is 1,450 m s^{-1}, find the depth at which the sunken ship is located.
    Ans : 1,812.5 m

(B) CHARACTERISTICS OF SOUND

7.11 CHARACTERISTICS OF SOUND

There are three main characteristics of sound that help in differentiating any two sounds. These characteristics are (1) *loudness and intensity*, (2) *pitch* and (3) *quality* or *timbre*. These characteristics of a given sound can be deduced from its wave pattern.

Loudness and Intensity

Loudness is a property of sound that depends on the *amplitude* of a sound wave. It is an auditory perception to the ears.

Take two similar tuning forks A and B such that their frequencies are same. Strike tuning fork A *gently* in a rubber pad and bring it close to your ear. You will hear a *feeble* sound. Now, strike tuning fork B *hard* on the rubber pad and bring it close to your ear. You will hear a *loud* sound. Now, take tuning fork A, which was hit gently, and put its stem on a small hollow wooden box. Again you will hear a *loud* sound. In each of these cases, sound is heard but the loudness of sound is less in the first case as compared to second and third cases. This happens because large amount of air is set into vibration in the second and third cases. This difference in loudness is due to the *difference in amplitudes of vibration in these cases*. The waves of louder sound are of larger amplitude than waves of soft sound, as shown in Fig. 7.9.

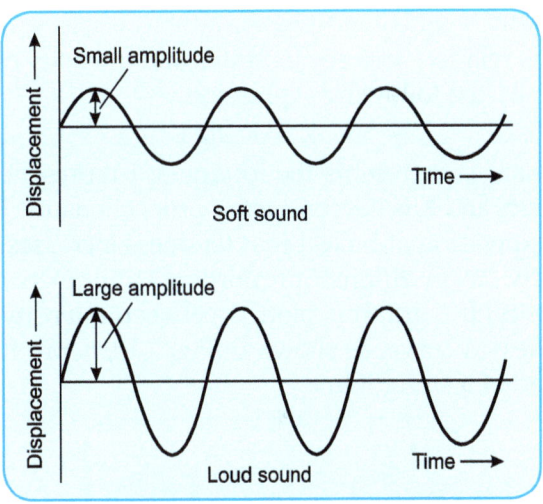

Fig. 7.9 : Soft and loud notes.

Loudness is the property of sound that enables to distinguish a loud sound from a faint sound when both the sounds have the same pitch and quality.

In general, the greater the mass of air that can be set into vibration, the louder will be the sound. Thus, *loudness of sound can be increased by increasing the mass of air.*

Example : The sound from a telephone earpiece is heard clearly only when it is placed close to the ear, whereas the sound from a loudspeaker can be heard from a much longer distance. The reason is that the telephone earpiece has only a small metal plate to vibrate for producing sound, while the loudspeaker has a large vibrating cone that sets a large mass of air into vibration.

The loudness of sound can be increased by increasing the input of energy.

Example : When we increase the volume control button on a TV set, the input of energy increases, resulting in louder sound.

Loudness is a *subjective quantity* that depends on the *response of the ear*. Its *objective measure* is called *intensity*.

Intensity of sound at a point of the medium is the amount of energy flowing per second normally across a unit area at that point.

Greater the energy carried by a sound wave, greater is the intensity of sound and hence louder to the ears.

Thus, *loudness and intensity are different*. Loudness depends on the energy as well as the response or sensitivity of the ears, whereas intensity is independent of the response of the ear. *Sound waves of different frequencies but same intensity have different loudness.* This may hold true even for a same listener as the sensitivity of ears is different for different frequencies. The maximum sensitivity for normal ears is at a frequency of 1 kHz.

The relation between loudness and intensity can be given by the following expression :

$$L = K \log I \qquad ...(7.7)$$

where L represents the loudness, I represents the intensity and K is the constant of proportionality. From this expression, it is clear that loudness increases non-linearly (*i.e.* in different proportions) with increase in intensity. If a graph is plotted between intensity and loudness, a curve, as shown in Fig. 7.10, is produced, instead of a straight line.

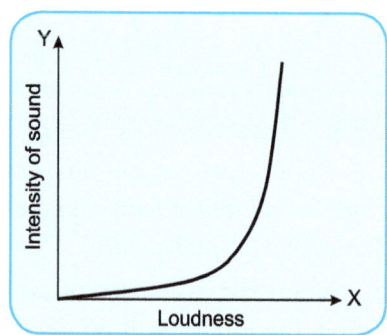

Fig. 7.10 : Intensity and loudness graph.

Factors Affecting the Loudness/Intensity of Sound

The following factors affect the loudness or intensity of sound at a given place :

1. Amplitude : Loudness (or intensity) is *directly proportional* to the square of amplitude of a given sound wave. Greater amplitude means a greater amount of energy and hence more intensity or louder sound.

2. Distance : Loudness is *inversely proportional* to the square of the distance of listener from the source.

Less is the distance between the source and the listener, louder or more intense is the sound. As the distance between the two (source and listener) increases, the loudness of sound decreases and becomes inaudible after a particular distance.

3. Surface area of vibrating body : Loudness is *directly proportional* to the surface area of the vibrating body. Larger the surface area, greater is the amount of energy and thus greater is the intensity and loudness. This is known from the examples of forced vibrations such as a tuning fork mounted on a soundbox or sound chamber in musical instruments. The large area of the box/chamber can accommodate a large volume of air and thus increases the loudness of sound.

4. Density of the medium : Loudness is *directly proportional* to the density of the medium, *i.e.* higher the density of the medium, greater is the loudness.

5. Resonant bodies : Loudness of a vibrating body depends on the presence of resonant bodies in its vicinity. If bodies with resonant vibrations are present near a vibrating body, then its loudness increases.

Units and Measurement of Loudness and Intensity

The unit for level of sound is *bel*. It signifies the *sound pressure* level. Each bel is subdivided into 10 decibels (abbreviated as dB). A change in sound level of 1 dB is the smallest change that a normal ear can detect.

The unit of loudness is *phon*. The phon and decibel scales are not identical. The two scales are equal for a sound of frequency 1,000 Hz or 1 kHz.

The unit of intensity is *watt per square metre* (W m^{-2}). The commonly used smaller unit of intensity is *microwatt per square metre* (μW m^{-2}).

The intensity of normal sound is approximately 10 μW m^{-2} and the minimum intensity of sound audible to the ears is 10^{-6} μW m^{-2}.

As described, loudness is related to intensity as follows :

$$L = K \log_{10} I$$

Let I_0 be the intensity and L_0 be the loudness of sound of a particular frequency f_0. At frequency f_1, let the intensity and loudness of sound be I_1 and L_1, respectively.

From the above relation,

$L_0 = K \log_{10} I_0$ and $L_1 = K \log_{10} I_1$

The difference in loudness of two sounds will be

$$L = L_1 - L_0$$

i.e. $\qquad L = K(\log_{10} I_1 - \log_{10} I_0)$

i.e. $\qquad L = K \log_{10}\left(\dfrac{I_1}{I_0}\right)$

The minimum intensity of sound audible to the ears is $10^{-6}\ \mu W\ m^{-2} = 10^{-12}\ W\ m^{-2}$. This value represents I_0, i.e. *reference intensity* at a frequency of 1 kHz. Hence, L represents the sound level, i.e.

$$L = K \log_{10}\left(\frac{I_1}{I_0}\right) \text{ bel}$$

If K is taken as 1, then

$$L = \log_{10}\left(\frac{I_1}{I_0}\right) \text{ bel}$$

i.e.
$$L = \left\{10\log_{10}\left(\frac{I_1}{I_0}\right)\right\} \times \frac{1}{10} \text{ bel}$$

i.e.
$$L = 10\log_{10}\left(\frac{I_1}{I_0}\right) \text{ decibel} \quad ...(7.8)$$

At the minimum intensity of audible sound, i.e. at I_0, the level of sound is zero, i.e. L = 0.

If sound level of 1 dB is considered, i.e. L = 1 dB, then

$$1 = 10\log_{10}\left(\frac{I_1}{I_0}\right)$$

i.e. $\log_{10}\left(\frac{I_1}{I_0}\right) = \frac{1}{10}$

i.e. $\left(\frac{I_1}{I_0}\right) = \text{anti log}(0.1) = 1.26$

i.e. $I_1 = 1.26\, I_0$ ...(7.9)

Thus, if $I_0 = 1\ W\ m^{-2}$, then $I_1 = 1.26\ W\ m^{-2}$, which implies that there is an increase in loudness of sound by 1 dB if intensity of sound increases by 0.26 W m^{-2} ($I_1 - I_0 = 1.26 - 1$) or 26 %.

From Equation (7.9) the decibel is defined as,

The change in level of loudness is said to be 1 dB when there is a 26% change in the intensity of sound.

If there is an increase in intensity by 100 times, the increase in sound level will be 20 dB (10 log 100 = 20). Similarly, if there is an increase in intensity by 10,000 times of the initial intensity, the increase in sound level will be 40 dB (10 log 10,000 = 40). Thus, if the intensity increases by 100 times (10,000/100), then loudness is doubled (40/20).

Table 7.1 : Various Sound Sources and their Sound Levels

Source of Sound	Sound level (in dB)
Dropping of pin	0
Breathing, rustling leaves	10
Broadcasting studio, ticking of watch	20
Whisper, library	30
Refrigerator	40
Normal conversation, moderate rainfall	50
Dishwasher, vacuum cleaner	60
Alarm clock, city traffic	70
Motorcycle, car	80
Truck	90
Noisy factory	100
Car horn, tools such as hammer	110
Rock concert, police car siren, thunder	120
Stadium crowd, ambulance siren	130
Jet aircraft	140
Shotgun blast	150

Do You Know ?

- The unit 'bel' was invented by engineers of the Bell telephone network in 1923 and named in honour of the inventor of the telephone, Alexander Graham Bell.
- Explosions create blast overpressure, which is the sudden pressure increase of the atmosphere. Blast overpressure also produces a loud noise, which at 160 dB will cause deafness, and at 200 dB can cause internal injuries, such as a ruptured lung, ultimately leading to death.

Pitch or Shrillness

Pitch of a sound, particularly a musical note, determines its sharpness and is related to the frequency of sound. This characteristic enables to differentiate between two sounds with equal loudness coming from sources of different frequencies.

Pitch is that characteristic of sound by virtue of which a sharp (or shrill) note can be differentiated from a flat (or grave) note.

A shrill sound is said to have a high pitch, whereas a *flat sound* is said to have a low pitch. The terms *treble* and *bass* are used to represent high and *low pitch*, respectively, in a television set or a tape recorder. The sound of a *tabla* is of low pitch and is represented by bass mode, whereas the sound of a *flute* is of high pitch and is represented by treble mode.

The pitch of a note depends on its frequency. The higher the frequency of a note, higher is the pitch or lower the wavelength of a note, higher is the pitch as frequency and wavelength are inversely related.

On a given instrument, two notes with same amplitude will differ in pitch if their vibrations are of different frequencies or wavelengths.

Take two tuning forks of different frequencies and hit them with a same amount of force on a rubber pad. The two forks will vibrate with same amplitude, but the sound of tuning fork of higher frequency will be shriller than the sound of tuning fork of lower frequency as shown in Fig. 7.11.

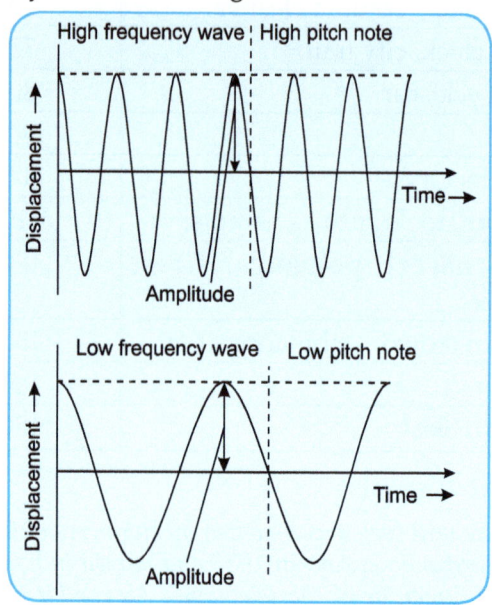

Fig. 7.11 : Waves of notes of different pitch.

Examples :

1. There are a number of strings in musical instruments such as piano, harmonium and guitar that are made up of varying thickness and of different tensions which results in different frequencies. If a thinner string or a string under high tension is made to vibrate, it will result in a note of higher pitch, whereas if a thicker string or a string under low tension is made to vibrate, it will result in a note of lower pitch.

2. In a flute, if the length of the vibrating air column is increased by closing one or more holes, then its frequency decreases, resulting in a note of lower pitch.

3. When a bucket is kept under a water tap, a sound of low pitch can be heard. As the level of water in the bucket rises, the length of air column decreases and causes increase in frequency of the sound. Due to increasing frequency, the pitch of the sound becomes higher and a shriller sound is heard. By hearing the sound from a distance, one can get an idea of the water level in the bucket. The sound is of high pitch (or high shrillness) when the water level is highest in the bucket.

4. A man with hoarse voice has a lower pitch, while a woman with shrill voice has a higher pitch.

Pitch is one's judgement on how high or low a sound is and is a *subjective entity* that is *non-measurable*, whereas *frequency* of a sound is an *objective entity* and is *measurable*.

The pitch of a sound is the sensation perceived by a listener; thus for a particular frequency, the pitch of a note may not be the same for different listeners. The frequency of sound depends on the source producing it and thus has a fixed value for a particular note. It will be same for different listeners.

Many people who are musically trained can detect a difference in frequency between two sounds that is as little as 2 Hz. Most people are capable of differentiating two sounds of frequency difference of more than 7 Hz, when played simultaneously.

Quality or Timbre

When different instruments such as guitar, violin and piano are played with same pitch (or same frequency) and same loudness, they can still be identified by hearing the sound even from a distance without seeing the instruments. The characteristic of musical sound that makes it possible is known as *quality* or *timbre*. This is because different waveforms are produced by different instruments. Thus, the quality of a sound depends on the waveform.

Quality is that characteristic of a sound by virtue of which two sounds of same pitch and same loudness, originating from two different sources (or instruments), can be distinguished.

A vibrating body has its characteristic waveform that is different from another vibrating body, and because of this characteristic, two sounds of same loudness and pitch can be differentiated.

Fig. 7.12 shows waveforms of three different sounds : *sine wave, square wave* and *triangular wave*. They have

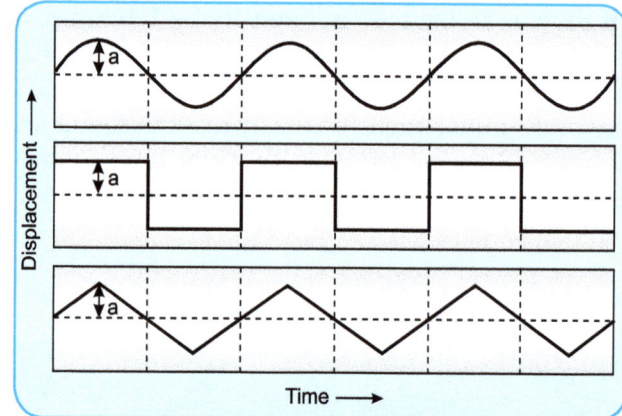

Fig. 7.12 : Different waveforms of different sounds with same frequency and same amplitude.

same amplitude and same frequency and thus same loudness and same pitch. Due to their difference in waveforms, a different sensation of sound is perceived by the ears.

Example : One can recognise the voice of a person even from a distance without seeing him, such as over a telephone, as the vibration produced by the vocal cords of every person has a typical waveform that differs from other persons.

In the case of musical instruments, the sound produced by them differ in (a) *wavelength (or frequency)*, (b) *loudness* and (c) *waveform*.

If the wavelength or frequency changes, it results in a change in pitch of the note. If the waveform changes, it results in a change in quality.

The sound produced by an instrument contains a number of vibrations of different frequencies and different amplitudes. The vibration of lowest frequency and maximum amplitude is known as *fundamental* or *principal vibration* and the vibrations that are integral multiple of this lowest frequency are known as *subsidiary* or *secondary vibrations* or *overtones*. Subsidiary notes have higher frequency and smaller amplitudes.

The presence of subsidiary vibrations along with the principal vibration (and thus their respective amplitudes) gives rise to a characteristic waveform of any sound.

Fig. 7.14 shows waveforms of different instruments. It can be seen from Fig. 7.13 that the note produced by a tuning fork is of a single frequency and thus is a pure note, generating a simple waveform or sine curve.

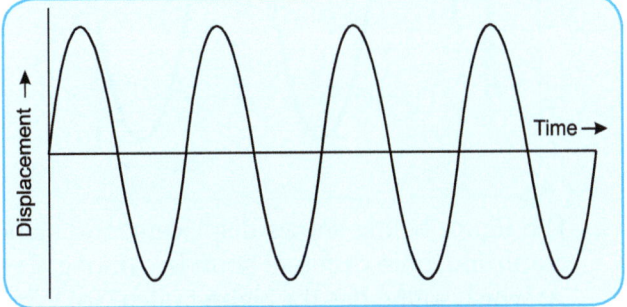

Fig. 7.13 : Waveform of a tuning fork.

Each of the waveforms of piano and guitar has same frequency and amplitude but consists of a mixture of subsidiary vibrations along with the principal vibration, making the waveform a complex one (Fig. 7.14). Also, it can be noticed that the waveform of guitar has more number of subsidiary vibrations as compared to that of a piano, and due to this, the sounds of these instruments can be easily distinguished even if they have same pitch and same loudness.

The quality of a sound is of subjective nature because it is not a measurable quantity, whereas the waveform is of objective nature.

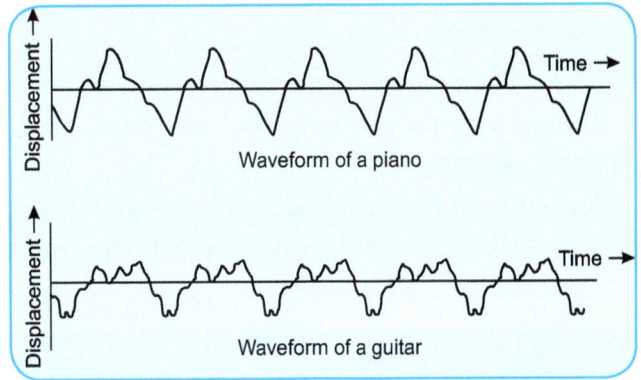

Fig. 7.14 : Waveforms of different instruments.

7.12 MUSIC AND NOISE

All audible sounds can be classified into two groups: (1) *music* and (2) *noise*. However, there is no sharp or clear distinction between the two types of sounds. It is a matter of perception of sensation to different people. For example, a loud peppy movie song might be music for youngsters but might be noise for elders. However, a loud religious or patriotic song might be music for elders but noise for youngsters. Thus, it is a subjective matter.

1. Music : A musical sound is that in which the vibrations of the sounding body are periodic, follow each other regularly and rapidly, so as to produce a pleasing effect on the ear without any sudden change in loudness. The waveform of musical sound is smooth as shown in Fig. 7.15(a). The sound level of music lies in between 10 dB and 30 dB.

Examples : Sound produced by a tuning fork, flute, sitar, harmonium, piano and so on.

2. Noise : Noise is an abrupt sound of a complex character with an irregular period and amplitude, originating from a source in non-periodic motion. It is unpleasant to the ears, and the waveform is irregular as shown in Fig. 7.15(b).

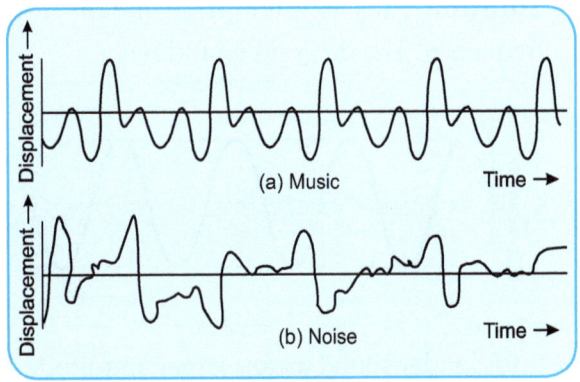

Fig. 7.15 : Waveforms of music and noise.

Examples : The horn of a motor car, the sound of a hammer striking a nail, the sound from a flying aeroplane, bursting of crackers and so on.

Noise Pollution

Noise pollution is the disturbance produced in the environment by undesirable, loud and harsh sound from various sources.

Normally, human ears can pick up sound from 10 dB to 180 dB. The level 0 dB represents the limit of hearing. A sound level of 10–30 dB is very soothing for the ears. The loudness of sound between 50 dB and 60 dB is considered normal. A normal human being can tolerate a loudness of 80 dB. However, when the loudness is greater than 120 dB, it is considered noise pollution as it causes health problems such as headache, stress and anxiety and might cause permanent damage to the ears, *i.e.* deafness. Sources of such loud sound are loudspeaker, moving vehicles, various machines, exploding crackers.

Difference between Music and Noise

Music	Noise
It is produced by periodic vibrations.	It is produced by irregular vibrations.
It is pleasant and acceptable to the ears.	It is unpleasant and undesirable to the ears.
There is no sudden change in amplitude, and all component waves are similar.	There is abrupt change in amplitude, and component waves are dissimilar.
The waveform is regular.	The waveform is irregular.
The level of sound is low and lies in the range of 10–30 dB.	The level of sound is high and lies above 120 dB.
Examples : Sounds produced by musical instruments such as piano, flute and guitar.	*Examples* : Sounds of vehicle horns, aeroplane, loudspeakers, crackers, etc.

ILLUSTRATIVE EXAMPLES

1. Study the adjoining diagram representing a musical note. Redraw the diagram for a note (a) with a higher pitch and (b) that is louder.

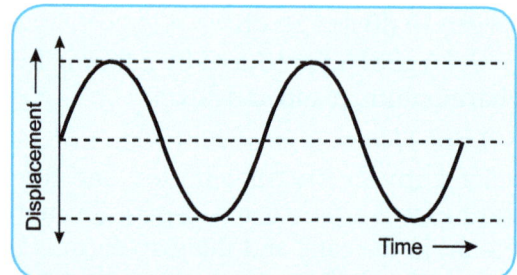

   Solution : (a) Higher pitch means higher frequency. The diagram would be

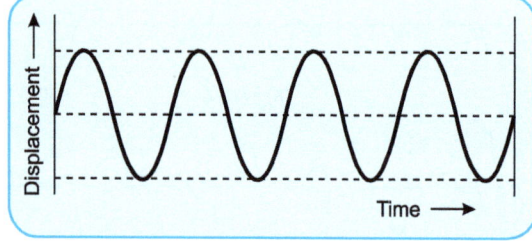

   (b) A louder sound means larger amplitude. The diagram would be

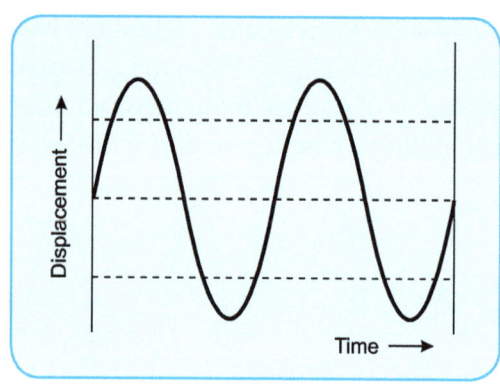

2. The figure below shows displacement-distance graph for three different sounds. Among these (a) which sound has the highest pitch? (b) Which is the loudest sound? (c) What is the ratio of wavelength of sound A to sound B? (d) How do the three sounds differ in quality?

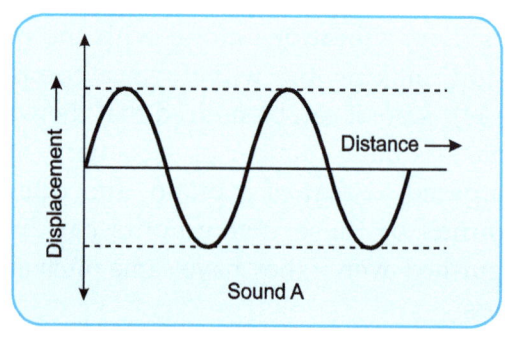

Sound A

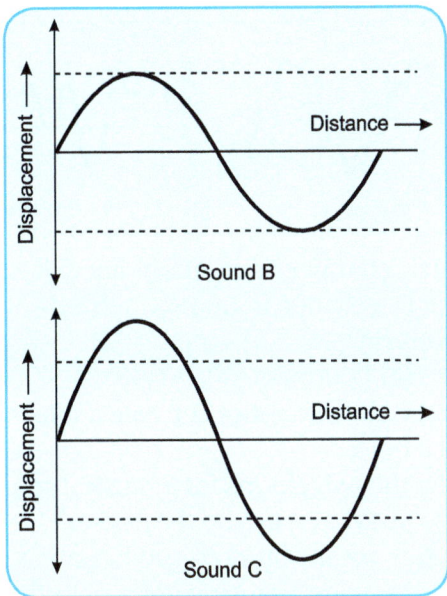

Solution :
(a) The frequency of sound A has the highest frequency among the three sounds. Hence, sound A has the highest pitch.
(b) The amplitude of sound C is larger among the three sounds and thus it is the loudest.

(c) From the figure, it can be seen that for every four vibrations of sound A, there are two vibrations of sound B for the same distance travelled.
   i.e. $\quad 4\lambda_A = 2\lambda_B$
   $\therefore \quad \lambda_A : \lambda_B = 2 : 4 = 1 : 2$
(d) All the three sounds have the same quality as their waveforms are same.

3. A person is listening to a song on a radio. At a point in the song, the singer hits a particular note and the person guesses the wavelength of that note to be 15 mm. Is this guess correct? Explain.
   Solution : Assuming the speed of sound = 330 ms^{-1}.
   Given : $\lambda = 15$ mm $= 0.015$ m.
   Then frequency of the note would be
   $\nu = v/\lambda = 330/0.015 = 22,000$ Hz.
   This frequency is beyond the human range of hearing. As the person would not be able to hear a note of such high frequency, his guess on the wavelength is wrong.

EXERCISE 7(B)

1. State the three characteristics of a musical sound.
2. What is meant by loudness of a sound?
3. Which factor determines the loudness of a sound wave?
   Ans : Amplitude
4. State any two ways by which the loudness of sound can be increased.
   Ans : By increasing the surface area of the vibrating body, by increasing the density of the medium
5. If the amplitude of a wave is doubled, what will be the effect on its loudness?
   Ans : Loudness will increase by four times
6. Draw a diagram to show the wave pattern of a loud note and a soft note. In what ways do they differ?
7. What is meant by intensity of sound? In what ways is it different from the loudness?
8. State the units of intensity and loudness of sound.
9. How is the loudness of sound related to the intensity of sound wave?
10. "Loudness of a sound is a subjective quantity while intensity is an objective quantity." Explain the statement.
11. State any three factors on which the loudness of sound depends.
12. Why does the loudness of sound of a vibrating tuning fork increase when it is mounted on a soundboard?
    Ans : The soundboard provides a larger volume of air to vibrate
13. The ratio of amplitude of two waves is 3 : 4. What is the ratio of their :
    (a) loudness ?
    (b) frequencies ?
    Ans : (a) 9 : 16, (b) 1:1
14. Name the unit used for measuring the sound level.
    Ans : decibel
15. Three different sound waves have amplitudes of magnitudes 14 mm, 10 mm and 12 mm. Which of these waves will produce the loudest sound?
    Ans : 14 mm sound wave
16. What is meant by the pitch of a sound?
17. Which quantity determines the pitch of a sound?
    Ans : Wavelength or frequency

18. Is pitch a subjective or an objective quantity?
    Ans : Subjective
19. Draw a diagram to show the wave pattern of a high-pitched note and a low-pitched note, each of same amplitude.
20. Three musical instruments deliver notes at the frequencies listed below :
    Flute : 400 Hz, Guitar : 200 Hz, Trumpet : 500 Hz. Which of these has the highest pitch?
    Ans : Trumpet
21. A bucket kept under a tap is filling with water. A person sitting at a distance is able to get an idea when the bucket is about to be filled. (a) What change takes place in sound to give this idea? (b) What causes the change in sound?
22. The figure below shows vibrations of a string in two different modes.

    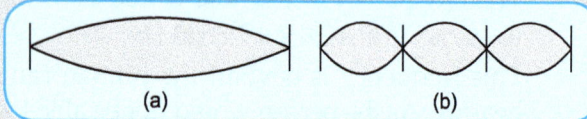

    (a) Calculate the ratio of frequency of note produced in mode (a) to note produced in mode (b).
    (b) Which note has a higher pitch?
    (c) What is the difference in quality of the two notes?
23. How can a note of lower pitch be generated from a given flute?
24. Name the characteristic of sound that enables one to distinguish notes from two different musical instruments even if they are of same pitch and same loudness?
    Ans : Quality
25. Draw any two different waveforms showing difference in quality of two sounds of same frequency and same amplitude.
26. How is it possible to recognise a person over a telephone without seeing him?
    Ans : From the unique quality of the person's voice
27. The figure below shows the wave patterns of two musical notes of same pitch and loudness generated by a violin and a flute. Explain why their waveforms are different?

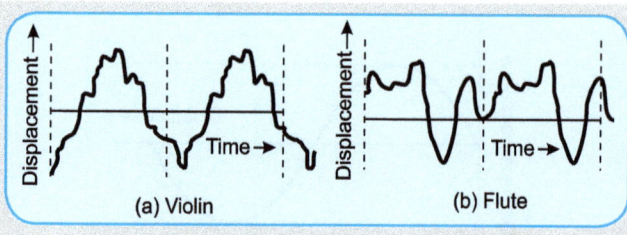

(a) Violin   (b) Flute

28. Which characteristic of sound will change if there is a change in (a) its amplitude and (b) its waveform?
    Ans : (a) Loudness, (b) Quality
29. What is the difference between a musical sound and a noise?
30. Draw the waveforms for a musical sound and a noise. In what ways do they differ?
31. What is meant by noise pollution? Name one source of sound causing noise pollution.
32. (a) State the safe limit of sound level in terms of decibel for human hearing.
    (b) Name the characteristics of sound in relation to its waveform.
    Ans : (a) 0 to 80 dB, (b) Quality or timbre.

MULTIPLE CHOICE QUESTIONS

1. If the amplitude of a sound wave is reduced to half, its loudness will :
   (a) increase by four times
   (b) increase by two times
   (c) decrease by four times
   (d) increase by four times
   Ans : (c)
2. The property by virtue of which a deep sound can be distinguished from a sharp sound is
   (a) loudness   (b) pitch
   (c) quality   (d) None of these
   Ans : (b)
3. Quality of sound of two notes of same frequency depends upon their :
   (a) amplitude   (b) waveforms
   (c) pitch   (d) intensity
   Ans : (b)
4. The frequency of four notes is A = 256 Hz, B = 120 Hz, C = 512 Hz and D = 400 Hz. Which of these notes have the lowest pitch?
   (a) A   (b) B
   (c) C   (d) D
   Ans : (b)

8

ELECTRIC CURRENT

LEARNING OUTCOMES

- Concept of electric current
- Electric potential and potential difference
- Resistance and Ohm's law
- Ohmic and non-Ohmic resistors
- Specific resistance and conductivity
- Electromotive force, terminal voltage and internal resistance of a cell
- Combination of resistors : series, parallel and both

8.1 CURRENT

Just as water flowing in a pipe constitutes water current or flowing air in the atmosphere constitutes air current, similarly flowing electric charges through a conductor constitute electric current.

If two charged bodies are connected by a metallic wire, electrons flow from a higher concentration area (body with maximum electrons) to a lower concentration area (body with minimum electrons). It is the flow of *free electrons* that constitutes an electric current.

Current is defined as the rate of flow of charge, i.e. charge flowing through a cross-sectional area of a conductor.

If a charge q flows through any cross-section of a conductor in time t, then electric current I is given as

$$\text{Current} = \frac{\text{Charge}}{\text{Time}}$$

i.e., $\quad I = \dfrac{q}{t} \quad$ ...(8.1)

The instrument used for measuring current in a circuit is known as *ammeter*. To measure the magnitude of current in a circuit, an ammeter is connected *in series* with the circuit with positive terminal of the ammeter connected to the positive terminal of the cell or battery (or source of current).

Flow of Current

The electric current flows due to both negative and positive charges. In metals, it is due to negatively charged electrons; in electrolytes, it is due to both positive ions (cations) and negative ions (anions); and in gases, it is due to positive ions and electrons.

Let n be the number of electrons that pass through the cross-section of a conductor in time t. The total charge flowing through the conductor will be

$$q = n\ e = ne$$

Hence, current in the conductor is

$$I = \frac{q}{t} = \frac{ne}{t} \quad ...(8.2)$$

Direction of Current

- **Conventional current :** In a conventional current, the direction of current is taken along the direction of flow of positive charges and opposite to the direction of flow of negative charges (electrons), that is, from a positively charged body to a negatively charged body.

- **Electric current :** The electric current or real current direction is taken along the direction of flow of negative charges (electrons), that is, from a negatively charged body to a positively charged body.

Unit of Current

The SI unit of charge is *coulomb*; thus, the SI unit of current is coulomb per second, which is known as *ampere* (A).

One ampere is defined as the current produced in a conductor when one coulomb of charge flows through its cross-section in one second.

$$1 \text{ ampere} = \frac{1 \text{ coulomb}}{1 \text{ second}}$$

i.e., $1 \text{ A} = 1 \text{ C s}^{-1}$

The charge on an electron is negative (*e*); it is equal to -1.6×10^{-19} C.

∴ The number of electrons in charge of 1 C is

$$1 \text{ C} = \frac{1}{1.6 \times 10^{-19}} = 6.25 \times 10^{18}$$

Thus, 1 ampere current in a conductor means the flow of 6.25×10^{18} electrons per second through the cross-section of the conductor.

i.e., $1 \text{ A} = 6.25 \times 10^{18}$ electrons s^{-1}

Some smaller units of current such as milliampere (mA) and microampere (µA) are used for measuring weak currents.

$1 \text{ mA} = 10^{-3}$ A and $1 \mu\text{A} = 10^{-6}$ A

Some bigger units of current such as kiloampere (kA) and megaampere (MA) are used for measuring very large currents.

$1 \text{ kA} = 10^3$ A and $1 \text{ MA} = 10^6$ A

8.2 ELECTRIC POTENTIAL AND POTENTIAL DIFFERENCE

Every object has a tendency to move from a position where its potential energy is high to a position where its potential energy is low.

This very tendency explain the flow of electrons.

Flow of charges : Let two charged conductors A and B, one negatively charged with excess of electrons (A), and another positively charged *i.e*, deficient in electrons (B), be connected by a metallic wire (Fig. 8.1). Electrons will flow from the conductor with more number of electrons to conductor with less number of electrons, that is, from A to B, until the concentration of electrons becomes equal in each conductor. This flow of electrons is determined by a quantity called the *electric potential*. The *negatively charged conductor* A is said to be at a *lower potential*, whereas the *positively charged conductor* B is said to be at a *higher potential*. Thus, electrons flow from a conductor at lower potential to a conductor at higher potential.

This seems to contradict from the above other examples discussed, where the flow of quantities (heat, water, etc.) is from higher level to lower level. However, to match with this convention, the flow of electrons is described in terms of flow of *electric current*. The direction of flow of electric current is opposite to the direction of flow of electrons. Thus, *electric current* flows from a conductor at higher potential to a conductor at lower potential, *i.e.* from conductor B to conductor A.

Potential can be defined as the electrical state of a conductor that determines the direction of flow of charge when two conductors are connected by a metallic wire or are kept in contact with each other.

To maintain the flow of electrons for a sufficiently long time, there has to be a constant difference in concentrations of electrons between the two conductors.

This happens in an *electric cell*. There are two electrodes in a cell, *anode* and *cathode*. The cathode has an excess of electrons while the anode has a deficit of electrons, and this is maintained by the chemical reactions within the cell for a long time. When a cell is connected in a circuit, the electrons flow from cathode to anode. Thus, an *electric cell* serves as a *source of electrons*.

Work Done in Transferring Charge

When electric charge moves through a conductor, an electric field is set up in the conductor. The electric field is a region around the charge within which a force is exerted on other charges. This force is repulsive between similar charges. Thus, some amount of energy is spent in moving the charges in the forward direction against the repulsive force. The measure of the energy spent is called the *electric potential*.

The amount of work done in moving a unit positive charge from infinity to a given point in an electric field is called the electric potential at that point.

Potential Difference

When a current flows through a conductor, it means that a charge is present in an electric field at some

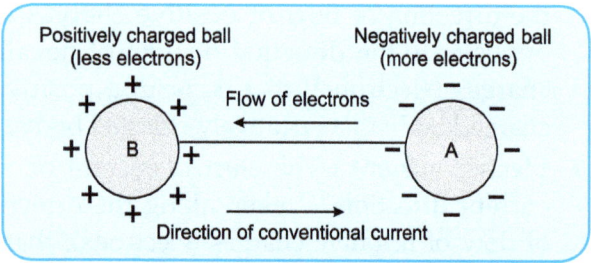

Fig. 8.1 : Flow of charges and direction of current.

point. So, work has to be done to move the charge from one point to other point in the same electric field. In this case, we need to know the difference in electric potential that exists between these two points and this is known as the *potential difference*.

The measure of work done in moving a unit positive charge from one point to another in an electric field is called the potential difference.

If a unit positive charge q is moved from one point, say A, to another point, say B, in an electric field or from one conductor to another, such that W is the work done and V is the potential difference between the two points,

where $\quad V = V_A - V_B$

Then,

$$\text{Potential difference} = \frac{\text{Work done}}{\text{Charge moved}}$$

i.e. $\quad V = \dfrac{W}{q} \quad$ ...(8.3)

In other words, the work done in moving a charge q from one point to another in an electric field where the potential difference between two points is V is

$$W = qV \quad ...(8.4)$$

Potential difference is a *scalar* quantity. It is measured by an instrument called *voltmeter* that is connected in *parallel* with the circuit, such that the positive terminal of the voltmeter is connected to the positive terminal of the cell or source of current.

Unit of Electric Potential / Potential Difference

Since the SI unit of work is *joule* (J) and that of charge is *coulomb* (C), the SI unit of potential or potential difference is JC^{-1}, which is known as *volt* (V).

One volt is defined as the potential difference between two points when 1 joule of work is done in transferring 1 coulomb of charge from one point to another.

$$1 \text{ volt} = \frac{1 \text{ joule}}{1 \text{ coulomb}} \text{ or } 1 \text{ V} = 1 \text{ J C}^{-1}$$

> **Do You Know ?**
> - *The units ampere and volt have been named in honour of scientists Andre Ampere and Alessandro Volta, respectively.*

8.3 RESISTANCE

The flow of current through a conductor, such as a metallic wire, is a result of motion of electrons. However, the movement of electrons is not a smooth continuous flow. An electron travelling through a wire encounters *obstruction* or *resistance*.

The opposition or obstruction offered by a conductor to the flow of current (or electrons) is called the electrical resistance.

Flow of Electric Current and Cause of Resistance

A conductor such as a metallic wire is composed of *free electrons*, which are capable of moving freely, and *positive ions*, which are fixed and thus do not move.

A metal wire has a large number of free electrons that drift randomly in various directions, but there is no net flow of electrons in any direction; hence no electric current flows in the wire. When this wire is connected to some electrical source such as a dry cell, its ends acquire different potentials. Because of this potential difference, electrons start drifting from negative to positive terminal of the cell through the metal wire, thereby setting up an electric current.

When the electrons start moving from negative terminal to positive terminal, they repel each other and also collide with the fixed positive ions of the wire in their path (Fig. 8.2). This leads to change in direction of motion and reduction in speed of electrons. The path of a typical electron through a wire could be described as a chaotic, zigzag path characterised by collisions with fixed positive ions. After collision, the electrons again

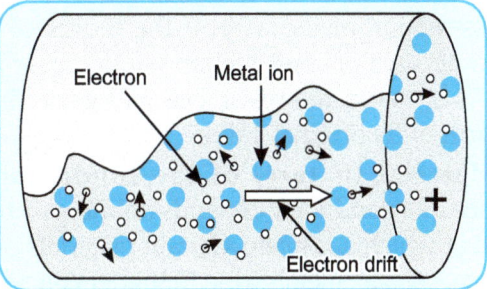

Fig. 8.2 : Flow of electrons in a conductor.

migrate towards the positive terminal due to the existing potential difference. They suffer repeated collisions, but their progress continues. Due to these collisions or resistance offered by the positive ions of the metal wire, there is no bulk movement of electrons with an accelerating speed rather they drift slowly towards the positive terminal. The overall effect of countless collisions of the electrons is that the net drift speed of an electron is very slow. But since there are a large number of electrons moving at once throughout the length of the wire, electric current is generated in the wire.

Factors Affecting the Resistance of a Conductor

The resistance of a conductor depends on the following *four* factors :

1. Length of the conductor : *The resistance of a conductor is directly proportional to its length.* It means longer the length of the conductor, greater is the resistance offered by it, as the number of collisions will be more in it than a conductor with short length. If R is the resistance of a conductor and l is its length, then $R \propto l$.

2. Area of cross-section or thickness of the conductor : *The resistance of a conductor is inversely proportional to its area of cross-section.* It means thicker the conductor, lesser is its resistance. This is because in a thicker conductor, the electrons get a larger area to flow than in a thinner conductor. If R is the resistance of a wire and a is its area of cross-section, then $R \propto 1/a$. From the relation of above factors, we can infer that if the wire of a given length is stretched, such that the length is *doubled* and the area of its cross-section is *halved*, then the resistance becomes *four times* the previous value. Similarly, if the wire is stretched such that the length becomes *three* times, then its resistance will become *nine times* its original value. However, if a wire is *doubled* on itself, its length will become *half* and its cross-section will get *doubled* so that the resistance will decrease by *four* times the original resistance.

Also area of cross-section of a conductor such as a metallic wire is $a = \pi r^2$, where r is the radius of the cross-section of the wire. If the radius of wire is doubled, its area of cross-section will increase by four times. As a result, the resistance will get reduced to one-fourth of its original value.

3. Material (nature) of the conductor : The resistance of a conductor depends on the nature of the material of which it is made. Certain materials offer less resistance, such as metals (due to higher concentration of electrons), compared to other materials, such as non-metals. Metals such as silver, copper and aluminium are called *good conductors* of electricity as they offer less resistance, whereas materials such as rubber, wood and glass are called *bad conductors* (or *insulators*) of electricity as they offer high resistance.

4. Temperature of the conductor : *The resistance of a conductor generally increases with the rise in temperature* (all metals), but there are a few exceptions where the resistance does not increase with increase in temperature (few metallic alloys, *e.g.* constantan). In general, as the temperature increases, the random motion of electrons increases, resulting in more collisions and thus offering more resistance to the flow of electric current.

8.4 OHM'S LAW

This law was named after the German physicist George Ohm who conducted experiments through simple electrical circuits and derived a relation between the potential difference applied at the ends of a conductor and current flowing through it.

Ohm's law can be stated as :

The current flowing through a conductor is directly proportional to the potential difference applied at its ends, provided all the physical conditions, including the temperature of the conductor, remain constant.

If I is the current flowing through a conductor when there is a potential difference of V across its ends, then according to Ohm's law,

$$I \propto V$$

i.e. $\quad \dfrac{V}{I} = \text{Constant} \quad \quad ...(8.5)$

or $\quad V = IR \quad \quad ...(8.6)$

Here R is the constant of proportionality and is the *resistance* of the conductor.

The resistance R is constant for a given conductor at a given temperature.

If $\quad I = 1$ A, then $V = R$.

When a unit current flows through a conductor, then its resistance is numerically equal to the potential difference applied at its ends.

Unit of Resistance

From equation (8.6), we have V = IR, *i.e.* R = V/I. The SI unit of potential difference is volt and that of current is ampere, so the unit of resistance is volt/ampere (VA^{-1}) and is called *ohm*. It is represented by the symbol Ω (omega).

$$1 \text{ ohm} = \dfrac{1 \text{ volt}}{1 \text{ ampere}}$$

i.e. $\quad 1 \Omega = 1 \text{ V A}^{-1}$

When a current of 1 ampere flows through a conductor on applying a potential difference of 1 volt at its ends, the resistance of the conductor is said to be 1 ohm.

The bigger units for measuring high resistances are kiloohm (kΩ) and megaohm (MΩ).

$$1 \text{ k}\Omega = 10^3 \, \Omega \text{ and } 1 \text{ M}\Omega = 10^6 \, \Omega$$

Conductance : The reciprocal of resistance is known as *conductance*.

$$\text{Conductance} = \dfrac{1}{\text{Resistance}} \quad \quad ...(8.7)$$

The unit of conductance is ohm^{-1} (Ω^{-1}), which was earlier also called *mho*.

I–V graph : If a graph is plotted between potential difference V taken along X-axis and current I taken along Y-axis for a metallic conductor, a straight line is obtained passing through the origin as shown in Fig. 8.3.

The slope of the I–V graph is $\Delta I/\Delta V$ and is equal to conductance of the conductor, that is, reciprocal of resistance.

Resistance of the conductor = $\dfrac{1}{\text{slope}} = \dfrac{\Delta V}{\Delta I}$ ...(8.8)

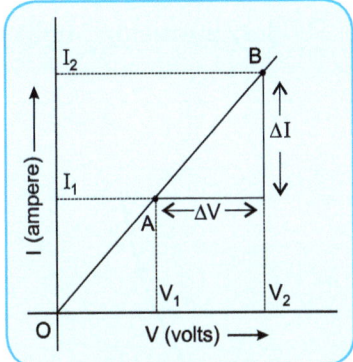

Fig. 8.3 : I–V graph for a metallic conductor.

NOTE

Ohm's law is valid only if the temperature of the conductor remains constant.

8.5 EXPERIMENTAL VERIFICATION OF OHM'S LAW

To verify Ohm's law, an electrical circuit as shown in Fig.8.4 is used. It consists of a resistor R, say a nichrome wire XY of unknown resistance connected in series to a battery through a key K, a rheostat Rh and an ammeter A. The positive terminal of the ammeter is always connected to the positive terminal of the battery. A voltmeter V is connected in parallel to the resistance wire such that its positive terminal is towards the positive terminal of the battery.

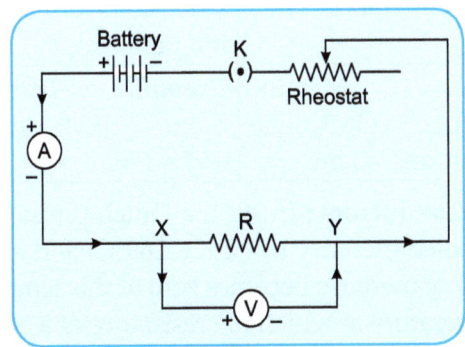

Fig. 8.4: Experimental set up for verification of Ohm's law.

Procedure : When the key is closed, the circuit is complete and current begins to flow from the battery. The ammeter shows the current flowing through the circuit and the voltmeter shows the potential difference across the ends X and Y of the resistance wire. The current in the circuit can be controlled by adjusting the slider of the rheostat. At first, the rheostat is adjusted in a way that minimum current flows through the circuit and is shown by the ammeter. The slider of the rheostat is then moved to increase the current gradually. Each time when the current is changed, the reading of voltmeter also changes correspondingly. In this manner, a few sets of values of I and V are recorded in an observation table as shown below. For each set of value, the ratio of V/I is calculated.

Observation no.	Current I (ammeter reading) in ampere	Potential difference V (voltmeter reading) in volt	Resistance R (V/I) in ohm
1.	I_1	V_1	V_1/I_1
2.	I_2	V_2	V_2/I_2
3.	..	..	
4.	..	..	..
5.	..	..	..
6.	I_6	V_6	V_6/I_6

It is found that the ratio is almost constant for each observation,

i.e. $V_1/I_1 = V_2/I_2 = \ldots = V_6/I_6$. This ratio gives the value of resistance of the wire.

Also, if a V–I graph is plotted, with V on Y-axis and I on X-axis, the graph is found to be a straight line as shown in Fig. 8.5. The slope of the graph ($\Delta V/\Delta I$) gives the value of the resistance of the wire. Greater the slope, greater is the resistance of a given conductor.

Slope of V–I graph : The slope of the straight line obtained on the V-I graph can be calculated by taking two points A and B on the straight line (Fig. 8.5). Draw two perpendiculars AP and BQ from points A and B, respectively, on the Y-axis. Similarly, draw two perpendiculars AS and BT from points A and B respectively on the X-axis. The difference in potentials at points P and Q is $V_P - V_Q = \Delta V$. Similarly, the difference in current at points S and T is $I_S - I_T = \Delta I$.

The slope of the graph $\Delta V/\Delta I$ gives the value of resistance (R) of the wire. This slope is found to be constant at different points on the graph.

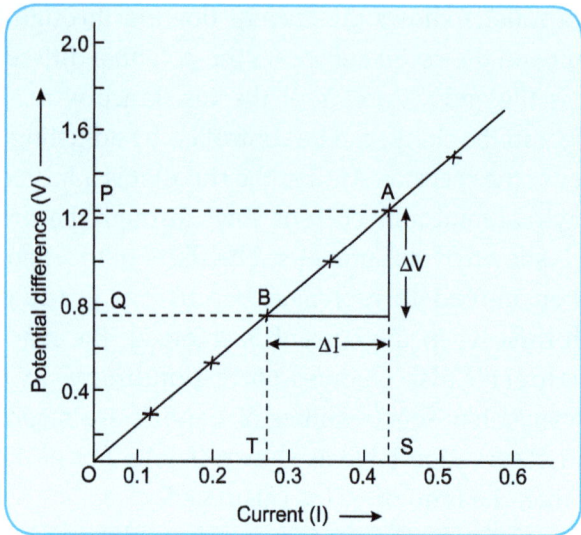

Fig. 8.5 : V–I graph for a resistance wire.

From the above observations and graph, it can be seen that $V \propto I$ or $V = RI$, thereby verifying ohm's law.

V–I graph for a conductor at different temperatures : If the temperature of a conductor is varied, its resistance will also vary. Fig. 8.6 shows V–I graph for a conductor at two different temperatures T_1 and T_2 such that $T_1 > T_2$. Since the resistance increases with increase in temperature, it is higher at T_1 as compared to T_2 and thus, the line 1 in the graph is steeper than line 2.

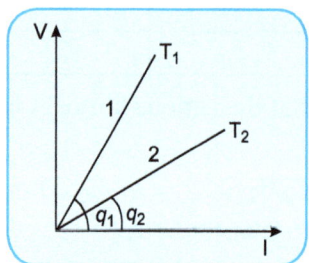

Fig. 8.6 : V–I graph at two temperatures of a conductor.

8.6 OHMIC AND NON-OHMIC RESISTORS

Conductors can be divided into two classes (1) Ohmic and (2) Non-ohmic resistors.

1. Ohmic resistors : The conductors or devices that obey Ohm's law are called *Ohmic resistors*. For these resistors, a V–I graph is a straight line (Fig. 8.5), which means the value of resistance (V/I ratio) remains constant with any change in the value of current or potential difference.

Examples : Metallic conductors, liquid electrolytes with suitable electrodes and so on at a constant temperature.

2. Non-Ohmic resistors : The conductors or devices that do not obey Ohm's law are called *non-Ohmic resistors*. For these resistors, a V–I graph is not a straight line as shown in Fig. 8.7. The resistance of these conductors does not remain constant and is different for different values of V or I. To calculate the resistance at a particular value of V or I, a tangent is drawn at that point on the curve and the slope of the tangent then gives the value of the resistance. The slope of the tangent (can be calculated as described earlier) gives a particular resistance which is known as *dynamic resistance* as the value of resistance is different for the different values of V or I.

Examples : Diodes, transistors, bulb filament and so on.

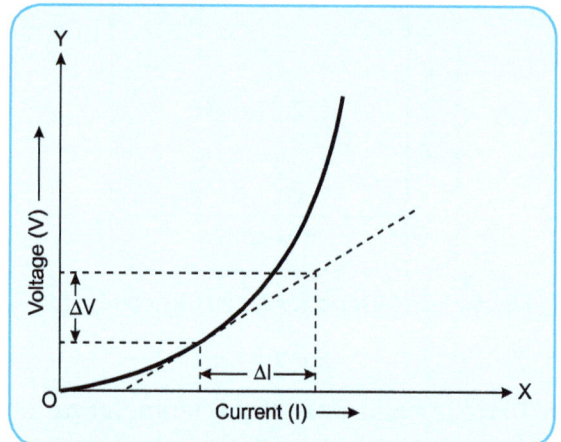

Fig. 8.7 : V–I graph for non-Ohmic resistors.

Difference between Ohmic and Non-Ohmic Resistors

Ohmic resistors	Non-Ohmic resistors
These obey Ohm's law, *i.e.* the resistance remains constant for all values of V or I.	These do not obey Ohm's law, *i.e.* the resistance is not constant for all values of V or I.
The graph of V versus I is a straight line.	The graph of V versus I is not a straight line.
The slope of V–I graph is same at all values of V or I at a given temperature.	The slope of V–I graph is different at different values of V or I at a given temperature.
Examples : Metallic conductors, electrolyte solutions, and so on.	*Examples* : Transistors, diodes, bulb filament, and so on.

Superconductors : In 1911, a Dutch physicist H. K. Onnes cooled mercury to 4.2 K (–269°C) and found the resistance of mercury becomes zero at this temperature. The temperature at which the resistance of a conductor becomes zero is called the *critical temperature* and the conductor is called a *superconductor*.

A conductor that offers zero resistance to the flow of electric current at a very low temperature is called a superconductor.

It has been experimentally found that the resistance of certain substances decreases with decrease in temperature and becomes almost negligible near absolute zero temperature (very low temperature).

Examples : Lead (7.2 K), niobium (9.25 K), tin (3.7 K), vanadium (5.4 K) and so on.

Due to zero resistance, the conductance of a superconductor is *infinite* and the current persists for a very long time without applying any voltage. However, it is difficult to achieve and maintain such low critical temperatures required for the phenomenon of superconductivity and so superconductors are not commonly used.

Research is in progress to produce superconductors at room temperature. If this could be achieved, then a lot of electrical energy that normally gets wasted as heat energy could be saved and power cables could then be made as thin as a single wire. Other promising *applications of superconductors* include induction heaters, transformers, power storage, motors and generators.

8.7 SPECIFIC RESISTANCE OR RESISTIVITY

As already stated, the resistance of a conductor is directly proportional to its length, $R \propto l$ and inversely proportional to the area of cross-section, $R \propto 1/a$.

If the conductor is a metallic wire of radius r, then its area of cross-section is $a = \pi r^2$.

Combining these above two factors, we obtain

$$R \propto \frac{l}{a}$$

or $$R = \rho \frac{l}{a} = \rho \frac{l}{\pi r^2} \qquad ...(8.9)$$

where ρ is the constant of proportionality and is called *resistivity* or *specific resistance*. Its magnitude depends on the nature of the material of the conductor.

From the above relation, we have

$$\rho = \frac{Ra}{l} \qquad ...(8.10)$$

If $a = 1, l = 1$, then $\rho = R$

The resistivity of the material may be defined as the resistance of the wire of that material of unit length and unit area of cross-section.

Unit of Resistivity

Resistivity, $\rho = \dfrac{Ra}{l}$

Unit of resistivity $= \dfrac{\text{ohm} \times \text{metre}^2}{\text{metre}}$

$= $ ohm metre (Ω m)

The unit of resistivity is ohm metre (Ω m) in SI system and ohm centimetre (Ω cm) in CGS system.

Factors Affecting Resistivity

The resistivity of a conductor is affected by the following *two* factors :

1. Material of the conductor : The resistivity is less for a good conductor of electricity and more for a bad conductor or insulator. The resistivity is least for metals (order of 10^{-8}), followed by alloys (order of 10^{-7}), semiconductors (wide range) and very high for insulators (order of 10^8–10^{16}).

2. Temperature of the conductor : The resistivity of a metallic conductor increases with increase in its temperature, but for a semiconductor, it decreases with increase in temperature.

The resistivity of a conductor is independent of its shape and size and does not depend on the current flowing through it or a potential applied on it.

Table 8.1 shows the values of resistivity of some common substances.

Table 8.1 : Resistivity of Substances at 20 °C

Substance	Resistivity (in Ω m)
Metals	
Silver	1.59×10^{-8}
Copper	1.68×10^{-8}
Gold	2.44×10^{-8}
Aluminium	2.65×10^{-8}
Tungsten	5.6×10^{-8}
Nickel	7×10^{-8}
Iron	9.7×10^{-8}
Mercury	9.8×10^{-8}
Platinum	10.6×10^{-8}
Lead	22×10^{-8}
Alloys	
Manganin	4.82×10^{-7}
Constantan	4.9×10^{-7}
Nichrome	11×10^{-7}
Semiconductors	
Graphite	2.5×10^{-6}–5.0×10^{-6}
Carbon	3.5×10^{-5}
Germanium	4.6×10^{-1}
Silicon	6.4×10^{2}
Insulators	
Pure water	2.5×10^{5}
Wood	10^{8}–10^{11}

Dry paper	10^{12}
Diamond	10^{12}
Glass	10^{10}–10^{14}
Common salt	10^{14}
Mica	10^{11}–10^{15}
Hard rubber	10^{13}–10^{16}
Air	10^{16}
Ebonite	10^{15}–10^{17}
Fused quartz	7.5×10^{17}

Difference between Resistance and Resistivity

Resistance	Resistivity
It is the obstruction offered by a conductor to the flow of electric current.	It is the property of the material of the conductor due to which it offers resistance to flow of current.
It is numerically equal to the potential difference applied on a conductor when a unit current flows through it.	It is numerically equal to the resistance offered by a unit length of conductor with a unit area of cross section.
The resistance of a conductor depends on the length, area of cross section, material and temperature.	The resistivity of a conductor depends only on the material and temperature and not on length and area of cross section.
The SI unit of resistance is ohm (Ω).	The SI unit of resistivity is ohm metre (Ω m).

Conductivity : *Conductivity is the reciprocal of resistivity.* It is represented by the symbol σ (sigma). It is a material's capability to conduct electric current.

$$\sigma = \frac{1}{\rho} = \frac{l}{Ra} \qquad ...(8.11)$$

The SI unit of conductivity is ohm^{-1} metre^{-1} (Ω^{-1}m^{-1}), also known as siemen metre^{-1} or S m^{-1}.

Effect of Temperature on Resistance and Resistivity

♦ Both resistance and resistivity increase with increase in temperature for a metallic conductor.

♦ Both resistance and resistivity remain unchanged with increase in temperature for alloys (such as constantan and manganin).

♦ Both resistance and resistivity decrease with increase in temperature for semiconductors (such as silicon and germanium).

8.8 ELECTROMOTIVE FORCE OF A CELL

To understand the concept of electromotive force (emf), consider the example of flow of water in a pipe. If a horizontal pipe is attached at one end to a water tank, water will not flow through it if there is no pressure difference between the two. Water will flow out only if there is a pressure difference, and it is the magnitude of pressure difference that determines the rate at which the water will flow out of the tube. Also, to maintain a constant rate of flow of water, the water flowing out need to be restored by a pump into the tank to maintain the pressure difference.

Similar to the flow of water, the flow of current across a conductor occurs only if a steady potential difference is maintained between its two ends. To maintain a steady current flow, an agent is needed, similar to the pump in the case of restoring of water in the tank. This agent which does work on the charges is called the *electromotive force* or *emf*.

The emf of a cell is the characteristic of a cell, but it is not a force as the name suggests. It is a measure of the cell's ability to do the work necessary to pump the charge for maintaining a steady current flow.

When a cell is in use, the flow of current is *from anode to cathode* in the external circuit in the form of flow of *electrons* and *from cathode to anode* inside the electrolyte of the cell in the form of *ions* to maintain a continuous flow of charges.

The electromotive force (or emf) of a cell is defined as the energy spent by the cell per unit charge in carrying a positive charge through its complete circuit (external as well as internal).

In other words, an emf of a cell is the *potential difference between the terminals of the cell when the cell is in open circuit, i.e. when no current is drawn from the cell* (Fig. 8.8).

It is the maximum potential difference between the two electrodes.

It is represented by the symbol ε (epsilon), and its unit is volt (V), same as that of potential difference.

If W is the work done in carrying a unit charge q_0 around the complete circuit of the cell, then the emf of cell is

$$\varepsilon = \frac{w}{q_0} \qquad ...(8.12)$$

Every cell has its own characteristic emf and thus, is different for different types of cells.

Examples : The emf of *voltaic* cell or a *Daniel* cell is 1.08 V, *Leclanché* cell is 1.5 V and lead accumulator is 2.05 V.

Factors Affecting the Emf of a Cell

The factors affecting the emf of a cell are as follows :
1. The material of the electrodes of the cell.
2. The nature and concentration of electrolyte used in the cell.
3. Temperature.

However, the emf of a cell is not affected by (a) the shape and area of electrodes, (b) the amount of electrolyte, (c) the distance between the electrodes and (d) the size of the cell.

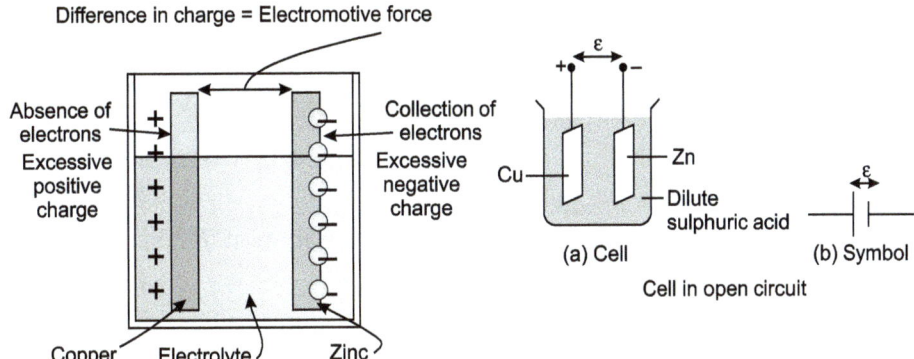

Fig. 8.8 : The emf of a cell in an open circuit.

8.9 TERMINAL VOLTAGE OF A CELL

The terminal voltage of a cell is defined as the work done per unit charge in carrying a positive charge around the external circuit of the cell i.e. circuit connected across the terminals of the cell.

In other words, the terminal voltage of a cell is the *potential difference between the electrodes of the cell when the cell is in a closed circuit, i.e. when a current is drawn from the cell* (Fig. 8.9).

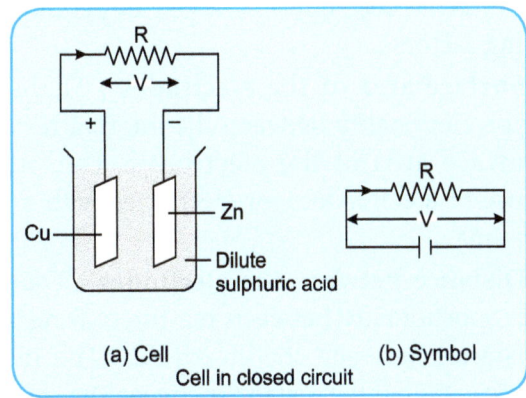

Fig. 8.9 : Terminal voltage of a cell in a closed circuit.

It is represented by the letter V and its unit is volt (V).

If W' is the work done in carrying a unit charge q_0 around the external circuit of the cell, then terminal voltage of the cell is

$$V = \frac{W'}{q_0} \qquad ...(8.13)$$

The terminal voltage of a cell is always less than its emf when a cell is in use. The difference between the two is equal to the amount of energy spent or work done in carrying a unit positive charge through the electrolyte (internal circuit) of the cell.

If w is the amount of work done in carrying a unit charge q_0 through the electrolyte inside the cell, then the difference between emf and terminal voltage is w/q_0 and is known as the *voltage drop in the cell*.

Voltage drop in the cell, $v = \dfrac{w}{q_0}$ ....(8.14)

Voltage drop in the cell is the amount of work done in carrying a unit charge through the electrolyte inside the cell.

From the law of conservation of energy, we obtain

$$W = W' + w \qquad ...(8.15)$$

$\dfrac{W}{q_0} = \dfrac{W'}{q_0} + \dfrac{w}{q_0}$ (on dividing Eq. 8.15 by q_0)

But $\qquad \dfrac{W}{q_0} = \varepsilon \; ; \; \dfrac{W'}{q_0} = V$ and $\dfrac{w}{q_0} = v$

i.e. $\qquad \varepsilon = V + v$

i.e. $\qquad V = \varepsilon - v \qquad ...(8.16)$

The terminal voltage V of a cell depends on the amount of current drawn from it. If a large current is drawn, it results in more voltage drop and thus, there is less terminal voltage.

NOTE

When a cell is not in use, that is, when no current is drawn, its terminal voltage is equal to the emf of the cell.

The terminal voltage is more than the emf of a cell under one condition, that is, when a cell is charged by passing current through it.

Difference between emf and Terminal Voltage of a Cell

Emf of a cell	Terminal voltage of a cell
It is the amount of work done in moving a unit positive charge around the complete circuit (internal and external) of the cell.	It is the amount of work done in moving a unit positive charge around the external circuit of the cell.
It does not depend on the amount of current drawn from the cell.	It depends on the amount of current drawn from the cell. More the current drawn from the cell, less is the terminal voltage.
It is always greater than the terminal voltage when a cell is in use.	It is always less than the emf when a cell is in use.

8.10 INTERNAL RESISTANCE OF A CELL

The flow of current inside the electrolyte of the cell is in the form of cations and anions. However, the electrolyte provides resistance to the flow of these ions.

The resistance offered by the electrolyte inside the cell to the flow of current is called the internal resistance of the cell.

It is represented by the letter r and its unit is ohm (Ω).

If the internal resistance provided by the electrolyte is r and I is the current drawn, then the voltage drop v of the cell is

$$v = Ir \qquad ...(8.17)$$

The internal resistance r of a cell can be considered to be connected in series with the cell (Fig. 8.10).

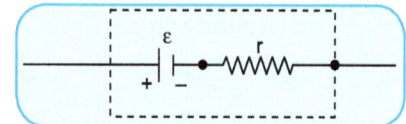

Fig. 8.10 : A cell with internal resistance.

Relation Between the emf, Terminal Voltage and Internal Resistance of a Cell $\left[r = \left(\dfrac{\varepsilon}{V} - 1\right)R\right]$

Let the emf of a cell be ε and its internal resistance be r. Let the current I be sent through the cell in an external resistance R across the cell (Fig. 8.11).

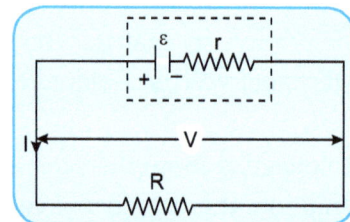

Fig. 8.11 : Current due to External and Internal Resistance.

Total resistance of the circuit = $R + r$ ...(8.18)
Current drawn from the cell is

$$I = \dfrac{\text{Emf of cell}}{\text{Total resistance}}$$

i.e. $\qquad I = \dfrac{\varepsilon}{R+r} \qquad ...(8.19)$

Emf of the cell, $\quad \varepsilon = I(R+r) \qquad ...(8.20)$

Now, terminal voltage of the cell is

$$V = IR \qquad ...(8.21)$$

and,

Voltage drop due to internal resistance is

$$v = Ir \qquad ...(8.22)$$

From Equation (8.20), we obtain

$$\varepsilon = IR + Ir \qquad ...(8.23)$$

Substituting values of IR and Ir from equation (8.21) and (8.22) respectively in equation (8.23), we get

$$\varepsilon = V + v$$

i.e. $\qquad v = \varepsilon - V$

Using these equations, we obtain the internal resistance of the cell as

$$r = \dfrac{v}{I} = \dfrac{\varepsilon - V}{I}$$

Since, $\qquad I = V/R$,

So, $\qquad r = \dfrac{\varepsilon - V}{V/R} = \left(\dfrac{\varepsilon}{V} - 1\right)R \qquad ...(8.24)$

Factors Affecting the Internal Resistance of a Cell

The internal resistance of a cell depends on the following factors :

1. Surface area of the electrodes : There is an *inverse* propotionality between the internal resistance and surface area of the electrodes. The internal resistance of a cell is less for electrodes with a larger surface area.

2. Distance between the electrodes : There is a *direct* proportionality between the internal resistance and distance between the electrodes. The internal resistance is high if the distance between the electrodes is more.

3. Concentration of the electrolyte : There is a *direct* proportionality between the internal resistance and concentration of the electrolyte. Higher the concentration of the electrolyte, greater is the internal resistance.

4. Temperature of the electrolyte : There is an *inverse* proportionality between the internal resistance and temperature of electrolyte. With increase in temperature, the internal resistance of a cell decreases.

8.11 COMBINATION OF RESISTORS

A number of resistors of different resistances can be combined in a circuit for drawing a current of desired value. The resistors can be combined in three possible ways : (1) series, (2) parallel and (3) both.

Combination of Resistors in Series

When two or more resistors are joined one after the other, they are said to be in series. Fig. 8.12 shows three resistors R_1, R_2 and R_3 in series combination. The resistor R_1 has one of its ends connected to point A and the other end to resistor R_2. Resistor R_2 has its other end connected to resistor R_3. The other end of resistor R_3 is connected to point D. The points A and D are connected to the positive and negative terminals of a battery respectively, through a key K.

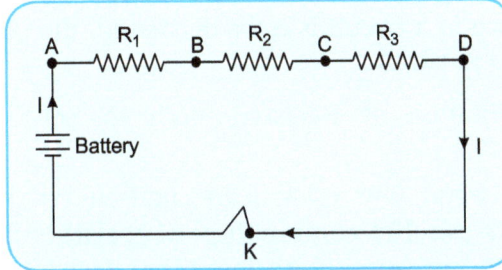

Fig. 8.12 : Resistors in series combination.

In a series combination,

1. The *same current* passes through each resistor, whereas the *potential difference varies* for each resistor.

2. The potential difference is maximum across resistor R_1 as it is connected to the positive terminal of the cell which is at a higher potential. The potential difference decreases across each resistor and is minimum at point of the last resistor.

Let V_A, V_B, V_C and V_D be the potentials at points A, B, C and D, respectively. In series connection, $V_A > V_B > V_C > V_D$. The potential difference across resistor R_1 is $V_1 = V_A - V_B$, across resistor R_2 is $V_2 = V_B - V_C$, across resistor R_3 is $V_3 = V_C - V_D$.

The potential difference across the entire circuit is equal to the sum of potential differences across each individual resistor, *i.e.*
$$V = V_1 + V_2 + V_3 + \ldots$$

Equivalent Resistance in Series

Let I be the current across each resistor, flowing from the battery to the entire circuit.

By Ohm's law, we obtain
$$V_1 = IR_1, \; V_2 = IR_2 \text{ and } V_3 = IR_3$$
$\therefore$
$$V = V_1 + V_2 + V_3$$
$$= I(R_1 + R_2 + R_3) \quad \ldots(i)$$

In series, the potential difference across a resistor is *proportional* to its resistance.

Let R_S be the equivalent resistance across the points A and D. Thus, potential difference across points A and D is
$$V = V_A - V_D = IR_S \quad \ldots(ii)$$

From Equations (i) and (ii), we obtain
$$R_S = R_1 + R_2 + R_3 \quad \ldots(8.25)$$

In series combination, the equivalent resistance is *equal* to the sum of individual resistances across each resistor.

If there are n resistors joined in series, their equivalent resistance is given as
$$R_S = R_1 + R_2 + R_3 + \ldots + R_n \quad \ldots(8.26)$$

If all the n resistors are equal, such that R is the resistance across each resistor, then
$$R_S = R + R + \ldots + n \text{ times} = nR \quad \ldots(8.27)$$

Example : If there are three resistors of resistances $2 \, \Omega$, $4 \, \Omega$ and $6 \, \Omega$ in series, the equivalent resistance R_S of the circuit will be
$$R_S = R_1 + R_2 + R_3$$
$$= 2 + 4 + 6 = 12 \, \Omega.$$

The value of the equivalent resistance is *always greater* than the value of the largest individual resistance in a series combination.

Combination of Resistors in Parallel

In a parallel combination, two ends of each resistor (R_1, R_2, R_3) are joined to two common points A and B, as shown in Fig. 8.13. The two points A and B are then connected to positive and negative terminals of a battery.

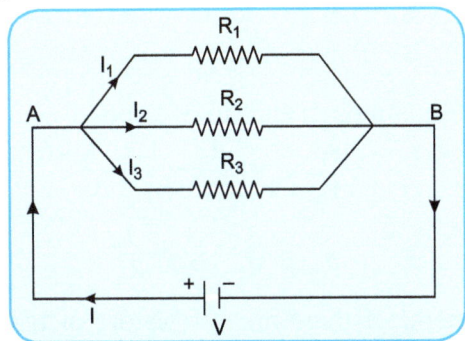

Fig. 8.13 : Resistors in parallel combination.

In a parallel combination,

1. The *potential difference* across each resistor is *same* and is equal to that across the terminals of the battery.

Let V_A and V_B be the potentials at points A and B, respectively. The point A is at a higher potential as it is connected to the positive terminal of the battery, while the point B is at a lower potential as it is connected to the negative terminal of the battery.

The potential difference across each resistor is equal to the difference in potentials across points A and B, i.e.
$$V = V_A - V_B$$

2. The *current* flowing across each resistor is *different*. If I is the current from the battery, then it gets divided in different branches at point A.

The current flowing through each branch is *inversely proportional* to the resistance, *i.e.* more current flows through the low resistance branch compared to the high resistance branch.

Let I_1, I_2 and I_3 be the currents flowing through the resistors R_1, R_2 and R_3, respectively. The sum of the currents flowing through individual branches of the circuit is equal to the current drawn from the cell, *i.e.*
$$I = I_1 + I_2 + I_3 + \ldots$$

Equivalent Resistance in Parallel

If the potential difference across two ends A and B is V, then by Ohm's law,

Current, $I_1 = \dfrac{V}{R_1}$

Current, $I_2 = \dfrac{V}{R_2}$

Current, $I_3 = \dfrac{V}{R_3}$

$\therefore \quad I_1 + I_2 + I_3 = \dfrac{V}{R_1} + \dfrac{V}{R_2} + \dfrac{V}{R_3}$ ...(i)

Let R_P be the equivalent resistance of the combination between points A and B, then total current is equal to
$$I = \dfrac{V}{R_P} \quad \ldots\text{(ii)}$$

From Equations (i) and (ii), we obtain
$$\dfrac{V}{R_P} = V\left(\dfrac{1}{R_1} + \dfrac{1}{R_2} + \dfrac{1}{R_3}\right)$$

i.e. $\quad \dfrac{1}{R_P} = \dfrac{1}{R_1} + \dfrac{1}{R_2} + \dfrac{1}{R_3}$ ...(8.28)

In general, if there are n resistors of resistances $R_1, R_2, R_3 \ldots R_n$ joined in parallel, then their equivalent resistance is given as
$$\dfrac{1}{R_P} = \dfrac{1}{R_1} + \dfrac{1}{R_2} + \dfrac{1}{R_3} + \ldots + \dfrac{1}{R_n} \quad \ldots(8.29)$$

In *parallel combination*, the reciprocal of equivalent resistance is *equal* to the sum of the reciprocals of individual resistances.

If the *n* resistors have an equal value of resistance R each, connected in parallel, then equivalent resistance is
$$\dfrac{1}{R_P} = \dfrac{1}{R} + \dfrac{1}{R} + \dfrac{1}{R} + \ldots + n \text{ times} = \dfrac{n}{R}$$

i.e. $\quad R_P = \dfrac{R}{n}$ ...(8.30)

Example: If there are three resistances of values 2 Ω, 20 Ω and 200 Ω connected in parallel, the equivalent resistance is

$$\dfrac{1}{R_P} = \dfrac{1}{R_1} + \dfrac{1}{R_2} + \dfrac{1}{R_3}$$
$$= \dfrac{1}{2} + \dfrac{1}{20} + \dfrac{1}{200} = \dfrac{111}{200}$$

i.e. $\quad R_P = \dfrac{200}{111} = 1.8 \, \Omega$

The value of equivalent resistance is *always less* than the value of smallest individual resistance. If the resistance in a circuit is to be decreased, the resistors are used in parallel.

Combination of Resistors both in Series and Parallel

In a circuit, few resistors are connected in parallel and this parallel combination of resistors is then connected in series with few other resistors. This combination is used to obtain a desired value of resistance from the given resistors.

In this combination, the equivalent resistance of parallel resistors is calculated at first. This equivalent resistance is then added to the resistances in series and the total resistance of the circuit is calculated.

In Fig. 8.14, two series–parallel combinations are shown.

In the first network, resistors R_2 and R_3 are in parallel combination. The equivalent resistance of these two is then in series with R_1.

In the second network, the combination of resistors R_2 and R_3 in series forms a simple parallel combination with R_1.

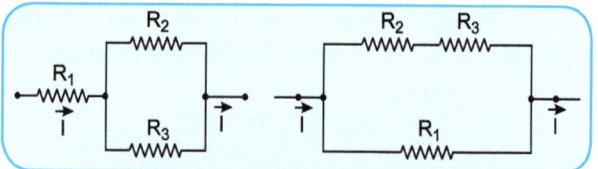

Fig. 8.14 : Resistors in both series and parallel combination.

Example: In Fig. 8.15, the resistances R_2 and R_3 are in parallel combination and the equivalent resistance of these two resistors will be in series to resistance R_1.

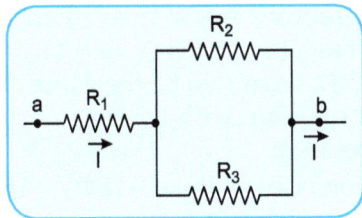

Fig. 8.15 : Series and parallel combination of resistors.
Suppose $R_1 = R_2 = R_3 = 2\,\Omega$
Then equivalent resistance of R_2 and R_3 will be

$$\frac{1}{R_P} = \frac{1}{R_2} + \frac{1}{R_3}$$

i.e. $\quad \dfrac{1}{R_P} = \dfrac{1}{2} + \dfrac{1}{2} = 1$

i.e. $\quad R_P = 1\,\Omega$

Now, R_P is in series with R_1. The equivalent resistance of these two will be
$R = R_P + R_1 = 1 + 2 = 3\,\Omega$. This is the total resistance of the circuit with resistances in both parallel and series combination.

ILLUSTRATIVE EXAMPLES

1. A conductor of resistance $4\,\Omega$ can pass a current of 2.5 A through it. Calculate the potential difference required across the conductor.
   Solution : Given, $R = 4\,\Omega$, $I = 2.5$ A
   From Ohm's law,
   $$V = IR = 2.5 \times 4 = 10\,V$$

2. Calculate the amount of work done in moving a charge of 5 C through a potential difference of 25 V. What will be the potential difference if this amount of work is done in moving a charge of 10 C ?
   Solution : Given : $q = 5$ C, $V = 25$ V
   Work done $W = qV = 5 \times 25 = 125$ J
   Now, $W = 125$ J, $q = 10$ C
   $\therefore \quad V' = \dfrac{W}{q} = \dfrac{125}{10} = 12.5$ V

3. A metallic wire of length 1 m is stretched to double its length in such a way that there is no change in density of the wire. Calculate the ratio of initial and final resistance.
   Solution : Since density is unchanged, it means volume is constant.
   So if the length is doubled, then the area of cross section has to be reduced by half its value so that volume remains the same.
   Let l and a be the initial length and area of the wire and ρ be the resistivity.

   Initial resistance $R_i = \rho \dfrac{l}{a}$
   New length $= 2l$, New area of cross section $= a/2$
   Final resistance $R_f = \rho \dfrac{(2l)}{(a/2)} = 4\rho\dfrac{l}{a} = 4R_i$
   $\therefore \quad R_i : R_f = 1 : 4$

4. A wire of length 15 m and uniform cross-section of 6×10^{-7} m² has a resistance of $5\,\Omega$. Calculate the resistivity of the material of the wire.
   Solution : Given : $l = 15$ m, $a = 6 \times 10^{-7}$ m², $R = 5\,\Omega$
   Resistivity, $\rho = R\dfrac{a}{l} = \dfrac{5 \times 6 \times 10^{-7}}{15} = 2 \times 10^{-7}\,\Omega\,m$

5. When a potential difference of 4 V is applied across the ends of a wire of 10 m length, a current of 2 A flows through it. Calculate (a) the resistance per unit length of the wire and (b) the resistance of 4 m length of this wire.
   Solution :
   (a) Given : $V = 4$ V, $I = 2$ A, $l = 10$ m
   $$R = \dfrac{V}{I} = \dfrac{4}{2} = 2\,\Omega$$
   Resistance per unit length $= \dfrac{2\,\Omega}{10\,m} = 0.2\,\Omega\,m^{-1}$
   (b) Resistance of 4 m length of the wire
   $= 0.2 \times 4 = 0.8\,\Omega$

6. A battery supplies a current of 0.8 A through a $2\,\Omega$ resistor and a current of 0.4 A through a $5\,\Omega$ resistor. Calculate the internal resistance of the battery.
   Solution : Let the emf of the battery be ε and internal resistance be r.
   Given, $I_1 = 0.8$ A, $R_1 = 2\,\Omega$, $I_2 = 0.4$ A, $R_2 = 5\,\Omega$
   $$\text{Current} = \dfrac{\text{emf}}{\text{Total Resistance}}$$
   $\therefore \quad I_1 = \dfrac{\varepsilon}{R_1 + r}$
   $\quad 0.8 = \dfrac{\varepsilon}{2 + r} \qquad \ldots(i)$
   and
   $\quad I_2 = \dfrac{\varepsilon}{R_2 + r}$
   $\quad 0.4 = \dfrac{\varepsilon}{5 + r} \qquad \ldots(ii)$
   Dividing equation (i) by equation (ii), we obtain
   $$\dfrac{\varepsilon/2 + r}{\varepsilon/5 + r} = \dfrac{0.8}{0.4}$$
   i.e. $\quad \dfrac{5 + r}{2 + r} = 2$
   or $\quad 5 + r = 4 + 2r$
   or $\quad r = 1\,\Omega$

7. What will be the equivalent resistance of three resistors of 4 Ω, 8 Ω and 16 Ω if these are connected in (a) series and (b) parallel?
   Solution : Given : $R_1 = 4\,\Omega, R_2 = 8\,\Omega, R_3 = 16\,\Omega$
   (a) In series, equivalent resistance will be
   $$R_s = R_1 + R_2 + R_3$$
   $$= 4 + 8 + 16 = 28\,\Omega$$
   (b) In parallel, equivalent resistance will be
   $$\frac{1}{R_P} = \frac{1}{R_1} + \frac{1}{R_2} + \frac{1}{R_3}$$
   $$= \frac{1}{4} + \frac{1}{8} + \frac{1}{16} = \frac{7}{16}$$
   $$R_P = \frac{16}{7} = 2.28\,\Omega$$

8. A lamp of resistance 800 Ω, a fire alarm of resistance 30 Ω and a vacuum cleaner of resistance 200 Ω are connected in parallel to the mains supply of 240 V. Calculate the current through each appliance and the total current supplied by the mains.
   Solution : Given : $R_{lamp} = 800\,\Omega, R_{f.alarm} = 30\,\Omega, R_{v.\,cleaner} = 200\,\Omega, V = 240\,V.$
   In parallel combination, the voltage remains same across each resistor.
   For lamp, current
   $$I_1 = V/R_{lamp}$$
   $$= 240/800 = 0.3\,A$$
   For fire alarm, current $I_2 = V/R_{f.alarm}$
   $$= 240/30 = 8\,A$$
   For vacuum cleaner, current
   $$I_3 = V/R_{v.cleaner}$$
   $$= 240/200 = 1.2\,A$$
   Total current $= I_1 + I_2 + I_3$
   $$= 0.3\,A + 8\,A + 1.2\,A$$
   $$= 9.5\,A$$

9. The effective resistance of two resistors is 25 Ω. If the resistance of one of the resistors is 10 Ω, what is the resistance of the other resistor?
   Solution : Given : $R_1 = 10\,\Omega$, effective resistance $R = 25\,\Omega$.
   Since the effective resistance is higher than the resistance of the given resistor, R_1 must be connected in series with R_2.
   In series combination,
   $$R = R_1 + R_2$$
   i.e. $$R_2 = R - R_1$$
   $$R_2 = 25 - 10 = 15\,\Omega$$

10. The effective resistance of three resistors connected to a battery is 5 Ω. If $R_1 = 10\,\Omega$, $R_2 = 15\,\Omega$, what will be the value of R_3? Draw a circuit diagram with the flow of current across each resistor.
    Solution : Given, $R_1 = 10\,\Omega, R_2 = 15\,\Omega$, Effective resistance $R = 5\,\Omega$
    Since the effective resistance is less than both R_1 and R_2, the three resistors must be connected in parallel combination.
    In parallel combination,
    $$\frac{1}{R} = \frac{1}{R_1} + \frac{1}{R_2} + \frac{1}{R_3}$$
    $$\frac{1}{5} = \frac{1}{10} + \frac{1}{15} + \frac{1}{R_3}$$
    or $$\frac{1}{5} = \frac{3R_3 + 2R_3 + 30}{30R_3}$$
    or $$30R_3 = 25R_3 + 150$$
    i.e. $$R_3 = 30\,\Omega$$
    The circuit diagram is given below :

    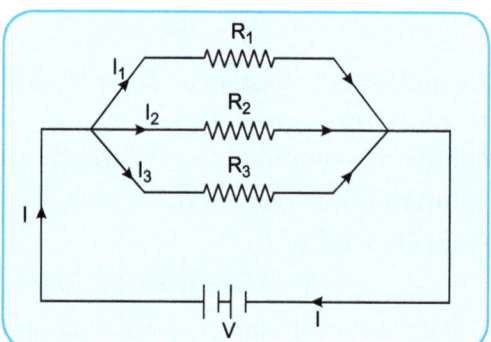

11. A parallel pair of resistors of values 4 Ω and 12 Ω are together connected in series with another resistor of value 3 Ω and battery of emf 24 V. Draw a circuit diagram and calculate the current across each resistor.
    Solution : The circuit diagram is shown below :

    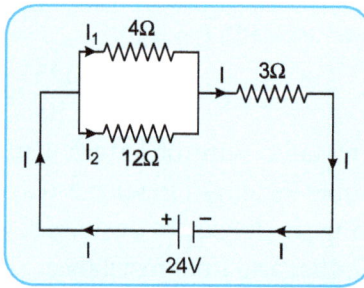

    The resistances of 4 Ω and 12 Ω are in parallel. Their equivalent resistance R_P will be
    $$\frac{1}{R_P} = \frac{1}{4} + \frac{1}{12}$$
    i.e. $$\frac{1}{R_P} = \frac{4}{12}$$
    or $$R_P = \frac{12}{4} = 3\,\Omega$$

Now, this equivalent resistance of 3 Ω is connected in series with the resistance of 3 Ω. The equivalent resistance of these two will be $R_s = 3\,\Omega + 3\,\Omega = 6\,\Omega$. This is the total resistance of the circuit.

Given emf of the battery = 24 V

∴ Total current across the circuit,

$$I = \frac{\text{emf}}{\text{Total resistance}}$$

$$= \frac{24}{6} = 4\text{ A}$$

The current flowing through the single resistor of resistance 3 Ω is equal to the total current in the circuit, which is 4 A.

However, for the other two resistors 4 Ω and 12 Ω in parallel, the current I = 4 A will get divided as I_1 and I_2, respectively, in inverse proportion to their resistance.

Thus, $\dfrac{I_1}{I_2} = \dfrac{R_2}{R_1} = \dfrac{12\,\Omega}{4\,\Omega} = \dfrac{3}{1}$

i.e. $I_1 = 3 I_2$

Now, $I_1 + I_2 = 4$

i.e. $3 I_2 + I_2 = 4$

i.e. $I_2 = 1\text{ A}$

∴ $I_1 = 3\text{ A}$

Thus, the current across 4 Ω resistor is 3 A and across 12 Ω resistor is 1 A.

12. The figure below shows V–I graphs of two metallic conductors for series and parallel combination. Which graph represents parallel combination?

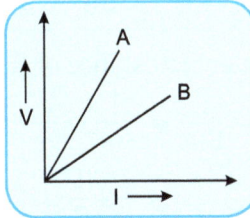

Solution : The effective resistance R = V/I is more in series than that in parallel combination. The slope of V–I graph represents the resistance. From the graph, we infer the slope of line A is more than the slope of line B, i.e. resistance for line A is more than for line B. Thus, line A represents series combination and line B represents parallel combination.

13. The lengths of three conducting wires of same material are in the ratio 1 : 2 : 3. The area of cross-section of each wire is same. If these wires are joined in parallel across a battery, what will be the ratio of currents in them?

Solution : In a parallel connection, potential difference V across each wire is the same.

Resistance of a wire, $R = \dfrac{\rho l}{a}$, i.e. $R \propto l$

Given a and ρ are constant (made of same material)

∴ $R_1 : R_2 : R_3 = l_1 : l_2 : l_3$

i.e. $R_1 : R_2 : R_3 = 1 : 2 : 3$

$$I \propto \frac{1}{R}$$

Now, $I_1 : I_2 : I_3 = \dfrac{1}{R_1} : \dfrac{1}{R_2} : \dfrac{1}{R_3}$

i.e. $I_1 : I_2 : I_3 = \dfrac{1}{1} : \dfrac{1}{2} : \dfrac{1}{3} = 6 : 3 : 2$

14. In the given circuit diagram, the emf of the cell is 5 V and its internal resistance is 2.5 Ω. Calculate the current flowing in the circuit.

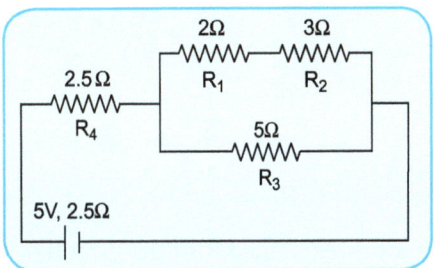

Solution : From the figure, we find resistors R_1 and R_2 are connected in series.

Equivalent resistance $R_s = R_1 + R_2 = 2 + 3 = 5\,\Omega$

R_S is in parallel with resistor R_3. The equivalent resistance of these two is

$$\frac{1}{R_P} = \frac{1}{R_s} + \frac{1}{R_3}$$

i.e. $\dfrac{1}{R_P} = \dfrac{1}{5} + \dfrac{1}{5} = \dfrac{2}{5}$

i.e. $R_P = \dfrac{5}{2} = 2.5\,\Omega$

Now R_P and R_4 are connected in series. Equivalent resistance,

$$R = R_P + R_4$$
$$= 2.5 + 2.5 = 5\,\Omega$$

Given : Internal resistance of the battery, $r = 2.5\,\Omega$, emf = 5 V

Total resistance of the circuit = R + r
$$= 5 + 2.5 = 7.5\,\Omega$$

∴ Total current across the circuit,

$$I = \frac{\text{emf}}{\text{Total resistance}}$$

$$= \frac{5}{7.5} = 0.67\text{ A}$$

15. Find the current flowing through the given circuit connected to a cell of supply 5 V.

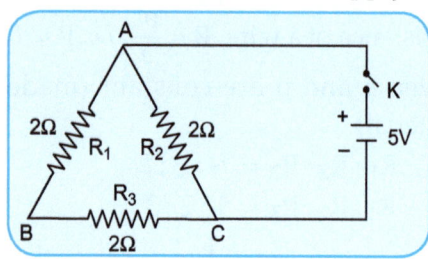

Solution : Given : $R_1 = 2\ \Omega$, $R_2 = 2\ \Omega$, $R_3 = 2\ \Omega$, $V = 5\ V$

From the diagram, resistors R_1 and R_3 are in series.
Equivalent resistance of the two resistors,
$R_S = R_1 + R_3 = 2 + 2 = 4\ \Omega$.
Now, R_S and R_2 are connected in parallel.
Equivalent resistance is
$$\frac{1}{R_P} = \frac{1}{R_S} + \frac{1}{R_2}$$
$$\frac{1}{R_P} = \frac{1}{4} + \frac{1}{2} = \frac{3}{4}$$
i.e. $R_P = \frac{4}{3}\ \Omega$

The total resistance R of the circuit is $4/3\ \Omega$.
Current through the circuit is
$$I = \frac{V}{R} = \frac{5}{4/3} = 3.75\ A$$

16. From the circuit flow diagram given below, calculate the current flowing through the circuit.

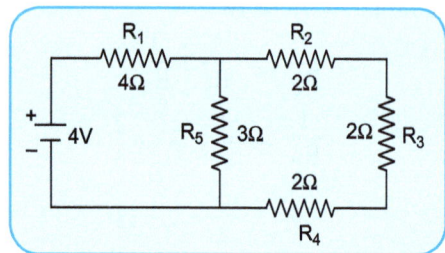

Solution : From the diagram, we know the resistances R_2, R_3 and R_4 are in series. Their effective resistance is
$$R_S = R_2 + R_3 + R_4$$
$$= 2 + 2 + 2 = 6\ \Omega$$
This effective resistance is in parallel to the resistance R_5. The effective resistance of these two is
$$\frac{1}{R_P} = \frac{1}{R_s} + \frac{1}{R_s}$$
i.e. $\frac{1}{R_P} = \frac{1}{6} + \frac{1}{3} = \frac{3}{6}$

i.e. $R_P = \frac{6}{3} = 2\ \Omega$

Now, this effective resistance of 2 Ω is in series with resistance R_1.
The total effective resistance of the circuit R
$= 2 + 4 = 6\ \Omega$
Given Potential difference = 4 V
∴ Current in the circuit is
$$I = V/R$$
$$= 4/6 = 0.67\ A$$

17. Three resistors of 8 Ω, 4 Ω and 2 Ω are connected together in such a way that the total resistance is greater than 8 Ω but less than 10 Ω. Suggest a suitable arrangement of how these resistors can be possibly combined and calculate the total resistance.

Solution : Given : $R_1 = 8\ \Omega$, $R_2 = 4\ \Omega$, $R_3 = 2\ \Omega$
Since the total resistance is greater than the greatest resistance R_1, so R_1 must be in series with the other resistors.
Since the total resistance lies between 8 Ω and 10 Ω, the effective resistance of the resistors R_2 and R_3 must be less than 2 (10Ω − 8Ω). Thus, R_2 and R_3 must be connected in parallel to obtain this. The diagram for this arrangement is given below.

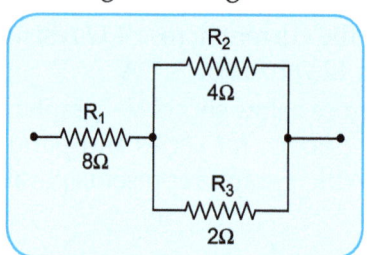

The equivalent resistance of R_2 and R_3 is
$$\frac{1}{R_P} = \frac{1}{R_2} + \frac{1}{R_3}$$
$$= \frac{1}{4} + \frac{1}{2} = \frac{3}{4}$$
$$R_P = \frac{4}{3} = 1.33\ \Omega$$

Now, R_1 is in series with R_P, as shown below.

$\begin{array}{cc} R_1 & R_P \\ \text{—WWW—WWW—} \\ 8\Omega & 1.33\Omega \end{array}$

Thus, the total resistance $= R_1 + R_P = 8 + 1.33$
$= 9.33\ \Omega$, which lies between 8 Ω and 10 Ω.

18. In the given diagram, A_1, A_2 and A_3 are three ammeters of negligible resistance. The reading of ammeter A_3 is 1 A. Calculate (a) the readings

of ammeter A_1 and A_2 and (b) the total resistance of the circuit.

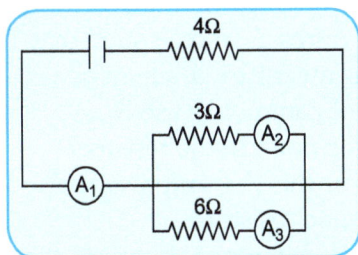

Solution : (a) Given : Reading of ammeter $A_3 = 1$ A. This is equal to current in 6 Ω resistor. Let it be I_3, *i.e.* $I_3 = 1$ A.
Potential difference across 6 Ω resistor = $I_3 \times 6$
= $1 \times 6 = 6$ V
Since 6 Ω resistor is connected in parallel to 3 Ω resistor, the potential difference across 3 Ω resistor will be same, *i.e.* V = 6 V.
Let current across 3 Ω resistor be I_2.
$$I_2 = V/R = 6/3 = 2 \text{ A}$$
This is the reading of ammeter A_2.
Since ammeter A_1 is in series connection, the current across it, I_1, will be equal to the total current I.
$$I_1 = I = 1 + 2 = 3 \text{ A}$$
(b) The equivalent resistance of 3 Ω resistor and 6 Ω resistor in parallel is
$$\frac{1}{R_P} = \frac{1}{3} + \frac{1}{6} = \frac{3}{6}$$
i.e. $\quad R_P = \frac{6}{3} = 2 \text{ Ω}$
Thus, R_P is in series with 4 Ω resistor.
Total resistance of the circuit = 2 + 4 = 6 Ω

19. The diagram below shows three resistors 5 Ω, 8 Ω and 10 Ω connected to a battery of emf 10 V. Calculate (a) the potential difference across the parallel resistors 8 Ω and 10 Ω and (b) the current through 8 Ω resistor.

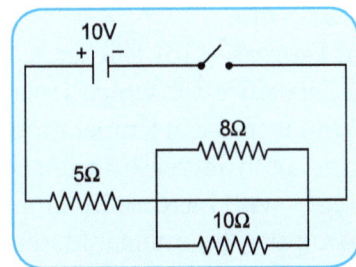

Solution : The equivalent resistance of the two resistors in parallel combination is
$$\frac{1}{R_P} = \frac{1}{8} + \frac{1}{10}$$
$$= \frac{9}{40}$$
i.e. $\quad R_P = \frac{40}{9} = 4.44 \text{ Ω}$
Now, R_P is in series with a 5 Ω resistor.
Total resistance of the circuit is = 4.44 + 5 = 9.44 Ω
Total current drawn from the battery is
$$I = \frac{\text{emf}}{\text{Total resistance}}$$
$$= \frac{10}{9.44} = 1.05 \text{ A}$$
(a) The potential difference across the parallel resistors will be
$$V = I \times R_P$$
$$= 1.05 \times 4.44 = 4.7 \text{ V}$$
(b) Let I_1 be the current through 8 Ω resistor.
$$I_1 = V/8 = 4.7/8 = 0.59 \text{ A}$$

20. A cell of emf 2.5 V and internal resistance 1.5 Ω is connected to resistors of 5 Ω and 15 Ω in series. Draw a circuit diagram and calculate (a) the current in the circuit, (b) the potential difference across each resistor and (c) the total potential difference across the cell.

Solution : The circuit diagram is given below.

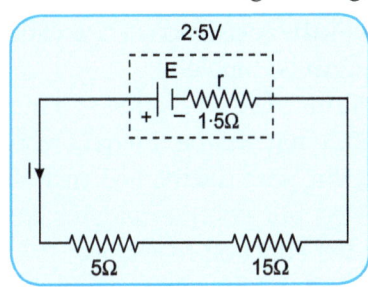

Given : emf = 2.5 V, $R_1 = 5$ Ω, $R_2 = 15$ Ω, $r = 1.5$ Ω
Total resistance of the circuit
$$= R_1 + R_2 + r$$
$$= 5 + 15 + 1.5 = 21.5 \text{ Ω}$$
(a) Current in the circuit
$$I = \frac{\text{emf}}{\text{Total resistance}}$$
$$= \frac{2.5}{21.5} = 0.116 \text{ A}$$
(b) Now, potential difference across R_1
$$V_1 = IR_1$$
$$= 0.116 \times 5 = 0.58 \text{ V}$$
Potential difference across R_2
$$V_2 = IR_2$$
$$= 0.116 \times 15 = 1.74 \text{ V}$$
(c) Total potential difference across the cell
$$= V_1 + V_2$$
$$= 0.58 + 1.74 = 2.32 \text{ V}$$

EXERCISE 8

1. What is meant by current? State its unit.
2. What is the difference between conventional current and electric current?
3. Define one ampere. State the number of electrons in 1 A current passing through a conductor in one second.
4. Which particles are responsible for current in conductors?
5. What is meant by the term 'electric potential'? Explain its analogy with flow of water in a pipe.
6. What is meant by the term 'potential difference between two points'? State its SI unit.
7. Name the devices used for measuring current and potential difference in a circuit.
8. 'The potential difference between two points is 1 V'. Explain the statement.
9. What is meant by the term 'resistance'? What is its SI unit?
10. Explain the flow of current through a conductor. What is the cause of resistance?
11. State any two factors on which the resistance of a conductor depends and how it depends on these factors.
12. How will the resistance of a metallic wire vary if its length is doubled?
13. If the radius of cross-section of a metallic wire is doubled, what will be the new resistance?
14. If a metallic wire is stretched such that its length is doubled but volume remains constant, what will be the effect on resistance?
15. Among metals and non-metals, which one offers more resistance to flow of electric current?
16. Why does the resistance of a metallic conductor increase with increase in temperature?
17. State Ohm's law.
18. Describe an experiment to verify Ohm's law.
19. Name the term given to the reciprocal of resistance. State its unit.
20. What is the condition essential for a conductor to obey Ohm's law?
21. The relationship between the potential difference and the current in a conductor is stated in the form of a law
    (a) Name the law.
    (b) What does the slope of V-I graph for a conductor represent?
    (c) Name the material used for making the connecting wire.
    Ans : (a) Ohm's law, (b) Resistance, (c) Copper.
22. Draw a V–I graph of a conductor at two different temperatures T_1 and T_2 such that $T_1 > T_2$.
23. What is meant by a superconductor? Why are these not commonly used?
24. What is a non-Ohmic resistor?
25. How will the V–I graph vary for a Ohmic and non-Ohmic resistor?
26. State few differences between Ohmic and non-Ohmic resistor.
27. The V-I graph for a series combination and for a parallel combination of two resistors is shown in the figure below. Which of the two A or B represents the parallel combination? Give a reason for your answer.

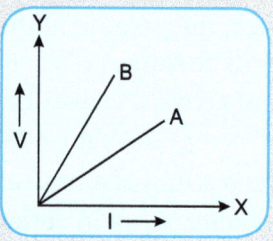

28. What is specific resistance? State its SI unit.
29. Write an expression for resistivity of a conductor.
30. State the two factors that affect the resistivity of a conductor.
31. Does the resistivity of a conductor depend on the current flowing through it?
32. Among two wires, one is made of copper and the other is made of nichrome, each of same length and same radius. Which one will have more resistance and why?
    Ans : Nichrome; because resistivity of nichrome is more than copper
33. (a) What happens to the resistivity of semiconductors with the increase of temperature?
    (b) For a fuse, higher the current rating ...... is the fuse wire.
    Ans : (a) Decreases, (b) Thicker.
34. Name a substance for which resistance (a) increases with increase in temperature, (b) remains unchanged with increase in temperature and (c) decreases with increase in temperature.
    Ans : (a) copper, (b) manganin, (c) silicon
35. Name the material used for making connection wires. Which property of this material makes it a choice for using it as a connecting wire?
    Ans : Copper; small resistivity and thus small resistance

36. Which material would you prefer for a resistance wire : copper or constantan? Give reason.
    Ans : Constantan; negligible effect of temperature on resistance in addition to low resistivity
37. Why is a tungsten wire used in a bulb filament? What will happen if it is replaced by an aluminium wire?
    Ans : High melting point and high resistivity; the bulb would fuse
38. Which alloy is used for making a fuse wire ?
    Ans : Lead and tin alloy
39. State the characteristics required in a material to be used as an effective fuse wire.
40. What is the use of a nichrome wire?
    Ans : Used in heating element of electrical appliances
41. What is meant by electromotive force of a cell? Explain it with the help of an example.
42. State the factors affecting emf of a cell.
43. Does the shape and size of electrodes affect the emf of a cell?
    Ans : No
44. Define terminal voltage of a cell. How is it different from the emf of a cell?
45. A cell is transmitting current in an external circuit. How does the terminal voltage compare with the emf of the cell?
46. What is meant by voltage drop across a cell?
47. What is internal resistance of a cell? State two factors affecting it.
48. Write an expression for emf, terminal voltage and internal resistance of a cell.
49. State the condition when (a) the terminal voltage is equal to the emf of a cell and (b) terminal voltage is greater than the emf of a cell.
    Ans : (a) When the cell is not in use, (b) when the cell is getting charged
50. How will the internal resistance of a cell vary if (a) the concentration of the electrolyte is increased and (b) the distance between the electrodes is increased?
    Ans : Internal resistance will increase in both cases
51. With the help of a diagram, explain how two resistors can be connected in a parallel and series combination respectively.
52. What would be the preferred combination if the effective resistance required is higher than the individual resistances?
53. Among the following statements, choose whether each one is applicable for series or parallel combination :
    (a) The equivalent resistance is less than any of the individual resistors in a circuit.
    (b) The current flowing through each resistor is equal to the current being drawn from the cell.
    (c) The potential difference across each resistor is same.
    Ans : (a) Parallel, (b) Series, (c) Parallel.

MULTIPLE CHOICE QUESTIONS

1. Which among the following metals is not a very good conductor of electricity?
   (a) copper (b) silver
   (c) platinum (d) iron
   Ans : (c)
2. Which of these substances acts as a non-Ohmic resistor?
   (a) nichrome wire (b) tungsten filament
   (c) copper wire (d) aluminium filament
   Ans : (b)
3. If the resistance of a copper wire of certain length is R, then on doubling the length, its resistance :
   (a) will get doubled
   (b) will become halved
   (c) will become quadrupled
   (d) will become $\frac{1}{4}$ th
   Ans : (c)
4. The resistance offered by a conductor is directly proportional to its :
   (a) length (b) area of cross-section
   (c) both (a) and (b) (d) neither (a) nor (b)
   Ans : (a)
5. With increase in temperature, the resistivity of manganin :
   (a) increases (b) decreases
   (c) remains unchanged (d) any of the above
   Ans : (c)
6. Two unequal resistances are connected in parallel across a cell. Which of the following statements is true?
   (a) Current flowing through smaller resistance is higher.
   (b) Current flowing through larger resistance is higher.
   (c) Current flowing through both the resistances is equal.
   (d) Current can be higher in any resistance depending on the emf of the cell.
   Ans : (a)

7. In a series combination of resistors :
   (a) the equivalent resistance is reduced
   (b) the potential difference across each resistor is same
   (c) the current across each resistor is same
   (d) both (b) and (c)
   Ans : (c)
8. The equivalent resistance of three resistors, each of 3 Ω resistance, when joined in parallel combination is :
   (a) 1 Ω   (b) 3 Ω
   (c) 6 Ω   (d) 9 Ω
   Ans : (a)

NUMERICAL PROBLEMS

1. If 3.2×10^{17} electrons pass through a wire in 0.5 s, calculate the current flowing through it.
   Ans : 0.1024 A.
2. Find the number of electrons passing in 1 s through the cross-section of a conductor if a current of 2μA is flowing through it.
   Ans : 1.25×10^{13}
3. A battery can supply a charge of 3×10^3 C. If a 1.5 A current is drawn from the cell, calculate the time in minutes in which the battery will get discharged.
   Ans : 33.33 min.
4. What is the electric potential at a point in an electric field when 30 J of work is done in moving a charge of 90 C from infinity?
   Ans : 0.33 V.
5. Calculate the potential difference required to allow a current of 0.5 A to pass through a wire of resistance 2 Ω.
   Ans : 1V.
6. A music system draws a current of 400 mA when connected to a 12 V battery.
   (a) What is the resistance of the music system ?
   (b) The music system is left playing for several hours and finally the battery voltage drops and the music system stops playing when the current drops to 320 mA. At what battery voltage does the music system stop playing ?
7. What will be the magnitude of current flowing through a conductor that has a resistance of 15 Ω when a potential difference of 10 V is applied at its ends? If the current passing through the conductor is made twice the original current, what will be the potential difference that needs to be applied?
   Ans : 0.667 A, 20 V.
8. The table below gives the readings obtained in an experiment done for verification of Ohm's law.

Observation Number	Current I (ammeter reading) in ampere	Potential difference V (voltmeter reading) in volt
1.	0.1	0.25
2.	0.2	0.50
3.	0.3	0.75
4.	0.4	1.00
5.	0.5	1.25

From the table, (a) draw a V–I graph and (b) calculate the resistance from the graph.

9. Calculate the length of a wire of resistance 5 Ω, if length of a similar wire is 50 cm and resistance 2 Ω.
   Ans : 125 cm
10. A metal wire of resistance 6 Ω is stretched so that its length is increased to twice its original length. Calculate its new resistance.
    Ans : 24 Ω
11. An electric current is passed through a circuit consisting of two wires of same material connected in parallel. If the length and radii of the wires are in the ratio 4 : 3 and 2 : 3, respectively, calculate the ratio of currents passing through the wire.
    Hint : The wires are made of same material and thus have same resistivity.
    Ans : 1 : 3
12. A wire of resistance 2 Ω and length 20 cm is stretched such that the length becomes 40 cm but its volume remains unchanged. Calculate the new resistance.
    Ans : 8 Ω
13. Calculate the resistivity of a wire if its radius is 1 mm, length is 200 m and resistance across it is 4 Ω.
    Ans : 6.28×10^{-8} Ω m
14. A cell supplies a current of 2.5 A when it is connected to a 5 Ω resistor and a current of 1.5 A when connected to a 10 Ω resistor. Find (a) internal resistance and (b) emf of the cell.
    Ans : (a) 2.5 Ω, (b) 18.75 V
15. When three resistors, each of resistances 2 Ω, are connected in parallel, what is the effective resistance?
    Ans : 0.67 Ω
16. Calculate the effective resistance if three resistors of 2 Ω, 4 Ω and 6 Ω resistances are connected in series.
    Ans : 12 Ω

17. Calculate the equivalent resistance between the points A and B for the following combination of resistors :

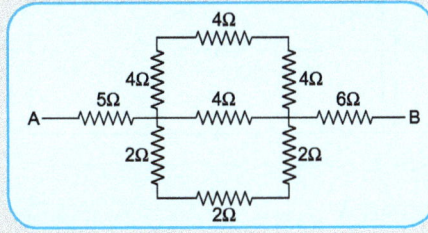

Ans : 13 Ω

18. Find the equivalent resistance between points A and B.

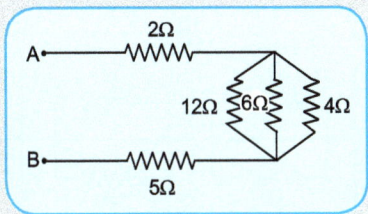

Ans : 9 Ω

19. Determine the effective resistance between points X and Y from the diagram given below.

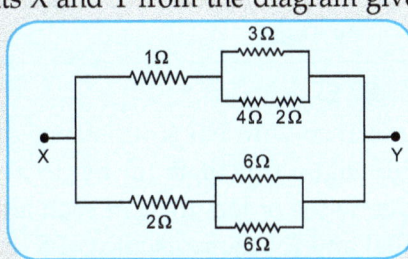

Ans : 1.87 Ω

20. Calculate the effective resistance between points A and F from the diagram given below.

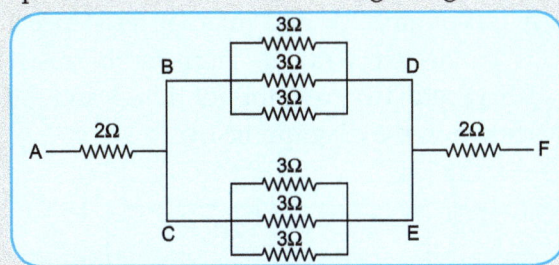

Ans : 4.5 Ω

21. Three resistors are connected to a 12 V battery as shown in the figure below.

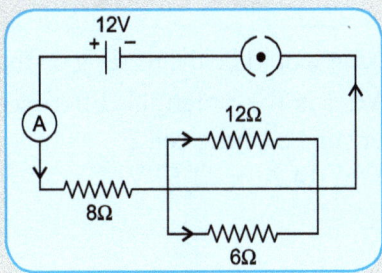

(a) What is the current through the 8 Ω resistor?
(b) What is the potential difference across the parallel combination of 6 Ω and 12 Ω resistor?
(c) What is the current through the 6 Ω resistor?
Ans : (a) 1 A, (b) 4 V, (c) 0.67 A.

22. Calculate the equivalent resistance between P and Q in the given diagram.

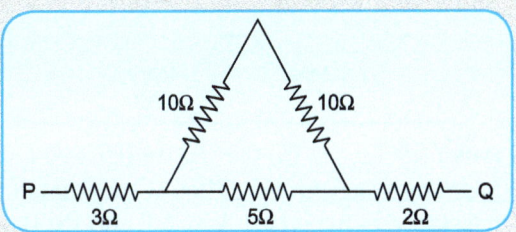

Ans : 9 Ω

23. A resistor of 6 Ω is connected in series with a resistor of 4 Ω. A potential difference of 20 V is applied across the combination. Draw the circuit diagram and calculate the current through the circuit and potential difference across 6 Ω resistance.
Ans : 2 A, 12 V

24. There are two sets of resistors joined in series in a circuit. Set 1 has two resistors of 10 Ω and 40 Ω in parallel combination. Set 2 has three resistors of 20 Ω, 30 Ω and 60 Ω in parallel combination. A potential difference of 12 V is applied across the combination. Draw a circuit diagram to represent this arrangement. Calculate (a) the total resistance and (b) the total current flowing in the circuit.
Ans : (a) 18 Ω, (b) 0.67 A

25. Three resistors are connected to a 6 V battery as shown in the diagram below. Calculate (a) the equivalent resistance of the circuit, (b) total current in the circuit, (c) potential difference across the 7.2 Ω resistor.

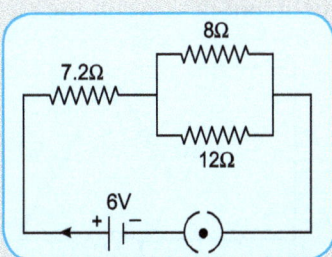

Ans : (a) 12 Ω, (b) 0.5 A, (c) 3.6 V

26. Four resistors are connected such that effective resistance is 50 Ω. If the resistance of three resistors is 5 Ω, 12 Ω and 15 Ω, respectively, calculate the resistance of the fourth resistor.
Ans : 18 Ω

27. The diagram given below shows a battery of emf 8 V. Calculate the (a) current drawn from the battery, (b) current flowing in the resistor of 4 Ω and (c) current flowing in the resistor of 12 Ω.

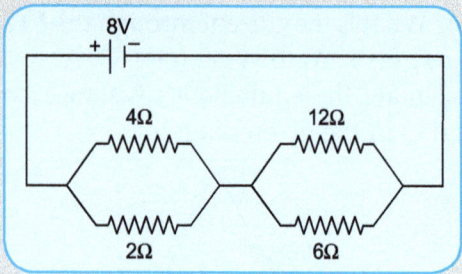

Ans : (a) 1.5 A, (b) 0.5 A, (c) 0.5 A

28. From the diagram given below, calculate the total resistance between (a) A and F and (b) B and E.

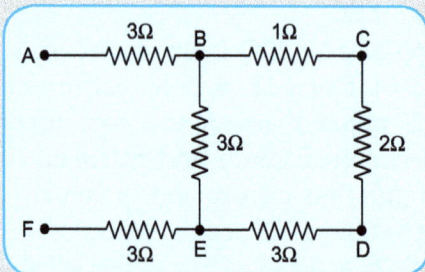

Ans : (a) 8 Ω, (b) 2 Ω

29. From the figure given below, calculate the resistance between the points (a) P and Q, (b) R and S and (c) A and B.

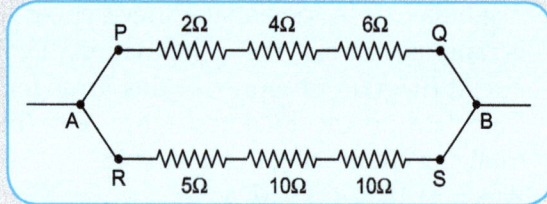

Ans : (a) 12 Ω, (b) 25 Ω, (c) 8.1 Ω

30. How can three resistors of 2 Ω, 3 Ω and 6 Ω be connected to give an equivalent resistance of 4 Ω? Explain with a diagram.

31. In the figure shown below, I_1 = 0.4 A. Calculate the total current flowing in the circuit.

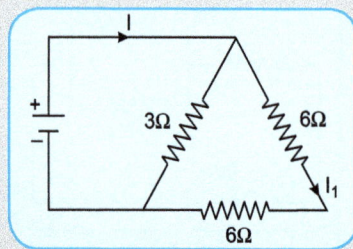

Ans : 2 A

32. In the diagram given below, the current across 4 Ω resistor is 1.2 A. Find the potential difference across points B and C.

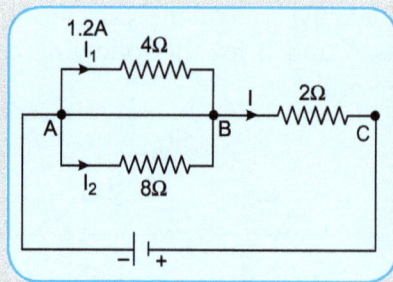

Ans : 3.6 V

33. Find the current drawn from a cell of emf 1 V and internal resistance 0.66 Ω connected to the combination of resistors shown in the figure below.

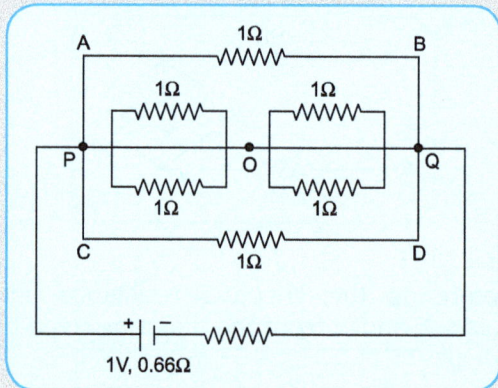

Ans : 4.5 Ω

34. A resistance wire has a resistance of 5 Ω per metre length. Calculate (a) the total resistance if three wires of length 2 m each are joined in parallel and (b) the resistance of 5 m length of wire of same material but double the area of cross-section.

Ans : (a) 3.33 Ω, (b) 12.5 Ω

35. A cell of emf 2 V and internal resistance 1.2 Ω is connected with an ammeter of resistance 0.8 Ω and two resistors of 4.5 Ω and 9 Ω as shown in the diagram below :

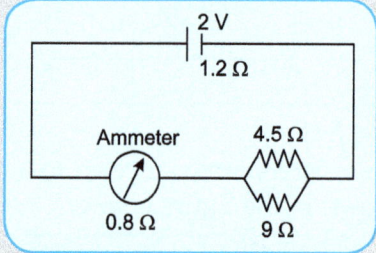

(a) What would be the reading on the Ammeter ?
(b) What is the potential difference across the terminals of the cell ?

Ans : (a) 0.4 A, (b) 1.52 V

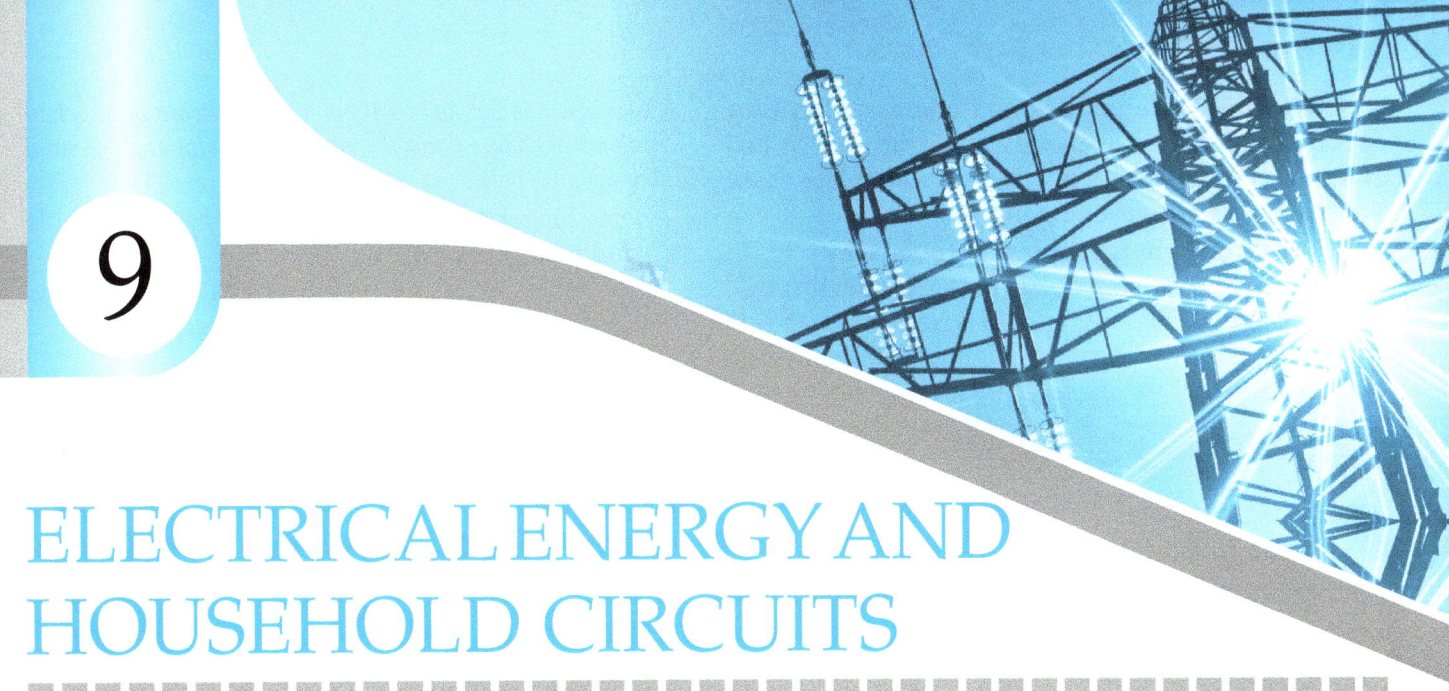

9

ELECTRICAL ENERGY AND HOUSEHOLD CIRCUITS

LEARNING OUTCOMES

- Electrical energy and power
- Power rating and household consumption of electrical energy
- Heating effect of current : Joule's law
- Power transmission and distribution
- Household circuits : Wiring systems
- Fuse and switch
- Plug and socket
- Earthing
- Colour coding of cable wires

(A) ELECTRICAL ENERGY AND POWER

9.1 ELECTRICAL ENERGY

By now, we are familiar with various forms of energy that exist, such as mechanical energy, chemical energy, heat energy and light energy. But the most commonly used energy form by everyone is the *electrical energy*. According to the law of conservation of energy, "Energy can neither be created, nor be destroyed, it can only be transformed from one form to another". All modern day devices make use of electrical energy where it is converted into various forms of energy.

Electrical energy is the energy spent in moving electric charges through a conductor, that is possessed by electric current.

Examples of Transformation of Electrical Energy to other Forms of Energy

1. Electrical energy to heat energy : This is one of the most common forms of energy conversion. Most electrical appliances, such as toaster, heater, oven and geyser, make use of electrical energy for their primary functioning. When current passes through the wires of these appliances, heat is produced due to the resistance of the wires, thereby transforming electrical energy to heat energy.

2. Electrical energy to light energy : It is one of the most important energy conversion required in our everyday life. A common example of this is an electric bulb. When current passes through the filament of a bulb, the filament is heated and begins to emit light. In this case, the electrical energy is converted to both light energy and heat energy.

3. Electrical energy to chemical energy : This kind of conversion occurs when an electrochemical cell is charged. Here, when electric current is passed through the electrolyte solution of the cell, a chemical reaction occurs and thus converts electrical energy into chemical energy.

4. Electrical energy to mechanical energy : When electrical energy is passed through the coils of an electric motor, mechanical energy is produced. In an electric motor, a couple acts on a freely suspended coil in a magnetic field due to which it rotates. The electric motor is used in many appliances such as an electric fan, a mixer and washing machine. Besides mechanical energy, a part of electrical energy is also converted to heat energy and results in appliances heating.

5. Electrical energy to sound energy : This type of conversion occurs in a loudspeaker, an electric bell and so on. In these devices, the electrical pulses cause vibrations, thereby resulting in sound.

6. Electrical energy to magnetic energy : In an electromagnet, an electric current passing through an insulated coil wound around a soft iron bar gets converted to magnetic energy and magnetises the iron bar.

Expression for Electrical Energy

Electrical energy is the total work done by an electric current when it flows through a conductor in a given time.

It is known to us that the amount of *work done* in carrying a *unit positive charge* from one point to another in an electric field is the *potential difference* in the given electrical circuit.

If W is the amount of work done in carrying Q charge from one point to another in an electric field such that V is the potential difference, then

$$V = \frac{W}{Q}$$

or $\quad W = VQ \quad$ ...(9.1)

If a current I flows through a conductor in time t, the charge Q is given by

$$Q = It$$

∴ $\quad W = VIt \quad$ ...(9.2)

It is the work that measures the electrical energy supplied by the cell/battery (source of electric current).

Electrical Energy in terms of Ohm's Law

According to Ohm's law, V = IR

Applying this relationship in equation (9.2), we obtain

$$W = I^2Rt \quad ...(9.3)$$

Further, as I = V/R, equation (9.3) can be written as

$$W = \left(\frac{V}{R}\right)^2 \times Rt$$

i.e. $\quad W = \frac{V^2 t}{R} \quad$ ...(9.4)

From equations (9.1) to (9.4), the expression of electrical energy supplied by a given source can be written as

$$W = QV = VIt = I^2Rt = \frac{V^2 t}{R}$$

Units of Electrical Energy

The SI unit of electrical energy is *joule* (J), similar to other forms of energy.

As,

$$W = QV$$

1 joule = 1 coulomb × 1 volt

One joule is defined as the amount of work done when 1 coulomb of charge flows through a conductor at a potential difference of 1 volt.

Some bigger units of electrical energy are kilojoule (kJ) and megajoule (MJ).

$$1 \text{ kJ} = 10^3 \text{ J and } 1 \text{ MJ} = 10^6 \text{ J}$$

The CGS unit of electrical energy is *erg*.

$$1 \text{ erg} = 10^{-7} \text{ J}$$

9.2 ELECTRICAL POWER

Electrical power is defined as the rate at which work is done by an electric current or the rate at which electrical energy is supplied by the source of electric current.

If W is the amount of work done in time t, then

Power, $\quad P = \frac{W}{t} \quad$ ...(9.5)

From equation (9.2),

$$W = VIt$$

∴ $\quad P = \frac{VIt}{t} = VI \quad$ ...(9.6)

Electrical power in terms of Ohm's law

From Ohm's law,

$$V = IR$$

or $\quad I = V/R$

Substituting value of I from Ohm's law in equation (9.6), we obtain

$$P = \frac{V^2}{R} \quad ...(9.7)$$

or $\quad P = \frac{(IR)^2}{R} = I^2R \quad$ ...(9.8)

From equation (9.5) to (9.8), the expression of electrical power can be written as

$$P = \frac{W}{t} = VI = \frac{V^2}{R} = I^2R$$

Units of Electrical Power

The SI unit of electrical power is J s^{-1} (work/time) or *watt*.

From equation (9.6),

$$P = VI$$

Hence, unit of power = *volt ampere* (VA).

P = 1 W, if V = 1 V and I = 1 A.

One watt is the electrical power consumed when a current of 1 ampere flows through a conductor at a potential difference of 1 volt.

Few bigger units of power are kilowatt (kW), megawatt (MW) and gigawatt (GW).

$$1 \text{ kW} = 10^3 \text{ W}$$
$$1 \text{ MW} = 10^6 \text{ W}$$
$$1 \text{ GW} = 10^9 \text{ W}$$

Smaller units of power are milliwatt (mW) and microwatt (μW).

$$1 \text{ mW} = 10^{-3} \text{ W}$$
$$1 \text{ μW} = 10^{-6} \text{ W}$$

Horsepower (h.p.) : It is another bigger unit of power that is used in auto industries and mechanical engineering.

$$1 \text{ h.p.} = 746 \text{ W} = 0.746 \text{ kW}$$

9.3 COMMERCIAL UNITS OF ELECTRICAL ENERGY

As, Power = Energy/Time

∴ Energy = Power × Time

The unit of power is *watt* and the unit of time is *second*, so the unit of energy is *watt × second* (Ws).

However, this unit is too small for measuring large quantities of energy. The bigger units of energy used commercially are watt-hour (Wh) and kilowatt-hour (kWh).

One watt-hour (1 Wh) is the amount of electrical energy consumed by a source of power 1 watt in 1 hour.

$$1 \text{ watt-hour (Wh)} = 1 \text{ watt} \times 1 \text{ hour}$$
$$= 1 \text{ Js}^{-1} \times 3{,}600 \text{ s}$$
$$= 3{,}600 \text{ J} = 3.6 \text{ kJ}$$

Thus, $1 \text{ Wh} = 3{,}600 \text{ J}$ ...(9.9)

One kilowatt-hour (1 kWh) is the amount of energy consumed by a source of power 1 kW in 1 hour.

$$1 \text{ kilowatt-hour (kWh)} = 1 \text{ kilowatt} \times 1 \text{ hour}$$
$$= 1{,}000 \text{ Js}^{-1} \times 3{,}600 \text{ s}$$
$$= 3.6 \times 10^6 \text{ J} = 3.6 \text{ MJ}$$

Thus, $1 \text{ kWh} = 3.6 \times 10^6 \text{ J}$ ...(9.10)

One unit of electricity or electrical energy consumed in houses and industries is equal to 1 kWh.

9.4 POWER RATING OF COMMON APPLIANCES

The commonly used electrical appliances in households such as a bulb, heater, oven, fan and juicer are rated in terms of power and voltage. A simple electric bulb is often rated as 100 W, 250 V, which means if the bulb is lighted up with a 250 V supply, it consumes 100 W of electric power. This also implies that 100 J of electrical energy is converted into heat and light energies in 1 s.

From the power-voltage rating of an appliance, (a) its resistance, and (b) the safe limit of current that can flow through it, can be calculated.

Since $P = \dfrac{V^2}{R}$

∴ $R = \dfrac{V^2}{P}$

i.e. Resistance = $\dfrac{\text{(Voltage rating of the appliance)}^2}{\text{Power rating of the appliance}}$ ...(9.11)

Since $R = \dfrac{V}{I}$

∴ $I = \dfrac{P}{V}$

i.e. Safe current = $\dfrac{\text{Power rating of the appliance}}{\text{Voltage rating of the appliance}}$ ...(9.12)

Example : The rating of a bulb is 100 W, 250 V. The resistance of the filament of the bulb will be

$$R = \dfrac{V^2}{P} = \dfrac{(250)^2}{100} = 625 \text{ Ω}$$

This is the resistance of the filament when the bulb is glowing, which is much higher than the resistance when the bulb is not glowing. This is because, the resistance of the filament increases with increase in temperature. A glowing bulb has a higher temperature and thus higher resistance than a cold non-glowing bulb.

The safe limit of current flowing though the filament of the bulb when it is glowing is

$$I = \dfrac{P}{V} = \dfrac{100}{250} = 0.4 \text{ A}$$

If the voltage supplied to the bulb is marginally higher than its voltage rating, then due to a slightly larger flow of current, the bulb will glow more brightly and will thus consume more power. Similarly, if the voltage supplied to the bulb is marginally lower than its voltage rating, due to smaller flow of current, the bulb will glow faintly and will consume less power. This is true only if the resistance of the filament in the electric bulb is taken as constant.

However, if the voltage supplied to the bulb is substantially higher than its voltage rating, then the current passing through the filament of the bulb would be quite higher than its safe limit. This would result in an increase in temperature of the filament, causing it to melt, and thus the bulb would fuse.

Example : Suppose a heater coil is rated as 2,000 W, 220 V. It means that the coil would consume 2,000 W power at a 220 V supply. The resistance of the coil would be

$$R = \dfrac{V^2}{P} = \dfrac{(220)^2}{2{,}000} = 24.2 \text{ Ω}$$

This is the resistance of the coil when it is hot. The resistance of the coil would be less than this when the coil is not hot.

If the heater is connected to a voltage supply of 110 V, the power consumed by it would be

$$P = \frac{V^2}{R} = \frac{(110)^2}{24.2} = 500 \text{ W}$$

The power consumed by the heater is much less than its rating.

In the example discussed, the calculation is based on the assumption that the resistance of the coil is same at both 110 V and 220 V. However, it is not true. At 110 V supply, the resistance of the coil would be less than 24.2 Ω and so the power consumed would be more than 500 W but less than 2,000 W.

Now, if the heater is connected to a higher voltage supply, say 250 V, the power consumed by it would be

$$P = \frac{V^2}{R} = \frac{(250)^2}{24.2} = 2,582.6 \text{ W}$$

Which is greater than its rating. Again this power would be consumed, assuming that the resistance remains constant. In actual practice, the resistance would be more than 24.2 Ω at 250 V supply and the power consumed would be less than 2,582.6 W but more than 2,000 W.

Table 9.1 presents the power rating of some common electrical appliances at 220 V.

Table 9.1 : Approximate power rating of common appliances

Appliance	Power (in W)
Tube light	36–52
Radio/tape recorder	50
Ceiling fan	75
Television	80
Electric bulb	100
Computer	300
Washing machine	230–320
Water pump	375
Refrigerator	100–400
Electric mixer	250–400
Vacuum cleaner	600
Electric iron	750
Toaster	750
Electric kettle	1,000
Room air conditioner	1,400–2,100
Geyser	2,000

In India, the current supplied for domestic use is at a voltage of 220 V.

9.5 HOUSEHOLD CONSUMPTION OF ELECTRICAL ENERGY

The amount of electrical energy consumed in houses is recorded by an *electrical meter* placed in the premises of each house. The meter measures the amount of electrical energy in the unit of kilowatt-hour (kWh) which is commonly referred to as *Board of Trade Unit* (BOTU). It is this unit in which the electrical energy or electricity is sold by the board and paid by the consumer.

$$1 \text{ kWh} = \frac{\text{watt (power)} \times \text{hour (time)}}{1,000}$$

i.e. $$1 \text{ kWh} = \frac{\text{volt} \times \text{ampere} \times \text{hour}}{1,000} \quad ...(9.13)$$

The electrical appliances used in households have their power ratings mentioned on them in the kW unit. The amount of energy consumed by an appliance can be obtained by multiplying its power rating with the duration of time in hours, for which it has been used. The cost of electricity consumed is given as rate in rupees per kWh unit of energy consumed. Hence, once the electrical energy consumed is calculated, its cost is paid accordingly in rupees.

In households, different appliances have different power ratings, and they might be used for same or different duration of time per day. For instance, an electric fan is used more per day than a juicer or mixer. So the energy consumed for each appliance is calculated separately and the total energy consumed by all appliances is then added up.

Example : An electric heater is rated as 2 kWh and it is used every day for 1 h, whereas an electric fan is rated as 1 kWh and is used for 8 h every day. Let the cost of electrical energy consumed be ₹ 3 per unit. We need to calculate the total operating cost for 1 month.

The total time for which the heater is used in 1 month = 30 × 1 h = 30 h.

The total electrical energy consumed by heater in 30 h = 2 × 30 = 60 kWh.

The operating cost of heater = 60 × 3 = ₹ 180.

Similarly, the total time for which the fan is used in 1 month = 30 × 8 = 240 h.

The total electrical energy consumed by fan in 240 h = 1 × 240 = 240 kWh.

The operating cost of fan = 240 × 3 = ₹ 720.

Hence, the total operating cost of both appliances is ₹ 180 + ₹ 720 = ₹ 900.

9.6 HEATING EFFECT OF CURRENT : JOULE'S LAW OF HEATING

We know that the current passing through a conductor such as a metallic wire results in heat production due to collisions of electrons with the fixed positive ions present in the conductor.

The amount of heat produced in a wire depends on the following *three* factors :

1. The amount of current passing through the wire : The amount of heat (H) produced in a wire is *directly* proportional to the square of current (I) passing through the wire, i.e. $H \propto I^2$. More current indicates the larger number of electrons drifting through the wire and thus more number of collisions with the positive ions. As the flow of current through a wire increases, it gradually heats up.

2. The time of flow of current through the wire : The amount of heat (H) produced in a wire is *directly* proportional to the time (t) for which current is passed in the wire, i.e. $H \propto t$. The longer the current is passed in the wire, greater is the heat produced.

3. The resistance of wire : The amount of heat (H) produced in a wire is *directly* proportional to the resistance (R) of the wire, i.e. $H \propto R$. Higher the resistance of the wire, larger is the number of collisions and thus greater is the heat produced.

From the above factors, heat produced in a wire can be written as

$$H = I^2Rt \qquad ...(9.14)$$

This relation is known as *Joule's law of heating*.

Thus, more heat will be produced in a given conductor if a stronger current is passed for a longer time through a conductor of large resistance.

The SI unit of heat produced is *joule* (J).

$$1 \text{ J} = 0.24 \text{ calorie (cal)}$$

Hence, $\qquad H = I^2Rt = 0.24 \, I^2Rt \text{ cal} \quad ...(9.15)$

ILLUSTRATIVE EXAMPLES

1. An electric motor draws a current of 5 A from a 220 V line. Determine the power of the motor and the energy consumed in 2 h.
   Solution : Given : I = 5 A, V = 220 V, t = 2 h = 2 × 60 × 60 = 7,200 s
   Power, P = VI = 220 × 5 = 1,100 W
   Energy consumed by the motor
   $$W = VIt$$
   $$= 220 \times 5 \times 7{,}200 = 7.92 \times 10^6 \text{ J}$$

2. A heater has a power of 1.1 kW at 220 V. (a) Find the resistance of the heater. (b) Calculate the energy in kWh consumed in a week if the heater is used daily for 4 h.
   Solution : Given : P = 1.1 kW = 1,100 W, V = 220 V, t = 7 × 4 = 28 h
   (a) Resistance of the heater
   $$R = \frac{V^2}{P} = \frac{(220)^2}{1{,}100} = 44 \, \Omega$$
   (b) Energy consumed by the heater in 1 week is
   $$W = P \times t$$
   $$= 1{,}100 \times 28$$
   $$= 30{,}800 \text{ Wh} = 30.8 \text{ kWh}$$

3. An electric heater draws 5 A of current for 10 min when connected to 230 V power supply. Find the heat energy developed.
   Solution : Given : I = 5 A, t = 10 min = 10 × 60 = 600 s, V = 230 V
   Heat energy developed by the heater is
   $$H = VIt = 230 \times 5 \times 600 = 6{,}90{,}000 \text{ J} = 690 \text{ kJ}$$

4. Find the current flowing through an electric bulb rated as 100 W, 220 V when connected to a 110 V supply. What will be the power consumed now?
   Solution : Given : P = 100 W, V = 220 V
   Resistance of the bulb
   $$R = \frac{V^2}{P} = \frac{(220)^2}{100} = 484 \, \Omega$$
   Now, R = 484 Ω, V = 110 V
   Current flowing through the bulb is
   $$I = \frac{V}{R} = \frac{110}{484} = 0.227 \text{ A}$$
   Power consumed, P = VI = 110 × 0.227 = 25 W

5. Three bulbs, A, B and C, are connected in parallel across a 110 V source. The rating of bulb A is 50 W, 110 V, bulb B is 20 W, 110 V and bulb C is 100 W, 110 V. (a) Calculate the current flowing in each bulb. (b) Which bulb will glow the brightest?
   Solution : Given : for bulb A, P = 50 W, V = 110 V
   For bulb B, P = 20 W, V = 110 V
   For bulb C, P = 100 W, V = 110 V
   (a) Resistance of bulb A,
   $$R_A = \frac{V^2}{P_A} = \frac{(110)^2}{50} = 242 \, \Omega$$
   Resistance of bulb B,
   $$R_B = \frac{V^2}{P_B} = \frac{(110)^2}{20} = 605 \, \Omega$$
   Resistance of bulb C,
   $$R_C = \frac{V^2}{P_C} = \frac{(110)^2}{100} = 121 \, \Omega$$

Since the bulbs are connected in parallel, the voltage across each bulb will be same, i.e., 110 V.

Current in bulb A = $I_A = \dfrac{V}{R_A} = \dfrac{110}{242} = 0.45$ A

Current in bulb B = $I_B = \dfrac{V}{R_B} = \dfrac{110}{605} = 0.18$ A

Current in bulb C = $I_C = \dfrac{V}{R_C} = \dfrac{110}{121} = 0.9$ A

(b) The voltage rating of each bulb is same. The maximum power consumed at this voltage is by bulb C, i.e. 100 W. Thus, it will glow the brightest.

6. Two resistors with resistances $R_1 = 5\,\Omega$ and $R_2 = 7\,\Omega$ are connected in series across a battery of emf 16 V. Draw a circuit diagram and find (a) the electrical energy consumed by each resistor in 30 s and (b) total power developed in the circuit.

Solution : The circuit diagram is shown below :

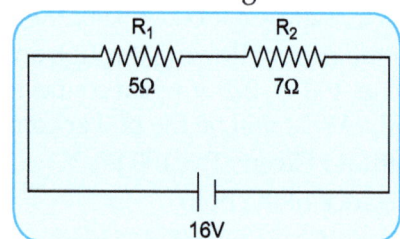

Given : $R_1 = 5\,\Omega$, $R_2 = 7\,\Omega$, $V = 16$ V, $t = 30$ s
Total resistance of the circuit in series
$= R_1 + R_2 = 5 + 7 = 12\,\Omega$

Current flowing in the circuit is
$$I = \dfrac{V}{R} = \dfrac{16}{12} = 1.33 \text{ A}.$$

In series connection, the current flowing through each resistor is same.

Electrical energy consumed by resistor R_1,
$W_1 = I^2 R_1 t$
$= (1.33)^2 \times 5 \times 30 = 265.33$ J

Electrical energy consumed by resistor R_2,
$W_2 = I^2 R_2 t$
$= (1.33)^2 \times 7 \times 30 = 371.47$ J

(b) Total power developed in the circuit,
$P = VI = 16 \times 1.33 = 21.28$ W

7. In the previous example, if the resistors are connected in parallel instead of series, what would be the electrical energy consumed by each resistor. Draw a circuit diagram for the same.

Solution : In parallel connection, the voltage across each resistor remains the same.

Electrical energy consumed by resistor R_1,
$$W_1 = \dfrac{V^2 t}{R_1} = \dfrac{(16)^2 \times 30}{5}$$
$= 1,536$ W

Electrical energy consumed by resistor R_2,
$$W_2 = \dfrac{V^2 t}{R_2} = \dfrac{(16)^2 \times 30}{7}$$
$= 1,097.14$ W

The circuit diagram is given below.

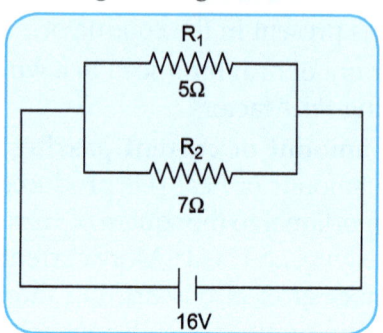

8. Two bulbs are rated as 40 W, 220 V and 40 W, 110 V, respectively. Compare the resistance of two bulbs.

Solution : Given : $P_1 = 40$ W, $V_1 = 220$ V, $P_2 = 40$ W, $V_2 = 110$ V

Resistance of bulb 1,
$$R_1 = \dfrac{V^2}{P_1} = \dfrac{(220)^2}{40} = 1{,}210\,\Omega$$

Resistance of bulb 2
$$R_2 = \dfrac{V^2}{P_2} = \dfrac{(110)^2}{40} = 302.5\,\Omega$$

Ratio of resistances of two bulbs = $R_1 : R_2$
$= 1{,}210 : 302.5 = 4 : 1$

9. A geyser is rated 1.5 kW, 250 V. It is connected to 250 V mains. Calculate (a) the current drawn by the geyser, (b) electrical energy consumed in 10 h in joules and (c) cost of energy consumed at ₹ 3.50 per kWh.

Solution : Given : P = 1.5 kW = 1,500 W, V = 250 V, $t = 10$ h $= 10 \times 60 \times 60 = 36{,}000$ s.

(a) Current drawn by the geyser is
$$I = \dfrac{P}{V} = \dfrac{1{,}500}{250} = 6\text{ A}$$

(b) Electrical energy consumed is
$VIt = 250 \times 6 \times 36{,}000$
$= 54 \times 10^6$ J

(c) Energy consumed in kWh is
$$\dfrac{54 \times 10^6}{3.6 \times 10^6} = 15 \text{ kWh}$$

Cost of energy consumed = $15 \times 3.50 = ₹52.50$.

10. Four tube lights of 40 W each, two fans of 100 W each and three bulbs of 60 W each operate on an average of 8 h per day. If the cost of energy is ₹ 2.50 per kWh, calculate the monthly bill.

Solution : Given : Power of each tube light = 40 W, Power of each fan = 100 W, Power of each bulb = 60 W, t = 8 h per day = 8 × 30 = 240 h per month.
Power of four tube lights = 4 × 40 = 160 W
Power of two fans = 2 × 100 = 200 W

Power of three bulbs = 3 × 60 = 180 W
Total power consumed = 160 + 200 + 180 = 540 W
Total energy consumed in a month
= P × t = 540 × 240 = 1,29,600 Wh = 129.6 kWh
Total cost = 129.6 × 2.50 = ₹324.

EXERCISE 9(A)

1. Give one example of conversion of (a) electrical energy to mechanical energy, (b) electrical energy to heat energy and (c) electrical energy to chemical energy.
2. Write an expression for the electrical energy in terms of its potential difference, resistance and time.
   Ans : V^2t/R, where V is the potential difference, R is the resistance and t is the time
3. Write an expression for the electrical energy spent in the flow of current through an electrical appliance in terms of I, R and t.
   Ans : $W = I^2Rt$
4. Define one joule.
5. Write an expression for electrical power spent by the flow of current through a conductor in terms of (a) current and resistance and (b) potential difference and resistance.
   Ans : (a) I^2R, (b) V^2/R
6. State the unit of electrical power. How would you define it?
7. What is horsepower? How is it related to watt?
8. What is the commercial unit of electrical energy? How is it related to one joule?
9. "The power of a heater is 1 kW." Explain the statement.
10. Name the two physical quantities that can be calculated from the power-voltage rating of an appliance.
    Ans : Resistance and safe limit of current.
11. "An electric bulb is rated as 60 W, 220 V." What would you infer from this statement?
12. The safe limit of current flowing through the filament of a bulb is 0.5 A when it is glowing due to a voltage supply of 250 V. What would be the effect on the bulb if (a) voltage is reduced to 220 V and (b) voltage is increased to 280 V?
13. The resistance of a coil of an electric heater is 25 Ω when it is hot. Will the resistance be more or less than 25 Ω if the coil is cold?
    Ans : Less
14. If the voltage supply to an appliance is reduced to half of its voltage rating, what would be the effect on the power consumed by it?
    Ans : The power consumed will be one-fourth.
15. What is the voltage of electricity that is supplied to a house in India?
    Ans : 220 V
16. Name any three electrical appliances used commonly in our houses. State its voltage and power rating. Calculate the approximate time for each appliance that is used in a day and find the electrical energy consumed by each appliance in a month.
17. What is meant by Board of Trade unit?
18. How is the cost of electricity consumed by an electrical appliance calculated from its power rating?
19. What is the expression for Joule's law of heating?
20. If current flowing through a wire is doubled, what will be the effect on amount of heat produced in it?
21. State any two factors on which the heat produced in a wire depends when current flows through it.

MULTIPLE CHOICE QUESTIONS

1. One watt-hour is equal to :
   (a) 36 J
   (b) 360 J
   (c) 3,600 J
   (d) 36,000 J
   Ans : (c)
2. An electric bulb is rated 100 W, 220 V. The resistance of the filament of the bulb when it is glowing is :
   (a) 2.2 Ω
   (b) 0.45 Ω
   (c) 45.45 Ω
   (d) 484 Ω
   Ans : (d)
3. One megawatt is equal to :
   (a) 10^{-3} W
   (b) 10^3 W
   (c) 10^{-6} W
   (d) 10^6 W
   Ans : (d)

4. Which of the following expressions is incorrect for electrical energy?
   (a) QV (b) VI
   (c) I²Rt (d) V²t/R
   Ans : (b)

5. The rating of a fan is 80 W, 250 V. The current flowing through it is :
   (a) 0.32 A (b) 3.12 A
   (c) 25.6 A (d) None of these
   Ans : (a)

NUMERICAL PROBLEMS

1. Calculate the energy consumed by a heater that draws a current of 5 A at 220 V for 2 min.
   Ans : 132 kJ

2. The power consumed by a geyser is 2 kW. If it is operated at 250 V, calculate (a) the current flowing through it and (b) the resistance offered by it.
   Ans : (a) 8 A, (b) 31.25 Ω

3. An electric bulb is marked 100 V, 250 W. What information does this convey? How much current will the bulb draw if connected to a 250 V supply?
   Ans : 6.25 A

4. Calculate the quantity of heat produced in a 20 Ω resistor carrying 2.5 A current in 5 minutes.
   Ans : 37.5 kJ

5. A current of 2 A passes through a conductor and produces 60 J of heat in 10 s. Find the resistance of the conductor.
   Ans : 1.5 Ω

6. The current flowing through a 10 V tungsten filament lamp connected to a 10 V battery of negligible resistance is 2 A. Calculate (a) the resistance of the filament, (b) the power of the lamp and (c) the electrical energy consumed in 3 h.
   Ans : (a) 5 Ω, (b) 20 W, (c) 60 Wh

7. A bulb rated 40 W, 120 V is operated at 80 V. Find the (a) current flowing through the bulb, (b) power consumed by it and (c) the safe current that can flow through the bulb without getting it damaged.
   Ans : (a) 0.22 A, (b) 17.77 W, (c) 0.33 A

8. An electric iron is rated as 1,000 W, 220 V. Calculate the electrical energy consumed by it in 10 h.
   Ans : 9.98 kW

9. An appliance with a resistance of 500 Ω is operated at 200 V. Calculate the energy consumed by it in 2 min (a) in joules and (b) in kWh.
   Ans : (a) 9,600 J, (b) 0.00266 kWh

10. An electrical appliance is rated at 1,000 kVA, 220 V. If the appliance is operated for 2 h, calculate the energy consumed by the appliance in (a) kWh and (b) joule.
    Ans : (a) 2 × 10³ kWh, (b) 7.2 × 10⁹ J

11. Two bulbs are marked 100 W, 220 V and 60 W, 110 V. Calculate the ratio of their resistances.
    Ans : 2.4 : 1

12. A battery of emf 12 V and internal resistance 2 Ω is connected with two resistors A and B of resistance 4 Ω and 6 Ω respectively joined in series.

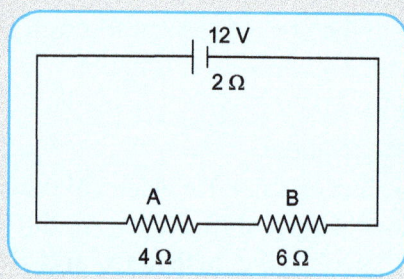

Find :
(a) Current in the circuit.
(b) The terminal voltage of the cell.
(c) The potential difference across 6 Ω resistor.
(d) Electrical energy spent per minute in 4 Ω resistor.
Ans : (a) 1 A, (b) 10 V, (c) 6 V, (d) 240 J

13. A table lamp of power 60 W consumed 9 units of electricity in the month of June. For how many hours per day was the lamp in use?
    Ans : 5 h

14. An electrical heater is rated 4 kW, 220 V. Find the cost of using this heater for 12 h if one unit of electrical energy costs ₹ 3.50.
    Ans : ₹ 168

15. Two resistors with resistances $R_1 = 5$ Ω and $R_2 = 15$ Ω are connected in series to a 10 V battery. Calculate (a) the heat produced in each resistor due to the flow of current in 20 s and (b) the power developed across each resistor.
    Ans : (a) 25 J, 75 J, (b) 1.25 W, 3.75 W.

16. From the given figure, calculate (a) the total resistance of the circuit, (b) the total current

flowing in the circuit, (c) power rating of resistor R_4 and (d) power consumed by resistor R_3.

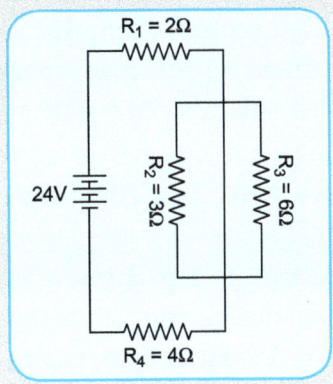

Ans : (a) 8 Ω, (b) 3 A, (c) 36 W, (d) 6 W

17. Determine the total amount of electrical energy used by the following devices when operated for the indicated times. Calculate the total cost of electricity consumed by these devices if the rate of electricity is ₹ 4.50 per commercial unit.

    (a) Hair dryer (1,500 W)—operated for 5 min
    (b) Electric heater (950 W)—operated for 4 h
    (c) Xrox (180 W)—operated for 6 h
    (d) 42-inch LCD television (210 W)—operated for 3 h

    Ans : (a) 0.125 kWh, (b) 3.8 kWh, (c) 1.08 kWh, (d) 0.63 kWh, cost = ₹ 25.35

18. A geyser has a label 2 kW, 240 V. What is the cost of running it for 30 min, if the cost of electricity is ₹ 3 per unit?
    Ans : ₹ 3.00

19. An electric kettle is rated 2.5 kW, 250 V, an electric fan is rated 100 W, 250 V and a bulb is rated 40 W, 250 V. If one kettle, three fans and four bulbs are operated for 5 h per day and the cost of electricity is ₹ 4 per commercial unit, calculate the monthly bill.
    Ans : ₹ 1,776

(B) HOUSEHOLD CIRCUITS

9.7 POWER TRANSMISSION AND DISTRIBUTION FROM GENERATING STATION TO HOUSEHOLDS

Electrical power or simply electricity is generated in bulk at the *power-generating stations* from various sources such as thermal power (coal, natural gas), hydropower, nuclear power and solar power. A power-generating station is generally located far from consumption areas over a vast area near the generating source (such as near a coal mine or a dam). Thus, there exists a large network of conductors between the power stations and the consumers. This network is divided into two parts : (1) transmission network and (2) distribution network.

Transmission Network

This network involves generation of electrical power at a power-generating station and its transmission to distribution substations.

A power station has three major components :

1. Boiler : The fuel such as coal and gas is burnt to produce heat (chemical energy to heat energy), which in turn is used to convert water into steam in the boiler.

2. Turbine : The steam produced drives the blades of the turbine (heat energy to kinetic energy).

3. Generator : It is a device that creates relative motion between a magnetic field and a conductor and converts the kinetic energy into electrical energy.

The electricity generated is an *alternating current* (a.c.) and has a frequency of 50 Hz, *i.e.*, the voltage generated changes direction twice in each cycle.

The electrical power is generated at 11,000 V (11 kV). This voltage is chosen because if the voltage is higher than 11 kV, it causes insulation problems, and if the voltage is lower than 11 kV, it involves heating problem. For a given amount of power, when the voltage is low, the current is high, as P = VI has to be constant. The greater the current flow, larger is the heat production, as H = I²Rt. Thus, at a high voltage of 11 kV, the current is low and heating effect in the wires reduces.

From the generating station, also known as the *grid*, the power needs to be transmitted to a *main substation*. For this purpose, the level of power needs to be increased and thus a *step-up transformer* is used, which increases the voltage level to 132 kV (or more as per requirement). From the main substation, it is transferred to substations. This power is carried through a network of high-voltage overhead lines that run into hundreds of kilometres and delivered to further substations. This is known as *primary transmission*. The use of overhead lines is preferred over underground lines as these are cheaper and easier to repair.

The grid is connected to a sub-transmission network consisting of three substations :

1. Main Substation : At this station, a *step-down transformer* is used to lower the level of voltage from 132 kV to 33 kV, a part of which is transmitted to heavy industries and the rest to the intermediate substations. This is known as *secondary transmission*. The conductors used for secondary transmission are called *feeders*.

2. Intermediate Substation : The level of voltage is further stepped down from 33 kV to 11 kV at this station using a step-down transformer. From here, the power is transmitted to light industries and to the next substation, *i.e.* the city substation.

3. City Substation : There is further reduction in the voltage level with the help of step-down transformer from 11 kV to 220 V, which is then supplied to the domestic consumers in the cities.

The whole process of power transmission is shown in Fig. 9.1 and 9.2.

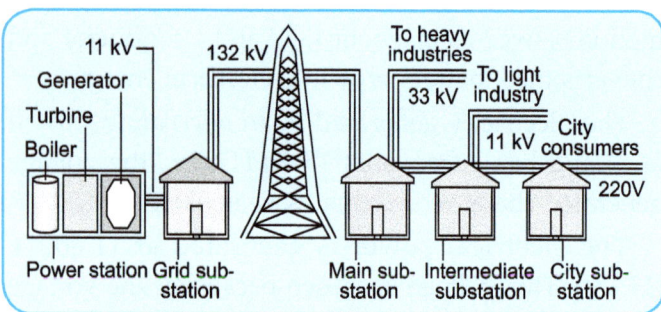

Fig. 9.1 : Transmission of electric power.

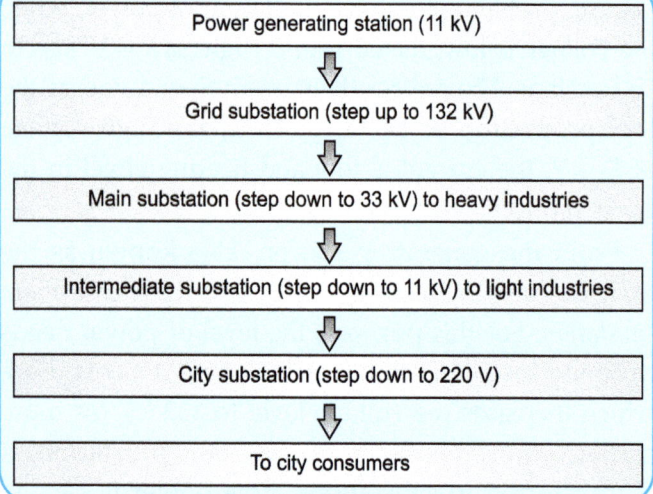

Fig. 9.2 : Flow chart with the steps in power transmission.

Distribution Network

From the city substation, power is transferred to local distribution centres. From distribution centres, power is supplied to the consumers through the overhead cables called *service mains*.

An overhead cable consists of three types of wires : (1) live wire (L), (2) neutral wire (N) and (3) earth wire (E).

1. The *live wire* is also known as *phase wire* or *hot wire* and carries current from the source to the distribution box or board of the house.

2. The *neutral wire* returns the current to the generator after it has passed through an appliance to complete the circuit.

3. The *earth wire* is for safety purpose and carries the current away when there is a fault.

The *neutral wire* and the *earth wire* are connected at the local substation, and both these wires have a *voltage of 0 V*. The wires are generally made of copper. The live wire is made from several wires twisted together and is thicker than the neutral and earth wire, in order to counter the wastage of electric current in the form of heat energy.

The overhead cable is connected to the *meter* of a house from a nearby pole via a *fuse* of high rating (generally of 50 A), which depends on the amount of load for which the connection is taken from the company. The fuse is connected to the live wire and is known as *company fuse* or *pole fuse*. From the fuse, the cable is connected to the meter which is generally mounted on the outside wall of the house or on the wall at the lowest floor of a building by the electricity supply department of the city (Fig. 9.3). The live and neutral wires emerging from the meter are connected to a *main switch* placed inside the distribution box. The main switch is a *double-pole switch*; it has two blades for opening or closing both lines, *i.e.* live wire and neutral wire, of a circuit simultaneously from the main supply. It has an iron covering that is connected to the earth wire. The earth wire from the meter is grounded or earthed in the premises of the house. There is another fuse called the *main fuse* connected with the live wire in the distribution box for consumer's safety. The fuse prevents from fire in case of overloading or short-circuiting. The wires go to the different parts of the house from the distribution box.

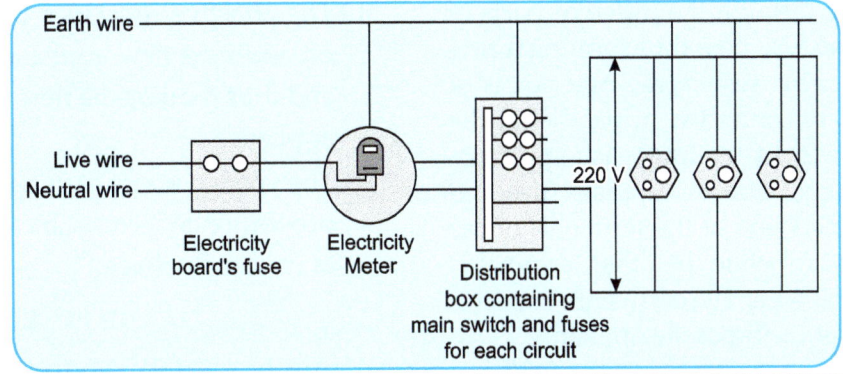

Fig 9.3 : A schematic diagram of one of the common domestic circuits.

> **Do You Know?**
> ♦ At present, the largest power-generating station is built over the Three Gorges Dam in China that has a capacity of 22,500 MW.
> ♦ The 4,620 MW Mundra Thermal Power Station located in the Kutch district of Gujarat is currently the largest operating thermal power plant in India. It is a coal-fired power plant owned and operated by Adani Power.

9.8 WIRING SYSTEM IN HOUSEHOLDS

The power from the main switch of the distribution box can be distributed in the house by either of the following two systems :

1. Tree system : In this system, different branch lines are taken out from the main supply line for different parts of the house, similar to the branches that extend from the trunk of a tree. Different circuits are taken out for different rooms or different parts of a house through a *fuse in the live wire* for each circuit (Fig. 9.4). The current rating of the fuse in any circuit depends upon the maximum load, which the circuit can bear. The fuses are placed in the live wire of the mains supply. The neutral and earth wire are common for all circuits. The current rating of the main fuse in the distribution box is slightly more than the sum total of the current rating of all the circuit fuses.

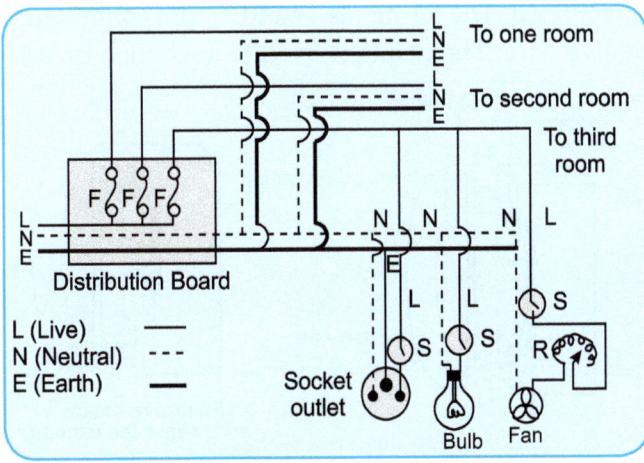

Fig. 9.4 : Tree system of house wiring.

The different distribution circuits from the main distribution board are connected in *parallel*. This is due to the following reasons :

(a) In case of any short circuit or overloading in one particular circuit, only the fuse of that circuit will melt and the power supply to all other circuits will remain intact.

(b) As the number of appliances increases, the effective resistance of the circuit decreases in a parallel connection and thus more current flows in different circuits depending on the resistances of the appliances.

(c) The voltage across each appliance remains the same, that is 220 V.

Each appliance is connected to the live wire and the neutral wire at two different terminals via a switch.

The live wire carries the current to the appliance and the neutral wire provides the return path for the current. In the socket outlet, the earth wire is also connected in addition to the live wire and neutral wire.

Disadvantages of tree system :

(a) If a fuse of any circuit blows, it disconnects all the appliances from the supply line in that particular circuit.

(b) The cost of this system of wiring is expensive.

(c) For different current-carrying capacities, it requires plugs and sockets of different sizes.

(d) If the rating of a particular circuit is lower than that of the current required by a new appliance to be installed in that circuit, then it would require new line wires from the appliance to the distribution box. This would lead to additional cost and also inconvenience.

2. Ring system : At present, this system of wiring is preferred over the tree system. This system has a ring-shaped circuit. The wires start from the main fuse box and, after running through the different parts of the house, return to the fuse box, thus forming a ring (Fig. 9.5). The rating of the fuse in the fuse box is of 30 A. All appliances are connected in parallel at the mains. From the live wire of the ring, each appliance is given a separate connection. A separate fuse and a separate switch connect one of the terminals of the appliance to the live wire while the other terminal is connected to the neutral wire. The earth wire connects to the metal covering or casing of the appliance.

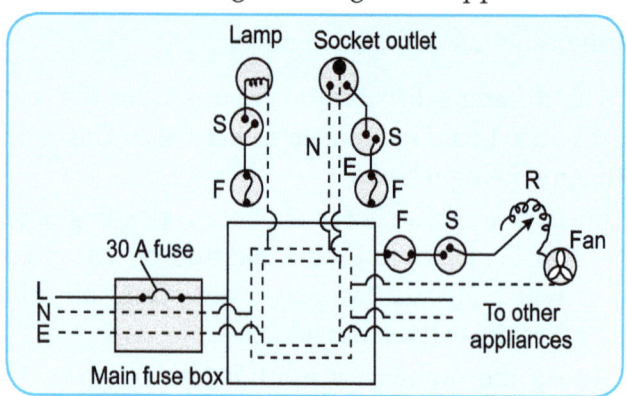

Fig. 9.5 : Ring system of house wiring.

Advantages of Ring System

(a) In this system, each appliance has a separate fuse. So, if the fuse of any one appliance burns due to fault, the other appliances still function without being affected.

(b) The plugs and sockets used can be of the same size, but the rating of each fuse should be suitable for the appliance to be connected with it.

(c) The current can travel through two different paths to an individual appliance, making the wire thick. This reduces the capacity of the wire required for the main ring than it would be required if directly connected to the mains. Thus, the cost is also reduced.

(d) In case, a new appliance is to be installed in a room of the house, it can be connected directly to the ring circuit of that room, ensuring that the total current drawn from the mains to the ring circuit does not exceed the main fuse rating. Thus, there is no need to set up a new line to the distribution box.

In the tree system and the ring system, the appliances are *connected in parallel* and not in series. This is because of the following *disadvantages of the series connection* :

(a) In series, all appliances work together. If any one of the appliance is short-circuited, then other appliances will be affected too and stop functioning.

(b) The effective resistance of the circuit increases on adding a new appliance in the same circuit and thus reduces the flow of current across each appliance.

(c) The voltage across each appliance is different, in proportion to its resistance, and not same as that of its rated voltage.

9.9 FUSE

A fuse is a safety device in an electric circuit which prevents the flow of excessive current due to overloading of a circuit or short circuit. Overloading occurs when the total load in a house exceeds the load limit for which the connection is taken in a house from the electricity company. Short circuit occurs when the open end of live wires comes in contact with the neutral wire. This occurs when a large current passing in the wires produces a large amount of heat that melts the insulation of wires. This results in a zero-resistance path and so a very heavy current passes through the wires, causing fire.

A fuse is a safety device that safeguards the circuit and the connected appliances from excessive flow of current and prevents them from damage.

A fuse is the weakest point in the electric circuit that is made up of a short wire of material of a low melting point around 200°C, such as an alloy of 65% tin and 35% lead. The resistivity of a fuse wire is more than that of the copper wire that carries the electric current so that its temperature rises rapidly as compared to the copper wires. Its thickness depends on its current rating, *i.e.*, the limit of flow of current through it. When there is an overload in the circuit, the fuse wire melts and breaks the electric circuit, preventing any damage.

A fuse is made up of the following two parts (Fig. 9.6) :

1. Porcelain casing : Porcelain is an *insulator* of electricity. It is used for making a rectangular hollow block in which two rectangular *brass terminals*, T_1 and T_2, are fixed. The terminals T_1 and T_2 are connected to the live wire. The casing is fixed to a wooden board.

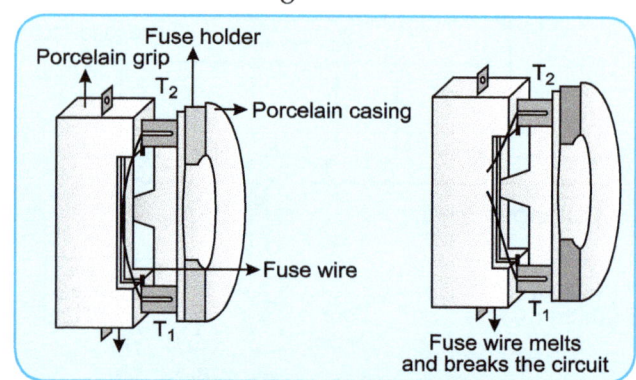

Fig. 9.6 : Electric fuse.

2. Porcelain grip : It is made up of a solid rectangular block and is provided with two rectangular *copper clamps* that can fit tightly on the terminals T_1 and T_2. In between the copper clamps, a *fuse wire* of appropriate value is fixed. The grip is inserted into the casing, and through the fuse wire, current flows from terminal T_1 to T_2.

Working of a Fuse

If a given circuit is short-circuited or overloaded due to some reason, then the fuse wire heats up and melts. Due to this, current cannot flow from terminal T_1 to T_2 and thus to the circuit. This prevents damage to the appliance due to high current flow. Once the fault is corrected, the circuit can be re-established by inserting a new fuse wire of same current rating in the fuse grip.

Every circuit can withstand a small amount of current beyond the safe limit without heating up. The fuse inserted in a circuit is thus made up of a value of current slightly higher than the maximum current that the circuit can tolerate.

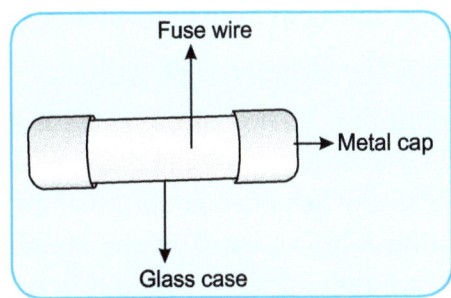

Fig. 9.7 : Cartridge fuse.

At present, the electrical appliances such as refrigerator, television, geyser and oven are expensive and sensitive to voltage fluctuations. If, by any chance, high current passes through them, they would burn. To protect these appliances, a *cartridge fuse* is used (Fig. 9.7). Cartridge fuses are of fixed value depending on the tolerance current and are fixed within the body of the appliance.

It is important to note that the *fuse* must be *connected to the live wire* and *not with the neutral wire* under any circumstance. The reason is that if the fuse is connected to the neutral wire, it will melt when overloading takes place, but the electrical appliances will continue to be in contact with the live wire even though the current is not flowing in the circuit. If such an appliance is touched by any person, the person will experience an electric shock which may prove fatal.

Current Rating of a Fuse

In general, in a lightning circuit, which consists of fan, bulb and so on, the maximum current drawn is of 5 A and thus a thin fuse wire of low current rating of 5 A is used. However, in the heating circuit, which consists of appliances such as geyser, washing machine, oven and air conditioner, the limit of current is 15 A and thus thicker fuse wires of higher current rating, that is 15 A, are used. The current rating of a fuse can be given by the relation,

Current rating of fuse

$$= \frac{\text{Total power of appliances in circuit}}{\text{Supply voltage}}$$

...(9.16)

Table 9.2 represents the current rating of fuses of various appliances.

Table 9.2 : Current Rating of Fuse for Various Appliances

Electrical Appliance	Power Rating (W) at 220 V	Current Drawn in Running Condition (A)	Fuse Rating (A)
Electric bulb	80	0.36	5
Electric fan	80	0.36	5
Television set	100	0.45	5
Refrigerator	200	0.90	5
Washing machine	300	1.36	5
Electric mixer	400	1.82	5
Electric iron	750	3.40	5
Electric kettle	1,000	4.54	5
Air conditioner	1,500	6.82	7
Geyser	2,000	9.10	10
Electric oven	3,000	13.6	15

Miniature circuit breakers (MCB) : Similar to a fuse, a circuit breaker is an automatically operated electrical switch designed to protect an electrical circuit from damage caused by overload or short circuit, but unlike a fuse, which operates once and then replaced, a circuit breaker can be reset to resume normal operation. An MCB is of a small size and switches off a circuit in a very short duration of time (25 ms), if there is an overload. Once the fault is repaired in the circuit, an MCB is again switched on. It has a quick response and is more convenient than a fuse.

9.10 SWITCHES

A switch is an electric device that can put on and put off an electric appliance in a circuit or conveniently helps in connecting and disconnecting the wires in the given circuit.

It is always connected to the live wire.

Switches are of various types and designs. They can be classified into two main types : (1) single-pole switch and (2) double-pole switch.

1. Single-pole switch : This is used in household appliances. It is used to start or stop the flow of current in an appliance. It disconnects *only the live wire* from the appliance.

2. Double-pole switch : It is used as a main switch in the distribution box to switch on or off the main supply. It disconnects *both the live and the neutral wires* simultaneously.

A Switch is Always Connected with a Live Wire

When a switch is on, the appliance receives current from the live wire as the circuit is complete (Fig. 9.8). The neutral wire provides the return path for the current. When the switch is off, the circuit is incomplete and the appliances does not receive current from the live wire. In 'off' position, both live wire and neutral wire connected to the appliance are at zero potential and so repair work can be carried out.

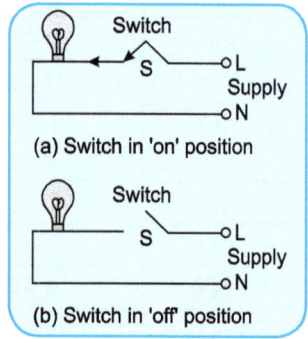

Fig. 9.8 : Switch connected to the live wire.

If however, instead of a live wire, a switch is connected to the neutral wire, as shown in Fig. 9.9, then in the 'off' position, no current will flow through the appliance, but the live wire is in contact with the appliance and thus, the potential of the appliance will be same as that of the live wire. It is not safe to carry out repair work in this condition. If a person touches the appliance in this case, the current from the live wire will flow through his body and may lead to a severe shock.

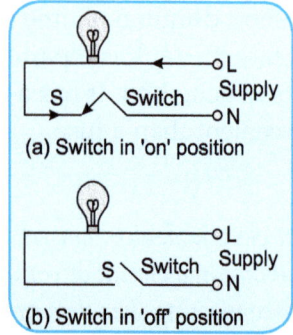

Fig. 9.9 : Switch connected to the neutral wire.

Safety Precaution While Handling a Switch

An electric switch should never be operated with wet hands because the presence of minerals in water acts as a conductor of electricity. Thus, if the moisture of the hand comes in contact with the terminals of the switch, it forms a conducting path through the body and a person will experience a severe shock.

9.11 STAIRCASE WIRING : DUAL CONTROL SWITCHES

The single-pole switches are generally used for putting on and putting off the electrical appliances in a house. However, in the houses, we often have dual control switches, which are a type of *double-pole switches*, used generally at the top and bottom of a staircase, at the opposite ends of a long hallway or a corridor or for lights in bathrooms that have a common entry and exit through two different rooms. These switches help to put on and put off an appliance such as a bulb or a tube light from two different places.

Working of Dual Control Switches

The circuit of a dual control switch is shown in Fig. 9.10. S_1 is a switch that is fitted at the bottom of a staircase, S_2 is a switch fitted at the top of the staircase for operating a bulb placed in the staircases and x, y and z are the points of connection of live and neutral wires. In the 'off' position as shown in Fig. 9.10(a), in switch S_1, the live wire connects between points x and y and in switch S_2, the neutral wire connects between points y and z. Thus, the circuit is incomplete.

The bulb can be switched on and off independently by either of the switches. If the switch S_1 at the bottom of staircase is switched on, the connection xy of the live wire changes to yz as shown in Fig. 9.10(b). This makes the circuit complete and the bulb glows. If the switch S_2 at the top of staircase is switched on, the connection yz of the neutral wire changes to yx as shown in Fig. 9.10(c).

This completes the circuit and makes the bulb light up. The glowing bulb can be switched off by operating either of the switches, S_1 or S_2. The connection can be changed from yz to yx or from xy to yz by either of the switches to break the circuit and thus put off the bulb.

ELECTRICAL ENERGY AND HOUSEHOLD CIRCUITS

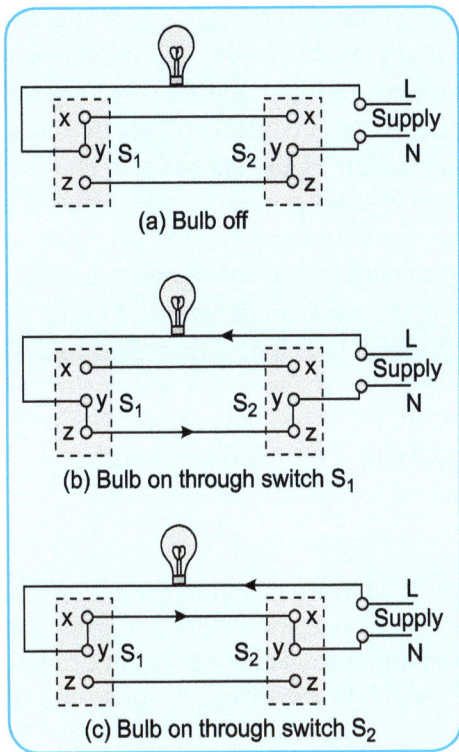

Fig. 9.10 : Working of a dual control switch.

Thus, while going upstairs, when a person presses switch S_1, the connection changes from xy to yz and the bulb glows. When he reaches the top of the stairs, he presses switch S_2 and thus the connection changes from yz to yx. This breaks the circuit and the bulb stops glowing.

Similarly, while returning from the top of the stairs, a person presses switch S_2 and the connection changes from yz to yx to switch on the bulb. After reaching the bottom of the stairs, he presses switch S_1 and the connection changes from yx to yz to switch off the bulb.

9.12 EARTHING

The process of *earthing* or *grounding* is a safety measure to pass off the excessive current through the earth wire deep into the ground or to the earth.

Earthing is done near the meter of the house as well as for the electrical appliances.

Local Earthing

For this process, a 2 m deep hole is dug in the ground near the kWh meter of the house. A thick copper wire or a rod surrounded by an insulating pipe is placed in the hole (Fig. 9.11). At the lower end of the copper rod, a thick copper plate is welded and buried in the ground. The plate is surrounded by a mixture of *charcoal* and *salt* and the ground near the plate is kept damp by pouring *water* through a pipe at regular intervals. The ions of charcoal and salt dissolve well in the water and form a low resistance path for the fault current and a good conducting medium between the plate and the ground. The upper end of the copper rod is joined to the earth wire at the meter.

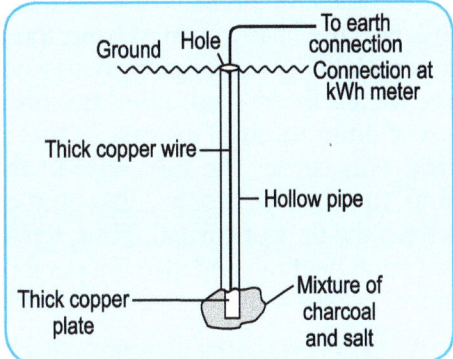

Fig. 9.11 : Local earthing.

Working : If, by any chance, such as due to short-circuiting, an excessive current flows through the line wires, it will pass to the ground (or earth) through the earth wire. The earth acts like an *electric sink* and thus can receive any amount of current without raising its potential. The process of local earthing protects the line wires from heating up due to excess current and prevents any accidental fire.

Earthing of an Appliance

Besides the local earthing, the electrical appliances that we come into contact physically, such as geyser, toaster, refrigerators, oven and iron, are also earthed. The live and neutral wires from the electricity source are connected to the electrical appliance through the insulation plugs, while the earth wire of the cable is connected to the outer metal casing of the appliance (Fig. 9.12). The switch and fuse are always connected to the live wire. The earth wire in turn is connected to the earth by the thick copper wire that is buried deep in the earth. To make the earth connection, a part of paint from the body of the appliance needs to be removed as the paint provides an insulating layer on the metal body of the appliance.

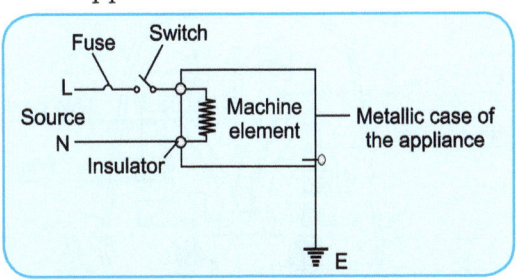

Fig. 9.12 : Earthing of an appliance.

Working : If, by any chance, the insulation of an appliance melts or damages due to wear and tear, the live wire comes in contact with the metal case of the appliance and as a result, acquires the high potential of the live wire. In such a condition, if a person touches the appliance, the electric current will rush through his body through the live wire and will cause a severe electric shock.

If the appliance is properly earthed, then as soon as the live wire comes in contact with the metallic case of the appliance, the heavy current from the live wire would immediately flow through the earth wire to the earth. Since the earth does not offer any resistance, a heavy current flows through the case of the appliance to the earth. This causes the fuse wire in the circuit to melt and the circuit breaks, disconnecting the appliance from the flow of current. Thus, the appliance is protected from heating, and also if a person touches the appliance, he/she will not receive a shock.

9.13 THREE-PIN PLUG AND SOCKET

Three-pin Plug

A plug is a fixture provided at one end of the cable to be connected to an electrical appliance. It consists of three metallic cylindrical brass pins, forming a triangle and embedded in a plastic casing. The upper pin is thicker than the two lower pins. The three pins are connected inside the body of the plug to three different wires. The *top pin* is connected to the *earth wire*, the *left pin* is connected to the *live wire* and the *right pin* is connected to the *neutral wire*. Often the words E, N and L are marked on the case of the plug for the three types of wires (Fig. 9.13). The pins have a split at the ends so that they fit tightly into the respective holes of the socket, preventing any sparking at the contacts.

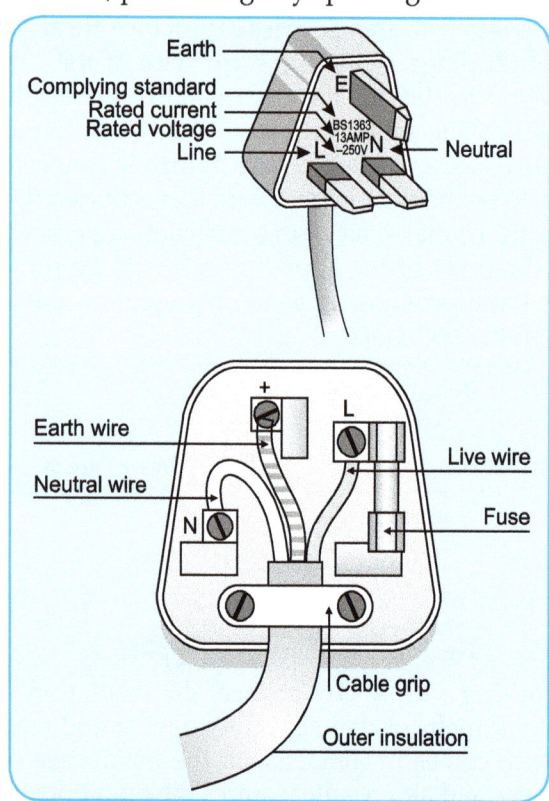

Fig. 9.13 : A three-pin plug and wires connected to its terminals.

The *earth pin is always made longer* and *thicker* than the other two pins due to the following two reasons :

1. The earth pin is made thicker to avoid the pin entering the live and neutral sockets by mistake when wrong orientation of the socket occurs. An electrical appliance will thus get connected only in a proper orientation, *i.e.* when the live pin connects to the live wire and the neutral pin to the neutral wire.

2. The earth pin is made longer to make connection to the earth terminal first, rather than to the live and neutral terminals. If there is a heavy flow of current due to any short circuit, the current would flow to the earth and would melt the fuse, ensuring the safety of the user.

Socket

A socket is a fixture in an electric circuit from which power can be tapped for electrical appliances such as heater, oven and iron. It consists of three holes, forming a triangle, which fit the three pins of a plug (Fig. 9.14). These holes are basically hollow cylinders made of brass and embedded in an insulating material such as plastic and porcelain. At the back, these brass cylinders form terminals that are connected to the live, neutral and earth wires of the cable. The *upper hole* is bigger in diameter than the other two holes and is for *earth* connection. The hole on the *right* side is for the *live wire*, while the hole on the *left side* is for *neutral wire* of the electricity supply.

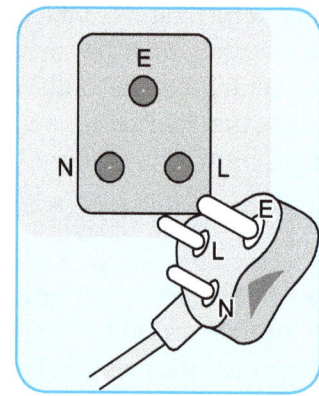

Fig. 9.14 : A socket and a three-pin plug.

Safety precautions while handling plug and socket : The hands must be completely dry while inserting the plug into the socket. The plug pin should fit tightly into the socket as loose connection might lead to sparking and burning of socket or plug.

9.14 SAFETY MEASURES WHILE USING ELECTRIC APPLIANCES

There are a few safety measures that should be followed by anyone handling electrical appliances to avoid electric shock or an event of fire.

1. All electrical gadgets should be disconnected when not in use.
2. Appliances such as an electric iron should never be left on while attending to other chores.
3. Ventilation holes in a television set should never be covered, for it may generate enough heat to cause a fire.
4. Electrical equipment should never be touched with wet hands.
5. All appliances must be provided with a fuse and their metallic casing should be earthed.
6. Proper maintenance of electric wiring and fuses is essential. Fuses should not be replaced with ones of higher amperage or with thick wires and the insulation of wires should be of good quality.
7. The wires used should have a current-carrying capacity higher than the total current that can flow through the circuit when all appliances are used together.
8. Faulty electric wires should never be used until repaired. Faulty appliances must be properly handled and repaired promptly.
9. Electric gadgets should be repaired only by an expert person who is qualified to handle them.
10. When working with electric appliances, one should never stand on metal, wet concrete or wet ground. It is wiser to stand on a rubber mat or a dry wooden platform as these are insulators of electricity.
11. In case of a fire due to electric short circuit or overloading, the first step is to cut off the current flowing through the mains supply and then steps should be taken to extinguish the fire.

9.15 COLOUR CODING OF WIRES AND HIGH-TENSION WIRES

An electrical appliance is provided with three core flexible cables, that is three insulated wires running parallel to each other in a common insulation. Further, the insulation of each wire; live wire, neutral wire and earth wire, is of a specific colour to distinguish them easily.

The old convention of colours of insulation is *red* for *live wire*, *black* for *neutral wire* and *green* for *earth wire*. According to the new international convention, the colour for *live wire* is *brown*, for *neutral wire* is *light blue* and for *earth wire* is *green* or *yellow*.

These three wires can withstand current of some specific value. If the current exceeds the value that these wires can tolerate, the plastic insulation on them melts, bringing the wires in contact and thus resulting in short circuit.

For high voltage and large current, instead of a single thick wire, a number of thin wires are twisted together to form *high-tension wires* that are provided with heavy insulation. A high-tension wire has a large surface area and low resistance. The large surface area allows the heat produced to be radiated readily as compared to a single thick wire, which might burn due to excess heat and cause fire.

ILLUSTRATIVE EXAMPLES

1. If you are given a battery, two bulbs, a switch and a wire, how would you join the two bulbs so that each bulb glows brightly? Draw a circuit diagram.

   Solution : The two bulbs would be joined in a parallel connection, as in parallel, the voltage across each bulb would be same as that of the battery. The power of each bulb would be thus high and both of them would glow brightly. The circuit diagram is given below.

   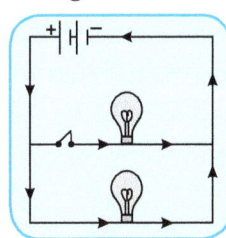

2. Draw a diagram showing connection of a fan and a bulb in a room from the mains supply. Show the location of a fuse and a switch for each appliance and the main fuse.

   Solution : The fan and bulb in a room are connected in parallel with the main supply. E, N and L represent earth wire, neutral wire and live wire, respectively, while S and F represent the switch and fuse for each appliance. The main fuse box has a 30 A fuse that is connected with the live wire.

   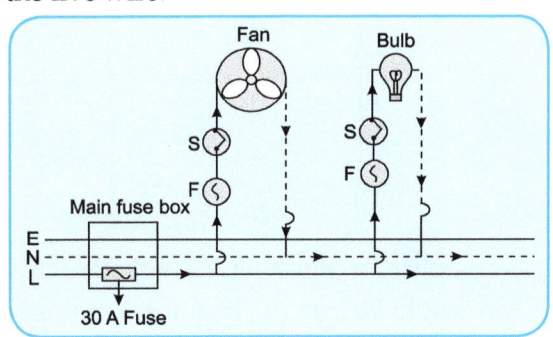

3. Two identical fans are connected in a series across a mains supply of 220 V. The rating of each fan is 220 V, 80 W. (a) Draw a diagram showing the arrangement.
(b) Calculate the resistance offered by the element of each fan. (c) Calculate the total power consumed by the two fans. (d) If the power is to be increased, what should be the alternate arrangement ? Draw the new arrangement and calculate the total power consumed.
Solution : (a) The diagram for the arrangement is shown below.

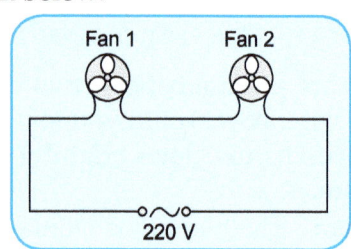

(b) Given : V = 220 V, P = 80 W
Resistance offered by the element of each fan is
$$R = \frac{V^2}{P} = \frac{(220)^2}{80} = 605 \, \Omega$$

(c) Since the two fans are connected in series, the voltage across each fan will be half of the total supply, i.e. V = 110 V.
Power consumed by one fan will be
$$P = \frac{V^2}{R} = \frac{(110)^2}{605} = 20 \, W$$
Total power consumed by both fans
$$= 20 + 20 = 40 \, W$$

(d) To increase the power, the two fans should be connected in parallel. The arrangement is shown in figure below.

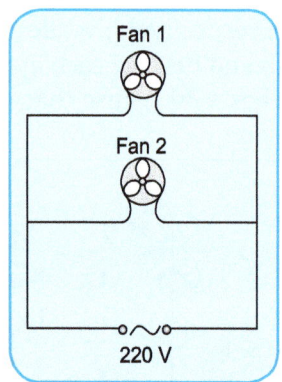

In parallel arrangement, the voltage across each fan would be same as that of the mains supply, i.e. 220 V, and thus, the power consumed by each fan would be 80 W.
Total power consumed by both the fans
$$= 80 + 80 = 160 \, W.$$

4. What fuse rating would you choose for (a) a table lamp of 100 W and (b) a kettle of 2,400 W, if the voltage supplied by the mains is 220 V. The options available are 3 A, 5 A and 13 A.
Solution : The current rating of a fuse is the maximum current that the fuse can carry without melting.
(a) Given : P = 100 W, V = 220 V
Current that can be drawn by the lamp is
$$I = \frac{P}{V} = \frac{100}{220} = 0.45 \, A$$
For the lamp, the fuse used should have a rating of 3 A.
(b) Given : P = 2,400 W, V = 220 V
Current that can be drawn by the kettle is
$$I = \frac{P}{V} = \frac{2,400}{220} = 10.9 \, A$$
For the kettle, the fuse used should have a rating of 13 A.

5. Under what circumstances does one get an electric shock from an electrical appliance?
Solution : A person can get an electric shock from an electrical appliance under two circumstances :
(a) *Absence of earthing :* When the outer metallic case of an electrical appliance is not earthed, the current from the live wire cannot flow to the earth and the live wire of an appliance comes in direct contact with its metal casing. The whole appliance attains the high potential of the live wire and thus any person who comes in contact with such a faulty appliance will experience a shock.
(b) *Use of wet hands :* When a person makes contact with a switch or a plug of an appliance with wet hands, water forms a conducting layer between the hand and the live wire of the appliance that causes heavy flow of current through the entire body of the person and leads to electric shock.

ELECTRICAL ENERGY AND HOUSEHOLD CIRCUITS

EXERCISE 9(B)

1. What are the two networks present between a power-generating station and the consumers?
   Ans : Transmission and distribution networks

2. Name the three components of a power-generating station and state the purpose of each component.

3. (a) Name the device used to increase the voltage at a generating station.
   (b) At what frequency is A.C. supplied to residential houses ?
   Ans : (a) Step up transformer, (b) 50 Hz.

4. At what voltage is the electric power generated at the power-generating station? Why a value of higher voltage than this is not generated?

5. What is the device that decreases the voltage level? At which station is it used?

6. (a) Name the transformer used in the power transmitting station of a power plant.
   (b) What type of current is transmitted from the power station ?
   (c) At what voltage is this current available to our household ?
   Ans : (a) Step up transformer, (b) Alternating current, (c) 220 V.

7. With the help of a simple flow chart show the transmission of electric power from the generating station to a house.

8. Name the three types of wires used in a household circuit. Which of these two wires are at the same potential?

9. What is meant by the pole fuse? State its current rating.

10. (a) To which wire of a cable in a power circuit should the metal case of a geyser be connected ?
    (b) To which wire should the fuse be connected ?
    Ans : (a) Earth wire, (b) Live wire

11. State the type of switch that is placed inside a distribution box. What is its function?

12. Where is the main fuse located? What is its purpose?

13. What are the two systems of wiring used in household? Which of these systems is preferred?

14. Why are the different circuits connected in parallel in the tree system of wiring?

15. Draw a simple diagram of a tree system of house wiring. State the disadvantages of this system.

16. Draw a simple diagram of a ring system of house wiring. State the advantages of this system.

17. With the help of a simple diagram, show how would you connect any three appliances, such as a bulb, a fan and a heater, from the main supply.

18. What are the disadvantages of connecting appliances in a series arrangement?

19. In a room, there are three tube lights glowing. One of the tubes fuses suddenly, but the rest two continue to glow. Explain why? What would be your justification if all the three tubes cease to glow when one of them fuses?

20. Three bulbs X, Y and Z are connected to a mains supply of 220 V in two different arrangements as shown in the figure below. (a) Name the two types of arrangements. (b) Which one of these is preferred in a household circuit? Justify.

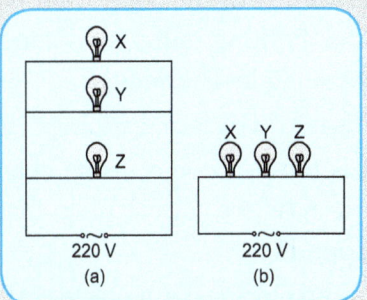

21. How should the electric lamps in a building be connected?
    Ans : In parallel

22. Name the device used to protect the electric circuits from overloading and short circuits. On what effect of electricity does the device work?

23. What are the characteristic properties of a fuse wire? Name the material from which it is made.

24. Why is porcelain casing used in a fuse?

25. Explain the working of a fuse?

26. What is a cartridge fuse?

27. Why should a fuse be always connected to the live wire and not to the neutral wire?

28. "The current rating of a fuse is 15 A." Explain the statement.

29. The rating of two fuse wires is 5 A and 15 A. Which of these two fuse wires is thinner? Give reason.
30. A fuse has a current rating of 5 A. Can it be used for a heater of rating 1 kW, 220 V?
31. An electric bulb is rated as 60 W, 110 V. What should be the rating of fuse that can be used for it : 1 A or 5 A. Justify.
32. How is a circuit breaker different from a fuse?
33. Name two safety devices that are connected to the live wire of a household electrical circuit. Give one important function of each of these devices.
34. Name the wire in a household electrical circuit to which the switch is connected.
    Ans : Live wire.
35. What is the purpose of a switch? State the two types of switches used?
36. Why is a switch always connected to the live wire?
37. What is the reason for not operating a switch with wet hands?
38. Explain the working of a dual control switch used for lighting bulbs in a staircase with the help of suitable diagrams.
39. What is meant by local earthing? How is it done?
40. What is the purpose of using charcoal and salt mixture near the copper plate that is buried in the ground?
41. How is an electrical appliance earthed?
42. Draw a simple diagram of a three-pin plug and label the pins.
43. Why are the plug pins splitted at their ends?
44. Why is the top pin of the plug thicker and longer than the other two pins?
45. Draw a simple labelled diagram of a socket of a three-pin plug.
46. What is the purpose of colour coding of the three wires of a cable?
47. What is the colour code for the insulation on the earth wire?
    Ans : Green
48. What are the old and new colour conventions of the three wires?
49. What is a high-tension wire? What is its purpose?
50. An electric gadget can give an electric shock to its user under certain circumstances. Mention two of these circumstances.
51. What preventive measure is provided in a gadget that can protect a person from an electric shock?
52. From the diagram below, explain what happens to the identical bulbs X and Y in the circuit shown when (a) only switch S_1 is closed, (b) only switch S_2 is closed and (c) both S_1 and S_2 are closed.

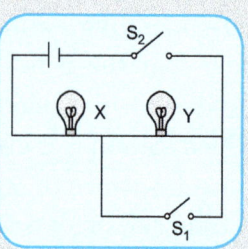

53. Draw a circuit diagram to show how three lamps can be lit from a battery in such a way that two lamps are controlled by the same switch while the third lamp has its own switch.
54. State few safety precautions that should be taken while using electricity.

MULTIPLE CHOICE QUESTIONS

1. The electric power to be transmitted is generated at :
   (a) 33 kV (b) 11 kV
   (c) 132 kV (d) 220 V
   Ans : (b)
2. Which of these two wires is at the same potential?
   (a) Earth wire and live wire
   (b) Earth wire and neutral wire
   (c) Live wire and neutral wire
   (d) None of the above
   Ans : (b)
3. Fuse wire is made of an alloy of :
   (a) iron and tin
   (b) copper and lead
   (c) tin and lead
   (d) copper and iron
   Ans : (c)

4. A fuse is rated 8 A. It means :
   (a) it will not work if the current is less than 8 A
   (b) it will work only if the current is 8 A
   (c) it will melt if the current exceeds 8 A
   (d) it will melt if the current is less than 8 A
   Ans : (c)

5. The top pin of a three-pin plug is for :
   (a) live wire
   (b) earth wire
   (c) neutral wire
   (d) any of the above
   Ans : (b)

6. The colour used for insulation of neutral wire is :
   (a) red
   (b) brown
   (c) green
   (d) blue
   Ans : (d)

NUMERICAL PROBLEMS

1. A house has a main fuse of rating 5 A. Four bulbs, each of 60 W, and four tube lights, each of 50 W, are glowing simultaneously. The voltage of mains supply is 220 V. (a) Calculate the current drawn from the mains. (b) How many more tube lights, each of 80 W, can also be lighted without blowing off the fuse?
   Ans : (a) 2 A, (b) 8

2. What fuse rating would you choose for (a) a heater of 1 kW and (b) an oven of 1,500 W, if the voltage supplied by the mains is 220 V?
   Ans : (a) 5 A, (b) 7 A

3. A fan consumes a power of 75 W from a 220 V mains supply. A fuse of rating 2 A is fixed in the main fuse box. Calculate the number of fans that can be safely operated in a house simultaneously without melting the fuse wire.
   Ans : 5

4. A household circuit has a fuse of 5 A rating. Calculate the maximum number of bulbs of rating 60 W, 220 V each which can be connected in the household circuit.
   Ans : 18

10

ELECTROMAGNETISM

LEARNING OUTCOMES

- Oersted's experiment to demonstrate the magnetic effect of electric current
- Magnetic field due to a current in a straight wire, the right-hand thumb rule and clock rule
- Electromagnets and permanent magnets
- Lorentz force : Force due to magnetic field on a current-carrying conductor
- Fleming's left-hand rule
- Simple DC motor : Principle and construction
- Electromagnetic induction : Faraday's laws
- Fleming's right-hand rule
- AC generator : Principle and construction
- AC and DC currents
- Transformers : Principle, construction and working, types and applications

(A) MAGNETIC EFFECT OF ELECTRIC CURRENT

10.1 OERSTED'S EXPERIMENT : DEMONSTRATION OF MAGNETIC EFFECT OF ELECTRIC CURRENT

In 1802, an Italian scientist G.D. Romagnosi observed that *a magnetic needle* is affected by *current flowing in a wire*. But his observation was ignored. Later, in 1820, the connection between electricity and magnetism was rediscovered by a Danish physicist Hans Christian Oersted.

Experiment

Take a thick and long insulated copper wire PQ and connect it to a battery through a key and a rheostat (variable resistor). Take a magnetic needle pivoted on a stand and place it under the wire so that the needle is parallel to the wire.

Observations

1. The magnetic needle points towards geographic north-south, along the Earth's magnetic field, when the key is open, that is, no current flows through the wire PQ [Fig. 10.1 (a)].

2. When the key is pressed, the current flows in a direction P to Q in the wire that is from south to north and the north pole of the needle deflects towards the west. [Fig. 10.1 (b)].

3. If the resistance is decreased by sliding the rheostat, so that the magnitude of current increases, the deflection of the needle increases, until the north pole of the needle points towards exact west, that is, the needle is perpendicular with respect to the wire.

4. The north pole of the needle deflects towards the east if the direction of flow of current through the wire is reversed. This is performed by reversing the connections at the terminals of the battery. The current now flows from Q to P, that is, from north to south [Fig. 10.1 (c)].

5. Similarly, if the magnitude of current is increased

by decreasing the resistance in this case, the needle points towards exact east.

6. If the needle is placed above the wire, instead of placing the needle below the wire, then the direction of deflection of needle is reversed. If the current flows from P to Q, and the needle is placed above the wire, it deflects towards east, and if the current flows from Q to P, with needle placed above, it deflects towards west [Fig. 10.1 (d) and 10.1 (e)].

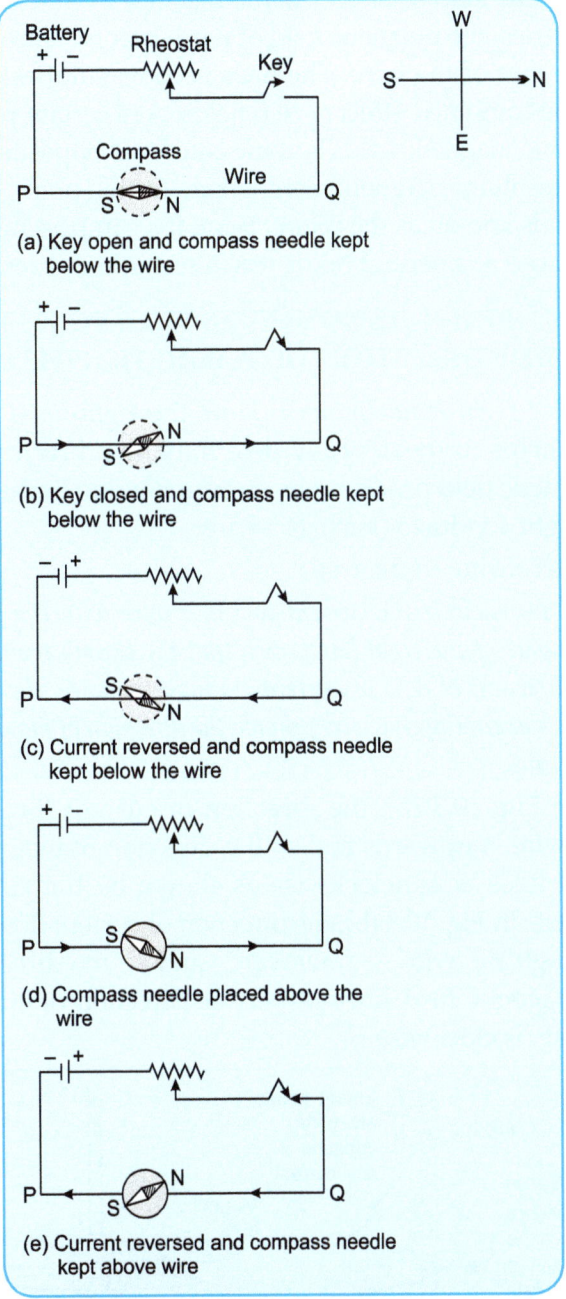

Fig. 10.1 : Oersted's experiment to show the magnetic effect of current.

Inferences

1. A conductor behaves like a magnet as long as the current flows through it.

2. A current-carrying conductor produces a magnetic field (represented by letter B) around it. A magnetic needle experiences a torque in this field and thus get deflected and aligned itself in the direction of magnetic field at that point.

3. When the direction of flow of current is reversed, the direction of magnetic field produced is also reversed and thus the deflection of magnetic needle is also reversed.

4. The strength of current flowing through a conductor influences the strength of magnetic field produced. Larger the current flowing through a conductor, greater is the magnetic field (*i.e.* $B \propto I$) and thus more is the deflection of the magnetic needle.

5. The magnetic field produced by a current-carrying conductor acts perpendicular to the direction of flow of current. When the current in a wire flows from south to north, the magnetic needle placed below it deflects towards west, that is, at right angle.

6. The direction of deflection of magnetic needle depends on the direction of flow of current through a conductor and on the relative position of the conductor with respect to the magnetic needle. When current flows from south to north (*i.e.* from P to Q in a wire), the magnetic needle deflects towards west if placed below the wire but deflects towards east if placed above the wire.

This phenomenon of deflection of magnetic needle due to the influence of electric current is known as *magnetic effect of current* or *electromagnetism*.

SNOW rule : The direction of deflection of a magnetic needle can be easily determined by the SNOW rule. SNOW stands for *south north over west*, that is, if current flows through a conductor from *south* to *north* and the wire is held *over* the magnetic needle, then the north pole of the magnetic needle deflects towards *west*.

10.2 MAGNETIC FIELD DUE TO CURRENT IN A STRAIGHT WIRE

From Oersted's experiment, it is known that when current flows through a wire, it behaves like a magnet and thus a magnetic field is produced around it. Similar to a bar magnet that has a magnetic field and field lines around it that can be mapped with the help of iron filings and a compass needle, the magnetic field lines of a current-carrying wire can also be mapped. The demonstration of magnetic field and mapping of its field lines around a wire can be performed by the following experiment.

Experiment

Take a stiff and smooth cardboard PQRS with a white sheet of paper fixed on it. Place the cardboard horizontally on a wooden stand and make a hole at its centre. Take a thick insulated copper wire AB and pass it vertically through the hole of the cardboard. Connect the ends of the wire to the terminals of a battery through a key and a variable resistance, as shown in Fig. 10.2. Sprinkle some fine iron filings on the cardboard evenly. Now, close the key to pass current through the wire and gently tap the cardboard.

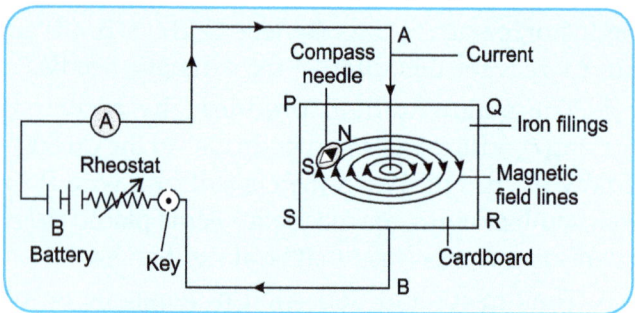

Fig. 10.2 : Magnetic field lines around a straight wire carrying current.

Observations

It is observed that the iron filings get arranged in the form of concentric circles around the wire, showing the existence of magnetic force around the wire. If a magnetic compass needle is placed along any of the concentric lines around the wire, it aligns itself in a geographic north-south. The direction in which the north pole of the magnetic needle points give the direction of magnetic field at that point. By keeping the compass needle at different points on the concentric circles, the direction of magnetic field lines can be traced.

Properties of Magnetic Field Lines Obtained

1. The plane of magnetic field lines formed around the wire is perpendicular to the plane of the wire, with their centres lying along the wire.

2. If the direction of flow of current is reversed, the iron filings still arrange in the pattern of concentric circles. However, the direction of alignment of magnetic needle is reversed. Now, the north pole of the compass points in the opposite direction from the former one. This shows that the direction of magnetic field has reversed.

3. If the magnitude of current is increased, the iron filings that form concentric field lines become more concentrated, *i.e.* the field lines become *denser* and the circles arrange up to a farther distance from the wire, *i.e.* the strength or intensity of magnetic field *increases*.

4. The iron filings spread in the form of *concentric circles* at points near the wire, but as the distance from the wire increases, the circular arrangement is not observed and the lines tend to become *elliptical*. The reason is that at points near the wire, the magnetic field due to current in the wire is stronger than the magnetic field of Earth. As the distance from the wire increases, the magnetic field of Earth becomes stronger than that of the wire. The lines become elliptical due to the combined effect of two fields. At a certain point, the two magnetic fields become equal and opposite and the resultant magnetic field is zero at this point. This point is known as the *neutral point*. If a compass needle is placed at a neutral point, it will rest in any direction.

10.3 RIGHT-HAND THUMB RULE TO FIND THE DIRECTION OF MAGNETIC FIELD

The *right-hand thumb rule* or the *right-hand grip rule* helps to theoretically determine the direction of magnetic field produced by current flowing through a straight conductor such as a wire.

According to the rule,

If we encircle the current-carrying wire with the palm or fingers of the right hand such that the thumb points in the direction of flow of current through the wire, then the fingers encircling the wire provide the direction of magnetic field lines.

In Fig. 10.3 (a), the direction of current through the wire is upwards and so the direction of magnetic field lines is anticlockwise as shown by the curled fingers. In Fig. 10.3 (b), the direction of current flowing through the wire is downwards and so the direction of magnetic field lines as per the direction of curled fingers is clockwise.

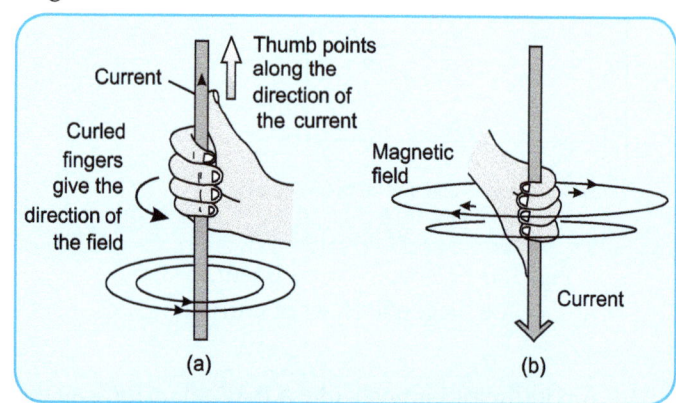

Fig. 10.3 : Right-hand thumb rule.

Maxwell's Corkscrew Rule

This is another rule to determine the direction of magnetic field around a current carrying conductor.

According to this rule,

Take a right-handed screw placed parallel to a straight current carrying conductor such that it advances in the direction of the flow of current on turning. Its direction of rotation gives the direction of magnetic field due to the current in the wire (Fig. 10.4).

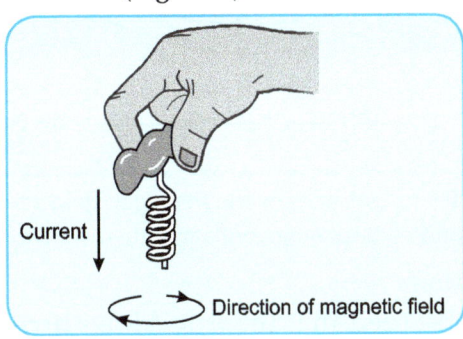

Fig. 10.4 : Maxwell's corkscrew rule.

10.4 MAGNETIC FIELD DUE TO CURRENT IN A CIRCULAR COIL

The magnetic field due to flow of current in a circular coil can be studied by the following experiment.

Experiment

Take a thick insulated copper wire and bend it in the form of a thick circular loop. Now take a stiff cardboard and make two holes in it such that the holes P and Q lie along the diameter of the coil and the plane of coil is perpendicular to the plane of cardboard. Pass the circular loop of wire through these holes and connect its ends to a battery through a key and a variable resistance, as shown in Fig. 10.5. Spread some iron filings on the cardboard evenly and tap the cardboard when current passes through the loop to trace the pattern of magnetic field lines. Now place a magnetic compass needle on the traced magnetic field lines to find the direction of these lines.

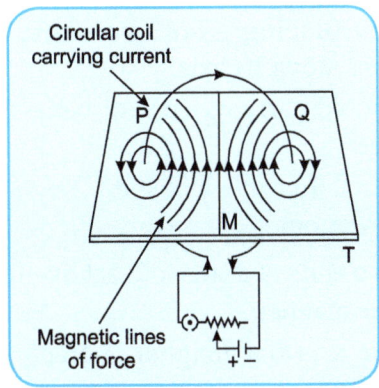

Fig. 10.5 : Magnetic field pattern around a circular loop.

Observations

It is observed that the iron filings arrange in a definite pattern around the coil, representing the magnetic field lines due to a current-carrying coil. The deflection of the north pole of the compass needle placed on the traced lines indicates the direction of the magnetic field. The direction is marked with arrows.

Properties of Magnetic Field Lines Obtained

1. The magnetic field lines are nearly circular around the points where current enters and leaves the coil, that is near points P and Q (Fig. 10.5).

2. The direction of magnetic field lines is same within the space enclosed by the coil, that is between points P and Q.

3. The magnetic field lines are almost *parallel* and thus *uniform* near the centre of the coil.

4. The plane of magnetic lines of force is at right angle to the plane of the circular coil at its centre.

5. If the direction of current flowing through the coil is reversed, the needle of the compass deflects in the opposite direction, that is the direction of magnetic field lines is reversed (Fig. 10.6).

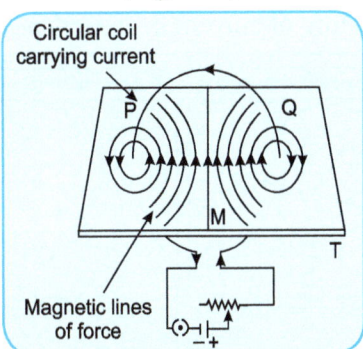

Fig. 10.6 : Magnetic field pattern around a circular loop when the current is reversed.

6. The *number* or *density of magnetic field lines increases* if (a) the strength of current flowing through the coil is increased, (b) the number of turns in the coil is increased (c) the circular loop of smaller radius is taken.

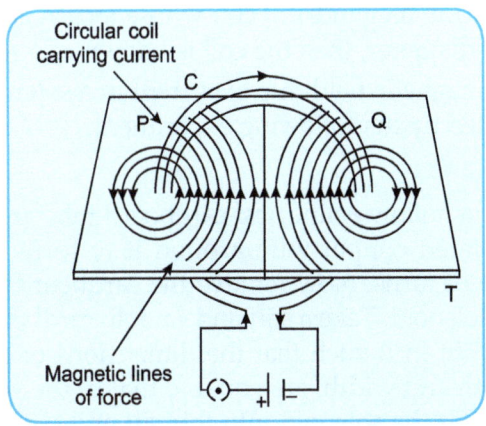

Fig. 10.7 : Magnetic field pattern around a circular loop when the number of turns is increased.

Direction of Current Determines the Polarity of the Coil

Considering the coil in a vertical plane, we can see that the magnetic field lines pass in the same direction in the region within the loop. One face of the loop acts like the *north pole* through which the field lines leave and the other face like the *south pole* through which the field lines enter. In other words, the coil acts like a *dipole*. The magnetic field of this coil or loop can be compared with that of a magnetised disc of same radius.

The direction of flow of current in the coil determines the polarity at the faces of the coil. This is determined by the *clock rule*.

Clock Rule

If an observer looking at the face of the coil finds the direction of current flowing around that face in clockwise direction, then the face has south polarity, but if the direction of current at that face is anticlockwise, then the face has north polarity. (Fig. 10.8).

Thus, *clockwise* flow of current is at *south pole* and *anticlockwise* flow of current is at *north pole*.

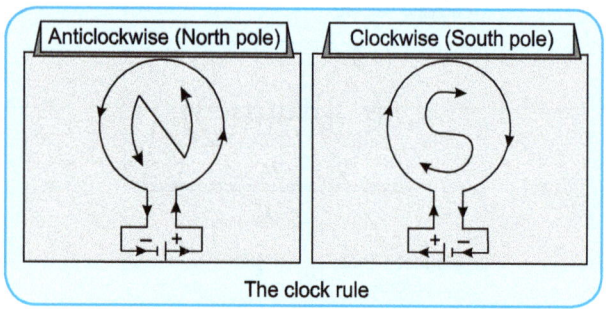

Fig. 10.8 : Polarities at the faces of a current-carrying coil or loop.

10.5 MAGNETIC FIELD DUE TO CURRENT IN A CYLINDRICAL COIL OR A SOLENOID

If a conducting wire is wound around a bottle or a tube to form a cylindrical coil whose length is greater than its diameter, then the coil is known as a *solenoid*.

The magnetic field due to current in a solenoid can be studied by the following experiment.

Experiment

Take a hollow cylindrical cardboard tube and wind an insulated copper wire around it to form a large number of turns. Now remove the cardboard tube to form a solenoid. Take a stiff and smooth cardboard and make a slit in it such that the dimensions of the slit, *i.e.* length and width, are equal to that of the solenoid formed. Fit the solenoid into this slit and connect the two ends of the wire to a battery through a rheostat and a key. Scatter some iron filings over the cardboard.

Let the current pass through the solenoid by closing the key and tap the cardboard gently (Fig. 10.9).

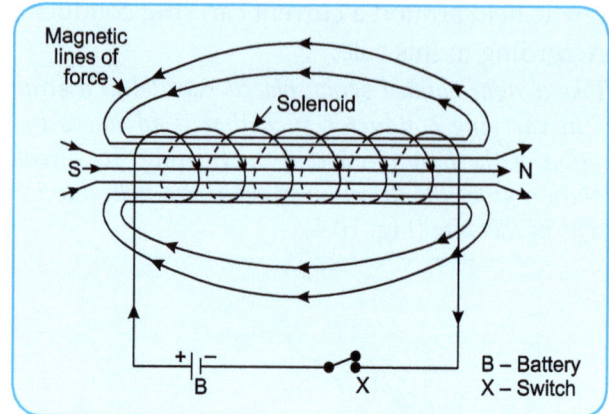

Fig. 10.9 : Field lines of the magnetic field through and around a current-carrying solenoid.

Observations

It is observed that the iron filings arrange in a definite pattern on the cardboard, representing the magnetic field lines due to a current-carrying solenoid. A magnetic compass needle can be placed on the traced lines to determine the direction of the magnetic field. The direction on a particular field line in which the north pole of the needle points is marked with an arrow, and this represents the direction of the magnetic field.

Properties of Magnetic Field Lines Obtained

1. The magnetic field lines within the solenoid are almost parallel to each other and to the axis of the solenoid and are thus *uniform*.
2. On reversing the direction of current flowing through the solenoid, the direction of magnetic field is also reversed. This can be detected by the deflection of the north pole of the magnetic compass needle in the opposite direction.
3. The *intensity* of magnetic field of a solenoid can be *increased* by (a) increasing the strength of current flowing through the solenoid, (b) increasing the number of turns of the solenoid and (c) placing a soft iron core within the solenoid along its axis.
4. A solenoid carrying current behaves like a bar magnet.

Similarities Between a Current-Carrying Solenoid and a Bar Magnet

1. The two ends of a solenoid act like the two poles of a bar magnet.
2. Similar to a bar magnet, a freely suspended solenoid comes to rest in north-south orientation (*directional property*).

3. Similar to a bar magnet, a current-carrying solenoid attracts iron filings (*attractive property*).
4. The magnetic field lines of a current-carrying solenoid are similar to those of a bar magnet, *i.e.* these start out from the north pole and end at the south pole.

Despite these similarities, a solenoid differs from a bar magnet in two ways.

Difference between a current-carrying Solenoid and a Bar Magnet

Current-carrying Solenoid	Bar Magnet
The strength of magnetic field due to a solenoid can be changed by increasing or decreasing the strength of current flowing through it.	The strength of magnetic field of a bar magnet cannot be changed.
The direction of magnetic field due to a solenoid can be reversed by reversing the direction of current flowing through it.	The direction of magnetic field of a bar magnet cannot be changed.

Do You Know ?

- Every person has a subtle electromagnetic field flowing through their bodies that they are unaware of. However, a lady named Brenda Allison has heightened electromagnetic field running through her body due to unknown reasons. As a result of the magnetic attraction, metallic objects, such as keys, jar lids, spanners and pins, stick to her body for a long time.
- A solenoid is used in a dialysis machine to control a person's blood flow during dialysis. It is also used in an automobile starter, automatic lock systems, air conditioner and so on.

10.6 ELECTROMAGNET

An electromagnet is a temporary strong magnet made of a soft iron piece within the core of a solenoid.

An electromagnet is an *artificial temporary magnet*.

Two common shapes of electromagnets that are used are (1) I-shaped and (2) U-shaped.

1. I-shaped (or bar) electromagnet : It is formed by either placing a soft iron core within the solenoid or winding a number of turns of a thin insulated copper wire around a soft cylindrical iron core (Fig. 10.10). The ends of the wire are connected to a battery through an ammeter, a rheostat and a key.

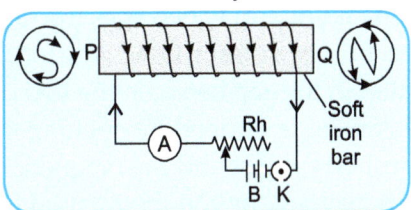

Fig. 10.10 : An I-shaped electromagnet.

The iron core increases the intensity of magnetic field of the solenoid as iron gets magnetised due to magnetic induction. Since it is a *temporary magnet*, it retains magnetic properties only as long as current flows through the solenoid. It loses the magnetic properties if current is switched off. The reason is that soft iron has low *retentivity* which is the capacity of the material to retain magnetic property in itself.

If the current is passed through the solenoid by closing the key and is viewed from the end P of the bar, it appears to flow in clockwise direction and so this end of the bar attains the south polarity. At the Q end of the bar, the current appears to flow in anticlockwise direction and thus this end attains the north polarity. In other words, P end becomes the south pole and Q end becomes the north pole.

2. U-shaped (or horse-shoe) electromagnet : A U-shaped soft iron core is taken and a thin insulated copper wire is spirally wound on its two arms such that the winding on the two arms appears to be in the opposite direction when viewed from the ends of the magnet. As shown in Fig. 10.11, the wire is wound around the P arm of the iron core starting from the lower end in a clockwise direction. Once the wire is wound around this arm and reaches the upper end, winding starts from back at the upper end of arm Q in an anticlockwise direction. The two ends of the wire are then connected to a battery through an ammeter, a rheostat and a key.

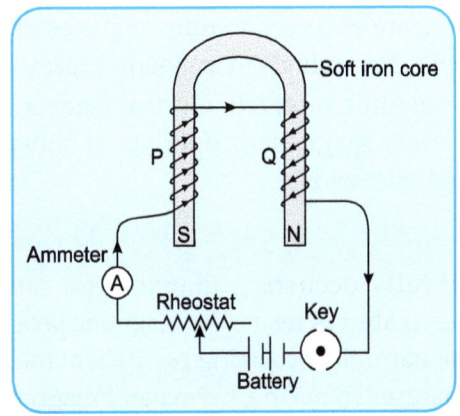

Fig. 10.11 : A U-shaped electromagnet.

When the key is closed to pass current through the wire, the open end of arm P becomes the south pole and the open end of arm Q becomes the north pole as per the direction of current flow. A strong magnetic field is created in the gap between the two poles. Once the flow of current is stopped by opening the key, the magnetic property is lost and the magnetic field cease to exist. Such magnets are commonly used in relay, DC motor and AC generator.

Ways to Increase the Strength of Magnetic Field of an Electromagnet

The strength of magnetic field of an electromagnet (bar or horseshoe) can be increased by the following two ways :

1. Increasing the number of turns of winding of the wire in the solenoid.

2. Increasing the strength of current flowing through the solenoid.

10.7 USES OF ELECTROMAGNETS

Electromagnets are used for a number of purposes, which are as follows :

1. Electromagnets are used in construction of electrical devices such as electric bell, electric fan, electric motor and generator, loudspeaker, relay switch, telephone and instruments.

2. These are used for separating magnetic substances such as iron and nickel from non-magnetic substances.

3. These are used to lift and transport heavy loads such as big machines, steel girders and scrap iron objects. It is easy to unload these heavy objects at the required place. This is performed by switching off the current in the solenoid of electromagnet.

4. Electromagnets are also used for magnetising steel bars.

5. These are also used to remove pieces of iron and steel from wounds in accidental cases.

6. In scientific research, electromagnets are used to study magnetic properties of substances in magnetic field.

10.8 PERMANENT MAGNET

A naturally occurring magnet is a permanent magnet, *i.e.* it always retains its magnetic property, but in general, naturally occurring permanent magnets are weak in nature. To make a permanent magnet, instead of an iron bar, a *steel bar* is used. When an insulated copper wire is wound around a steel bar and electric current is allowed to flow through it, the steel bar gets magnetised. Its *retentivity is higher* than that of soft iron, and so once magnetised, it does not lose its magnetism quickly and thus becomes a permanent magnet.

Uses : Permanent magnets are used in the needles of compasses that are used in navigation of ships and airplanes. These are used in refrigerator door seals to keep the doors closed, microphones and loudspeakers (these require both permanent and electromagnets to work). Other uses include audio cassettes, floppy disks, hard disks, credit cards and so on. All these devices have a thin magnetic coating or strip. These magnets are used in electric meters (galvanometer, ammeter, voltmeter).

10.9 ELECTROMAGNET VERSUS PERMANENT MAGNET

An electromagnet is a temporary magnet with a number of advantages over a permanent magnet. It differs from a permanent magnet in a number of ways and is preferred over it for various applications.

Difference between an Electromagnet and a Permanent Magnet

Electromagnet	Permanent Magnet
It is made up of soft iron.	It is made up of steel.
The magnetic field produced is temporary. It is produced as long as the current flows through its coils.	The magnetic field produced is permanent.
It produces a very strong magnetic field.	It does not produce a very strong magnetic field.
The strength of magnetic field produced can be altered.	The strength of magnetic field cannot be altered.
The polarity of an electro-magnet can be easily changed by reversing the direction of current.	The polarity of a permanent magnet is fixed and cannot be reversed.
It can be easily demagnetised by stopping the flow of current.	It cannot be easily demagnetised.

ILLUSTRATIVE EXAMPLES

1. A straight vertical wire passes through the centre of a horizontal cardboard on which some iron

filings are sprinkled. Plot the directions in which the iron filings will align themselves when the wire carries an electric current (a) in the upward direction and (b) in the downward direction.

Solution : The magnetic field lines along which the iron filings will align themselves is shown in the figure below. Figure (a) shows the direction of field lines when current flows in the upward direction. According to right-hand thumb rule, if current in a straight wire flows upwards, the direction of magnetic field lines is anticlockwise. Similarly in figure (b), when current flows through the straight wire in downward direction, the direction of magnetic field lines is clockwise.

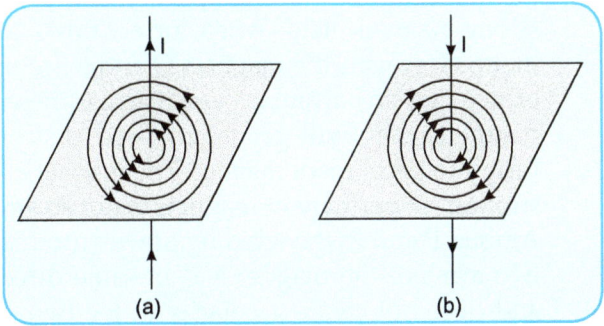

2. A circular coil penetrates a horizontal cardboard at two diametrically opposite points. If the coil carries a current in the clockwise direction from the viewing end, plot the direction of magnetic field lines along the horizontal plane of the cardboard.

Solution : The magnetic field lines on the cardboard are shown below :

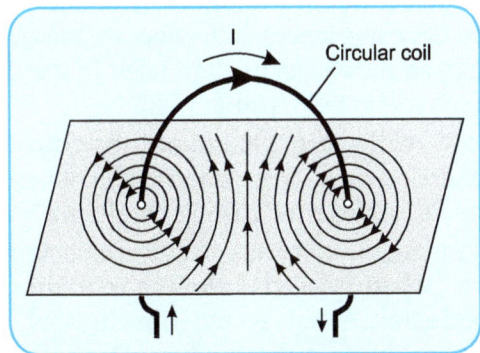

(i) The magnetic field lines are exactly circular at the points where the coil cuts the cardboard. At the point where the current direction is upward, the field is anticlockwise and at the point where the current is directed downwards, the field is clockwise. This is as per right hand grip rule.

(ii) The radii of curvature of the magnetic field lines increases as we go away from the point where the coil cuts the cardboard.

(iii) At the centre of the coil, the magnetic field line is a straight line and is perpendicular to the plane of the coil.

3. A circular coil of radius 10 cm, 50 turns, carrying a current of 2 A has a magnetic field strength of X. Will the magnetic field strength be less than, equal to or more than X if (a) radius is 20 cm, (b) number of turns are 75 and (c) current passing is of 5 A ?

Solution : The strength of magnetic field is directly proportional to the strength of current and the number of turns of the coil but inversely proportional to the radius of the coil. Thus, the magnetic field strength will be (a) less than X as radius is increased, (b) more than X as number of turns are increased and (c) more than X as the strength of current is increased.

4. In the given figure, P and Q are two straight conductors carrying current of equal strength in opposite directions as shown. O is a point located midway between the two conductors.

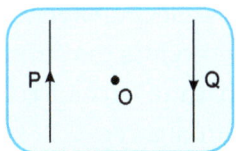

(a) Draw the pattern of magnetic field lines around the conductors P and Q.
(b) What will be the direction and strength of magnetic field at point O?
(c) How will you prove that the direction of magnetic field drawn by you around the point O is correct?
(d) What will be the magnetic field at point O if current in conductor Q is reversed?

Solution :
(a) The pattern of magnetic field lines around the conductors P and Q is shown in the figure below.

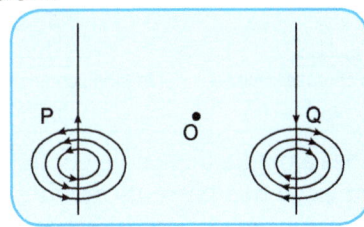

(b) The magnetic field at point O will be in inward direction. As shown in the figure, the direction of magnetic field at point O due to the conductors P and Q is same. The magnetic field due to both conductors being in the same direction is added up and thus, the strength of magnetic field at point O is higher than around P or Q alone.

(c) The direction of magnetic field can be proved by keeping a magnetic compass needle at the point O. Its north pole will face upwards and south pole will face downwards.

(d) If the current in conductor Q is reversed, the direction of magnetic field lines around it will also be reversed. As a result, around point O, the direction of magnetic field due to conductor Q will be opposite to that of conductor P. Since the point lies midway between the two conductors and the strength of current through the two conductors is equal, the two magnetic fields acting around O will be equal and opposite. As a result, the resultant magnetic field at point O will be zero.

5. Which of the electromagnets in the figure given below will produce the strongest magnetic field if the strength of current is equal in each case? Explain your answer.

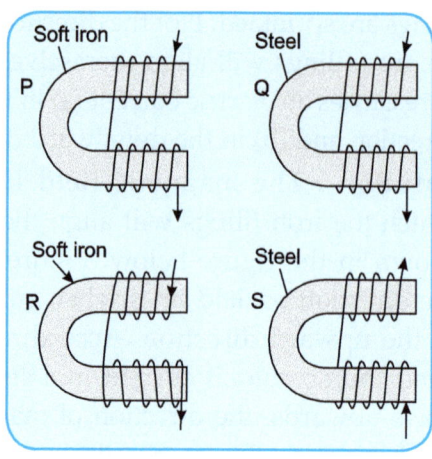

Solution : The strongest magnetic field will be produced by electromagnet P.

Reason : Electromagnets P and R are made of soft iron; these are temporary and produce strong magnetic fields when current flows across them. However, the magnets Q and S are made of steel. When current is passed across these two magnets, they will get magnetised easily and turn into permanent magnet. The magnetic field strength of permanent magnets is not so strong. Among P and R, the winding of wire around the two arms of the magnet R is in same direction and does not create a polarity at the two ends, whereas the winding of wire around the two arms of magnet P is in opposite direction and thus opposite polarities are developed across the two ends when current is passed. Thus, magnetic field produced by electromagnet P is the strongest.

EXERCISE 10(A)

1. Describe Oersted's experiment to show that a current-carrying conductor produces a magnetic field around itself.

2. In the diagrams given below, what would be the direction of the deflection of the magnetic compass needle placed below the conductor?

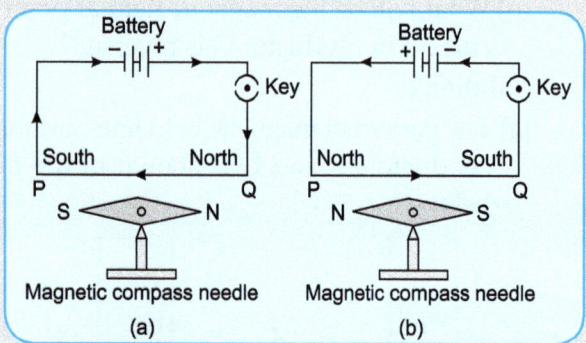

3. Why does a magnetic needle get deflected when brought close to a current-carrying conductor?

Ans : A current-carrying wire produces a magnetic field around it and the magnetic needle experiences a torque in this magnetic field, so it deflects to align itself in the direction of magnetic field at that point.

4. How will you determine the direction of deflection of a magnetic needle when placed close to a current-carrying conductor?

5. A magnetic compass needle deflects towards east when placed below a current-carrying conductor. What is the direction of flow of current through the conductor?

Ans : North to south

6. Draw a diagram showing the direction of magnetic field lines due to a straight wire carrying current. Also show the direction of current flowing through the wire.

7. What is the effect on magnetic field due to a

straight current carrying wire if the current in the wire is

(a) reversed and (b) increased?

Ans : The direction of magnetic field will get reversed, (b) the strength of magnetic field will increase

8. What is the pattern of magnetic field lines due to a straight current carrying wire (a) at points very close to the wire and (b) at some distance away from the wire?

Ans : The field lines are (a) circular, (b) elliptical

9. P and Q are two straight wires carrying current in the same direction as shown in the figure below. O and R are two points located on either side of the conductor P at an equal distance. (a) Draw the magnetic field lines and show their direction around P and Q. (b) Where would the magnetic field be greater—around point O or point R? (c) What would be the effect on magnetic field around points O and R if the direction of current in wire P is reversed?

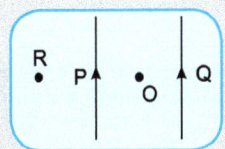

10. What is a neutral point?
11. Name the rule that helps to determine the direction of magnetic field around a straight conductor carrying wire. State the rule.
12. Draw a diagram showing the direction of magnetic field lines of a circular loop carrying current in an anticlockwise direction.
13. The diagram below shows a current-carrying loop or a circular coil passing through a sheet of cardboard at the points M and N. The sheet of cardboard is sprinkled uniformly with iron filings.

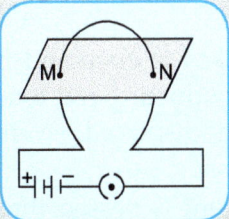

(a) Copy the diagram and draw an arrow on the coil to show the direction of current flowing through it.
(b) Draw the pattern of arrangement of the iron filings when current is passed through the loop.

14. What is clock rule?
15. A wire is bent into a circular loop and carries current in a clockwise direction. What is the polarity of this face of the loop?
16. Where are the magnetic field lines uniform for a current-carrying circular coil?

Ans : Near the centre of the coil

17. (a) Why does a current carrying, freely suspended solenoid rest along a particular direction ?
    (b) State the direction in which it rests.
18. What is an electromagnet? Draw a simple circuit diagram showing the construction of an I-shaped electromagnet.
19. With the help of a diagram, show how a wire is wound around a U-shaped soft iron piece to make an electromagnet. Complete the circuit diagram and label the necessary components.
20. Name two factors on which the strength of magnetic field of an electromagnet depends.
21. The figure given below shows current flowing through the coil wound around a U-shaped soft iron piece. What is the polarity developed at the ends X and Y?

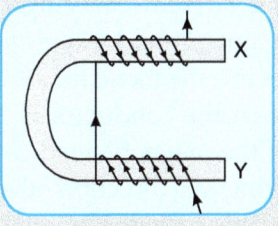

22. State any three uses of an electromagnet.
23. Give any two uses of a permanent magnet.
24. Write a few differences between an electro-magnet and a permanent magnet.

MULTIPLE CHOICE QUESTIONS

1. If the strength of current flowing through a wire is increased, the strength of magnetic field produced by it
   (a) remains unchanged
   (b) increases
   (c) decreases
   (d) first increases and then decreases

   Ans : (b)

2. Which of the following will decrease the strength of a magnetic field due to current through a circular loop?
   (a) increasing the number of turns in the coil
   (b) increasing the strength of the current flowing through the coil

(c) increasing the radius of the coil
(d) none of these
Ans : (c)

3. If the resistance of the rheostat attached in the circuit providing current to a wire is increased, its magnetic field strength will
   (a) remain same
   (b) increase
   (c) decrease
   (d) cannot decide on this parameter alone
   Ans : (c)

4. A permanent magnet is made of
   (a) soft iron   (b) nickel
   (c) steel   (d) copper
   Ans : (c)

(B) FORCE DUE TO MAGNETIC FIELD AND ITS APPLICATION

10.10 FORCE DUE TO MAGNETIC FIELD ON A CURRENT-CARRYING CONDUCTOR : LORENTZ FORCE

From Oersted's experiment, it was demonstrated that a current-carrying conductor exerts a force on a magnet and thus deflects the magnetic needle from its usual north-south orientation. Meanwhile, a French physicist A.M. Ampere suggested that the reverse should also be true, i.e., a magnet should also be able to exert an equal and opposite force on the current-carrying conductor.

Later, it was a Dutch physicist H.A. Lorentz who observed that a current-carrying conductor when placed in a magnetic field experiences a force, i.e., moving charges in a magnetic field experiences a force. This occurs when the conductor is not in parallel to the direction of the magnetic field, which implies that a charge is moving in a direction other than that of the magnetic field. This force is known as *Lorentz force*.

The following experiment will demonstrate the force experienced by a current-carrying conductor in a magnetic field.

Experiment

Take a small conducting rod such as an iron or aluminium rod (about 5 cm long) and suspend it horizontally with the help of two copper wires wound around its ends from a stand. Place a strong horseshoe magnet such that the rod lies between the two poles of the magnet. Place the magnet with its north pole vertically below and south pole vertically above the aluminium rod. In this position of the magnet, its magnetic field will be directed upwards, i.e. the rod lies normal to the magnetic field lines of the magnet. Connect the two wires at the ends of the aluminium rod to the two terminals of the battery through a rheostat and a key. Now allow the current to pass from the battery by closing its key. The direction of current is from end B of the rod to end A (Fig. 10.12).

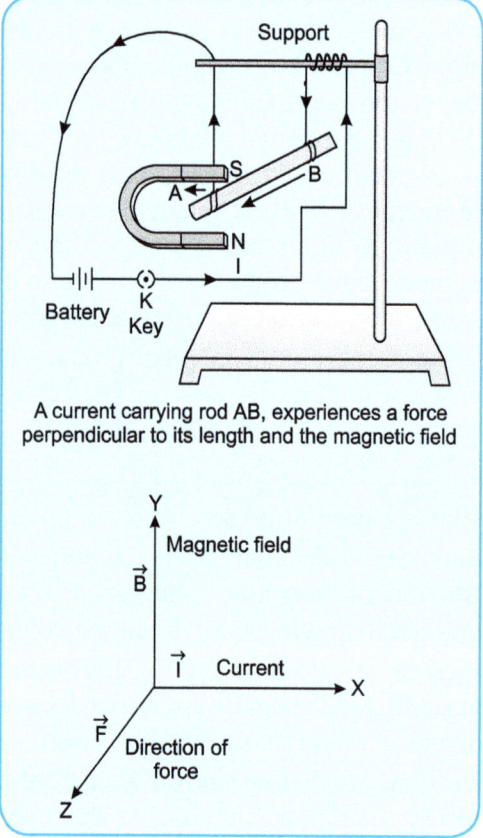

A current carrying rod AB, experiences a force perpendicular to its length and the magnetic field

Fig. 10.12 : Force due to magnetic field on a current-carrying conductor.

Observations

1. When the key is open and no current flows in the circuit, the conducting rod remains at its position and does not gets displaced, i.e., no force acts on the conductor.

2. When current is passed through the rod from end B to A, it is observed that the rod gets displaced towards the left side. This suggests that a force acts on the conductor in a direction perpendicular to both the direction of current flowing through the conductor and the direction of magnetic field of the horseshoe magnet. If the direction of current is taken along X-direction and direction of magnetic field along Y-direction, then the

direction of force acting on the rod is along Z-direction, i.e., normal to the plane of paper in outward direction (Fig. 10.12).

3. If the direction of current flowing through the conducting rod is reversed, so that it flows from A to B, then the rod is displaced towards right, i.e., the direction of force acting on the conductor is also reversed. Thus, if the direction of current is taken along X-direction and direction of magnetic field along Y-direction, then the direction of force acting on the rod is along Z-direction, i.e., normal to the plane of papers in inward direction.

4. If the direction of magnetic field is reversed, by placing the horseshoe magnet with north pole above the rod and south pole below the rod, and current flows from end B to end A of the rod, then the direction of force acting on the rod also reversed the rod also gets reversed. The rod gets displaced towards right, instead of left.

Magnitude of Lorentz Force

It has been experimentally determined that the magnitude of force due to the magnetic field acting on a current-carrying conductor in a perpendicular direction depends on *three* factors :

1. Current flowing through the conductor : The force F is directly proportional to the current flowing in the conductor, *i.e.* $F \propto I$.

2. Magnetic field strength : The force F is directly proportional to the strength of magnetic field, *i.e.* $F \propto B$.

3. Length of the conductor : The force F is directly proportional to the length of the conductor, *i.e.* $F \propto l$.

Combining the above three factors, we obtain
$$F \propto IBl \text{ or } F = KIBl,$$
where K is the constant of proportionality. In SI unit, the unit of B is such that K = 1.

Thus, $\quad F = IBl \quad$ ...(10.1)

From Equation (10.1), we obtain
$$B = \frac{F}{Il} \quad ...(10.2)$$

Unit of Magnetic Field

From Equation (10.2), we obtain the SI unit of magnetic field as

$$B = \frac{\text{Unit of force}}{\text{Unit of current} \times \text{Unit of length}}$$
$$= \frac{\text{newton}}{\text{ampere} \times \text{metre}} = NA^{-1} m^{-1}$$

This unit is named as *tesla* (T) and is also called *weber/metre²* (Wb m^{-2}).

10.11 FLEMING'S LEFT-HAND RULE : TO DETERMINE DIRECTION OF FORCE ACTING ON A CURRENT-CARRYING CONDUCTOR

According to Fleming's left-hand rule,

Stretch the thumb, the forefinger and the middle finger of the left hand mutually perpendicular to each other (Fig. 10.13), such that the forefinger points in the direction of magnetic field and the middle finger in the direction of flow of current through the conductor then the thumb gives the direction of motion of the conductor, i.e. direction of force acting on the conductor.

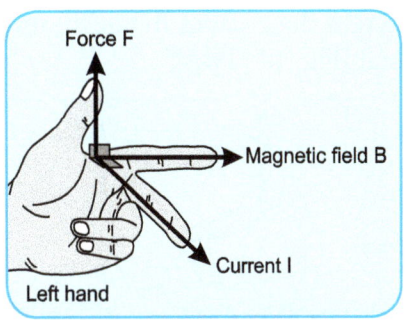

Fig. 10.13 : Fleming's left-hand rule.

10.12 SIMPLE DC MOTOR

An electric motor is a device that converts electrical energy (direct current) into mechanical energy.

An electric motor is used to produce rotational motion with the help of electricity in electrical appliances such as fan, mixer, juicer and washing machine.

Principle : When an electric current is passed through a conductor placed perpendicularly in a magnetic field, a force acts on the conductor and produces motion in it. Thus, the conductor begins to move, converting electrical energy to mechanical work or energy.

Construction : A DC motor consists of the following parts as shown in Fig. 10.14(a).

1. An armature : It is a rectangular coil made up of insulated copper wire wound around a soft iron core.

2. A split ring commutator : It is a device that is used to reverse the direction of flow of current through the armature after every half rotation of the coil. It is a copper ring split into two parts S_1 and S_2.

3. Brushes : Two small strips of carbon, B_1 and B_2, are attached to the two split rings of the commutator.

These are known as *brushes*. The function of these brushes is to make contact with the rotating rings of the commutator and through them to supply current to the coil.

4. A horseshoe magnet.

5. A battery, which is a source of direct current (DC).

The armature coil ABCD is wound around a soft iron core that is mounted on an axle such that the coil can freely rotate about its axis. The armature is placed between the two pole pieces of a horseshoe magnet NS as shown in Fig. 10.14 (b). The two ends of the coil, A and D, are connected to the two split rings S_1 and S_2, respectively, of the commutator. A battery is connected across the brushes B_1 and B_2 through a key and a rheostat [Fig. 10.14 (b)].

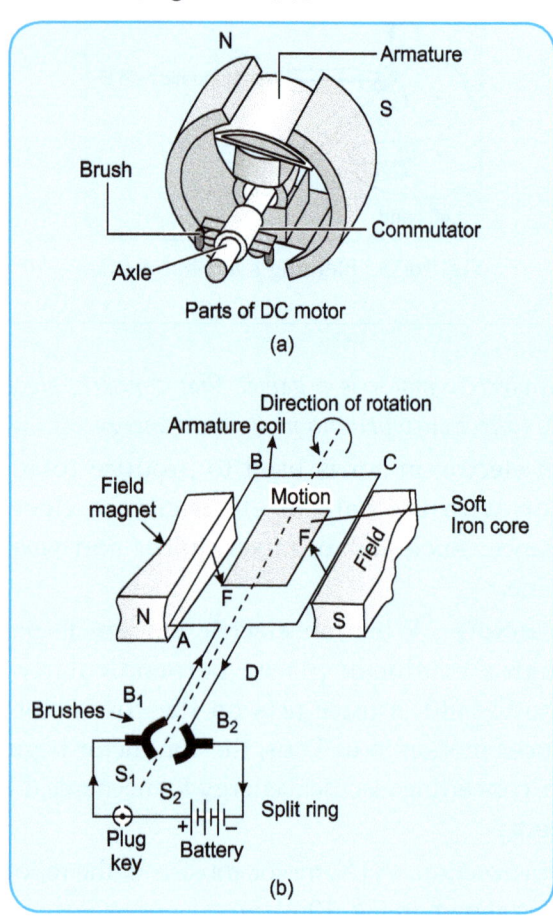

Fig. 10.14 : Construction of a DC motor.

To understand the working of the DC motor, it is essential to understand the working of the commutator.

Working of commutator : The two split rings S_1 and S_2 are joined by an insulating material so that they are not in contact with each other, and the ring is mounted on an axle. A resistance wire R is connected across the two rings. The carbon brushes B_1 and B_2 press against rings S_1 and S_2, respectively (Fig. 10.15), and allow the motion of the two rings. The brush B_1 is connected to the positive terminal of the battery and the brush B_2 is connected to the negative terminal.

When the current is passed from the battery to brush B_1, it flows to ring S_1 and from S_1 through the resistance wire R to ring S_2 (Fig. 10.15). From S_2, the current returns through the brush B_2. Now, if the ring is rotated in clockwise direction, the direction of the current in the resistance wire is along S_1RS_2 as long as strip S_1 touches the brush B_1 and strip S_2 touches the brush B_2. This would continue until half rotation of the ring, *i.e.* 180° turn. After half rotation, the strip S_2 touches the brush B_1 and strip S_1 touches brush B_2. Now the strip S_1 is connected to the negative terminal of the battery and strip S_2 to the positive terminal. This reverses the direction of current from S_1RS_2 to S_2RS_1.

As the ring continues its rotation about the axle after every half rotation, the direction of current changes automatically. This property of commutator of reversing the direction of current is employed in the DC motor.

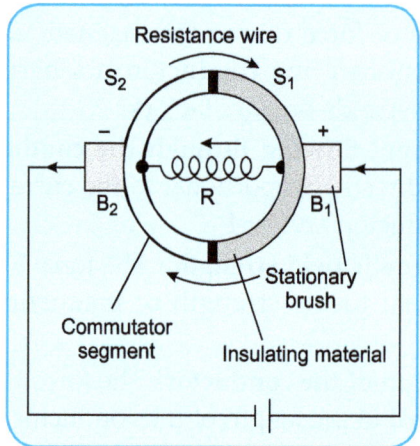

Fig. 10.15 : Working of a commutator.

Ways to increase the power of a DC motor : The power of a DC motor can be increased by increasing the speed of rotation of the coil. This can be performed by the following ways :

1. Increase the number of turns in the coil.
2. Increase the area of cross-section of the coil.
3. Increase the strength of current flowing through the coil.
4. Increase the strength of magnetic field by inserting a soft iron core within the coil.

Type of energy transfer in DC motor : In DC motor, the electrical energy supplied by the battery to the coil is transferred to mechanical energy which rotates the coil.

ILLUSTRATIVE EXAMPLES

1. The given figure shows a rectangular coil ABCD connected with a commutator and a battery between its ends A and D and is placed between the pole pieces of a strong magnet.

   (a) State the direction of current flowing in the coil.

   (b) What is the direction of force on each arm of the coil?

   (c) What will be the direction of rotation of the coil?

   (d) What will be the effect if the terminals of the battery across A and D are interchanged?

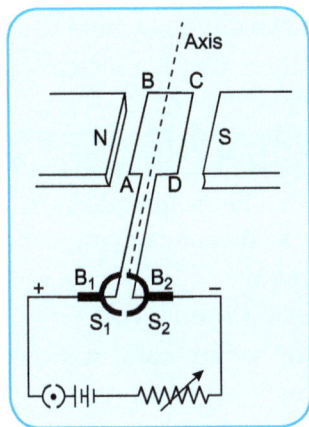

Solution :

(a) The direction of current in the coil is along ABCD.

(b) According to Fleming's left-hand rule, the direction of force on the arm AB is inwards, perpendicular to the plane of the coil. On the arm CD, the direction of force is outwards, perpendicular to the plane of the coil. No force acts on the arms BC and AD, as the direction of current flow is parallel to the magnetic field.

(c) According to right-hand thumb rule, the direction of the rotation of coil will be anticlockwise, with arm AB entering and arm CD leaving.

(d) If the terminals of the battery are interchanged, the direction of current through the coil will reverse and will be along DCBA and so the coil will rotate in a clockwise direction.

2. The given figure shows the diagram of a commutator. (a) Label its parts. (b) State the functions of its parts.

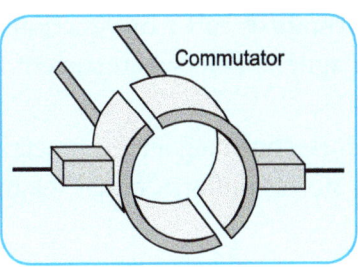

Solution :

(a) The parts of commutator are labelled below.

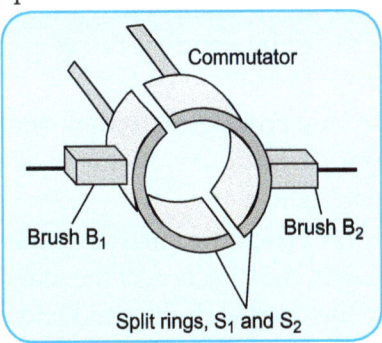

(b) The function of split rings is to reverse the direction of current through the coil of a DC motor after every half rotation so that the direction of rotation of the coil remains unchanged.

The function of the brushes is to supply a continuous current to the rotating coil. These are attached to the terminals of the current source.

3. State the effect if (a) the area of cross-section of the coil of a DC motor is decreased, (b) the strength of current passing through the coil is increased and (c) the direction of current through the coil is reversed.

Solution :

(a) If the area of cross-section of the coil is decreased, the speed of rotation of the coil will decrease.

(b) If the strength of current through the coil is increased, the speed of rotation of the coil will increase.

(c) If the direction of current is reversed, the direction of rotation of the coil will also get reversed.

4. State the functions of the following in a DC motor : (a) battery, (b) armature coil, (c) horseshoe magnet and (d) commutator.

Solution :

(a) **Battery :** Its function is to provide current to the coil of the motor, which in turn converts electrical energy to mechanical energy.

(b) Armature coil : Its function is to set up a magnetic field when current flows through it.

(c) Horseshoe magnet : Its function is to provide a strong uniform radial magnetic field that interacts with the magnetic field of the coil to provide mechanical energy.

(d) Commutator : Its function is to reverse the direction of the current after every half rotation of the coil.

EXERCISE 10(B)

1. What do you understand by Lorentz force?
2. Describe an experiment to demonstrate the force experienced by a current-carrying conductor in a magnetic field.
3. State the condition when the force on a current-carrying conductor is at (a) zero and (b) maximum

   Ans : (a) When the current in the conductor is flowing in the direction of the magnetic field, (b) when the current in the conductor is flowing in a direction normal to the magnetic field.
4. Name the three factors on which the magnitude of Lorentz force depends. State how these factors affect the Lorentz force.
5. What happens to the direction of force if the direction of current flowing through the conductor is reversed when placed in a magnetic field?

   Ans : The direction of force also get reversed.
6. State the two conditions that reverse the direction of current flowing through the conductor when placed in a magnetic field.
7. State the SI unit of magnetic field.
8. Name and describe the rule that is used to determine the direction of force acting on a current-carrying conductor in a magnetic field.
9. State the energy change that takes place in a DC motor.

   Ans : Electrical energy to mechanical energy
10. Draw a simple labelled diagram of a DC motor. What is the function of the split rings in a DC motor?
11. State the principle of working of a DC motor.
12. What is a commutator?
13. Name any two electrical appliances in which a DC motor is used.

    Ans : Fan, washing machine
14. State any three ways of increasing the power of a DC motor.

MULTIPLE CHOICE QUESTIONS

1. The rule that helps to find the direction of force acting on a current-carrying conductor is
   (a) Lenz's law
   (b) right-hand thumb rule
   (c) Fleming's right-hand rule
   (d) Fleming's left-hand rule
   Ans : (d)
2. A coil carrying current when placed between the pole pieces of a magnet experiences a :
   (a) pressure (b) couple
   (c) electrical force (d) none of these
   Ans : (b)
3. The energy conversion in a DC motor is :
   (a) magnetic to electrical
   (b) mechanical to electrical
   (c) electrical to magnetic
   (d) electrical to mechanical
   Ans : (d)

(C) ELECTROMAGNETIC INDUCTION AND ITS APPLICATION

10.13 ELECTROMAGNETIC INDUCTION

From Oersted's experiments, it became evident that an electric current flowing across a conductor produces magnetic field. Michael Faraday, an English physicist, wondered if the reverse phenomenon could take place. In 1831, Faraday and Henry conducted experiments to demonstrate that a changing magnetic field can induce an electric current.

The phenomenon of production of electric current by moving a conductor in a magnetic field is known as electromagnetic induction.

The necessary condition for electromagnetic induction to occur is that there must be *relative motion* between the conductor and the magnetic field. This results in a development of *electromotive force* (emf) between the ends of the conductor.

The phenomenon of electromagnetic induction can be demonstrated by the experiment given below.

Experiment

Take an insulated copper wire and wind it around a cardboard cylinder to form a solenoid. Connect the two ends of the solenoid to a galvanometer G that has a zero mark in the centre. It is a device that detects the presence of electric current. Take a bar magnet NS and place it at some distance from the solenoid along its axis.

Observations

1. When the magnet is not moved, *i.e.*, it is stationary, there is no deflection in the galvanometer. The pointer remains at zero mark [Fig. 10.16 (a)].

2. When the magnet is moved towards the solenoid, such that its north pole faces the solenoid, there occurs a deflection in the galvanometer towards right, indicating that current flows in solenoid in the direction B to A [Fig. 10.16 (b)].

3. If the motion of the magnet is stopped, the pointer of galvanometer returns to zero mark, indicating that current in the solenoid flows as long as the magnet is in motion. [Fig. 10.16 (c)].

4. If the magnet is moved away from the solenoid, the galvanometer deflects towards left, indicating that current flows across the solenoid but in opposite direction, *i.e.* A to B [Fig. 10.16 (d)].

5. If the magnet is moved with a greater speed, the deflection in the galvanometer increases and the direction remains the same. This suggests a greater strength of current flowing in the solenoid.

6. If the direction of magnet is reversed, *i.e.* its south pole facing the solenoid is brought closer, the direction of deflection of galvanometer becomes opposite to that shown in fig. 10.16 (e), suggesting reversal in the direction of flow of current *i.e.*, A to B.

Similar observations are recorded if the magnet is kept stationary and the solenoid is moved towards or away from the magnet. Thus, it is the *relative motion* between the solenoid and the magnet that produces a flow of current.

Explanation

Faraday provided an explanation based on his observations.

When both the coil and the magnet are stationary, no emf is induced in the coil. This is because the total number of magnetic field lines due to the magnet passing through the coil remains constant. The amount of magnetic field lines passing through a surface is known as *magnetic flux*. Thus, when there is no relative motion between the magnet and the coil, the magnetic flux remains constant and thus the galvanometer does not show any deflection.

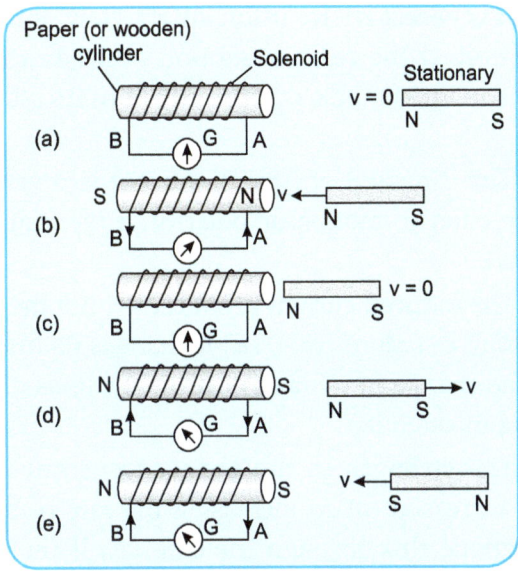

Fig. 10.16 : Demonstration of an Electromagnetic Induction.

When either the coil or the magnet is moved, *i.e.*, there occurs a relative motion between the two, the magnetic flux changes. When the north pole of magnet is moved towards the coil, the magnetic flux through the coil increases, but when the magnet is moved away from the coil, the magnetic flux decreases (Fig. 10.17). It is the change in magnetic flux that induces an emf in the coil due to which current flows across it.

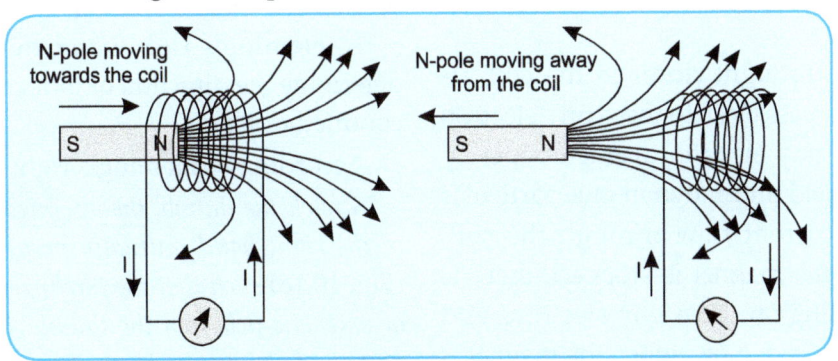

Fig. 10.17 : Change of magnetic flux through a coil.

Electromagnetic induction is the phenomenon in which an emf, and thus a current, is induced in the coil if there is a change in magnetic flux linked with it.

In this phenomenon, *mechanical energy is transformed to electrical energy*, which means that the energy spent in moving the coil or the magnet to cause a change in magnetic flux is transformed to current in the coil.

Conclusions

Faraday made the following conclusions from his experiments on electromagnetic induction :

1. A relative motion between the coil and the magnet is necessary for inducing the flow of current in the coil. If the relative motion between the coil and the magnet stops, no current is produced in the coil.

2. The direction of flow of current is reversed if the direction of motion or polarity of the magnet is reversed.

3. The induced current produced within the coil is *alternating* in nature (AC), *i.e.*, it changes its direction with the change in number of magnetic lines of force passing through it.

4. The strength of the induced current in the coil is increased (a) by increasing the rate of change of magnetic flux through the coil, *i.e.*, if the speed of motion of magnet or coil is increased; (b) if the magnet used is stronger, *i.e.*, there are more number of magnetic field lines passing through the coil; and (c) if the number of turns and area of cross-section of the coil are increased.

Reason for current induced in the coil : A copper coil has a very large number of free electrons that spin about their own axis and thus behave like tiny magnets with a definite north and south poles and a magnetic field. In a coil, millions of these tiny magnets move in all random directions.

When a magnet is brought closer to the coil, its magnetic lines of force pass close to these tiny electron magnets. Thus, these tiny electron magnets repel by the strong magnetic field and move in one particular direction, inducing current flow through the coil. When the motion of the magnet is stopped, there is no magnetic force acting on these tiny electrons and hence no current is induced. Now, when the magnet is moved away from the coil, the force of magnetic field on the electron magnets decreases and the electrons return to their original position, resulting in flow of current in the opposite direction.

10.14 FARADAY'S LAWS OF ELECTRO-MAGNETIC INDUCTION

Based on the above observations, Faraday stated the following two laws of electromagnetic induction :

1. *Whenever the magnetic flux linked with a coil changes, an emf is induced in the coil, which lasts as long as the change in magnetic flux associated with the coil continues.*

As a result of induced emf, an induced current flows, if the circuit is complete.

2. *The magnitude of the induced emf is directly proportional to the rate of change of magnetic flux linked with the coil.*

A steady emf is produced if the rate of change of magnetic flux remains uniform.

Thus, Induced emf

$$= \frac{\text{Change in magnetic flux}}{\text{Time in which the magnetic flux changes}} \quad ...(10.3)$$

Thus, *two* factors affect the magnitude of induced emf : (a) the change in magnetic flux and (b) the time in which the magnetic flux changes.

With more change in flux, more emf is induced in a given time.

10.15 DIRECTION OF INDUCED EMF OR INDUCED CURRENT

It is the increase or decrease of magnetic flux that determines the direction of induced emf or the induced current.

The direction of induced current can be determined by the following two rules :

1. Fleming's right-hand rule : This rule helps to determine the direction of induced current in a straight conductor or a coil.

According to Fleming's right-hand rule,

Stretch the thumb, the forefinger and the middle finger of the right hand mutually perpendicular to each other (Fig. 10.18) such that the forefinger points in the direction of magnetic field and the thumb points in the direction of motion of conductor. Then, the middle finger will give the direction of induced current.

ELECTROMAGNETISM 217

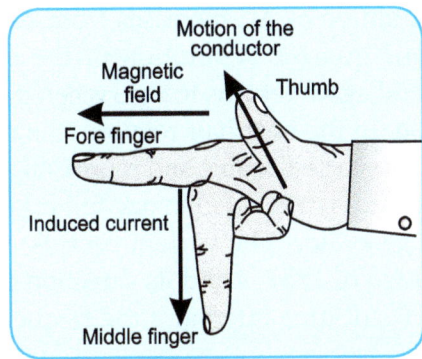

Fig. 10.18 : Fleming's right-hand rule.

2. Lenz's law : This rule helps to determine the direction of induced current in a solenoid.

According to Lenz's law,

The direction of induced current is such that it always tend to oppose the cause (the motion of conductor or magnet) that produces it.

When the north pole of a magnet is moved towards one of the ends of the solenoid, the direction of induced current opposes the motion of north pole of the magnet towards this end. Hence the end of the solenoid close to the magnet acquires the north polarity and repels the magnet [Fig. 10.19(a)]. Thus, the induced current opposes the cause (motion of magnet towards it) producing it. As this end of the solenoid becomes north pole, the induced current at this end will be in anticlockwise direction.

Alternatively, when the north pole of the magnet is moved away from one end of the solenoid, the direction of induced current should be such that it opposes the motion of north pole of the magnet away from this end [Fig. 10.19 (b)]. Hence this end of the solenoid acquires south polarity and attracts the magnet towards it. The induced current opposes the cause (motion of magnet away from it) producing it. Due to south polarity, current at this end of the solenoid begins to flow in clockwise direction.

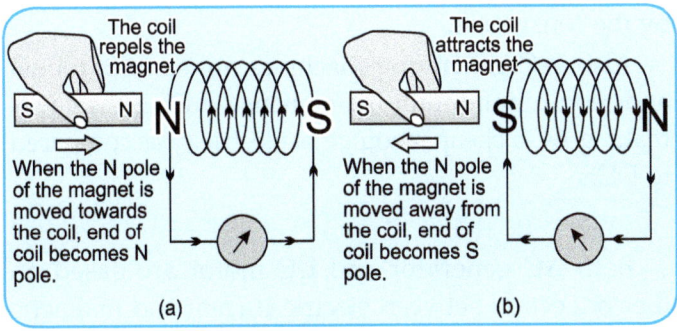

Fig. 10.19 : Lenz's law

Lenz's law obeys the *law of conservation of energy* in case of electromagnetic induction. The mechanical energy spent in opposing the motion of the magnet (or the coil) is transformed into electrical energy of the coil due to which current flows through it. The total energy remains conserved.

10.16 AC GENERATOR

An *AC generator* is a device that works on the principle of electromagnetic induction and converts *mechanical energy into electrical energy.*

It produces a large amount of electric power and hence is commonly known as a *generator*. Commonly, when the supply from the mains fails to provide electricity, an AC generator is used as an alternative source.

Principle : An AC generator is based on the principle of *electromagnetic induction*. When a closed coil is rotated in a magnetic field, its magnetic flux changes and thus induces an emf between the ends of the coil. Due to this emf, an electric current begins to flow in the coil.

Construction : An AC generator consists of the following parts (Fig. 10.20) :

1. Field magnet : It is a powerful horseshoe permanent magnet NS that produces a radial magnetic field which is highly concentrated in the middle and acts along the radius of curvature of magnets that causes maximum emf generation.

For bigger generators, an electromagnet powered by a DC source is generally used.

2. Armature : It consists of a soft iron core, from whose centre passes a steel axle to rotate it. A rectangular insulated copper coil ABCD of large number of turns is wound over the core.

3. Slip rings : There are two coaxial slip rings S_1 and S_2 that are made of gunmetal. These are connected to the two ends of the armature coil. The rings are insulated from each other and rotate with the coil along the same axis.

4. Brushes : There are two brushes B_1 and B_2 made of carbon or gunmetal. One of the ends of these brushes is pressed gently with slip rings S_1 and S_2, respectively. The other ends of the brushes are connected to an external load R. *These brushes are stationary but allow the rotation of slip rings along with the coil.* These act as the terminals of the generator for the external load.

Frequency of AC : In one complete rotation of the coil, we get one cycle of alternating emf in the external circuit. The alternating emf thus produced has frequency equal to the frequency of rotation of the coil.

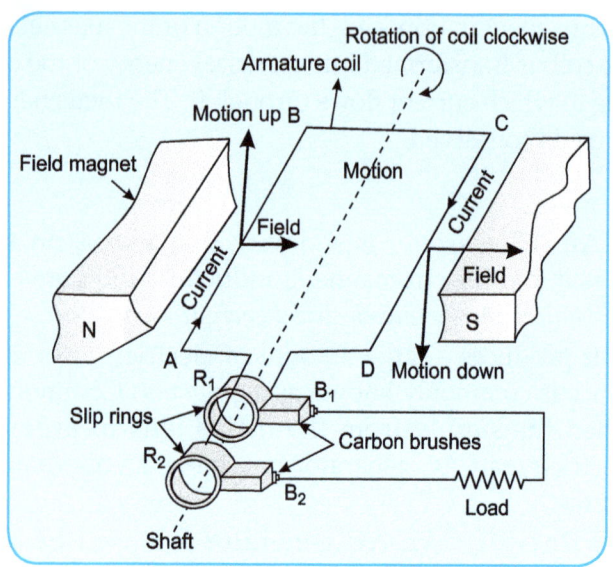

Fig. 10.20 : AC generator

If the coil makes n rotations per second, the magnitude of induced emf is given as

$$e = e_0 \sin 2\pi nt$$

and the current is expressed as

$$i = i_0 \sin 2\pi nt$$

where e_0 and i_0 represent the maximum values of emf and current respectively.

When the coil rotates through complete 360°, or one rotation, one cycle of alternating emf is generated in the external circuit. In other words, the frequency of *alternating emf* is *equal* to the frequency of *one complete rotation of the coil*. If the coil rotates 50 times in 1 s, then the frequency of alternating current is 50 Hz (50 cycles). In our houses, the voltage supplied has a frequency of 50 Hz, *i.e.*, the polarity at the supply terminal changes 100 times a second (50 times + and 50 times –).

10.17 DISTINCTION BETWEEN DC AND AC

When the source of current is a *dry cell* (primary electrochemical cell) or an *accumulator* (secondary electrochemical cell), the current generated has no change in magnitude and direction.

Direct current is a current in which the magnitude and direction remain *constant* with time.

When the source of current is a *generator* or the *mains* in our house, the magnitude and direction of current does not remain constant but changes periodically.

Alternating current is a current in which the magnitude and direction *vary* with time (change periodically).

The magnitude of AC increases from zero to peak value in one quarter of rotation of the coil of the generator and again returns to zero when it completes half rotation. In the next half rotation, the magnitude again increases to peak value and returns to zero. Thus, one cycle of AC is completed in one full rotation of the coil of the generator. The current repeats its cycle in a time interval of 1/50 s and its direction changes in every 1/100 s of time interval if the frequency of AC is 50 Hz.

Difference between DC and AC

Direct current (DC)	Alternating current (AC)
This current has constant magnitude.	The magnitude of this current varies with time.
The direction of this current is constant.	The direction of this current reverses periodically.
Source : Cell or a battery.	Source : AC generator and mains supply.

Advantages of AC over DC

The electric power that we receive in our house is the alternating current (AC). The use of AC is preferred over DC as wide range of voltages can be obtained in case of AC by using a transformer. At the power-generating station, a step-up transformer is used to increase the voltage of the AC generated before transmitting it to the substation. This reduces the loss of electrical energy in the form of heat in the line wires. In the case of DC, it is not possible to increase its voltage for transmission through a transformer and thus a lot of heat would be generated in the wires, resulting in loss of electrical energy during transmission. It is easy to step down the voltage in the case of AC using step-down transformers for safe use by the consumers.

Also, AC generating machines are simple, robust and require minimum maintenance during their use, making AC a cheaper source of electricity as compared to DC.

Comparison between AC Generator and DC Motor

Both AC generator and DC motor are based on the connection between electric current and magnetic field. In both these devices, a coil undergoes motion in a magnetic field produced by the pole pieces of a powerful horseshoe electromagnet. However, the basic process of working is converse in the two devices.

Difference between AC generator and DC motor

AC generator	DC motor
It works on the principle of electromagnetic induction.	It works on the principle of Lorentz force (force acting on a current-carrying conductor placed in a magnetic field).
In this device, mechanical energy is converted into electrical energy.	In this device, electrical energy is converted into mechanical energy.
There are two separate coaxial slip rings in a generator.	There is a single slip ring divided into two parts (split rings) in a DC motor which act as commutator.
In this device, the coil rotates in a magnetic field to produce AC.	In this device, DC flows into the coil placed in a magnetic field and produces rotation of the coil.

10.18 TRANSFORMER

A transformer is a device that is used to increase or decrease the emf of an alternating current.

A transformer is used to increase or decrease the voltage supplied from the mains (220 V) as per the need for a particular device, without affecting the frequency of the AC.

Example : A small device such as an electric bell requires only 10 V while the picture tube of a television requires several thousand volts.

Principle : A transformer is based on the principle of *mutual induction in which two coils with different number of turns are used.* Mutual induction is a special case of *electromagnetic induction.* In mutual induction, when an alternating current is passed through a coil (called primary coil) wound on a soft iron core, an induced emf is produced in another coil (secondary coil) wound on same soft iron core.

When there is change in magnetic field lines linked with the primary coil due to an applied AC, it causes change in magnetic field lines linked with the secondary coil, which in turn produces a current of same frequency but different magnitude in the secondary coil, depending on the number of turns in this coil.

Since there is no change in magnetic field lines in the primary coil connected with a direct current (DC) source, it cannot induce any change in magnetic field lines in the secondary coil and thus no current is induced in it. Thus, a transformer cannot be used with a DC source.

Construction : A transformer consists of three main parts (Fig. 10.21) :

1. A rectangular soft iron core : It is made up of thin laminated sheets insulated from each other by paint or varnish. The sheets are held tightly using clamps. The advantage of using a soft iron core is that due to its high magnetic permeability, the magnetic field lines are highly concentrated and energy loss due to *magnetic hysteresis* is less. The lamination of iron core prevents the formation of *eddy currents* and thus prevents energy losses.

Magnetic hysteresis : It refers to the retention of magnetisation by the core when the applied current is removed.

Eddy currents : These are circular currents flowing in a solid conductor such as a metallic plate moving in a magnetic field. A metal plate acts like a closed coil. The free electrons of the plate are disturbed when placed in a varying magnetic field. This sets up an induced emf in the plate. Since there are no free ends on the plate, the currents induced cannot flow and thus heats up the plate. Eddy current is a nuisance as it heats up the core of the transformers, generators and so on.

2. Primary coil : On one arm of the iron core, an insulated copper wire is wound. This coil is called *primary coil* and is connected to the source of an alternating emf, *i.e.*, the *input* voltage.

3. Secondary coil : The insulated copper wire wound on the other arm of the iron core is called the *secondary coil*. Across the terminals of this coil, an induced alternating emf of required *output* voltage is obtained.

Since the two coils are wound on the same iron core, it provides a closed path for magnetic field lines produced by the current flowing in the primary coil. These field lines remain linked with the secondary coil and thus energy loss is prevented.

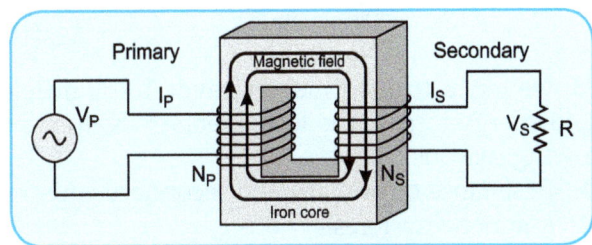

Fig. 10.21 : A transformer.

Working : The terminals of the primary coil are connected to the source of alternating emf and the terminals of the secondary coil are connected across an external load in which the required (high/low) voltage is generated. Suppose a current is flowing in the primary coil in an anticlockwise direction. Due to the flow of varying current, a varying magnetic flux is induced in the soft iron core. When this changing magnetic flux passes through the secondary coil, it induces an emf in it. Due to the induced emf, current begins to flow in the secondary coil in a clockwise direction (Lenz's law). The *induced emf* in the secondary coil has the *same frequency* as that of the *input emf* in the primary coil.

The magnitude of induced emf depends on two factors :

1. The ratio of number of turns in the secondary coil to the number of turns in the primary coil. This ratio is called the *turns ratio*.

Turns ratio (n)

$$= \frac{\text{Number of turns in the secondary coil } N_s}{\text{Number of turns in the primary coil } N_P}$$

...(10.4)

2. The magnitude of the emf applied in the primary coil. It is given as

$$\frac{\text{Emf across the secondary coil } (E_s)}{\text{Emf across the primary coil } (E_P)} = \frac{\text{Number of turns in the secondary coil } (N_s)}{\text{Number of turns in the primary coil } (N_P)}$$

i.e.
$$\frac{E_S}{E_P} = \frac{N_S}{N_P} = \text{Turns ratio } (n)$$

....(10.5)

In an *ideal transformer*, where there is no loss of energy, the output power is equal to the input power.

Power in the secondary coil = Power in the primary coil

i.e. Emf induced in secondary coil × Current induced in secondary coil = Emf applied in primary coil × Current flowing in primary coil

i.e. $\qquad E_S I_S = E_P I_P \qquad$ ...(10.6)

or $\qquad \dfrac{E_S}{E_P} = \dfrac{I_P}{I_S} \qquad$ ...(10.7)

From Equations (10.5) and (10.7), we get

$$\frac{N_S}{N_P} = \frac{I_P}{I_S} \qquad ...(10.8)$$

However, a transformer is never 100% efficient due to energy losses. The loss of energy is due to the following reasons :

1. Resistance of primary and secondary coils
2. Magnetic hysteresis
3. Eddy currents

Types of Transformers

Transformers are of two types : (1) step-up transformer and (2) step-down transformer.

1. Step-up transformer : A step-up transformer is used to convert a low-voltage alternating emf to a high-voltage alternating emf of same frequency (Fig. 10.22).

The number of turns in the primary coil of a step-up transformer is less than the number of turns in the secondary coil, *i.e.* $N_P < N_S$ or $N_S/N_P > 1$. The turns ratio is greater than 1.

From Equation (10.8), since $N_S > N_P$, hence $I_S < I_P$, *i.e.*, a large current flows in the primary coil. Due to this, the primary coil is made up of thick wire as compared to the secondary coil. Due to the thickness of the wire, the resistance is reduced and thus prevents energy loss in the form of heat (also known as *copper loss*).

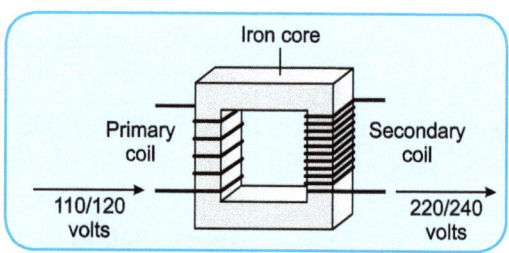

Fig. 10.22 : Step-up transformer.

2. Step-down transformer : A step-down transformer is used to convert a high-voltage alternating emf to a low-voltage alternating emf of same frequency (Fig. 10.23).

The number of turns in the primary coil of a step-up transformer is more than the number of turns in the secondary coil, *i.e.* $N_P > N_S$ or $N_S/N_P < 1$. The turns ratio is smaller than 1. Since $N_S < N_P$, hence $I_S > I_P$, *i.e.*, a large current flows in the secondary coil. In this case, the secondary coil is made up of thick wire as compared to the primary coil to prevent heat loss.

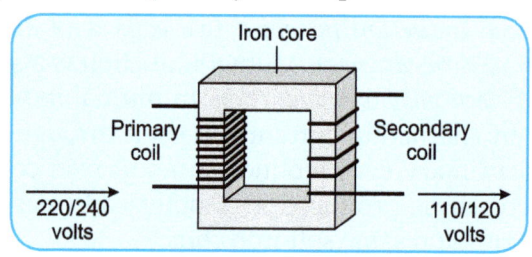

Fig. 10.23 : Step-down transformer.

Uses of Transformers

Step-up transformer

1. In grid (power-generating station) transmission, it is used to step up the voltage from 11 kV to 132 kV to save energy during power transmission.

2. At home, in electronic equipment such as television sets and wireless sets.

3. In discharge tubes and X-ray tubes.

Step-down transformer

1. In power sub-stations, to decrease the voltage before supplying to the consumers.

2. At home, in devices such as electric bells, night bulbs, radio sets, transistors and battery chargers.

Difference between Step-up Transformer and Step-down Transformer

Step-up transformer	Step-down transformer
This device converts low AC voltage to high AC voltage.	This device converts high AC voltage to low AC voltage.
It decreases the output current.	It increases the output current.
The turns ratio is greater than 1, *i.e.* there are more number of turns in the secondary coil than in the primary coil.	The turns ratio is less than 1, *i.e.* there are less number of turns in the secondary coil than in the primary coil.
The primary coil is made up of thicker wire as compared to that of the secondary coil.	The secondary coil is made up of thicker wire as compared to that of the primary coil.
These are used at power-generating station, television sets, X-ray tubes, etc.	These are used at power substations, night bulbs, electric bells, etc.

ILLUSTRATIVE EXAMPLES

1. The given figure shows a coil connected to a sensitive galvanometer G and a magnet NS placed close to it. (a) What will you observe if the magnet is dropped into the coil? (b) What will be the observation if the magnet is taken out of the coil? (c) What will be the effect if the number of turns in the coil is decreased?

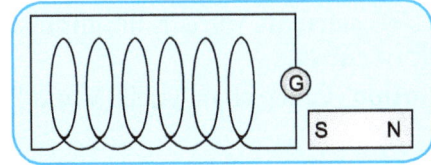

Solution :

(a) When the magnet is dropped in the coil, a momentary deflection is observed in the galvanometer as long as the magnetic field lines linked with the coil increases. The deflection is towards the left as the end of the coil close to the south pole of the magnet acquires south polarity and current begins to flow in the coil in clockwise direction.

(b) If the magnet is taken out from the coil, the magnetic field lines linked with it decreases and a momentary deflection is observed in the galvanometer in the opposite direction, *i.e.* towards the right side, as long as the magnetic field lines linked with the coil decreases.

(c) If the number of turns in the coil is decreased, the deflection observed in the previous cases will be less.

2. The given figure shows two coils A and B wound around a soft iron core. (a) State the polarity at end P and end Q when switch S is closed. (b) What is the effect in the galvanometer attached to coil B when the switch S is closed? (c) What will be the effect if resistance R is reduced and then switch is closed? (d) What will be observed if coil B is moved away from coil A with the switch closed?

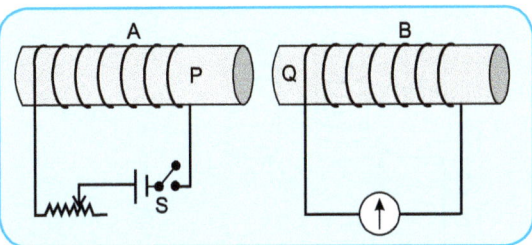

Solution :

(a) When the switch S is closed, current begins to flow in anticlockwise direction in the coil A. Hence, the left end becomes north pole and the end P of the coil acquires south polarity. The magnetic field of coil A will induce a current in coil Q. The end Q is close to end P and hence by using Lenz's Law, the coil Q will acquire south polarity to oppose the source producing the current in it.

(b) When the switch S is closed, a current is induced in coil B due to the magnetic effect of current flowing in coil A. Since Q end acquires south polarity, current begins to flow in clockwise direction at point Q of coil B and so the galvanometer shows a momentary deflection towards left. Once the current becomes steady in coil A, there is no varying magnetic field to induce current in coil B and so the galvanometer will return to its zero position.

(c) If the resistance is decreased, large current will flow across coil A and thus the intensity of its magnetic field will be higher, resulting in a greater induced current in coil B. Hence, the deflection in galvanometer towards left will be more than previous case before it returns to zero position.

(d) With the switch of coil A closed, if coil B is moved away, the Q end would acquire north polarity to attract the P end of coil, as per Lenz's law. The induced current would flow in anticlockwise direction at point Q of coil B and the deflection of the galvanometer would be towards right.

3. The given figure shows a coil A wound around a soft iron core with its terminals connected to an AC source through a lamp A and a switch S. Another coil B wound around an iron core has a lamp B connected to its terminals and is placed close to coil A. (a) What will happen in coil A when the switch is closed? (b) What will be the effect on coil B? (c) Will the lamp B glow constantly?

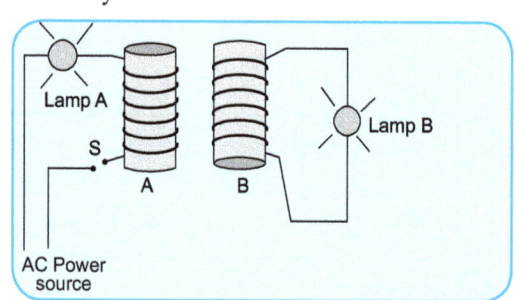

Solution :
(a) When the switch is closed, the current will flow from the power source through the coil A to the lamp A and lamp A will glow.
(b) Due to the varying magnetic field produced by AC flowing in the coil A, an emf will be induced in coil B and thus current will begin to flow across it and the lamp B will glow.
(c) As the current induced is alternating type, the emf becomes zero, then increases and becomes maximum and again falls to zero. This cycle continues and hence the bulb will not glow continuously but would pulsate, *i.e.* flicker. However, since the frequency of AC is 50 Hz, *i.e.* it alternates 50 times in 1 s, but the pulsating effect of lamp would not be visible to the naked eyes.

4. (a) Draw a simple labelled diagram of a step-up transformer.
(b) On which principle a transformer work?
(c) Can a transformer work with DC source?

Solution :
(a) The figure below shows a labelled diagram of a step-up transformer.

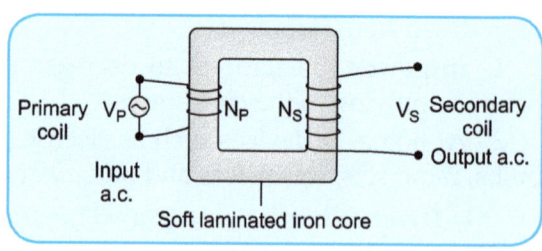

(b) A transformer works on the principle of electromagnetic induction.
(c) No, a transformer cannot work with a DC source as there is no change in magnetic flux linked with the secondary coil when a DC source is applied to a primary coil.

5. (a) Draw a simple schematic representation of the circuit of a step-down transformer.
(b) What is the function of a step-down transformer?
(c) What is the turn ratio of a step-down transformer?

Solution :
(a) The schematic representation of the circuit of a step-down transformer is shown below :

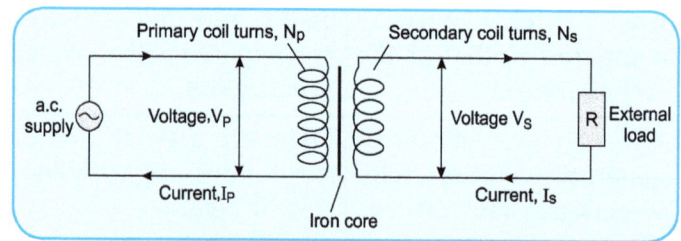

(b) The function of a step-down transformer is to convert a high AC voltage to a low AC voltage.
(c) The turn ratio of a step-down transformer is less than 1 as the number of turns in secondary coil is less than that of the primary coil.

6. At the generation station, voltage is generated at 11 kV and then it is stepped up to 132 kV. If the input power and output power is same equal to 11 kW, calculate turns ratio, input current and output current.

Solution : Given : $E_P = 11,000$ V and $E_S = 1,32,000$ V.
The turns ratio will be
$$n = \frac{N_S}{N_P} = \frac{E_S}{E_P} = \frac{1,32,000}{11,000} = \frac{12}{1}$$
The number of turns in the secondary coil will be 12 times the number of turns in the primary coil.

For an 11 kW input power, the current in primary coil will be
$$I_P = \frac{P}{V} = \frac{11,000}{11,000} = 1 \text{ A}$$

For the same output power, current in the secondary coil will be

$$I_S = \frac{P}{V} = \frac{11,000}{1,32,000}$$

$$= 0.083 \text{ A} = 83 \text{ mA}$$

7. If the voltage at mains supply is 220 V and an electric bell requires 11 V to operate, which type of transformer should be used ? Also calculate its turns ratio.

Solution : Given : $E_P = 220$ V and $E_S = 11$ V

Since, $E_P > E_S$

Step-down transformer should be used.

Turns ratio $(n) = \dfrac{E_S}{E_P} = \dfrac{11}{220} = \dfrac{1}{20}$

EXERCISE 10(C)

1. What is meant by electromagnetic induction?
2. Describe an experiment to demonstrate the phenomenon of electromagnetic induction.
3. The figure below shows a bar magnet NS placed close to a solenoid connected with a galvanometer.

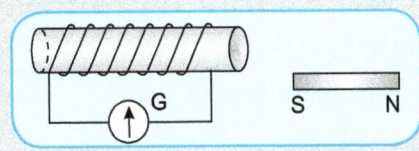

   (a) Why does the galvanometer shows deflection when the south pole of the bar magnet is brought close to the solenoid?
   (b) What will be the effect if the magnet is reversed and its north pole is brought close to the solenoid?
   (c) What will be the effect if, instead of the magnet, the solenoid is moved closer to the magnet?
   (d) When will the pointer of the galvanometer show zero reading?

4. From the diagram below, what will you observe when (a) the magnet is dropped into the coil, (b) the number of turns of the coil is increased and (c) the magnet is moved with twice the speed?

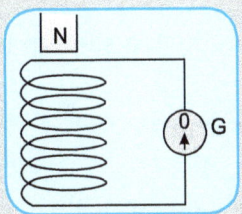

5. Why is current induced in a coil when a bar magnet is brought closer to it?
   Ans : Due to the change in magnetic flux linked with the coil
6. State two ways of increasing the strength of induced current in a coil.
   Ans : By rapid motion of coil or magnet and by increasing the number of turns in the coil

7. State Faraday's laws of electromagnetic induction.
8. State the two factors that affect the magnitude of induced emf.
   Ans : The change in the magnetic flux and the time in which the magnetic flux changes
9. State the energy change that takes place in the phenomenon of electromagnetic induction.
   Ans : Mechanical energy to electrical energy
10. In which of the following cases does electromagnetic induction occur :
    (a) A magnet is moved inside a solenoid.
    (b) A stationary coil is placed beside a stationary magnet.
    (c) A current-carrying loop of wire is kept beside a solenoid with open ends.
    (d) A closed loop of wire kept near a magnet is moved away from it.
    Ans : (a) and (d)
11. Name two laws that help to determine the direction of induced current in a conductor.
    Ans : Fleming's right-hand rule and Lenz's law
12. State Fleming's right-hand rule.
13. Explain Lenz's law.
14. Does Lenz's law violate the law of conservation of energy? Justify your answer.
15. A magnet is moved towards (a) a coil with few turns and (b) a coil with large number of turns. In which case, is it difficult to move the magnet? Give reason.
16. In the figure given below, a bar magnet is moved away from a closed coil. (a) What will be the deflection in the galvanometer? (b) What will be the direction of current induced in the solenoid? (c) What will be the effect if the magnet used is more powerful? (d) What will be the effect if the magnet is rapidly moved towards the coil?

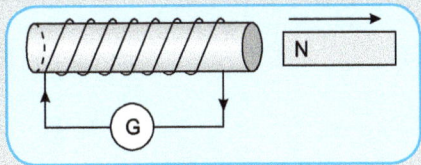

17. Two coils A and B are facing each other as shown in the figure. A current I flows through the coil A. (a) What will be the effect on coil B? (b) What will happen if the current I is increased in the coil?

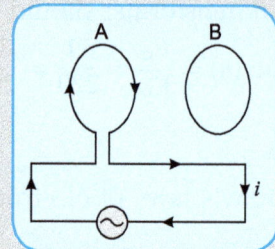

18. What is AC generator or dynamo used for? Name the principle on which it works.
19. Draw a simple labelled diagram of an AC generator.
20. State the energy conversion taking place in an AC generator.
    Ans : Mechanical energy to electrical energy
21. State any two factors that will increase the magnitude of induced current in an AC generator.
22. State one advantage of AC over DC.
    Ans : The AC voltage can be increased or decreased by the use of a transformer, whereas DC voltage cannot be changed
23. Name two sources of AC and DC.
24. Give two similarities between an AC generator and a DC motor.
25. What is a transformer? State the principle on which it is based.
26. What are eddy currents? How can these be avoided in a transformer?
27. Why a transformer cannot be used with a DC source?
28. What is turns ratio? For which transformer is it greater than 1?
29. How are the emf and current in the primary and secondary coils of a transformer related with the number of turns in these coils?
30. Draw a simple labelled diagram of a step-down transformer and explain its working.
31. Name the device used to transform a 6 V AC to 220 V AC. What is the turns ratio of this device?
32. Explain the working of a step-up transformer.
33. A device is used to transform a 33 kV AC to 220 V AC. Name the device and state its two uses.
34. Is an ideal transformer practically possible? If not, give reason.
35. Which coil of a step-up transformer is made thicker and why?
36. How can the efficiency of a transformer be increased?
37. State few differences between a step-up transformer and a step-down transformer.

MULTIPLE CHOICE QUESTIONS

1. The rule that gives the direction of induced current in a conductor is :
   (a) Fleming's left-hand rule
   (b) Fleming's right-hand rule
   (c) Right-hand thumb rule
   (d) Lenz's law
   Ans : (b)

2. The energy conversion taking place in an AC generator is :
   (a) mechanical to electrical
   (b) electrical to mechanical
   (c) magnetic to electrical
   (d) electrical to magnetic
   Ans : (a)

3. The frequency of AC current supplied at our houses has a frequency of 50 Hz. The number of times the polarity of the current changes in 1 s is :
   (a) 25   (b) 50
   (c) 100   (d) none of the above
   Ans : (c)

4. The turns ratio in a step-up transformer is :
   (a) less than 1
   (b) greater than 1
   (c) equal to 1
   (d) could be any of these
   Ans : (b)

11

HEAT

LEARNING OUTCOMES

- Heat and temperature
- Heat capacity and specific heat capacity
- Principle of calorimetry
- Determination of specific heat capacity of a substance
- Applications of high specific heat capacity of water
- Change of state : Melting, freezing, boiling, and condensation
- Latent heat and specific latent heat
- Heating and cooling curves

(A) CALORIMETRY

11.1 HEAT AND TEMPERATURE

Heat

Heat is one of the different forms of *internal energy* possessed by a body, resulting from a random motion of molecules of the body.

Every substance or a body comprises molecules that are in a state of *random motion*. Every molecule in motion possesses *kinetic* and *potential* energies.

The sum of kinetic and potential energies of all molecules is the total internal energy of a body and is called heat.

Units of Heat

Since heat is a form of energy, its SI unit is joule (J) and its CGS unit is erg, where

$$1 J = 10^7 \text{ erg}$$

The commonly used unit of heat is *calorie* (cal).

One calorie is the quantity of heat energy required to raise the temperature of 1 g of water (pure) from 14.5 C to 15.5 C i.e., by 1 C.

For practical purposes, calorie is a smaller unit of heat energy. Thus, a bigger unit called *kilocalorie* is used to measure heat.

One kilocalorie is the quantity of heat energy required to raise the temperature of 1 kg of water (pure) from 14.5 C to 15.5 C i.e., by 1 C.

Kilocalorie is also called *doctor's calorie* as it is used to measure the energy value of foods and fuels.

Relation of calorie and kilocalorie with joule

1 calorie (cal) = 4.186 J = 4.2 J (approximately)

1 kcal = 1,000 cal = 4,200 J (approximately)

Temperature

When certain amount of external heat energy is supplied to a body, the random motion of its molecules increases which results in an increase in the average kinetic energy of the molecules. This average kinetic energy is measured as *temperature*. Thus, when heat is supplied to a body, there is an increase in temperature. Conversely, if certain amount of heat is removed from a body, there is a decrease in body's temperature. This is because there is a decrease in random motion of molecules, which in turn causes a decrease in the average kinetic energy of the molecules. Thus,

Temperature of a body is the measure of average internal kinetic energy of the molecules of a body.

When two bodies at different temperatures are brought in contact, heat flows from a body at a higher temperature to a body at lower temperature, until an equilibrium temperature is attained. Thus, the *temperature* of a body is the *parameter* that determines the *direction of flow of heat energy.*

Units of Temperature

The SI unit of temperature is *kelvin* (K). The other commonly used unit of temperature is *degree Celsius* (°C). Relation between K and °C is given by the following equation :

$$T(K) = 273 + t(°C) \quad \ldots(11.1)$$

However, 1 unit of rise in temperature in Kelvin scale is equal to 1 degree rise in temperature in Celsius scale and vice-versa.

Heat and temperature are measurable quantities. The temperature of a body is measured using a *thermometer* and the heat of a body is measured by the *principle of calorimetry.*

It must be noted here that heat and temperature are different, even though they are commonly used together. *Heat* is a *form of energy*, whereas *temperature* is a *measure of heat* contained in the body. It can be said that 'heat is the cause and temperature is the effect'.

However, temperature is not the only factor, rather one of the factors, that determines the amount of heat contained in the body.

Factors Determining the Quantity of Heat Required to Raise the Temperature of a Body

There are *three* factors that determine the quantity of heat required to raise the temperature of a body.

1. Mass of the body : The amount of heat (Q) required to raise the temperature of a body is *directly* proportional to the mass (m) of the body, *i.e.*, $Q \propto m$. Thus, different masses of a same substance require different amounts of heat energy to raise the temperature by same amount.

2. Material of the body : The amount of heat energy required to raise the temperature of a body depends on the nature of the material used. It is expressed in terms of *specific heat capacity*, and will be discussed in subsequent topics.

Due to different specific heat capacities of various bodies, different amounts of heat is required to raise the temperature of equal masses of different bodies.

Example : If equal masses of mercury and water are heated, the amount of heat required for water is almost 30 times the heat required for mercury to raise the temperature by the same amount.

3. Rise in temperature of the body : The amount of heat energy required to raise the temperature of a body is *directly* proportional to the rise in temperature (Δt). Equal masses of same substance require different amounts of heat energy to raise their temperature by different amounts. If Δt is the rise in temperature of a body, then $Q \propto \Delta t$.

From the above relations, we obtain

$$Q \propto m \text{ and } Q \propto \Delta t$$

i.e. $$Q = cm\Delta t \quad \ldots(11.2)$$

Here, c is the constant of proportionality and is called the *specific heat capacity* of the body.

Difference between Heat and Temperature

Heat	Temperature
Heat is a form of energy obtained due to random motion of molecules of a body.	Temperature is a quantity that determines the direction of flow of heat when two bodies at different temperature come in contact.
It is the total internal energy of the molecules of the body.	It is the measure of average kinetic energy of the molecules of the body.
Heat is the cause.	Temperature is the effect.
The SI unit of heat is joule (J).	The SI unit of temperature is kelvin (K).
When two bodies are brought in contact, the total amount of heat produced is equal to the sum of heat of two bodies, *i.e.* it is an additive quantity.	When two bodies at different temperatures make contact, the resultant temperature is any temperature in between their temperatures, *i.e.* it is not an additive quantity.
Heat is measured by the principle of calorimetry with the help of a calorimeter.	Temperature is measured by a thermometer.

11.2 HEAT (OR THERMAL) CAPACITY (C')

If 1 kg of water and 1 kg of copper are supplied heat to raise their temperature by 1°C, then the amount of heat required for water is nearly 10 times the amount of heat required for copper because of the difference in their heat absorbing capacities. Different substances have different capacities to absorb heat, and this is known as their thermal capacity. If a body absorbs large amount of heat, it is said to have a high thermal capacity, *i.e.* a large amount of heat is required to raise the temperature of this body, compared to a body (of equal mass) that has a low thermal capacity.

Heat (or thermal) capacity is defined as the amount of heat required to raise the temperature of a given mass of a body by 1 C or by 1 K.

It is represented by the symbol C'. It is equal to the ratio of the total heat supplied to the total rise in temperature of a body.

$$\text{Heat capacity, } C' = \frac{\text{Amount of heat energy supplied}}{\text{Rise in temperature}}$$

If Q is the amount of heat energy supplied to a body such that its temperature rises by Δt (°C) or Δt (K), then

$$\text{Heat capacity, } C' = \frac{Q}{\Delta t} \qquad ...(11.3)$$

In heat capacity, the mass of the substance is not stated. Hence, different masses of same substance will have different heat capacities.

Example : The heat capacity of 1 kg, *i.e.* 1,000 g, of water is 4,200 J °C^{-1}, whereas the heat capacity of 10 g of water is 42 J °C^{-1}.

Units of Heat Capacity

$$\text{Heat Capacity} = \frac{\text{Heat}}{\text{Rise in temperature}}$$

The SI unit of heat capacity is JK^{-1}.

It is also written as J °C^{-1}, as the rise in temperature of 1 K is equal to a rise in temperature of 1°C.

If the amount of heat is expressed in calorie or kilocalorie, then the unit of heat capacity is cal K^{-1} (or cal °C^{-1}), or kcal K^{-1} (or kcal°C^{-1}).

$$1 \text{ kcal °C}^{-1} = 1,000 \text{ cal °C}^{-1}$$
$$1 \text{ cal K}^{-1} = 4.2 \text{ J K}^{-1}$$

11.3 SPECIFIC HEAT CAPACITY (c)

When a unit mass of a substance is specified in describing its heat capacity, it is called the *specific heat capacity*.

Specific heat capacity is defined as the amount of heat required to raise the temperature of unit mass of a substance (1 kg or 1 g) by 1 K or 1 C.

Relation between Heat Capacity and Specific Heat Capacity

Specific heat capacity of a body is the heat capacity per unit mass of that body.

It is represented by the symbol *c*.

If Q is the amount of heat energy supplied to a body of mass *m* such that its temperature rises through Δt (°C) or Δt (K), then specific heat capacity is given as

$$\frac{\text{Specific heat}}{\text{capacity, } c} = \frac{\text{Amount of heat energy supplied}}{\text{Mass of the body} \times \text{Rise in temperature}}$$

i.e. $$c = \frac{Q}{m \times \Delta t} \qquad ...(11.4)$$

i.e. $$Q = m \times c \times \Delta t \qquad ...(11.5)$$

$$\frac{\text{Specific heat}}{\text{capacity, } c} = \frac{\text{Heat capacity of the body}}{\text{Mass of the body}}$$

i.e. $$c = \frac{C'}{m} \qquad ...(11.6)$$

or $$C' = m \times c \qquad ...(11.7)$$

Heat capacity = Mass × Specific heat capacity

Units of Specific Heat Capacity

In SI system, the unit of specific heat capacity is J kg^{-1} K^{-1} or J kg^{-1} °C^{-1}.

If cal and kcal units of heat are considered, the units of specific heat capacity are cal g^{-1} °C^{-1} and kcal kg^{-1} °C^{-1}.

$$1 \text{ cal g}^{-1} \text{ °C}^{-1} = 4.2 \text{ J g}^{-1} \text{ °C}^{-1}$$
$$1 \text{ kcal kg}^{-1} \text{ °C}^{-1} = 4,200 \text{ J kg}^{-1} \text{ °C}^{-1}$$

Also, 1 cal g^{-1} °C^{-1} = 1 kcal kg^{-1} °C^{-1}

Example : The specific heat of mercury is 139 J kg^{-1}K^{-1}, which means that 139 J of heat is required to raise the temperature of 1 kg of mercury by 1 K or 1°C.

Difference between Heat Capacity and Specific Heat Capacity

Heat capacity	Specific heat capacity
It is the amount of heat energy required to raise the temperature of a body by 1°C.	It is the amount of heat energy required to raise the temperature of unit mass of the body by 1°C.
Its SI unit is JK^{-1}.	Its SI unit is J kg^{-1}K^{-1}.
It depends both on the substance and mass of the body. Greater the mass of the body, larger is the heat capacity.	It is the characteristic property of the material of the body. It does not depend on the mass of the body.

Specific Heat Capacity of Some Common Substances

The specific heat capacity is the characteristic property of a substance. When heat is supplied to equal masses of two different substances, the rise in temperature for the two substances in a given interval of time is different due to their different specific heat capacities.

Table 11.1 represents the value of specific heat capacity of some common substances.

Table 11.1 : Specific Heat Capacity of Some Common Substances

Substance	Specific Heat Capacity		
	$J\ kg^{-1}\ K^{-1}$	$J\ g^{-1}\ °C^{-1}$	$Cal\ g^{-1}\ °C^{-1}$
Water	4,186	4.186	1.0
Seawater	3,900	3.90	0.95
Alcohol	2,400	2.40	0.57
Ice	2,100	2.10	0.50
Kerosene oil	2,100	2.10	0.50
Steam	2,000	2.00	0.47
Turpentine oil	1,760	1.76	0.42
Air (50°C)	1,046	1.046	0.25
Aluminium	882	0.882	0.21
Glass	670	0.67	0.16
Carbon	500	0.50	0.12
Iron	483	0.483	0.115
Copper	399	0.399	0.095
Brass	380	0.380	0.092
Silver	236	0.236	0.056
Mercury	139	0.139	0.033
Tungsten	135	0.135	0.032
Lead	130	0.130	0.031

The specific heat capacity of water is very high, approximately 4,200 J kg^{-1} K^{-1}. The specific heat capacity of a substance varies with *change in phase*. From Table 11.1, it can be seen that the specific heat capacity of ice (solid phase) is 2,100 J kg^{-1} K^{-1}, water (liquid phase) is 4,186 J kg^{-1} K^{-1} and steam (gaseous phase) is 2,000 J kg^{-1} K^{-1}.

11.4 CALORIMETER

A *calorimeter* is an instrument used for measuring the heat gained or lost by a body.

It consists of a cylindrical vessel made up of thin copper sheet with highly polished inner and outer surfaces to prevent loss of heat due to *radiation* (Fig. 11.1). Copper vessel is chosen because it is a *good conductor* of heat and has a *low specific heat capacity*. Due to its good conducting property, the vessel quickly gains the temperature of the content placed in it, and also due to its low specific heat capacity, the heat energy taken from the contents to acquire the temperature is very less.

The cylindrical copper vessel is placed in a rectangular wooden jacket for insulation. The inner side of this jacket is lined with a material, such as wool, cotton, glass or asbestos, which being a poor conductor of heat, prevent its loss due to conduction. The top of the calorimeter is covered with a wooden lid to prevent heat loss by *convection*. The lid has two holes, one for the *thermometer* to measure the temperature of the contents and the other for a copper *stirrer* for mixing the contents of the calorimeter.

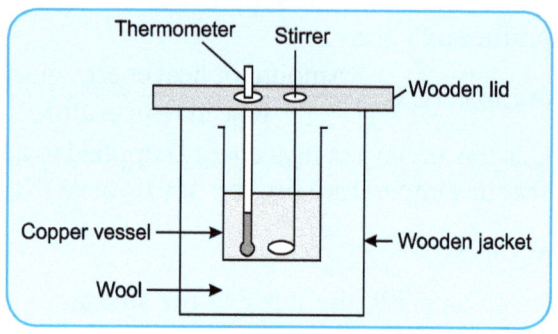

Fig. 11.1 : Calorimeter.

11.5 PRINCIPLE OF CALORIMETRY

The principle of calorimeter is based on the *law of conservation of energy*. According to the law of conservation of energy, "Energy in a system can neither be created nor be destroyed but can be transformed from one form to the other". Hence, the total energ of the system remains constant.

We know that heat flows from a body at higher temperature to the body at lower temperature until it attains a state of equilibrium. Thus, when a hot body makes contact (or combines) with a cold body, heat energy flows from the hot body to the cold body until both the bodies attain the same temperature. If the system is completely insulated, then there is no loss of heat to the surroundings. Thus,

Heat energy lost by the hot body = Heat energy gained by the cold body

This is the principle of calorimetry and is also known as the *principle of mixtures*.

Consider a hot substance X with mass m_1, specific heat capacity c_1 and at a higher temperature t_1. It is mixed with a cold substance Y with mass m_2, specific heat capacity c_2 and at a lower temperature t_2. When these two substances are mixed, let the final temperature be t.

Fall in temperature of hot substance X = $t_1 - t$
Rise in temperature of cold substance Y = $t - t_2$
Heat lost by the hot substance X = $m_1 \times c_1 \times (t_1 - t)$
Heat gained by the cold substance
$$Y = m_2 \times c_2 \times (t - t_2)$$

If there is no loss of heat to the surroundings, then by the principle of calorimetry,

Heat lost by the hot substance X = Heat gained by the cold substance Y

i.e. $m_1 \times c_1 \times (t_1 - t) = m_2 \times c_2 \times (t - t_2)$ ...(11.8)

11.6 EXPERIMENTAL DETERMINATION OF SPECIFIC HEAT CAPACITY OF A SOLID

Procedure

The following steps are to be followed to find the specific heat capacity of a solid (such as a metal) that is insoluble in water.

1. Take the given solid, whose specific heat capacity is to be determined and break it into small pieces. Weigh a piece of the solid and then suspend it with the help of a thread into a beaker containing boiling water.

2. Take an empty and dry calorimeter and weigh it along with its stirrer. Fill one-third of the calorimeter with water and weigh it again. The difference in the two measurements will give the mass of the water.

3. Record the temperature t_1 of the water in the calorimeter with the help of a thermometer.

4. Record the temperature t_2 of the heated solid, once it has attained a steady temperature, by placing a thermometer in the boiling water bath.

5. Drop the piece of heated solid into the calorimeter gently to avoid splashing of water.

6. Stir the contents of the calorimeter properly. Let the temperature of the contents stabilise and note the final temperature t of the mixture with a thermometer.

Observations

Mass of the solid piece = m g
Mass of empty calorimeter = m_1 g
Mass of calorimeter + Water = m_2 g
Temperature of water in calorimeter = t_1°C
Temperature of heated piece of solid = t_2°C
Temperature of mixture = t°C
We know,
Specific heat capacity of water c_w = 4.2 J g^{-1} °C^{-1}
Specific heat capacity of copper (calorimeter) c_c = 0.4 J g^{-1} °C^{-1}.
Let Specific heat capacity of solid = c_s

Calculations

Mass of water = $(m_2 - m_1)$ g
Rise in temperature of water and calorimeter
$= (t - t_1)$°C
Heat energy gained by water
$= (m_2 - m_1) c_w (t - t_1)$ J ...(i)
Heat energy gained by calorimeter
$= m_1 c_c (t - t_1)$ J ...(ii)
Total heat energy gained by water and calorimeter
$= \{(m_2 - m_1) c_w (t - t_1) + m_1 c_c (t - t_1)\}$ J ...(iii)
Fall in temperature of solid
$= (t_2 - t)$°C
Heat energy lost by solid
$= m c_s (t_2 - t)$ J ...(iv)

By the principle of calorimetry,

Heat energy lost by solid = Heat energy gained by water and calorimeter

i.e.
$$m c_s (t_2 - t) = \{(m_2 - m_1) c_w (t - t_1) + m_1 c_c (t - t_1)\}$$

i.e.
$$c_s = \frac{\{(m_2 - m_1) c_w (t - t_1) + m_1 c_c (t - t_1)\}}{m(t_2 - t)} \text{ Jg}^{-1}\text{°C}^{-1}$$
...(11.9)

If we substitute the values of specific heat capacity of water and of calorimeter (i.e. copper) in equation (11.9), we obtain

$$c_s = \frac{\{(m_2 - m_1) 4.2 (t - t_1) + m_1 0.4 (t - t_1)\}}{m(t_2 - t)} \text{ Jg}^{-1}\text{°C}^{-1}$$

$$\therefore \quad c_s = \frac{(t - t_1)\{4.2(m_2 - m_1) + 0.4 m_1\}}{m(t_2 - t)} \text{ Jg}^{-1}\text{°C}^{-1}$$
...(11.10)

From this expression, the specific heat capacity of the solid can be calculated.

11.7 EXPERIMENTAL DETERMINATION OF SPECIFIC HEAT CAPACITY OF A LIQUID

The procedure for determining the specific heat capacity of a liquid is similar to that of a solid described in Sec. 11.6. In this case, a solid of known specific heat capacity that does not react chemically is used with the given liquid whose specific heat capacity is to be determined. This liquid is taken in the calorimeter instead of water.

If c_L is the specific heat capacity of the given liquid, then

Heat energy lost by solid = Heat energy gained by liquid and calorimeter

$$m c_s (t_2 - t) = \{(m_2 - m_1) c_L (t - t_1) + m_1 c_c (t - t_1)\}$$

i.e.
$$c_L = \frac{\{m c_s (t_2 - t) - m_1 c_c (t - t_1)\}}{(m_2 - m_1)(t - t_1)} \text{ Jg}^{-1}\text{°C}^{-1}$$
...(11.11)

An expanded polystyrene cup, instead of a calorimeter, can also be used to determine the specific heat capacity of a substance. The expanded polystyrene cup has very low heat capacity due to its small mass and thus absorbs negligible heat from the contents. The expression for heat energy taken by calorimeter can be neglected if this cup is used. Thus, the equations (11.9) and (11.11) for solid and liquid, respectively, will be modified as follows :

$$c_s = \frac{(m_2 - m_1) c_w (t - t_1)}{m(t_2 - t)} \text{ Jg}^{-1}\text{°C}^{-1} \quad ...(11.12)$$

$$c_L = \frac{m c_s (t_2 - t)}{(m_2 - m_1)(t - t_1)} \text{ Jg}^{-1}\text{°C}^{-1} \quad ...(11.13)$$

Electrical Method for Determination of Specific Heat Capacity

This method uses an electric heater of known power to supply heat energy for a specific period of time to a known mass of a substance (solid/liquid) to raise its temperature by a definite value. If there is no loss of heat energy, then the energy supplied by the heater is equal to the energy absorbed by the substance in raising the temperature.

If m is the mass of substance, c is the specific heat capacity and Δt is the rise in temperature, then heat absorbed by the substance will be $m\ c\ \Delta t$.

If P is the power of the heater and t is the time for it works, then the energy supplied by the heater is P t. Thus,

$$mc\,\Delta t = Pt$$

Specific heat capacity of the substance is given by

$$c = \frac{Pt}{m \times \Delta t}\ \text{Jg}^{-1}\,{}^\circ\text{C}^{-1} \qquad ...(11.14)$$

11.8 CONSEQUENCES OF HIGH SPECIFIC HEAT CAPACITY OF WATER

The specific heat capacity of water is high; it is 4.2 $\text{Jg}^{-1}\,{}^\circ\text{C}^{-1}$, which implies that every 1 g of water absorbs 4.2 J of heat energy with only 1°C rise in temperature. By virtue of this fact, water has wide range of application in everyday life.

1. Fomentation : The swollen parts of a body are heated at a moderate temperature to provide relief. This is known as *fomentation*. Hot water bags are used for fomentation because water has a high specific heat capacity and therefore, can retain the heat energy for a long period of time even at a moderate temperature (50°C).

2. Coolant : Water is used as a coolant in car radiators, thermal power stations and so on. Water can absorb a large amount of heat from the engine of the car without much rise in its temperature due to its high specific heat capacity.

3. Thermal radiator : Water is used for internal heating of houses in cold countries. Hot water carrying a good amount of heat energy due to high specific heat is made to flow through a radiator. The heat radiated from the radiator then warms the surroundings of the house.

4. Protection of crops during winter : During winters, the temperature at night-time falls below 0°C. At such low temperature, there are chances of bursting of veins and capillaries of crops due to expansion of water contained in them upon freezing. This would damage the crops. To protect the crops from this damage, farmers fill the fields with water. As water has high specific heat capacity, it liberates good amount of heat energy and does not let the temperature of its surroundings fall below 0°C. This prevents damage and death of crops.

5. Protection of bottled wines : In cold countries, water is used as a reservoir to store wine and juice bottles. Due to the high specific heat capacity of water, it radiates good amount of heat and prevents the surrounding temperature from falling below 0°C. This prevents the bottles from freezing.

11.9 NATURAL PHENOMENON INVOLVING SPECIFIC HEAT

1. Moderate weather due to land and sea breezes near seashores : The specific heat capacity of sand is about five times less than that of seawater and therefore, sand is heated or cooled rapidly as compared to seawater.

When the Sun shines during daytime, both sand and water absorb the heat energy, but the sand is heated faster than water due to its low specific heat capacity. Therefore, the temperature of air above the sand increases quickly. This hot and light air then rises up and creates a pressure difference and hence cold air from the sea starts blowing towards the land, thereby forming the sea breeze.

At night time, both sand on the shores and the sea radiate heat. Due to low specific heat capacity of sand, as compared to water, it radiates heat quickly and its temperature falls rapidly compared to seawater. The warm air above seawater rises and thus air pressure drops over the sea. As a result, the cold air from the land starts blowing towards the sea, thereby forming the land breeze.

These breezes help in moderating the weather near the seashores.

2. Internal heat regulation in plants and animals : Nearly, 70–90% of bodies of all plants and animals contain water. The high specific heat capacity of water helps to regulate the body temperature of living organisms in different seasons.

11.10 APPLICATIONS OF HIGH AND LOW HEAT CAPACITIES

1. The vessel in calorimeter is made of thin sheet of copper : Copper has a low specific heat capacity. When a thin layer of copper is used, it absorbs negligible amount of heat energy from the contents and thus affects less the measurement of the heat energy of contents.

2. The bottom of cooking utensils is made of thick layer of copper : When a thick layer of copper is used at the base of cooking utensils such as frying pan, pots and kettles, it increases the thermal capacity of the utensil and thus a large amount of heat energy is available for the food to be cooked at a low temperature and also keeps the food warm for a long period of time.

3. The base of an electric iron is made thick and heavy : A thick and heavy layer increases the thermal capacity of the base of the electric iron and thus retains good amount of heat for a long period of time when the current source is switched off.

4. Mercury is used as thermometric liquid : The specific heat capacity of mercury is very low and therefore, can detect even a small change in temperature with great rapidity and accuracy.

ILLUSTRATIVE EXAMPLES

1. To raise the temperature of a substance by 15°C, the amount of heat energy required is 3,500 J. Calculate the heat capacity of the substance.
   Solution : Given, $Q = 3,500$ J, $\Delta t = 15°C = 15$ K
   Heat capacity, $C' = \dfrac{\text{Heat energy required} Q}{\text{Rise in temperature } \Delta t}$
   i.e. $C' = \dfrac{Q}{\Delta t} = \dfrac{3,500}{15} = 233.33$ JK^{-1}.

2. A 1,000 cal of heat energy is required to raise the temperature of 0.060 kg of a liquid from 10°C to 50°C. Find the specific heat capacity of the liquid (a) in kcal kg^{-1} °C^{-1} and (b) in J kg^{-1} K^{-1}.
   Solution : Given, $Q = 1,000$ cal $= 1$ kcal
   $\Delta t = (50 - 10) = 40°C = 40$ K, $m = 0.060$ kg
   (a) Heat absorbed by the liquid $Q = m\, c\, \Delta t$
   i.e. $c = \dfrac{Q}{m \times \Delta t} = \dfrac{1}{0.060 \times 40}$
   $= 0.416$ kcal kg^{-1}°C^{-1}
   (b) 1 kcal $= 4,200$ J
   i.e. $c = \dfrac{Q}{m \times \Delta t} = \dfrac{4,200}{0.060 \times 40}$
   $= 1,750$ J kg^{-1}K^{-1}

3. Calculate the heat energy required to raise the temperature of 500 g of copper from 30°C to 50°C. Take specific heat capacity of copper as 400 J kg^{-1} K^{-1}.
   Solution : Given, $m = 500$ g $= 0.5$ kg
   $\Delta t = (50 - 30) = 20°C = 20$ K, $c = 400$ J kg^{-1} K^{-1}.
   Heat energy required,
   $Q = mc\,\Delta t = 0.5 \times 400 \times 20$
   $= 4,000$ J

4. An electric immersion rod is switched on for 5 min. The heat supplied by it raises the temperature of 1 kg of water from 30°C to 90°C. Calculate (a) the power of heater and (b) heat capacity of water, if the specific heat capacity of water is 4.2 Jg^{-1} °C^{-1}.
   Solution : Given, $t = 5$ min $= 5 \times 60 = 300$ s, $m = 1$ kg $= 1,000$ g, $\Delta t = (90 - 30) = 60$ °C
   (a) Heat energy absorbed by water,
   $Q = mc\, \Delta t = 1,000 \times 4.2 \times 60 = 252,000$ J
   If P is the power of the heater, then energy supplied by the heater
   $= \text{Power} \times \text{Time}$
   $= P\ 300$
   If heat lost to the surroundings is neglected, then by law of conservation of energy,
   $P\ 300 = Q$
   i.e. $P = 252,000/300$
   $= 840$ J s^{-1} or 840 W
   (b) Heat capacity of water
   $= \text{Specific heat capacity} \times \text{Mass}$
   $= 4.2 \times 1,000$
   $= 4,200$ JK^{-1}.

5. The temperature of 250 g of water rises by a certain value, when some amount of heat is supplied to it. When the same amount of heat is supplied to 125 g of kerosene oil, its temperature rises by four times the temperature rise of water. If the specific heat capacity of water is 4,200 J kg^{-1} K^{-1}, calculate the specific heat capacity of kerosene oil.
   Solution : Given, $m_w = 250$ g $= 0.25$ kg, $m_K = 125$ g $= 0.125$ kg, $c_w = 4,200$ J kg^{-1} K^{-1}.
   Let the rise in temperature of water be t K, then rise in temperature of kerosene oil $= 4t$ K
   Heat energy given to water,
   $Q = m\ c\, \Delta t$
   $= 0.25 \times 4,200 \times t = 1,050\, t$
   The same amount of heat energy is given to kerosene oil.
   Specific heat capacity of kerosene oil
   $c_k = \dfrac{Q}{m_k \times \Delta t_k}$
   $= \dfrac{1,050}{0.125 \times 4t} = 2,100$ Jkg^{-1}K^{-1}

6. A 100 g of water at 70°C is poured into a beaker containing 60 g of water at 20°C. The final temperature of the mixture is 35 °C. If the specific heat capacity of water is 4.2 Jg^{-1} K^{-1}, calculate the thermal capacity of the beaker.
   Solution : Given, Mass of hot water $m_1 = 100$ g, $t_1 = 70°C$, Mass of cold water $= 60$ g, $t_2 = 20°C$, Final temperature $t = 35°C$, $c = 4.2$ J g^{-1} K^{-1}.

Fall in temperature of hot water
$$= (t_1 - t) = 70 - 35 = 35°C$$
Heat energy lost by hot water
$$= m_1 \times c \times 35$$
$$= 100 \times 4.2 \times 35 = 14{,}700 \text{ J}$$
Rise in temperature of cold water
$$= (t - t_2) = 35 - 20 = 15°C$$
Heat energy gained by cold water
$$= m_2 \times c \times 15$$
$$= 60 \times 4.2 \times 15 = 3{,}780 \text{ J}$$
Let the thermal capacity of the vessel be C' J K^{-1}
Heat energy gained by the vessel = Thermal capacity of the vessel × Rise in temperature
$$= C' \times (35 - 20) = 15\,C' \text{ J}$$
Assuming, there is no loss of heat energy to the environment,
Heat energy lost by hot water = Heat energy gained by cold water + Heat energy gained by the vessel
i.e. $\quad 14{,}700 = 3{,}780 + 15\,C'$
or $\quad C' = 10{,}920/15 = 728$ J K^{-1}.

7. Some amount of hot water is poured in a vessel containing cold water at 10°C temperature whose mass is three times the mass of hot water. The final equilibrium temperature is found to be 30°C. Calculate the temperature of hot water. Neglect the heat energy absorbed by the vessel.

Solution : Let mass of hot water be m kg. Then mass of cold water = $3m$ kg. Let c be the specific heat capacity of water.
Let the temperature of hot water be t_1°C, temperature of cold water is $t_2 = 10$°C and equilibrium temperature $t = 30$°C.
Fall in temperature of hot water
$$= (t_1 - t) = (t_1 - 30)°C.$$
Heat energy lost by hot water $= m \times c \times (t_1 - 30)$
Rise in temperature of cold water
$$= (t - t_2) = 30 - 10 = 20°C$$
Heat energy gained by cold water $= 3m \times c \times 20$
By law of conservation of energy,
Heat energy lost by hot water = Heat energy gained by cold water
i.e. $m \times c \times (t_1 - 30) = 3m \times c \times 20$
or $\quad t_1 - 30 = 60$
∴ $\quad t_1 = 60 + 30 = 90°C$

8. A solid of mass 50 g is heated to a temperature of 80°C. It is dropped into a copper calorimeter containing 150 g of water at 20°C. The mass of calorimeter is 50 g and the specific heat capacity of copper is 0.4 Jg^{-1} K^{-1}. The final temperature of the mixture after stirring is 30°C. If the specific heat capacity of water is 4.2 Jg^{-1} K^{-1}, find the specific heat capacity of the solid.

Solution : Let the specific heat capacity of the solid be c Jg^{-1} K^{-1}.
Heat energy lost by the solid
$$= \text{Mass of solid} \times c \times \text{Fall in temperature}$$
$$= 50 \times c \times (80 - 30) = 2{,}500\,c$$
Heat energy gained by the calorimeter = Mass of calorimeter × Specific heat capacity of copper × Rise in temperature
$$= 50 \times 0.4 \times (30 - 20) = 200 \text{ J}$$
Heat energy gained by water in the calorimeter
= Mass of water × Specific heat capacity of water × Rise in temperature
$$= 150 \times 4.2 \times (30 - 20) = 6{,}300 \text{ J}$$
Total heat energy gained by water and calorimeter = 200 + 6,300 = 6,500 J
Since there is no loss of heat to the surroundings,
Heat energy lost by the solid = Heat energy gained by water and calorimeter
$$2{,}500\,c = 6{,}500$$
or $\quad c = 2.6$ Jg^{-1} K^{-1}

9. A liquid A of specific heat capacity 1,600 Jg^{-1} K^{-1} at 80°C is mixed with a liquid B of specific heat capacity 900 Jg^{-1} K^{-1} at 30°C. The final temperature of the mixture is 50°C. Calculate the ratio of masses of the liquid.

Solution : Let mass of liquid A = m_A and mass of liquid B = m_B.
Given, $c_A = 1{,}600$ Jg^{-1} K^{-1}, $c_B = 900$ Jg^{-1} K^{-1}
Fall in temperature of liquid A = 80 − 50 = 30°C
Heat energy lost by liquid
$$A = m_A \times 1{,}600 \times 30 = 48{,}000\,m_A$$
Rise in temperature of liquid B = 50 − 30 = 20°C
Heat energy lost by liquid B = $m_B \times 900 \times 20$
= 18,000 m_B
Assuming there is no loss of heat to the surroundings,
Heat energy lost by liquid A = Heat energy lost by liquid B
i.e. $\quad 48{,}000\,m_A = 18{,}000\,m_B$
$$m_A : m_B = 18{,}000 : 48{,}000 = 3 : 8$$

10. A hot cube of iron of mass 200 g is dropped into 600 g of water at 20°C. The final temperature attained is 40°C. Calculate the temperature of the hot ball. Specific heat capacity of iron is 0.483 Jg^{-1} K^{-1} and specific heat capacity of water is 4.2 Jg^{-1} K^{-1}.

Solution : Given, Mass of iron cube m_1 = 200 g, Mass of water m_w = 600 g, Specific heat capacity of iron c_i = 0.483 J g^{-1} K^{-1}, Specific heat capacity of water c_w = 4.2 J g^{-1} K^{-1}.

Let the temperature of iron cube be t°C

Fall in temperature of hot cube = $(t - 40)$°C

Heat energy lost by hot cube
$$= m_i \times c_i \times (t - 40)$$
$$= 200 \times 0.483 \times (t - 40)$$
$$= 96.6 (t - 40) \text{ J}$$

Rise in temperature of water = 40 − 20 = 20°C

Heat energy gained by water
$$= m_w \times c_w \times 20$$
$$= 600 \times 4.2 \times 20 = 50,400 \text{ J}$$

Assuming there is no loss of heat to the surroundings,

Heat energy lost by hot cube = Heat energy gained by water

i.e. $96.6 (t - 40) = 50,400$

or $96.6 t - 3,864 = 50,400$

or $96.6 t = 54,264$

∴ $t = 54,264/96.6 = 561.74$°C

EXERCISE 11(A)

1. What is heat? State its SI unit.
2. What is temperature? State its SI unit.
3. Some heat is provided to a body to raise its temperature by 25°C. What will be the corresponding rise in temperature of the body as shown on the Kelvin scale?
   Ans : 25 K
4. Why does the temperature of a body rise when heat is supplied to it?
5. Differentiate between heat and temperature.
6. Define calorimetry.
7. Name the three factors that determine the quantity of heat required to raise the temperature of a body.
   Ans : Mass, material and rise in temperature of the body
8. Define calorie. State its relation with joule.
9. Name the unit of heat used to measure the energy value of foods and define it.
10. Define the term 'heat capacity' and state its SI unit.
11. What is meant by specific heat capacity?
12. How is the heat capacity of the body related to its specific heat capacity?
13. What is meant by the statement "The specific heat capacity of iron is 483 J kg^{-1} K^{-1}"?
14. A certain amount of heat Q will warm 1 g of material X by 3°C and 1 g of material Y by 4°C. Which material has a higher specific heat capacity?
    Ans : Material X
15. Differentiate between heat capacity and specific heat capacity.
16. State two factors upon which the heat absorbed by a body depends.
17. What is a calorimeter? Why is it madeup of copper?
18. (a) What is the principle of method of mixtures ?
    (b) What is the other name given to it ?
    (c) Name the law on which the principle is based.
19. Describe an experiment to determine the specific heat capacity of a metal such as iron piece.
20. Describe an experiment to determine the specific heat capacity of a liquid such as kerosene oil.
21. How can you determine the specific heat capacity of a solid substance using an electric heater of a known power?
22. How does the high specific heat capacity of water help in maintaining a moderate climate in the coastal areas?
23. Specific heat capacity of substance A is 3.8 Jg^{-1}K^{-1} whereas the specific heat capacity of substance B is 0.4 Jg^{-1} K^{-1}.
    (a) Which of the two is a good conductor of heat? Give reason.
    (b) If substances A and B are liquids, then which one would be more useful in car radiators?
24. Describe any two applications of high specific heat capacity of water.
25. Why is hot water used in bags for fomentation?
26. Give one example where high specific heat capacity of water is used (a) as a heat reservoir and (b) for cooling purpose.
27. Which property of water makes it an effective coolant ?
28. Explain the following :
    (a) Farmers fill the field with water during night in winters.
    (b) The bottom of a cooking pan is made of thick layer of copper.

MULTIPLE CHOICE QUESTIONS

1. The SI unit of thermal capacity is :
   (a) J °C^{-1} (b) J K^{-1}
   (c) cal °C^{-1} (d) cal K^{-1}
   Ans : (b)

2. The principle of calorimeter is based on :
   (a) law of conservation of mass
   (b) law of conservation of energy
   (c) law of conservation of temperature
   (d) None of the above
   Ans : (b)

3. If temperature rises by 10°C, what is its equivalent rise in the Kelvin scale?
   (a) 273 K   (b) 283 K
   (c) 10 K   (d) 0 K
   Ans : (c)

NUMERICAL PROBLEMS

1. The specific heat capacity of glass is 670 J kg^{-1} K^{-1}. What will be the heat capacity of a glass beaker of mass 50 g?
   Ans : 33.5 J K^{-1}

2. A piece of iron of mass 5.5 kg has a thermal capacity of 2,656 J°C^{-1}. (a) What is its specific heat capacity in SI units? (b) How much heat in kJ is needed to warm it by 50°C?
   Ans : (a) 483 J kg^{-1} K^{-1}, (b) 132.8 kJ

3. Calculate the amount of heat energy required to raise the temperature of 200 g of lead from 30°C to 60°C. Specific heat capacity of lead is 130 J kg^{-1} K^{-1}.
   Ans : 780 J

4. A 2,000 J of heat energy is supplied to 200 g of copper to raise its temperature from 30°C to 55°C. Calculate the specific heat capacity of copper.
   Ans : 0.4 J g^{-1} °C^{-1}

5. In an experiment to measure the specific heat capacity of copper, 0.02 kg of water at 70°C is poured into a copper calorimeter (with a stirrer) of mass 0.16 kg at 15°C. After stirring, the final temperature is found to be 45°C. If the specific heat of water is 4,200 Jkg^{-1} °C^{-1}, (a) what is the quantity of heat released per kg of water per 1°C fall in temperature? (b) Calculate the heat energy released by water in the experiment in cooling from 70°C to 45°C. (c) Assuming that the heat released by water is entirely used to raise the temperature of calorimeter from 15°C to 45°C, calculate the specific heat capacity of copper.
   Ans : (a) 4,200 J, (b) 2,100 J, (c) 437.5 J kg^{-1}°C^{-1}

6. A hot liquid of mass 40 g at 80°C is placed in 100 g of water at 20°C. The final steady temperature recorded is 30°C. Find the specific heat capacity of the liquid. Take specific heat of water 4.2 Jg^{-1} °C^{-1}.
   Ans : 2.1 Jg^{-1} °C^{-1}

7. A metal of mass 250 g is heated to a temperature of 65°C. It is then placed in 50 g of water at 20°C. The final steady temperature of water becomes 25°C. By neglecting the heat taken by the container, calculate the specific heat capacity of the metal.
   Ans : 0.105 J g^{-1} °C^{-1}

8. A 150 g of water is boiled using an electric heater that is labelled as 250 W. Calculate the time, in minutes, required to raise the temperature of water from 32°C to its boiling point. (Specific heat capacity of water = 4.2 J g^{-1} °C^{-1})
   Ans : 2.85 min

9. A 200 g of hot water at 80°C is added to 300 g of cold water at 10°C. Calculate the final temperature of the mixture of water. Consider the heat taken by the container to be negligible (Specific heat capacity of water is 4,200 J kg^{-1} °C^{-1}).
   Ans : 38°C

10. A hot solid of mass 60 g at 100°C is placed in 150 g of water at 20°C. The final steady temperature recorded is 25°C. Calculate the specific heat capacity of the solid. (Specific heat capacity of water is 4,200 J kg^{-1} °C^{-1})
    Ans : 700 J kg^{-1} °C^{-1}

11. A calorimeter of mass 50 g and specific heat capacity 0.42 J g^{-1} °C^{-1} contains some mass of water at 20°C. A metal piece of mass 20 g at 100°C is dropped into the calorimeter. After stirring, the final temperature of the mixture is found to be 22°C. Find the mass of water used in the calorimeter. (Specific heat capacity of the metal piece = 0.3 J g^{-1} °C^{-1}, specific heat capacity of water = 4.2 J g^{-1} °C^{-1})
    Ans : 50.71 g

12. A heater rated 1 kW is used to heat 1.5 kg of water at 40°C to its boiling point. Calculate the time in which the water comes to boil. Specific heat capacity of water is 4,200 J kg^{-1} °C^{-1}.
    Ans : 378 s

13. A power drill of 200 W makes a hole in a lead ball of specific heat capacity 130 J kg^{-1}°C^{-1} in 120 s. If the rise in temperature of lead is from 50°C to 300°C, calculate the mass of the lead ball.
    Ans : 738.46 g

(B) LATENT HEAT

11.11 CHANGE OF STATE

Matter can exist in three different phases *i.e.*, solid, liquid, gas depending on the temperature and pressure conditions. When heat is supplied to a solid (*e.g.* ice), its temperature rises until it starts melting. Upon melting, it turns into liquid (water). When heat is supplied to liquid state, its temperature begins to rise until it changes to vapour or gaseous form (steam).

When the change of state occurs at a *constant temperature* by the exchange of heat, it is called *change of phase* (Fig. 11.2).

The process of conversion of a material from its solid phase into its liquid phase is known as *melting*. Its reverse process, *i.e.* from liquid to solid, is known as *freezing* (or *fusion*).

The process of conversion of a material from its liquid phase into its gaseous form is known as *vaporization*, and its reverse process, *i.e.* from gas to liquid, is known as *condensation*.

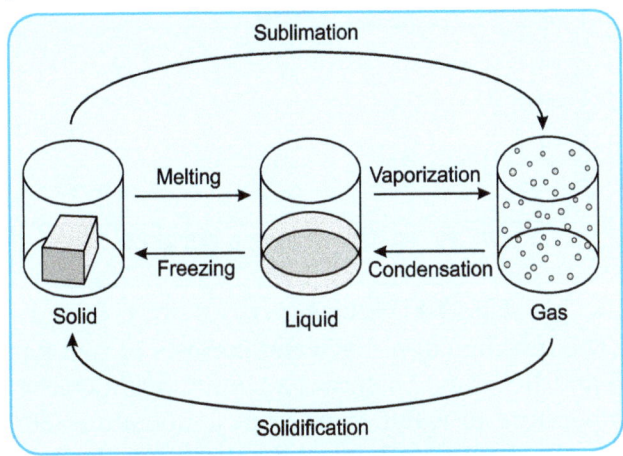

Fig. 11.2 : Changes of phase.

The process of conversion of a material from its solid phase into its gaseous form (vapour) directly is known as *sublimation*, and its reverse process, *i.e.* from vapour to solid, is known as *solidification*.

11.12 MELTING AND FREEZING

Melting is the process of conversion of a substance from solid to liquid phase with absorption of heat at a constant temperature.

The constant temperature at which a solid changes to a liquid is called the *melting point* of the solid.

Freezing (or *fusion*) is the reverse process where a liquid matter is converted to solid with the release of heat at a constant temperature.

The constant temperature at which a liquid changes to a solid is called the *freezing point* of the liquid.

The process of melting involves absorption of heat and is known as *endothermic process*, while the process of freezing involves release of heat and is an *exothermic process*.

The numerical value of melting point and freezing point for a pure substance of a given mass is identical.

Example : If the melting point of a certain mass of ice is 0°C, then the freezing point of same mass of water is 0°C. The amount of heat energy absorbed during melting is equal the amount of heat energy released during freezing.

On melting, *the volume of most substances increases*, *i.e.* the material expands during solid to liquid conversion.

Examples : Wax, lead, copper and so on.

However, some substances, such as *ice*, *contract* on melting instead of expanding, *i.e.* when ice converts to water, its volume decreases.

Heating and Cooling Curves

A *heating curve* represents the change in temperature with respect to time when a substance is heated.

A *cooling curve* represents the change in temperature with respect to time for a substance which loses heat to its surroundings.

Heating Curve for Ice when its Phase Changes from Solid to Liquid (*i.e.* from Ice to Water)

The following experiment can be conducted to observe the melting of ice at different temperatures and plot a heating curve.

Procedure :

1. Take a test tube half filled with ice cubes. Insert a thermometer gently into the tube and note the temperature of ice. It is found to be 0°C.

2. Now dip the test tube in a hot water bath (beaker containing hot water) and heat the bottom of the tube over a flame. Start a stopwatch and note the temperature using a thermometer for regular interval of time, say after every 30 s, until whole the ice melts into water and the temperature of water rises to 30°C.

3. Plot a graph with temperature on Y-axis and time on X-axis. The graph or the heating curve obtained is shown in Fig. 11.3.

The graph obtained is a straight line but after a certain interval of time. The graph consists of two portions : AB and BC. In part AB, from 0 s to 100 s, the temperature of ice remains constant. In this interval of time, the heat supplied is used in melting of ice.

Once whole of the ice melts and changes to water, the temperature of water begins to rise, as shown in part BC of the graph. From 100 s to 180 s, the temperature of water increases constantly until it reaches 30°C. The constant temperature at which a solid melts is its melting point. Thus, melting point of ice is 0°C.

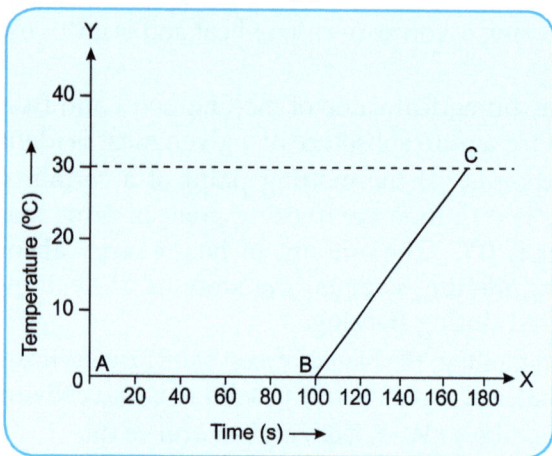

Fig. 11.3 : Heating curve for ice.

Factors Affecting Melting Point of a Solid

The following two factors affect the melting point of a solid :

1. Pressure : The melting point of substances that expand on melting (wax, lead, etc.) increases by increase in pressure.

In the case of substances that contract on melting (*e.g.* ice), the melting point decreases by increase in pressure. The melting point of ice decreases by 0.0072°C for rise in pressure by 1 atm.

2. Impurities : The melting point of a substance decreases if impurities are present in it.

Example : If salt is added to ice in a proper proportion, its melting point decreases from 0°C to –22°C.

11.13 VAPORIZATION OR BOILING

Vaporization or *boiling* is the process of conversion of a substance from liquid to gas (or vapour) phase with absorption of heat at a constant temperature.

The constant temperature at which a liquid changes to a gas is called the *boiling point* of the liquid.

Condensation is the reverse process where a substance in gaseous form is converted to liquid state with the release of heat at a constant temperature.

The constant temperature at which a gaseous substance changes to liquid is called the *condensation point* of the vapour.

The process of boiling involves absorption of heat and is known as *endothermic process*, while the process of condensation involves release of heat, thus, is an *exothermic process*.

The boiling point and condensation point are same for a pure substance.

Heating Curve for Water

The following steps are followed to plot a heating curve for water.

Procedure :

1. Take a flask containing water at room temperature. Suppose the room temperature is 30°C. Suspend a thermometer in the flask.

2. Keep the flask over a moderate flame of Bunsen burner and note the temperature using a thermometer after every 30 seconds until the water starts boiling and some vapours appears on the neck of the flask. (Bubbles are formed when the water boils, and these bubbles are observed in the whole of water, indicating that the process of boiling occurs throughout the volume of water.)

3. Plot a graph of temperature on Y-axis and time on X-axis.

The heating curve for water is shown in Fig. 11.4.

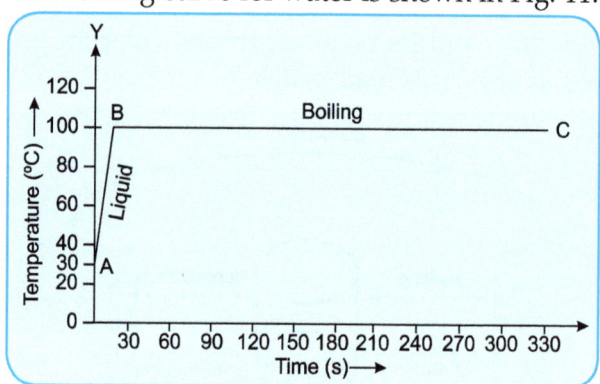

Fig. 11.4 : Heating curve for water.

The heating curve for water consists of two parts, AB and BC. Part AB shows a continuous increase in temperature of water from room temperature (30°C) with absorption of heat. AB represents the liquid phase. At point B, boiling starts, and part BC represents change of liquid to vapour form with absorption of heat but at a constant temperature. The temperature at point B is 100°C and represents the boiling point of water.

The volume of all liquids increases on boiling, *i.e.* there occurs an expansion when liquid changes to vapour state. In the case of water, the volume expands by 1,700 times when it changes from liquid to steam, *i.e.* the volume of 1 cm³ of water at 100°C increases to 1,700 cm³ of steam.

Factors Affecting the Boiling Point of a Liquid

1. Pressure : The boiling point of a liquid *increases* with increase in pressure and vice-versa.

The boiling point of water is 100°C when the pressure is 1 atm.

This property of boiling of water is employed in a *pressure-cooker*. In a pressure-cooker, steam is not allowed to escape, and thus its internal pressure increases. Due to this increase in pressure, the boiling point of water increases to about 125°C, and also the vegetables inside the cooker receive good amount of heat energy before water begins to boil and thus cooking becomes faster.

However, in higher altitudes, the atmospheric pressure decreases, which in turn decreases the boiling point of water. Therefore, as water begins to boil below 100°C, the heat energy available to the food for cooking is less and thus the process of cooking becomes slower.

2. Impurities : The boiling point of a liquid *increases* if impurities are added to it.

To boil water at a temperature greater than 100°C, a little amount of common salt is added. This is especially done during cooking to provide enough heat energy to the food before water begins to boil.

11.14 LATENT HEAT

In the process of change of phase, heat energy is either absorbed (endothermic process) or released (exothermic process).

Heat energy is *absorbed* when a solid changes to liquid during *melting* or when a liquid changes to gas during *boiling* with constant temperature.

Heat energy is *released* when a liquid changes to solid during *freezing* or when a gas changes to liquid during *condensation* with constant temperature.

The heat energy absorbed or released during the phase change is stored in the form of potential energy within the molecules of the substance and does not cause a rise or fall in temperature. This heat energy is known as *latent heat*. Thus,

Latent heat is the amount of heat energy absorbed or released during the process of phase change with constant temperature.

Explanation of Latent Heat

Latent heat of melting : The total internal energy of a molecule is the sum of its kinetic energy and potential energy. The kinetic energy occurs due to the vibration of the molecules about their mean position, whereas the potential energy is a result of force of attraction and the distance between the molecules (intermolecular separation).

When there is a change of phase from solid to liquid, with temperature being constant, the average kinetic energy of the molecules remains unchanged. It is the potential energy of the molecules that changes because of an increase in the distance between molecules and disruption of attractive force between them. The heat energy (latent heat) absorbed is utilised in increasing the potential energy of the molecules.

Latent heat of vaporization : The average kinetic energy of the molecules, similar to the process of melting, does not change in the process of vaporization *i.e.*, when a liquid changes to vapour phase. In gas or vapour phase, the volume increases due to increase in distance between the molecules and against the force of attraction between the molecules. Thus, the heat energy supplied is used up in increasing the potential energy of the molecules and the volume of the gas (*i.e.* expansion).

11.15 SPECIFIC LATENT HEAT

The amount of heat energy required for the phase change at its melting point or boiling point depends on the mass of the substance. Larger the mass, greater is the heat energy required to change the phase. The same substance will have different latent heats depending upon its mass.

To know the definite amount of heat energy required by a substance for phase change, we take a unit mass of the substance. Thus,

Specific latent heat is the amount of latent heat required by a unit mass of substance to undergo a phase change.

It is represented by the symbol L. During the change of phase, if Q is the amount of heat absorbed or released by mass m of a substance at a constant temperature, then its specific latent heat is given as

$$L = \frac{\text{Heat absorbed or released during the phase change}}{\text{Mass}}$$

$$L = \frac{Q}{m} \qquad \ldots(11.15)$$

The amount of heat energy absorbed or released by a given amount of substance for the change of phase can be given as

$$Q = \text{Mass} (m) \times \text{Specific latent heat (L)}$$
$$\ldots(11.16)$$

Units of Specific Latent Heat

Since specific latent heat is heat absorbed or released per unit mass, its SI unit is J kg^{-1}. If heat energy is expressed in calorie or kilocalorie, then the unit of specific latent heat is cal g^{-1} and kcal kg^{-1}.

Relation between different units

1 kcal kg^{-1} = 1 cal g^{-1}

1 cal g^{-1} = 4.2 J g^{-1} = 4,200 J kg^{-1}

11.16 SPECIFIC LATENT HEAT OF FUSION OF ICE

The amount of heat energy required to convert unit mass (1 kg or 1 g) of a solid to liquid state at its melting point without any change in temperature is known as the *specific latent heat of melting*.

On the other hand, specific latent heat of fusion of ice is the heat energy released when a unit mass of water at 0°C freezes to ice at 0°C without any change in temperature.

For a pure substance, the specific latent heat of fusion is same as the specific latent heat of melting.

For ice, the specific latent heat of fusion is very high which is 336,000 J kg^{-1} in the SI system and is equivalent to 80 cal g^{-1}, which means that 1 kg of ice at 0°C requires absorption of 336,000 J of heat energy to convert into water at 0°C.

Similarly, 1 kg of water at 0°C will release 336,000 J of heat energy to convert into ice at 0°C.

Thus, 1 kg of water at 0°C contains 336,000 J of more heat energy than 1 kg of ice at 0°C.

Table 11.2 represents the specific latent heat of fusion of some common substances.

Table 11.2 : Specific latent heat of fusion of common substances

Substance	Latent heat of fusion	
	J kg^{-1}	cal g^{-1}
Ice	336,000	80
Copper	180,000	43
Paraffin wax	146,000	35
Silver	88,000	21
Sulphur	37,700	9
Lead	27,000	6.42
Mercury	12,500	3

11.17 NATURAL CONSEQUENCES OF HIGH SPECIFIC LATENT HEAT OF FUSION OF ICE

1. In cold countries, waterbodies do not freeze suddenly : The specific latent heat of freezing of ice is quite high (336 J g^{-1}) and therefore, a large amount of heat energy needs to be radiated by waterbodies such as lakes, rivers and oceans to freeze. Thus, water freezes slowly into ice and not rapidly. Also when it freezes, due to release of heat energy, the surrounding weather becomes moderate.

2. Snow melts slowly on the mountains : Due to high specific latent heat of fusion of ice, large amount of heat from the Sun is required to melt the snow. As the snow melts gradually, there are no episodes of floods and there is sufficient water in the rivers throughout the year. If the latent heat of fusion would have been low, the snow would have melted quickly from the heat of the Sun, resulting in floods.

3. The weather becomes colder after a hailstorm : During a hailstorm, ice begins to melt by absorbing heat energy from the surroundings. This decreases the temperature of the surroundings. Thus, the surroundings become colder after a hailstorm than before a hailstorm.

4. The weather becomes mild during a snowstorm : During a snowstorm, water vapour freezes to form ice. Thus, a large amount of heat is released to the surroundings that raises the temperature and makes the weather moderate.

11.18 GENERAL APPLICATIONS OF HIGH SPECIFIC LATENT HEAT OF FUSION OF ICE

1. Soft drinks are cooled by adding pieces of ice rather than cold water : 1 g of ice at 0°C takes up 336 J of energy from the soft drink to melt. The drink loses this heat to the ice and gets cooled. The cooling produced by ice at 0°C is more than water at 0°C due to additional 336 J of energy absorbed by each gram of ice from the soft drink.

2. Protection of vegetables and fruits from damage in sub-zero temperature : During cold weather, fruits and vegetables are stored with tubs of water around them to prevent them from damage. The reason is that as water starts freezing in the sub-zero temperature, it liberates a large amount of heat to the surroundings. This increases the temperature of the vicinity and protects the vegetables and fruits from damage.

3. Ice candy feels colder than water at same temperature : When an ice candy is placed in the mouth, it extracts heat from the mouth to melt into water, whereas water at the same temperature does not require this amount of heat for melting purpose. Hence, ice candy feels colder than cold water.

ILLUSTRATIVE EXAMPLES

1. The graph given below represents the heating curve of a substance that starts as a solid below its freezing point.

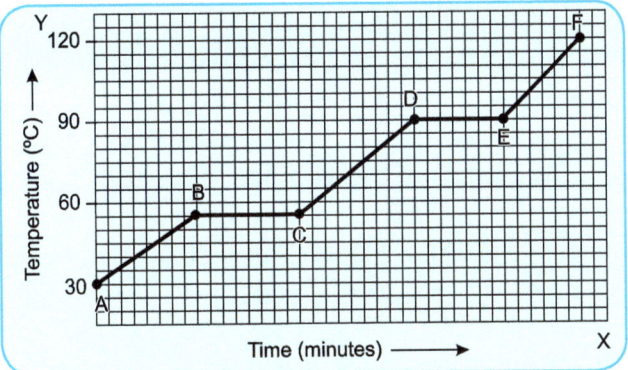

(a) What is the melting point of this substance?
(b) Which process is represented by the line segment DE of the curve?
(c) In which line segment is the average kinetic energy increasing?
(d) What is happening to the average kinetic energy of the molecules in part BC of the curve?
(e) What is the boiling point of the substance?

Solution :
(a) Point B represents the melting point of the substance, *i.e.* 55°C.
(b) The line segment DE represents boiling or vaporization, *i.e.* conversion of liquid to gas state.
(c) In segments AB, CD and EF, the average kinetic energy of the molecules is increasing and thus, (vapour) the temperature is rising.
(d) In part BC, since there is no change in temperature, hence the average kinetic energy of the molecules is constant. The heat absorbed by the substance is stored as the potential energy of molecules.
(e) Point D represents the boiling point of the substance, *i.e.* 90°C.

2. The graph given below shows two curves, one for water and the other for benzene of same mass, with variation of temperature with amount of heat supplied.

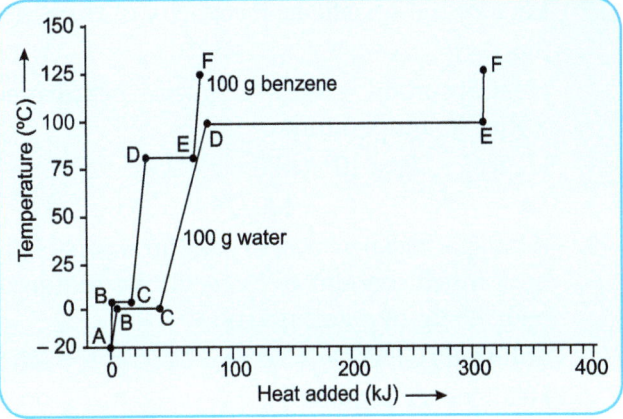

(a) Calculate approximately the latent heat of fusion of water and benzene.
(b) Calculate approximately the latent heat of vaporization of water and benzene.
(c) Calculate approximately the specific heat capacity of benzene.

Solution :
(a) Part BC of the graph represents the latent heat of fusion.

For water : Approximate heat energy absorbed in part BC = 35 kJ = 35 × 10³ J
Given, Mass = 100 g
Hence, Specific latent heat of fusion
$= Q/m = 35 \times 10^3 / 100$
$= 350 \text{ J g}^{-1}$

For benzene : Approximate heat energy absorbed in part BC = 20 kJ = 20 × 10³ J
Given, Mass = 100 g
Hence, Specific latent heat of fusion
$= Q/m = 20 \times 10^3 / 100$
$= 200 \text{ J g}^{-1}$

(b) Part DE of the graph represents the latent heat of vaporization.

For water : Approximate heat energy absorbed in part DE = (310 – 80) = 230 kJ = 230 × 10³ J
Given, Mass = 100 g
Hence, Specific latent heat of vaporization
$= Q/m = 230 \times 10^3 / 100$
$= 2,300 \text{ J g}^{-1}$

For benzene : Approximate heat energy absorbed in part DE = (70 – 30) kJ = 40 kJ = 40 × 10³ J
Given, Mass = 100 g
Hence, Specific latent heat of vaporization
$= Q/m = 40 \times 10^3 / 100 = 400 \text{ J g}^{-1}$

(c) In part CD of the benzene curve, heat energy absorbed = (30 – 20) kJ = 10 kJ = 10 × 10³ J
Approximate rise in temperature = (80 – 5) = 75°C

Let c be the specific heat capacity of benzene.
Since
Heat absorbed = Mass × Specific heat capacity × Rise in temperature
Hence, $10 \times 10^3 = 100 \times c \times 75$
i.e. $c = 100/75 = 1.33$ J g^{-1} °C^{-1}

3. If the specific latent heat of paraffin wax is 146 Jg^{-1}, how much amount of heat will be required to melt 1.5 kg of paraffin wax?

Solution : Given, $m = 1.5$ kg $= 1,500$ g, L $= 146$ Jg^{-1}
Heat energy required
$= mL = 1,500 \times 146$
$= 219,000$ J $= 219$ kJ

4. Calculate the quantity of heat required to convert 2 kg of ice at 0°C to water at 15°C.
Given : Specific latent heat of ice = 336 Jg^{-1}, specific heat capacity of water = 4.2 J g^{-1}°C^{-1}.

Solution : Given, $m = 2$ kg $= 2,000$ g, L $= 336$ Jg^{-1}, $\Delta t = 15 - 0 = 15$°C, $c = 4.2$ Jg^{-1}°C^{-1}.
Heat energy required to convert ice at 0°C to water at 0°C = $m \times L = 2,000 \times 336 = 672,000$ J
= 672 kJ.
Heat energy required to convert water at 0°C to water at 150°C = $m \times c \times \Delta t = 2,000 \times 4.2 \times 15$
= 126,000 J = 126 kJ
Total heat energy required = 672 + 126 = 798 kJ

5. A piece of metal at 10°C has a mass of 50 g. When it is immersed in a current of steam at 100°C, 0.7 g of steam is condensed on it. Calculate the specific heat of metal. (Take latent heat of steam = 540 cal g^{-1}).

Solution : Given, Mass of metal = 50 g, $\Delta t = 100 - 10 = 90$°C, Mass of steam = 0.7 g, L = 540 cal g^{-1}. Let c be the specific heat capacity of metal.
Heat absorbed by the metal = Heat released by the steam.
Heat absorbed by the metal
$= m \times c \times \Delta t$
$= 50 \times c \times 90 = 4,500\ c$ cal
Heat released by steam
$= m \times L = 0.7 \times 540 = 378$ cal
Now, $4,500\ c = 378$
∴ $c = 378/4,500$
$= 0.084$ cal g^{-1} °C^{-1}

6. A 30 g ice cube at 0°C is dropped into 200 g of water at 30°C. Calculate the final temperature of water when the entire ice cube has melted. Take : Latent heat of ice = 80 cal g^{-1}, specific heat capacity of water = 1 cal g^{-1} °C^{-1}.

Solution : Given, Mass of ice = 30 g, Mass of water = 200 g, $t_1 = 0$°C, $t_2 = 30$°C, t°C = Final temperature, L = 80 cal g^{-1}, $c = 1$ cal g^{-1}°C^{-1}
Heat gained by ice at 0°C to melt into water at 0°C = $m \times L = 30 \times 80 = 2,400$ J
Heat gained by water at 0°C to reach the final temperature = $m \times c \times \Delta t = 30 \times 1 \times (t - 0) = 30\ t$
Total heat gained = $2,400 + 30\ t$
Heat lost by 200 g water
$= m \times c \times \Delta t$
$= 200 \times 1 \times (30 - t)$
$= 6,000 - 200\ t$
By the law of conservation of energy,
Heat lost = Heat gained
$6,000 - 200\ t = 2,400 + 30\ t$
or $230\ t = 3,600$
∴ $t = 15.65$ °C

7. A 500 g of ice slab at 0°C is provided with heat energy at a constant rate. It gets converted to water in 4 min. Calculate the time required to raise the temperature of water from 0°C to 80 °C. Take specific latent heat of ice = 336 J g^{-1}, specific heat capacity of water = 4.2 J g^{-1} K^{-1}.

Solution : Given, $m = 500$ g, $t = 4$ min $= 240$ s, $\Delta T = 80 - 0 = 80$°C, L = 336 J g^{-1}, $c = 4.2$ Jg^{-1} K^{-1}
Heat energy gained by ice at 0°C to melt into water at 0°C in 240 s
$= m\ L = 500 \times 336$
$= 168,000$ J
Heat energy gained by ice in 1 s
$= 168,000/240 = 700$ J s^{-1}
Heat energy required to raise the temperature of water to
80°C $= m \times c \times \Delta T$
$= 500 \times 4.2 \times 80 = 168,000$ J
Let t be the time required to raise the temperature of water. So heat energy supplied in time $t = 700 \times t$ s
$700 \times t = 168,000$
or $t = 240$ s $= 4$ min

8. A 20 kW electric heater with 60% efficiency is used to melt 400 g of ice at 0°C. Calculate the time required by the heater to do so if the specific latent heat of ice is 336 J g^{-1}.

Solution : Given, P = 20 kW = 20×10^3 W, Efficiency = 60%, $m = 400$ g, L = 336 Jg^{-1}.
Effective power of the heater
$= \dfrac{60}{100} \times 20 \times 10^3$
$= 12 \times 10^3$ W

Energy supplied by the heater
$$= P \times t = 12 \times 10^3 \times t$$
Heat energy required by ice to melt
$$= m \times L = 400 \times 336 = 134{,}400$$
Now, $12 \times 10^3 \times t = 134{,}400$
i.e. $t = 11.2$ s

9. **How much amount of ice will melt if 300 g of ice at 0°C is mixed with 400 g of copper strips at 400°C? What is the extra amount of heat energy needed to melt the whole of ice? (Specific heat capacity of copper = 0.4 J g^{-1} K^{-1}, Latent heat of ice = 336 J g^{-1})**

    Solution : Given, Mass of ice = 300 g, Mass of copper strips = 400 g, $\Delta t = 400 - 0 = 400°C = 400$ K, $c = 0.4$ J g^{-1} K^{-1}, L = 336 Jg^{-1}

    Heat energy lost by the copper strips to ice = $m \times c \times \Delta t = 400 \times 0.4 \times 400 = 64{,}000$ J
    It is this amount of energy that will melt m_1 g of ice.
    Heat energy gained by m_1 g of ice = $m \times L = 336\, m_1$
    Heat energy gained by ice = Heat energy lost by copper strips
    $$336\, m_1 = 64{,}000$$
    i.e. $m_1 = 64{,}000/336 = 190.47$ g
    Total heat energy required to melt whole of ice
    = Mass of ice × L
    = 300 × 336 = 100,800 J
    ∴ Extra amount of heat energy required to melt whole of ice = 100,800 − 64,000 = 36,800 J

10. **A vessel of negligible heat capacity contains 60 g of ice in it at 0°C. 100 g of water at 80°C is passed into the ice to melt it. (a) Find the amount of heat absorbed by ice to melt into water at 0°C. (b) Find the final temperature of the contents of the vessel. (Specific latent heat of fusion of ice = 336 Jg^{-1}, specific heat capacity of water = 4.2 J g^{-1} °C^{-1})**

    Solution : Given, Mass of ice = 60 g, Mass of water = 100 g
    Let the final temperature of the vessel be t°C.
    Δt for 100 g water = $80 - t$, Δt for a 60 g ice converted into water = $t - 0 = t$, L = 336 J g^{-1}, $c = 4.2$ J g^{-1} °C^{-1}

    (a) Heat gained by ice at 0°C to melt into water at 0 °C = $m \times L = 60 \times 336 = 20{,}160$ J

    (b) Heat lost by water to melt the ice
    $$= m \times c \times \Delta t$$
    $$= 100 \times 4.2 \times (80 - t)$$
    $$= (33{,}600 - 420\, t) \text{ J}$$

    Heat gained by water at 0°C to reach final temperature t°C = $m \times c \times \Delta t = 60 \times 4.2 \times t = 252\, t$
    By principle of conservation of energy,
    Total heat gained = Total heat lost
    i.e. $20{,}160 + 252\, t = 33{,}600 - 420\, t$
    or, $672 - t = 13{,}440$
    ∴ $t = 20°C$

11. **In a laboratory experiment for finding the specific latent heat of ice, 100 g of water at 30°C was taken in a calorimeter made of copper of mass 10 g. When 10 g of ice at 0°C was added to the mixture and kept within the liquid until the ice melted completely, the final temperature of the mixture was found to be 20°C. (a) What is the total quantity of water in the calorimeter at 20°C? (b) If specific heat capacities of water and copper are 4.2 Jg^{-1} °C^{-1} and 0.4 Jg^{-1} °C^{-1}, respectively, what quantity of heat would each calorimeter and water release in cooling down to 20°C from the initial stage? (c) Calculate the heat gained by ice on melting. (d) Calculate the value of the latent heat of fusion of ice from the data discussed above.**

    Solution : Given, Mass of water $m_w = 100$ g, $c_w = 4.2$ J g^{-1} °C^{-1}, $\Delta t_w = 30 - 20 = 10°C$, Mass of calorimeter $m_c = 10$ g, $c_c = 0.4$ Jg^{-1}°C^{-1}, $\Delta t_c = 30 - 20 = 10°C$, Mass of ice $m = 10$ g
    Let L be the latent heat of ice.

    (a) Total quantity of water in calorimeter at 20°C = 100 g + 10 g (ice that melts into water) = 110 g

    (b) Heat released by water in calorimeter
    $= m_w \times c_w \times \Delta t_w = 100 \times 4.2 \times 10 = 4{,}200$ J
    Heat released by calorimeter
    $= m_c \times c_c \times \Delta t_c$
    $= 10 \times 0.4 \times 10 = 40$ J

    (c) Heat gained by ice to melt = Heat released by water in calorimeter + Heat released by calorimeter
    $= 4{,}200 + 40 = 4{,}240$ J

    (d) Heat gained by ice to melt into water at 0°C
    $= m \times L = 10$ L
    Heat gained by water at 0°C to rise to 20°C
    $= m \times c_w \times \Delta t$
    $= 10 \times 4.2 \times (20 - 0) = 840$
    Total heat gained by ice = $(10\,L + 840)$ J
    By principle of calorimetry,
    Total heat lost = Total heat gained
    i.e. $10\,L + 840 = 4{,}240$
    or $L = 3{,}400/10 = 340$ Jg^{-1}

EXERCISE 11(B)

1. Name the three states of matter.
   Ans : Solid, liquid and gas
2. What is meant by change of phase of a substance?
3. What is meant by melting of a substance? What is the reverse process of melting called?
4. What is meant by vaporization? Does it involve absorption or release of heat?
5. What is melting point of a substance? State its value for ice.
6. Give an example of (a) endothermic process and (b) exothermic process.
   Ans : (a) Melting, (b) Freezing
7. What happens to the volume of a substance on melting?
   Ans : The volume of a substance increases on melting; exception is melting of ice.
8. State the energy change that takes place when a substance undergoes a change in phase (a) without increase in temperature and (b) with increase in temperature.
   Ans : (a) The average potential energy of molecules change, (b) The average kinetic energy of the molecules change.
9. What are heating and cooling curves?
10. Describe an experiment for determination of heating curve for ice.
11. What is the effect of increase in pressure on the melting point of ice?
12. State an easy way of decreasing the melting point of ice.
13. Some ice is heated at a constant rate, and its temperature is recorded after every few seconds, till steam is formed at 100°C. Draw a temperature time graph to represent the change. Label the two phase changes in your graph.
14. A sample of water is heated at 40–110°C. The temperature-time graph obtained is given below :
    (a) In the graph, label the three portions, QR, RS and ST.
    (b) For the section QR of the graph what is happening to the molecules as heat is added?
    (c) Why is the temperature constant for the part RS of the graph, even though heat is being supplied constantly?

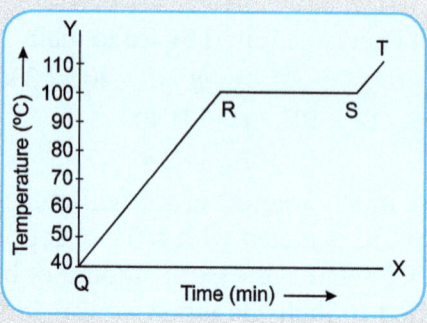

15. What is meant by the boiling point? Is it same as condensation point?
16. How does food get cooked easily in a pressure-cooker?
17. What happens to the boiling point of water as one goes to a hill?
18. Rishi is surprised when he sees water boiling at 115°C in a container. Give reasons as to why water can boil at the above temperature.
19. Name the two factors that affect the melting and boiling point of a substance.
    Ans : Change in pressure and addition of impurities
20. What is the effect of adding impurities on the boiling point of a substance?
21. The graph given below represents the heating curve of a substance starting as a solid below its melting point and being heated at a constant rate over time.

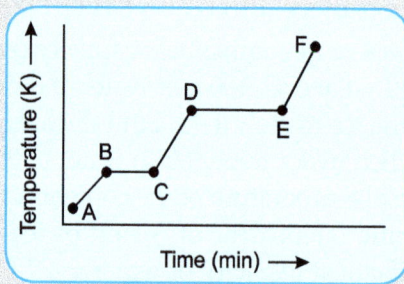

   (a) Which segment of the graph represents change of phase from liquid to gas?
   (b) What is happening to the average kinetic energy of the molecules in segment BC of the graph?
   (c) Which point in the graph represents the boiling point of the substance?
   (d) How does the curve illustrate that latent heat of vaporization is greater than the latent heat of fusion?
22. A 500 g of steam at 150°C is subjected to condensation. The water so formed is allowed

to cool down to 0°C. Draw a temperature-time graph to represent the phase changes during this cooling process. Label the melting and boiling point in the graph.
23. What is meant by latent heat ?
24. What is specific latent heat ? State its SI unit.
25. What is meant by specific latent heat of fusion of ice? Give its value in SI system.
26. How will you explain the latent heat of melting at molecular level?
27. Which among the two carries more heat energy : 50 g of ice at 0°C or 50 g of water at 0°C?
    Ans : 50 g of water
28. What is meant by the statement "The specific latent heat of ice is 80 cal g^{-1}"?
29. What happens to the average kinetic energy of the molecules as ice melts at 0°C?
    Ans : It remains unchanged.
30. What happens to the heat supplied to a substance when the heat supplied causes no change in the temperature of the substance?
    Ans : It is used up in increasing the average potential energy of the molecules.
31. When 1 g of ice at 0°C melts to form 1 g of water at 0°C, is the latent heat absorbed or released by ice?
    Ans : Latent heat is absorbed
32. State the effect of an increase of impurities on the melting point of ice.
33. Name the two method of determination of specific latent heat of fusion of ice.
34. Which of these two will require more heat energy to rise to a temperature of 50°C : 10 g of ice at 0°C or 10 g of water at 0°C?
    Ans : 10 g of ice
35. Explain why the weather becomes very cold after a hailstorm?
36. It is observed that the temperature of the surroundings drops when the ice in a frozen lake starts melting. Give a reason for the observation.
37. Why does a bottle of soft drink cool faster when surrounded by ice cubes than by ice-cold water, both at 0°C?
38. Water in lakes and ponds do not freeze at once in cold countries. Give a reason in support of your answer.
39. Explain the following :
    (a) An ice candy feels colder in the mouth than water at 0°C.
    (b) Fruit merchants keep water tubs besides the fruits in sub-zero weather.

MULTIPLE CHOICE QUESTIONS

1. The melting point of a substance is numerically equal to its :
   (a) boiling point   (b) freezing point
   (c) condensation point   (d) none of these
   Ans : (b)
2. Which of the following statements is true about line segment 3 in the graph given below?

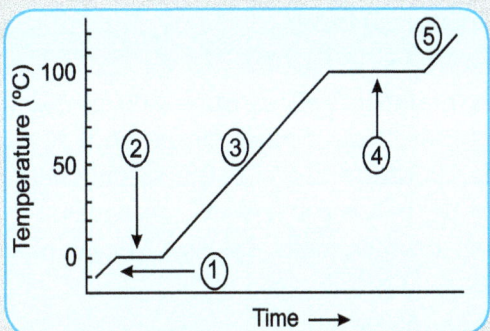

   (a) a solid is melting with constant temperature
   (b) a solid is melting with rise in temperature
   (c) a liquid is heating with rise in temperature
   (d) a liquid is boiling with constant temperature.
   Ans : (c)
3. Which of these carries the maximum amount of heat energy?
   (a) 1 g of ice at 0°C
   (b) 1 g of water at 0°C
   (c) 1 g of water at 100°C
   (d) 1 g of steam at 100°C
   Ans : (d)
4. The specific latent heat of fusion of ice is :
   (a) 2,260 J g^{-1} (b) 80 J g^{-1}
   (c) 336 J g^{-1} (d) 4,200 J g^{-1}
   Ans : (c)

NUMERICAL PROBLEMS

1. How much heat energy is released when 5 g of water at 20°C changes to ice at 0°C? (Specific heat capacity of water = 4.2 Jg^{-1} K^{-1}, specific latent heat of ice = 336 J g^{-1})
   Ans : 2,100 J
2. If 20 g of ice absorbs 8,000 J of energy at 0°C to melt into water, calculate the temperature at which it changes to water. (Specific heat capacity of water = 4,200 J kg^{-1} °C^{-1}, specific latent heat of fusion of ice = 336 × 10^3 J kg^{-1})
   Ans : 15.23°C
3. A 40 g of ice at 0°C is used to reduce the temperature of a certain mass of water at 60 °C

to 10 °C. Find the mass of water used. (Specific heat capacity of water = 4,200 J kg^{-1} °C^{-1}, specific latent heat of fusion of ice = 336 × 10^3 J kg^{-1}).
Ans : 72 g

4. A metal cube of mass 400 g and at 500°C is placed on a block of ice. It is able to melt 357 g of ice and not the whole block. If the specific heat capacity of the metal is 0.6 J g^{-1} °C^{-1}, calculate the specific latent heat of ice.
Ans : 336.13 J g^{-1} °C^{-1}

5. A metallic ball of mass 300 g and at 700°C is placed on a block of ice until it attains the temperature of ice. If the specific heat capacity of the ball is 800 J kg^{-1} °C^{-1}, calculate the amount of ice which melts. Take specific latent heat of ice as 336 J g^{-1}.
Ans : 500 g

6. A vessel of mass 50 g and specific heat capacity 0.7 J g^{-1} °C^{-1} contains 200 g of water at 40°C. Calculate the amount of ice at 0°C that must be added to it so that the final temperature is 10°C. (Take specific latent heat of ice = 340 J g^{-1}.)
Ans : 68.71 g

7. An immersion heater of power 30 W keeps 600 g of a molten metal at its melting point. When the heater is switched off, the temperature begins to fall in 6 min. Calculate the specific latent heat of fusion of the metal.
Ans : 18 J g^{-1}

8. 50 g of ice at –10 °C is heated by a heater of power 300 W, such that water formed after melting attains the temperature of boiling point. Find the time duration for which the heater is switched on. (Specific heat capacity of ice = 2 J g^{-1} °C^{-1}, specific latent heat of ice = 336 J g^{-1}, specific heat capacity of water = 4.2 J g^{-1} °C^{-1})
Ans : 129.33 s

9. Heat energy is supplied at a constant rate to 100 g of ice at 0°C. The ice is converted into water at 0°C in 2 min. How much time will be required to raise the temperature of water from 0°C to 20 °C? (Given : Specific heat capacity of water = 4.2 J g^{-1} °C^{-1}, specific latent heat of ice = 336 J g^{-1})
Ans : 30 s

10. 80 g of water at 35°C is taken in a calorimeter made of copper of mass 20 g. When 17 g of ice at 0°C is added to the mixture and kept within the liquid until the ice melts completely, the final temperature of the mixture is found to be 15°C. (a) If specific heat capacities of water and copper are 4.2 J g^{-1} °C^{-1} and 0.4 J g^{-1} °C^{-1}, respectively, what quantity of heat would each release in cooling down to 15°C from the initial stage? (b) Calculate the heat gained by ice on melting. (c) Calculate the specific latent heat of fusion of ice.
Ans : (a) Heat released by water = 6,720 J, Heat released by calorimeter = 160 J, (b) 6,880 J, (c) 341.7 J g^{-1}

11. A copper vessel of mass 100 g contains 150 g of water at 50°C. How much ice is needed to cool to 5 °C ?
Given :
Specific heat capacity of copper = 0.4 J g^{-1} °C^{-1}
Specific heat capacity of water = 4.2 J g^{-1} °C^{-1}
Specific latent heat of fusion of ice = 336 J g^{-1}
Ans : 84.45 g

12. A refrigerator converts 100 g of water at 20° C to ice at – 10°C in 35 minutes.
Calculate the average rate of heat extraction in terms of watts.
Given :
Specific heat capacity of ice = 2.1 J g^{-1} °C^{-1}
Specific heat capacity of water = 4.2 J g^{-1} °C^{-1}
Specific latent heat of fusion of ice = 336 J g^{-1}
Ans : 21 watts

12

MODERN PHYSICS

LEARNING OUTCOMES

- Structure of atom and its nucleus
- Isotopes, isobars and isotones
- Radioactivity : Emission of α, β and γ radiations
- Properties of α, β and γ radiations
- Changes in the nucleus of atom in α, β and γ emissions
- Uses of radioactivity
- Sources and harmful effects of radiations
- Safety precautions while handling radioactive elements
- Background radiations
- Nuclear energy
- Nuclear fission
- Nuclear fusion
- Difference between nuclear fission and fusion

(A) RADIOACTIVITY

12.1 STRUCTURE OF THE ATOM

After the discovery of electrons by Sir J. J. Thomson and protons by Rutherford, an atomic model was proposed by Rutherford that was further refined by a Danish physicist Niels Bohr. After the study done by various scientists, the following model of an atom has been proposed :

- An atom is composed of three subatomic particles : *protons*, *neutrons* and *electrons* (Fig. 12.1).
- The protons and neutrons together form the central core of the atom called the *nucleus*.
- The nucleus is surrounded by *electrons* which revolve in some definite stationary paths called *orbits* or *shells*. These shells have some amount of energy associated with them.
- The shells are numbered (n), starting from the one closest to the nucleus and then moving away as 1, 2, 3, 4, 5 and so on. These shells are named K, L, M, N, O, P and so on, with shell K ($n = 1$) being closest to the nucleus.
- The radius of the outermost shell determines the size of an atom and it is of the order of 10^{-10} m.
- The maximum number of electrons that can be accommodated in a shell is given by $2n^2$, where n is the number of the shell. According to this formula, shell K ($n = 1$) can have maximum 2 electrons, shell L ($n = 2$) can have maximum 8 electrons. Thus, the maximum number of electrons that can be accommodated in the shells in ascending order of their radius is 2, 8, 18, 32, 50, 72, 98 and so on.
- The total number of electrons in an atom determines the place of an atom in the periodic table.
- All electrons carry same negative charge, *i.e.* -1.6×10^{-19} C. This charge is the smallest charge that cannot be subdivided.
- Its mass is extremely small as compared to a proton or a neutron. The mass of an electron is equal to 9.1×10^{-31} kg.

- An atom is generally neutral, with the number of electrons being equal to the number of protons. An atom can gain or lose electrons from its outermost shell, thereby becoming a negatively or a positively charged atom respectively.

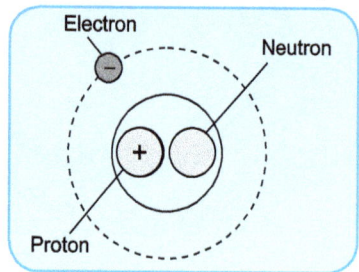

Fig. 12.1 : Structure of an atom.

12.2 STRUCTURE OF THE NUCLEUS OF ATOM

- The nucleus forms the central core of an atom and consists of the *protons* and the *neutrons*. The protons and neutrons are also known as *nucleons*; the particles forming the nucleus.
- The size of the nucleus is of the order of 10^{-15}–10^{-14} m; it is 10^{-5}–10^{-4} times the size of an atom.
- The nucleus carries a positive charge due to the positive charge of protons. The charge on a proton is equal and opposite of the charge on an electron; *i.e.* $+1.6 \times 10^{-19}$ C. A neutron is electrically neutral; it does not carry any charge.
- Since the mass of electrons is extremely small, the mass of an atom is due to the mass of its nucleus. The mass of a proton is equal to 1.67×10^{-27} kg (1,840 times the mass of an electron) and is equal to the mass of a hydrogen atom. The mass of a neutron is almost equal to the mass of a proton.
- The number of protons in the nucleus of an atom is called its *atomic number*; it is same as the number of electrons in a neutral atom. It is represented by letter Z. Every element has different number of protons and the chemical properties of an element depends on its atomic number.
- The total number of the nucleons (*i.e.* protons + neutrons) in the nucleus of an atom is called the *mass number* or *atomic mass* of an element. It is represented by letter A.

Atomic number (Z) : The number of protons in the nucleus (which is same as the number of electrons) of an atom is called the *atomic number*.

Mass number (A) : The total number of the nucleons (protons + neutrons) in the nucleus of an atom is called the *mass number*.

Table 12.1 : Symbol, Mass and Charge of Subatomic Particles

Subatomic particle	Symbol	Mass (in kg)	Charge (in C)
Electron	e	9.1×10^{-31}	-1.6×10^{-19}
Proton	p	1.67×10^{-27}	$+1.6 \times 10^{-19}$
Neutron	n	1.67×10^{-27}	Zero

12.3 REPRESENTATION OF ATOMIC STRUCTURE OF AN ELEMENT

An atom is electrically neutral, *i.e.*, the number of protons in the nucleus of an atom is equal to the number of electrons revolving around the nucleus.

Number of electrons = Number of protons
= Atomic number (Z)
Number of protons + Number of neutrons
= Mass number (A)
i.e. Atomic number + Number of neutrons
= Mass number
Thus, Number of neutrons
= Mass number – Atomic number
i.e. Number of neutrons = A – Z

An atom is represented as $_Z^A X$. Here X represents the chemical symbol of an element, A is its mass number and Z is its atomic number.

Examples :

1. Hydrogen : It is the first element in the periodic table. It is the lightest atom with mass number A = 1 and atomic number Z = 1. It is represented as $_1^1 H$. It has only 1 proton in the nucleus and 1 electron in the K-shell. It does not have any neutron (A – Z = 0).

2. Helium : It is the second element in the periodic table. Its mass number is A = 4 and its atomic number is Z = 2. It is represented as $_2^4 He$. It has 2 protons and 2 neutrons (A – Z = 4 – 2 = 2) in the nucleus and 2 electrons in the K-shell.

3. Carbon : The mass number of carbon is A = 12 and its atomic number is Z = 6. It is represented as $_6^{12} C$. It has 6 protons and 6 neutrons (A – Z = 12 – 6 = 6) in the nucleus and 6 electrons revolving around the nucleus in two shells. Out of the 6 electrons, 2 are in the K-shell and 4 in the L-shell.

4. Magnesium : It is represented as $_{12}^{24} Mg$, its mass number is A = 24 and atomic number is Z = 12. The number of protons is 12 and the number of neutrons is also 12 (A – Z = 24 – 12 = 12). The 12 electrons revolve around in three shells, K, L and M. The K-shell consists of 2 electrons, the L-shell consists of 8 electrons (since maximum electrons = $2n^2$) and the remaining 2 electrons are present in the M-shell.

12.4 ISOTOPES

Isotopes are the atoms of the same element with the same atomic number (Z) but different mass number (A).

The difference in mass number of different atoms is due to the different number of neutrons in the nuclei of atoms. These atoms have the same number of electrons and so their chemical properties are same. They vary in physical properties such as mass and density.

Most elements have one or more isotopes occurring in different proportions.

For some elements, the isotopes can be of two types : (1) *stable isotopes*—these atoms have nearly equal number of protons and neutrons in their nuclei and (2) *unstable isotopes* (also known as *radioactive isotopes*)—these atoms have more number of neutrons than the number of protons in their nuclei.

Examples of Isotopes

1. Hydrogen : It has *three* isotopes : protium ^1_1H (or ordinary hydrogen), deuterium ^2_1H (or heavy hydrogen) and tritium ^3_1H. Each of these isotopes has one proton and one electron. The number of neutrons in protium is 0, in deuterium is 1 and in tritium is 2 (Fig. 12.2).

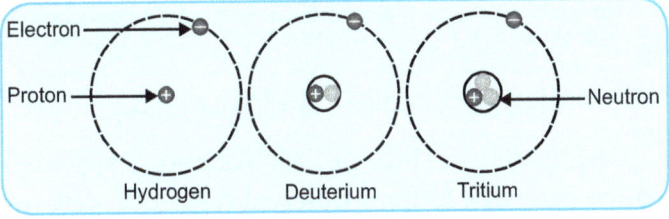

Fig. 12.2 : Isotopes of hydrogen.

2. Carbon : There are *three* isotopes of carbon : $^{12}_6C$, $^{13}_6C$ and $^{14}_6C$. Each isotope has 6 protons and 6 electrons. The number of neutrons in isotope $^{12}_6C$ is 6, in isotope $^{13}_6C$ is 7 and in isotope $^{14}_6C$ is 8.

3. Chlorine : There are *two* isotopes of chlorine : $^{35}_{17}Cl$ and $^{37}_{17}Cl$. Each isotope has 17 protons and 17 electrons. The number of neutrons in isotope $^{35}_{17}Cl$ is 18 and in isotope $^{37}_{17}Cl$ is 20.

4. Uranium : It has two isotopes : $^{235}_{92}U$ and $^{238}_{92}U$ each with 92 protons and 92 electrons. The number of neutrons is 143 and 146, respectively, in isotopes $^{235}_{92}U$ and $^{238}_{92}U$.

The largest number of isotopes is 10 for the element tin (Sn).

12.5 ISOBARS

Isobars are the atoms of different elements with the same mass number (A) but different atomic number (Z).

The atoms of isobars have same number of nucleons in their nuclei. However, the number of protons and neutrons are different in each atom. The total number of nucleous in one atom remains the same as that in its isobar. The number of electrons in different atoms of isobars is different but is equal to the number of protons in a given atom.

The atoms of isobar have different chemical properties, but the physical properties such as mass and density are same for different atoms.

Examples of Isobars

1. $^{13}_6C$ and $^{13}_7N$: The atom of carbon contains 6 protons, 6 electrons and 7 neutrons. The atom of nitrogen has 7 protons, 7 electrons and 6 neutrons. The total number of nucleons is 13 in each case.

2. $^{23}_{11}Na$ and $^{23}_{12}Mg$: The sodium atom consists of 11 protons, 11 electrons and 12 neutrons. The magnesium atom consists of 12 protons, 12 electrons and 11 neutrons. The total number of nucleons is same, *i.e.* 23 in each case.

As in the above case, if the number of protons and neutrons interchanges inside the nucleus, such atoms are called *mirror isobars*.

3. Other examples are $^{40}_{18}Ar$, $^{40}_{19}K$ and $^{40}_{20}Ca$, $^{58}_{26}Fe$ and $^{58}_{27}Ni$ and so on.

12.6 ISOTONES

Isotones are the atoms of different elements with different mass number (A) and different atomic number (Z). These atoms have different number of electrons and protons but same number of neutrons (A − Z).

The atoms of isotones vary in both physical and chemical properties.

Examples of Isotones

1. $^{23}_{11}Na$ and $^{24}_{12}Mg$: Both atoms contain 12 neutrons in their nucleus. The number of protons is 11 in sodium but 12 in magnesium.

2. $^{39}_{19}K$ and $^{40}_{20}Ca$: Both potassium and calcium atoms contain 20 neutrons in their respective nucleus, but the number of protons is different. Potassium has 19 protons, whereas calcium has 20 protons.

3. Other examples are $^{16}_8O$, $^{15}_7N$, $^{14}_6C$ and $^{31}_{14}Si$, $^{32}_{15}P$ and so on.

12.7 RADIOACTIVITY

Radioactivity is the phenomenon in which the nucleus of an unstable atom disintegrates and loses energy by emitting invisible ionising radiations.

The phenomenon of radioactivity was discovered in 1896 by a French scientist Prof. Henri Becquerel in Paris. He was working on the nature of *phosphorescent* substances, which are materials that glow in the dark after exposure to light. He wrapped a photographic plate with a phosphorescent salt (potassium uranyl sulphate crystals) on it in a black paper and kept it inside a drawer. A few days later, when he took out the photographic plate to develop it, he found that the plate was already affected. He conducted the experiment with various other salts of uranium and found the same result.

From these observations, he concluded that uranium and its various salts are capable of emitting some kind of invisible radiations that can pass through certain substances such as black paper, glass and wood and can affect the photographic plate. He named these radiations as *Becquerel rays*. Later on, these radiations were classified into three types : (1) *alpha radiations* (α) : positively charged, (2) *beta radiations* (β) : negatively charged and (3) *gamma radiations* (γ) : uncharged.

The elements that disintegrate upon spontaneous emission of radiations are called *radioactive elements*.

The isotopes of elements with atomic number greater than 82 (lead) are radioactive as these atoms have more number of neutrons compared to the number of protons in their nuclei (*i.e.* unstable isotopes).

Examples of radioactive elements : Uranium, radium, polonium, thorium and so on.

Radioactivity is a *stochastic* or *random* process as it is not possible to predict when a particular atom of a radioactive substance will decay. But there are several radioactive laws which tries to describe the probable rate of disintegration of nucleus of an atom. Any nucleus can undergo radioactive decay at any time.

The phenomenon of radioactivity is a *property of the nucleus of the atom* and not due to its electrons. This is because the rate of decay of radioactive substances is not altered by either physical changes, such as change in temperature and pressure, or chemical changes, such as heating, freezing, electric and magnetic fields and oxidation.

NOTE

A *chemical change* in an atom occurs if there is a change in the number of electrons in the orbits of the atom and a *nuclear change* occurs if there is a change in the number of nucleons inside the nucleus of an atom. A much higher energy is required for a nuclear change as compared to a chemical change.

12.8 RUTHERFORD'S EXPERIMENT : EMISSIONS OF ALPHA (α), BETA (β) AND GAMMA (γ) RAYS

Rutherford did experiments to study the radiations emitted by radioactive substances.

Experiment

A small lead cube was taken and a cavity was drilled in it, as it was found that a lead cube could absorb the radiations emitted by the radioactive substances (Fig. 12.3). A small amount of radioactive material was placed in the cavity and the cavity was covered from the top with a lead plug. The cube was then placed in a glass vessel with two copper plates kept at its sides to provide an electric field perpendicular to the path of the radiations emitted by the radioactive substance. The copper plates were connected to a source of very high electric potential. Above the cavity was placed a photographic plate. The glass vessel was evacuated and then the lead plug was removed. The radiations from the radioactive substance were allowed to fall on the photographic plate for some time and then got developed.

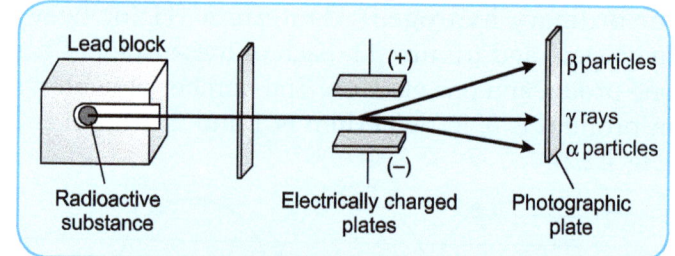

Fig. 12.3 : Emission of α, β and γ rays.

Observations : Three distinct black spots appeared on the plate due to three different types of radiations emitted. The spot that appeared near the negative copper plate must have been due to deflection of positively charged particles and the spot near the positive plate must have been due to negatively charged particles. The spot in the middle must have been due to uncharged particles.

Similar observations were made when a magnetic field was applied in a direction perpendicular to the path of emitted radiations, instead of an electric field in the experiment. The direction of deflection in a magnetic field is given by the Fleming's left-hand rule (Fig. 12.4).

Conclusions : The positively charged radiations were named the *alpha particles*. These deviated by a smaller angle compared to the negatively charged radiations, which were named *beta particles*. Thus, α-particles must have been heavier than the β-particles. The radiations that remained undeviated were uncharged and were named *gamma radiations*.

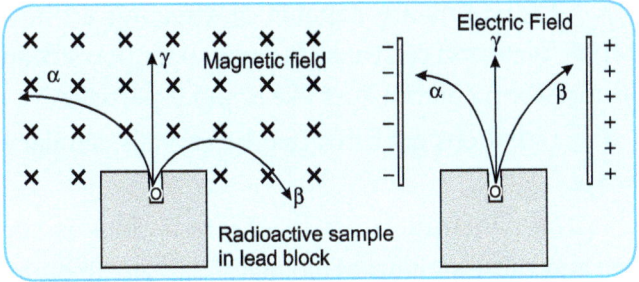

Fig. 12.4. : Deflection of radioactive radiations in magnetic and electric field.

12.9 CHARACTERISTIC PROPERTIES OF ALPHA (α) PARTICLES

1. An α-particle is a doubly ionised helium (He^{++}) nucleus, *i.e.* a helium nucleus consisting of two protons and two neutrons. It is represented as $^4_2$He. A neutral helium atom also has two electrons. If an α-particle gains two electrons, it becomes a neutral helium atom (He).

2. The mass of an α-particle is 6.68×10^{-27} kg, it is four times the mass of a proton.

3. The charge of an α-particle is $+ 3.2 \times 10^{-19}$ C, it is twice the charge of a proton.

4. Since α-particles are positively charged, these are deflected by electric and magnetic fields. An α-particle is heavier than a β-particle, it has more mass and thus its deflection is less compared to a β-particle.

5. The speed of α-particles is different for different radioactive substances and also for different nuclei of same radioactive substance. However, it lies in the order of 10^7 m s^{-1}.

6. The penetration power of an α-particle is very small as it rapidly loses energy on passing through a medium. An α-particle can penetrate from 2.7 cm to 8 cm in air and can be easily stopped by a thick paper. The penetration power of an α-particle is 10^{-2} times that of a β-particle and 10^{-4} times that of γ-radiation.

7. The ionising power of an α-particle is very strong. It is around 100 times that of a β-particle and 10^4 times that of γ-radiation.

8. α-particles are capable of affecting a photographic plate and cause fluorescence upon striking a fluorescent material.

9. α-particles undergo scattering when they pass through thin gold foils.

10. α-particles are used to convert one element into another by bombarding the nuclei of atoms due to their large kinetic energy.

11. α-particles can penetrate the uppermost layers of the skin, thereby causing biological damage. To avoid this damage, a radioactive substance is stored in a thick-walled lead container, and a person working with these substances is advised to wear a protective apron which has a thick lining made of lead.

12.10 CHARACTERISTIC PROPERTIES OF BETA (β) PARTICLES

1. β-particles are electrons with high velocity emitted from the nucleus of an atom when a neutron changes into a proton. It is represented as $^0_{-1}e$.

2. The mass of a β-particle is 9.1×10^{-31} kg.

3. The charge of a β-particle is -1.6×10^{-19} °C.

4. β-particles are negatively charged and get deflected by electric and magnetic fields. The deflection of a β-particle is in opposite direction to that of an α-particle and more than an α-particle as its mass is less than that of an α-particle.

5. The speed of β-particles is different for different atoms of same radioactive substance. It lies in the order of 10^8 ms^{-1}. It is 0.9 times the speed of light.

6. The penetration power of β-particles is more than that of α-particles. They can penetrate through 5 m in air, through thin cardboard, 5 mm in thin aluminium sheet and 1 mm in lead.

7. The ionising power of β-particles is 100 times more than that of γ-radiations but 100 times less than that of α-particles.

8. Similar to α-particles, β-particles too are capable of affecting a photographic plate. They also cause fluorescence upon striking a fluorescent material.

9. β-particles produce X-rays if they are stopped by certain metals such as tungsten that have a high atomic number and a high melting point.

10. As the penetration power of β-particles is more than that of α-particles, these cause more biological damage. They can invade deeper layers of skin and thus proper precautions need to be taken while handling radioactive substances.

12.11 CHARACTERISTIC PROPERTIES OF GAMMA (γ) RADIATIONS

1. γ-radiations are electromagnetic waves, similar to X-rays, UV rays and so on. These are given out from the nucleus. These rays differ in wavelength from other electromagnetic waves. The wavelength of γ-rays is the smallest, in the range of $10^{-12} - 10^{-14}$ m, while the wavelength of X-rays is in the range of $10^{-8} - 10^{-11}$ m.

2. γ-radiations have no charge or mass but possess high energy.

3. These radiations are not deflected by magnetic and electric fields.

4. The speed of γ-radiations is equal to the speed of light, i.e. 3×10^8 ms^{-1}.

5. The penetration power of γ-radiations is high, it is 10^4 times that of α-particles and 10^2 times that of β-particles. These radiations can pass through 500 m in air, 30 cm in iron sheet and 10 cm in lead.

6. The ionising power of γ-radiations is low. It is 10^{-4} times that of α-particles and 10^{-2} times that of β-particles.

7. γ-radiations are capable of affecting a photographic plate and can cause fluorescence upon striking a fluorescent material, just like α and β-particles.

8. γ-radiations get diffracted by crystals, similar to X-rays.

9. The penetration power of γ-radiations is very high and cause significant biological damage to human body and thus require proper precautions while handling radioactive substances.

Difference between γ-rays and X-rays

γ-rays	X-rays
The wavelength of γ-rays is shorter. It lies in the range of 10^{-12}–10^{-14} m.	The wavelength of X-rays is longer, in the range of 10^{-8}–10^{-11} m.
γ-rays are emitted by the nucleus of the atom.	X-rays are emitted when there is transition of electrons in the inner orbits of an atom.
It has more penetration power.	It has less penetration power.

Difference between α, β and γ radiations

Characteristic	α-particle	β-particle	γ-radiation
Composition	A helium nuclei consisting of two protons and two neutrons.	High-energy electron particle.	High-energy electromagnetic radiation.
Charge	Positive, twice that of a proton ($+2e$) = $+3.2 \times 10^{-19}$ C.	Negative, equal to that of an electron ($-e$) = -1.6×10^{-19} C.	Neutral, no charge.
Mass	Four times the mass of a proton = 6.68×10^{-27} kg.	Same as the mass of an electron = 9.1×10^{-31} kg.	No mass.
Speed	About 3.33% the speed of light = 10^7 m s^{-1}.	About 90% the speed of light = 2.7×10^8 m s^{-1}.	Same as the speed of light = 3×10^8 m s^{-1}.
Magnetic and electric field effect	Deflected towards negative plate or terminal.	Deflected towards positive plate or terminal.	No deflection.
Relative angle of deflection	Less	More	Zero
Penetration power	Small, 2.7–8.0 cm in air.	Large, 5 m in air.	Very large, 500 m in air.
Absorbed or stopped	Thin cardboard, human skin.	5 mm thick aluminium sheet, 1 mm thick lead.	30 cm thick iron sheet, 10 cm lead.
Ionising power	Highest, 10^4 times that of γ-radiations and 10^2 times that of β-particles.	Moderate, 100 times less than α-particles but 100 times more than γ-radiations	Low, 10^{-4} times of β-particles and 10^{-2} times that of β-particles.
Biological damage	Less damage.	More damage.	Immense damage.

12.12 CHANGES WITHIN THE NUCLEUS IN ALPHA, BETA AND GAMMA EMISSION

Cause of radioactivity : In an atom, the nucleons are held together by an attractive force called the *nuclear force*. This force operates in the range of very small distance, around 10^{-15} m. With increase in number of protons and neutrons, the magnitude of nuclear force also increases but only up to atomic number 82, that is lead. Beyond this atomic number, as the number of nucleons further increase, the nuclear force becomes weaker as the repulsive force of protons becomes greater and the nucleus of an atom becomes unstable. This instability is due to the increase in number of neutrons in an atom. In order to stabilise itself, it ejects α-particles, β-particles or γ-radiations (Fig. 12.5).

The process of disintegration of an unstable atom by the emission of ionising particles such as α and β-particles or γ-rays is termed as *radioactive decay* or *nuclear decay*.

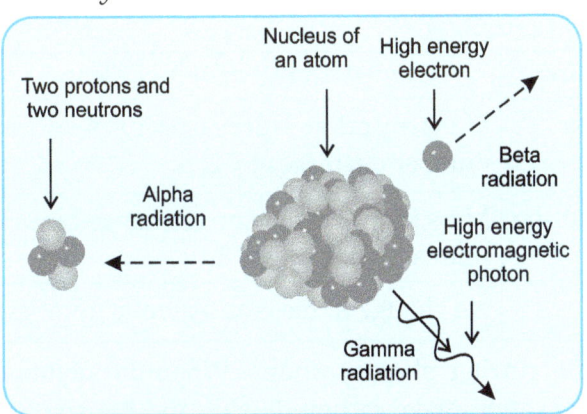

Fig. 12.5 : Different types of emissions.

Alpha emission : If the number of neutrons is greater than the number of protons in the nucleus of an unstable atom, it tends to emit two protons and two neutrons tightly bound together as a single particle called the *alpha particle* along with the release of energy (Fig. 12.6). A stream of many α-particles is known as α-rays. This changes the mass number and atomic number of the *parent nucleus*, and the new element so formed after the release of α-particle is called *daughter nucleus*. It generally occurs for nuclei of atoms whose atomic number is greater than 82.

Consider a radioactive element X of mass number A and atomic number Z. If it emits an α-particle, a new element Y is formed and has mass number equal to A – 4 and atomic number equal to Z – 2. The new element Y formed (also called the daughter nucleus) has its position two places behind in the periodic table compared to the position of the parent nucleus. The reaction can be expressed as

$$^{A}_{Z}X \rightarrow\ ^{A-4}_{Z-2}Y +\ ^{4}_{2}He\ (\alpha\text{-particle}) + \text{Energy}$$

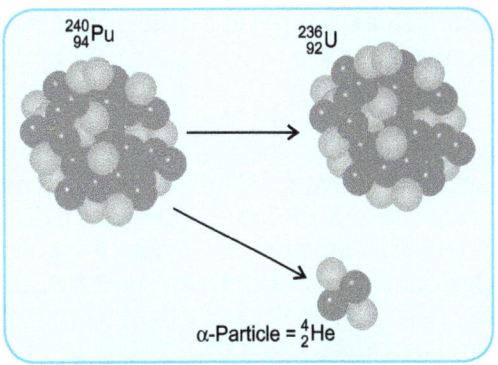

Fig. 12.6 : Alpha emission.

Examples :

1. $^{238}_{92}U \rightarrow\ ^{234}_{90}Th +\ ^{4}_{2}He$ (α-particle) + Energy

The nucleus of radioactive element uranium consists of 92 protons and 146 neutrons. When it emits an α-particle, a new element thorium is formed and consists of 90 protons and 144 neutrons.

2. $^{198}_{86}Rn \rightarrow\ ^{194}_{84}Po +\ ^{4}_{2}He$ (α-particle) + Energy

A radon atom changes to polonium by emitting an α-particle.

Beta emission : β-emission takes place in nucleus of atoms that have more number of neutrons than protons. In these nuclei, a neutron may transform into a proton with emission of an electron and a particle with no charge and negligible mass called *anti-neutrino*. The electron so emitted has a high speed and is called a *β-particle*. A stream consisting of a number of β-particles is called *β-rays*.

During β-emission, the number of neutrons decreases by 1, whereas the number of protons increases by 1. Thus, the number of nucleons inside the nucleus remains the same. The mass number of an atom does not change, but its atomic number increases by 1 upon emission of a β-particle. The new element formed has its position one place higher in the periodic table. The daughter nucleus formed is an *isobar* of the parent nucleus.

Consider a radioactive element X of mass number A and atomic number Z. If it emits a β-particle, the daughter element Y formed has mass number equal to A and atomic number equal to Z + 1. The reaction can be expressed as :

$$^{A}_{Z}X \rightarrow\ ^{A}_{Z+1}Y +\ ^{0}_{-1}e\ (\beta\text{-particle}) + \text{Anti-neutrino}$$

Examples :

1. $^{14}_{6}C \rightarrow\ ^{14}_{7}N +\ ^{0}_{-1}e$ (β-particle) + Anti-neutrino

Radioactive carbon consists of 6 protons and 8 neutrons (14 nucleons). When it emits a β-particle, it is transformed to nitrogen nucleus consisting of 7 protons and 7 neutrons (14 nucleons).

2. $^{24}_{11}Na \rightarrow\ ^{24}_{12}Mg +\ ^{0}_{-1}e$ (β-particle) + Anti-neutrino

A sodium atom changes to a magnesium atom upon emission of a β-particle.

NOTE

The β-particle, *i.e.* the electron emitted during a β-decay, is created when one neutron gets transformed into a proton. It does not exist in the nucleus and is instantaneously released once formed.

Under conditions of extreme temperature and pressure, when the nucleus of a lighter atom absorbs a proton, it becomes unstable. To stabilise itself, the nucleus ejects a particle called *positron* along with another particle called *neutrino*. Positron is a particle of mass equal to the electron but it is positively charged $^{0}_{+1}e$.

Neutrino is a neutral particle of negligible mass carrying extremely high energy.

α and β particles are never emitted together in a single radioactive decay. In any reaction, either of these particles is released and may be accompanied by a γ-radiation.

Gamma emission : In most cases of α and β-emissions, the daughter nucleus formed from the parent nucleus contains excess of energy. This energy is released in the form of electromagnetic radiation called the γ-radiation. During γ-emission, there is no change in mass number and atomic number of an atom, *i.e.* there is no loss or gain of protons or neutrons in the nucleus. It is represented as

$$^{A}_{Z}X^* \to {}^{A}_{Z}X + \gamma\text{-radiation}$$

The asterisk (*) indicates the excited state of the nucleus. Upon release of energy in the form of γ-radiation, the excited nucleus returns to its ground state.

Examples :

1. $^{137}_{56}Ba^* \to {}^{137}_{56}Ba + \gamma$-radiation
2. $^{12}_{5}B \to {}^{12}_{6}C^* + {}^{0}_{-1}e$(β-particle) + Anti-neutrino
3. $^{12}_{6}C^* \to {}^{12}_{6}C + \gamma$-radiation

Summary of α, β and γ Emissions

Type of emission	Representation by a common equation	Change in the daughter element
Alpha	$^{A}_{Z}X \to {}^{A-4}_{Z-2}Y + {}^{4}_{2}He$ (α-particle) + Energy	Mass number decreases by 4, atomic number decreases by 2.
Beta	$^{A}_{Z}X \to {}^{A}_{Z+1}Y + {}^{0}_{-1}e$ (β-particle) + Anti-neutrino	Mass number remains unchanged, atomic number increases by 1.
Gamma	$^{A}_{Z}X^* \to {}^{A}_{Z}X + \gamma$-radiation	No change in mass and atomic number.

12.13 USES OF RADIOACTIVITY : RADIOISOTOPES

Radioisotopes are the isotopes (same atomic number, different mass number) of elements with atomic number Z < 82. The nucleus of these elements becomes radioactive when the number of neutrons inside the nucleus is greater than the number of protons.

Examples :

Carbon $^{14}_{6}C$, Potassium $^{40}_{19}K$, Phosphorus $^{32}_{15}P$, Cobalt $^{60}_{27}Co$ and so on.

Besides naturally occurring radioisotopes, these can also be prepared artificially by bombarding neutrons, protons, α-particles and so forth on the nucleus of atoms of various elements. This process is called *nuclear transmutation*. It has many applications in various different fields.

Uses in Scientific Field

1. Carbon-14 is used in biological research, agriculture, pollution control, archaeology and so on.

Carbon dating : Carbon-14 is present in carbon dioxide along with carbon-12, which is used by living plants during photosynthesis. When the plants die, they cannot intake carbon dioxide and the amount of carbon-14 present in the dead remains of plants decays slowly. The rate of decay of carbon-14 in the dead remains of plants is used to study the age of plants and woods. This process is called *Carbon dating*.

Argon dating : Potassium-40 is an unstable isotope found in rocks. It decays to form argon gas. The ratio of amount of trapped argon gas to the amount of potassium in the rocks helps to determine the age of the rocks. This process is called *Argon dating*.

2. Tritium is used to ensure the safety of potential new drugs so that they are metabolised without forming harmful by-products.

3. Selenium-75 is used in protein studies in life science research.

4. Radioisotopes are also used in agricultural science for producing high yielding crop seeds, for producing fertilisers, to trace minerals (*e.g.* phosphorus) in body of plants, for pest management, food preservation and so on.

5. α-particles are used in determining the size of the nucleus, nature of nuclear forces, as projectiles for nuclear reactions and so on.

Uses in Medical Field

Radioisotopes are used for diagnosis as well as treatment of various diseases, besides sterilization of surgical instruments.

1. Diagnosis of diseases : Cobalt-57 ($^{57}_{27}Co$) is used for diagnosing pernicious anaemia, iodine-123 for thyroid disorders, gallium-67 for tumour location, indium-111 for brain diagnosis and so on.

2. Studying processes in human body : Certain radioisotopes such as radio-sodium chloride and radio-iron are called *tracers* as these are used to study natural processes in human body. Radio-sodium chloride along with common sodium chloride is injected into human body to study blood circulation through different parts of the body. This technique is known as *radio cardiology*.

Strontium-85 is used to study bone formation and metabolism. Various other radioisotopes are used for studying lung ventilation, for genetic analysis and so on.

3. Treatment of diseases : Iodine-131 is used in treatment of thyroid disorders and cobalt-60 is used to treat cancer cells; other isotopes are used in dental fixtures, for relieving arthritis pain and so on.

4. Radioisotopes that emit γ-radiations are used for sterilizing bandages, syringes, dressings, surgical instruments and so on. This method is quick, more efficient, convenient and less expensive than heat sterilization.

Uses in Industries

1. There are a wide variety of uses of radioisotopes in various industries such as smoke detectors, identification of sources of soil erosion and deposition, in blast furnaces and to locate flaws in metal components.

2. Radioisotopes such as gold-198 are used to study sewage and liquid waste movements, for tracing factory waste causing ocean pollution, to trace sand movement in riverbeds and so on.

3. Certain radioisotopes such as nickel-63 are used in light sensors in cameras and television displays and for electronic discharge prevention.

4. Uranium-235 is used as fuel for atomic energy reactors.

5. The penetrating power of β-radiations emitted from radioisotopes is used to control the thickness of paper, plastic, metal sheets (*e.g.* steel), rubber, textile and so on. In the manufacturing industry, for determining place for drilling oil wells and so on.

6. Thorium-229 makes the life of fluorescent lights longer. Thorium-230 provides colouring and fluorescence in glassware.

12.14 SOURCES AND HARMFUL EFFECTS OF RADIOACTIVITY

Among the three types of radiation, the penetration power of γ-radiations is maximum and thus these are the most harmful radiations, causing damage to biological tissues.

There are two main sources of radiations reaching us : (1) leak from nuclear power plants and (2) nuclear waste disposal.

1. Leakage from nuclear power plants : Worldwide, the nuclear power plants are used largely for generation of electricity. A variety of failure modes might occur in a nuclear power plant despite taking all precautions, which might cause leakage of radiation from the radioactive material into the nearby surroundings. This leakage can spread to far distances by air and water currents. It results in damage to the plant itself, to the persons working in the plant, to persons living in the vicinity of the plant as well as to crops and animals.

Around the world, a number of accidents have taken place at nuclear power plants : while some are minor (with no casualties), others are major and have resulted in casualties. One of the world's major nuclear disasters took place in 1986 at *Chernobyl* in Ukraine due to the rupture of a reactor vessel that led to a series of steam explosions that spread to surrounding regions of Europe. It led to a number of deaths, injuries and several long-term and short-term effects. Other significant accidents that took place were in 1957, *Kyshtym* in Russia due to explosion of a high activity waste tank; in 1979, the *Three Mile Island* accident in the USA due to loss of coolant and operative errors; and in 2011, the *Fukushima Daiichi* nuclear disaster in Japan due to a tsunami that flooded and damaged the nuclear plants.

2. Nuclear waste disposal : Nuclear wastes can be solids, liquids and gases and are classified into three types, low, intermediate and high-level waste, based on the level of radioactivity contained in them. Depending on the category, each type of waste is disposed as per the norms set up in a nuclear power plant. The high-level wastes require extra care for their disposal as these contain the maximum level of radioactivity. It includes the used fuel that is not meant for further reprocessing, waste containing α-emitters and so on. If these wastes are not disposed properly, then there are chances of contamination of air, water and soil, which in turn affects all living organisms, including humans.

Biological Effects of Nuclear Radiations

Some effects of radiation on human health are *stochastic* or *random*, *i.e.* their severity is independent of the radiation dose.

Examples : Cancer, abnormal physiological development, heart diseases and so on.

However, some effects are *non-stochastic* or *deterministic* or dose dependent, *i.e.* their severity increases with the increase in radiation dose.

Examples : Radiation burns, thyroiditis, gastrointestinal effects and so on.

The biological effects are classified into three types : (1) *short-term recoverable effects*—headache, dizziness, vomiting, nausea, diarrhoea, abdominal pain, loss of appetite, loss of hair, fever, skin damage and so on; (2) *long-term irrecoverable effects*—haemorrhage, cancer and infertility; and (3) *genetic effects*—mutations in genes.

While the first two types of effects are limited to individuals who are exposed directly to the radiations, the genetic effects are indirect effects. These occur in the later generations of the persons when the genes in their cells are altered and are passed to their progeny and subsequent generations.

12.15 SAFETY PRECAUTIONS TO BE TAKEN WHILE USING NUCLEAR ENERGY

There are certain safety rules that are required to be followed while establishing a nuclear power plant and while disposing the waste by the people working with radioactive substances.

Safety Measures during Establishment of Nuclear Power Plants

1. In a nuclear power plant, lead and steel walls are used to shield the nuclear reactor of the plant to avoid radiations escaping to the environment.

2. A strong concrete structure is used for housing the nuclear reactor to protect the reactor from earthquakes, fires, explosions and so on.

3. *Emergency core cooling system :* These are designed as a backup system if the prevailing cooling system fails or to safely shut down a nuclear reactor during accidental conditions.

4. *Emergency electrical system :* Under normal conditions, nuclear power plants receive power from off-site. However, during an accident, a plant may lose access to this power supply and thus may be required to generate its own power to supply its emergency systems. These electrical systems usually consist of diesel generators and batteries.

5. *Containment systems :* These are designed to prevent the release of radioactive material to the environment. A sealed metallic or ceramic layer is used to protect the spreading of nuclear fuel.

Safety Measures during Disposal of Nuclear Waste

Nuclear waste is the radioactive material left after its use. The nuclear wastes obtained from various sources such as the nuclear power plant, laboratories and hospitals are stored in sealed steel casks and are then buried in deep underground pits or boreholes far away from populated areas or in deep mined tunnels. The boreholes and tunnels are then sealed after storing the casks. The boreholes dug are few metres deep for low and intermediate-level radioactive waste and hundreds of metres deep for high-level radioactive wastes.

Safety Measures While Working with Radioactive Materials

1. The radioactive substances must be stored in long lead containers with a narrow opening and lead lid to absorb the radiations that strike its walls.

2. Any person who needs to handle a radioactive material should wear disposable aprons or laboratory coats and gloves which are lined with lead.

3. The material should not be handled directly. Forceps, tongs and custom-designed holders should be used to maintain a safe distance between the hand and the source.

4. Hand must be properly sanitized or sterilized after the operation is over.

5. Mirrors, transparent shields or lead glass windows should be used to view the operations. Direct viewing should be avoided.

6. Regular checks should be made for skin exposure to radiation by using special film badges. This is to ensure that no person is exposed beyond the safe limit of radiation.

12.16 BACKGROUND RADIATIONS

Background radiations are the radioactive radiations present universally all around the Earth to which all people are exposed and these cannot be avoided. They include both natural and artificial sources.

1. Natural sources include solar radiations, cosmic rays, radioactive materials in soil, rocks, water, air, vegetation and so on. One significant contribution is from radon gas released from the Earth's crust. It decays into radioactive atoms that become attached to airborne pollutants.

Solar radiations, cosmic radiations and radon-222 are *external sources*.

2. Artificial sources include X-rays used in medical imaging, cigarette smoke, nuclear testing, accidents at nuclear power plants, burning of fossil fuels, fluorescent dials and signs and so on.

Radioactive substances such as potassium-40 and carbon-14 are obtained by humans from the food they eat and are present inside their body. These are *internal sources*.

The effect of different radiations on human tissue is measured in a unit called *sieverts* (Sv). The worldwide average natural dose to humans per year is about 2.4 mSv. In general, the total radiation from internal and external sources that forms the background radiations is within the safe limit of permissible dose for humans and thus is not a matter of much concern.

Do You Know?

'*Radium girls*'—*In 1917, in New Jersey, female workers working in United States Radium factory contracted radiation poisoning while painting watch dial with a fluorescent paint. These girls ingested radioactive radium present in the paint thinking it was harmless and later began to suffer from a number of diseases such as anaemia and necrosis of teeth.*

ILLUSTRATIVE EXAMPLES

1. From the following elements, choose the atoms that are (a) isotopes, (b) isobars and (c) isotones : $^{12}_{6}C$, $^{13}_{6}C$, $^{14}_{6}C$, $^{13}_{7}N$, $^{14}_{7}N$.

    Solution :
    (a) Isotopes : $^{12}_{6}C$, $^{13}_{6}C$ and $^{14}_{6}C$ are isotopes. These elements have same atomic number but different mass number.

    (b) Isobars : $^{13}_{6}C$ & $^{13}_{7}N$ and $^{14}_{6}C$ & $^{14}_{7}N$ are two pairs of isobars. These elements have same mass number but different atomic number.

    (c) Isotones : $^{12}_{6}C$ & $^{13}_{7}N$ and $^{13}_{6}C$ & $^{14}_{7}N$ are two pairs of isotones. These elements have different mass number and atomic number but same number of neutrons.

2. What is the effect of freezing a radioactive element on the radiations emitted by it?

    Solution : Radioactivity is a random nuclear phenomenon. It remains unaffected by any physical or chemical change. Hence, there would be no effect on the radiations emitted by the radioactive material if it is subjected to freezing.

3. Compare γ-rays with UV rays.

    Solution : Similarities between the two types of rays :

    (a) Both are electromagnetic waves.

    (b) Both travel with an equal speed in air/vacuum = 3×10^8 ms^{-1}.

    Differences between the two types of rays :

    (a) The wavelength of γ-rays is shorter, *i.e.* < 0.01 nm, whereas the wavelength of UV rays is longer, *i.e.* lies between 10 nm and 400 nm.

    (b) **Source of γ-rays :** Cosmic radiations and nuclear changes in radioactive atoms.

    Source of UV rays : Solar radiations, electric arcs and mercury vapour lamps.

    (c) The penetration power of γ-rays is greater than that of UV rays.

4. Complete the table given below :

Change in property of element	α-emission	β-emission	Positron emission	γ-emission
Mass number				
Atomic number				

Solution :

Change in property of element	α-emission	β-emission	Positron emission	γ-emission
Mass number	Decreases by 4	No change	No change	No change
Atomic number	Decreases by 2	Increases by 1	Decreases by 1	No change

5. State the properties that are common to α, β and γ radiations.

    Solution :
    (a) All the three radiations originate from the nucleus of a radioactive atom.

(b) All the three radiations affect a photographic plate and cause fluorescence on striking a fluorescent material such as zinc sulphide.

6. An element X has a mass number 40 and atomic number 19. (a) Write the symbolic representation of the element. (b) What are the number of protons, electrons and neutrons in it? (c) Write an equation if the element undergoes a β-emission reaction.

   Solution :

   (a) Symbolic representation : $^{40}_{19}X$

   (b) No. of electrons = 19, No. of protons = 19, No. of neutrons = 21 (40 − 19)

   (c) Upon β-particle emission, the atomic number of the daughter element increases by 1 while the mass number remains unchanged. It can be represented in the form of an equation as
   $^{40}_{19}X \rightarrow {}^{40}_{20}Y + {}^{0}_{-1}e$.

7. The nucleus of a thorium atom $^{234}_{90}Th$ undergoes several α and β disintegrations and ultimately decays to form a lead atom $^{206}_{82}Pb$. Calculate the number of α and β particles emitted.

   Solution : In α-decay, the mass number decreases by 4 and the atomic number decreases by 2. In β-decay, the mass number remains constant and the atomic number increases by 1. When $^{234}_{90}Th$ disintegrates to $^{206}_{82}Pb$, its mass number decreases by 234 − 206 = 28, which means the number of α-particles emitted is 28/4 = 7.

   For 7 α-particles, the atomic number should decrease by 7 × 2 = 14. But from $^{234}_{90}Th$ to $^{206}_{82}Pb$ disintegration, the atomic number has decreased by 90 − 82 = 8.

   The increase in atomic number by 14 − 8 = 6 suggests emission of 6 β-particles.

   Thus, in total 7α and 6β particles have been emitted in the given disintegration.

8. Complete the following equations of radioactive disintegrations :
   $X \xrightarrow{\alpha} X_1 \xrightarrow{\beta} X_2 \xrightarrow{\gamma} X_3 \xrightarrow{\beta} {}^{234}_{92}X_4$

   Solution : To complete the entire equation, we need to start it from backwards. $^{234}_{92}X_4$ is formed after a β-particle emission from X_3, so the atomic number of X_3 will be 1 less than X_4 while its mass number will be the same, i.e. X_3 is $^{234}_{91}X_3$.

   $^{234}_{91}X_3$ is in turn formed after a γ-emission from X_2. During γ-emission, the atomic number and mass number remain unchanged but the atom is in an excited state, i.e. X_2 is $^{234}_{91}X_2^*$.

   $^{234}_{91}X_2^*$ is formed after a β-particle emission from X_1, so the atomic number of X_1 will be 1 less than X_2 while its mass number will be the same, i.e. X_1 is $^{234}_{90}X_1$.

   $^{234}_{90}X_1$ is formed after an α-particle emission from X, so the mass number of X will be 4 more than X_1 and atomic number will be 2 more than X_1, i.e. X is $^{238}_{92}X$.

   Thus, the complete equation is
   $^{238}_{92}X \xrightarrow{\alpha} {}^{234}_{90}X_1 \xrightarrow{\beta} {}^{234}_{91}X_2^* \xrightarrow{\gamma} {}^{234}_{91}X_3 \xrightarrow{\beta} {}^{234}_{92}X_4$

9. An element A undergoes two α-decays and the daughter element B undergoes a β-decay forming an element C. The element C is in an excited state and undergoes a γ-radiation to form element D. Represent the series in the form of an equation.

   Solution : In one α-decay, the mass number decreases by 4 and atomic number decreases by 2. Thus, in two α-decays, the mass number will be reduced by 8 and atomic number will be reduced by 4. If A is represented as $^{A}_{Z}A$, then B will be $^{A-8}_{Z-4}B$. When B undergoes a β-decay, its mass number remains unchanged and atomic number increases by 1. The element C formed is in an excited state. Thus, C is represented as $^{A-8}_{Z-3}C^*$. C undergoes γ-radiation in which both mass number and atomic number remain unchanged. Only energy is released. Thus, D is same as C in ground state, i.e. D is $^{A-8}_{Z-3}D$. The series can be represented as

   $^{A}_{Z}A \xrightarrow{2\alpha} {}^{A-8}_{Z-4}B \xrightarrow{\beta} {}^{A-8}_{Z-3}C^* \xrightarrow{\gamma} {}^{A-8}_{Z-3}D + Energy$

10. State two harmful and two beneficial effects of radioactivity for human beings.

    Solution :

    Harmful effects

    (a) Short-term recoverable effects such as loss of hair, loss of blood, headache, vomiting, fever and nausea.

    (b) Genetic defects which affect the next generations.

    Beneficial effects

    (a) Radioisotopes can be used for diagnosis of diseases such as thyroid and tumours.

    (b) γ-radiations are helpful in killing cancerous cells.

EXERCISE 12(A)

1. What are the three particles of an atom ? State the charge of each particle.
   Ans : Electrons (negative), protons (positive) and neutrons (neutral).

2. Name the subatomic particle that revolves in definite orbits.
   Ans : Electrons

3. What is the maximum number of electrons that can be accommodated in K, L and M shells?
   Ans : 2, 8, 18

4. What is the mass of (a) a proton, (b) an electron and (c) a neutron?

5. Name the particles forming the nucleus of an atom. What is the net charge on (a) the nucleus and (b) on an atom?

6. Define atomic number and mass number.

7. State the number of electrons, protons and neutrons in the following elements : (a) $^{23}_{11}Na$, (b) $^{14}_{7}N$ and (c) $^{235}_{92}U$.

8. State the number of electrons distributed in different shells for these elements : (a) $^{24}_{12}Mg$ and (b) $^{40}_{20}Ca$.

9. What is the basic difference between a chemical change and a nuclear change occurring in an atom?

10. What are isotopes? Give an example.

11. What are the three isotopes of hydrogen? State the number of neutrons in each of these isotopes.

12. Two atoms have same mass number but different atomic number. What are these atoms called? Give an example.

13. What are isotones? Give an example.

14. Classify the following pairs of elements as isotopes, isobars and isotones : (a) $^{24}_{12}Mg$ and $^{23}_{11}Na$, (b) $^{23}_{11}Na$ and $^{23}_{12}Mg$ and (c) $^{35}_{17}Cl$ and $^{37}_{17}Cl$.

15. Define radioactivity?

16. Give two examples of radioactive substances.

17. A radioactive substance is oxidized. Will there be any change in the nature of its radioactivity? Give a reason for your answer.

18. Name the three types of radiations emitted from radioactive substances.

19. Describe Rutherford's experiment on detection of α, β and γ-radiations.

20. (a) Complete the diagram as given above by drawing the deflection of radioactive radiations in an electric field.

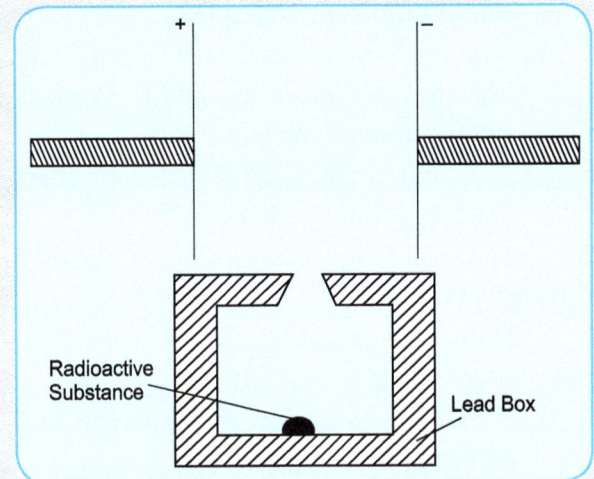

   (b) State any two precautions to be taken while handling radioactive substances.

21. The figure below shows a radioactive substance present in a lead-walled container with a small opening. The radiations emitted from the substance are allowed to pass through a magnetic field, represented by dots, acting perpendicular to the plane of the paper outwards. X, Y and Z are the paths of three radiations. (a) Label the three radiations. (b) Which rule helps in determining these radiations?

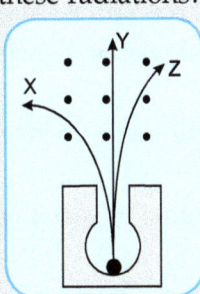

22. State the composition of α, β and γ-radiations.

23. Read the following statements, choose the type of radiation that satisfies the given statement :
    (a) This radiation does not get deflected by magnetic or electric field.
    (b) This radiation has the lowest ionising power.
    (c) This radiation deflects towards the positive plate in an electric field.
    (d) This radiation has the intermediate penetration power.
    (e) This radiation has the lowest speed.
    Ans : (a) γ, (b) γ, (c) β, (d) β, (e) α

24. An atomic nucleus A is composed of 84 protons and 128 neutrons.
    (a) The nucleus A emits an alpha particle and is transformed into nucleus B. What is the composition of nucleus B ?
    (b) The nucleus B emits a beta particle and is transformed into a nucleus C. What is the composition of nucleus C ?
    (c) Does the composition of nucleus C change if it emits gamma radiations ?

25. A mixture of radioactive substance gives off three types of radiations.
    (a) Name the radiation that travels with the speed of light.
    (b) Name the radiation that has the highest ionising power.
    Ans : (a) γ, (b) α

26. Why is it not possible to detect γ-radiations using a magnetic or electric field?

27. State any two similarities and two dissimilarities between the three types of radiations : α, β and γ.

28. What is the ratio of (a) ionising power and (b) speeds of α, β and γ-radiations?

29. Arrange α, β and γ rays in ascending order with respect to their (a) penetrating power, (b) ionising power, (c) biological effect.
    Ans : (a) $\alpha < \beta < \gamma$ (b) $\gamma < \beta < \alpha$ (c) $\alpha < \beta < \gamma$.

30. What is the similarity between γ-radiation and visible light?

31. What is the difference between γ-radiation and X-rays?

32. What is the value of speed of γ-radiations in air or vacuum?

33. Which of the radioactive radiations (a) cause severe genetic disorders and (b) are deflected by an electric field?
    Ans : (a) γ, (b) α and β

34. What is meant by radioactive decay?

35. When an α-particle takes two electrons, it becomes neutral and becomes an atom of an element that is a rare gas. What is the name of this rare gas?
    Ans : Helium

36. Express the change in the form of an equation when an α-particle is emitted from the nucleus of an atom.

37. What is the difference between the parent nucleus and the daughter nucleus formed after emission of an α-particle?

38. Which number remains the same during emission of a β-particle?
    Ans : Mass number

39. What happens inside the nucleus that causes the emission of β-particle? Express this change in the form of an equation.

40. When a certain particle is emitted from the nucleus of a radioactive atom, the mass number of the atom remains unchanged but atomic number increases by 1. Name the particle.
    Ans : β-particle

41. What happens to the mass number and atomic number of an element $_Z^AX$ when (a) an α-particle, (b) a β-particle and (c) γ-radiation are emitted?
    Ans : (a) A decreases by 4, Z decreases by 2, (b) No change in A, Z increases by 1, (c) No change in both A and Z

42. An element $_Z S^A$ decays to $_{85}R^{222}$ after emitting 2α particles and 1 β particle. Find the atomic number and atomic mass of the element S.

43. A certain nucleus X has a mass number 14 and atomic number 6. The nucleus X changes to $_7^{14}Y$ after the loss of a particle. (a) Name the particle emitted. (b) Represent the change in the form of an equation.

44. A radioactive nucleus undergoes a series of decays according to the following sequence :
    $X \xrightarrow{\beta} X_1 \xrightarrow{\alpha} X_2 \xrightarrow{\alpha} X_3$. If the mass number and atomic number of X_3 are 172 and 69, respectively, what is the mass number of X ?

45. An element X is composed of 88 protons and 134 neutrons. The nucleus of this element emits an α-particle and gets transformed to element Y. State the mass number and atomic number of Y.

46. (a) Represent the change in the nucleus of radioactive element when a β particle is emitted.
    (b) What is the name given to elements with same mass number and different atomic number ?
    (c) Under which conditions does the nucleus of an atom tend to be radioactive ?

47. An element X is composed of 92 protons and 146 neutrons. It undergoes two successive decays. After first decay, its atomic number decreases by 2, and after the second decay, its atomic

number increases by 1. Represent the decays in the form of an equation and state which are the two particles that are emitted in the two decays.

48. Complete the following nuclear changes :
    (a) $^{238}_{92}U \rightarrow Th + ^4_2He$
    (b) $^{226}_{88}Ra \xrightarrow{\alpha} Rn + ?$
    (c) $^{218}_{84}Po \xrightarrow{\alpha} Pb \xrightarrow{\beta} Bi$
    (d) $^{40}_{19}X \rightarrow \beta + ?$
    (e) $^A_Z X \rightarrow 2\alpha + ? \xrightarrow{2\beta} ?$

49. An element A undergoes an α-decay and the daughter element B undergoes two β-decays, forming an element C. Represent this in the form of an equation and state how are A and C related?

50. What are radioisotopes? Give one example.

51. What is meant by artificial transmutation?

52. Choose the radioisotope among the following pairs : (a) $^{12}_6C$ and $^{14}_6C$ and (b) $^{35}_{16}S$ and $^{32}_{16}S$. Give reason.

53. Explain the use of (a) carbon dating and (b) argon dating.

54. State two uses of radioisotopes in industrial field.

55. State the medical use of radioactivity.

56. What are the two major sources of nuclear radiations?

57. What is the difference between stochastic and non-stochastic effect of radiations on human tissues?

58. State any two harmful effects of nuclear radiations.

59. What is meant by nuclear waste? Suggest one effective way for the safe disposal of nuclear waste.

60. State any two safety precautions that a person should take while handling a radioactive substance.

61. What are background radiations?

62. Give any two important sources of background radiations.

MULTIPLE CHOICE QUESTIONS

1. Which of these particles do not carry any charge?
   (a) Proton and β-particle
   (b) Neutron and γ-radiation
   (c) Electron and α-particle
   (d) Positron and α-particle
   Ans : (b)

2. Which of these pairs of elements are not isobars?
   (a) $^{40}_{19}K$ and $^{40}_{20}Ca$ (b) $^{58}_{26}Fe$ and $^{58}_{27}Ni$
   (c) $^{35}_{17}Cl$ and $^{37}_{17}Cl$ (d) $^{23}_{11}Na$ and $^{23}_{12}Mg$
   Ans : (c)

3. Which of these radiations has the least ionising power?
   (a) α-radiations   (b) β-radiations
   (c) γ-radiations   (d) all of these
   Ans : (c)

4. Which of these is not an electromagnetic radiation?
   (a) γ-radiation   (b) X-rays
   (c) UV radiation   (d) α-radiation
   Ans : (d)

5. When an α-particle is released from the nucleus of an element, its mass number :
   (a) increases by 2   (b) decreases by 2
   (c) increases by 4   (d) decreases by 4
   Ans : (d)

(B) NUCLEAR FISSION AND FUSION

12.17 NUCLEAR ENERGY

Everything around us is made up of tiny objects called atoms. Most of the mass of each atom is concentrated in the centre (which is called the nucleus) and the rest of the mass is in the cloud of electrons surrounding the nucleus. Protons and neutrons are subatomic particles that comprise the nucleus.

Under certain circumstances such as radioactive decay splitting of nucleus of very large atom etc., nuclear change occurs. In this process, the total sum of masses of product nuclei is always less than the total sum of the masses of reactant nuclei. Thus, there is a loss in mass. This loss in mass is converted to pure energy following Einstein's famous equation of relativity i.e.,

$$E = (\Delta m)c^2$$

Here Δm is the loss in mass in kg, c is the speed of light (3×10^8 m s^{-1}) and E is the energy in joule (J).

When 1 kg of mass is lost, the amount of energy released is

$$E = (\Delta m)c^2$$
$$= 1 \times (3 \times 10^8)^2 = 9 \times 10^{16} \text{ J}$$

Hence, 1 kg lost mass is equivalent to 9×10^{16} J of energy. This energy is called the *nuclear energy*.

We have already studied in previous classes that mass of atomic particles is expressed in *atomic mass unit (a.m.u.)* which is defined as $\frac{1}{12}$th the mass of the carbon-12 atom.

$$1 \text{ a.m.u.} = \frac{1}{12} \times \text{Mass of one C-12 atom}$$
$$= 1.66 \times 10^{-27} \text{ kg}$$

Due to loss in mass $\Delta m = 1$ a.m.u., the energy released is

$$E = (1.66 \times 10^{-27}) \times (3 \times 10^8)^2 \text{ J}$$
$$= 1.49 \times 10^{-10} \text{ J}$$

But $\quad 1 \text{ MeV} = 1.6 \times 10^{-13}$ J

$$\therefore \quad E = \frac{1.49 \times 10^{-10}}{1.6 \times 10^{-13}} \text{ MeV}$$
$$= 931 \text{ MeV}.$$

Thus, 1 a.m.u. of mass is equivalent to 931 MeV of energy.

12.18 NUCLEAR FISSION

Nuclear fission is a process in which a heavier nucleus gets split up into two or more lighter nuclei with the release of a large amount of energy.

The reason for the release of energy is the loss of mass in this reaction. This loss in mass is converted into energy by the Einstein's equation i.e., $E = (\Delta m)c^2$. Fission was discovered in 1938 by the German scientists Otto Hahn, Lise Meitner and Fritz Strassmann, who bombarded a sample of uranium $^{235}_{92}U$ with slow neutrons in an attempt to produce new elements with Z > 92. They observed that a most unstable isotope $^{236}_{92}U$ is formed which splits into two lighter nuclei *i.e.* barium ($^{144}_{56}Ba$) and krypton ($^{89}_{36}Kr$) with the release of three neutrons and a large amount of energy. The fission reaction is given by

$$^{235}_{92}U + ^{1}_{0}n \longrightarrow {}^{236}_{92}U \longrightarrow {}^{144}_{56}Ba + {}^{89}_{36}Kr + 3{}^{1}_{0}n + \text{Energy}$$

NOTE

$^{236}_{92}U$ isotope decays not only into $^{144}_{56}Ba$ and $^{89}_{36}Kr$ fragments, but it can decay in different pairs of nuclei such as ($^{148}_{57}La$, $^{85}_{35}Br$); ($^{140}_{54}Xe$, $^{94}_{38}Sr$) etc.

Nuclear energy released during fission reaction of $^{235}_{92}U$ nucleus :

The fission reaction of $^{235}_{92}U$ is given as follows :

$$^{235}_{92}U + {}^{1}_{0}n \longrightarrow {}^{144}_{56}Ba + {}^{89}_{36}Kr + 3{}^{1}_{0}n + \text{Energy}$$

In the above reaction, the total mass of Ba, Kr and three neutrons was found to be less than the total mass of uranium and one neutron. This loss in mass appears as energy.

If we take the mass of neutron = 1.01 a.m.u.
Mass of uranium-235 nucleus = 234.99 a.m.u.
Mass of barium-144 nucleus = 143.87 a.m.u.
Mass of krypton-89 nucleus = 88.90 a.m.u.

Loss in mass in fission reaction is given by

Δm = (Mass of $^{235}_{92}U$ nucleus + Mass of 1 neutrons) − (Mass of $^{144}_{56}Ba$ nucleus + Mass of $^{89}_{36}Kr$ nucleus + Mass of 3 neutrons)

$= [(234.99 + 1.01) - (143.87 + 88.90 + 3 \times 1.01)]$ a.m.u.
$= (236.00 - 235.80)$ a.m.u. $= 0.20$ a.m.u.

But $\quad E = (\Delta m)c^2$

1 a.m.u. = 931 MeV

∴ Energy released

$E = 0.20 \times 931$ MeV
$= 190$ MeV

Thus, in the fission of $^{235}_{92}U$, 190 MeV energy is released. Most of this energy appears in the form of kinetic energy of fission fragments. The remaining part is carried by β-rays, γ-rays and neutrinos.

Uncontrolled and Controlled Chain Reaction

When uranium-235 ($^{235}_{92}U$) nucleus is bombarded by slow neutrons, it splits into two fragments i.e., $^{144}_{56}Ba$ and $^{89}_{36}Kr$ with a release of three new neutrons and nearly 190 MeV of energy. The three neutrons released during fission, can be used to effect fission in other nuclei, producing nine neutrons. These nine neutrons can cause fission in nine uranium nuclei and so on. This self sustaining series of nuclear fission reaction proceeds fill the whole of the fissile material is disintegrated. This is called *uncontrolled chain reaction*. Due to this chain reaction, a sudden explosion takes place with the release of tremendous amount of energy, in the form of heat and light. This uncontrolled chain reaction is the principle of working of *atom bomb.*

The chain reaction is *controlled* by absorbing some of the neutrons emitted in the fission process by means of moderators like graphite, heavy water etc. This is the principle of working of a *nuclear reactor*.

Uses of Nuclear Fission

1. The process of nuclear fission is used in making **atom bombs** where the energy released is fast and uncontrolled.

2. This process is also used in making **nuclear reactor** where the rate of release of energy is slow and controlled.

12.19 NUCLEAR FUSION

When two or more light nuclei combine to form a heavy stable nucleus, part of the mass disappears and is converted into energy. This phenomenon is called nuclear fusion.

Nuclear fusion is the opposite of nuclear fission, it is the joining together of two light nuclei to form a heavier one (plus a small fragment).

Example : When two ^2_1H (deuterium) nuclei fuse, a helium isotope (^3_2He) is formed with a release of 3.3 MeV of energy. When this helium isotope (^3_2He) again gets fused with one deuterium (^2_1H) nucleus, a helium nucleus (^4_2He) is formed with a release of 18.3 MeV of energy. The nuclear reactions are :

$$^2_1H + ^2_1H \longrightarrow ^3_2He + ^1_0n + 3.3 \text{ MeV}$$
(deuterium) (deuterium) (helium isotope) (neutron)

$$^3_2He + ^2_1H \longrightarrow ^4_2He + ^1_1H + 18.3 \text{ MeV}$$
(helium isotope) (deuterium) (helium) (proton)

Hence in all, three deuterium nuclei fuse to form a helium nucleus with a release of 21.6 MeV energy. A part of this energy is obtained in the form of kinetic energy of neutron (^1_0n) and proton (^1_1H).

Examples of other fusion reactions which occur more rapidly are given below :

(1) $^1_1H + ^1_1H \longrightarrow ^2_1H + 0.42 \text{ MeV}$
(proton) (proton) (deuterium)

(2) $^2_1H + ^2_1H \longrightarrow ^3_1H + ^1_1H + 4.0 \text{ MeV}$
(deuterium) (deuterium) (tritium) (proton)

(3) $^2_1H + ^3_1H \longrightarrow ^4_2He + ^1_0n + 17.6 \text{ MeV}$
(deuterium) (tritium) (helium) (neutron)

(4) $^2_1H + ^2_1H \longrightarrow ^3_2He + ^1_0n + 3.3 \text{ MeV}$
(deuterium) (deuterium) (helium isotope) (neutron)

(5) $^3_2He + ^2_1H \longrightarrow ^4_2He + ^1_1H + 18.3 \text{ MeV}$
(helium isotope) (deuterium) (helium) (proton)

Nuclear fusion reactions take place only at high temperature and pressure. The reason is that when two reacting nuclei come close to each other then due to their positive charge, the electrostatic force of repulsion between them becomes more strong. So they do not fuse. Hence, this high temperature ($\approx 10^7$ K) and pressure is required for fusion reaction because then only they will have sufficient energy to overcome the Coulomb's electrostatic force of repulsion. Due to this reason, the nuclear fusion reactions are also known as thermo-nuclear reaction.

Nuclear Fusion Process in Nature

The Sun which gives us heat and light derives its energy from the fusion of hydrogen nuclei into helium nuclei, which is going on inside it, all the time.

The nuclear fusion reaction taking place inside the sun is

$$4\,^1_1H \xrightarrow[\text{(Inside the Sun)}]{\text{Nuclear fusion}} ^4_2He + 2\,^0_{+1}e + \text{Tremendous}$$
Hydrogen nuclei → Helium nucleus + Positrons + amount of energy

The total energy produced by the fusion of hydrogen into helium is tremendous. All this energy is released in the form of heat and light which makes the sun shine and gives us heat and light.

Hence, nuclear fusion reactions of hydrogen are the source of Sun's energy. Just like the Sun, the stars also obtain their energy from the nuclear fusion reactions of hydrogen.

Uses of Nuclear Fusion

1. The nuclear fusion reactions are used in making hydrogen bomb which is a weapon of mass destruction.

2. The nuclear fusion reactions are used in making electricity. It can provide a safe, clean energy source for future generations with several advantages over current nuclear fission reactors.

12.20 DIFFERENCE BETWEEN THE NUCLEAR FISSION AND NUCLEAR FUSION

Nuclear Fission	Nuclear Fusion
It is the process in which a heavy nucleus is splitted into two light nuclei by bombarding it with slow neutrons.	It is the process in which two light nuclei combine to form a heavy nucleus.
It is a chain reaction.	It is not a chain reaction.
It takes place at normal temperature.	It requires extremely high temperature ($\approx 10^7$ K).
Large amount of energy is released.	Energy released is much more than that of fission reaction.
It can be controlled.	It can not be controlled.
It leaves behind radioactive wastes.	It does not leave behind any radioactive wastes.
Nuclear bomb is based on the uncontrolled fission reaction.	Hydrogen bomb is based on the uncontrolled fusion reaction.

ILLUSTRATIVE EXAMPLES

1. Calculate the loss in mass equivalent to the energy 3.0×10^{10} kWh.
   Solution : Given, E = 3.0×10^{10} kWh, $c = 3 \times 10^8$ m/s
   Since 1 kWh = 3.6×10^6 J
   ∴   E = $3.0 \times 10^{10} \times 3.6 \times 10^6$ J
             = 1.08×10^{17} J
   Using Einstein's mass energy equivalence,
   $$E = \Delta mc^2$$
   Loss in mass,
   $$\Delta m = \frac{E}{c^2}$$
   $$= \frac{1.08 \times 10^{17}}{(3 \times 10^8)^2}$$
   $$= \frac{1.08 \times 10^{17}}{9 \times 10^{16}} = 1.2 \text{ kg}$$

2. Calculate the amount of energy released in MeV due to loss of 4 kg mass.
   Solution : Given, $\Delta m = 4$ kg, $c = 3 \times 10^8$ ms^{-1}
   Using Einstein's mass energy equivalence,
   $$E = \Delta mc^2$$
   $$E = 4 \times (3 \times 10^8)^2$$
   $$= 3.6 \times 10^{17} \text{ joule}$$
   But 1 MeV = 1.6×10^{-13} J
   ∴ $E = \frac{3.6 \times 10^{17}}{1.6 \times 10^{-13}}$ MeV
           = 2.25×10^{30} MeV

3. Calculate the loss in mass equivalent to the energy 12×10^{16} joule.
   Solution : Given, E = 12×10^{16} J, $c = 3 \times 10^8$ ms^{-1}.
   Using $E = \Delta mc^2$
   ∴ Loss in mass,
   $$\Delta m = \frac{12 \times 10^{16}}{(3 \times 10^8)^2}$$
   $$= 1.33 \text{ kg}.$$

4. In a nuclear fusion reaction, the loss in mass is 0.56 a.m.u. Calculate the energy released.
   Solution : Given, $\Delta m = 0.56$ a.m.u.
   We know that, 1 a.m.u. = 931 MeV
   ∴ Energy released,
   $$E = 0.56 \times 931 \text{ MeV}$$
   $$= 521.36 \text{ MeV}.$$

5. In a nuclear fission reaction, uranium-235 is split into two lighter nuclei. During this process 0.20 a.m.u. of mass is lost. Calculate the energy released.
   Solution : Given, $\Delta m = 0.20$ a.m.u.,
   We know that, 1 a.m.u. = 931 MeV
   ∴ Energy released,
   $$E = 0.20 \times 931 \text{ MeV}$$
   $$= 186.2 \text{ MeV}$$

EXERCISE 12(B)

1. Define nuclear energy. What is responsible for its release?
2. Write the expression of Einstein's mass-energy equivalence relation, and calculate the amount of energy released due to a loss of mass of 1 kg.
3. Explain 1 a.m.u. of mass is equivalent to 931 MeV of energy.
4. What is nuclear fission ? Explain with an example. Write the equation of the nuclear reaction involved.
5. What is an uncontrolled chain reaction ? How is it controlled.
6. A nuclear reaction is represented by the following equation :
   $$^{235}_{92}U + ^{1}_{0}n \longrightarrow ^{144}_{56}Ba + ^{89}_{36}Kr + xy + E$$
   (a) Name the process represented by this equation.
   (b) Identify the particle y and the number x of such particles produced in the reaction ?
   (c) What does E represent ?
   (d) What type of bomb is based on similar type of reactions ?
7. Explain the uses of nuclear fission.
8. What is nuclear fusion ? Explain with an example. Write the equation of the reaction involved.
9. Why are very high temperatures required for nuclear fusion to occur ?
10. A nuclear reaction is represented by the equation :
    $$^{2}_{1}H + ^{2}_{1}H \longrightarrow ^{3}_{2}He + xy + E$$

(a) Name the process represented by this equation.
(b) Identify the particle y and the number x of such particles produced in the reaction.
(c) What does E represent ?
(d) What type of nuclear bomb is based on similar reactions ?

11. Differentiate between nuclear fission and fusion.
12. Name the following nuclear reactions :
    (a) $^{235}_{92}U + ^{1}_{0}n \longrightarrow ^{115}_{44}Ru + ^{118}_{48}Cd + 3^{1}_{0}n + $ Energy
    (b) $^{2}_{1}H + ^{6}_{3}Li \longrightarrow ^{4}_{2}He + ^{4}_{2}He + $ Energy
    Ans: (a) Nuclear fission
    (b) Nuclear fusion
13. What type of nuclear reaction is responsible for the liberation of energy in the Sun and Stars ?
14. Why nuclear fusion reactions are also known as thermonuclear reactions ?
15. The mass numbers of four elements A, B, C and D are 2, 20, 135 and 235 respectively. Which one of them will be most suitable to make :
    (i) an atom bomb and (ii) a hydrogen bomb.

MULTIPLE CHOICE QUESTIONS

1. One atomic mass unit is equivalent to an energy of :
   (a) 9.31 MeV   (b) 1 MeV
   (c) 931 MeV   (d) 931 eV
   Ans: (c)

2. The type of nuclear reaction which is involved in the working of atom bomb is :
   (a) Nuclear fusion   (b) Nuclear fission
   (c) Both (a) and (b) (d) None of these
   Ans: (b)

3. Which of the following can undergo nuclear fission reaction ?
   (a) Uranium   (b) Deuterium
   (c) Barium   (d) Krypton
   Ans: (a)

4. The energy released during nuclear fission and fusion is due to the :
   (a) conversion of stored chemicals into energy
   (b) conversion of momentum into energy
   (c) conversion of mass into energy
   (d) conversion of magnetism into energy.
   Ans: (c)

NUMERICALS

1. In a nuclear fusion reaction, the loss in mass is 0.6%. How much energy is released in the fusion of 1 kg mass ?
   Ans: 5.4×10^{14} J

2. If in nuclear fission of a piece of uranium, 0.8 g mass is lost, how much energy in MeV is obtained ?
   Ans: 4.5×10^{26} MeV.

www.ingramcontent.com/pod-product-compliance
Ingram Content Group UK Ltd.
Pitfield, Milton Keynes, MK11 3LW, UK
UKHW050418240426
12048UKWH00014B/698